Curriculum Studies Guidebooks

Studies in the Postmodern Theory of Education

Shirley R. Steinberg
General Editor

Vol. 498

The Counterpoints series is part of the Peter Lang Education list.
Every volume is peer reviewed and meets
the highest quality standards for content and production.

PETER LANG
New York • Bern • Frankfurt • Berlin
Brussels • Vienna • Oxford • Warsaw

Marla Morris

Curriculum Studies Guidebooks

VOLUME 1

Concepts and Theoretical Frameworks

PETER LANG
New York • Bern • Frankfurt • Berlin
Brussels • Vienna • Oxford • Warsaw

Library of Congress Cataloging-in-Publication Data
Morris, Marla.
Curriculum studies guidebooks: concepts and theoretical frameworks / Marla Morris.
volumes; cm. — (Counterpoints: studies in the
postmodern theory of education; vols. 498–499)
Includes bibliographical references and index.
Contents: v. 1. Introduction—Historical Curriculum Concepts, Part One—
Historical Curriculum Concepts, Part Two—Historical Curriculum Concepts,
Part Three—Political Curriculum Concepts—Multicultural Curriculum Concepts—
Gender Curriculum Concepts—Literary Curriculum Concepts—
v. 2. Introduction—Aesthetic curriculum concepts—Spiritual curriculum concepts—
Cosmopolitan curriculum concepts—Ecological curriculum concepts—
Cultural studies curriculum concepts—Postcolonial curriculum concepts—
Poststructural curriculum concepts—Psychoanalytic curriculum concepts.
1. Education—Curricula—United States—Philosophy. I. Title.
LB1570.M685   375'.001—dc23   2015022031
ISBN 978-1-4331-3126-4 (v. 1, hardcover)
ISBN 978-1-4331-3125-7 (v. 1, paperback)
ISBN 978-1-4539-1658-2 (v. 1, e-book)
ISBN 978-1-4331-3128-8 (v. 2, hardcover)
ISBN 978-1-4331-3127-1 (v. 2, paperback)
ISBN 978-1-4539-1659-9 (v. 2, e-book)
ISSN 1058-1634

Bibliographic information published by **Die Deutsche Nationalbibliothek**.
Die Deutsche Nationalbibliothek lists this publication in the "Deutsche
Nationalbibliografie"; detailed bibliographic data are available
on the Internet at http://dnb.d-nb.de/.

Cover image: ©iStock.com/gemenacom

The paper in this book meets the guidelines for permanence and durability
of the Committee on Production Guidelines for Book Longevity
of the Council of Library Resources.

© 2016 Peter Lang Publishing, Inc., New York
29 Broadway, 18th floor, New York, NY 10006
www.peterlang.com

All rights reserved.
Reprint or reproduction, even partially, in all forms such as microfilm,
xerography, microfiche, microcard, and offset strictly prohibited.

Printed in the United States of America

DEDICATION

To William F. Pinar. My friend and my teacher.

TABLE OF CONTENTS

Acknowledgments	ix
Chapter 1. Introduction	1
Chapter 2. Historical Curriculum Concepts, Part 1	21
Chapter 3. Historical Curriculum Concepts, Part 2	77
Chapter 4. Historical Curriculum Concepts, Part 3	155
Chapter 5. Political Curriculum Concepts	245
Chapter 6. Multicultural Curriculum Concepts	295
Chapter 7. Gender Curriculum Concepts	339
Chapter 8. Literary Curriculum Concepts	371
References	401
Index	435

ACKNOWLEDGMENTS

I would like to thank Mary Aswell Doll for her ongoing support of this project. Through the ups and downs she stuck with me the whole way. Special thanks to Chris Myers who believed in this project and was there every step of the way. I would like to thank Shirley Steinberg for her support and words of wisdom throughout the process. I would like to thank John Weaver who taught me the virtue of perseverance. Special thanks to William Schubert who gave detailed feedback on the history chapters. I would like to thank Naomi Rucker who gave thoughtful suggestions and listened to me for endless hours on the difficulties of working on this project. Finally, I would like to thank all the reviewers and the copyeditor for helping make this book a better one.

· 1 ·

INTRODUCTION

The concept of a guidebook evokes travel through unknown terrain. The purpose of this guidebook is to introduce students, professors, and teachers to current concepts and theoretical frameworks in the field of curriculum studies. Both undergraduates and graduate students will benefit from reading this book. Students, after studying this book, will broaden their knowledge base and better understand current debates around curriculum studies and education. In this chapter I explore the notion of travel as a metaphor for studying curriculum theory. I unpack my general approach to this book. I discuss various scholars who have influenced my thinking. Finally, brief chapter outlines will conclude this chapter.

Travel as Metaphor

The terrain of the field of curriculum studies is vast. Indeed, a guide is needed. Studying the configurations of the field can be bewildering. These configurations are always on the move. The field changes as new ideas arrive on the scene, as new scholars enter the field. Travel is an apt metaphor for a field that is in flux. It is difficult to write about something that changes continually. But this is the nature of academic work. I have tried to capture current discussions in the field even though I know that in the future the field will be different. Pinar et al. (1995) put it this way:

> Movement. From different traditions toward different ends each of the contemporary discourses points to an understanding of curriculum in terms of movement, even, we might say, velocity, knowledge prompting questioning that moves the student...from one "location" to another. (p. 858)

The aim of this guidebook is to evoke questions, not to settle things once and for all. Questions about the field of curriculum studies are always on the move. Scholars who work in this field raise a variety of questions that turn the field in different directions. Concepts and theoretical frameworks that shape the field shift over time. The student of curriculum studies is a traveler. A guidebook such as this one helps travelers find their way across difficult terrain. Ingrid Johnston (2003) states

> The very notion of travel presupposes a movement away from some place, a displacement, a rupture, a crossing of boundaries. A journey, like good research, has a powerful ability to dislodge the framework in which it is placed; it always takes us somewhere, but not necessarily where we planned to go. (p. 3)

Intellectual travel moves scholars and students "away" from the taken-for-granted. This field is theory-rich, deep, wide, and exciting. Getting ready to travel somewhere should be exhilarating. As Johnston suggests, traveling leads to places that "dislodge." Thought "dislodged" is what makes this field so exciting. Stanley Fish (2011) writes about the "twists and turns in the journey" of scholarship (p. 8). Curriculum studies has many "twists and turns" because it is a broad field with a variety of competing theoretical frameworks. And these frameworks change over time; none is written in stone. This guidebook explores the interstices of curriculum and history, politics, multiculturalism, gender, and literary studies. The second volume of the guidebook examines the interstices of curriculum with aesthetics, spirituality, cosmopolitanism, ecology, cultural studies, poststructuralism, and psychoanalytic theory. The terrain of curriculum studies is vast, as I mentioned earlier.

Sven Birkerts (2006) argues that thought is "a kind of narrative travel" (p. 13). Thinking through these competing theoretical frameworks in curriculum studies is an experience in "narrative travel." The narratives of each of these theoretical frameworks differ and change over time. Each different narrative tells a different tale. Travelers in the field of curriculum are introduced here to the complex intersections of current theories. John Sallis (2006) tells us that "travel narratives are oriented to...disclosive openings" (p. 1). Curriculum studies in all of its complexity encourages "openings" in interdisciplinary study. This is a wide open field. And this field could be configured in numerous ways. Every time a new theoretical framework is introduced new "openings" in thought emerge. Frederic Gros (2014) writes

> Walking through these new megalopolises [or new theoretical frameworks]...you passed through districts that were like different worlds, separate, apart. Everything could vary: the size and architectural style of the buildings, the quality and scent of the air, the way of living, the ambiance, the light, the social topography. (p. 176)

Curriculum in the interstices of history or the interstices of politics, for example, is akin to being in "different worlds." Each chapter of the guidebook takes travelers to different worlds, different "social topograph[ies]." And indeed "the size and architectural style" of theoretical frameworks "vary." For example, curriculum in the intersections of history is dauntingly enormous and "architecturally" speaking it is labyrinthine. Conversely, the "size and architectural style" of curriculum in its intersection with literary studies, for example, differ in "social topography" as it is smaller in size and has a different "ambience" than curriculum in the intersections of history. All of the chapters in this guidebook vary in size and ambience, if you will, depending on the current discussions in these areas.

Michel Serres (2000) writes

> No learning can avoid the voyage. Under the supervision of a guide, education pushes one to the outside. Depart: go forth. Leave the womb of your mother, the crib, the shadow cast by your father's house and the landscapes of your childhood. (p. 8)

This guidebook serves to "push" intellectual boundaries. Every chapter explores different aspects of curriculum which require, on the reader's part, an open mind. The guidebook pushes readers to travel outside their comfort zone. This voyage hopefully changes the way readers think. And changing thought and undoing habit are the purpose of education.

Curriculum studies is an interdisciplinary field. The notion of interdisciplinarity evokes travel between one's home discipline and fields outside of curriculum. Curriculum scholars travel back and forth between the field of curriculum studies and fields other than curriculum. Curriculum scholars are generalists, not specialists. Working in the interstices between, say, curriculum and psychoanalytic theory does not mean that one is a specialist or an expert in psychoanalysis. Curriculum scholars work in a third space between these two disciplines. Terry Eagleton (2003) captures the work of interdisciplinarity as he suggests that scholars are

> inside and outside a position at the same time [which I call the third space]—to occupy a territory while loitering…on the boundary—[this is]…where the most intensely creative ideas stem from. It is a resourceful place to be. (p. 40)

Curriculum scholars, then, travel between their own territories while moving toward a boundary. Not only do curriculum scholars move toward a boundary, say, in psychoanalysis, but cross over the boundary, with care, to do interdisciplinary work. There is always danger once crossing over the boundary because, again, curriculum theorists are generalists, not specialists in other fields. According to J. E. Malpus (2007), Ludwig Wittgenstein (1977) writes

> I am trying to conduct you on tours in a certain country. I will try to show that the philosophical difficulties [or curricular difficulties]…arise because we find ourselves in a strange town and do not know our way about. So we must learn the topography by going from one place to another, and so on. (cited in Malpus, p. 41)

Like philosophers, curriculum theorists too "find" themselves "in a strange town" while working in other fields. To some extent these strange towns remain strange. Interdisciplinary work is strange because one never finds a home in other fields but remains, in some sense, on the outskirts. Studying curriculum theory means that scholars travel "from one place to another," as Wittgenstein puts it. In this guidebook students are required to travel between curriculum and a variety of other fields. This is not easy work. But it is exciting work. Jacques Derrida (2002) writes

> Whether one wants it or not, one is always working in the mobility between several positions, stations, places, between which a shuttle is needed. The first image that comes to mind when one speaks of negotiation is that of the shuttle, *la navette*, and what the word conveys of a to-and-fro between two positions. (p. 12)

In interdisciplinary work scholars "negotiate" between "two positions." There is, in a way, a certain give and take when negotiating. For Derrida, negotiating means never finding one's home in any one discipline. But I find this rather problematic. It seems to me that Derrida does, in fact, have an intellectual home in poststructural philosophy. And, too, curriculum theorists have an intellectual home in curriculum studies. Interdisciplinary work is tricky because if the traveler-scholar spends too much time in other fields, she might

INTRODUCTION 5

lose her way and forget her home. This is why William Pinar (2007a) calls for more focus on disciplinarity because he worries that some curriculum scholars lose their way in other fields. At any rate, curriculum scholars must travel hither and yon—and then—come home again. Derrida (2002) suggests that this movement requires a "shuttle" (p. 12). What would that shuttle be? Perhaps the shuttle is a state of mind. Alain de Botton (2004) speaks to this issue as he says

> What, then, is a travelling mind-set? Receptivity might be said to be its chief characteristic. Receptive, we approach new places with humility. We carry with us no rigid ideas about what is or is not interesting. (p. 242)

Students of curriculum studies, then, must be receptive and humble when approaching other fields. Students interested in the intersections between curriculum and politics are sometimes not, for example, open to studying psychoanalytic literature because they think it is not a science. But as psychoanalyst Adam Phillips (2013) puts it, psychoanalysis is a form of poetics. Sometimes scientifically oriented students are not open to poetics. If students are wedded, for instance, to cognitive psychology, they have a difficult time thinking in metaphors. What kind of a shuttle, as Derrida puts it, is needed for students who are not receptive to new ideas? That remains an open question. Like de Botton (2004), Wittgenstein (1977) suggests that intellectual work requires a particular sort of mind-travel if you will. He states: "If you want to go down deep you do not need to travel far, indeed, you don't have to leave your most immediate and familiar surroundings" (p. 50e). For Wittgenstein, then, travel is an inner, psychological metaphor. Intellectual work demands soul searching—or inner travel. But unlike the philosopher, the curriculum theorist must leave her "familiar surroundings" and venture forth into other fields.

General Approach to this Guidebook

My approach to this guidebook is subjective. The chapters reflect my position on the state of the field. If someone else had written this book, different chapters would probably appear. This study is perspectival. This is by no means a comprehensive document on the field of curriculum studies. I write about what strikes me. I take the conversation in myriad directions and suggest ways in which the field might advance. Again, someone else would take the discussions in different directions. Jeffery Gray (2001) puts it this way: "Few serious readers believe any longer in a view from nowhere" (p. 51). This guidebook is, indeed, "a view" from somewhere. I take positions. I argue. I make suggestions. I explore new terrain and retrace old terrain in my own way. Madeleine Grumet (2006) writes

> I recognize that subjectivity is suspect. Our ways of speaking of it reveal the distrust and uneasiness that it evokes when it emerges in public discourse, as if some private internal fluid has begun to leak and threatens to leave a permanent stain. (pp. 71–72)

Traditional scholars who worked in the social sciences, say, twenty years ago prided themselves on objectivity. More poststructural social science scholars today argue that discourse is situated, partial, and incomplete. Objectivity is impossible. Surprisingly, these debates in the social sciences are not over, not finished. At any rate, I write from my perspective which is, again, situated, partial, and incomplete. William Pinar (2012) argues that curriculum scholars should have "subjective engagement with what we study" (p. 6). And as feminists remind us the personal is political. I have particular interests, particular tastes, and work in particular areas of the discipline. My worldview is limited of course. But I attempt in both volumes of these guidebooks to see things from a broad perspective. I have, for example, a particular interest in history, although I am not a curriculum historian. This explains why there are three rather lengthy chapters on curriculum in its intersection with historiography in volume 1. I also have a particular interest in psychoanalytic theory, which teaches that subjectivity and the study of the self are paramount to understanding scholarship. As Derrida might say traces of my personhood and personality are everywhere in these guidebooks. Robert Nash (2004) speaks to these issues as he states

> Ralph Waldo Emerson once said that it is impossible to utter even two or three sentences without letting others know where you stand in life, what you believe, and which people are important to you.... It's the recognition that you can never be fully outside your writing. (p. 24)

I write about theorists whom I find important in the field of curriculum studies; I write about theorists whom I find important in other fields as well. Books that evoke, that provoke, are the texts with which I grapple. There is nothing wrong with "letting others know where you stand in life." David Bleich and Deborah Holdstein (2001) argue that "one's own experience may well matter in one's way of announcing knowledge" (p. 2). How does one detach one's experience from one's writing? Is that even possible? And if so, why would a scholar want to do that? Scholarship is shot through with personal experience, even if that personal experience is not explicit in the text at hand. Alberto Manguel (1996) speaks to these issues here:

> Like every reader, [and I would add any writer] Rilke was also reading [and writing] through his own experience. Beyond the literal sense and the literary meaning, the text we read acquires the projection of our own experience, the shadow, as it were, of who we are. (p. 267)

Reading and writing about curriculum studies and fleshing out a variety of theoretical frameworks reflects my experience. For example, I write in this guidebook about the intersections of curriculum and politics. I am not a political scholar, but I have written about political implications of the Holocaust (Morris, 2001) and European history during the fin-de-siècle (Morris, 2006). These books inform my take on issues of representation, on European debates about fascism, and on Jewish identity. Thus, my previous books shape my writing of this guidebook. Sven Birkerts (2006) remarks that "serious reading [and writing] is above all an agency of self-making" (p. 87). Writing these guidebooks has been a daunting endeavor to say the least. I believe that the experience of delving into many areas has broadened my perspective not only of the field but in life. Harold Bloom (2001) writes that "one of the uses of reading [and writing] is to prepare ourselves for change" (p. 21). I must say that writing these guidebooks has changed me, especially in my writing practices, especially in the revision stages. Endless revisions taught me much about the virtue of patience. And more important I see the world differently now. I have a broader perspective on life. I understand the field better now. I think more about the craft of language and the care of words. Not that I didn't do this before, but now these issues have become more focused. Wittgenstein (1977) states

> Working in philosophy [and I would add curriculum studies]—like work in architecture in many respects—is really more a working on oneself. One's own interpretation. On one's way of seeing things. (p. 16e)

Like Wittgenstein, William Pinar, throughout his work, suggests, too, that scholarship is about working on the self. The self-work, if you will, becomes public when the work is published. Thus, working on the self is not merely a narcissistic exercise. David Jardine (1998) writes that "the interpretation is thus unavoidably linked to *me*" (p. 44). My interpretation of the texts examined in this guidebook is "unavoidably linked to me." My interpretation might be very different from someone else's interpretation. This might seem commonsensical but it is not. Interpretation is personal and political. Interpretation is psychological. Interpretation is socially constructed and culturally mediated. Terry Eagleton (2013) says

> Literary works [and here too I would add work done in curriculum studies] may best be seen not as texts with a fixed sense, but as matrices capable of generating a whole range of possible meanings. They do not so much contain meaning as produce it. (p. 144)

The purpose of interpreting texts is indeed to produce knowledge. Scholars, by fleshing out passages, by arguing certain points, by comparing and contrasting other texts are producing knowledge. But again these knowledges are perspectival and, in fact—as Eagleton (2013) suggests—texts can "generate a whole range" of "meanings." There is little consensus, for example, in curriculum studies on theoretical frameworks. The way I see the field is very different from the way someone else sees the field. The theoretical frameworks that I have chosen for these guidebooks are not fixed in stone. There are many ways of seeing the field. The theoretical frameworks that I chose to work on were ones that I thought represented the current scene in curriculum studies. But different scholars might have chosen different theoretical frameworks. I chose books that I thought were notable in the field. Others might have chosen different books to work on. Nadine Gordimer (2003) states:

> A journey through realms of how far, wide and deep writing can venture in the endless perspectives that you have to find your way to yours, at the urge of the most powerful sense of yourself—creativity. (p. 60)

There are endless perspectives on what constitutes the discipline of curriculum studies. There are endless perspectives on which theoretical frameworks should be used when talking about curriculum. At the end of the day, as Gordimer explains, it is creativity above all that allows writers to write what they do. I see scholarship, at bottom, as a creative adventure. I do think that to advance a field scholars must be creative in finding new ways of talking about issues. Interpretation, too, is a creative adventure. In fact, Umberto Eco (2012) says that "a text is a machine conceived for eliciting interpretations" (p. 6). I hope this guidebook opens spaces for a multitude of interpretations.

Theorizing Curriculum

There are many ways of theorizing curriculum. And there are many things to think about when it comes to theory, generally speaking. In fact, Verlyn Klinkenborg (2013) says

> Every work of literature [or curriculum studies] is the result of thousands and thousands of decisions. Intricate, minute decisions—this word or that, here or where, now or later, again and again. It's the living tissue of a writer's choices. (p. 33)

Scholars—like novelists or poets—make "thousands and thousands of decisions." It is not enough to have ideas. One must write about these ideas. One must communicate these ideas. Not only that. Scholars might think about writing more eloquently or even poetically. But most scholars do not concern themselves with eloquence or poetics. Finding the right words is a beginning. This is difficult. And as Klinkenborg puts it, writers have an infinite amount of choices to make. Revisions are about making new choices. To revise means to change your mind. This guidebook, for example, went through many, many, many revisions! My goal in rewriting passages was to make for a more readable book. I do not consider myself a writer per se, but a scholar who struggles with language. And what a struggle it is. John Dewey (1991) remarks in his book *How We Think*

> Thinking [or curriculum theorizing] begins in what might be called a *forked-road* situation, a situation which is ambiguous, which presents a dilemma, which proposes alternatives. As long as our activity glides smoothly along from one thing to another, or as long as we permit our imagination to entertain fancies at pleasure, there is no call for reflection. Difficulty or obstruction in the way of reaching a belief brings us, however, to a pause. In the suspense of uncertainty, we metaphorically climb a tree. (p. 11)

Theorizing curriculum is that "*forked-road* situation." There are times when scholars do not know which road to take. There are many dead ends. And there are many false starts. It is interesting to note that Dewey suggests that thinking takes place in difficulties and in uncertainty. Nothing is clear cut in scholarship. Oftentimes you cannot find your way. But then—after much study and work—you do find your way. Patience and frustration are, at least for me, the root of theorizing. Perseverance helps. Yet one can still be unsure of where one is going.

Like Dewey, Jorge Luis Borges—according to Umberto Eco (1995)—also uses the metaphor of forking paths when it comes to writing. This way, or that, which road to take? Sometimes it is so hard to know where to go next. Alberto Manguel (1996) and Geoffrey Hartman (1982) talk about the labyrinthine nature of reading and writing. This image is of importance to me because in the first three chapters on history in this guidebook, I wanted to make the experience of reading feel like being in a labyrinth, to somehow capture the nonlinearity of history. This more postmodern approach reflects lived experience. Nothing happens in a straight line. Life is like an ongoing tangent. Nothing is finished. Things seem chaotic. History is happening all around us but to try to capture the past—as well as the present—is nearly impossible. Madeleine Grumet (2006) says, "Theory is in constant flux" (p. 67). History is in constant flux. So is life. So too are academic fields. Curriculum theory is continually changing. Theoretical frameworks, too, are continually changing. But, as Jonathan Culler (2011) points out, there is more to theory than change. He states

> Treating contemporary theory as a set of competing approaches or methods of interpretation misses much of its interest and force, which comes from its broad challenge to common sense, and from its explorations of how meaning is created and human identities take shape. (p. xi)

Theorizing evokes, provokes, and even surprises. Theorizing interrupts "common sense."

Janet Miller (2005) suggests that "theoretical frameworks and perspectives enable curricularists to analyze, critique [and] rewrite" (p. 207). Theoretical frameworks help scholars not only to rewrite texts but advance the field by doing novel things. Theoretical frameworks help scholars to organize thoughts. Petra Munro Hendry (2011) writes that "curriculum is constituted of infinite discourses" (p. 6). Students might feel overwhelmed by the sheer number of ways to talk about curriculum. Janet Miller seems unmoored by what she calls a "riotous array of theoretical stances" (p. 207) in curriculum studies. There are indeed many ways of theorizing curriculum, and this is what makes the field so exciting and vibrant. Michel Foucault (1994) suggests that ordering concepts—or I would add putting into place theoretical frameworks—is completely arbitrary. Foucault states that "there is nothing more tentative, nothing more empirical…than the process of establishing an order among things" (p. xix). Thus, Foucault suggests that, in fact, there is no order to anything. Scholars impose order where there is chaos. Scholars impose order to attempt to make sense of a complex world. Alberto Manguel (2006) speaks to this point. He says

> And yet, with bewildering optimism, we continue to assemble whatever scraps of information we can gather in scrolls and books and computer chips, on shelf after library shelf, whether material, virtual or otherwise, pathetically intent on lending the world a semblance of sense and order, while knowing perfectly well that, however much we'd like to believe the contrary, our pursuits are sadly doomed to failure. (p. 3)

The world, for Manguel, does not make sense and there is no order to it. However, most chaos theorists believe that there is both order and chaos in the universe. But lived experience can seem rather chaotic. Sometimes the more one plans things, the more things fall apart. Teachers can have great lesson plans but sometimes things unravel in the classroom. One wonders if there is any order to thinking. Probably not. And this is why academic writing is so difficult. Scholars must impose order on thought.

John Sallis (2006) asks: "How is it that thoughts arrive, that they come as if from nowhere" (p. 71)? But thoughts do come from somewhere. They arrive out of our own subjectivities. Who you are, how you've lived, what experiences you've had all go into the arrival of thoughts. Scholars put thoughts to work and order thoughts so as to make sense of the world even though little sense can be made. Niran Abbas (2005) says that in order to begin to understand the world, it might be helpful to map things out. Abbas tells us

> Acts of mapping are creative, sometimes anxious, moments in coming to knowledge of the world, and the map is both the spatial embodiment of knowledge and a stimulus to further cognitive engagements. (p. 1)

Theoretical frameworks serve to map the discipline of curriculum studies. If scholars do not map their worlds or organize their worlds, fields would not advance.

The (Post)Reconceptualization

I approach the material in this guidebook from a position dubbed the (post) reconceptualization. William Pinar reconceptualized the field of curriculum studies in the 1970s. A groundbreaking book on the reconceptualization was initially released in the 1970s called *Toward a Poor Curriculum*, co-written by

William Pinar and Madeleine Grumet. This book has recently been reissued. In the 2006 reissue of this text, Pinar states

> We wrote these essays to express our resistance to the mind numbing bureaucracy of the accountability of the times: behavioral objectives, and to propose a humanities methodology as an alternative to the social science inquiries that were dominating educational research. (p. vii)

Pinar and Grumet wanted to move away from curriculum design toward understanding curriculum in a more phenomenological, psychological sense. In *Toward a Poor Curriculum* Grumet and Pinar (2006) introduce also the importance of integrating politics, spirituality, existential, phenomenological, and psychoanalytic theoretical frameworks into curriculum studies.

In *Toward a Poor Curriculum* Pinar introduces the concept of *currere*. This is the Latin root of curriculum. Currere has four psychological movements: the regressive, progressive, analytical, and synthetical. Currere is a psychological concept that points to examining one's past, one's future, to take apart and study one's life, and then synthesize and put things back together again. This is a foundational concept for curriculum studies. The upshot of currere is that scholars must look inward to do curriculum work. One must understand the self before engaging in theory. In 1995 William Pinar, William Reynolds, Patrick Slattery, and Peter Taubman co-wrote *Understanding Curriculum*, which expanded theoretical frameworks in order to understand curriculum in more complex ways. To reconceptualize the field in more depth and breadth Pinar et al. (1995) fleshed out the following theoretical frameworks: history, politics, race, gender, phenomenology, poststructuralism, deconstruction, autobiography, biography, aesthetics, theology, institutionalized text, and internationalized text. It is interesting to note that Pinar (1998a) points out in his edited collection *Curriculum: Toward New Identities* that "new configurations are now appearing" (p. x). Notice that the field had already begun to change three years after *Understanding Curriculum* was written. Pinar suggests, in fact, that as time marches on "another reconceptualization" might emerge in the future. Today a new generation of curriculum scholars are calling the present field the post-reconceptualization. Erik Malewski (2010) suggests that the post-reconceptualization is "moving away from traditional representations of the field and toward juxtapositions of perspectives in order to incite a multiplicity of readings" (p. xiii). Malewski points out that the post-reconceptualization does not mean that the reconceptualization is over, that is, post. Malewski says that he wants to "disrupt the notion that next moments in the field belong to a single generation or that post-reconceptualization necessarily be interpreted as that which comes after reconceptualization" (p. xiii). I would concur with Malewski's position. For me the concept (post)reconceptualization suggests that, in a sense, the reconceptualization is over and yet traces of it exist and new configurations of the field continually emerge and change. Thus I prefer to use (post) to designate the overlap between what occurred in the initial phases of the reconceptualization and the work being done today. (Post) does not mean the reconceptualization is gone, it merely means that it has changed and will continue to change. Postcolonial scholar Homi K. Bhabha (1994) states

> It is the trope of our times to locate the question of culture in the realm of the *beyond*.... . Our existence today is marked by a tenebrous sense of survival, living on the borderlines of the "'present'", for which there seems to be no proper name other than the current and controversial shiftiness of the prefix "'post'": postmodernism, postcolonialism, postfeminism. (p. 1)

Like Bhabha, N. Katherine Hayles (2005) writes about the posthuman and even the postbiological (p. 2). The posthuman does not mean that the human is dead, obviously. What it does mean is that humanism is problematic for many reasons. Humans are not the center of the world. Rather, for posthuman scholars, human beings are in continuum with nonhuman animals and with machines. Humanism does not take into account other creatures or machines and the ways in which humans are enmeshed in a complicated world. Similarly, postcolonialism does not mean that colonization is dead. It still exists but in different forms. Even if the colonizers have left, the impact of colonialization is still alive as it damages generations of people psychologically.

For me the (post)reconceptualization overlaps with the reconceptualization in some ways as curriculum scholars still draw on theoretical frameworks fleshed out in 1995 in *Understanding Curriculum*. More specifically, history, politics, gender, race, poststructuralism, and aesthetics are still strong configurations of the field. As I see it, though, (post)reconceptualization scholars also draw on such theoretical frameworks as the literary, the cosmopolitical, postcolonialism, spirituality, cultural studies, ecology and psychoanalytic theory. I explore all of these frameworks across both volumes of the guidebooks.

A Note on Style

Curriculum theorists do not usually talk about their style of writing. It seems to be a taken for granted assumption that academics write in the same style. But this is not so. There are many ways to write academic papers and books. Yet not many pay attention to how they write, they just write. However, over the years I have been wondering about this issue. This topic could make for an interesting debate. At any rate, I think that social scientists and academics coming out of the humanities do have different styles. I have never considered myself to be a social scientist. Most of my training has been in the humanities. And as I see it curriculum studies is more like the humanities than the social sciences. William Pinar (2012) tells us that curriculum studies is "informed by theory in the humanities, arts, and interpretive social sciences" (p. 1).

Talking about style in academe seems to be beside the point. But I think this is an important debate that scholars should have. Truman Capote (*Paris Review*, 2006) speaks to this issue as he says: "What is style? And what, as the Zen Koan asks, is the sound of one hand? No one really *knows*; yet either you *know* or you don't.... . I suppose style is the mirror of an artist's [and I would add curriculum scholar's] sensibility" (p. 29). Capote suggests that style is not "consciously arrived at, any more than one arrives at the color of one's eyes" (p. 30). The question of style remains a mystery. I write the way I write. My background has shaped the way I write.

Helen Sword (2012) comments

> For many academics, "stylish academic writing" is at best an oxymoron and at worst a risky business. Why, they ask, should we accessorize our research with gratuitous stylish flourishes? Doesn't overt attention to style signal intellectual shallowness... . And won't colleagues reject as unserious any academic writing that deliberately seeks to engage. (p. vii)

Some social scientists feel that scholars who are unserious do not draw on statistics. Some social scientists feel that scholars who use the pronoun 'I' are not being scientific. Some social scientists feel that academic work should be flat, transparent, and to the point. As Sword says above if you engage texts with personal flair, you won't be taken seriously. I do engage with texts in my own personal style. I work diligently to make my scholarship readable, clear, and sometimes poetic. Geoffrey Hartman (1982) remarks that "the question of style, literary or philosophical, is crucial, for there are many who still insist that the best philosophers [and I would add curriculum scholars] have no style" (p. xxiv). What is the style of no style, I wonder? A flat, dry unreadable text is not my idea of good scholarship.

Eric Hayot (2014) says

> I don't care whether you write just like me. I care whether you write just like you— that you come to scholarly prose with both purpose and intention, that you take it seriously as a craft, that you understand how and why you do what you do, that you strive to do more than reproduce the stylistic average of your age and experience. And that you follow, in the long run, the path that you make. (p. 4)

The path that I have made has perhaps been an eccentric one. My writing style is perhaps idiosyncratic. I want to write who I am. Certainly there are people who have influenced my style and there are writers I love to read because I love their style and I identify with what they say. Adam Phillips, Donna Haraway, Jacques Derrida, Michel Serres, Christopher Bollas, Mary Aswell Doll, and William Pinar are all writers I love to read. These individuals write beautiful books and take great care with language and are thoughtful and speak to issues with which I identify. Still, at the end of the day, I do not write like any of these scholars. I write who I am.

Unlike most academics, Michel Serres (2000) feels that having a style is a good thing, not a bad thing. Serres tells us that style is something one attains only after hard work. He states that "the writer does not attain style until after such preliminary traversals, in the same way that a philosopher arrives at a thought after long journeys in the country of the encyclopedia" (p. 72). Serres has a controversial style. He is a philosopher of science but he does not write like a traditional scientist. His style is poststructural and even at times nonsensical or playful. Playful prose in academe is frowned upon. He certainly has his own unique style.

Some scholars might think that guidebooks, handbooks, textbooks should have no style. Some feel that these kinds of books should be written from the third person. Some feel that the writer's personality gets in the way of the 'facts.' I engage in interpretation, I take positions. I write from my gut and feel strongly about taking care with language. For me scholarly writing is not that much different from writing imaginative literature. Scholars must use imagination to write. For me scholarship is an art form.

The Influence of Others

This guidebook did not come out of nowhere. There are several books in the field that have influenced my thinking, and it is important to acknowledge them here. Michel de Certeau (1988) writes about the scholar who forgets his history. He states:

> In "forgetting" the collective inquiry in which he is inscribed, in isolating the object of his discourse from its historical genesis, an "author" in effect denies his real situation. He creates the fiction of a place of his own… . In spite of the contradictory ideologies that may accompany it, the setting aside of subject-object relation or of the discourse-object relation is the abstraction that generates an illusion of "authorship." It removes the traces of belonging to a network. (p. 44)

Scholarship is deeply communal. Of course writing is a lone act, but books keep us company and inform the work at hand. Graduate students are profoundly influenced by their professors; students are profoundly influenced by their teachers. Colleagues influence thought. An acknowledgement of gratitude is in order. Scholars do not write in a vacuum. As de Certeau points out writers "belong to a network."

Curriculum scholars belong to a network. I want to mention books in the field that have influenced my thinking while working on this guidebook. Connelly, He, and Phillon's (2008) book, *The SAGE Handbook of Curriculum and Instruction*, maps out the field of curriculum in a very different way than I do. But this difference inspired me. Briefly, the *Sage Handbook* is rather traditional in that its focus is on curriculum design. There are, however, some chapters that deal with postcolonialism, multiculturalism, and politics. Most of the chapters in the book have little in common with the work being done by (post)reconceptualization scholars. Yet, there is one chapter on internationalization by William Pinar—who founded the reconceptualization. David Flinders and Stephen Thornton co-edited the book *The Curriculum Studies Reader*, and its second edition was printed in 2004. This text is closer to what one might expect to see in the (post)reconceptualization literature. In the second edition, these editors added Jane Addams as a curriculum historian of note alongside Dewey, Counts, Bobbitt, and Kliebard. In Flinders and Thornton's section on the reconceptualization, they include Mortimer Adler's *Paideia Proposal* and Nel Nodding's critique. Adler's "proposal" is a throwback to the classics or what is called the Great Books Tradition. Why Flinders and Thornton included Adler's work under the heading of the reconceptualization is curious. In the last part of the book these co-editors include scholars who discuss a variety of important issues such as AIDS education, women's issues, gender issues, gay issues, literacy, multiculturalism, and issues of place. I treat some of these issues in the guidebook. Dan Marshall (2007) heads up the book *Turning Points*, which contextualizes curriculum history in current affairs. This is certainly an interesting way to write about the history of curriculum. My approach to curriculum history is very different from Marshall's. However, it is important to remember that history is always written from the present. William Schubert (2002) headed up a work called *Curriculum Books: The First Hundred Years*. This is a good reference book for students. This book has some interesting commentary on curriculum books and serves as an important bibliographic and archival source. Another impressive bibliographic and archival source is Craig Kridel's (2010) *Encyclopedia of Curriculum Studies*, Volumes 1 and 2.

The most influential book—for me—was co-written by William Pinar, William Reynolds, Patrick Slattery, and Peter Taubman (1995) called *Understanding Curriculum: An Introduction to the Study of Historical and Contemporary Curriculum Discourses*. The organization and structure of my guidebooks were influenced by the organization and structure of *Understanding Curriculum*. However, in my guidebooks the content, approach, and style differ significantly from *Understanding Curriculum*. The configuration of the field has changed since 1995 and my guidebooks reflect some of those changes. It is important to note that my take on the field is probably different from someone else's. If someone else had written these guidebooks the theoretical frameworks, more than likely, would be different from mine.

Brief Chapter Outlines

In chapter 2, "Historical Curriculum Concepts, Part 1," I theorize curriculum historiography. I do this because the field of curriculum studies has been—historically—atheoretical and ahistorical. Most historians do not theorize their subject matter. As a curriculum theorist, I feel very strongly that history should be theorized. In the second section of this chapter I drive a wedge between what I call traditional educational history and curriculum historiography. I also address questions around what counts as curriculum historiography.

In chapter 3, "Historical Curriculum Concepts, Part 2," I explore issues of gender and race in the context of the common school. I argue that many traditional educational historians exclude women and minorities from their discussions. I discuss women's contributions to progressive education through examining case studies as well as biographies. In this chapter I introduce some debates around progressive education.

In chapter 4, "Historical Curriculum Concepts, Part 3," I suggest that scholars broaden what counts as curriculum historiography. Here, I move beyond traditional histories that deal primarily with the schoolhouse. In this chapter I write about what I call biography as history of the other, autobiography as history of the self. I unpack what I call intellectual retrospectives of notable books on curriculum. Finally, I examine historical trauma and unpack the concept of "witnessing" and its relevance to curriculum.

In chapter 5, "Political Curriculum Concepts," I look at the problematics of neoliberalism and the ways in which neoliberalism has affected schooling practices, as well as neoconservatism and the battles over whose knowledge is of most worth. I explore poststructural politics, drawing on the works of Michel Foucault and Jacques Derrida and then turn to critical theory and Marx to further deepen the discussion on neoliberalism and neoconservatism. I also examine debates around the concepts of fascism, authoritarianism, and militarism as they relate to neoliberal politics. Finally, I examine the politics of postformalism, school shootings, and what I call the politics of emotion.

In chapter 6, "Multicultural Curriculum Concepts," I outline a brief overview of multicultural education. I discuss some of the origins of multiculturalism and theoretical frameworks for studying multiculturalism. Many scholars organize multicultural education differently than I have. I write about what I consider to be some of the most pressing issues educators must grapple with today. The major threads of multiculturalism that I examine here are whiteness studies, Latino/a studies, Islamophobia, Black/Feminist/Womanist studies, and disability studies.

In chapter 7, "Gender Curriculum Concepts," I take the discussion in three directions. Here I briefly look at feminism, as the main concept for feminism is gender. Then I explore what is called masculinity studies, and finally I write about queer theory. I argue that—at the end of the day—feminism, masculinity studies, and queer theory should be thought of together but for the sake of organization I separate them out for clarity.

In chapter 8, "Literary Curriculum Concepts," I write about the interconnections among reading, writing, and thinking, writing and the imagination, what I call eco-poesis, identity and difference, and memory and history as they pertain to the literary. I discuss the possible cathartic effects of reading, writing, and thought. It is important to note that this chapter is not on literacy, but on the literary. For me, literacy means the study of how to read and better comprehend. The literary, contrarily, is about studying literary texts, that is, imaginative fiction, in their relation to curriculum studies.

· 2 ·
HISTORICAL CURRICULUM CONCEPTS, PART 1

Theorizing Curriculum Historiography

The aim of the first section of this chapter is to theorize curriculum historiography. The second section deals with outlining differences between what I call traditional educational history and curriculum historiography. What counts as curriculum historiography and who writes historiography are serious questions that will be addressed. My approach to curriculum historiography is perspectival and theoretical.

The Curriculum Scholar Thinking through the Past

When I think through what it means to be a curriculum scholar, many things come to mind. Although there might be little agreement on what it means to be a curriculum scholar, one thing is clear. William Pinar (2010) points out that "what we curriculum studies scholars have in common is not the present but the past" (p. 528). Curriculum scholars owe a debt of gratitude to those who have gone before us. Younger generations need to understand that the work that is being done today in curriculum studies has been made possible by generations of scholars who took risks in their careers to challenge the status quo and do new things.

Doing what is new in the academy is not easy nor is it welcomed. Younger generations need to continue to take risks to keep this field vibrant and alive and pave the way for future generations. But in order to pave the way, younger scholars must know their curriculum history. Without a sense of the past, the present and future make little sense. Madeleine Grumet (2010) emphasizes that "we do not only point forward, we also point back to interpret our histories" (p. 407). What strikes me in Grumet's passage is the call toward interpretation. Historiographies are interpreted. What story (of the past) scholars choose to tell depends upon particular interests.

The telling of history depends on who the teller is. Curriculum history, first and foremost, is a task not of reporting but, as William Pinar points out, of understanding (Pinar, Reynolds, Slattery, & Taubman, 1995). Pinar (2007) states, "The intellectual labor of understanding—the labor of comprehension, critique, and reconceptualization—constitutes the discipline of disciplinarity" (p. xii). The word "understanding" is profound. How many of us really understand in a deep sense our own histories, let alone the history of a field as complex as curriculum studies? The undertaking of understanding—when grappling with the complexity of this field—is enormous. This undertaking requires discipline. To understand a discipline requires erudition and that takes a tremendous amount of commitment. I am reminded of Hannah Arendt (1994) who says, "What is important for me is to understand. For me, writing is a matter of seeking this understanding, part of the process of understanding [is that]...[c]ertain things get formulated" (p. 3). What strikes me about Arendt is her suggestion that understanding, first off, must be sought out. The act of understanding means writing about that understanding. Writing is no easy task! But through writing, thoughts begin to emerge. As Arendt points out, understanding means formulating ideas. However, formulating ideas does not mean that they are neat and tidy or even clear. Scholars must attempt to make sense of ideas but the act of understanding is always limited. Jerome Kohn (1994) comments that Arendt

> was not primarily concerned with solving problems; her ceaseless ventures in understanding were for her no more "instrumental" than life itself. What is more difficult to grasp is that the activity of understanding afforded her a measure of reconciliation to the world in which she lived. (p. x)

The point of understanding curriculum history is not instrumental. I am not writing about the history of curriculum in order to solve problems, to get answers, to fix the schools. However, studying curriculum history is worth doing because it educates us about our past. The field has no future if it does not have a past.

The Notion of the Past

The notion of the "past" is not a simple one. This is a notion that demands theorization. What does the past mean? Our relation to the past is not simple. This relation to the past is a generational one. Understanding links between generations is highly problematic. When studying historiography scholars are studying a certain rendition of the past, a certain interpretation of that history. Petra Munro Hendry (2010) asks: "What makes this history possible, what identities does it make available" (p. 498)? Interesting questions indeed. Munro Hendry is asking what makes certain configurations of the past possible and how representations of identity shape those configurations. Alongside Munro Hendry, I would ask, what makes this *interpretation* of this history possible and what does that interpretation do to one's subjectivity? It is the interpretation of that history that is important. As researchers work through their scholarship it changes them. How does studying one's history change the self? How does studying curriculum historiography change the curriculum theorist? Where do our interpretations come from? Why do scholars interpret the past in the way they do? Scholars work in the present to think through the past. This is a complex undertaking. What is the relation between the present and the past, between working in the now and thinking about the "then" of history? According to Michael Jennings (2008), for Walter Benjamin—whose work is primarily about thinking through historicity—

> who we are, the character of the physical environment in which we move, and the character of the historical moment in which we live—are in fact denied to us. (p. 11)

How is it that people do not understand the "historical moment" of the present? If the present is difficult to grasp, how are people to understand the past? Here is the complication that Benjamin sets up. When you are in the middle of a forest, you cannot see through the trees; sometimes you cannot find your way out. Being thrown into the middle of the present historical moment presents certain difficulties. How, for example, to explain to our children and grandchildren that horrible day when the World Trade Center Towers were destroyed? How is one to explain the feeling of that dreadful day and how to make sense of it now that it is in the past? The event, perhaps, is still too close in time to make much sense of it. Present generations have lived through the worst attack on American soil. How to make sense of the magnitude of this historical catastrophe? It will take generations to sort out this catastrophe, and yet still, in generations to come, there will always be questions, confusion, and anger over what happened. Being thrown into the middle of a catastrophe confounds, especially when one is too close historically to the event at hand. Yet, on the other hand, scholars should attempt to study historically what has happened and attempt to understand, even at the limits of understanding. The future forever in the United States—and the world for that matter—is one of grave uncertainty because of the rise of global terrorism. Thus, understanding the present in relation to the past is highly problematic because of the limits of understanding of either the present or the past. Through study and patience, the past can reveal certain things. The present moment is not all a haze of confusion. There are some illuminations at hand, although most of what is experienced is dimly understood.

Curriculum Studies and the Historical

It has been noted by many in curriculum studies that the field has historically been ahistorical. Pinar and colleagues (1995) mention this in *Understanding Curriculum*. Pinar also stresses this fact in a more recent work, stating,

> Despite its centrality in efforts to understand the present, curriculum history remains underdeveloped in a field traumatized by malevolent politicians and undermined by opportunistic colleagues. The present field is not entirely ahistorical…it remains, however, plagued by an ameliorative orientation. (2010, p. 528)

My project here is about historicality. I deal specifically with texts that concern the history of the field and texts that deal with issues on doing historiography. William Pinar's (2007) turn toward what he calls "verticality"—or the historicity of the field—must be considered seriously. It is our professional obligation to make sure that students understand the history of this field. Interdisciplinarity, Pinar (2007) points out, has become a problem for our field. It would behoove curriculum scholars to study our field before venturing out to other disciplines. Of course, interdisciplinarity is important: curriculum studies is also an interdisciplinary field. But first and foremost, curriculum scholars must know their own history. Dwayne Huebner (1999) complained about this very problem in 1967. He states: "The curriculum person needs to be chided for his ahistoricalism" (p. 133). Huebner points out that Jim Macdonald began the work toward making this field more historical. Huebner explains

> Jim [Macdonald] began his work before interest developed in the history of curriculum. In fact, it was the next generation of curriculum scholars, the students of Jim and of his colleagues and peers, who attended to the history of the field. They did so, in part because of the questions that Jim was asking. His work might have taken a different tack if the historical work had seriously started before the 1950s. (p. 354)

As students of curriculum know, Macdonald's (1995) work is about "theory as a prayerful act." Perhaps scholars can think of theorizing curriculum history as a prayerful act as well. The theorizing of this history is crucial. Too much historical writing tends toward being atheoretical, a fact long pointed out by feminist historians such as Joan Scott (1999) and Sue Morgan (2006). Historians are suspicious of theory just as they are suspicious of victim narratives (Morris, 2001). Theory and victim narratives have something in common; however, they both disturb the flow of the "facts" of history, the "facts" of a positivistic history. History is socially constructed. This does not mean events did not occur, but what it does mean is that events get interpreted and those interpretations are socially constructed narratives. This doesn't make the event any less real. Events happen. But the way in which events get interpreted is highly complex.

The Time of Historicality

Dwayne Huebner (1999) has taught much about the importance of thinking historically when thinking through curriculum theory. Huebner states, "It does seem obvious that education must be concerned with man's temporality" (p. 135). As I read Huebner I see the influence of Martin Heidegger's *Being and Time* (1962). Heidegger's major theme in that text is that if being is really becoming and becoming is always on the move, then being is inextricably related to time and time is inextricably related to historicality. Studying Huebner, I have found at least thirteen references to historicality in his collection of essays. Obviously, this was a major issue for him.

The difference between history as a discipline and the discipline of curriculum theory is that when curriculum theorists think through history, they think *theoretically* through it. Thinking history theoretically is something

I want to emphasize here to make a point. Historiography is not mere description, although description is important. But historiography, too, is about theorizing that description. Speculative thought, however, seems foreign to most historians, since their method of analysis works against this. But a historiography without theory is not thought through enough. Thick description—the catchphrase for anthropologists and ethnographers—needs theorizing. Much thickly described history tends to remain undertheorized. Curriculum theorists can work to correct this problem as they think history theoretically. Curriculum scholars must ask questions about the traditional categories and language in which historiography is written; otherwise, our own historical work becomes unthought and problematic, mired in presuppositions. Historiography remains forever stuck in a rut if researchers do not ask questions about the way the past gets talked about. What is the past? This is the kind of question that many historians take for granted and do not ask at least explicitly. Petra Munro (1998a) tells us that "Hannah Arendt (1954) maintains [that] history is itself a concept that must be historicized" (p. 285).

Doing history today is different from doing history during Herodotus's time, for example. Today embellishments and flowery language are considered anathema for traditional historians. Not so for Herodotus. Perhaps scholars—who are not bound by the rules and methods of traditional historians—are freer to do what they want when interpreting the past. Curriculum historians (who are historians by training) are bound by certain rules and methods that do not bind others of us who are not historians per se. The historian gathers her evidence in the archives and uses primary source documents to make a case. The scholar who thinks historically might also draw on primary sources but in addition pulls from secondary literature and draws on her own theoretical talents to glean what she can from the texts at hand. Again, traditional historians are wary of theorizing.

Time and the Archive of the Past

Time is a complex idea. One has to be a mathematician to really understand what time means. Or time can be felt phenomenologically. The feeling of time is always in flux. So too is a narrative of history. Archives are collections of material that are gathered up at a certain time in history. But what exactly does the archive mean or what is its purpose for the scholar? The archive continually changes, as Jacques Derrida (1996) tells us. As soon as a particular aspect of history is grasped, things change. How to capture a changing narrative? That is the conundrum. Trying to capture what has gone on in the field of curriculum studies since 1996, say, is like trying to capture a wild horse running. The past is continually changing as more and more of the archive-of-the-past is uncovered via study. But at every corner a new book has been written; another journal article needs to be read and deconstructed and then there is always more. As Dwayne Huebner (1999) tells us, "There is more than we know, can know, will ever know. It is a 'moreness' that takes us by surprise when we are at the edge and end of our knowing" (p. 403). This "moreness" about which Huebner speaks is profound and mystical. Can historical time and the archive of that historical time also be considered mystical time? For a historian, perhaps not: there is little about traditional historiography that is mystical. But let this historiography be mystical, let the knowing as well as the unknowing be a mystery. Honoring the ancestors in many spiritual traditions is a ritual not taken lightly. This kind of a textbook is a way to honor our curriculum studies ancestors. The archive then is about our ancestors.

Archiving the Ancestors: A Plurality of Time(s)

The archive of the ancestors eludes—at times—because it is, in reality, a multiple archive. Think about a field of study; much goes on at the same time(s). Time is not singular but plural; history is not linear but labyrinthine. Sylviane Agacinski (2003) addresses this point. She declares:

> The permanent kinetic flux [of historical time] is animated by an infinite number of movements, that is, by different temporalities and also by separate rhythms. Not only does nothing escape time, but there also are an infinite number of times, or *tempos*, which makes it hard for us to define an epoch, or a history, since they go together. (p. 15)

What is striking in Agacinski's passage above concerns the notion of rhythms in historical time. After studying the field of curriculum studies in depth, it becomes evident that various segments of the field have their own rhythms. Each configuration of the field differs in feel, scope, and breadth. Some segments have longer histories than others, some have more breadth than others. This book, then, will reflect these variations, so the chapter lengths in the book will depend on the breadth of that particular segment. What I propose to do in the various sections of this book is make suggestions about where the field might be broadened or deepened by drawing on other literatures and suggesting further reading in these literatures so as to advance the field. If the various segments of the field are represented seemingly unevenly it is because the segments are uneven and move along at different paces and rhythms. Some of the segments are larger than others, some are less fleshed out, but all are of importance. Thus, I will try to make suggestions about where curriculum scholars might look to find source material to broaden and deepen the field.

Histories as Multiplicities

Again, as Agacinski (2003) discusses, the feel of historical time is various. Different historical times move along beside one another; this makes for a complex problem. Like Agacinski, Sol Cohen (1999) remarks that history happens in multiplicities. Cohen teaches us

> At this point, I think we have to acknowledge, first, the multidimensionality of historical reality and, second, we have to say that those who have no knowledge of histories of education [I would add here histories of curriculum studies] can believe any history of education [or any history of curriculum studies]. Which is to say that not only writers of histories have to make choices; readers have responsibilities as well. (p. 81)

Cohen makes an important point in this passage: he claims that any historiography can be believed. This presents a problem because not all historiographies are believable or worth reading. Cohen is right to point out that both writers and readers of historiography have responsibilities. These responsibilities concern reading broadly to try to figure out which historiographies advance the field and which do not. Of course, this is a personal choice that the reader has to make. Historiographies are political. It is important that readers understand what that political agenda might be. The only way to understand that agenda is to keep reading and keep studying.

One of the striking things about the field is that it is not monolithic by any means. Some of the more traditional historiographies as opposed to historiographies from below, or social and cultural historiographies, are radically different. And then there are collections of historically intuitive narratives that are theoretical. Students of curriculum must know what they are reading and must know the history behind the history, as it were. These varying types of historiographies I mention above are highly political and strain the field. But strain is simply the way in which fields are built. As Andre Green (1999) says, people must work the negative—as the title of his book suggests. Working the negative (of strained historical narratives) is what I plan to do here.

Historical Analysis

Huebner (1999) stresses in his writing on historicity and temporality that the job of the writer is "to participate responsibly in history [by]...criti[cizing] and creat[ing]" (p. 433). The job of the historian is not merely to report. To theorize history, critique is necessary. Scholars must speculate and analyze and be honest and forthcoming about political positions. Some will see this as an unnecessary intrusion into the text at hand. But I do not see analysis and critique as intrusion; rather, I see it as a call toward honesty and integrity of academic work.

The notion of the theoretical always implies the practical: the practical is not split off from what is theoretical. This probably does not need saying here, but maybe it does. Scholars of curriculum theory are also practitioners. Those who call for the practical forget that theory is needed to undergird practice.

Petra Munro (1998a) says, "Historical narratives work to suppress contradictions (multiple stories)" (p. 271). I will not suppress the multiple stories that make up curriculum history and curriculum studies. The generational, gendered, raced, and classed arguments that scholars have with each other (e.g., see the Purdue Conference 2006 in Malewski, 2010) demonstrate these contradictions and multiple stories. Part of the problem at hand is that some do not like to think through contradictions or to think in multiples. One nation under God, *One Best System* (Tyack, 1974), monotheism: it is easier to think one thing, one story, one country, one God, one kind of curriculum history, one kind of school system. Standardization is all about the one answer on a test. But life is not about the one answer on a test. And curriculum studies is not about one subject, the schoolhouse. But again, this does not mean that curriculum scholars are not interested in what goes on in school. Curriculum studies is also about culture and education inside and outside of formal institutions; it is about organic intellectuals (Gramsci, 2005) and academics inside of formal institutions; it is about the production of knowledges, not the production of one kind of knowledge. And these knowledges (or various segments of the field) are going on simultaneously, which is what makes writing about this field so difficult. Antonio Novoa (2001) calls for a new kind of educational history that takes into account the multiple.

> I am convinced that we have to introduce more complex conceptions to historical reflection that will allow us to understand the coexistence of distinct dimensions of time. "History is not a time period, it is a multiplicity of time periods that are linked to and contain each other. It is necessary to substitute the old notion of time with the notion of multiple duration" (Foucault, 1994, vol. II: 279). (p. 61)

As against Novoa, we do not think that dimensions of time are, in fact, distinct. Curriculum studies is a field with many overlapping and hybrid dimensions all going on simultaneously. One of the difficult tasks I have had during the writing of this book is trying to separate out these overlaps by categorizing curriculum theorists in certain sectors and configurations. This is done for the sake of organization and not to simplify a scholar's work. Many curriculum scholars belong to many areas; that is, many of us could be categorized in many sectors simultaneously. Some of us work in autobiography, psychoanalysis, cultural studies, ecology, and gender and queer theory. Eric Malewski (2010) claims that the field is primarily composed of hybrids. That may be the case for some, but I do think that most scholars fall into primarily one or two sectors of the field. There are, as I see it, at least thirteen sectors to this field. These sectors can be likened to what—according to Thomas Popkewitz (2001)—Wittgenstein called "historical conjunctions" (p. 170). Popkewitz explains.

> Wittgenstein (1966) who provided a way of understanding historical change as multiple rates developing across different institutions at different times that come together in what can be called a historical conjunction. Wittgenstein likened historical change to a thread made up of many fibers. The strength of the thread does not reside in the fact that some fibers run its entire length but in fact that many fibers overlap. (p. 170)

A historical conjunction is what I would consider to be, say, autobiography or gender or ecology. However, these sectors, too, are hybrid "fibers," as Wittgenstein put it, and "overlap" at times. And fibers can tear or break; they can be long or short. Fibers are not even, but rather circular and webbed, curled up in each other and sometimes disjointed and unrelated. Fibers can also become—as Stephanie Polsky (2005) points out about the writings of Walter Benjamin—"blockages" (p. 82). These blockages Benjamin calls "constellations," which is a term—as Werner Hamacher (2005) says—Benjamin borrowed from Mallarmé (p. 56) What does Benjamin (2006) mean then by constellation? He contrasts positivist history—which he calls "universal" historiography—with "materialist" historiography. Universal historiography is additive and linear: smooth. Materialist history, on the other hand, is constructive and thought through (p. 396). Benjamin (2006) states

> Universal history has no theoretical armature. Its procedure is additive: it musters a mass of data to fill the homogeneous, empty time. Materialist historiography, on the other hand, is based on a constructive principle. Thinking involves not only the movements of thought, but their arrest as well. Where thinking suddenly comes to a stop in a constellation saturated with tensions, it gives that constellation a shock by which thinking is crystallized as a monad. (p. 396)

The thought (of history) gets constructed; when it comes to a stop, a constellation—when things gather round each other, like a sector of the field. That monad would be a particular segment of the field where thoughts have gathered round each other to form a particular idea, like autobiography or gender. Even though these things cannot actually be separated out, I think of them separately for the sake of organization. Years before Foucault arrived on the intellectual scene, Benjamin was talking about the problems of homogeneous time. For Benjamin, time was not in fact linear or chronological, but rather complex and jagged. Universal history, as he called it, pretended to be linear, neat, clear, and tidy. But Benjamin called this kind of time empty. Because historical time and the writing of history are complex, it is, as Sue Morgan (2006) puts it, "neither innocent nor transparent" (p. 3).

History as Social Construction

The writing of history is always political. Politics are not innocent. The writing of history is always constructed socially and therefore it is not transparent. It is not clear even to the historiographer why certain materials seem to gather round each other. It is not clear why scholars deem certain materials important and others not. When materials seem to gather round each other—to become a segment or sector of the field—this does not imply closure. Rather, the gathering round of materials is ongoing and continues through time(s). These gatherings and continuation of gatherings are always perspectival. Hayden White (1999) puts it this way:

> It is the metaphoric nature of the great classics of historiography that explains why none of them has ever wrapped up a historical problem definitively; rather, they have always opened up a prospect on the past that inspires more study. It is this fact that authorizes us to classify historical discourse primarily as interpretation, rather than explanation or description. (p. 7)

What constitutes a great classic, as White puts it, is political. Historically, great classics were thought to be written by European or Euro-American white men. Who deems a book a classic is an issue of power. At any rate, I do agree with White that good historiography is never a closed text but rather opens up further discussion. Hopefully this book, too, will open up more discussion rather than close things down. Opening up a discussion about what counts as curriculum history could lend to very important intellectual avenues.

White is right to point out that what historiography should do is not explain but interpret. To explain is to repeat without analysis what is in the text. Explaining does this: that this is what is said here and this is what is said there and this is that. The idea that history is merely explanation is—as Jacques Rancière (1991) puts it—the function of the "ignorant schoolmaster" (which is the title of his book). Let us not be ignorant! Rather, Sol Cohen (1999) suggests that "we reconstruct the past…so that we can, if we want to, converse with it" (p. 27). Reconstructing the past is not explaining but interpreting and gathering together in idiosyncratic ways texts that explore what historically came before us. And to converse with what came before us, scholars need to deconstruct what has been reconstructed.

The Historical Archive as Movement

Robert Alter (1991) discusses Walter Benjamin's oeuvre as one that was "to preserve the fragmentariness of his materials through the mobility of montage" (p. 11). Benjamin's writings certainly reflect both this fragmentary nature and the nature of montage as he shifts quickly from one artifact of history to another seemingly without transition. Perhaps the seemingly jumbled-up nature of his writing was a way to mimic the historical process. History feels like a jumbled-up and confusing duration of events that are always on the move and always split off and fragmentary. And the issue of mobility makes the writing task all the more complicated: catching a moving target (i.e., history) is no easy task. Werner Hamacher (2005) reminds us that "history can be missed" (p. 46). It is inevitable that the writer of a historiography is going to miss things. One person can only write about so much. Books, at one point, have to end. Books are limited by page numbers. I do my best here within the confines of a book to capture a moving target and to write about a very complex field that is constantly on the go and complicated by all the competing segments. I do my best here to be as comprehensive as possible and yet I know that what I am doing is of necessity fragmented and partial.

The notion of "shifting" is also something I want to address. Here I take my lead from Kathleen Weiler (1998), who, in her marvelous study titled *Country Schoolwomen: Teaching in Rural California 1850–1950*, tells us that for her what is important is to take into account "shifting historical representations" (p. 9). History teaches that things always change and representations of history always change.

Issues of Competing Representations

I argue in my book on the Holocaust that representations shift according to who is doing the writing (Morris, 2001). I found that former East Germans and former West Germans re-presented the history of the Holocaust in competing ways. (A re-presentation is to tell the story again, to re-present it.) That is, their re-presentations of this event radically differed. And even more so, Jewish representations of the Holocaust were radically different still. I do not mean here to essentialize these groups of people, but I want to point out that geography, religion, and ethnicity all impact how someone understands historical events. Representations shift and so what readers get are shifting histories (Weiler, 1998). Because something shifts does not mean that it is any less true or any less real; perspectives do not undermine the truth of an event. What does undermine the truth of a historical event is what Holocaust historians call revisionings. Now, revisionism can take on different meanings in different disciplines. In educational history, Joel Spring revisioned history in a good way so as to include marginalized peoples; in psychology James Hillman revisioned psychology so as to get back to Carl Jung's project but in new ways. However, in Holocaust history the word revision takes on a negative connotation. Revisionist Holocaust histories tend to unwrite history (Morris, 2001) and rewrite history to twist it into something that it was not. History can be gotten wrong. Interpreting events can become misinterpretations if the truth is not told. Politics again comes into play here. National shame tends to get rewritten or unwritten. Americans, too, have whitewashed history by making invisible shameful events like the genocide of the Native Americans, lynching, slavery, and the internment of Japanese during WWII.

Historical Trauma

Curriculum history also includes the broader study of trauma as reflected in the work of Roger I. Simon (2005), Simon, Rosenberg, and Eppert (2000),

Sharon Rosenberg (2000), and Claudia Eppert (2002) as they explore with other writers a variety of traumatic incidents around the globe and their educational impact. Again, this opens up the conversation to what counts as curriculum history. Should trauma studies be included in curriculum history? The 20th and 21st centuries have been extremely violent so I think that violence is something around which curriculum history needs to focus. The Simon, Rosenberg, and Eppert (2000) book, *Between Hope and Despair: Pedagogy and the Remembrance of Historical Trauma*, is important because it teaches us to examine what is unthinkable and shows how pervasive the unthinkable is on a global scale. Education must take into account the unthinkable and events that are not traditionally seen as part of the canon of curriculum history.

John Weaver (2001), in his book on *Rethinking Academic Politics*, works through the traumatic history in Germany by examining the reunification of Germany and the historians' debates that followed. Here, Weaver shows that German historians—especially former East German historians—revisioned history to suit their own purposes. History was rewritten to erase the national shame of the Holocaust. What counts as curriculum history? Historiography of trauma and the politics of that historiography count as curriculum history. Why do scholars unwrite history, Weaver asks? This is a question that historians of curriculum need to examine globally because everywhere history is being unwritten for political purposes.

History and Power

The writing of history is, as Foucault (2003) teaches, about power. Who has the power to tell a certain story? Which version of history gets passed down and why? What counts as history? Who decides? There are a number of curriculum books that deal with informal education, that is, education that happens outside of the public school. Who decides what education is? What kinds of education count? Does informal education count as education? These are all questions of power.

Reconfiguring What Counts as Curriculum History

Scholars need to rethink what it means to be educated and reconfigure possibilities of doing curriculum history. For example, Petra Munro Hendry's

(2011) *Engendering Curriculum History* is a fascinating study of the ways in which gender and education work to create alternative sites of education. Munro Hendry spends a good deal of time making the case that for women—since colleges and universities were not always places where women could get an education—other sites of education such as monasteries served educational purposes. Munro Hendry argues that during the medieval period in Europe, for example, the place that many women turned to get an education was the Church. Women medieval mystics, Munro Hendry suggests, were educated in monasteries. Munro Hendry's study opens up a much broader vision of what counts as curriculum history, especially when we are talking about the history of women and education. It is sometimes overlooked that women and minorities could not attend colleges and universities in the United States or in Europe up until roughly 1920. M. Carey Thomas had to go to Europe—to the University of Zurich—to get her PhD. There were very few colleges and universities that granted PhDs to women at the turn of the century.

Like Munro Hendry's (2011) work, William Pinar's (2009b) *The Worldliness of a Cosmopolitan Education* moves the curriculum conversation into the public sphere by suggesting that Jane Addams, Laura Bragg, and Pier Paolo Pasolini (an Italian filmmaker) all changed what it means to be educated, because their "classrooms" were the world stage. Pinar argues, for example, that Pasolini taught through the medium of film. Sol Cohen (1999) also argues that the cultural history of education should include the study of film because film has something to teach about education. And, of course, in the area of cultural studies—which will be teased out in volume 2—film can be a serious venue for study.

Paula Salvio's (2007) study of the poet Anne Sexton is another example of the way in which curriculum scholars open up the conversation outside of the traditional history of the school. Salvio's book can be considered biography. And as I see it biography is a form of history. Anne Sexton was a poet and a professor. What strikes me about Salvio's book is her focus on the poet-as-pedagogue. What does a poet teach curriculum theorists? The book is a fascinating study of mental illness, and the not good enough teacher. This is no heroine teacher. Sexton is a problematic antihero who crossed many boundaries. Again, Salvio's text opens the conversation on what counts as curriculum history. Anne Sexton, the poet-teacher, taught us to value the eccentric.

Like Paula Salvio's work, my work in *Jewish Intellectuals and the University* concerns the study of European Jewish intellectuals—before the rise of Nazi Germany—and their struggles against anti-Semitism and the academy (Morris, 2006). Anti-Semitism is not usually a topic found in discussions on curriculum history (with the exception of perhaps Alan Block's 2004 work). My book on Jewish intellectuals is about organic intellectuals—those not connected to the academy—as well as those connected to the academy, for example, Sigmund Freud, who had much trouble because of the anti-Semitic nature of the university, especially in Austria and Germany during the early part of the 20th century.

William Watkins's (2001) important historical study, *The White Architects of Black Education: Ideology and Power in America, 1865–1954*, deals with issues of race, discrimination, the problem of eugenics, and the ways in which the eugenics movement was complicit with progressive education. Watkins's book opens the conversation of what counts as curriculum history by dealing with issues of power and race; he questions philanthropic gestures of whites. Most of the traditional histories of American education deal little with issues of race or gender and hardly any of them deal with the issue of eugenics with the exception of Watkins and the work of Winfield (2007) and Selden (1999).

The more traditional path of curriculum history focuses on the schoolhouse. I list some books here that later I will explore in more detail. Many books on curriculum history deal only with the history of the school. See, for example, Cuban and Shipps (2000) on the history of what is meant by the common good in public schools and where that common good has gone wrong; Kliebard (1999) on vocational education and how vocational education has wrecked our public schools and turned education into the quest for the bottom line; Kliebard (2002) on the history of schools and a variety of other subjects like the Eight-Year Study and the Committee of Ten; Larry Cuban (2003) on trying to define what a good school is all the while demonstrating that schools have become "arm[s] of the economy" (p. 23); William J. Reese (2005) on the history of the common school to No Child Left Behind (NCLB); Barry Franklin (2000) on the work of Herbert Kliebard and the "promise" of schooling; Joseph Watras (2002, 2004, 2008) on the history of education (mostly schooling) from the 16th century up to the present; Alan Sadovnik and Susan Semel (2002) on the founding of progressive schools and on the founding mothers of progressive schools; David Tyack (2003) on common ground and public schools.

Curriculum History: Fiction, Memory, and Subjectivity

Competing representations of curriculum history—whether that history is, strictly speaking, about the schoolhouse or not—are subjectively filtered. To interpret a competing representation is to acknowledge that the scholar who writes the historiography makes a difference. Different scholars approach historiography in different ways. Historiography is not Truth with a capital T, although dogmatic approaches to historiographies presuppose just that. As Petra Munro (1998a) points out, "History is not the representation of reality, it never has been" (p. 267). Likewise, Walter Benjamin (2006) teaches that "articulating the past historically does not mean recognizing it 'the way it really was'" (p. 391). Historians never write the past the way it actually happened, for that is impossible. However, writing about the past is possible within the limits of what representations can do, how the past is revealed, and whether or not the historian is ethically bound to get at the past in a way that honors people who lived in that past. Just because a representation shifts—depending on who is doing the writing—does not mean that the event is false. It means that the event is interpreted. But does interpretation (of history) make it fiction? Some would say yes. Petra Munro (1998a) argues that all history is fiction. But is it? Hayden White (1999) also says that all history is fiction. But he points out that even if we call history "fiction"—because of the way it is constructed through language and exclusion—this does not mean that history has nothing to do with what is real. White tells us,

> It is absurd to suppose that, because a historical discourse is cast in the mode of narrative, [or that it is constructed from the choice of materials and documents] it must be mythical, fictional [in the sense of being made up ex nihilo], substantially imaginary, or otherwise "unrealistic" in what it tells us about the world. To suppose this is to indulge in the kind of thinking that results in belief in contagious magic or guilt by association. If myth, literary fiction, and traditional historiography utilize the narrative mode of discourse, this is because they are all forms of language use. This in itself tells us nothing about…truthfulness—and even less about their "realism"… Anyway, does anyone seriously believe that myth and literary fiction do not refer to the real world. (p. 22)

Historiography is like literary fiction because of the way in which both are constructed and put together. However, as against Munro and White, I argue alongside Dominick LaCapra (2001) that history is not the same as literary fiction because of the methods by which the historian is constrained. Novelists are not constrained. If you make the claim that history is fiction, then you play into the hands of the Holocaust revisionists who say that the Jews made the Holocaust up to get Israel, or that they exaggerated the number of people who were annihilated. I suggest, then, that historiography has some of the features of literary fiction but the two cannot be collapsed for ethical reasons.

The Shifting Archive of Memory and History

The problem of history and fiction deepens when we add into the mix the notion of memory. Again, I have dealt in detail with these problems elsewhere (Morris, 2001) but feel it is important to tease out these issues in the context of this book—*Curriculum Studies Guidebook*—primarily because I am dealing with both the history of a past that many of us did not live through (e.g., biographies of Jane Addams or Ida B. Wells) as well as the recent past (say, the last ten–fifteen years). When one can remember the past and write about it, those memories have a way of shaping the way the past gets represented. When scholars write about the past that is distant, that historiography is written differently because the impact of memory is not the same. If scholars can remember the past they are writing about, memory changes the way that that history is understood.

All historians have memories. These memories impact what they write and why they write what they do. A question that has come up especially in German historiography concerns this very issue of memory of the recent past and the impact memory has on the writing of historiography. During what was called the "historians' debates" of the 1980s Martin Broszat, a German non-Jewish historian, called for the erasure of memory in order to write history more objectively (Morris, 2001). What he wanted to erase was his own memory of German complicity in the Holocaust. How can you erase your memories and why would you want to? What was behind this so-called plea for historicization? If a historian remembers his or her past, those memories become part of the construction of the document, even if they are not explicit. Erasing memory—or the attempt to do so—is a form of psychological splitting off. If the historian suffers from a split-off psyche, the historiography suffers. Memory impacts history. History writing is entangled with memory if writing about the recent past; no amount of splitting off will make the history any more objective.

Another problem with traditional historiographies is that traditional historians do not draw on first-person testimony—especially of trauma—because it is thought that first-person witnessing is not reliable. Memory falters. But who would know better than Holocaust survivors what it was like to suffer internment in a concentration camp? Historians' methods—as John Weaver (2002) points out—blind them to the history around which they are writing. The very people that historians are writing about get erased from history because their voices are "unreliable." Even if memory falters, and it does, this faltering does not make the past any less real or less important. If researchers dismiss memory as being unreliable, then researchers also dismiss autobiography and biography. Autobiography and biography are ways of getting at the past that especially have to do with memory. Is autobiography an invalid form of writing because people draw on their memories? Do biographies reconstruct the lives of their subjects? Does that reconstruction make the work any less real or valuable? Human fragility makes historians nervous. Historians should include the fragility of memory in their work and not disregard it as something false or invalid.

Memory Is Political

Memory is always already political. What one chooses to remember and what one chooses to forget are implicated in the political. Embarrassing histories and issues of national shame tend to be either whitewashed or forgotten. In the United States, traditional curriculum history rarely, if ever, deals with the fact that David Sneeden, Franklin Bobbitt, and W. W. Charters were all involved in eugenics organizations as Winfield (2007) points out. These "fathers" of curriculum are an embarrassment to our field. Curriculum historians have a selective memory when it comes to these issues. As John Weaver (2001) points out "the struggle over the creation of palatable memories of the past is often at the heart of academic politics" (p. 9). It is unpalatable to think that the fathers of curriculum were also racist and probably misogynist too. In the context of German historiography, palatable memories were hard to come by (Weaver, 2001). Shifting the blame or making a history seem less awful by whitewashing it are methods to control the way the past is remembered. In the United States, conservative writers of social studies textbooks erase embarrassing historical events. And when these textbooks do explore national shame they do so in a very superficial manner. The genocide of Native Americans, slavery and lynching, the internment of Japanese Americans during WWII, for example—if treated at all—are dealt with in very superficial manners. The control of historical memory is about power. Foucault (2003) puts it this way: "History is an operation of power, an intensifier of power" (p. 66). Who gets to say what about whom is an issue of power. Feminist historians have long been interested in issues of power and the misrepresentation of women by male historians. African Americans and other minority groups also know that when Eurocentric historians write about them, they tend to misrepresent them. This is why Native Americans are so fiercely protective of the telling of their pasts.

Curriculum History as Memory Work

Curriculum theorists are ethically responsible for doing the work of historical memory. Many of us write historically about the recent past and so we write out of our memories. It is imperative that scholars do not attempt to erase memories to make for a more useable past. And too, historians who write on the distant past also work out of memory to form interpretations of a past that they did not literally live through. However, they do live through the past as they work out of their memories of the present. Memory and history are inextricably tied no matter how you turn the discussion. And the issue of memory becomes even more heated in autobiography and biography, especially when they are dealt with as forms of historical texts. An important point that Dwayne Huebner (1999) makes about memory work is that memory work is a public act. What is private becomes public when scholars write about it. The purpose of memory, says Huebner, is the "building of public, or shared worlds" (p. 186). Writing about memory is made public by publications. And writing those memories tells us much about the history into which the writer is thrown. Autobiographies—even if not explicit—always clue us into a particular historical period in which the subject is born. If researchers are careful readers, much can be gleaned about history from reading autobiographies. So autobiography is not just a solipsistic act: the writing of a life is, as Huebner points out, a sharing of a world. Writing an autobiography makes a private life public. And when a private life becomes public it makes memory history. Curriculum history as memory work ensures that. Those memories, as Huebner puts it, are "protected from loss or forgetfulness" (p. 187). And this is why it is imperative that academics write. Publishing means passing down to the next generation our memories, our histories, what is deemed important and what is deemed worthy of conversation. The scholarly life must be a writerly life. Historical archives of curriculum cannot be built but through writing. Roger Simon (2005) writes about the obligations of testimony. Simon states:

> As the enactment of historical memory, the movement of testimony is always caught up in the obligations expected by the transitive testamentary act—the act of writing, speaking, imaging—so as to bear an educative inheritance to those who "come after." (p. 5)

Writing curriculum history, as Simon declares, is our responsibility so as to educate the next generation. What survives is the archive. Scholars must work to make sure that the archiving of curriculum history continues into the next generation and beyond.

Theorizing Curriculum History as Biography and Autobiography

As I said earlier in the chapter curriculum history also includes biography and autobiography. I want to theorize what biography and autobiography might be (as forms of history) as a way to introduce ideas that I will deal with in detail later.

The issue at hand here is that memories and histories are written by people. Memories and histories therefore are embodied. And it is this sense of embodiment that is striking. Andrew Benjamin (2005) states,

> History, once freed from the hold of dates, involves bodily presence. The presence of those bodies is positioned within a nexus of operations. If that nexus can be named then it is the locus of moods. (p. 156)

All writing is embodied. Traditional historians might not like to think this way because bodies falter, leak. Bodies get tired and—as Andrew Benjamin reminds us—are subject to moods. Bodies get depressed especially when working on depressing history. Walter Benjamin was certainly aware of these things as he tried to escape the Nazis. His ideas about historiography came about because of the historical context into which he was thrown. He witnessed the eclipse of freedom and intuited what was to come as the Nazis annihilated European Jewry. Benjamin's life ended tragically since he committed suicide when he thought that his capture was inevitable. And yet his capture was not, in fact, inevitable. His moods got the best of him. Benjamin felt that history was a continual catastrophe, and this influenced the way he saw the world and what he wrote about. So the point here is that historiography—as embodied and en-mooded if you will—is, as William Pinar (2009b) points out, "subjectively stimulated" (p. xi).

What could better demonstrate this subjective dimension of historiography than biography and autobiography? Pinar (2009b) builds his book on cosmopolitanism on three biographic sketches: Jane Addams, Laura Bragg, and Pier Paolo Pasolini. In a breathtaking move, Pinar shows that to get a sense of the world (cosmopolitanism) one must get a sense of the individual (via biography). What is missing in discussions on cosmopolitanism, Pinar tells us, is the turn to toward subjectivity.

Earlier in the history of curriculum, it was Dwayne Huebner who argued that biography and autobiography should be considered forms of history. Huebner (1999) states:

> Education is a manifestation of the historical process, meshing the unfolding biography of the individual with the unfolding of history of his society. The past becomes the means by which the individual can project his own potentiality for being. (p. 139)

The "unfolding biography" of a person is also related to an unfolding autobiography of the biographer. Biography is always related to autobiography. And these two genres, Huebner points out, are part and parcel of "the unfolding of history" (p. 139). Thus, I take my lead from both Pinar and Huebner to argue that if one is to write about historiography, it is imperative to understand that biography and autobiography are forms of history. Again, there is a depth in these genres that one doesn't find in traditional historiographies. The depth of the personal against the face(lessness) of history is a lure—as Huebner would put it—for those of us interested in the personal side to the scholarly life. Theorizing the subjective and theorizing our own relations to others is what makes our intellectual lives rich and vital. History is not merely a collection of dates and documents. History is about peoples' lives and our relation to those lives.

Who Gets Left Out

What is curious is that when studying traditional curriculum historiographies one does not find many references to women or minorities. This is not a new thought of course. Petra Munro talks about this problem in some detail in her works as do other feminist curriculum theorists and historians. The question, then, is where does one find work on women and minorities? In biographies and autobiographies. I found a parallel problem in the literature on the Holocaust (Morris, 2001). Most of the traditional historiographies were top down, military histories that dealt with male figures and with perpetrators. The victims' voices were rarely heard in the traditional historiographies; the stories of women and gay and lesbian victims were found in different literatures: in memoirs, biographies, autobiographies. Traditional historians tend to split off women and minorities from the mainstream of historical thought. Feminists warn, however, that splitting off women and minorities from historical texts is problematic. This is the same problem with teacher education programs offering separate courses for multiculturalism. Multicultural ideas should be embedded throughout the curriculum. Likewise, ideally, women and minorities should be integrated into traditional historiography, but still there is a grave imbalance in the literature. When women are written about they get ghettoized in women's histories. Women and men should be analyzed together, in the same books. But it seems that they are not. This is another reason why I turn to biographies and autobiographies as forms of historiography because this is where researchers learn about women and minorities. More traditional historians do not include women in their studies and the history of curriculum tends to be the history of white males. Although in curriculum studies, as William Pinar (2010) points out, scholars have devoted thirty years of work to the study of race and gender.

Biography as It Relates to History

Curriculum historians Craig Kridel and Vicky Newman (2003) have much to say about the genre of biography as it relates to history. Kridel and Newman discuss what counts as curriculum history and argue that we need to broaden what this kind of work entails. Kridel and Newman argue,

> We designate eight contexts for curriculum history research: curriculum history of social/educational history, subject areas, case studies, synoptic introductions, memoirs and oral histories, archival documents, biography, and unsilencing voices. (p. 641)

Notice in this passage that Kridel and Newman include both biography and autobiography—what they call memoirs and oral histories. Biography and autobiography are ways to make audible those voices that have been silenced. The point here, though, is primarily that these curriculum historians recognize biography and memoir as forms of history. In fact, in another text edited by Kridel (1998), *Writing Educational Biography*, he reminds us that "Emerson stated, 'There is properly no history: only biography,' and Yeats said, 'Nothing exists but a stream of souls, that all knowledge is biography'" (p. 7). Emerson and Yeats make extremely profound statements about the nature of historiography. However, as Kridel points out, biography, for example, is still not treated "extensively" in education.

Freud's Suspicions of Biography

Freud was suspicious of biography and so too are traditional historians. Biographies, like autobiographies, are based on the art of storytelling. How does the biographer know that her subject is telling the truth? Freud thought that every biography was basically a lie; he had no use for biography. But he did tell his story, he did write his autobiography. Ah, the contradictions in Freud abound! Isn't autobiography a form of biography, the study of someone's life? Do autobiographers tell the truth? This is an open question. But then again one can ask the same questions about the writings of traditional historians. If they draw on primary source documents, how would one know if those documents are falsified or not? I reiterate the question raised earlier: is history really fiction? Some seem to think so. But if all historical writing is socially constructed, does that mean that it is shot through with lies? No. From the study of psychoanalysis, one learns that all of life is shot through with fantasy and fantasy structures subjectivity. Does this, then, make our stories any less real or any less important? No. The problem here is an old one and comes up to haunt us from the ghosts of positivism. No document is directly related to reality; everything is filtered through our subjectivities. There is no direct relation to objective facts. When Freud talked about the importance of dreams he suggested that the plot of the story is not important and literally getting back to childhood is impossible. Rather, what is important is what one does with the dream, what meaning is made of it. Freud called this dream work. The word "work" implies that one does something with the dream psychologically. And this relates to history-biography-autobiography. Perhaps the plot of the story as it is told in history-biography-autobiography is not as important as the meaning made of it. The question is what does the scholar psychologically do with the study of history, biography, and autobiography? What meanings and associations can be drawn from the study of these genres? What meanings are drawn from the past in relation to our own lives?

What Is Educational Biography?

What counts as "educational" biography? Tom Barone (2000) uses the phrase "educational biography" when he states, "Certainly educational biographies are legitimate focal points for curriculum criticism" (p. 56). But what is meant by the phrase "educational biography?" Why not just say biography? Do educational biographies mean stories of teachers? Are biographies of organic intellectuals (Gramsci, 2005) educational biographies? What kind of biography is educational? Must scholars of curriculum study only teachers? Who counts as a teacher?

Kridel (1998) has a helpful way of thinking about what biography means by breaking down the term in the following way. He tells us:

> Perhaps more important than definition is the tradition from which a writer speaks—history or literature, humanities or social sciences, art or craft, or a variety of subspecialties as feminist biography, psychobiography, prosopography (group biography), or "new" biography a la postmodernism. (p. 8)

If someone writes a biography from the tradition of the humanities, say, about a filmmaker, say Pasolini, does that make it an educational biography? What relevance does Pasolini the filmmaker have to education? Pinar (2009b) makes this connection clear in his work on cosmopolitan education, as I mentioned earlier. But Pasolini was not an educator in the traditional sense, although at one point in his life he was a schoolteacher. But his worldly teachings—as Pinar puts it—were via filmmaking. What counts as educational biography depends on how one defines what it means to be an educator.

Organic Intellectuals as Educators

Organic intellectuals (Gramsci, 2005) are educators, but they do not work in a traditional classroom. Think of the figure of the flaneur about whom Walter Benjamin wrote. I think the flaneur was Benjamin himself. A flaneur is a man (or woman) who lives in coffeehouses and walks the streets of, say, Paris trying to understand the historical value of all culture. From the arcades to photography, Benjamin demonstrated that these cultural phenomena were important to study. Traditional scholars tend to overlook the everyday and popular culture. Contrarily, the flaneur is the teacher of the streets. The flaneur is the cosmopolitan educator who is unattached to an institution; he or she is a free-floating intellectual. Walter Benjamin was not affiliated with any institution since his PhD thesis was not accepted by prospective employers in the European university system. If the PhD thesis was not deemed acceptable in Europe—at least during Benjamin's lifetime—no job prospects were possible. It is possible that he was not hired as faculty because of anti-Semitism. And it is also possible that he was not hired because the faculty who reviewed his thesis could make little sense of what he was doing.

Bringing History to Life

Traditional historiography tends to be written in a lifeless way. Again, this is because historians are supposed to write without embellishment. History writing was not always this way though. Biographies and autobiographies bring history to life. As a matter of fact, Alan Wieder (1998) says most eloquently that "biography is described as the 'human heart of history'" (p. 113). Certainly, biographies can also be lifeless if they are poorly written. But for the most part biographies capture peoples' imagination. Biographies sell. Biographies are popular with laypersons. Because the genre of biography is popular, though, doesn't devalue its scholarly worth. A scholarly biography is scholarly, popular or not. But if a biographer gets to be too famous, traditional scholars tend to think that he or she is not scholarly enough. What is popular, these traditional scholars might think, cannot be scholarly. People like biographies because they are personal. What do these personal stories teach? The better written biographies teach us much about the larger historical and political context in which they are written. William Ayers (1998b) remarks that biography is about

> the search for identity and meaning within multiplicity. It embraces active choice making at the intersection of private and public. It resists objectification, portraying the importance of individual experience and personal narrative inside a social surround, a cultural web, an historical flow. (p. 242)

There is something profound about telling the life story of an individual if that individual has a story to tell. And that story also tells us something about the history into which that person finds herself. All biographies are webbed inside of history, as Ayers (1998b) suggests.

Biography and Culture

Barbara Finkelstein (1998) tells us,

> Biography provides a unique lens through which one can assess the relative power of political, economic, cultural, social and generational processes on the life chances of individuals, and the revelatory power of historical sense-making. (p. 45)

Recall Paula Salvio's (2007) biography of Anne Sexton teaches how the politics of her time worked to squash her. The reason Sexton is such an important poet is that she broke ground for women. She wrote about women in ways that nobody dared to before her. Sexton's style of writing was called confessional and was often looked down upon by the formalists (like T. S. Eliot) because they thought confessional writing was too feminine and that personal revelations had little to do with poetic insight.

Is autobiography (which can be considered as confessional) thought today to be effeminate? Is autobiography considered soft by social scientists? Perhaps. Is biography also considered soft? And if it is, one must wonder whether the resistance to studying biography in the larger field of education has something to do with misogyny.

Theorizing Autobiography as Historical Text

William Pinar (2004) brought the genre of autobiography into the field of curriculum studies some thirty years ago. It continues to be a strong and vital segment of the field. Pinar's work is devoted to the intersections of self and society, politics and understanding curriculum. Pinar insists that studying the self is also studying the social; hence studying the self is an inherently political act. He speaks here to the power of African American autobiography and its relation to history and politics:

> In African-American autobiography, we discern not mindless egoism or asocial subjectivism (characteristics sometimes associated with European and European-American autobiographical practices), but, rather, first-person accounts composed by remarkable individuals whose subjective struggles were simultaneously collective ones. (p. 46)

Writing the self is also writing the social, Pinar suggests, especially when that self has something to say about the fight against oppression. In my book *Teaching Through the Ill Body* I studied many pathographies (autobiographies of illness) and was particularly struck by the political power of the personal in the writings of Audre Lorde, who was a black lesbian poet (Morris, 2008). Lorde's (1997) autobiography, *The Cancer Journals*, became very well-known because she not only allowed the readers into her life and into her struggles with cancer, but she also critiqued the medical establishment and made disturbing remarks about the inhumane treatment that sick people sometimes get while being "cared for" by physicians. Pinar (2004) tells us, "Nikki Giovanni [a black poet] has pointed out that black women's autobiographies have been inextricably linked to changing political conditions" (p. 46). Autobiographical writing—when it is political—can be powerful. Writing about the self is always political. Political autobiography oftentimes deals with struggle. When autobiographies capture a particular struggle in a particular time—say in the work of Audre Lorde—one gets a sense of the historicity of that struggle and the personal then is made historical. Denise Taliaferro-Baszile (2010) comments that "all work is autobiographical" (p. 483). Scholars write out of their own subjectivities, even if they argue that their work is objective.

To write the self through autobiography is a daunting task. It is not as easy as it looks. Think about writing the story of your own life. Where to begin? What to include, what to exclude? What is too private to make public? Who to include, what to say about whom? What relations to others shape us? Autobiography turns out not to be about the self only. Autobiography is also about the relations of the self to others across time and history. Thus, it is a very complex undertaking to write about the self. To make what is private public, too, opens one up to vulnerabilities. Audre Lorde certainly opened herself up to vulnerabilities as she was facing death. But at that point in a life, what does it matter if the writing makes one more vulnerable? What is there to lose in the face of mortality? Many people turn toward autobiographical writing when they are experiencing limiting situations like grave illness. The story must be told. And the telling of the story is also an ethical act because in the telling the writer helps others who suffer.

When writing an autobiography, memory becomes key. The autobiographer works out of her memory. And the concept of memory is not so easy to understand. James Olney (1998) comments:

> Indeed, I have at times claimed that the narrator of a life-story remembers in reverse chronological order as he or she has lived and narrates in forward chronological order. I am not sure this is altogether wrong, but I do feel that the matter is considerably more complicated than this rather simple formulation would suggest. (p. 10)

The idea of chronological order comes apart when writing about the self. Memory does not work chronologically and to impose a chronology on the writing only constrains the narrative at hand. Aharon Appelfeld (1994), a Holocaust survivor, comments that when he tried to write his autobiography chronologically—in an attempt to get the facts straight—the more constrained he felt and the less able he was to write. Writing trauma is particularly difficult because memory has ways of protecting itself from collapse. Blanks occur when attempting to remember traumatic situations. What to do with a blank? And then there is the question of getting it right. What we remember is probably different from what actually happened. When studying autobiographies of survivors of catastrophe—whether that catastrophe is illness or war—one gets a sense not only of the political but also of the historical, even if these things are not stated explicitly.

Other Kinds of Autobiography: Race and Gender

What of other kinds of autobiography? Traditionally, as many commentators point out, the genre of autobiography was taken up by European white males, and the plot of many of these was the successful and heroic adventures of the white man. When men—particularly heterosexual white men—write autobiographies, they are deemed important. When women and minorities write autobiographies they are deemed—by white men—as narcissistic. The reception of autobiography has its own history and that history is engendered and raced.

Again, autobiography is always historical. Now, there are some, like Ivor Goodson (1998), who drives a wedge between autobiography and what he calls "life history." Goodson argues that autobiography does not reflect history and is narrowly about the self. He states that life history is different. Goodson argues:

> In the life history, the intention is to understand the patterns of social relations, interactions, and constructions in which lives are embedded. The life history pushes the question of whether private issues are also public matters. The life story individualizes and personalizes; the life history contextualizes and politicizes. (p. 11)

As against Goodson, I argue that the life story is always already a life history and that there is little difference between autobiography per se and life history. How can one write an autobiography that does not, for instance, deal with social relations? The self is constructed out of relations with the other.

These relations are inherently political and the political is already embedded in the personal and in the historical. Whether the political intentions of the writer are stated explicitly or not, they can be gleaned from the text at hand.

Who Counts as a Teacher?

Goodson (1998), when writing about life history, refers to the "teacher's life and work" (p. 11). I ask, again, who counts as teacher? Who can write a teacherly autobiography? Who teaches us? Only classroom teachers? Or are there organic intellectuals and flaneurs and cosmopolitan intellectuals who do not have a classroom of their own but who can teach through their autobiographical writings? I think that when scholars talk about autobiography and biography, it is important not to make our subject so narrow as to only refer to classroom teachers. Augustine, for example, has something to teach. His work educates. A classroom teacher? No, but a teacher of the public. White European and white Euro-American males have things to teach us just as black poets do. It is important to study the canon and the countercanon together. Cameron McCarthy (1998a) makes this point when he talks about reading "contrapuntally".

Autobiography Is Historical and Literary

Autobiography—whether undertaken by white men or black women poets—is both historical and political but it is also literary. How can autobiography be all these things at once? Laura Marcus (1994) tells us that the "traditional" view of autobiography is that it is a "sub-category of history" (p. 8). She wants to take autobiography out of this subcategory and put it inside of the literary tradition. As I see it, autobiography is both historical and literary. I make this claim because I argue that all history is literary. In curriculum studies, the issue is not so much to move autobiography out of the "sub-category of history" (Marcus, 1994, p. 8) but to move it back into that subcategory. Historical texts are narratives and narratives are literary. Of course, most traditional historians do not feel that their writing is in the least bit literary. But how can it not be? Curriculum scholarship is both historical and literary. This is of particular importance because one of the defining characteristics of curriculum scholarship since the Reconceptualization has been the conscious move to draw on the humanities as well as the social sciences. Now, social scientists probably do not think that their writing has anything to do with what is literary, but I argue to the contrary. It is all literary. The minute you put pen to paper, or fingers to keyboard, you are doing the work of the literary.

Autobiography and Interiority

In curriculum studies autobiography came into being with the writings of William Pinar starting in the 1970s. What autobiography can do for the individual, Pinar (2004) suggests, is to "democratize one's interiority" (p. 38) while simultaneously working the political. But in order to work the political, one must work the self. If the self is not democratized, as Pinar puts it, the political cannot be worked. To work the self is to work on the self, to work the social is to work on the social. When the self is too much under the shadow of the object, stultification is at hand. Working the self and working the social become an imperative if one is to make any changes for the common good.

Autobiography and the Common Good

David Tyack (2003) suggests that the point of the common school is to work for the common good. The purpose of the common school is equality and justice for all. But not only this, the common school and the common good can be realized in a broader sense. Tyack's point is that the problem of the notion of the "common" is that people have little in common to begin with. Scholars write about the notion of difference, but how to bridge difference and what is common for the common good? Well, autobiography is a place to start. To work the self is to work the social. Democratization of one's interiority, as Pinar (2004) puts it, also means the democratization of what Chet Bowers (1995) calls "the commons." The complexity of the commons comes about because of the difference that is inherently inside of the commons—Tyack's point. The genre of autobiography fosters the common good. One cannot arrive at the commons without working the self first. And one cannot work the commons without working difference. The common good is the polis and the polis is that political sphere around which educators work. I bring together the insights of David Tyack and William Pinar to suggest that the common good is what is good for both self and other. And it is in the relation of the difference between self and other that education happens.

The "Auto" in Biography

The relation between the "auto" in biography is a curious one that needs some unpacking. The self who writes about the other has an investment in writing about that other. Who scholars write about is no accident. There are reasons for choosing particular subjects, but these reasons might be unconscious. William Pinar and Anne Pautz (1998) tell us that "the biographer's autobiographic voice sounds in the biographical subject" (p. 67). A good example of this conundrum is Wayne Urban's work on Horace Mann Bond. Urban (1998) comments, "I decided to do more than just a biography: I wished to write the biography of an historian of education. I made this decision because I wanted to study a life that was in some ways similar to my own" (p. 104). Urban is a historian of education. His biography is about a historian of education. Do scholars write about people with whom they identify? Probably. And if that is the case then the "auto" is always already in the biography. It is interesting that these two genres were more blurred in earlier historical periods, as Laura Marcus (1994) points out. She says, "Recent critics have tended to argue that the conceptual separation of biography and autobiography… occurred from the mid-nineteenth century onwards" (p. 142). It is interesting to note that the separation of the auto from the biography has a history, one that perhaps is not thought through enough. Historically, autobiography and biography weren't always split into two neat and tidy categories just as the disciplines of history, science and literature, for that matter, were at one time merged with philosophy. The separation of the disciplines occurred in the academy with the rise of scientism. And perhaps the separations of the disciplines were foreshadowed by Descartes's clear and distinct categories and his search for a method, as Sartre might put it. Disciplinary boundaries presuppose that areas of knowledge production are clear and distinct. And these disciplinary boundaries are also political. Turf wars among the varying disciplines become obvious in the academy when engaging in interdisciplinary scholarship. For more traditional scholars, it seems anathema to step outside the bounds of one's own field of study. Each discipline has its own sort of method of approaching its subject matter.

Descartes's Dilemma

Descartes wanted to find one philosophical method that would clear away complexities and reduce things to their most basic elements. And when scholars talk about the problematics of method in education—as William Doll (1998) has done in much of his work—Descartes comes to mind. But as Gadamer (1975) notes in his book *Truth and Method*, there is no truth in method, and this is the problem with Descartes and the problem with methods courses in education. Interestingly enough, Isaiah Berlin (1997) reminds us that Descartes did not think that the study of history was worth bothering about. There are no clear and distinct ideas in history, according to Descartes. Descartes felt that the study of history was too uncertain and ambiguous. Isaiah Berlin puts it this way:

> Descartes had already denied to history any claim to be a serious study. Those who accepted the validity of the Cartesian criterion of what constitutes rational method could (and did) ask how they could find the clear and simple elements of which historical judgments were composed, the logical transformation rules, the rules of inference, the rigorously deduced conclusions? (p. 17)

It is interesting to note that positivist historians, such as Leopold Von Ranke, who is considered to be the father of modern history (Weaver, 2001), felt they could meet the Cartesian criterion (be clear and distinct) when doing historiography. And this is where history as a discipline made a wrong turn. No historiography is clear and distinct; no historiography is objective.

The Postmodern Turn

Postmodern historians feel that Descartes was off the mark on every point. Postmodern versions of history embrace the ambiguous. The different theoretical problems posed in this chapter are postmodern ones. The discussions about history and fiction, the literary and the historical, memory, truth, and representation are all issues that are unclear, ambiguous, and reflect our postmodern era. Attempting to articulate what history is while living in the postmodern era is an uncertain and daunting task. What you see is not what you get for the postmodern historian. Representations are filtered through perspectives and those perspectives are changing all the time. The lines between the historical, the biographical, the autobiographical are unclear as well. These categories are all interrelated and intertwined. There are no clear and distinct separations between biography, autobiography, literature and history. And this presents a problem for historians who still have a Rankean or Cartesian mindset.

On a related note, Leigh Gilmore (2001) writes about authors who write more than one autobiography. If autobiography is multiple then, too, are selves, and this is a postmodern idea completely foreign to Descartes. Gilmore tells us:

> Several writers have taken the project of self-representation to be open-ended, susceptible to repetition, extendible even, perhaps, incapable of completion. In their sustained multibook projects, the notion of an "end" to autobiography becomes ironic with each new publication. The multivolume autobiographies of Maya Angelou, Lillian Hellman, and Mary McCarthy, among others, demonstrate this pattern of returning to the autobiographic scene. (p. 96)

Like Maya Angelou, Lillian Hellman, and Mary McCarthy, curriculum scholars who have written multiple volumes—whether specifically autobiographic or not—are also engaged in a kind of ongoing autobiography as their scholarship reflects who they are. Every book is a twist on a few ideas near and dear to that thinker. Every scholarly book is another autobiographic portrait whether explicitly stated or not. Ironically, one does not have to write an "autobiography" to write an autobiography. For example, Maxine Greene's work is clearly Greene's! She has a unique and unmistakable style. She does not call her books autobiographies per se, but her writing tells us who she is and what is important to her. Her writings are autobiographical in that Greene is telling us a story about her interests and what she is invested in by drawing on the work of others.

Theorizing Curriculum History as Autobiographic Text: The Embodiment of Gender, Race, and Class

Traditional historiography deals little with gender, race, or class. Top-down history deals with white male heroes, wars, battles won, and victors. History from below deals with everybody else and everything else. And this separation in curriculum history literature becomes rather evident and troubling when studying someone as well respected as Herbert Kliebard. In his historiographies—see, for example, his books *Schooled to Work* (1999) and *Changing Course* (2002)—his main areas of interest turn on white men only. He might deal here and there with others but those others are dealt with in passing. Why is it that women still get left out of history? Where are women and minorities in Kliebard's version of curriculum history? Again, he does treat issues of

African American education here and there, but his overall focus is on people like W. W. Charters, David Sneeden, Harold Rugg, and Franklin Bobbitt. There is certainly more to curriculum history than the study of white men.

Women are written about in separate histories like Alan Sadovnik and Susan Semel's (2002) work *Founding Mothers* or in feminist treatments of curriculum like Petra Munro Hendry's (2011) *Engendering Curriculum History*; or one can find the stories of women and minorities in biographies and autobiographies. Few books in curriculum history manage to integrate men, women, and minorities. And so when it becomes obvious that there is this split in curriculum historiography questions of gender, race, and class demand interrogation. Now, what I propose to do at this point in the book is to raise some preliminary questions about gender, race, and class in relation to historiography generally. Later in the book, I devote entire chapters to race, gender, and class.

William Pinar (2001), in his book *The Gender of Racial Politics and Violence in America*, points out that both gender and race are "historical, ideological process[es] (Bederman, 1995a)" (p. 4). I would argue, too, that the concept of class is also a "historical, ideological process." "Gender," "race," and "class," as concepts, all have their own histories. Each term needs its own deconstruction and historical analysis. Pinar argues that scholars must think, especially, of gender and race together. I would add that we must think of the concept class together with these categories as well. Pinar (2001) argues that race is gendered and gender is raced and depending on what is emphasized (gender or race), each is political. This is not easy to think through because when studying these concepts they all belong to different sets of literatures. Students of gender might study feminism and masculinity studies; students of race might study critical race theory or multiculturalism; students of class might study neo-Marxism or cultural studies. To try to intertwine these literatures is extremely difficult, but Pinar points out that this might be a necessary task, especially when talking of race and gender. Of course, these are all socially constructed terms that change meaning over time. And so that is why it behooves students to always study concepts historically.

Kathleen Weiler (2001) points out that "theoretical stances continue to be profoundly gendered" (p. 11). I would add that theory is also raced and classed. Abstractions are always already concretized by race, class, and gender and scholars must work abstractions concretely. Race, class, and gender have real material consequences that need to be explored. Sexism is a real-world issue that affects both men and women negatively. Historians, those who are rather traditional, seem to forget these things or deem them unimportant. However, curriculum studies as a field has not—as a whole—forgotten or left out completely the story of women and minorities. William Pinar (2010) stresses to those who would argue to the contrary,

> While prominent participants in early 20th century curriculum studies (as in practically every other academic discipline) were male and of European descent, women and African Americans were not entirely absent nor are these historic figures invisible today. (p. 531)

Since the 1970s at least, curriculum studies scholars have been working in the areas of race, class, and gender but still more work needs to be done. Curriculum theorists need to continually unpack what is problematic about historiographies when they do not address in a theoretical or concrete way race, class, and gender.

Traditional curriculum historiographies, Petra Munro (1998a) tells us, present a variety of problems, and one of those problems is erasure (p. 264). The grand master narratives of the more traditional curriculum historiographies, according to Munro (1998a), take the following masculine trajectory:

> It is the quintessential hero's tale predicated on separation (lone schoolmaster), individualism (common school movement), and control (reforms, progressivism, technical rationalism, and professionalization are conspicuously masculine discourses that focus on individuality and autonomy). (p. 268)

Munro's point is that more traditional historiographies are mostly coming-of-age stories of the white male hero, which has little to do with the way that history really gets played out. The history of curriculum is much more complex than this. Who gets erased? Women and minorities. Munro also argues that to begin curriculum history with the common school movement is a way to erase the fact that women and minorities had little opportunity to be educated in an educational institution before the late 19th century.

The Erasure of Gender and Race

Another notable problem concerning erasure is when race and gender both are present; when for example, African American women get left out of historical narratives. The problem here is the erasure of both gender and race. Cally Waite (2001) points out that although W. E. B. Du Bois was sympathetic to the struggle of black women, he rarely cited them in his work. He mentions neither Anna Julia Cooper (by name) nor Ida B. Wells, both of whom he read or had contact with. This is how women get written out of history. This is not an uncommon occurrence. Men often do not cite women or write about them. This exclusion has much to do with misogyny. Since the 1960s, though, as Kathleen Weiler (1998) tells us, feminists have tried to address this problem of erasure by doing two things. First, feminists argue that scholars must add in missing women to the historical mix. But more than that, feminists must demonstrate that women are not just passive pawns in the face of history. Weiler explains:

> In the 1960s, historians writing from an explicitly political, feminist perspective began a project to recover women's lives from the oblivion to which they had been relegated. These histories tended to emphasize the oppression of patriarchal practices and existing ideologies. Subsequent women's historians turned to the question of resistance and the ways in which women created meaning in the past. (p. 5)

But are recovery and agency enough? Maybe not. Petra Munro Hendry (1998, 2011) argues that scholars must be careful to not merely do compensatory history. Sue Morgan (2006) concurs. Morgan states: "The limitations of a 'compensatory' and 'separatist' approach to feminist history had already become increasingly apparent by the 1990s" (p. 10). What are the limitations of "compensatory" history? Well, first off, merely adding in the absent voices does not mean that the overall structure of traditional historiography is addressed. Munro Hendry argues that scholars must work to continually deconstruct the way in which traditional historiography takes for granted concepts that only serve to further undermine women and minorities. The grand metanarratives of historiography must be unpacked to see what the hidden agenda of those narratives might be. Concepts must be studied historically and terms teased out so as not to make category mistakes when doing an analysis of history. If scholars leave in place history as it is—in the traditional fashion—merely adding in missing people does little to address the ongoing problematics of doing historiography. For example, Petra Munro (1998a) unpacks the notion of "progressive" in the context of progressive education. What does "progressive" mean, she wonders? Munro asks: "What, then, makes it thinkable or possible to conceive of the progressive era as progressive" (p. 278)? Who was the progressive era progressive for? Women were still held to certain gender roles and if they stepped outside of those roles they were deemed mannish. Women were still second fiddle to male progressive educators, according to Munro, and were seen as little more than "dutiful daughters" (p. 269). Progressive education was not progressive for blacks, as Sadovnik and Semel (2002) point out. Progressive schools, for the most part, were not open to black children. Also progressive schools were mostly private and so the poor had no place in them either. And Sadovnik and Semel also comment on the fact that some of the women founders of progressive schools ran these schools in an autocratic manner. Is an autocrat a progressive? On the other hand, as Munro (1998a) teaches, there were things about the progressive era that were liberatory. What is striking about Munro's work here is that she is thinking through two things at once about progressive education. It was both good and bad, both oppressive and liberating. And progressive education, as Kliebard (2002) points out, was not monolithic; he admits that it was full of contradictions. What seems odd is that what was deemed progressive in the 1920s and 1930s (social efficiency) does not in the least seem progressive now. But to say that progressive education was of no use or is not really progressive is reactionary (e.g., see Diane Ravitch, 2001). Some of the ideas and concepts that came out of progressive education were forward thinking and helped people to think through complex educational issues in open ended and creative ways. Why is it that William Heard Kilpatrick's project method is not children's educative experience today? Even in college, students are so highly structured that projects are not options. Still, the bulk of traditional instruction is a throwback to the days of recitation and memorizing textbooks. Contrarily, Margaret Naumburg, in the very early years of the 20th century, argued for a psychoanalytic education (for more on this, see Blythe Hinitz's work in Sadovnik and Semel, 2002). Lucy Salmon, the famed woman historian, argued that students must study primary sources and explore the everyday way before it was fashionable. Today this is called cultural history or history from below. During her lifetime, Salmon was not taken seriously by more conservative scholars. During the 1960s social and cultural history—what Lucy Salmon was doing back in the early part of the 20th century—became popular (for more on this, see Sol Cohen, 1999). John Dewey's work, especially *Democracy and Education* (1916/1966), *The School and Society* (1899), and *The Child and the Curriculum*, (1902), was progressive. Jane Addams, another progressive, founded Hull House and worked for the common good of the people. Harold Rugg was another progressive who stands out because of the courage it took for him to write social studies texts that had a socialist slant. There was much progressive about the progressive era. But there was also much about it that was problematic. But the problems do not overshadow the promises of the progressive movement. Later, we will treat these issues in more detail.

Educational History versus Curriculum Historiography

I hope that this theoretical background gives the student of curriculum some ideas on what he or she would like to research further. I have explored some theoretical issues—as they pertain to doing historical research—that are in need of deepening of course. But this backdrop should give the student new to curriculum studies an introduction to the kinds of debates that are of interest when talking about curriculum as a historical concept.

I divide historiography as it pertains to education into three broad groups: (1) educational history (these are histories of the schoolhouse); (2) curriculum historiography (these are histories that deal with broader themes and do not necessarily have to do with school per se; i.e., the organic intellectual, the flaneur, the cosmopolitan; histories of trauma; histories of informal sites of education; historians' debates); (3) curriculum historiography as biography and curriculum historiography as autobiography.

It should be noted that scholars divide up the historical terrain differently. For example, Petra Munro (1998a) suggests that curriculum historiography differs from what she calls the "history of teaching and education" (p. 285). Munro explains:

> I would like to delineate the history of curriculum theory from the history of teaching and education. Although these fields are interrelated, the history of teaching and education is primarily concerned with the history of the profession itself and its role in shaping what we consider the institution of schooling. The history of curriculum theory is more specifically concerned with the question of how education (more general than schooling) shapes and is shaped by ideology and culture. (p. 285)

More traditional educational historians seem to be narrowly focused on the schoolhouse with the exception of, say, Lawrence Cremin (1988); who contextualizes his work around social and political movements, as Kliebard (1995) reminds us. Cremin's masterpiece titled *American Education: The Metropolitan Experience 1876–1980* is extremely broad. He is not narrowly focused on the schoolhouse but situates education with larger social movements such as progressivism.

Many educational historians, however, do not write broad historiographies, as did Cremin. The educational historiographies that will be examined here are narrowly focused on the school. And it is this narrow focus that sets educational history apart from curriculum historiography. What Cremin did in his work is closer to what I call curriculum historiography.

Why study both the narrow (what I call educational history) and the broad (what I call curriculum historiography)? I follow Craig Kridel and Vicki Newman's (2003) lead as they tell us that what is included in "curriculum history research" is "social/educational history" (p. 641). I argue that curriculum historiography is the broader, more expansive field of study under which educational history is subsumed. So in order to understand the varying ways to theorize curriculum it is imperative that students know something about educational history as it relates to curriculum historiography. The question is how does the narrow relate to the broad; how does the broad encompass that which is narrow?

Engaging with Historical Texts

I would like to make some general comments again on theorizing history and think through some thoughts about what it is we are studying. I find useful here a remark by William James (1998) who says that "the history of philosophy [and I would add the history of curriculum] is to a great extent that of a certain clash of temperaments" (p. 11). Historiography is built on these "clash[ing] of temperaments." Books are written out of strong emotional convictions and these emotional convictions split on ideological lines. These splits are what become segments and configurations. These configurations of curriculum historiography do not come out of nowhere, they are emotionally and intellectually driven by varying ideologies. Historiography is highly political and it behooves students to know what kind of politics is getting played out in the text. What comes to mind here is Diane Ravitch's (2001) book *Left Back*. I will discuss this later in the context of progressive education, but I will say here that it behooves the student to know that Ravitch's ideology is rightwing. I argue that Ravitch misunderstands Dewey and the progressive dream. Her book works to re-*right* history wrongly. Most curriculum historiography that I explore here is driven from the political left. Historiography is politically motivated, and different writers will represent different events according to their own political "temperament" to use James's word.

I find useful here a remark by John Dewey (1974) who states:

> The mentally active scholar [I would add curriculum scholar] will acknowledge, I think, his mind roams far and wide. All is grist that comes to his mill, and he does

not limit his supply of grain to any one fenced off field. Yet the mind does not roam abroad. It returns with what is found, and there is constant exercise of judgment to detect relations, relevancies, bearings upon the central theme. (p. 424)

What richness is found in Dewey's writing! Dewey encourages us to be generalists, and yet he also states that scholars must come back from general studies to one's specific discipline. Studying educational history and curriculum historiography certainly encourages students to roam far and wide. I attempt here to demonstrate "relations, relevances, [and the] bearings upon a central theme" (Dewey, 1974, p. 424). What I would like to do here is to have a discussion that turns on various themes that have given us grist for the mill, food for thought, ideas and pause.

I approach texts and engage with these texts to arrive at certain themes that have emerged from the readings. I engage with the texts at hand not as a historian but a curriculum theorist. I engage with the texts as a curriculum theorist and that means that I theorize and talk with these texts. Or as Bill Readings (1999) puts it, "Thought take place besides thought" (p. 192). What strikes me here is the notion of the "beside." Texts beside other texts. My work here is interpreting texts alongside other texts.

Many historians approach their material in such a way as to not talk with their texts. Dominick LaCapra (2000) explains the problematic of approaching texts from the historian's perspective. He states,

> History in accordance with a self-sufficient research paradigm gives priority if not exclusive status to accurate reconstruction, restricts exchange with other inquirers to a subordinate, instrumental status (signaled textually by a relegation to footnotes or a bibliography), and is forced to disguise a dialogic exchange as reconstruction, often in a manner that infiltrates values into a seemingly objective or value-neutral account. (p. 65)

What I am writing here is a history of histories, a sort of metahistory on the books in the curriculum field that deal with history. This metahistory is one where I plan on engaging actively with these texts in what LaCapra calls a "dialogic exchange" (p. 65). I want to talk with these texts. In no way is this writing value-neutral. As Ellen Condliffe Lagemann (2000) puts it: "Discipline histories investigate the changing ecology of knowledge and politics that have been part of that" (p. xiv). This entire project is a history of the discipline of curriculum theory and certainly the various configurations that have emerged have done so because of social and cultural politics.

Emerging Themes from Educational History: An Unfinished Portrait

The educational histories I discuss here represent major trends. I want to tease out themes and trends in ways that open dialogue, give pause, and hopefully make readers think differently. I emphasize also in the above heading that this is a portrait, it is not an encyclopedic approach by any means. I want to paint a portrait that is open to change and contestation. This is an unfinished portrait, because the story of educational history is ongoing.

Educational History: The Common School and the Hunt for the Common Good

A common theme that emerges in many current educational historiographies is the common school in relation to the common good. This theme is by no means new, it has been emerging in historiographies for decades. In fact, Larry Cuban and Dorothy Shipps (2000) have co-edited an interesting collection titled *Reconstructing the Common Good in Education: Coping with Intractable American Dilemmas*. A writer in their collection, William J. Reese, says that the search for the common good is an elusive one. Does one really know what the common good is? What is the good? What is common? Friedrich Nietzsche (1967) tells us that "we are unknown to ourselves, we men [and women] of knowledge—and with good reason" (p. 2). We are unknown to ourselves because to know the self—to use Cuban and Shipps's word—is an intractable problem. The self is built in relation to the other, but people are not alike—ever—so the notion of the common good becomes problematic. There is nothing common about us and that is the beginning of the problematics with the notion of the common good. Another way to turn this issue is to relook at an old philosophical debate between the one and the many. Much of the notion of the common good is entangled in the problems of the one and the many. People are individuals (the one) and when people come together a group is formed (the many). The question is how to reconcile the one with the many. In *The One and the Many*, William James (1998) asks the following question:

> Philosophy [and educational history] has often been defined as the quest or the vision of the world's unity [think of the common school in its relation to the common good]. We never hear this definition challenged.... But how about the *variety* in things? Is that such an irrelevant matter? (p. 64).

James, although a straddler on most issues, says that "pragmatism must turn its back on absolute monism" (p. 78). The issue of the common school and the hunt for the common good are issues of "absolute monism." The common school will never be common and the common good will never be found. Emmanuel Levinas (2001) tells us that what is, absolute alterity and not simply James's variety. If you have a variety, you might have some things in common. But for Levinas, on an ontological level, people never have anything in common, and none of us speaks the same language, as it were. People are absolutely Other to each other. But if that is the case, how can Levinas talk about issues of social justice? There has to be some common ground upon which people can do good deeds and fight for social justice. A just cause must be agreed upon to make it just. But then again a single individual can do a good deed and fight for a just cause without having to appeal to authority. People are not one thing and groups are not monolithic. This is yet another intractable problem as Cuban and Shipps (2000) might say. The intractable problem, too, is that Americans are, as Michael Kammen (1990) points out, a "people of paradox" as the title of his book suggests. America is a complex country and many of our ideals are contradictory. There isn't one America, there are many. Every state differs. One side of the country is completely different from the other. The North and the South couldn't be more different. The common good is of necessity paradoxical because what is good for one person might not be good for another person.

David Tyack (2003) is an educational historian who does address these issues in his book *Seeking Common Ground: Public Schools in a Diverse Society*. What drove people apart during the emergence of the common school was a serious problem of not seeing eye to eye. Tyack explains.

> Racism, religious bias, ethnocentrism, and self-interest marred the search for a common denominator of civic instruction. But that is only part of the story. It is hard to find another reform in American history that spread as fast as the common school, had such an egalitarian rationale, and aroused so little dissent nationwide. In a society that offered few other government services Americans created the most comprehensive system of public schooling in the world. During the 19th century at least, civic education was the public school's crucial purpose. (p. 12)

Civic education as a goal gets thwarted because of racism. Public schools were built for white Protestant children. Others were not welcomed in the schoolhouse. I will talk more about this later but for now let us focus on the problem of what the hunt for the common good means and why it is problematic. Like

Tyack, William Reese (2000) points out that one of the main purposes of the common school was the "elevation of civic values and ideals above individual self-interest" (p. 14). The elevation of the civic is a noble idea. However, this noble pursuit—in reality—never got played out.

Ella Flagg Young (1900) drives a wedge between the uniform and unity to argue that common schools (and I might add the hunt for the common good) are more about unity than uniformity. The real goal of the common school is unity and this unity has everything to do with civic ideals. For Young, unity suggests "comradeship in experience," "the democratic experience," and that which is "humanitarian" (p. 47). These are lofty ideas indeed. But schooling today is hardly about humanitarianism with the onslaught of NCLB and Race to the Top. At any rate, Young recognizes the problem of confusing unity with uniformity and tries to address this issue, as she says that uniformity is a problem and is certainly not what is meant by unity. Young states, "For teachers and pupils to become parts of an 'incoherent homogeneity' is for them to be lost in their school life and individuality which is the inherent right of every soul" (p. 48).

The problem of the one (the individual) and the many (the common good, or unity) is hard to reconcile, perhaps impossible. The will of the individual is often in contradistinction to the will of the group. And as Young points out, often the soul can get squashed under the weight of the will of the group, especially when that will is at odds with the will of the individual. Lawrence Cremin (1988) talks about the problems of the will of the powerful as the problem of Americanization. To Americanize those who are not Americans or those who are not considered American enough was the purpose of the common school; to reshape individuals, to homogenize people—as Young put it—was the goal of the common school. Cremin says,

> School systems across the country [in 1921] organized comprehensive Americanization programs for immigrant children (and often their parents as well). Such programs ordinarily involved a complex process of socialization that went far beyond instruction in English and civics to include training in personal cleanliness, middle-class values, and factorylike discipline. (p. 237)

What is striking in this passage is the issue of cleanliness. Many thought that immigrants were less than "civilized" and maybe even thought to be vermin. In fact, William Reese (2000) says that in the 1830s "Horace Mann and his allies regularly complained that the rich stubbornly refused to send their children to public schools, fearing social contamination" (p. 20).

Contamination is the key word in this passage. Vermin contaminate. So there are two issues here, one of race and one of class. To clean up the self is to make the self more white, more Anglo-Saxon. Immigrants were not seen as white or white enough. And certainly the poor were feared as if poverty could rub off on people. Students of European history know how the notion of contamination played out for Jews. When people think of others as contaminated they find a way of getting rid of that contamination by exiling or annihilating them. Too, in the United States we have our own history of genocide as the Native Americans were decimated by white settlers and African Americans were enslaved, tortured, murdered, and lynched. The civic virtues of the common school were overshadowed by hatred and fear of the Other.

Fear of the Other

William Reese (2005) comments that social harmony was a goal of the common school in the 1800s. But how can you have harmony when there is so much hatred and fear of the Other? An underlying problem with the common school turned on managing psychological projections, containing the fear of the Other. Issues of contamination, as Reese put it, are psychological issues. People project (or spit out) what they feel is contaminated about themselves (what Jung would call the shadow) and project that shadow onto Others.

The issue of cleanliness is not a literal one, but has everything to do with fantasies of purity (Anglo-Saxon) and impurity (non-Anglo-Saxon). The longing to clean up the other is at bottom the longing to get rid of (project or spit out) the psyche's own feelings of impurity, dirtiness, the shadow. What is dirty in the psyche is what one doesn't like about oneself. But in order to psychologically manage the negative many project the dirt outside themselves onto Others so as not to face their own shadow within. European Jews and Gypsies were often compared with vermin (Morris, 2001), as vermin are (1) not human and (2) are dirty. Fantasies of the unclean and impure are dangerous.

Most historians of the common school, though, do not touch upon the psychological problems of projection because psychohistory has fallen out of fashion in the historical community since the 1970s. But the psychological aspects of historiography are necessary to discuss, especially since they are absent in most discussions of the common school.

Perhaps the notion of the common is the problem. In fact, Henry David Thoreau (2000) remarks that "it is time that we had uncommon schools" (p. 114). In rich language Thoreau declares that getting an education outside of formal institutions is very important. He states,

> It is time that villages were universities, and their fellow inhabitants the fellows of universities, with leisure—if they are indeed so well off—to pursue liberal studies the rest of their lives. Shall the world be confined to one Paris or one Oxford forever? Cannot students be boarded here and get a liberal education under the skies of Concord? Can we not hire some Abelard to lecture to us? Alas! [W]hat with foddering the cattle and tending the store, we are kept from school too long, and our education is sadly neglected. (p. 114)

Thoreau foreshadows what curriculum studies scholars suggest today. The idea here is that education happens elsewhere, outside of formal institutions, and maybe scholars should look more closely at informal sites of education. This is a topic of concern that is taken up by curriculum studies scholars and by curriculum historians. Dewey also talks about the importance of informal education, calling for a balance of formal and informal education. Petra Munro Hendry (2011) addresses this issue, too, as she claims that when educational history begins with the narrative of the common school, historians exclude all sorts of places where women and minorities could get an education. There are other sites of education outside the schoolhouse. For Munro Hendry, women's religious orders were educative places, in fact, monasteries were educational refuges for the medieval women mystics. Where else could they get educated? They were not allowed to attend university so the monasteries were the only places that they could be supported in their studies.

Containing Psychological Projection: Morality, Religion, and the Common School

In many educational historiographies it is noted that the hidden curriculum of public schooling turned on inculcating Protestant morality. In fact, Carl Bankston and Steven Caldas (2009), in *Public Education: America's Civil Religion*, argue that the civic purpose of the common school was actually religious. Colin J. Marsh and George Willis (2007) point out that in colonial America

> most settlers were Christians who saw the value of at least some religious training in order to make people more godly despite their inherently sinful nature. The most

common model for the few formal schools that existed throughout the colonies thus became the Latin grammar school, for it provided the beginnings of a literary education necessary for males to enter the clergy. (p. 30)

The separation of church and state in public institutions is not clear at all. State institutions seem to have a religious underpinning, even though they are not supposed to. The religious and moral slant to public education is really about containing and controlling psychological projections. The purpose of the Protestant ethic is to keep at bay psychological fears about the self.

Containing the self means containing a sexualized self. The Other is often portrayed as sexually out of control, especially in the case of Jews and blacks (Morris, 2001). A sexually out-of-control self is a dirty self. Martin Luther punished himself for even thinking about sex as he thought that even the thought of sexuality was bad. Schooling, I argue, is partly, then, about desexualizing the self and pretending that children do not have sexualities.

One of the most interesting books on Protestantism and public schooling is by Douglas McKnight (2003). He argues that the goals of the common school get emplotted by an underlying Protestant narrative. He talks about some key ideas such as progress as a form of transcendence. What is it that people need to transcend? Our sinful nature. Martin Luther thought that people are innately bad. Original sin is part and parcel of Protestantism. So children need to transcend original sin through schooling, McKnight tells us. Students need, in fact, to be redeemed. And schooling will redeem us. McKnight explains:

> Part of this process is to instruct students [in the history textbooks] in the symbolic narrative of America, specifically its historical tale of redemption and transcendence. This has been the call of the historian from the first histories written by the colonial Puritans (p. 5).

So the story of coming to America is a Protestant morality tale. Children must learn this morality tale, make sure they get their thoughts in order, and clean up any thoughts that might be impure or sinful. What McKnight does not address, nor do other historians of education, is that at bottom what the Protestant morality tale is attempting to redeem us from is our own sexualities. The Puritans wanted to be pure (that is asexual). And this is why sexuality issues in the United States are still taboo. Gender bending and sex change operations are hardly acceptable in this very Protestant country.

The Common Curriculum: The "Classics"

McKnight (2003) tells us that William Torrey Harris (who I call a traditionalist) was known for advocating the classical curriculum. Diane Ravitch (2001) says that he is unjustly called conservative. But he was conservative. He was a Great Books man. The only proper study for students would be the classical. There is nothing wrong with studying the classics, as Dewey (1974) suggested. The problem is that these classical texts—if unrelated to life—become meaningless for students. William Torrey Harris is one of Diane Ravitch's heroes in the story of who got "left back" in educational history. The implication of her book is that what teachers should be doing today is what William Torrey Harris suggests. Teachers should be teaching our children the Great Books tradition. There is nothing wrong with reading the Great Books, but there is so much more to the curriculum. One could make the claim that if all we teach our youngsters are the Great Books we are also inadvertently perhaps teaching them to be racist and sexist. The curriculum is much broader than the Great Books Tradition and scholars should work to integrate women and minorities into the canon and also to critique the canon. At any rate, William Torrey Harris, McKnight (2003) tells us, felt that a child should study the Great Books so as to "surpass" his "animal, depraved self" (p. 99). Torrey Harris thought that children were animals and were highly impure, dirty, and tempted by sexuality. What else is the "animal" self but the sexualized self? What else would "depraved" mean but the sexual? The 19th and 20th century idea of the child is full of contradictions as he is innocent, asexual and also animal, evil, and sexually crazed. Is studying the Great Books a way to contain the "animal" in the child? Or is the study of the Great Books a way to erase thoughts of sexuality? Strengthening the mind (faculty psychology) for Torrey Harris was a way to overcome the weakness of the body. So, too, for religiously minded educators, strengthening the mind through adherence to religious discipline was a way to overcome the body. Philosophers and theologians alike—especially during the 17th and 18th centuries—believed that the body was evil. The study of the Great Books Tradition for the traditionalists like Harris was a way to insure the separation of mind from body, for the Great Books do not address the body at all.

Keeping the Body in Check

Religion is hardly rational. The leap of faith has little to do with reason; the purpose of religion is to keep in check the emotions and the body. The common school is a tale of keeping emotions and the body in check and the tale is partly a religious one. In fact, Donald and Jo Ann Parkerson (2001) remind us that school prayer was not unusual in the 1800s. They state,

> Religion, of course, would continue to play a role in the moral education of American children well into the 1800s. As we have seen, many common school classes recited a short, nonsectarian prayer at the beginning or end of the day. (p. 128)

Whether the prayer was sectarian or not, it was still a prayer, which is still religion. What is the purpose of the prayer? To pray that children do not fall back into original sin? To pray that the mind can overcome the body? Morality is not a benign idea. What is immoral to think about? Doing bad things. And what is bad? For the Puritans, it was sex. William Reese (2005) comments that the common schools emerged during a time of "evangelical Protestantism" (p. 3). Today the term "evangelical" means ultra-rightwing fundamentalists. They are, in a word, religious zealots. The schoolmaster is zealous. The schoolmaster image is harsh; the school master is a strict disciplinarian who wouldn't hesitate to beat children into submission. The Puritans, in fact, did beat school children. Peter Hlebowitsh (2007) claims:

> Some of the schoolrooms were equipped with whipping posts, which were used with unruly students (Cubberly, 1947). But even the use of the whipping post had an ecclesiastical rationale. Because children were believed to be born sinful, they periodically had to have "old Adam beaten out of them" (Knight, 1951, p. 127). The wisdom of the schoolmasters was that children were better off whipped than eternally damned. (p. 153)

Like Hlebowitsh, Tanner and Tanner (2007) tells us that teachers "taught—rote and recitation, supported by the rod" (p. 5).

The common school was mired in a sort of evangelicalism, as Reese (2005) suggests. The American curriculum field has always been based, as Alan Block (2004) points out, on Christian principles. Block explains,

> The field of curriculum has been forever dominated by the discourses derived from Greek, Roman, and Christian principles and by practices and methods that derive from these principles. These are the principles found in the works of Socrates, Plato, Aristotle, Augustine, Aquinas and Descartes. (p. 10)

These are the Great Books men. Block's point is that studying the Great Books Tradition is studying principles that are hardly Jewish. Block calls for a reexamination of the curriculum and the ways in which it has excluded non-Christian peoples. Like Block, Leon Fink (1997) points out that academic disciplines are shot through with "Protestant moral values" (p. 16). Fink explains.

> If secular humanism offered one prop to democratic educational change, a more widespread stimulus was religion. In his interpretation of progressivism as "a climate of creativity," historian Robert M. Crunden has highlighted the diffusion of Protestant moral values into secular professions including social work, journalism academia, the law, and politics. Creative individuals from the middle-class backgrounds, Crunden argues, found conventional outlets inadequate for the quest for religious perfectionism instilled in them during childhood. (pp. 16–17)

Religious perfectionism here also means Christian religious perfectionism because people of other religious backgrounds were not invited into these various professions until around the mid-20th century. What is striking is the way in which mostly all the professions were shot through with religion. One must wonder what it is about religion that so attracts people, that so inflames their imaginations and permeates their worldviews.

Americans of course weren't the only ones who cleaved to religious ideas. In Europe many intellectuals talked about the moral and religious purposes of education. Although Immanuel Kant tried to separate religion from reason, one can see traces of the religious in his golden rule imperative. Too, Kant, according to Michael Hofstetter (2001) believed that "man must be made moral" (p. 27). Hofstetter traces many instances of European thinkers who mixed the religious with the study of academic disciplines. In fact, the aim of the European university was a moral or religious one in the 1800s. Hofstetter tells us that "Fichte, Schelling, von Humboldt and Coleridge (among others) were all in agreement here. Universities could make society more moral, more cultured and (in Coleridge's eyes, at least) more Christian" (p. xii). Americans, then, aren't alone in their quest for making education more religious.

Redemption, Race, and Gender: The Common School Undone

Scholars talk about the notion of redemption as a goal of public schooling (McKnight, 2003). Who are people being redeemed from and for what purpose? What is a redemptive education? Is the quest for building a moral character about being redeemed from something immoral? And what would that immoral thing be? Recall that the Puritans, Western philosophers, and theologians thought the body evil. People are, therefore, schooled to hate the body, and our redemption comes when we get over our bodily impulses, our emotions, and our sexualities.

But there are other things about which redemption might refer. Here I want to talk about two issues: race and gender. Some white Anglo-Saxons, when talking about redemption, are also talking about redemption from the Other and that Other is both nonwhite and female. White supremacy and misogyny go hand in hand.

I take my lead in this discussion from Lawrence Cremin (1988), who tells us that there were "two views of redemption" (p. 212) for Southerners in the context of schooling. To save themselves, Cremin suggests that after Reconstruction, Southerners were to embrace the Northern idea of the common school and therefore embrace "northern values and culture" (p. 212). Why would Southerners want to buy into Northern culture? More than likely, most Southerners wanted nothing to do with the North. Cremin then argues that redemption in this case meant "the redemption of the South from the Northern blight of universal schooling" (p. 215). This ties directly into issues of race. Southerners feared blacks. Jonathan Zimmerman (2002) says,

> Neo-Confederates promoted a distinct, rigidly pro-southern set of texts for white students. Refusing to concede even a scintilla of Dixie honor to the invading Yankee horde, these orthodox [I would say racist] books dominated white schools for at least forty years [after Reconstruction].... Confederate loyalists controlled the entire history curriculum in thousands of White [schools]...As early as 1913 the historian William Dodd could report with horror—and with only slight hyperbole—that "two distinct histories are taught in the schools: one above the Mason-Dixon Line, and one below it." (p. 34)

Southern whites clearly rewrote history to suit them and also to redeem them from any lingering guilt they might have had over slavery. The white-controlled history textbooks served to erase and unwrite the past; they served to erase shame and guilt. Rewriting history is a way to control whose past will be remembered, and clearly this is an issue of politics and power. Ted Mitchell (2000) points out that this unwriting of history was going on all over the South, and he discusses the case of New Orleans in particular. It took "military authority" (p. 38) to deal with miseducating youth. Mitchell explains:

> In occupied New Orleans, the replacement of civil authority by military authority in educational affairs was barely masked by the appointment of a civilian Bureau of Education. That board proceeded rapidly to develop loyalty tests for teachers, to replace Confederate texts currently in use with "sound" Northern ones, and, as we have seen, to require patriotic performances in schools. [The Northern military wanted to]... eliminate Confederate loyalty by rooting out disloyal and "neutral" teachers. (p. 38)

Even if the military forced the Southerners to change their textbooks to reflect a more accurate portrayal of slavery and even if the military worked to "root out disloyal" teachers, still the Southern mentality held firm with the rise of the Ku Klux Klan, Jim Crow, and lynchings (Pinar, 2001). What disturbs is that many Southerners held firm also to their religious convictions, especially if they were evangelicals. The evangelical mindset fueled racism.

If the common school, then, was really an evangelical morality tale (as Reese (2005) suggests), then the common school came undone because evangelical morality cannot be separated out from racism. The common school was in no way common for blacks or for other races for that matter. To bring history to life let us for a moment dwell on what is reported by Donald and Jo Ann Parkerson (2001) about Southerners' struggle to redeem the Old South.

> Throughout the entire period of Reconstruction (1865–1877) states in the South fought desperately to bring back [or redeem] their conservative [racist] governments, destroy the Freedmen's Bureau, and generally return things to the way they were prior to the war. In North Carolina, for example, white Democrats waged a campaign of intimidation and terror on Freedman's Bureau representatives, Republicans, and former slaves. A white Republican had his throat cut and a black organizer was hanged in a courthouse square with a sign pinned to his shirt reading "Beware, ye guilty, both black and white." Moreover, countless African Americans were whipped, tortured, and their homes burned. (p. 42)

This is the kind of history that gets erased. High school history texts work to sanitize the past so as not to offend readers, parents, and schoolteachers. But this is the very kind of history that needs to be told so as not to redeem the Old South and erase the truth of the past. Students of history need to consult especially William Pinar's (2001) book on lynching and violence in America. Here is a book that does not work to erase or sanitize. I will discuss in more detail Pinar's work later, but for now it is enough to say that historians need to be told not to redeem an unusable past but to tell the truth of what happened, to represent history in all its gruesomeness.

The commonality of the common school was the Anglo-Saxon Protestant male. Racists believed that the common school was contaminated, as Reese (2000) put it, by blacks and other nonwhite races. Mexicans, Chinese, Japanese, Blacks, and Native Americans all "contaminated" the common school, and it was this so-called contamination that made the common school unravel.

Oppressions

Mexicans, too, have had their problems in common schools due to racism and discrimination. It is not too well known that Mexicans were actually segregated from white schools in various parts of the country for many years. Mary S. Black (2005) says that Mexican children had very different kinds of public schools than did white children. She explains,

> Those schools [for Mexican children in Texas during the 1920s] were strictly segregated and generally had very poor facilities, a basic curriculum, a short school year, and few enrichment activities. For example, the typical one-room, country school for Mexican immigrant children in Texas in the 1920s concentrated on teaching pupils oral English skills to the exclusion of most other subjects. Mastery of reading, writing, and mathematics was not considered important, nor, some argued, desirable for these students. Many of these schools only operated half days for 5 or 6 months a year. (pp. 262–263)

A good way to miseducate youth is to teach them a basic curriculum. That in this case means teach them basically nothing. If you don't teach someone to read, he or she cannot find a way to fight back. Reading is a way to construct a language that allows one to fight oppression. Without learning to read and write what are your options in life? How can you ever think your way out of a horrible situation if you don't have the language to do so? By not teaching people to read and write, oppressors have a way of keeping people down, controlling them, and doing them further harm. The other thought that comes to mind, when reading the above passage by Mary Black, is how little non-Mexicans know about Mexican history or the history of Mexican immigrants in America. If scholars do not seek out and study these histories of oppression, we are complicit with undoing and unwriting the racist past that is America. Scholars need to work to deepen the history curriculum in order to not miseducate our youth and make sure that they know that the history of common schooling has not been equitable. Texas wasn't the only state where Mexican or Latino/a children were segregated. Joel Spring (2010) tells us about Chicano children in California and how they too were segregated during the 1920s from white children. Spring reports,

> In *Chicano Education in the Era of Segregation*, Gilbert Gonzalez finds that the typical attitude in California schools was reflected in the April 1921 minutes of the Ontario, California, Board of Education: "Mr. Hill made the recommendation that the board select two new school sites; one in the southeastern part of the town for a Mexican school; the other near the Central School." Gonzalez reports that a survey conducted in the mid-1930s found that 85 percent of the districts investigated in the Southwest were segregated. (p. 91)

Joel Spring also points out that Native Americans, Chinese, and Japanese children were all discriminated against. Spring points out that William Torrey Harris argued that Native Americans needed to be taken from their homes so as to become less Indian and more American. Spring tells us,

> In 1889, U.S. Commissioner of Indian Affairs Thomas J. Morgan wrote a bulletin on Indian Education that outlined the goals and policies of Indian schools. The bulletin was distributed by the U.S. Bureau of Education with an introduction written by the Commissioner of Education, William T. Harris. In the introduction, Harris praised what he called "the new education for our American Indians," particularly the effort "to obtain control of the Indian at an early age, and to seclude him as much as possible from tribal influences." (p. 99)

Native American children were forcibly taken away from their families in order to be schooled to become more like the white man. This is also what happened to "the stolen generation" in Australia. British colonizers stole Aboriginal children from their homes to try to make them more white and "breed" them to get the Aboriginal out of them so that they could become more white (see the film *Rabbit-Proof Fence* [2002] for more on this). Native Americans and the Aboriginal children suffered at the hands of colonizers.

Cultures are decimated by schooling. Spring calls this "deschooling." What happened to the common good in our story of the common school? What happened to the noble ideas that Ella Flag Young (1900) had about schooling as a "humanitarian" act? If the purpose of schooling is to colonize the Other, it is hardly humanitarian. On another related note, William Torrey Harris, who was an advocate of the classics, was also an advocate of schooling for colonization. Racism was also evident, as Joel Spring (2010) points out, in the shocking "lynching of 22 Chinese men by Los Angeles mobs [in 1871]" (p. 94) and also the fact that "more than 100,000 Japanese Americans" were put in "concentration camps" (p. 95) during WWII. These are little known histories for school students. Joel Spring, more so than any other educational historian, has worked hard to bring these little known histories to light. His historiography works to undo racism on many levels. Many educational historians spend little time addressing the issues of race, but not Spring. Spring has done some of the most important historical work of our generation. Like Spring, William Reese (2005) comments on the situation faced by many minorities in the context of public schooling. Reese tells us:

> In San Francisco in the 1860s and 1870s Chinese American children were often excluded from public schools, and Japanese children later faced exclusion and severe discrimination as immigration increased their numbers. Assimilation was not a universal policy, since some marginalized groups were segregated into often inferior school facilities or were excluded entirely. (pp. 52–53)

Ming Fang He, JoAnn Phillion, Elaine Chan, and Shijing Xu (2008) report that often when talking about discrimination and schooling, Asians get left out of the discussion. And, too, these writers suggest that Asians get lumped together as if they are one monolithic group, when in fact there are many kinds of Asians. Oftentimes Asian students are not thought of as people of color, and they are not talked about because of the stereotype that Asians are overachievers and always do well in school. So when an Asian student has a learning disability, educators are puzzled. I will be devoting an entire chapter to multiculturalism and will flesh out issues on race and equity there, but for now I wanted to drive home the point that these so-called common schools were not common for everyone and that the common good was not, in fact, good at all. The noble goal of democracy in schooling has never been a reality. Political writers in curriculum studies address these issues in much depth and detail still, perhaps following the lead of people like Ella Flagg Young (1900), who so often gets left out of the story of curriculum history. Our tale of morality and character building has gotten lost in the midst of the realities of the racism and colonialism that schooling has fostered. William Watkins (2001) holds nothing back when he states,

During the nineteenth century, America's racial and ethnic attitudes hardened. More than 2 centuries of slavery, territorial conquest, and international isolation fed notions of White supremacy, ethnocentrism, and great-nation chauvinism. The concept of morality came to be associated with the triumphant White American character. (p. 12)

The morality tale of the public school is not a good one. And there is nothing common about the common school. The school has been a place to be indoctrinated and colonized. It is striking and ironic that today there are so many books on democracy and schooling because there is little democracy in schools. These institutions are simply not democratic.

· 3 ·
HISTORICAL CURRICULUM CONCEPTS, PART 2

Introduction

The aim of this chapter is to examine the concept of gender in the context of the erasure of women from traditional historiographies. John Dewey and debates around the Progressive movement will be explored. Progressive women educators will be discussed against the backdrop of their interests in politics and the arts. Here, too, I will engage in a discussion of the importance of race, class, and gender in the context of Progressive education.

Gender and Redemption

Like issues of race, gender issues in the context of schooling are disturbing. In this section I want to talk about general ideas related to gender, redemption, and the common school. Recall that William Reese (2000) wrote about the notion of "contamination" (p. 20) and the way in which wealthy parents did not want to send their children to public schools because they feared the poor. The poor were treated as if they were contaminated. I suggested that the issue of race in the previous chapter be treated alongside class—as nonwhites had been treated historically as if they were contaminated as well. And so, too, women have historically been treated in public schools and universities, as if they were contaminated.

So in this section of this chapter I want to raise some general questions about issues that turn on gender in the context of school. Later I will discuss in more detail women's contributions to Progressive education through examining both case studies as well as biographies, but here I want to talk about some issues, generally speaking, that will help set the scene for later discussions.

Recall, one of the themes that has emerged in many recent educational historiographies concerns the intersections of religion and schooling and the way in which religion has set the tone for what goes on in the common school—even though church and state are supposed to be separate in the United States. When I address issues of gender, again, religion plays a role in the way that women are portrayed. Women have historically been treated like second-class citizens, in part, because in the Bible, Eve is considered the temptress; Eve is short for evil. Misogyny comes, in part, from religion. And in the United States, during the emergence of the common school, it was the Christian interpretation of Eve (as temptress) that set the stage for the way women have been treated. Women are "contaminated" because they are temptresses, hence they are sexual creatures. The repression of sexuality in both women and men is the Puritan heritage. Women are blamed for the downfall of men because Eve tempted Adam.

Women and Erasure

In recent historiographies of the common school (and of universities) it is reported by many scholars that women had been treated badly by men. What surprises is how intensely women have been discriminated against. First, it is a well-known fact that many historiographies—even recent ones—leave women out of the story of the common school. If women are discussed they are discussed in passing. Recall, two of the most well-known and well-respected educational historians—Herbert Kliebard and Lawrence Cremin—deal little with the contributions of women in education. In Herbert Kliebard's (1995) *The Struggle for the American Curriculum: 1893–1958*, women are left out. Ella Flagg Young is mentioned in passing. The same problem occurs in the work of Lawrence Cremin (1988). In his interesting book *American Education: The Metropolitan Experience 1876–1980*, women are not in the story. Here is an example from a brief passage about Progressive schools. Cremin (1988) states

> Beyond a great variety of changes in public schooling, the Progressive school movement, particularly between 1910 and 1930, became an important stimulus to the founding of independent schools. Some, like the Walden School in New York City or the Chevy Chase School in Maryland, were established by individual teachers seeking to apply particular pedagogical theories. (p. 240)

Cremin mentions Caroline Pratt as the founder of a Progressive school but her name is the only one mentioned in the context of these schools. When talking of the Walden School in the above passage, he doesn't mention Margaret Naumburg. He does not flesh out, in any way, what her contribution was or that she was not only a school founder but also an intellectual who wrote books that advanced the progressive field not only in education but in art therapy as well as in psychoanalysis. I will talk in more detail about Naumburg later. But for now notice also in the above passage Cremin says that these schools were founded by "individuals." Almost all of the Progressive schools were founded by individuals who were women. Alan Sadovnik and Susan Semel (2002)—who have done a marvelous job in bringing women into the discussion in their book *Founding Mothers and Others: Women Educational Leaders during the Progressive Era*—tell us

> Historians of progressive education have often overlooked the contributions of women to the movement. Although the women chronicled in this book are mentioned in various histories, this is more often than not in the context of brief discussions of the schools that they founded, rather than a discussion of their lives and careers. More importantly, histories of progressive education tend to be histories of great men, including John Dewey, William Heard Kilpatrick, Harold Rugg, and George Counts. (p. 253)

More than just talking about women's contributions to Progressive education, it is important to note that these women were also intellectuals. This is a point driven home in the work of Petra Munro Hendry (2011). The term "intellectual" has historically only been attributed to white men (Morris, 2006). School teachers, too, are not thought of as intellectuals because of the feminization of the profession. Again, part of the problem is that the feminine (which is a social construct) is relegated to temptress or, in the case of schooling, schoolmarm (an asexual person). Petra Munro Hendry writes much about the social construction of the "spinster" teacher (the unmarried and perhaps asexual person) and how this construct served to oppress and denigrate. One of the missing discussions among recent educational historiographies of Progressive women educators who founded schools is that many of them were lesbians. This is an important point not to pass over. Lesbianism (as a social construct) is still a taboo topic for historians. Educational historians don't, for the most part, address this in any way. Some of the historians talk in a de-sexualized way about women—who founded Progressive schools—as having lifelong relationships with other women, or they talk about lesbian partnerships as friendships. But it is long past due that scholars acknowledge that the sexuality of these women is something worth talking about. The social construct of the spinster is also a code word for lesbian. One of the points I am trying to drive home here is that not only were women marginalized in historiographies but so too were sexualities of the women who made history. One wonders whether homophobia plays a part in the absence of discussion of homosexuality and Progressive schools. This is an important discussion to have because when scholars talk about women as a category—another social construction, of course—they are talking about all kinds of women, including nonheterosexual women.

Kathleen Weiler (1998) tells us that when historians talk about the school teacher, the assumption is that she is white. Weiler says

> Native American and African-American women teachers have been ignored in white discourse, both in nineteenth- and twentieth-century constructions of the "woman schoolteacher" and in later historical studies of teaching. Discussions of the woman schoolteacher have almost always focused on white women teachers' experience. (p. 19)

There are, today, more books that focus on nonwhite teachers, but still this omission remains a problematic issue. However, more liberal historians and curriculum theorists do address women and race in their work. For example, Alan Sadovnik and Susan Semel (2002) include a discussion of Charlotte Hawkins Brown in their case studies of women Progressives; William F. Pinar (2001) talks extensively about Ida B. Wells in his book *The Gender of Racial Politics and Violence in America: Lynching, Prison Rape, and the Crisis of Masculinity*; Petra Munro Hendry (2011) in her book *Engendering Curriculum History* talks about Ida B. Wells, Anna Julia Cooper, Charlotte Hawkins Brown, and others. Race, again, has been a major category of discussion in curriculum theorizing since at least the 1970s. But in the context of more traditional educational historiographies gender and race issues are not treated as much as they should be.

Women as Contaminants

As I suggested earlier, to be a woman (and certainly there are different kinds of women along the race/class/gender/sexuality/disability spectrum) historically has meant to be perceived as almost less than human. Women have been thought to be contaminated. In the context of schooling, Kathleen Weiler (1998) talks about one James Barr, who, in 1906, claimed that boys were in "danger" (read the fear of contamination) because of the "overfeminization of the schools" (p. 43). Weiler says

> According to Barr, the British were struck by the large number of women teachers in American public schools, and seven of the twenty-seven members of the [Moseley Educational] commission "deplored the preponderance of women teachers" in the United States. Their concern was expressed most strongly by one Professor Armstrong, who deplored the plight of American boys: "The boy in America is not being brought up to punch another boy's head or to have his own punched in a healthy manner; there is a strange indefinable feminine air coming over America. (pp. 43–44)

The dangerous influence of women on men is stated over and over again throughout these historiographies. These issues are, at root, about the fear of sexuality and the fear also of gender bending or even the fear of homosexuality.

What is astounding is that despite misogyny, it was—for the most part—women who founded Progressive schools, not men. Maybe they founded these schools because they felt unwelcome in other educational settings and had to carve out their own space. Wayne Urban (2000) points out that women were prohibited from speaking in National Education Association (NEA) meetings in the late 1800s. Urban tells us "Women teachers and other women were allowed to be present at NEA conventions but were *forbidden* [emphasis mine] to speak at them or to otherwise participate actively until the twentieth century" (p. 1). It is disturbing that men (in the NEA) made certain that women had no say in their own lives and careers. This trend seems still to go on today as government officials decide what teachers should or shouldn't do in their own classrooms (read NCLB and Race to the Top as patriarchal and misogynist mandates). School teachers (who are mostly women) have no say in what they teach or how they teach. The punitive measures taken by the government (i.e., to fire teachers whose students' test scores are too low) and to print in the newspaper schools that have low test scores (read *The Scarlet Letter*) are highly misogynist as well.

At the NEA the Pledge of Allegiance caused controversy. The controversy, Joel Spring (2010) reports, turned on misogyny and racism. Spring explains

> In 1892, Francis Bellamy wrote the Pledge of Allegiance and introduced it in the same year to educators attending the annual meeting of the National Education Association. A socialist, Bellamy wanted to include the word "equality" in the Pledge but this idea was rejected because state superintendents of education opposed equality for women and African Americans. (p. 9)

The writer of this pledge, Bellamy, was a socialist. One must remember that in 1892 women and minorities had little in the way of civil rights. So the fact that the superintendents rejected the pledge because of the word "equality" should come as no surprise.

Donald and Jo Ann Parkerson (2001), in their book *Transitions in American Education: A Social History of Teaching*, tell us about one particular meeting at the NEA that should raise eyebrows for our feminist readers. Margaret Haley (who was president of the Chicago Teachers Federation) had a run in with William Torrey Harris. Harris, according to the Parkersons, argued that schools should align themselves with businesses. Margaret Haley had no truck with business. Parkerson and Parkerson report,

> Clearly frustrated by these remarks, Haley jumped to her feet and protested that increasing the salaries of teachers should be the top priority of the NEA. Harris's response to Haley was abusive, patronizing, and revealed the low opinion that the administrative leadership typically had of elementary school teachers. [Harris said to the NEA]…"Pay no attention to what that teacher down there has said, for I take it that she is a grade teacher, just out of her school room at the end of the year, worn out, tired and hysterical." (pp. 181–182)

For Harris, an elementary school teacher was childish and hysterical. The contention that women teaching children are childlike themselves is another stereotype that many men have of women. The hysteria that Harris accuses Haley of is not hysteria at all but a plea for equal pay. Still women and men do not have equal pay whether they are elementary school teachers or university professors. When a woman speaks out she is hysterical but when a man speaks out he is macho. The lesson here is that women are not supposed to speak their minds. When they do they are also called witches. Petra Munro Hendry (2011) tells us that "in 1913, when several members of the School Board [in Chicago] tried to unseat her [Ella Flagg Young], she and Margaret

Haley [once again] were both accused by Chicago school board member John Harding of being 'witches'" (p. 170). Ella Flagg Young and Margaret Haley were two Progressive women educators who did great things for this country and especially for women and the Progressive movement. They were both intellectuals and both dedicated to humanitarian causes.

Chicago was home to many settlement houses, most famously Jane Addams's settlement house. Her settlement house work was also demonized, especially after she made statements about being a pacifist and inviting union leaders to speak. At one time Addams was called upon to run for president of the United States, but then was excoriated when her work became too well known and she was thought to be too powerful (Elshtain, 2002).

William Schubert (2009a) tells us that Jane Addams and Ella Flagg Young had a strong influence on John Dewey. Schubert declares

> Now, Dewey had admitted that he learned most about teaching and schooling from his wife, Alice, and from Ella Flagg Young. Dr. Young was his doctoral student and longtime teacher and administrator (including the first female superintendent) in the Chicago public schools, and later President of the National Education Association.... Dewey's larger view of education...was forged at...Hull House, under the tutelage of its founder Jane Addams. (p. 47)

Schubert points out a very important theme here. These women—Jane Addams and Ella Flagg Young—influenced Dewey's work. Mostly, this influence goes unnoticed by educational historians.

Women and the University

Women were not permitted to attend most colleges and universities in the 19th century and even in the early 20th century. Some people had the foresight to open women's colleges—a move made for the same reason that women started Progressive schools. But then, the women's colleges—which most would consider prestigious (the Seven Sisters Colleges)—were thought not to be prestigious by male historians. Helen Lefkowitz Horowitz (1999) says, "Most historians of higher education have seen women's colleges as *retrograde* [emphasis mine] institutions" (p. xiii). When women attended colleges and universities—especially the non-Ivy League institutions—during the late 1800s they did not have the same privileges and rights that their male peers had. Jana Nidiffer (2003) claims

> This antagonism toward women students was tangibly manifested in the inequitable distribution of resources that universities bestowed on them. In general, coeducational universities did not provide women with housing, medical care, or physical education facilities, despite the fact that such facilities existed for men by the 1870s. (p. 23)

These gross inequities are so remarkable that they need to be remarked upon to remind us of what most of us now take for granted. It wasn't always the case that women students had healthcare or housing on a college campus.

Ellen Condliffe Lagemann (2000), in a very important and engaging book called *An Elusive Science: The Troubling History of Educational Research*, points out that colleges of education have suffered from a poor reputation because they have always been considered places where scholars did "woman's work" (p. 16). Lagemann says that Teachers College even suffered this reputation at the turn of the century (and probably still does today). Lagemann tells us

> The association of education with "woman's work" marginalized the new "ed schools" relative to other faculties. The extreme instance of this was Columbia, whose board of trustees would accept a contractual affiliation with Teachers College, but would not accept the college as a regular faculty of the university. Instead, like Barnard College, the Columbia-affiliated college for women, it remained legally and geographically just outside of Columbia's gates: (p. 16)

It is astounding that these colleges are literally "geographically" set apart. Columbia had a history of anti-Semitism as it had a quota for Jewish students and faculty. Jews did not serve on the faculty until around the 1930s. Some faculty said that if they had known Horace Kallen was Jewish they wouldn't have hired him (Morris, 2006). Many people felt that Jews could not possibly be "intellectuals" because they were imitators (Morris). English and history were two disciplines in American universities that fought against Jewish hires during the early and mid-twentieth century.

The Disciplines as Gendered

Ivor Goodson and Colin Marsh (1996) write about school subjects and how they have also been stereotyped as either feminine or masculine. Subjects thought to be feminine are of less worth in the eyes of a misogynist. Biology as a school subject, Goodson argues, was marginalized in the 19th century in Britain because it was thought to be soft (read feminine). Goodson and Marsh claim that "the contested and belated development of biology is related to the gendered character of grammar school science" (p. 76). The crowning branches of the sciences were thought to be physics and chemistry because they are associated with doing lab work (read male). Ellen Condliffe Lagemann (2000) suggests education is "an elusive science." Trying to make education "scientific," as Lagemann points out, was one way to masculinize the discipline. The move toward quantification was a move toward making education more male.

Another discipline that was once thought too soft was educational history. Lagemann tells us that during the rise of the discipline of education as a field of study at the university, educational history was once vibrant but quantification and the social efficiency movement emerged and educational history was more or less history. Lagemann explains that when education increasingly became more "scientifically" oriented (W. W. Charters, Franklin Bobbitt, David Sneeden, E. L. Thorndike), those who studied and wrote educational history were looked down on as not being scientific, so doing history became unfashionable. Lagemann says that "even at Teachers College, history eventually lost its initially premier place as the method of choice for doctoral dissertations. By the 1920s, it had been replaced by studies based on school surveying" (p. 76).

Work and Redemption

A theme in current historiographies of education is vocational education. Of course this is not a new theme, it has been talked about for many years. Pinar, Reynolds, Slattery, and Taubman (1995) state, "*The Cardinal Principles of Secondary Education* provided additional support for the social-efficiency movement. Relatedly, it argued for increased emphasis upon vocational education which by 1907 had become a dominant educational issue" (p. 99). It is important to note here that vocational education is a natural outcome of the social efficiency movement, which for Pinar et al. is a "rival" reform movement (pp. 116–117). The Progressives, for Pinar, are considered to be a different kind of reform movement from social efficiency. This is an important point to make because others, like Ravitch (2001), collapse social efficiency with the Progressives. The social efficiency scholars were reactionary and so too was their "related" cry for the practical and vocational education. Herbert Kliebard (1999) and William Watkins (2001) argue that vocational education serves to oppress. Watkins says of the Hampton Institute that

> Armstrong's vision for Hampton [he was the founder of the Hampton Institute, which was focused on vocational education for blacks] was multidimensional. It would be a manual labor school. It would provide badly needed teachers for a mostly illiterate, alienated, and displaced Black population. It would provide training in character building, morality, and religion to "civilize" the "childlike"…"impetus." (p. 48)

Manual labor is hardly educative. The purpose of industrial education is to contain the Other. Industrial education or vocational education is an education for colonization, not for liberation. Herbert Kliebard (1999), in his important book *Schooled to Work: Vocationalism and the American Curriculum, 1876–1946*, argues that, for many, vocational education was a form of redemption. He talks about the "myth of the dignity of work" (p. 23) and goes on to talk about the ways in which vocational education was racist. Kliebard says "African Americans and Indians as well as other outsider groups, such as immigrants and the poor, could be redeemed from moral squalor. Here again, manual training was being proposed as a remedy" (pp. 23–24). Notice the phrase "moral squalor." Here again minorities were often seen as contaminated. Work would serve to clean them up "morally." And Kliebard mentions that religion ties directly into vocational education in that the Protestant work ethic was about getting cleaned up morally. Manual labor is in no way freeing or liberating. The Protestant work ethic is an ethic of control. If work is nothing more than alienated labor, as Marx put it, it is hideous. Working-class life is not to be romanticized. There is nothing about it that sets anybody free. Kliebard's (1999) book on vocational education is a very important one and is recommended for students to study especially if they are interested in questions about alienated labor and control. William Reese (1999) says of Kliebard that "he laments the continual erosion in this century for academic, humanistic education and the undemocratic consequences that often resulted" (p. x). More important, Reese points out that for Kliebard the deeper tragedy is what Kliebard calls "vocationalization—the idea that every school subject had to be justified by its occupational utility" (p. x). The idea that disciplines have to be tied to the market is not new.

Gender and Vocational Education

Vocational educators tend to polarize gender. To make sure that girls don't get too manly, they must learn sewing and housework, how to cook and clean for their husbands. To make sure that boys don't get effeminate, they must learn the masculine crafts of woodworking, drafting, and metal works. Kliebard (1999) comments on how these gender issues were also raced. He states,

> One study reported in 1931 that in twelve southern states, 85 percent of black high schools required home economics of their girls, whereas only 30 percent of the white high schools did. Home economics was also considered to be particularly desirable for girls in rural areas. (p. 136)

Vocational education was raced and classed. That is, teaching girls to be housewives is a way of keeping them down; it is a way of keeping them under the thumb of the patriarchy. Vocational education keeps minorities contained.

Kliebard (1999) also talks about a kind of crisis of masculinity (Pinar, 2001) that goes hand in hand with the Protestant work ethic and vocationalism. Kliebard writes about vocational education and the "bare-armed" man, who became good through his work (p. 6). He says that this image of the "bare-armed" man was in contradistinction to the "bookish" (read effeminate) man (p. 6).

Anti-intellectualism is partly about the crisis of masculinity. William Reese (2005) states that in the depression of the 1870s when "workers lost their jobs, went on strike, and sometimes engaged in mass violence, capitalists conveniently blamed unemployment on the laziness of employees and on the overly "literary" qualities of the school" (p. 102). Blaming the schools for the state of the economy is irrational. What does education have to do with money? Nothing. If only the curriculum would be more about work, then the economy would be healthier. The same kind of irrational critique was aimed at the humanities during WWII. Gerard Giordano (2005), in his book *Wartime Schools: How World War II Changed American Education*, says that conservatives

> criticized liberal teachers, many of whom were progressive educators, for disregarding civic responsibilities, patriotism, and the menace of Communism. They censured them for their allegiance to the creative arts and the humanities rather than mathematics, science, physical conditioning, career training. (p. 239)

During times of war and economic downturns it seems that the humanities and the arts get demonized. Spending too much time playing music or reading books might thwart the war effort. But there is more to it than that. Again these issues are gendered. The humanities and the arts are seen as soft (read effeminate) and the sciences are seen as hard (read masculine). War time means muscle, and the arts and humanities are hardly muscular disciplines.

During times of war and economic downturns what one tends to see is what Dewey (1974) disparagingly calls "the cry for the practical" (p. 290). In the late 1800s, during the depression, William Reese (2000) tells us that "as labor strife worsened...calls for a more practical education intensified" (p. 28). Likewise, during WWII, Gerard Giordano (2005) tells us that even Teachers College Columbia instituted a more practical curriculum. Giordano tells us:

> New York City's Teachers College was the institution of higher education with the most prominent reputation for radical, liberal politics during this period [WWII]. However, even this bastion of liberalism sponsored a prewar symposium on teacher-centered defense activities ("Schools and Defense," 1941). The symposium's agenda comprised topics such as promoting nationalism among immigrants, pre-induction curricula, physical fitness, vocational education, and school diet as a critical component of total defense. (p. 5)

As Giordano suggests, Teachers College caved under pressure as it offered an anti-intellectual curriculum. It is interesting also to note how work and nationalism go hand in hand during times of war. War makes even the most thinking people unthinking. Any study of education that draws only on the practical at the expense of the theoretical is anti-intellectual. And even the thought that the theoretical cannot also be practical is anti-intellectual because the theoretical always has practical implications. Scholars of teaching and learning tend to be highly anti-intellectual if their focus is on the "how to" of teaching and if they do not theorize on what they are doing. The study of teaching in and of itself tends to be parochial. And as Dwayne Huebner (1999) said, the focus on "learning" trivializes the complex act of becoming educated. The study of teaching divorced from culture is anti-intellectual because it is a study in method. Methods reduce the complex experience of education to simple. Ellen Condliffe Lagemann (2000) comments on this problem by putting anti-intellectualism in the context of the larger American landscape, and she is especially critical of "instrumental knowledge, know-how" (p. xiii). This, too, is Herbert Kliebard's complaint about vocational education. Kliebard (1999) states

> Under vocationalism, academic subjects of study are reconstructed or adapted in order to meet the demands of the labor market. The subject of English becomes infused with writing job applications and preparing resumes; mathematics becomes business arithmetic. When literature, geometry, or a foreign language cannot demonstrate its relationship to the demands of commerce or industry, it is relegated to a kind of ritual status. (p. 121).

When a discipline is reduced to a business it also gets reduced to a how-to: how to market your art, how to make learning expedient, how to apply science to practical projects, how to put mathematics to military use. There are ethical implications here, especially for the instrumentalization of science and mathematics. To instrumentalize curriculum is to reduce its richness and complexity to the trivial. This is not only an American problem. It is a European problem as well. Michael Kammen (1990) tells us that practicality, then, is not a peculiarly American virtue; and the commitment to practicality, as Peter Gay (1998) observes, "is after all itself an idea in fact with a long and honored history" (p. 20). One could even argue that Aristotle's empiricism could be an early move toward the practical. Empirical studies reduce the complexity of experience to what you observe. If you can't see it, it can't be tested, measured, or evaluated. Empirical studies are highly problematic because they tend toward the anti-intellectual, especially when there is little theory involved when looking at phenomena. When education scholars go into school classrooms and observe teachers to find out what they do and how they do it, what intellectual richness can come of that? Well, if one theorizes richly around what is observed there is great intellectual value in the endeavor. But mostly, as William Pinar points out (personal communication), many ethnographies—whether quantitative or qualitative—suffer from a lack of theorization. The problem with doing classroom observations is that what you see is not always what you get. The whole idea of lived experience is highly complex, and the notion of experience, as Dewey points out, is difficult to untangle. Philip Jackson (2002) does a marvelous job of unpacking for us Dewey's difficulty with unpacking the concept of experience. Jackson tells us that Dewey was troubled with the "slipperiness" of experience (p. 1). Dewey wasn't really sure what experience meant. Experience is a highly complex notion that is not easily deconstructed.

The Practical and the Theoretical

The upshot of this discussion is twofold. I want to emphasize that, on the one hand, there has always been the problem of the practical in the field of education. On the other hand, there has always been the promise of the theoretical and the intellectual. This duality represents the larger American culture. Michael Kammen (1990) comments on what he calls the paradox of American culture, as the title of his book suggests. He tells us that America has always been both anti-intellectual *and* intellectual. Kammen states

> Hence from the very beginning there may have been two main currents running parallel through American minds: the transcendental current, elevated by Jonathan Edwards, refined by Ralph Waldo Emerson; and the practical current which Benjamin Franklin made into a philosophy of common sense. (p. 111)

Philip Jackson, as William Pinar (1998a) points out, comments on these two trends—the practical and the theoretical—and argues that the call toward the practical is problematic because it does not advance knowledge. Jackson calls the more practically oriented curriculum scholar a "curricularlist-as-consultant"—as Pinar (1998a) shows—and the more theoretical-oriented curriculum scholar is "moving toward the academy" (Pinar, p. xi). Theoretical scholars attempt to advance knowledge rather than merely reorganize the curriculum, Pinar (2009b) suggests.

I belabor the point of anti-intellectualism in the context of educational history and in particular in the context of vocational education to make several broader points. Vocational education, as I suggested earlier, is (following Pinar et al., 1995) an extension of social efficiency and aligned with industry and business. Vocational education as an extension of social efficiency is in no way intellectual or progressive, although historically the social efficiency scholars called themselves Progressives.

Diane Ravitch's (2001) historiography of education is a dismissal of Progressive education as she calls it anti-intellectual (p. 16). The mistake Ravitch makes is one of misunderstanding the complexity of the Progressive movement of education. One simply cannot reduce all of Progressive education to vocational education, which she seems to imply in her book. And one cannot reduce all of Progressive education to social efficiency either. Even if the social efficiency scholars thought of themselves as Progressive, clearly they were not. Cremin (1961)—a scholar Ravitch critiques—says it best when talking about the Progressive work of people like Jane Addams. Cremin puts it this way:

> Jane Addams, the noble lady who founded Hull House and led its efforts for fully forty years, once remarked: "We have learned to say that the good must be extended to all of society before it can be held secure by any one person or any one class... ." Here was the spiritual nub of progressive education, and it simply negates contemporary nonsense about the movement being narrowly practical and nothing else. (p. ix)

As Cremin says, Progressive education meant a lot of things to a lot of people but one thing is clear: its meaning could be construed in contradictory ways. Ravitch seems to want to bash Progressives and blame them for the failure of today's schools, which is absurd.

Dewey: A Brief Snapshot

I want to flesh out some of Dewey's writings. I return to Dewey because he is considered by many to be the founder of the Progressive movement in education, although Dewey attributes the founding of the movement to Francis Parker. First off, Dewey addressed the idea of vocation but not in the same way as the word was used in the context of vocational education. Dewey theorized around the concept so as to make it intellectual. He did not reduce the idea of the vocational to the instrumental.

John Dewey: The Intellectual and the Progressive Era

The Progressive era is of great interest to us because curriculum studies scholars see our roots there. I want to take a brief detour through Dewey to argue that Progressive education—as it is explored by Dewey (and the women who founded Progressive schools)—is indeed intellectual. Upon returning to Dewey, one might be struck by the sheer number of times he uses the term "intellectual" and the word "intellect" throughout his work. Pragmatism—where scholars situate Dewey's work—gets misread as a turn toward the practical. Dewey (1916/1966) addresses this misreading in his work and often argues that pragmatism is not about the "narrowly practical" (p. 307). Dewey wanted to ground the intellectual in experience and in community. Some scholars misread Dewey because they think that the appeal to experience is the practical. But for Dewey the idea of experience is highly complex, as I mentioned earlier when talking about Philip Jackson's (2002) read on Dewey.

What is striking about Dewey is that a vocation can be an intellectual endeavor. For Dewey, the idea of a vocation has little to do with industry or efficiency. For Dewey (1916/1966), a vocation is a "calling," and this calling is "an organizing principle for information and ideas; for knowledge and intellectual growth" (p. 309). A vocation, however, is not a calling if it is alienated labor—as Marx put it. But a vocation, or calling, is chosen out of love and passion—a point Jim Garrison (1997) makes. There is almost something spiritual about vocation—if thought of as a calling. For Dewey a calling is not a leap of faith but a leap of intellect. Dewey (1916/1966) says that a vocation is an "appeal to thought" (p. 309). If you truly love what you do, you *think* about your work all the time. Good work demands thought. Now, Dewey defines the notion of work, or "occupation," very broadly. He suggests that a vocation can be manual labor but it can also be thought of as the work of the artist and the work of the novelist or teacher (1916/1966, pp. 312–313). Dewey states that the vocation of the artist is also intellectual. The artist is a thinker. Dewey (2005) says that it is "an odd notion that the artist does not think" (p. 14). Many people might think that playing a musical instrument, for example, is all about emotion and getting lost in the music. Well, certainly emotion is part of music making. But there is deep thought that goes into the way in which music gets interpreted and phrased. The artist is a thinker and art is a vocation. When art is thought through and it is thought of as a calling it is intellectual and spiritual. Dewey makes the point, too, that the thinker is an artist. He (2005) puts it this way: "The thinker has his esthetic moment when his ideas cease to be mere ideas and become the corporate meanings of objects. The artist has his problems and thinks as he works" (p. 14). Both the artist and the thinker are called by their vocations. So for Dewey a vocation is both artistic and intellectual. Even the mechanic can make his job both artistic and intellectual, says Dewey. Vocations do not have to be alienated labor. Jim Garrison (1997) points out that "many of the new scholars have called attention to Dewey's aesthetics. Some even suggest that it is the unifying theme of his entire philosophy" (p. xix). Certainly, for Dewey, aesthetic experience should, in some way, permeate the everyday. But there is a lot more to Dewey than this. Dewey was a generalist, thus, it is hard to say what exactly the center of his thought was. At any rate, the point here is that even when he talks about the idea of vocation, it too can be thought of as an intellectual concept. However, most vocational education is not about the intellectual; it is about controlling and draining thought.

For Dewey intellectual work means trying to see things anew, beginning again, and giving new direction to old ideas. The intellectual, Dewey (1974) states, "opens up a new field, raises new questions, arouses the demand for further knowledge" (p. 178). And too, Dewey thought of teachers as intellectuals. Laurel Tanner (1997) says that in Dewey's lab, school teachers were expected to build their own knowledge base, work from primary sources, and take "intellectual responsibility" (p. 72) to heart. Tanner says that the disciplines around which the curriculum was built at Dewey's lab school "seem rather surprising" (p. 66). Tanner remarks:

> This is Dewey's School? We ask. Somehow we expected something different. History, geography, literature, French, Latin (foreign languages were introduced early), science, mathematics, music, art, wood shop, cooking, and physical education seem to reflect a subject-centered view of the curriculum. (p. 66)

People who do not bother to study Dewey, or to study what his lab school was all about, think that Progressive education means letting the child go wild. That is not it at all. Dewey expected children to explore the academic disciplines but not in a rote or utilitarian fashion. Making the disciplines relevant to the child's life does not water down the academic rigor of the disciplines. The intellectual content of the disciplines is of importance to Dewey. The teacher has to make connections between the child's interests and the discipline. Making an academic discipline relevant to a life does not make for anti-intellectualism. Integrating a discipline into a life means contextualizing it. To make meaning from study, the discipline at hand must be made relevant. Dewey (1974) states that "traditional education" was too "rigid" and "too remote from the experiences of the child" (p. 9). He goes on to say

> What is needed in the new education [another phrase for progressive education] is more attention, not less, to subject matter.... But when I say more, I do not mean more in quantity of the same old kind. I mean an imaginative vision which sees that no prescribed and ready-made scheme can possibly determine the exact subject-matter that will best promote educative growth. (p. 9)

The life of the mind is not to be stultified but rather opened to an ongoing exploration of ideas. The universe of ideas is vast. Nothing should constrain the search for meaning. But traditional education, according to Dewey, constrains meaning and exploration. The integrity of the disciplines must stay intact. Dewey is not dismissing canon(s) of knowledge but he is critiquing the way that these canon(s) are constrained. Dewey is speaking from the position of a scholar, and he understands that the scholarly life is composed of a vast universe of living ideas. Living ideas have histories, have meaning, have content and substance. They give to life depth. This is the gift that teachers need to give to students, to children who begin to study the disciplines at an early age. But more often than not the disciplines are taught as dead things without life or depth. Even in college the disciplines are taught as subjects to memorize for a test. If the disciplines are taught in this fashion the richness of a field gets reduced to multiple choice tests where there are right and wrong answers. This has nothing to do with the life of the mind and intellect. Testing for the right answer kills disciplines and the mind and kills the spirit of the child, too. David Jardine, Sharon Friesen, and Patricia Clifford (2006) write eloquently about this in their work. They argue, for example, that mathematicians work with and in a living discipline, one with depth and meaning. But when children learn mathematics in school this subject is taught in a dead way. What is taught to children in school—to memorize formulas for tests—is certainly not what mathematicians do in their everyday work. We are, in essence, miseducating children if we do not treat the discipline the way that a working mathematician treats the work. Jardine, Friesen, and Clifford put it this way:

> The Pythagorean Theorem is part of a *living discipline* despite how it often appears in the classroom. It is precisely this character of a living discipline that is occluded by regimes of scarcity [i.e., memorizing formulas for standardized tests] and their consequent impoverishment of our ability to imagine and understand the curriculum topics entrusted to us as teachers. (p. 39)

Pay close attention to the words "scarcity" and "impoverishment" in the above passage. Mathematics becomes a dead thing when it is taught to be spit back on a test. One way to bring mathematics to life is to teach the history of mathematics. When students study a discipline historically, the figures and characters of the discipline come to life. Who was Pythagoras? When did he live? How did he live his life? These kinds of questions might help to nourish the discipline of mathematics.

This is Dewey's point, too. Dewey wanted to nourish the disciplines and bring them to life. Doing philosophy—as a philosopher does it—is not what is taught in philosophy classes in college if the professor makes the student memorize and take tests. Students should be learning to "do" philosophy as a philosopher does it. Philosophers do not take tests, nor do they memorize things. Doing philosophy means thinking thoughts and making connections.

Lawrence Cremin (1961) writes about the way in which Dewey thought teachers should know fields in order to make them come alive for students. Cremin writes about studying mathematics. It is interesting that Cremin says, for Dewey, the teacher should have a

> thorough acquaintance with organized knowledge as represented in the disciplines. To recognize opportunities for early mathematical learning, one must know mathematics; to recognize opportunities for elementary scientific learning one must know physics, chemistry, biology, and geology; and so on down the list of fields of knowledge. In short, the demand on the teacher is twofold: thorough knowledge of the disciplines and the common experiences of childhood that can be utilized to lead children toward the understandings represented by this knowledge. (p. 138)

Dewey had great respect for the study of the disciplines and he had great respect for the rigor of study and of knowledge. His lab school was rigorous. Dewey (1974) drives the point home that Progressive education must be intellectual when he says that it "is a fitting time to raise the intellectual, the theoretical problem of the relation of the Progressive movement to the art and philosophy of education" (p. 170). Progressive education is a "theoretical problem," Dewey says. This is an important claim to make, especially against the charges that Progressive education is anti-intellectual. It is only anti-intellectual if you make it so.

Dewey and the Notion of Experience

Abstract ideas must be grounded in the concrete, Dewey says. Much of his philosophy turns on the notion of experience. Experience, for Dewey, is a difficult concept to grasp. Dewey conceptualizes experience as movement, of temporality and of historicity. This is why it is difficult to capture an experience, because it is always on the move, and we are always already in the middle of it. When one is in the middle of an experience it is difficult to articulate what that experience means. This is a phenomenological problem. The biggest problem for a phenomenologist is describing experiences to others. The experience is always vanishing as one tries to describe its meaning. Against a vanishing horizon, people try to communicate experiences to one another. At any rate, for Dewey experience is a kind of movement in time. When studying disciplines what students are actually studying is the past because disciplines have histories. And it is this history that students should be studying. Dewey (1916/1966) states, "The subject matter of education consists primarily of the meanings which supply content to existing social life. The continuity of social life means that many of these meanings are contributed to present activity by past collective experience" (p. 192). The disciplines, then, are made up of "past collective experience." Hence disciplines are on the move and should be studied historically. This is not always the way disciplines are treated. Mathematics and science are not often treated historically. This gives the student the wrong idea about math and science. If these disciplines are not treated historically, students get the impression that these fields are static. When disciplines are not studied historically, it becomes difficult to untangle things or to understand how ideas change shape and form over time. A scholar does not understand a field if the study of its history is not taken seriously. Dewey's point is that disciplines have histories and these histories are made up of experiences. When students begin to understand a discipline as a way to experience life, it brings that discipline to life. Dewey (1974) puts it this way:

> Organized subject matter represents the ripe fruitage of experiences like theirs [students'], experiences involving the same world, and powers and needs similar to theirs. It does not represent perfection or infallible wisdom; but it is the best command to further new experiences which may, in some respects at least, surpass the achievements embodied in existing knowledge and works of art. (p. 361)

Students can advance knowledge by thinking about the concept of experience in the context of the disciplines and the past. Disciplines do not advance if they are not worked on historically. Dewey suggests here that students must also seek "new experiences" but that these new experiences—although rooted in "existing knowledge"—can surpass that knowledge. Fields and disciplines do advance with rigorous study.

Dewey and the Everyday World

For Dewey, knowledge is built in the everyday world, even if it is highly abstract. Knowledge is built on and in experience. That which is intellectual is always already experiential. And as Philip Jackson (1998) points out, for Dewey, experience "exists in time and changes over time. It always has a history" (p. 4). Experience not only has a history, it is history. And this is why empirical studies are highly problematic. As one observes something it changes. As one thinks through an issue and theorizes that issue, thoughts move quickly. It is difficult to catch moving thoughts. Not only this, the mind has the capacity to think many thoughts at once and for the theorist this presents the problem of organizing and selecting which thoughts to theorize.

Dewey makes the point that the abstract must be made concrete to have meaning. Thoughts are embodied and therefore must be situated in experience. For Dewey, there is no separation between thought and experience or mind and body. Everything is interconnected. And it is this interconnection and flow between and among things that complicate.

More important for Dewey, the everyday must be appreciated and lived fully. He makes an interesting argument in his book, *Art as Experience*: "The task [of living] is to restore continuity between refined and intensified forms of experience that are works of art and the everyday events" (2005, p. 2). Life should, in other words, be lived artfully. As Philip Jackson (1998) puts it, "Dewey points out that the arts provide us with exemplary instances of an experience" (p. 4). One should try to live life as if every moment were tuned to the pitch of that exemplary and artful experience. That is no easy task. The mundane is hard to overcome. The life of the mind, however, and the scholarly and teacherly life can be lived in this exemplary way if teachers and professors are true to their callings and do their work with passion. Easier said than done when working inside of anti-intellectual institutions. Dewey's point, though, is an interesting one that needs some time to digest. The experience of the artist at work is an elusive one. The musician who has a good practice day is at one with her instrument and the everyday is made artful. The profane becomes sacred in those moments where time slips without notice. But for the musician many days of practice can be torture. The working out of phrases and the ongoing repetition can become intensely tedious and even boring. When Pablo Casals—a world renowned cellist—was a young man, he fell down a hill and broke his arm and actually was relieved that he wouldn't have to practice anymore (Morris, 2009). Even for Casals, practice could be torture. Too, for writers, sometimes the writing is bliss, other times it is hell. But for Dewey, what people must strive for is to live in moments where the work is artful, where the work is generative. But these moments are hard to come by in a chaotic world. Perhaps Dewey did not address the negative enough in his work. The question becomes how to push through the negative to keep the work alive. Andre Green (1999) argues, "Free association, that is, the mimetic figuration of the dream, is still the most prototypical expression of the negative. What does free association mean if not loosening the noose of the positive which constrains consciousness" (p. 37)? Green is speaking psychoanalytically here. Perhaps pragmatists, as a whole, did not confront the negative enough. William Schubert (2009a) points out that Dewey "strangely...rarely referred to the psychoanalytic tradition, despite the fact that his contemporaries led the movement" (p. 6). At any rate, what is interesting in Green's passage above is that he suggests that in the everyday life—when things seem to be going along smoothly—or positively—consciousness is actually constrained. There is always something else going on—unconsciously—that needs digging up in order to break free from the constraints that bind thinking and hold us back.

Dewey and Chaos

These are chaotic times. Dewey's time was not so different. Wars seem always to be going on. Poverty is always awful. Violence and meanness are always a part of life. These issues are rarely addressed by Dewey. Educating young people against the larger social context of war and meanness is no easy task. But for Dewey, progress could be made and he was always hopeful about the future of the young. And he wanted us to feel good about our experiences in life. But it is hard to be positive and feel good when war, poverty, and social injustices abound.

Dewey suggests thought, as it is experienced, should work to improve our lives. Dewey (1916/1966) says that education should become a "direct transformation of the quality of experience" (p. 76). He also uses the word "enrichment" (p. 76) in the context of education. Transformation and enrichment are words that imply progress and upward movement. Education should make us better, brighter, happier even. Dewey also says that experience—that is, to really experience something—might feel like "heightened vitality" (p. 18). Education—as an experience—should bring life and movement to thought. All of the words Dewey uses are of the transcendent. His descriptions of what experience can be are images of moving up, of progressing higher. Progression is about overcoming something. For Dewey (1951), progress is not made without overcoming "doubt" and "suspense" (p. 348). It is interesting that Dewey suggests that people need to embrace doubt and suspense rather than "be shut of it" (p. 348). The work of progress is made only by moving through doubt and moving through obstacles. And these are experiences that can make one uncomfortable. Dewey explains:

> Here is where ordinary thinking and thinking that is scrupulous diverge from each other. The natural man is impatient with doubt and suspense: he impatiently hurries to be shut of it. A disciplined mind takes delight in the problematic and cherishes it until a way out is found. (p. 348)

Theorizing experience can be highly frustrating. Between the thought and the experience of the thought is an abyss, and the scholar must jump over that abyss artfully if one follows Dewey's advice. The point of the life of scholarship is to find a way out of problems. That way out is not easily found. But scholarship can help work through issues of both a personal and social nature and this is what Dewey was concerned with. For Dewey the personal and the social are intertwined, and so too is experience and the theorizing of it. Diving into the abyss is part of the transformation brought on by the organization of knowledge and the advance of knowledge. Many are not willing to take the risk. The artist and philosopher, the thinker and the poet, for Dewey, all take risks to find a way out and make the everyday rich and not dull.

Pragmatism and Real Life

One of the issues that the pragmatists brought to philosophy was the need to make philosophy matter in real life. What this means is that thought, as it is situated in experience, must be made social. The social problems of the early 20th century were on the minds of the pragmatists. This way of doing philosophy differs radically from positivism or idealism. Bringing philosophy into the realm of experience and real-world problems was what made pragmatism so different from European philosophy. Of course, existentialism was about the problems of the world. But for the most part European philosophy had little to do with real-world problems. Because philosophy takes on real-world problems does not make it anti-intellectual. Dewey's way of doing philosophy was more sociological than anything. Like Dewey, George Herbert Mead (1964) claims that the self is social. Jane Addams's work was highly sociological. And Dewey was influenced by her work at Hull House. The emergence of social work as a field and sociology as a discipline came into being around the same time that Dewey was working on philosophical problems. Josiah Royce (1951), another pragmatist philosopher, was concerned about "the nature of community" (p. 200). And like Dewey, Royce thought that the nature of community was primarily temporal. Royce says, "But a true community is essentially a product of a time-process. A community has a past and will have a future. Its more or less conscious history, real or ideal, is part of its very essence" (p. 203). The social like the personal is also historical and Dewey felt this strongly. Thus, what the individual thinker thinks is situated in experience, which means that thought is situated in the larger sociohistorical landscape. For Dewey (1899), remember that the school is situated in society and hence individuals live in a social situation. The history of the school, too, should be couched in the larger history of society. When historiographies of the school are too narrow and do not take into account larger historical and social trends, one can lose sight of things and get lost in the details of the schoolhouse. Dewey (1961/1966) tells us that the "reconstruction of experience may be social as well as personal" (p. 78). He also sees "education as reconstruction" (p. 76). So what is it that educators are reconstructing? Educators are reconstructing thoughts as they are experienced both on a personal and communal level. This is a very complex move that Dewey is making here. Thought, experience, and the social are all interconnected and highly complex. How the individual is thrust into the world is a deep philosophic problem. Being situated always in the world means that people are always in the middle of things. And it is hard to make sense of being in the middle of a vastly complex world. The reconstruction of knowledge and the advance of knowledge, for Dewey, happen in experience and in the world of that experience. Thought, in other words, is not stuck in the head. In no way is thought a solipsistic act. Thought is always social. And for Dewey, thought must work to change the social for the better. Changing the social is what progress is about. Changing the world is done not by one person but by many. Dewey (1951) puts it this way:

> The problem of restoring integration and cooperation between man's beliefs about the world in which he lives and his beliefs about the values and purposes that should direct his conduct is the deepest problem of modern life. It is the problem of philosophy [and I would add education] that it is not isolated from that life. (p. 361)

The point of doing philosophy for Dewey is not that much different from Marx. For both the point of philosophizing was to change the world. The history of Western philosophy—for the most part—is a history of disinterest in worldly things. However, existentialists changed that. Marx changed that. And so too did Dewey. The debates that most of the pragmatists had, had real-world consequences. C. S. Peirce was perhaps the most difficult to understand and the most abstract. But for the majority of pragmatists, philosophy served to unpack worldly issues. Pragmatism is quintessentially American. And one can see from unpacking Dewey—even in brief—that pragmatism is not about the "narrowly practical" as Dewey put it. Too often the word "pragmatic"—in the commonsense meaning—is collapsed with the philosophical movement of pragmatism. Pragmatism—as a movement of thought and as a philosophical tradition—is not the same thing as the practical. Unpacking worldly problems does not mean that scholars do so in an anti-intellectual way.

Dewey and the Social

For Dewey, vocations, art, and academic disciplines are all situated in the social. Dewey (1916/1966) states that "an occupation is the only thing which balances the distinctive capacity of an individual with his social service" (p. 308). To work means to work in the service of the social. If a person is true to her calling, accordingly, the work that gets done is ultimately to help others. Work should not be a Gradgrindingly awful thing. Unfortunately for many people, work is little more than Gradgrinding. One wonders whether the work of the corporate world is about helping others. Is big business about helping others or about making a few wealthy at the expense of the many? Wall Street as a metaphor is in contradistinction to Main Street; big business has never been about social service; it has been about oppression and the creation of poverty and suffering. Andrew Carnegie, J. P. Morgan, and the rest exploited workers, to say the least. Carnegie was, no doubt, a philanthropist, but for the most part his wealth came at the expense of the poor. Industry has never been a friend to the poor. As Michael McGerr (2003) points out, the larger Progressive movement in America came about as a protest against big business. McGerr tells us that during the rise of industrialism, in the era of Carnegie and J.P. Morgan,

> If workers survived the threat of unemployment, they still faced the twin specters of injury and early death. Every working-class occupation had its difficulties and dangers, from the explosions [in plants, mines, and mills], fires, cave-ins, debilitating "miner's lung," and other notorious perils of hard-rock mining in the West to the "Monday morning sickness," asthma, byssinosis, tuberculosis, and maimings in the textile mills of the East. While the upper ten [like Carnegie] seemed to last into their sixties, hard labor and poor diets aged workers quickly. An iron puddler was "old at forty." (pp. 16–17)

This quote is important in the context of what Dewey and other Progressive educators were fighting against. Dewey grew up during a time when work meant early death and horror. The Progressive movement in the United States was, in part, a fight against the abuses of big business. These kinds of occupations—steel workers, coal miners, textile workers—were the kinds of occupations that killed. When Dewey talks about a vocation as a calling and as a way to do social service, he is not talking about living in a coal mine and dying from black lung disease. He was highly critical of industry and worried about the fate of the worker.

One must wonder if Dewey and other academics were, in a way, blinded by their own upper-class privilege. Certainly the social reconstructionists—like George Counts and Harold Rugg—critiqued Dewey and the other pragmatists for not being political enough, although Jane Addams was certainly political. Dewey wasn't primarily a political scholar. Perhaps he did not take on the Babbitts of the world. But some, like Jay Martin (2002), see Dewey as a "social critic" (p. 377) and place him in the company of other social critics of his time. Martin explains:

> Long before the economic crash, American writers had put together a case against the spiritual poverty of contemporary society. The public had listened to these writers in the 1920s but refused to take their criticisms so seriously. After the crash, however, the prewar literary traditions of muckraking and reform revived in popular esteem. Whether calling themselves Marxists, progressives, historians, or novelists, such writers as John Dewey, Michael Gold, Max Eastman, Edmund Wilson, Matthew Josephson, and John Dos Passos all could be termed social critics. (p. 377)

There were also women who were social critics as well. Emma Goldman, Jane Addams, Ida B. Wells, Eleanor Roosevelt, Mary McCloud Bethune, Rosa Luxemburg, Ellen Gates Starr, and Caroline Pratt, among others, were also social critics.

Dewey and Art

Dewey (2005) suggests that like other vocations art was in "commerce with the world" (p. 18). Art is not a solipsistic act for Dewey, it happens in the midst of the world and its purpose should be to serve the world. Like Dewey's work, arts-based education—an exciting contemporary outgrowth of Dewey's philosophy of art—concerns the political aspects of art. Tom Barone (2000) and Landon Beyer (2000) both suggest that art is also political, that art should have a political function. Maxine Greene (1995) often makes the point that art and social justice should be related. Art doesn't always have a political function of course, but these scholars—coming from the Deweyan tradition—suggest that politics and art might go hand in hand.

Academic Disciplines and the Social

Vocations, art, and the academic disciplines, Dewey suggests, are all situated in the social. Dewey (1916/1966) speaks here about the problem of subject matter when it is not contextualized in the social. He states

> Isolation of subject matter from a social context is the chief obstruction in current practice to securing a general training of mind. Literature, art, religion, when thus dissociated are just as narrowing as the technical things which the professional upholders of general education strenuously oppose. (p. 67)

Putting schooling in the context of the social is crucial in order to understand what is going on (Kincheloe, Slattery, & Steinberg, 2000; Chiarelott,

2006). Understanding the context of a problem—what Kincheloe, Slattery and Steinberg call "contextualizing"—is necessary in order to understand the problem. Teaching must occur in context of the larger sociohistorical backdrop.

Culture must be studied in order to understand any academic discipline. In order to advance knowledge, one must put that knowledge in context of the larger social background. The technical, about which Dewey speaks, is synonymous with "methods." To understand education students need to understand culture and not be overwhelmed by issues of the technical or of method. Curriculum theorizing is about studying the broader culture and studying contexts against which education happens. Theorizing around curriculum means studying culture.

Speaking of school subjects more directly, Dewey (1916/1966) argues,

> There is a standing danger that the material of formal instruction will be merely the subject matter of the schools, isolated from the subject matter of life-experience. The permanent social interests are likely to be lost from view. Those which have not been carried over into the structure of social life, but which remain largely matters of technical information expressed in symbols, are made conspicuous in schools. (p. 8)

Dewey drives the point home that the academic disciplines must be made relevant to student's lives, otherwise these disciplines will not have much meaning and they will make little sense against the larger historical backdrop around which they are formed. Schooling happens in society and not apart from it. If schooling happens seemingly apart from culture and the school subjects are not contextualized against history and the sociopolitical, students are being miseducated.

This detour into Dewey is part of the theorizing of educational and curriculum history. If we are to understand our Progressive roots curriculum theorists must always return to Dewey.

Our Progressive Inheritance: The Debate and Controversy

One of the best books on the Progressive movement of education is Lawrence Cremin's (1961) *The Transformation of the School: Progressivism in American Education 1867–1957*. First, Cremin suggests that he does not have a good definition of Progressive education because the movement was "frequently, contradictory" (p. x). And second, he states that he is writing a "social and intellectual history" (p. x), suggesting that American Progressive education

> was clearly part of a much larger response to industrialism, and that while the American movement proceeded in terms of the American experience, many of its elements were similar to, and indeed, influenced by, contemporary developments in other industrial nations. (p. x)

Cremin does exactly what Dewey calls for: he contextualizes his study of the "transformation of the school" against the larger backdrop of the movement of progressivism in American politics. It is important to follow up on Cremin's advice by trying to understand the larger American progressive movement before talking about what Progressive education meant in the early 20th century. Here I touch on some key aspects of progressivism to better understand how education fits into the larger social scene and explore the historical relation that reconceptualization has with this larger Progressive movement. Scholars might agree on certain aspects of American progressivism as a political movement in the early 20th century, but there are many disagreements as to who was and was not a Progressive. Richard Hofstadter (1955) makes an interesting point about American progressivism writ large. He tells us

> By "Progressivism" I mean something more than the Progressive (or Bull Moose) Party formed by the Republican insurgents who supported Theodore Roosevelt for the Presidency in 1912. I mean rather that broader impulse toward criticism and change that was everywhere so conspicuous after 1900, when the already forceful Agrarian discontent was enlarged and redirected by the growing enthusiasm of the middle-class people for social and economic reform. (p. 5)

It is important to note that the Bull Moose Party, according to Sidney Milkis (2009), was the largest third political party in United States history. Bull Moose reforms were far reaching as many of them "anticipated that New Deal political order in prescribing an expansive welfare and regulatory state" (Milkis, p. 5). Teddy Roosevelt—who headed up the Bull Moose Party—was seen by some, conversely, not as Progressive but as reactionary in that his conservation movement was really a symptom of a crisis of masculinity (Haraway, 1989). Donna Haraway argues that Roosevelt really wanted to conserve manhood more than nature. Killing wild game was a way to show people how much of a man he was. And yet, Teddy Roosevelt, according to Douglas Brinkely (2009), did many remarkable things as he "quadrupled America's forest reserves.... He established five national parks.... Courtesy of an executive decree, Roosevelt saved the Grand Canyon...set aside...over 234 million acres [of land]" (p. 19). And yet he remained the hunter; while he worked to save species, he also shot and killed them. Brinkley remarks that this behavior on Roosevelt's part has puzzled historians. Brinkley tells us, that "Nothing has baffled Roosevelt scholars over the decades more than how Theodore, who vehemently opposed cruelty to animals, could nevertheless kill wildlife with such ease" (p. 58). So one could say that Roosevelt was both Progressive (in his efforts at conservation) and reactionary (in his killing of animals). William Pinar (2001) points out too that Teddy Roosevelt was a "(sometimes) progressive reformer" (p. 72).The key word here is "sometimes." Roosevelt was sometimes liberal (on worker's rights) and sometimes reactionary (in his racism). Roosevelt fought big business and fought for equal rights for workers but he also "pandered" to the "rape myth" that "justified" lynching (Pinar, p. 72) of blacks. But then, schizophrenically—as Douglas Brinkley (2009) remarks—Roosevelt "fought to end racial segregation in public schools, and demanded antiracism efforts in schools" (p. 373). David Southern (2005) says of Teddy Roosevelt:

> Some contemporaries described him as a man "drunk with power," a self-aggrandizing politician, a malevolently self-righteous prude, and a radical rabble-rouser. Yet one historian portrayed Roosevelt as a deeply conservative "stabilizer of the status quo." (p. 113)

And yet Roosevelt's vision was also Progressive in that he wanted to regulate big business, grant better working conditions to people, work to make child labor laws just, and more than any other president, he worked to protect wild life and was one of the earliest members of the conservation movement. Joshua David Hawley (2008) says that "Roosevelt made the progressive era possible" (p. xvii) but—in many ways—he was not liberal. In fact, Hawley contends that Roosevelt was a "social conservative" (p. 107). Roosevelt, says Douglas Brinkley, was "reminiscent of Dr. Jekyll and Mr. Hyde" (p. 274), especially when it came to issues of race. Brinkley (2009) comments that "Commissioner Roosevelt (unlike the historian Roosevelt) said that the Indians deserved a 'square deal'" (p. 274). Roosevelt did write historical books on the West and throughout them racist statements are made about the Indians. He "seemed to loath Indians" (Brinkley, p. 275), too.

Roosevelt reflects the contradictions inherent in the Progressive reform movement. He was a character of contrasts. Raised in Manhattan, he longed for the rough and tumble of the West. And his love of the land allowed him to be sympathetic with the plight of farmers who were not happy with the rise of industrialization. Roosevelt had no great love for industry. In fact, Douglas Brinkley points out that "somehow or other Roosevelt found a way to be at war with the Standard Oil Company for his entire life" (p. 383). After reading Upton Sinclair's novel *The Jungle* (1906), it was Roosevelt who went after the meat packing industry in Chicago (Brinkley).

Progressive reform was a symptom of agrarian discontent—as Michael McGerr (2003) puts it—and this discontent concerned the rise of industrialism. The rise of industry, in many ways, shattered lives and it was this shattering that the Progressives critiqued. Were agrarian populists Progressive? Or were they something else? Hofstadter (1955) drives a wedge between populists and Progressives, but at some points in his text he uses the phrase the "Populist Progressives," which clearly puts these two groups together. Glenda Elizabeth Gilmore (2002) tells us that according to Elizabeth Sanders, there was indeed a connection between the Populists and Progressives:

> She traces the major national legislation of the Progressive Era to the farmer's revolt of the 1890's, known as the Populist Movement. In a stunning analysis of legislation, Sanders draws parallels between agrarian complaints and urban remedies, as she credits the Populists with inspiring reform that far outlived their original political organization. (p. 20)

What is striking here is that people often think of rural and urban problems as separate. But in fact, they are interrelated. It is as Dewey taught: everything is interrelated. What affects the urban also affects the rural. Mostly, though, when people think of the progressive movement they think of urban intellectuals who critiqued the corrupt power of industry. Leon Fink (1997) seems to separate out the populists from the Progressives but says that their mission was the same: to root out corruption and improve the living conditions of working-class people. Not surprisingly, too, as Gilmore (2002) points out, "Socialists saw themselves as progressives" (p. 10). Were Socialists, Populists, and Progressives three different groups? Can one drive a wedge between these? Students of history have to also remember that not all socialists were liberals. Ross Wetzsteon (2002) reminds us that there were "right wing elements in the Socialist party...still advocate[ing] segregation" (p. 66). And not all populists were liberal either. Many were anti-Semitic. However, each of these groups had liberal strains as well, and all were fighting against workers being, as Leon Fink (1997) puts it, "powerless in a machine age" (p. 9). Robert Wiebe (1967) argues that the Progressives and Populists were, in fact, two separate groups and that they were at loggerheads. Wiebe points out, "Narrowness, which characterized the towns and farms as well as the smaller cities, also stood in marked contrast to late-nineteenth century reform. Very few of these progressives had looked kindly upon Populism or its near relations" (p. 178). Populists, for Wiebe, were the parochial farmers or small-town people who were only looking out for themselves and were in no way cosmopolitan in outlook. Joshua David Hawley (2008) tells us that Teddy Roosevelt was suspicious of the Populists because he saw them as anarchists (p. 97). Roosevelt hated the anarchists partly because McKinley was assassinated by an anarchist (Brinkley, 2009). And yet the Populists were calling for many of the same reforms that Roosevelt wanted.

Some intellectuals who thought that they were Progressives (but were not) were just as parochial and racist as some of the Populists. David Southern (2005) tells us that "American historians who came of age during the Progressive Era…combined so-called scientific history with scientific racism" (p. 53). What Southern tells us next disturbs. He states

> Professor Herbert Baxter Adams led the way by mentoring graduate students at prestigious Johns Hopkins University in the late nineteenth century. Trained in Germany in the scientific method of history, Adams harped on Teutonic superiority. John W. Burgess, a Tennessean who studied law, history, and political science at several German universities, disseminated theories of Teutonic superiority at Columbia University from 1880 until his retirement in 1912. (p. 54)

Historians are not immune to racist ideology. They are not immune to sexism or homophobia. One of the biggest problems with some sectors of the Progressive movement was racism. As David Southern points out, "Democratic reform and racism went hand-in-hand in the Progressive Era" (p. 3). Clearly Roosevelt was racist as were many of the reformers of his generation. Hence, some things about the Progressive movement weren't progressive at all.

The Progressives and Women

On the other hand, the Progressive party was the only party in the early 1900s that welcomed women. Sidney Milkis (2009) tells us

> Many women in both social work and the women's movement considered the position of Roosevelt and the Progressives on equal suffrage to be a decisive point in their

> favor. The National American Women Suffrage Association had sent delegations to the Republican and Democratic conventions, only to be spurned by both parties. The Progressive Party, by contrast, not only adopted an equal suffrage plank but practiced what it called an "open door policy" toward women who wanted to participate in its organization. At its national convention an unprecedented number of women took part as delegates. (p. 162)

It is astonishing that neither the Democrats nor the Republicans welcomed women into their parties. The Progressive Party was not wholly open to the participation of black women nor to immigrant women. And at bottom, Teddy Roosevelt was more than likely a misogynist and had little tolerance for the Other. He was so incredibly consumed by his own crisis of masculinity (Pinar, 2009b) that one wonders whether he had any room in his psyche for the nonmasculine. So one might wonder whether the Progressive Party really did embrace women's causes or just appeared to embrace women's causes.

Politicians like Woodrow Wilson, who was considered a Progressive by some, might have had some Progressive policies—but he was also simultaneously reactionary. John Milton Cooper (2009) points out that Wilson, when president, started progressive programs such as

> the Federal Reserve, the income tax, the Federal Trade Commission the first child labor law, the first federal aid to farmers, and the first law mandating an eight-hour workday for industrial workers, as well as the appointment of Brandeis to the Supreme Court. (p. 8)

There were hints of all of these policies during Teddy Roosevelt's administration, and certainly women like Jane Addams and Margaret Haley began the discussions around child labor laws and eight-hour workdays. So the power of women should not be underestimated here.

Woodrow Wilson—who some considered Progressive—was highly sexist, as can be attested by Lucy Salmon who was a student in one of his history classes while he was teaching at Bryn Mawr (Bohan, 2004). Chara Bohan tells us that Wilson thought that "women's intellectual abilities were inferior" (p. 20), and that he actually said that he "would prefer to teach young men" (p. 21). He had no use for women and did not like teaching them. And he did not support women's suffrage during his first term as president but surprisingly enough—during this first term—many left wing intellectuals, including women like Jane Addams, supported him perhaps because of his record on reform (Cooper, 2009). It wasn't until the United States entered WWI that he felt the pressure to pass the suffrage amendment. John Cooper tells us that many women were calling him "a hypocrite who professed to promote freedom abroad while not extending it to women at home" (p. 411). Under pressure, he finally began to see the importance of passing the suffrage amendment, but I am not convinced that he really believed women should have the right to vote.

Wilson was not only sexist, he was also racist. His record on race relations is abysmal. John Cooper tells us that "he turned a stone face and deaf ear to the struggles and tribulations of African Americans" (p. 11). And even worse, Cooper tells us that Wilson

> allowed some of his cabinet secretaries to try to introduce segregation into the federal workplace, and he permitted them to reduce the number of African Americans employed by the government. When vicious racial violence broke out during and after the war, he said nothing, except once, when he belatedly but eloquently denounced lynching. (p. 11)

So like Teddy Roosevelt, Woodrow Wilson was both reactionary and Progressive. These contradictions are not easy to square. When running for a second term as president, Wilson said in a speech, "We have in four years come very near to carrying out the platform of the Progressive Party as well as our own: for we also are progressives" (Cooper, p. 348). On another occasion, Wilson proclaimed: "I am a progressive. I do not spell it with a capital P, but I think my pace is just as fast as those who do" (Cooper, p. 351). And yet, some did not believe he really was a true Progressive. What is a progressive with a small p? John Cooper suggests that this small p progressive was nothing more than opportunism (p. 106). Cooper claims

> Opportunism unquestionably played a part in swinging Wilson toward progressivism. The popularity of Roosevelt's anti-trust and regulatory policies, growing reformist insurgency in both parties, and repeated defeats of conservative Democrats—all pointed to the direction in which the political winds were blowing. (p. 106)

Astonishingly, Wilson himself even claimed to be an opportunist as he said: "A politician, a man engaged in party contests, must be an opportunist" (Cooper, p. 106). One can admire Wilson's record on reform. But his record on racism is abysmal. Wilson allowed for the showing of the film *Birth of a Nation* at the White House. As John Cooper points out, this film "glorifie[d] the Ku Klux Klan" (p. 172). Cooper argues that Wilson was a sort of unknowing dupe. That is, he argues that Wilson did not know what the film was about before its showing at the White House. Even if he were an unknowing dupe, he did not say much about the fiasco afterwards. Cooper tells us that because of this incident, "even more than segregation policies, Wilson's involvement with *The Birth of a Nation* would make him anathema to African Americans" (p. 273).

This leads us to Leon Fink's (1997) comments about our contemporaries who dismiss the Progressive movement altogether. Fink tells us that there is a certain condescension (p. 11) that contemporary writers have when looking back at the Progressive era in America. This attitude of condescension is one that needs some thought. Fink puts it this way:

> Yet there are problems with this standard "history of ideas" approach to intellectual reformers as a social group. A tone of glib condescension all too often sneaks into the critiques of Progressive reformers, as if from some newfound heights of wisdom we have somehow resolved the classic issues of democracy and industrial civilization that they first confronted. (p. 11)

To say that the Progressives were mere dreamers is unfair and historically inaccurate. Looking back to the accomplishments of scholars like Dewey, Addams, and Ida B. Wells, one can only be in awe and astonished at their bravery. Who today has accomplished what, say, Jane Addams, accomplished at Hull House? To say that the Progressives accomplished little or to say that the Progressive movement was merely patronizing, backhanded philanthropy is unfair and historically inaccurate. These Progressive reformers left their mark historically and changed the way we think about American history, and they opened doors to future generations to change our thoughts, hearts, and minds about what it might mean to think about the notion of the common good and why it has to continually be thought through. Not only this, but one can argue that people like Jane Addams changed the social landscape of American politics and charted the way for later New Deal programs during Franklin Roosevelt's administration. Jason Scott Smith (2006) tells us that the New Deal was a "reforming impulse that stretched back to William Jennings Bryan" (p. 6). But Smith does not give women enough credit for their work in starting social welfare programs. Smith does say, however, that women who came after Jane Addams and worked on the New Deal like "Hilda Worthington Smith, Sue Shelton White and Ellen Woodward… [shared] an abbreviated moment" (p. 15) in history. But I do not think that Jane Addams's moment was, in fact, abbreviated. Of all the women who worked on social welfare programs, Addams, by far, is cited by historians more than any other. Her accomplishments were historic and lasting. If it weren't for Jane Addams, one might wonder whether the New Deal would have happened at all. Perhaps that statement is a bit bold, but FDR's ideas did not come out of a vacuum.

Intellectuals, as Dewey suggests, must work toward changing the public and the way in which scholars go about thinking about our public work and the work of public education. Scholars owe a debt of gratitude to the likes of Dewey, Addams, and Wells, among many others. To dismiss these public intellectuals out of hand, as Fink (1997) warns, is irresponsible. Let us build on Dewey's progressivism, critique it, and take it in new directions. This is what the Reconceptualization in curriculum studies has been all about.

Who Counts as Progressive

Against the larger scene of American political progressivism—whether we call it Populist, Socialist, or reformist—American educators too, during the early 20th century, were responding to the call of the problems of industrialism and big business, as Cremin (1961) reminds us. When studying different historiographies of American education students should note that Progressives get classified in a variety of ways. Cremin struggles when attempting to explain what Progressive education was. He says mostly it was contradictory. One of the interesting and rather lengthy footnotes in the back of his book concerns whether or not he wanted to include Thorndike as a Progressive (p. 369). Well, he did. He argues that the more scientifically oriented thinkers of the time (the social efficiency scholars) should be included as Progressives even though politically they were reactionary. This is clearly a contradiction. Many of the social efficiency scholars were also involved in eugenics organizations, which is extremely disturbing. Kliebard (1995) addresses this problem in the afterword of his book (which is worth studying carefully) *The Struggle for the American Curriculum 1893–1958*. He states that most educational historians can be divided into two groups on this issue. He explains:

> The two dominant approaches to interpreting progressive education have been (1) to define progressive education in broad terms, often acknowledging obvious inconsistencies and contradictions (e.g., Cremin); and (2) to single out a particular subgroup or program of reform and to exclude everything that may be inconsistent with it from what may be legitimately defined as progressive education (e.g., Zilvermit). (p. 246)

A similar problem is pointed out by Richard Hofstadter (1955) when talking about the American Populist Progressives and how reactionary they were. He states:

> The Populist Progressives were frank to express their dislike of the immigrant and to attack unrestricted immigration with arguments phrased in popular and "liberal" language. Many labor leaders stood with them on this issue, and so did a number of academic scholars. Men like Edward A. Ross, John R. Commons, and Edward Bemis, all three of whom were considered radicals and lost academic jobs on this ground that they gave support to the anti-immigrant sentiment. (p. 179)

Hofstadter points out how complicated and contradictory the notion of progressive is historically. Our idea of what progressive is today, is not the same as what progressive meant to differing groups during the Progressive era.

The way in which educational historians classify groups of people depends on how they view who was Progressive and who wasn't. It is clear that Cremin (1961) is hesitant to even make these classifications. However, I do think that it can be helpful to understand common threads among groups of people. I suggest that there were three broad groups of educationists working in the early 20th century. The first group I call the Traditionalists (the Great Books scholars); the second group I call the Industrialists (social efficiency scholars), and the third group I call Progressives. Progressives are politically liberal, not reactionary. Just because someone calls himself a Progressive doesn't mean that he really is. Just because a government calls its country democratic doesn't mean that it really is. Hitler was elected by the people in a "democratic" country. But certainly National Socialism was in no way democratic.

Now, interestingly enough, Petra Munro Hendry (2011) says that all the fuss about who fits where into what category—in the debate about the Progressives—is wrong-headed to begin with. She claims the argument of who fits where is, in fact, an engendered argument that tends to confuse more than clarify and serves to police gender. Who fits into what category is a male story, she says. The categorizing of people into groups (i.e., like our grouping of Traditionalists, Industrialists, and Progressives) is a sort of Oedipal drama about sons killing fathers. This debate really concerns only male struggles. This is the Oedipal struggle. This entire conversation, Munro Hendry says, leaves women and minorities completely out of the picture and erases what contributions women and minorities have made to American education. So the whole discussion is wrong-headed. Maybe students of history should be asking different questions that help us better understand how complicated history is. Categorizing people simplifies history, according to Munro Hendry. Is the question who counts as a Progressive any longer relevant? History is not about categorizing people and categories erase our contradictions. People are full of contradictions, so how can we categorize anybody?

Curriculum Historiography and Women Progressive Educators: A Theoretical Matrix

I offer here what I call a theoretical matrix that explores stories of women educators of the Progressive era. Recall what was discussed earlier concerning the overall structure of this chapter. I drive a wedge between educational history and curriculum historiography. This will be important to keep in mind here. I argue that curriculum historiography is the larger category under which educational history falls. And both need to be examined when talking about doing curriculum historiography. Let us clarify. Curriculum historiography differs from educational history in that curriculum historiography deals with broader issues than only the schoolhouse. Here I want to turn to the issue of curriculum historiography to explore what those broader issues might entail. William Pinar (2001) says, "I join my colleague Petra Munro and her co-authors Margaret Crocco Smith and Kathleen Weiler (1999) in broadening the scope of curriculum history, what counts as the 'canon' of curriculum knowledge" (p. 26). Again, most educational historians focus narrowly on the schoolhouse. Pinar, Munro, Crocco Smith, and Weiler go beyond the schoolhouse to talk about who has gotten left out of curricular conversations: women, minorities. But further still, the conversation gets broadened as these writers question who counts as a teacher and what counts as a classroom. Pinar (2009b) argues that for people like Jane Addams and Ida B. Wells, their classroom was the world. Although Addams was not a teacher per se, she taught us much through her scholarly work as well as her work at Hull House. Ida B. Wells taught the world about the evils of lynching. William Pinar (2001) says that when educational theorists "reduce the discipline of education to schooling [this has] often meant the exclusion of educational phenomena that occur outside the school, such as those pedagogical elements of political and social movements" (p. 26).

The work of opening up this discussion beyond the confines of the schoolhouse leads us into exciting and important new terrain when curriculum theorizing. This more open conversation is what sets curriculum theorists apart from, say, more traditional educational historians. When the discussion is narrowed to what goes on inside of institutions, scholars miss what is going on in the world. The study of culture was what Dewey called for and this is what curriculum theorists do. The study of the larger culture helps us not to become myopic and narrow. Narrow studies of the schoolhouse could potentially lead to what Russell Jacoby (1997) called "social amnesia." He states that "social amnesia is society's repression of remembrance—society's own past" (p. 3). This past is a forgotten one because it is in some way too painful to remember. A painful past is easier to gloss over, repress, or simply ignore. It is painful to read the ways in which women get left out of the history of education, or if they do get mentioned, they get footnoted or they get mentioned in a sentence or two or maybe in a paragraph. Not all educational historians are guilty of these omissions, but still the history of education is largely a history written by men about men. Of course, things have changed and scholars are now writing about women but still more work needs to be done. In the past ten or fifteen years, there have been many biographies of women educators that I want to explore here and talk about the ways in which these must be studied as part of our educational inheritance. Lest students of history not develop social amnesia, historical narratives about the work and intellectual labor of women Progressives must be studied.

Now, this is not to say that all women Progressives share the same history, or that women and men share the same history. Gisela Bock (2006) says,

> The difference between women's and men's history does not imply that the history of women is identical for all women: women do not all have the same history. Awareness of the Otherness, the difference, the inequality between female and male history has been complemented by an awareness and historical study of the Otherness, the differences and inequalities among women themselves. (p. 105)

When studying women Progressive educators, scholars should note that race, class, and gender make a difference in how experience gets played out.

Race, class, and gender are social constructions whose meanings change over time. But that is not to say that because these terms are social constructions that they don't matter materially. Susan Kingsley Kent (2006) says that in *Comparative Studies in Society and History* a piece appeared titled "If 'Woman' Is Just an Empty Category, Then Why Am I Afraid to Walk Alone at Night?" (p. 184). If "gay" is just a social construction, why is it that gay people are afraid of being bashed in the parking lot? If "black" is just a social construction, why are black people afraid to pull over for gas in rural Georgia? The point here is that these social constructions, although changeable categories, do have meaning in real-world situations. So although feminists question the term "woman" and critical race theorists question the term "black" and queer theorists question the word "gay," they all matter in the danger that is real-world politics.

The Complexities of Doing History

Doing history means making historical discussions complex and questioning the terms that shape who gets represented in historical texts. Sue Middleton and Kathleen Weiler (1999) "consider the ways in which the historian as author is implicated in the choice of what is represented" (p. 3). There is a psychological investment made when one identifies with certain texts and not others. Why that identification is made is not always obvious. Elisabeth Young-Bruehl (1998) suggests that biographers "are drawn to subjects who are like themselves, usually in ways that the biographer is not consciously aware of" (p. 21). The biographies that will be discussed here were written by scholars who have had certain psychological identifications with the people they write about. The reader will not know what those identifications are about, unless the biographer tells us. But it is important for the reader as well as the writer to try to drive a psychological wedge between the writer's own subject(ivity) and object of writing. As Michael Shanks (2001) says, "the past is ineffable in its difference" (p. 138). The subjectivity of the writer can get somehow mixed up with the object of study. And this mixing up of self and Other is what psychological identification is about. But it is important to try to untangle self from Other when reading or writing or studying Others as texts of the past.

Christopher Bollas (1997) suggests that objects process us. He states, "When we choose an object, we very often pick something that will process us.... when we make use of objects, when we select a book to read or a novelist to explore, we're going to be processed by the integrity offered us by the object" (p. 54). That the object under study processes us means that that object is in psychological relation to our subject(ivity). Or, as Michael Shanks (2001) puts it, "the past looks back" (p. 138). The objects under study, then, "look back" at the subjects studying them, figuratively of course. Keeping this in mind, the writer of a biography must work to keep the integrity—as Bollas puts it—of the object intact. The scholar must honor the subject in such a way that she is honest in her analysis of that subject, which means not falling into the trap of writing a "myth of the heroic individual" (p. 7), as Crocco, Munro, and Weiler (1999) put it. Biographers do not have to paint a false picture to cover for their object of study. Honesty about one's object of study is a question of ethicality. When biographers talk about their objects of study, sometimes they tell us that point blank they did not like who they studied. Others fall in love with their subjects. Both are problems. Falling in love with a subject is also a way of mixing up the subject and object of study. A sort of love (what Freud called neurotic) transference is going on that obscures the representation of the past. Whether one likes or does not like the objects of study, one thing is clear. Students of history must, as Michael Shanks (1991) points out, "go beyond the object we have found, follow it in becoming something else" (p. 135). Studying the past is a curious phenomenon. Thus, the writing of curriculum history is about keeping the past past *and* making use of it today. The past as interpreted in the present is no longer, strictly speaking, the past. The past that one interprets through scholarship is part of our present circumstance and yet it is still past. But as scholars interpret the past, the past gets changed and what is interpreted changes us as well. In talking about doing archaeology, Michael Shanks says

> A lot of people are fascinated by excavating the past, the slow painstaking process, the allure of discovery. But it appears in report form; the experience is lost and hardly evoked. It is fixed as an image of the site; in spite of the inclusion often of the sequences of excavation in reports, process is absent from the figures, the photographs, lists, comments. Yet excavation [and I would add curriculum history as a form of textual excavation] is all about process, unfolding, growth, the cultivation of ideas. (p. 183)

My work here is an exploration of ideas and evocations. What evokes or stuns or shocks or surprises? What omissions, exclusions, reversals, and dismissals are apparent? What does it mean to omit somebody from history? What does it mean to gloss over an uncomfortable idea or event from the past? There are certainly things about the Progressive movement that make readers uncomfortable. Many Progressives were highly racist and turned their heads when told of lynchings. Drawing on a citation from Anna Julia Cooper—an African American Progressive educator I will talk more about in a while—William Pinar (2001) points out

> Once captured, public notices were circulated usually a day or two in advance of the lynching event itself. Sometimes the notices were distributed in distant communities. Sometimes trains made special trips, adding extra cars to meet the demands of crowds wishing to travel in order to watch the spectacle (Harris 1984). Anna Julia Cooper recalls: "Excursion trains with banners flying were run into place and eager children were heard to exclaim: "We have seen a hanging, we are now going to see a burning!" (quoted in Lemert and Bhan 1998, 210]). (p. 53)

This history disturbs and should not be glossed over or excluded from the larger discussion. This is why Cremin's (1961) message to historians is so important: scholars must always contextualize studies against the larger social backdrop or what is elaborated upon will be naïve.

There is no one-to-one correspondence between our writing and the subject written about. The subject written about is mediated by text, psychology, and other unknowns. Biographers write about their subjects but never get at the object of their study with Truth (with a capital T). Interpretation slips. The subject of the past is slippery, just as John Dewey said that the notion of experience is slippery.

A Sociocultural Portrait of Women Educators During the Progressive Era

I call my approach a sociocultural one because I am interested in the larger sociocultural scene around which and against which these women worked. My approach—as a more sociocultural one—will raise questions about what it means to be an educated person and the ways in which gender and race have direct impact on getting an education or becoming an educator. Because I am more interested in following the stories of these women's lives and what they contributed to the larger educational landscape, I argue that a sociocultural analysis always includes an intellectual analysis. The intellectual analysis is part and parcel of the sociocultural. What women Progressives did during their lives sprang from their intellectual work. But here I am not interested in doing a textual exegesis of, say, Jane Addams' speeches. That approach is too narrow for the larger picture that I want to paint here. I suggest that students look to these and other important primary sources for future studies. My task here is to paint in broad strokes the ways in which women Progressives changed lives.

The Forgotten Ones

Perhaps it should come as no surprise that many women Progressive educators have been forgotten because most history books are written by men and are about men. Margaret Smith Crocco, Petra Munro, and Kathleen Weiler (1999) tell us, "Of course, the stories of male progressive educators are far better known today than those of their female counterparts. This uneven recollection reflects the gendered dimension of traditional historical representation and cultural transmission" (p. 3). This "uneven recollection" is more than uneven, it is out of joint. One must wonder why our culture is so out of joint when it comes to remembering the accomplishments of women. Karen Johnson (2000) has written about the life and work of Anna Julia Cooper and Nannie Helen Burroughs and states, "Even though Cooper's and Burroughs's contributions to the field of education were distinctive, their accomplishments, experiences and 'voices' have remained ignored and forgotten by educational historians" (p. xi). What is striking about Anna Julia Cooper is that she was born a slave and took her PhD at the Sorbonne when she was well into her 60s. This is a remarkable accomplishment. Why is it not noted more often in educational historiographies?

Who Gets Left Out

The study of history must also be a study of who gets left out of history. If people get left out of it, then what exactly is history? It is a particular past written for a particular reason. Any historiography is necessarily exclusive. Of course, one can't write about everybody. But still it seems that even today there are major omissions in traditional historical accounts of education. The history of the common school is the history of the way men wanted to control women and children. Perhaps an unspoken part of the issue of control is to make invisible those who are being controlled. Is schooling about making people invisible? Perhaps. Think about standardized testing as it works to make invisible peoples' thoughts and lives. Personalities and idiosyncratic ideas (which most of us have but are afraid to voice) are squashed with standardization. Test taking is a way to control and make invisible subjectivities and lives. It is no accident that people like Anna Julia Cooper are not remembered in traditional historical accounts of schooling. It is a clear instance not only of sexism that she is left out but also racism. African Americans, for one, were pushed out of the common school because they were not white. The experience of school was only common for white people. Segregated peoples, hence, have segregated histories. These histories should not be segregated. Scholars must work to bring back to the discussion the stories of forgotten women. Mary Helen Washington (1988) argues that Anna Julia Cooper is "far less well known" than other African American women (p. xxvii). Washington states

> One of her biographers, Dr. Paul Cooke, suggests that Cooper's role as a scholar limited her public profile: "Cooper was continually the scholar. She was in the library when Mary Church Terrell was picketing drugstores and cafeterias in downtown Washington D.C. She chose the lesser limelight, while Terrell chose the Civil Rights route and carried the media." (p. xxvii)

African American male scholars have name recognition, while many African American female scholars do not. W. E. B. Du Bois is a name that is highly recognized today and he was a scholar. So being a scholar does not necessarily make you invisible. Anna Julia Cooper is as unknown as Mary Church Terrell is today by most academicians who are not experts in African American studies. Both of these women are unknown because (1) they were women and (2) they were African American. Both misogyny and racism play into who gets known and who disappears from history. Even Ida B. Wells—who was an activist like Terrell and a scholar like Cooper—as William Pinar (2001) points out, today is "underappreciated" (p. 433). Why might Wells still be underappreciated today? History is his-story, not her-story. There is a certain amount of repression too associated with the memory of what Wells did to uncover the evils of lynching. White Americans do not want to know this history so they tend to repress the memory of Ida B. Wells.

Vivian May (2007) declares that "the question remains: Why have Cooper's astute ideas and methods not been given the attention they deserve…. Does she continue to be overlooked because she was Black and female?" (p. 2). The question does remain as to why being black and female means also disappearing in the historical archives. Another scholar of note who has been forgotten is Lucy Maynard Salmon who was a history professor at Vassar for forty years. Chara Haeussler Bohan (2004) writes

> Lucy Maynard Salmon, a pioneer in American education, is a name not recognized today. As has been the case with other notable early female pioneers in education, Lucy Salmon's life unfortunately has been marginalized and largely forgotten in the pages of history… . An inspiring, progressive educator, an advocate of suffrage and women's rights, a scholarly researcher and prolific author, Salmon pushed the boundaries of human understanding. (p. 1)

Salmon changed the way scholars write about history but was dismissed by her male contemporaries. She argued for what she called "history in the round" (Bohan, p. 59). History in the round—as Salmon called it—is a sociocultural history, not a narrow parochial history. Salmon was one of the first historians to do what today is called social and cultural history, or history from below, the peoples' history. This way of approaching history was not fashionable in her time at all. But today it is. She paved the way for historians to do sociocultural studies. It is remarkable that she taught at Vassar for forty years. Vassar, as Lynn Gordon (1990) points out, had a long history of Progressive ideology. Of the Seven Sisters schools, Vassar was clearly one of the most progressive.

Like Vassar, Bryn Mawr had its star in M. Carey Thomas, its second president. She too has "fallen into eclipse" (Horowitz, 1999, p. xiii). Helen Lefkowitz Horowitz tells us that Thomas was also involved in developing the Johns Hopkins School of Medicine, two remarkable achievements for anybody, let alone a woman of her time. Thomas couldn't find a place to get a PhD in the United States because of sexist policies of most universities. Thus, she took her PhD at the University of Zurich. In those days women were banned from lectures (Horowitz). What is also remarkable about M. Carey Thomas is that according to historian Lillian Faderman (1991),

> The Ph.D. program she instituted at Bryn Mawr—the only women's college with such a program—was meant not only to produce female Ph.D.s but also to provide role models for undergraduates. In this way, Thomas believed, a female tradition of scholarship would begin to be perpetuated. (p. 210)

Many women of our generation take it for granted that they can get PhDs in any subject of their choosing. This wasn't always the case. Intellectuals owe a debt of gratitude to people like M. Carey Thomas for having the vision to open the doors so that women could earn doctorates.

Another remarkable woman is Mary McLeod Bethune who, like M. Carey Thomas, broke ground in higher education. Audrey McCluskey (1999) tells us that "her unprecedented role in education and public affairs has been shrouded in anecdote and hagiography" (p. 3). Bethune was an African American woman who founded Bethune-Cookman College. This is a remarkable accomplishment. Think of what she was up against during those hard years from the early 1900s through the mid-twentieth century. Racism was intense during those years as lynchings and other "southern horrors," as Ida B. Wells puts it, were all around her. In the midst of racial tension Bethune not only founded this college but was also its president for many years. Even today, there are not many African American women college presidents.

On another front, Elsie Ripley Clapp should be remembered for her work in Progressive education, but she is mostly forgotten. Sam Stack (2004) tells us that one of the most important things about Clapp is that she "brought progressive education to two rural public schools in Appalachia, in Kentucky and West Virginia" (p. 4). Most of the Progressive schools were not public institutions but private ones, and they were mostly located in the Northeast and served mostly upper-middle-class children. It is remarkable that during the mid-1930s that Clapp was able to bring to poor children Progressive education. These were the children of coal miners. Clapp, who came from wealth and shopped at Tiffany's growing up (Stack), wanted to teach poor children. Many of the women Progressive educators came from money; many attended Ivy League schools. Jane Addams came from money but she served the working class.

Other reformers who worked with the poor were the Social Gospelers. Robin Berson (2004) comments that Social Gospelers were "easily tainted by righteousness and condescension" (p. 35). The Social Gospel movement was a Christian one that was built on helping others, namely the poor. The Social Gospel movement could be considered part of the Progressive movement from the Christian perspective, but many were suspicious of its religious undertones. There was a missionary bent to the Social Gospel movement and socialists especially would see this as colonizing.

Jane Addams, too, according to Jean Bethke Elshtain (2002), has "gone largely unrecognized" (p. xxii). Elshtain says, "Although Jane Addams has had her day, she has yet to receive her due" (p. xxii). There are two curriculum theorists, though, who have done extensive work on Jane Addams: William Pinar (2009b) and Petra Munro (1999). Most people associate Addams with social work and not education. But both Pinar and Munro make the argument that Addams was an educator. Pinar (2009b) claims that Addams's classroom was the world, especially as she brought her message of peace to international audiences. Addams was excoriated for being a pacifist during a time of war. But she was also excoriated because she was a woman who took a stand and spoke loudly about what she believed. In the early 20th century this was unacceptable behavior for a woman. Addams won the Nobel Peace Prize in 1931 despite being demonized in the United States. People are threatened by women who speak loudly and take strong positions. I am thinking here too of Ida B. Wells and the enemies she had in the white (racist) community. Wells took her campaign to the United Kingdom and got the attention of the international community because in the United States people would not listen to her. Both Addams and Wells were international educators as they traveled the globe with their messages of peace and antilynching. Wells slept with a Winchester rifle near her bed. So, unlike Addams, she was not a pacifist (Giddings, 2008). But Wells was working toward the same end as Addams. Both fought against social wrongs. Disturbingly, both women have gotten the short shrift in the historical archive. Paula Giddings reports that Wells-Barnett (as she was then married) was left out of many historical accounts of antilynching campaigns, even the accounts of the well-known African American historian Carter Woodson. Giddings tells us

> Carter G. Woodson, the black Harvard-educated "father of African American history" who conceived the idea of setting aside the week every year to focus on the contributions of people of African descent.... Woodson's book had failed to mention her own [Wells-Barnett's] contributions to the campaign against lynching. (p. 5)

Ida B. Wells started the antilynching campaign but is not recognized in Woodson's work. This is a glaring example of sexism. Likewise, W. E. B. Du Bois, according to Mary Helen Washington (1988), left out Anna Julia Cooper's name when using her words to talk about women's oppression. Washington explains,

> In a compassionate and generally progressive essay called "On the Damnation of Women", Du Bois sympathetically analyzes the oppression of black women, but he makes no effort to draw on the writings of black women intellectuals for their insights.... In fact, in a remarkable oversight in this essay, Du Bois quotes Cooper's brilliant observation that "only the black woman can say 'when and where I enter'" and attributes the statement *not* to Her but *anonymously* to "one of our women." (pp. xli–xlii)

This is another clear instance of sexism as Cooper's name is made invisible by Du Bois. Women get left out, forgotten, eclipsed; they are oversights, underappreciated, dismissed, and swept into the ashbins of history.

The (Mis)Recognition of Women Progressive Educators

When Progressive women educators were recognized by others their accomplishments were thought of always in relation to men. For example, Anna Julia Cooper, according to Karen Johnson (2000), "was considered the female

Du Bois" (p. xxiv). Likewise, Mary McLeod Bethune, according to Audrey Thomas McCluskey (1999), was "dubbed the female Booker T. Washington" (p. 4). Women are considered little more than "sidekicks" (Crocco, Munro, & Weiler, 1999, p. 3) to men. Or as Petra Munro Hendry (2011) points out, women like Jane Addams were seen as dutiful daughters of Dewey. If students study the life and work of any of these women, they will see that they were neither the female versions of the men they supposedly imitated, nor were they sidekicks or dutiful daughters. All of these ways of talking about women's accomplishments are dismissive and belittling not to mention sexist. Perhaps one of the reasons that Caroline Pratt "refused to be associated with any paternalistic doctrine of progressive education that was espoused by John Dewey and William Heard Kilpatrick"—according to Mary Hauser (2006, p. 79)—was that she wanted to carve out her own identity and did not want to be seen as yet another sidekick (Crocco, Munro, & Weiler, 1999, p. 3) of Dewey's. Clearly, Pratt must have been influenced by some of the other Progressive thinkers of her time as she studied at Teachers College, Columbia. Her motives for wanting distance between herself and the men of Columbia are certainly understandable.

Many men worried that if women studied academics they would become like men and this was seen as a problem. Lynn Gordon (1990) points out

> Founders and supporters of the eastern women's colleges, later known as Seven Sisters, argued that their schools met the demand for women's higher education without sacrificing femininity. At single-sex Colleges, women, they promised, could develop their minds without becoming like men. (p. 26)

Margaret Haley and Ida B. Wells took strong positions on things. Kate Rousmaniere (1999) tells us that Haley was called "lady labor slugger" (p. 149) and Ida B. Wells, Paula Giddings (2008) tells us, felt that "dignity…came through the authentic voice of militant protest and, sometimes, the barrel of a gun" (p. 244). The social construction of the image of the Victorian "lady" does not square with Haley and Wells. G. Stanley Hall, Lillian Faderman (1999) reports, called women scholars "amazons" (p. 210).

Many of the women Progressive educators did have same-sex partners. In the early 20th century the word "homosexual" was not used. Heteronormativity and homophobia were strong forces with which to contend. Women who loved women were thought of as "sexually deviant" (Gordon, 1990, p. 39). Despite homophobia, Caroline Pratt and Helen Marot were partners (Hauser, 2006); Lucy Salmon had a lifelong companion named Adelaide Underhill

(Bohan, 2004, p. 48); M. Carey Thomas had two partners over her lifetime, one was Mamie Gwinn and the other was Mary Garrett (Horowitz, 1999). Jane Addams also had two partners: Ellen Gates Starr and Mary Rozet Smith (Elshtain, 2002). Lillian Faderman (1999) comments on Addams and Rozet Smith's relationship. She states

> Almost every biographer of Jane Addams has recognized the importance of her relationship with Mary Rozet Smith, yet it has been difficult for most of them to discuss it as lesbian, since, as Blanche Cook has pointed out, a "conventional lady with pearls" (as both Jane and Mary were) has generally not been thought of in terms that the twentieth century has associated with perversion. (p. 127)

Were Addams and Rozet Smith less mannish than the heterosexual Ida B. Wells or the lady labor slugger Margaret Haley? Because Addams was a "lady with pearls" perhaps she could pass as straight and she was more acceptable than lady labor slugger.

The Curriculum Is Gendered

Petra Munro Hendry's (2011) phrase "engendering the curriculum" suggests that the curriculum has always already been engendered. Everything is gendered. Debra Newman Ham (2005) says of Mary Church Terrell that while at Oberlin, she wanted to "pursue the 'Gentleman's course,' which meant four years of classical studies" (p. 11). Today this notion of a gentleman's course seems ridiculous. What makes the so-called classics gentlemanly? Or manly? The classics are considered classic partly because they are books written by white men.

Anna Julia Cooper, according to Karen Johnson (2000), was fired from the famous M Street High (an African American high school) for teaching a classical curriculum. The board accused her of having an affair at the time, but the real reason for the firing—according to Horace Mann Bond, Johnson tells us—was because she refused to teach a vocational, or industrial curriculum. What was it about the classical curriculum that seemed a threat to the board of M Street High? Was this too an issue of gender?

Are the humanities seen as effeminate? If so would the classical curriculum—ironically—make the boys at M Street High effeminate? Interestingly, Lynn Gordon (1990) tells us that men at the University of California in the early 20th century "Shared the fears common on other campuses that women were driving men out of the humanities. Many believed that sexually segregated classes would prevent the effeminization of the University" (p. 70). Were the women by their very presence in humanities classes driving men away? Is subject matter engendered? Is the production of knowledge masculine or feminine? Or is it both? The problem isn't whose knowledge is of most worth, but who gets discriminated against for studying certain knowledge. Lillian Faderman (1991) reminds us

> In Boston from 1789 to 1822, for example, girls were allowed to attend the public schools during the summer only, and for a time for two hours in the afternoon during the school year, after the boys had gone home. (p. 175)

When girls did go to school the subjects they took were always suspect if the subjects were thought to be male. Faderman remarks

> Emma Willard's Troy Female Seminary, which opened in 1821, was revolutionary in its intention to provide serious study for girls, including courses such as physiology and algebra, but it was met with general disfavor. Though Mrs. Willard tried to be assuring in her "Address to the Public" that her school would not "masculinize" girls, many were not convinced. (p. 175)

How is the subject of physiology masculine? Is algebra a masculine subject too? If the classics include the study of languages, are they too considered masculine? If so, what does it mean when a woman studies Greek or Latin? Does she become mannish? This sounds ridiculous but this was an issue for Anna Julia Cooper who, according to Vivian May (2007),

> Wanted access to the full curriculum at St. Augustine's, [but] the administration attempted to deny Cooper the right to take courses in Greek and Latin (offered exclusively to boys studying to become ministers since, as Cooper recounts it, the principal presumed that the girls were only at school to find a husband). (p. 15)

It is interesting that during the era of the Social Gospelers, it was noted that some of the "New Presbyterians" (Hawley, 2008, p. 17) feared the "feminization" of the church. They called for a "muscular Christianity" (p. 18) and argued that because "Jesus was a carpenter [he] had been a strong and vigorous man" (p. 18).

Women Progressive Educators: Politics and the Arts

It is no wonder that many of the women Progressive educators became highly political. People become political when they have to. That is, when life is a constant battle against discrimination there comes a time to fight back. Margaret Smith Crocco, Petra Munro, and Kathleen Weiler (1999) have it right when they call for "pedagogies of resistance." Munro Hendry (2011) points out that one of the stereotypes of child-centered education is that women teachers focus on the well-being of children and pay little attention to the political. But many of these Progressive educators (even if they didn't call themselves child centered) were highly political; they became political for a reason. When you are pushed into a corner you fight back and that is exactly what these women did.

The second trend among these women Progressive educators is that many of them were interested in the arts. Perhaps for some of these women the arts were seen as political. Can the arts be thought of as another example of a "pedagogy of resistance?" Are politics and aesthetics strange bedfellows or a natural fit? Art can also be thought of as psychological; it can be used in the service of a defense against pain (Segal, 2000). In this brief section, then, I want to talk about two things: the political and the aesthetic in the context of women Progressive educators.

The Personal Is the Political

As I tried to show in the previous section, many women Progressives were belittled, dismissed, insulted, and discriminated against. The personal becomes political when the pain of discrimination becomes overwhelming. One becomes political when things become unbearable.

Many people do not know that Ida B. Wells was a school teacher for many years. She was fired for speaking out against the horrid conditions of the schools for African American children (Duster, 1970). She never really felt comfortable teaching school, instead she would teach the world about the "southern horrors" of lynching. William Pinar (2001) states

> Wells's genius in igniting British public sentiment during her controversial tours of Great Britain in 1892 and 1894 is an example of this strategy—I argue it qualifies as a form of pedagogy—conducted on an international scale. Her pedagogical and political success [was]…redirecting the American discussion of lynching. (p. 432)

For Pinar, Wells's classroom was the world. Munro Hendry (2011) calls Wells a curriculum theorist. Many historians of American education don't often include Wells in the canon. But clearly Pinar and Munro want to do so, and this move has advanced the field of curriculum history because it gets us to think otherwise about who counts as an educator and curriculum theorist.

Alfreda Duster (1970) says that Wells's "pen would not be silenced" (p. xix). Duster tells us that Wells "was perhaps the first person to recite the horrors of lynching in lurid detail" (p. xi). In the history of curriculum, William Pinar (2001) is one of the first curriculum scholars to unpack the horrors of lynching. This marks a radical turn in the way race gets discussed in the field of curriculum theorizing and curriculum history. One of Pinar's overall points is that when talking about racism students need to study this issue historically, in all its graphic and horrid detail, so as to understand what racism means. It is not enough to talk about changing attitudes and beliefs as so much multicultural literature suggests. Students will never understand racism if they do not study it historically, and if they don't understand it historically they will never be able to undo their own racism or work to dismantle racist institutional structures.

Jane Addams as Political Educator

Like Ida B. Wells, Jane Addams is also excluded from most of the traditional historiographies of education. However Pinar and Munro insist that she must be included in the history of curriculum. Like Wells, Addams was a political educator of the world (Pinar, 2009b). Pinar makes the interesting claim that Addams became political because she engaged in "self-reflective academic study," which enabled her to have a "sustained, critical, and creative engagement with the world" (p. 62). Pinar says, "Study does not just yield new 'information,' it restructures one's subjectivity, animating and focusing one's engagement of the world" (p. 65). Political labor, in other words, is only possible in connection with intellectual labor. Hull House wasn't only a place for labor leaders to meet, it was also, as Jean Bethke Elshtain (2002) says, "a place for the life of the mind" (p. 92).

The Political and Literary

Hull House was not only a place of political engagement it was also a place of literary engagement. Addams offered reading circles to people who would not have had the opportunity to read (with others) elsewhere. Together people studied important literary works. The literary, Pinar (2009b) teaches, opened doors to politics for Addams. And Addams's penchant for the literary is something that is not missed on Elshtain (2002) either who states

> What nearly all scholars and critics of Addams have missed or given short shrift to is just how much hers was a literary mind. Her sensibilities were forged in the generous company of literary personages who became companions in her struggles personal and political. (p. 28).

Jane Addams's reforms were revolutionary. What Elshtain calls "Hull House Firsts" (p. xix) are too lengthy to list here, but some of the unions that organized at Hull House include the "Women Shirt Makers Union, Dorcas Federal Labor Union, Woman Cloak Makers, [and the] Chicago Woman's Trade Union League" (p. xix).

Women and Labor Unions

Kate Rousmaniere (1999) tells us,

> Margaret Haley is one of the most popular and popularized icons of American teachers' history, heralded as a radical school reformer, labour activist, and feminist. In the first three decades of the twentieth century, Haley led the Chicago Teacher's Federation to be the first teachers' labor union in American history. (p. 147)

Labor unions came about during the Progressive era because of poor working conditions, unfair treatment, and abuse of workers (and in this case women teachers). It is important to note that for women, labor union issues were different from the labor issues men had. Women always had it harder than men and had little access to the rights that male workers had. Even when women were involved in labor unions, they were not treated as equals. Andrea Nye (1994) comments, "Marxist labor unions refused to admit women, the Soviet Union disbanded Alexandra Kolontai's Women's Bureau, the Progressive Labor party in the United States assigned women to coffee making" (p. 9). Lillian Faderman (1991) comments, "According to the AFL's newspaper, *American Federationist*, organized labor had a duty to 'keep women out of the trades, and if not, out of the unions'" (p. 105). Many labor unions were not only sexist, they were also racist. Michael McGerr (2003) tells us about the AFL. He states that in the 1890s:

> To many in the AFL, black workers were dangerous competitors, scabs who threatened white jobs and white unions. Blacks had, Gompers declared, "so conducted themselves as to be a continuous whip placed in the hands of the employers to cow the white men and to compel them to accept abject conditions of labor." The solution to black competition was to keep African-Americans out of craft unions—and out of skilled jobs—as much as possible. (p. 130)

So being pro-labor does not necessarily mean being also pro-black. McGerr tells us many Socialists were also racists. Just because people want class equality does not necessarily mean they also want racial equality too. And historically many Socialists—both European and American—were also anti-Semitic (Morris, 2001).

During the turn of the century, strikes were more common than not. Michael McGerr (2003) calls the United States the "most strike-torn nation in the world" (p. 120) from 1889 through 1901. He states that in 1901 there were more than three thousand strikes. Against this background, it is crucial to note that women's labor unions organized at Hull House were so important. These women were fighting not only for better working conditions but also they were fighting against discrimination, sexism, and the patriarchy.

Alongside Margaret Haley, Helen Marot and Caroline Pratt (who founded the City and Country Progressive School in Greenwich Village, New York) were very active in labor union work. Caroline Pratt called herself a "radical socialist" and her partner Helen Marot was involved with the Women's Trade Union (the WTUL). Lillian Faderman (1991) explains the importance of this union:

> The WTUL played a prominent role in the establishment of unions among garment workers, retail clerks, paper box makers, waitresses, laundresses, and many other female occupational groups. Its members helped lead strikes, such as the 190 women shirt makers' "Uprising of the Twenty Thousand," which eventually involved about 40,000 strikers and was the largest strike of female workers in history. (p. 106)

It is stunning to note the sheer numbers of strikers. This tells us something about the horrid treatment of workers and the horrid condition of factories and the abuse of workers.

Elsie Ripley Clapp and Labor Disputes

Like Caroline Pratt, Elsie Ripley Clapp was also involved in labor disputes, which is surprising because she was not "a political revolutionary nor a radical feminist" (Stack, 2004, p. 5). But she got involved in a silk workers strike and made acquaintances with Jack Reed, who was a well-known radical revolutionary Socialist. Sam Stack tells us that "well documented by labor historians, the Paterson Silk Workers Strike officially began on February 25th, 1913, when six thousand silk workers left their mills" (p. 92). Stack suggests that one of the reasons that Elsie Ripley Clapp got involved in this strike is that she failed her comprehensive exams in graduate school and was looking for a way to heal from that defeat. Perhaps there was more to it than that. Clapp, although not a "political revolutionary" (Stack, p. 5), did have a deep sense of helping the poor and those struggling for basic human rights.

Mary Church Terrell and the Lynching Crisis

Like Ida B. Wells, Mary Church Terrell got involved in politics because of the lynching crisis. Debra Newman Ham (2005) tells us

> The primary event that drove Terrell back into the political and professional arena was the 1892 lynching of her lifelong friend from Memphis, Tom Moss, who was murdered by Whites jealous of his grocery store. Never before had such blatant injustice struck Terrell so personally. She and Frederick Douglass were able to make an appointment with President Benjamin Harrison to urge him to speak out forcibly about such racial violence. Although the president gave them a sympathetic hearing, he made no public statement. (p. 14)

Whites in power hardly ever spoke out against lynching. The ongoing silence on the part of whites is an admission of racism. Teddy Roosevelt responded the same way to lynchings; he was silent about them. And Ida B. Wells had to travel abroad to get people to listen to her, and it was only because of the pressure the British placed on Americans that anything at all was done about lynching (Giddings, 2008).

Mary McLeod Bethune and Politics

Black women educators had a tremendous amount to deal with during the Progressive era. They had to deal with the ongoing problem of lynchings, silence on the part of whites, and the Ku Klux Klan. Mary McLeod Bethune, Audrey Thomas McCluskey (1999) tells us, "faced down the Ku Klux Klan at least once when they staged a late night march on her campus" (p. 8). McCluskey also reports that Bethune, "[in] a newspaper interview...[said] 'How long will you kick us, shoot us and burn us without your conscience speaking to you?'" (p. 80.). This statement was remarkably brave knowing what kind of retaliation Bethune could have suffered from making her views public.

M. Carey Thomas

When scholars talk about the idea of difference (in the context of being a woman) one can see here how black women, like Bethune, had totally different experiences, from, say, the privilege of M. Carey Thomas who was white and was the president of an upper-class, wealthy, white Ivy League institution. Thomas had her own struggles to be sure—especially with the male Quaker board with whom that she had to contend. But Thomas did not have to face down the Klan. Race and gender matter. And this is William Pinar's (2001) point in his book on lynching and violence in America as he says, "The racial crisis is gendered, and, in the United States at least, the crisis of gender is racialized" (p. 2). It seems counterintuitive to think of women suffragists as racists, but many of them were—hence race and gender are not easily separable. Here I am thinking of Mary Church Terrell's struggle with white suffragists. Debra Newman Ham (2005) says that while marching for the women's right to vote in front of the White House, "she and her daughter were sometimes mistreated by the White suffragists or made to march in the back of the line" (p. 15). Being liberal on issues of gender does not necessarily make one liberal on issues of race. M. Carey Thomas was racist and virulently anti-Semitic (Horowitz, 1999). Most of the Ivy League schools were racist and anti-Semitic (Morris, 2006; Gordon, 1990).

Margaret Haley

Kate Rousmaniere (1999) contends that Margaret Haley—who was liberal on women's issues and founded the first teachers union—was not liberal on issues of race. In fact, Haley was quite racist. Rousmaniere tells us

> One group of reformers that Haley refused to work with were African American club women. By the turn of the century, more than 50 black women's clubs in Chicago were organized for community reform. Education was the single most important area of activism for these women, primarily because of the poor educational conditions that the city offered African American children... . [Haley] generally ignored the Black community and the significant problems that Black teachers and students faced. (p. 156).

Haley might have been the "lady labor slugger" but she certainly had no truck with the civil rights of blacks.

Conflicting Views on Race and Gender

Many of these women had conflicting views on issues of race and gender. Just because someone is liberal on one issue does not mean that that person will be liberal on other issues. And this is difficult to understand. One of the mistakes that is easy to make when trying to understand these figures of our collective past is to smooth over their conflicted personalities and make them into something they were not. Russell Jacoby (1997) reminds us that Freud was "a theoretician of contradictions" (p. 27), while the ego psychologists were into "the business of harmonizing the unpleasant" (p. 29). Political positions taken on issues of race and gender are often, uncomfortably, conflicted as one can see from studying historical figures—both women and men—during the Progressive era. Students of history must not project ideas onto these women for the sake of smoothing out their difficult personalities. Some of the women Progressives were difficult women, as Sadovnik and Semel (2002) remind us. In particular, Helen Horowitz (1999) begins her biography of M. Carey Thomas by saying that she really didn't like Thomas. The legacy of Thomas is conflicted because she seemed to be ruthless and underhanded but then again she was a woman fighting against a board of men who tried at every turn to destroy what she was building at Bryn Mawr. People become defensive because they are pushed into corners. Thomas probably felt that she was in a corner much of the time.

Women who attended a university, especially in the early 1900s, were up against resistance from their male counterparts. Lynn Gordon (1990) says, "Hostility, ridicule, and neglect characterized the experiences of pioneer women students at Michigan, Wisconsin, and Cornell" (p. 22). M. Carey Thomas was an undergraduate student at Cornell; one wonders what kind of experience that was for her.

Women involved in the political realm came under fierce attack from men because it was here that men felt particularly threatened. I am thinking here of Rosa Luxemburg. Andrea Nye (1994) claims that Luxemburg, the radical Socialist, came under fire from her male compatriots. Like the ridicule women students received at universities in the States, Luxemburg received ridicule in Europe. Nye reports

> Ridicule, sarcasm, crude irony, personal insult are often the rule when one socialist criticizes the errors of another, but the male leaders of the European social democracy in the early decades of this century were particularly venomous when it came to their intractable colleague, Rosa Luxemburg... . She was a phenomenon, not a person, as she disrupted socialist opinion, transgressed the superior wisdom of the leaders of the party...worst of all, refused to take Marxist doctrine as fixed or unquestionable. (p. 3)

Luxemburg was murdered by her own party in 1919 because she was too outspoken and challenged Marxist orthodoxies. She was too much of a threat. Luxemburg is the European counterpart to many of the women Progressives in the States. All of the American women Progressives challenged the status quo and patriarchy. And like the American women Progressives, Luxemburg has been relegated to footnotes (p. 7), as Nye tells us. She fought for the rights of working-class people and called for revolution. She was killed for her beliefs.

I wonder how someone like Ida B. Wells managed not to get killed for her antilynching campaigns as she was threatened repeatedly by white Supremacists. It is amazing that she avoided getting lynched. Paula Giddings (2008) says of Wells that "she herself had been threatened with lynching. She was receiving urgent telegrams telling her that whites were posted at the railway station waiting for her return" (p. 1). She did not go back to Memphis.

Anna Julia Cooper, Vivian May (2007) tells us, was a "woman of rare courage and conviction" (p. 1). May says

> Cooper theorizes from her own experiences as a Black woman to highlight how race and gender politics are interlocking, to speak out against myriad forms of violence and domination, and to insist upon the right of all marginalized people to self-determination and self-definition. (p. 1)

These Progressive women educators were political educators. Political educators such as these women, however, are usually left out of the canon of the history of American education. Students learn about George Counts and Harold Rugg as early pioneers of social reconstruction in many histories of education. Very few traditional educational historians have focused on the political educators mentioned here. The divide between traditional educational history and curriculum historiography becomes clear. Curriculum historians have opened up the discussion to include these women who have previously been erased from the history of education.

Education and the Arts

One of the things that is striking about some of these women Progressive educators is their interest, not only in politics, but in the arts. In a moment, I will explore some of the art interests of Anna Julia Cooper, Margaret Naumburg, Marietta Johnson, Jane Addams, and Caroline Pratt. But first to historically contextualize this discussion it is important to look at broader Progressive artistic and educational movements.

Chautauqua, Salons, and Ashcan Art

Chautauqua is an often overlooked Progressive site that dovetailed both education and the arts, and it was an event in which both Jane Addams and John Dewey participated. People would gather during the summer at Chautauqua to hear music, listen to lectures, and to talk politics. Andrew Rieser (2003) argues that Chautauqua was really a woman's movement, although men were involved. Perhaps one of the reasons Chautauqua has been ignored in most traditional educational histories is that it was of primary interest to women. Women's interests have historically been ignored. I will talk about rural Chautauqua and contrast it to the work that women were doing in urban settings—in relation to education and the arts—in salons and women's clubs, which served as educational sites outside the institution of schools. Here I will look at the salons held by Mabel Dodge in Greenwich Village and also look at a club in New York City called the Heterodoxy Club. Both the salon and the club served as sites of education mostly ignored by educational historians. In relation to both the salon and club, I want to talk about urban art (mostly male art) that best reflects the early days of the Progressive era. Here I want to touch on what was called the Ashcan Art Movement and contrast it to what women were doing in salons and clubs during the Chautauqua movement.

Chautauqua as a Rural Movement

Andrew Rieser (2003) makes an important point when he argues that one of the reasons Chautauqua—as a Progressive movement—gets ignored is because it was primarily a rural movement. Most of the Progressives lived and worked in urban areas and many associate Progressivism with the Northeast. Rieser tells us, "It is not coincidence that Chautauqua's role in Progressive reform…

falls between the cracks of the existing scholarship. Historians tend to locate the heart of Progressivism in the urban middle class" (p. 264). Chautauqua is ignored by historians probably because it is not considered a major historical event. But if students of history are to understand the Progressive movement it behooves them to study Chautauqua as it relates to progressivism.

Music at Chautauqua

The music at Chautauqua was of all sorts. Victoria Case (1948) wrote that one could hear "popular singers, violinists, ensembles, and finally in 1912, the New York Symphony, directed by Walter Damrosch, to play a full six weeks' engagement" (p. 15). Today there are many summer music festivals and music camps for aspiring young classical musicians—for example, Aspen, Tanglewood. But Chautauqua was different because it offered the entire spectrum from lectures to speeches to concerts. It offered a liberal arts curriculum.

Literary Circles at Chautauqua

The literary circles at Chautauqua are of interest here because there was certainly a gendered component to them. It was primarily women who ran these literary clubs, much to the dismay of men. As Victoria Case (1948) points out, "Colleges and universities…roughly prior to 1900 held fast to…classical education, [which was] mostly closed to women" (p. 15), but Chautauqua was an alternative site where women could get an education. These literary clubs—mostly run by women—could be found not only at the mother institution (in Chautauqua itself), but around the country as the Chautauqua movement expanded to what was called assemblies or circuits all over the United States. Mostly women joined these literary circles and were actually awarded degrees of completion after four years of study. Remarkably, Rieser (2003) points out,

> At the CLSC's [Chautauqua Literary and Scientific Circle's] height in 1887, its enrollment eclipsed that of the nation's largest universities: 4,468 people received diplomas for completing the four-year course of study, 18,000 were enrolled in the course and untold tens of thousands more unreported (non-dues paying) readers were participating. (p. 167)

Academic men felt threatened by the sheer number of women involved in these literary circles. And part of this threat was the fear of the feminization of literature. Male academics felt, as Rieser tells us, that academic departments of literature were being undermined and "the new discipline of literary criticism sought to undo the work of women's literary societies" (p. 170). The sheer numbers of women involved in these literary societies are remarkable. As Paulo Freire taught us, reading is not just about reading, it can also lead to revolution and heightened political consciousness.

Rieser says about the literary circles that "these crucibles of organized womanhood are increasingly viewed as political instruments linking club movement and later agitation for women's suffrage, urban reform, and consumer rights" (p. 164). So reading in literary circles is not just about reading. Reading is dangerous and the men who opposed these groups knew this. But also I want to emphasize that studying literature is not just about forming political opinions. Studying literature is also being engaged in the arts, a point that Maxine Greene (1995) drives home when she talks about "releasing the imagination" through literature. One should not reduce literature or reading to politics because it is much more than that.

What is striking about the Chautauqua movement is that it had a home base in rural New York, and it spread all over the country in what were called mini-Chautauquas. At the home base in rural New York one could attend lectures, go to plays, study literature, and hear music. Most festivals today, like the Spoleto Festival, are narrower in scope. One can hear music, see dance performances, watch plays but there are no lectures on labor unions or lectures on working-class issues. At Chautauqua all of that went on. Teddy Roosevelt said of Chautauqua that "'It was the most American thing in America'" (quoted in Rieser, 2003, p. 133). But America at the turn of the century was also racist, reactionary, as well as progressive, and Chautauqua reflected this. Victoria Case (1948) tells us that "Grant, Theodore Roosevelt, Hayes, McKinley, and Taft spoke in the pavilion by the lake [at Chautauqua and]... the magnificent voice of William Jennings Bryan soared out over the lake" (p. 14). Rieser points out, too, that Chautauqua was mostly for white people. And lectures that were delivered were not always progressive; some were reactionary. So while attending the rural New York mother institute (p. 243) one might hear

> a Jane Addams appeal for subjective understanding or a Booker T. Washington speech on self-reliance [who also] might share the stage haphazardly with Willard F. Mallalieu's "March of the Anglo-Saxon," a warning from Josiah Strong on the threat of "the heathen world," or a John Commons diatribe on the "inroads of alien stock." (pp. 128–129)

These lectures reflected the larger, complex, and contradictory American culture of the fin-de-siècle and the contradictory nature of the Progressive movement itself.

Chautauqua and Popular Education

The thing that makes Chautauqua so interesting is that it was a place where "popular education" (Rieser, 2003, p. 218) happened. And the idea of Chautauqua as a place of popular education spread all over the country. Now, it had its critics, William James being one, as Rieser, tells us. James thought that the Chautauqua idea was breezy and anti-intellectual. But his critique was elitist.

Chautauqua is a fascinating study for all sorts of reasons. First, Chautauqua has been for the most part forgotten. Second, women were powerful movers and shakers in the literary circles. Third, it democratized the arts. Victoria Case (1948) tells us that "fiddles and harmonicas and parlor organs and an occasional '"gramophone'" (p. 43) were common fare as well as "yodelers," (p. 40) "saws, bottles, sleigh bells" (p. 48) and symphony orchestras. The vast range of music—both popular and classical—made Chautauqua an unusual experience. The classical and popular arts were both part of the summer programs. And this was a way to democratize the arts. This was something about which Dewey was passionate. Classical music has always been an upper-class phenomenon. Concert tickets are usually expensive so working-class people cannot attend. But at Chautauqua working-class people could pick and choose. Tickets were inexpensive. In rural towns around the country, traveling musicians who came to these mini-Chautauquas brought with them music that people would not have been able to hear otherwise. So the mini-Chautauquas that were held around the country also helped to democratize music and make it available to all kinds of people, rather than just urbanites and the upper classes.

Problems with Chautauqua

Chautauqua had its problems, too, one of which was race. Chautauqua was reactionary in its "anti-urban[ness]" and "pastoral aesthetic" (Rieser, 2003 p. 54). Back to nature movements are often reactionary. Nostalgia is always reactionary, and perhaps part of the problem with Chautauqua was that it was a nostalgic institution. It was a reaction against industry and dirt, smoke stacks and the ongoing mess of pollution, and degradation of labor. But again, there were lectures given at Chautauqua by people like Jane Addams who addressed these issues. Chautauqua, in many ways, was not dissimilar to settlement houses. Settlement houses, like Hull House, were places where people could also get a popular education. At Hull House, Jane Addams saw to it that people were exposed to lectures of all sorts, reading circles, the arts, and politics.

Lawrence Cremin (1988) tells us that the people who were working toward their four-year reading program that Chautauqua offered read

> John Richard Green's *A Short History of the English People*, Charles Merivale's *A General History of Rome*, Henry White Warren's *Recreations in Astronomy, with Directions for Practical Experiments and Telescope Worked*, and J. Dorman Steele's *Fourteen Works in Human Physiology*... Richard T. Ely's *An Introduction to Political Economy* and *The Strength and Weakness of Socialism*, Jane Addams's *Twenty Years at Hull House*, and *The Autobiography of Lincoln Steffens*. (p. 435)

These reading circles are astounding considering that they were located all over the United States. America is usually thought to be a nonreading and anti-intellectual culture (Hofstadter, 1963). But there have always been segments of American culture that have engaged in intellectual labor.

Urban Progressives, the Arts, and Education

Like the rural Progressives, urban Progressives were also interested in the intersection between the arts and education. Much urban Progressive work was done in Greenwich Village. Lawrence Cremin (1988) writes that "the Village [was] a crossroads of avant-garde ideas and a mecca of creative writing, painting, sculpture, and theater" (p. 600). Interestingly enough, Cremin notes that Harold Rugg was influenced by Village intellectual life. He states

> Harold Rugg, a professor at Teachers College, Columbia University who had imbibed the heady brew of Village intellectual life...wrote a series of social studies textbooks...embodying interpretations of American life that had become prevalent among Village intellectuals. (p. 603)

Rugg's books were banned in many schools because they were thought to be too radical and even un-American (Evans, 2007). The Village was also home to Caroline Pratt and Helen Marot, as I have discussed earlier. Their work with the City and Country School must be understood against the larger backdrop of Village life. Alongside these educators, the Village was home to writers. Lawrence Cremin (1988) tells us "Floyd Dell, Waldo Frank, Theodore Dreiser, Willa Cather, Sinclair Lewis, Edmund Wilson, Edna St. Vincent Millay, and William Rose Benet" contributed to the Village intellectual scene. Cremin (1988) points out that publishing houses "were markedly conservative" (p. 600) and it took a while for them to pick up these writers.

Village Intellectuals and Curriculum Theorists

The experimental work that was done in the Village during the early 20th century strikes a chord because not only does it inspire but one also can find historical antecedents to what it is that curriculum theorists are doing today. It is important to study the Village intellectuals because not only do curriculum theorists have much in common with them, but one might argue that our work has been made possible because of the doors that the Village intellectuals opened to educators, artists, and writers. The reconceptualization as a movement is kin to the movement of the Village intellectuals during the early 20th century.

One aspect of Village life that was really interesting was the salon. Mabel Dodge opened her Greenwich Village apartment to the most influential of the intelligentsia of her time. These salons were educational in that people discussed all sorts of things, talked about the arts, the theater, intellectual ideas, and so forth. Salons were indeed Progressive, especially the ones that Mabel Dodge held. Gerald McFarland (2001) tells us

> On Wednesday evenings (or at other times on Thursdays) Dodge opened the rooms of her Fifth Avenue apartments to a kaleidoscopic array of guests of every ideological hue—Socialists, Trade-Unionists, anarchists, Suffragists, Poets, Lawyers, Murderers, 'Old Friends', psychoanalysts, I. W. W.s, Single Taxers, Birth Controlists, newspapermen, Artists, Modern-Artists, Clubwomen.... At the height of their success, most of Dodge's Evenings were organized around a topic or special guest, such as A. A. Brill on psychoanalysis, Big Bill Haywood on the I. W.W., Emma Goldman on anarchism. (p. 194)

It is remarkable that people of all stripes gathered at these salons to talk about such a wide variety of issues. The salons served an educational function and should be thought of as sites of curriculum history. Education happens outside of the walls of the schoolhouse, and it is important to include these other sites in our study of curriculum history.

Maxine Greene—the well-known philosopher of education—held many a salon in her New York City apartment. Here teachers gathered to talk about things literary, philosophical, and educational. Greene (1998) tells us

> I have been holding what we call "educational salons" at my home once a month. Teachers come from various parts of the city for discussion with each other and visitors like Lisa Delpit...Valerie Polakow...Wesley Brown...Rene Arcilla and Wendy Kohli [talked] about the canon and the curriculum. Another time we went to the Studio Museum in Harlem for our salon, for a remarkable discussion of the blank spaces where African-American painters must be discovered and named at last. (p. 12)

Greene's New York City apartment was located near the Guggenheim Museum and the Metropolitan Museum of Art. Central Park was not far from her apartment. One can only imagine how excited these teachers must have been to have engaged in discussion with Greene on all things educational. For Greene, education has always been thought of as something beyond school walls and certainly she has brought to our attention the importance of the arts through her work with the Lincoln Center Institute and through her many writings on the intersections between aesthetics and education.

Mabel Dodge, Women's Clubs

Ross Wetzsteon (2002) tells us, "Among her [Mabel Dodge's] many guests [at her salons] were Bernard Berenson, Roger Fry, Gordon Craig, Eleanora Duse, Andre Gide, Norman Douglas, Paul and Muriel Draper, and Lord and Lady Ashton" (p. 27). These salons, like the tradition of the European coffeehouses, served curricular purposes. One of the things Dodge is known for is her support for the art exhibition called the Armory Show held in 1913. Wetzsteon claims,

> As for Mabel, she could at least take some of the credit for introducing Picasso, Matisse, Van Gogh, Cezanne, Gaugin, Braque, Brancusi, Seurat, and Kandinsky to the New World. "Many roads are being broken—what a wonderful word—broken!" she exulted. (p. 29)

Curriculum history is also about the aesthetic and breaking roads, breaking through intellectual barriers.

Dodge was also a member of a women's group called the Heterodoxy Club in New York City. This club is important because it was a place where women could meet to discuss issues of the day and educate one another. These kinds of women's clubs should not be dismissed as frivolous. The Heterodoxy Club was quite a phenomenon. Ross Wetzsteon (2002) tells us that it lasted for thirty years! These women met for

> biweekly lectures, and more important, to talk, to argue, to proselytize, and even more important, to break down isolation, provide emotional support [and those who engaged in discussion]...were Democrats, Republicans, radicals, socialists, and anarchists. They might be teachers, journalists, lawyers, or sociologists, settlement house workers or popular novelists, labor organizers or stockbrokers, Freudian or Jungian. (p. 175)

These women's clubs were important educational sites that should not be overlooked in the history of curriculum. Since women have not had the same opportunities as men, they have had to carve out alternative spaces to discuss ideas. Many of the women who attended these meetings at the Heterodoxy Club are well known, such as Emma Goldman the anarchist and revolutionary, Charlotte Perkins Gilman, Henrietta Rodman, Crystal Eastman, and of course Mabel Dodge and more (Wetzsteon, 2002). One must make a distinction, though, between what people today call book clubs and women's clubs such as the Heterodoxy Club. This was not a book club per se. This was a club where women met to talk about intellectual issues. Not all book clubs are intellectual. The Heterodoxy Club was a place where women heard lectures and were involved in discussions about social issues such as labor strikes.

Ashcan School of Art

In response to the horrid conditions of labor—for both men and women—it is important to note that the art community did not turn a deaf ear or a blind eye, if you will. Here I want to mention the work of the Ashcan School of Art. The Ashcan School of Art best reflects the rise of industrialization and the horrors that went along with it. These artists were all male, and some were quite well known, like George Bellows who painted the grit and dirt of urban street life. He captured working-class sports, especially in his famous painting of boxers. Rebecca Zurier (2006) tells us,

> Commerce, the city's diverse population, changing mores, and above all looking proved to be subjects of fascination and meditation for [John]Sloan and five colleagues—George Bellows, William Glackens, Robert Henri, George Luks, and Everett Shinn—who later became known as the Ashcan School. (p. 4)

The Ashcan School can be thought of in contradistinction to the Chautauqua movement. The Ashcan School was urban, male, and gritty. These artists were interested in depicting the hard lives of the working class. The word "ashcan" suggests ashes (the dirt and grime) and the garbage (cans) and trash of city living. Chautauqua was hardly about garbage. It was a "pastoral aesthetic" (Rieser, 2003, p. 54), while the Ashcan School was more of a garbage aesthetic, or a depiction of "urban realism," as Zurier (2006, p. 4) puts it. Robert Henri, one of the teachers of the Ashcan School, "encouraged every artist to be a metropolitan reporter. He sent his students in New York to visit pool halls, restaurants, and other sites described in the urban press" (Zurier, p. 26). Interestingly, Zurier claims that "Ashcan artists picked up the debris that other painters overlooked" (p. 29). This "debris" symbolizes the horrors of industrialization and the horrid conditions that faced factory workers. Bellow's painting of boxers are bleak. Bellow's paintings are stark representations of the harshness of life in the city. This was clearly a response to poor working conditions and labor unrest during the early years of the 20th century. Also what comes to mind here is that these painters painted subjects previously thought to be irrelevant. They were paintings from below (like doing history from below a la Lucy Maynard Salmon). Recall, Bohan (2004) points out that Salmon taught her students to do what she called "history in the round" (p. 59). She taught history from below as she encouraged her students to look to the everyday and to study neglected subjects of history. And like the Ashcan artists, she was most concerned with "the education of the working classes," as Chara Bohan (p. 17) points out. The Ashcan artists' subject was the working class and they were determined to capture the harshness of that life. They were doing a sort of painting "in the round," as Salmon might say.

I discuss the Ashcan School because it is important to contextualize women Progressives in relation to their male counterparts. The Ashcan School reflects, in part, the early days of the Progressive movement and what the Progressives were most concerned about. And, too, it is important to show that alongside the "pastoral aesthetic" (Rieser, 2003, p. 54) of Chautauqua, the Ashcan School painted a different picture of life during the early 20th century. These competing narratives, if you will, of modern life must be thought of together, otherwise we get a narrow and parochial picture of the Progressive era.

Education and the Arts: Anna Julia Cooper, Jane Addams, Marietta Johnson, Caroline Pratt, and Margaret Naumburg

Once contextualized against the larger historical landscape of the Progressive era and the arts, students can begin to understand better the work of the women Progressive educators that are named above. Their work must be seen against this larger backdrop, otherwise our picture of them becomes too narrow. These women are interesting and important for various reasons and all, in one way or another, tie into the larger historical art scene. Their work was primarily educational. And again, there were educational elements both in the Chautauqua movement as people came to hear lectures, and in the Ashcan School as these artists indirectly taught about the tough conditions of working-class life through their paintings.

What students begin to understand, when studying the Progressive era and studying the forgotten ones—the women and minorities of the Progressive era—is that curriculum studies as a discipline is indebted to the work that these women did. I argue that these Progressives opened doors to what curriculum studies scholars do today.

Anna Julia Cooper and the Literary

I return again to Anna Julia Cooper whose work and life continues to inspire. Cooper, according to Vivian May (2007), was born a slave and graduated with a PhD from the Sorbonne when she was 66 years old. She was also a graduate of Oberlin College. May reports, "Following graduation, Cooper became chair of languages and science at Wilberforce University" (p. 18). Then she moved on to teach at M Street High, the well-known school for African Americans where many important African American scholars taught, such as Mary Burrill, Angelina Weld Grimké, Mary Church Terrell, and Carter G. Woodson (May). From M Street High Cooper moved on to Lincoln University, returned to M Street High, and then moved on to become the president of Frelinghuysen University (May). Cooper was a teacher and a scholar and is perhaps most well known for her book *A Voice from the South*, which was published in 1892. Perhaps her most famous lines from this book are: "Only the Black Woman can say 'when and where I enter, in the quiet, undisputed dignity of my womanhood, without violence and without suing or special patronage, then and there the whole Negro race enters with me'" (p. 31). This book is a remarkable critique that addresses racism and sexism, social issues, and literature. American literature was important for Cooper. Cooper talks about misrepresentations of blacks in literature, especially in the book *Harold* by an unknown writer. She critiques *Harold*, which is about the value of industrial education for blacks. Cooper felt that industrial education for blacks was oppressive. For Cooper, industrial education kept people ignorant; industrial education teaches little more than obedience to the white man. Cooper, in commenting about the book *Harold*, says,

> It gives the picture of a black Englishman cultured and refined, brought in painful contact with American,—or un-American, color prejudice. The point of the book seems to be to show that education for the black man is a curse, since it increases his sensitiveness to the indignities he must suffer in consequence of white barbarity. (Cooper, 1988/1892, p. 210)

Education, then, for Harold, only made things worse because he felt that he couldn't do anything about his position in life as he faced white supremacy. As Cooper points out, the author of *Harold* suggests that it is better not to educate blacks because it makes life worse. Clearly this was not Cooper's position and she takes great offense at this.

Her love for literature is clear in *A Voice from the South* as she goes on to talk about many well-known people in the literary canon. She argues that there are writers who are poetic and then there are preachers. She claims that the poets "will be the ones to withstand the ravages of time" (p. 182). The poets include people like "George Eliot…Robert Browning…Longfellow… Howells" (p. 182). The preachers include "Milton…Carlyle…Whittier… Lowell…Roe, Bellamy, Tourgee" (p. 183). Cooper argues that those who stand the test of time "paint what they see, as naturally, as instinctively, and as irresistibly as the bird sings—with no thought of an audience" (p. 181). The preacherly writers, on the contrary, "warp a character or distort a face in order to prove a point" (p. 181). Most commentators on Cooper point to her political side, to her social commentary about racism and sexism, but she also loved literature and the arts. In fact, like Mabel Dodge and Maxine Greene, Cooper and Charlotte Forten Grimke held salons, as Vivian May (2007) tells us, and these salons "prefigure[d] the better known 'Black Renaissance' salons held by poet and playwright Georgia Douglas Johnson in the 1920s" (p. 28). These salons are interesting because they "focused on art and literature…

[and] music [and]…were attended by local and international Black and white educators, artists, politicians, writers, and musicians" (p. 28). Salons seemed to be a rather popular forum for the intelligentsia, both black and white during the fin-de-siècle. Again salons were alternate sites of education where people gathered to talk, listen to music, discuss issues of the day, engage in politics, and learn from each other.

Anna Julia Cooper was not only a teacher per se in a schoolhouse. She also educated in many ways, the salon being one of these. The tradition of the salon, especially for women educators, must not be overlooked or forgotten in the history of curriculum. These alternative sites of education served many purposes and formed many an intellect and artist. These gatherings were educational and in some ways more important than traditional forms of schooling, especially for women because traditional forms of schooling came up short because women were banned from lectures, or from taking courses in mathematics or languages. Salons were a way to circumvent these discriminatory restrictions that women faced.

Jane Addams and the Arts

Like Anna Julia Cooper, Jane Addams was interested in the arts and education. This is an overlooked aspect of the contributions made by Addams. Most scholars tend to focus on her political accomplishments. Recall, earlier I suggested that Addams had a great love of literature and was quite well read. Studying literature was a large part of what went on at Hull House. But there was more. Jean Elshtain (2002) tells us

> It is not surprising that Addams and Starr from the start put so much emphasis on Hull-House as a place of interior beauty and grace, on teaching the arts and giving children the opportunity to participate in a variety of artistic activities. These goals were realized in part by the creation at Hull-House of the Butler Art Gallery and by the extensive instruction provided in theater, dance, orchestral music, folk music, sculpting, painting, pottery and literature. (p. 127)

It is remarkable that Addams—who was mostly known for her political activism—had such broad interests. To be both politically and artistically driven is unusual, to say the least. Many musicians, for example, are not interested in politics, unless of course they are forced to become political. Here I am thinking of the rise of the Third Reich and the way in which musicians had to make decisions about becoming Hitler's musicians. Some made a deal with the devil and stayed on; fame was more important to them than principle. Carl Orff became one of Hitler's musicians. Orff could have left Germany in protest, but he chose to stay and to conduct and perform. Musicians with principle—and a sense of the political—fled Germany as they watched their Jewish colleagues disappear (Morris, 2001).

Like musicians, artists too, are not always interested in the political. The abstract expressionists like Jackson Pollock and his cohorts, Ross Wetzsteon (2002) tells us, "showed little interest in radical politics (or politics of any kind)" (p. 568). They were not interested in history either. Wetzsteon says, "The only past that concerned them was art history" (p. 568). Artists and musicians tend to focus on their art and music and not on the larger world around them. But there are exceptions to this, like Pablo Casals who refused to play the cello in Fascist Spain and was dubbed the "cellist of conscience" (Morris, 2009).

Like Casals, Jane Addams was remarkable in that she was able to embrace both politics and the arts. Robin Berson (2004) comments on the place of the arts in Addams's work. She states,

> Both Addams and Starr were deeply convinced that the arts could play a central role in ennobling the lives of both residents and guests. The first major gift to Hull-House was used to build an art gallery, which opened in 1891. The first year Hull-House welcomed 50,000 visitors. (p. 34)

That an art gallery would draw such a large number of people is quite astonishing considering the hard economic times. There is a richness that is missed when people are not exposed to the arts. Jane Addams appreciated this because most of her residents were struggling financially, and yet it was important to Addams that they make time for reading, studying, listening to music, going to plays, and so forth. The arts should not only be for the wealthy. And this was the point that Dewey made. The arts need to be democratized. What is also remarkable too is that Addams was working under awful conditions politically, especially with the outbreak of WWI. She was under scrutiny from the Wilson administration and was accused of being a radical, a Socialist, and un-American because labor union leaders met at Hull House. Robin Berson (2004) reports, "From 1918 throughout the 1920s, the Department of Justice [during Wilson's presidency] supported nongovernmental Super-patriot groups and vigilantes like the American Protective League, who spied on their neighbors, opened other people's mail, led extralegal raids" (p. 100). Jane Addams was increasingly under surveillance because of her support for immigrants, labor unions, and freedom of speech. A list of so-called radicals was compiled by the government, mainly consisting of reform workers. Many were arrested, and as Berson (2004) points out, "Jane Addams was at the top of the list" (p. 103). Addams was a pacifist and this was not a popular position during WWI. Ironically, it was her position on peace that finally did her in. Jean Elshtain (2002) tells us that Addams's

> years of unpopularity were also years of political blacklisting by The Daughters of the American Revolution (of which Addams was a member) and the publications of the famous "Spiderweb Chart" of putative conspiracy against the government of the United States, with Addams as [sic] the very heart of the intricate web. (p. 245)

But Addams wasn't the only one in trouble. The Greenwich Village Progressives were also in trouble. Max Eastman and his sister Crystal Eastman both were active politically. Eastman's well-known magazine *The Masses* was shut down by the government (Wetzsteon, 2002), Crystal Eastman—who did the "first comprehensive study of industrial accidents" (p. 194) in the Pittsburgh Mills and "led the suffrage movement in New York" (p. 196)—was also on the government hit list of "dangerous reds" (p. 200). The Wobblies—the labor union headed up by the famous "Big Bill" Haywood—were also under attack from the government (Cooper, 2009, p. 399). Cooper reports,

> Agents of the department's Bureau of Investigation, with the cooperation of local police, raided IWW offices in thirty-three cities, seizing files and records—more than five tons of material. At the end of September, the department secured indictments in Chicago against 166 IWW leaders, including Haywood. (p. 400)

Notably these arrests were happening in Jane Addams's own Chicago. In fact, right in Addams's neighborhood immigrants were being willy-nilly deported by the thousands (Elshtain, 2002). It is important to understand the larger American scene and war craziness that was occurring during Addams's tenure at Hull House. She was not working under easy conditions. In the midst of all of this, the arts played a role in her work. This is what is so astonishing. She worked in a very chaotic and troubled time. War changes everything. One of the things that came out of censorship during WWI was the development of the American Civil Liberties Union, an idea that Crystal Eastman and others nurtured (Wetzsteon, 2002). And not only this, John Dewey was involved in the development of the American Association of University Professors (AAUP) because of the pressures of censorship of professors, especially during WWI (Martin, 2002).

Marietta Johnson and the Arts

Even though Jane Addams never called herself a socialist, many of the people whom she supported were Socialists. Progressive educator Marietta Johnson was a Socialist. Joseph Newman (2006) writes about the Socialist community in Fairhope, Alabama, of which Johnson was a part. Newman comments,

> From the very start, Fairhope won a well-deserved reputation as an intellectual group united in their belief that the economic system of the United States was flawed. Beyond that spirited conviction, the early residents agreed to disagree. Spirited debates broke out in the many organizations they formed, societies like the Progressive League, Socialist Club, and School of Philosophy. (p. 69)

It is important to take note that this Progressive League and Socialist Club were not in a metropolitan, urban setting, but rather in a rural backwater. And this is what makes Marietta Johnson's accomplishments—that is, as the founder of the Organic School—even more remarkable. The South, especially in 1903 when she founded the Organic School, was not exactly a welcoming place for radical politics or Progressive ideas, although there were some Progressive schools in the South. But compared to the Northeast, the South lagged behind on all fronts, including education.

What strikes me about Marietta Johnson's Organic School is that it was Progressive, its politics Socialist, and like Jane Addams, Johnson fostered the arts. This is an overlooked aspect of the Organic School. Newman (2006) tells us that Johnson was

> just beginning to extend her experiment to older students when Dewey visited, Johnson tried to ensure that the high school curriculum continued the organic emphasis on folk music, folk dancing, drama and handwork. These subjects were no less important than the academic subjects, she insisted, going into detail to explain how the daily work students did in the manual arts, for instance, helped promote balanced development of body, mind, and spirit. (p. 79)

Johnson loved folk music and folk dancing. Jane Addams was also interested in folk music. And, too, one of our contemporaries, Tom Barone (2001), has written a very interesting book on the use of folk art in a rural school. Barone writes about a school in Swain County, North Carolina. Here students do "weaving, quilting, and batik making" (p. 26). The school supports these "arts and crafts" because they are an "escape route from poverty" (p. 17). The students sell what they make to the community. Interestingly enough, Barone explains that the students do not see their work as craft but as art (p. 26).

Black children did not attend Marietta Johnson's school. Remember the Organic School was in the South, and blacks and whites were not integrated. In fact, Joseph Newman (2006) points out, "The Organic School's enrollment did reflect public school conditions—which meant African-American children were not welcome. Racial segregation was so widely accepted throughout the nation during the early twentieth century, not even John Dewey saw fit to comment" (p. 74). Most of the Progressive schools that were founded at the turn of the century were for white children. And that too is part of the larger problem with Progressivism. However, as Katherine Reynolds (2002) reminds us, Charlotte Hawkins Brown founded the Parker Institute, which was a Progressive school for African American children and it was in the South. Reynolds comments that "as summarized by Joseph Kett, regional differences confronted Progressive-minded reformers meant that 'southern Progressives had to swim in a different ocean'" (pp. 7–8). And this different ocean was hostile (p. 7) to say the least. Most people do not often associate Progressivism with the South, but there were small pockets in the South of forward-looking people who tried to change education and make things better for both blacks and whites.

Another interesting thing students learn about Marietta Johnson's Organic School—as I briefly commented on before—is that it had a noteworthy folk dance program run by Charles Rabold (Newman, 2006). Newman tells us,

> A student of the noted English Folklorist Cecil Sharp, Rabold left a position in the music department at Yale to teach at the Organic School. During the 1920s he turned the already well-established dance program (which Sharp himself had helped Johnson create) into one of the school's defining features. (p. 81)

It is astonishing that someone would leave Yale to teach at a school in the South. In fact, Newman tells us that Johnson was able to get many people from Ivy League institutions to teach at the Organic School. It is to Johnson's credit that she was able to assemble such talented faculty. Perhaps folk music and dance interested Johnson because of her Socialist politics. Folk means the art of the people and is quite different from what one would consider fine art. But still today, the art world is highly classist. Schools of fine art tend not to teach folk music and folk art. Rather, the emphasis is on the European tradition, the European canon of classical music and dance. Conservatories like Juilliard and Curtis are clearly schools where students learn the classical canon. Music programs—in most conservatories—are built on the European tradition. Music history is all about European classics. And this is a problem. Perhaps music conservatories could learn from Marietta Johnson that folk art and folk music have a place in the curriculum.

Caroline Pratt and the Arts

Another socialist who was also interested in the arts was Caroline Pratt. Mary Hauser (2006) tells us that Caroline Pratt's City and Country School—which was located in Greenwich Village—offered art classes and, in fact, placed much "emphasis on the creative arts" (p. 15). Hauser comments,

> In New York City, Greenwich Village was the center of expressionism that was flourishing in the bohemian and intellectual enclaves of the U.S. major cities. Creative artists in all fields were attracted to this neighborhood and were delighted to send their children to a school that emphasized the kind of individual expression that they were trying to accomplish with their own art. (p. 15)

Recall, Pratt and her partner, Helen Marot, were not only interested in the arts but were actively engaged in politics and in fighting for labor unions and for the rights of workers. And this is what is so interesting about them. Again, this dual interest of politics and the arts today is quite unusual.

Unlike Marietta Johnson's Organic School, however, Caroline Pratt's City and Country School hired the likes of Jackson Pollock who was an abstract expressionist artist. She and Helen Marot were friends with Pollock and gave him a job at the school when he needed money. In the early days of his career, he couldn't sell his work for much. But today, as Henry Adams (2009) tells us, his painting titled

> Number 5, 1948—described by one writer as "a nest-like drizzle of yellows and browns on fiberboard"—recently sold for $142 million, not only setting a record for a piece of American art but making it the world's most expensive art object, the most costly painting ever sold. (p. 7)

So Caroline Pratt had the vision to hire Pollock when he was still relatively unknown, but she understood his talent and contribution to the art world. Pollock was hardly political, as Ross Wetzsteon (2002) points out. Pratt, on the other hand, was highly political and called herself a "radical socialist" (Hauser, 2006, p. 77). Mary Hauser talks about the relation Pollock had, especially with Caroline Pratt's partner, Helen Marot. Hauser tells us

> Marot became Jackson Pollock's confidante and friend until death. She provided a sympathetic ear and practical advice about treatment and recovery from alcoholism. He would often come to Marot and Pratt's house in the early morning hours, wanting to talk. Marot seemed to be a maternal figure for Pollock. (p. 48).

This is an interesting relationship between a highly political person—Marot—and an artist who had no interest in politics whatsoever—Pollock. Pollock never did recover from his alcoholism; it ravaged him his entire life. Pollock was not exactly a nice person either. He was violent, threw fits, tore up other people's paintings, destroyed things in social gatherings, and treated women abominably (Wetzsteon, 2002). And yet he was a genius. From Ross Wetzsteon students learn about Pollock's philosophy of painting. Wetzsteon tells us that Pollock "wasn't interested in subjects outside himself. He experimented with many modes moving toward symbols, myths, archetypes" (p. 523). William Pinar (1994) says that theorists must "work from within" (p. 7) and, in fact, was influenced by Pollock. Now, Pinar, unlike Pollock, is also interested in "subjects outside himself" as his work is clearly historical and political, as well as autobiographical. Pinar tells us that Pollock did not have final aims or objectives or even outlines for his paintings. Rather, he let his unconscious and feelings guide him. Pinar tells us that when teaching a class he too lets the class take on its own life as he does not have "a preconceived lesson plan" (p. 7). Pollock's way of working was an attempt to "be" (Pinar, 1994, p. 9) with his paintings. And so, too, Pinar wants to "be" with his students. Jackson Pollock was interested in painting his inner psychic world. And yet, his paintings speak in a worldly (Pinar, 2009b) way. One might argue that Pollock was a cosmopolitan painter. Ironically he had no interest in being in the world—that is, being a political creature—and yet the world has taken note of his painterly world. Wetzsteon (2002) comments that Pollock "grew steadily more subjective, more direct" as he grew older (p. 527). Pinar (1994) comments on this direct aspect of Pollock's painting and says that he too tries to be direct with his students, that is he tries to "be" "with [his] students in a direct way" (Pinar, 1994, p. 9). This, too, is Pinar's point about doing curriculum theory. In order to be direct with one's work, to be in the work at the moment, to connect to the ideas at hand and to connect to the ideas of others the scholar must move inward and even, at times, withdraw from the world (Pinar, 2009b). But withdrawing from the world does not mean removing one's self from the world. As Pinar puts it, distance is necessary in order to write in a direct way, in order to be "immersed in the moment" (Pinar, 1994, p. 9). The more deeply and subjectively immersed the scholar becomes the more able she is—ironically—

to make connections with others. A scholar cannot talk about the political unless she is in touch with the personal and works the personal—in a psychological way. Like Pinar, Pollock said that he was "particularly impressed with [the]…concept of the source of art being the unconscious" (Pollock, cited in Wetzsteon, 2002, p. 529). For Pinar, too, working intellectually means working the unconscious. Pinar has always had an interest in psychoanalysis—as a study of the unconscious. It is the unconscious that drives scholarship. The experimental nature of both Pinar and Pollock becomes possible because they are able to tap into the unconscious by a certain letting "be." An interesting facet of Pollock's painting is that he "kept a painting 'open' for days and weeks at a time—waiting for the moment when the canvas and the vision he'd been seeking suddenly coincided. His goal?—'memories arrested in space'" (Wetzsteon, 2002, p. 529). "Memories arrested in space." Let us dwell on that phrase for a moment. Recall that Pollock was part of a school of painters who were called "abstract expressionists." These painters looked inward, into the abstractness, if you will, of the psyche. What else is the psyche but memory? "Memories arrested in space." There is something almost mystical about Pollock's painting and so too the work of Pinar.

Margaret Naumburg and the Inner World

Margaret Naumburg was one of the first psychoanalytically oriented educators to arrive on the scene. Naumburg was one of the Progressive women educators who founded the Walden School in 1915. Naumburg began her career as a Socialist, but, as Cremin (1961) points out, she became disillusioned with it (p. 211). Petra Munro calls her a pragmatist. Perhaps. But more to the point she was a psychoanalytically oriented educator.

Margaret Naumburg, as Blythe Hinitz (2002) tells us, was analyzed by both a Jungian and a Freudian. Naumburg was more interested in unconscious processes than in conscious ones. She talks about the use of art in therapy as a way to unlock associations that are blocked. Consciousness blocks unconscious material. Like other Progressive women educators, Naumburg was especially interested in the educative value of art, which became the focus of her work in psychoanalysis. Naumburg (1953) states, "Art therapy is psychoanalytically oriented, recognizing the fundamental importance of the unconscious as expressed in the patient's dreams, daydreams and fantasies" (p. 3). When a patient experiences resistances to a psychic problem, the best way to get at that problem, Naumburg teaches, is not through words but through pictures, through images.

This too was the lesson of Jung, she tells us. Words get in the way of translating unconscious images and making the unconscious conscious. Naumburg (1987) tells us, "As patients picture such inner experiences, they frequently become more verbally articulate. Through the use of graphic or plastic expression, those who are originally blocked in speech often begin to verbalize in order to explain their art productions" (p. 1).

Naumburg understood the use of art in psychoanalysis and, in fact, was the founder of art therapy. Naumburg was a fascinating person who is often overlooked in the history of American education. Cremin (1961) is one of the few educational historians who studied and wrote about Naumburg. He tells us interestingly enough that Naumburg was influenced by Marietta Johnson. Recall that Johnson, too, was interested in the arts as her children were introduced to folk music and folk dancing. Naumburg, Cremin tell us, while at Barnard, was one of Dewey's students. More recently, Blythe Hinitz (2002) has done work on Naumburg and brings to light many interesting facets of Naumburg's biography. For example, Naumburg was interested in Dalcroze Eurhythmics. Hinitz explains that Naumburg

> published an article about Dalcroze Eurhythmics, in which she explained the adaptation of a system originally developed to assist musicians in more accurate feeling for rhythm, for all children and adults. She connected the "idea of bringing out the inner sense of rhythm that all people have hidden within them." (p. 43)

It is interesting to note that Eurhythmics is part of the music curriculum at Carnegie Mellon University. It is a course offered to musicians to teach them how to be in touch with music via movement.

Naumburg's Walden School was one of the only Progressive schools where teachers were encouraged to undergo psychoanalysis (Hinitz, 2002). Like Marietta Johnson and Caroline Pratt, Margaret Naumburg was able to attract high-powered faculty to her school. Cremin tells us, "For a time Lewis Mumford taught English, Hendrik Van Loon, history, and Ernest Bloch, music. During 1924 and 1925 the twelve-year-olds studied anthropology with Alexander Goldenweiser of the New School for Social Research" (p. 213). For Naumburg, the overarching focus of the curriculum was the use of art in education and its therapeutic value. For Naumburg, then, school was about helping the child to understand her unconscious issues in order to become a healthier and artistically sensitive person. Aesthetics, the psyche, and education were all of a piece for Naumburg.

Hinitz (2002) sums up Naumburg's contribution to Progressive education as she says:

> The knowledge that Margaret Naumburg gained regarding children's direct use of free art expression and the psychoanalytic interpretation of the art "products" at Walden School formed the foundation for her later moves to art education and further study of and work in the field of psychology. It surely was one of the bases for her pioneering work in art therapy. (p. 50)

There are interesting parallels between Naumburg's work, Pinar's and Pollock's work. All three take note of the inner psyche and expression of that inner psyche. What could be more important than taking care of the psyche of a child?

· 4 ·
HISTORICAL CURRICULUM CONCEPTS, PART 3

Introduction

The aim of this chapter is to broaden what counts as curriculum historiography. This chapter moves beyond educational history, which is primarily about the schoolhouse. Here I want to explore biography as history of the Other, autobiography as history of the self. I examine texts that deal with what fiction teaches us about history. I unpack what I call "intellectual retrospectives" of notable books on curriculum. I explore notable books on teaching practices. Finally, I look at historical trauma and examine the concept of "witnessing" and its relevance to curriculum.

Hilda Taba, Laura Zirbes, Florence B. Stratemeyer, and Alice Miel: Biography as Memory

So here I begin with what I call biography as memory. I suggest students consult in its entirety the book upon which I draw, titled *Teachers and Mentors: Profiles of Distinguished Twentieth-Century Professors of Education*, edited by Craig Kridel, Robert V. Bullough Jr., and Paul Shaker (1996). I highlight four women who are discussed in the book: Hilda Taba, Laura Zirbes, Florence B.

Stratemeyer, and Alice Miel. What I want to do is to share with you some memories that people had of these scholars.

Kridel et al. have put together an interesting and important book that captures memories of "mentors" and suggest that mentoring is "fragile and somewhat sacred" (p. 3). Mentorship is often an overlooked art of working with students. Mentorship for Kridel, Bullough, and Shaker is a historical phenomenon not often talked about in educational literature. Mentorship is about those unspoken relationships between teachers and students. These unspoken relationships are often only memory traces and often forgotten.

Elizabeth Hall Brady's (1996) memories of Hilda Taba include: "In January 1945, Hilda Taba began the six-month exploratory phase of the Intergroup Education in Cooperating Schools project, sponsored by the American Council on Education from 1945 to September 1948" (p. 59). Taba's work was an early form of multicultural education. Now, students know from studying the Progressive era that talking about race and ethnicity in the early part of the 20th century was no easy task. Racism prevailed in the South as Brady tells us that "there were no cities in the deep South in the Intergroup Project" (p. 60). It is a remarkable testament to Hilda Taba that she began this conversation at all, considering the racism of American culture during the 1940s. This project was a large scale attempt to get teachers talking across difference. Brady explains

> During the first nine months the pilot study included Cleveland, Milwaukee, Pittsburgh, and South Bend—all large industrial cities.... The second period—from September 1945 to September 1947—was devoted chiefly to developing a variety of programs on a fairly broad scale with eighteen school systems. (p. 60)

Beyond this, there were, as Brady reports, summer workshops that became a feature of the Eight Year Study (which I will discuss later on).

Brady tells us that Taba took her doctorate at Teachers College under the direction of John Dewey. She also reports that "many people found Hilda demanding, forceful, difficult" (p. 65). Women who carved out their places in academe—especially in the 1940s—did not have it easy. So if Taba was "difficult" there was a reason for it that probably had something to do with the larger sociopolitical backdrop of working in an academic setting as a woman.

Like Hilda Taba, Laura Zirbes's work was also recorded in the Eight-Year Study. Paul Klohr (1996) remembers Zirbes "as a significant influence in [his] own professional life" (p. 139). He reminds students that Zirbes's interests, especially in the arts, need to be recognized because her work opened the doors to many curriculum scholars who incorporate the arts into their work. Klohr suggests that often "historically significant work and what we see as currently promising ideas tend not to be recognized" (p. 139). What tends to get erased from the historical archives are the contributions made by women.

Zirbes's work was done mostly at The Ohio State University School, Klohr reminds us, which was "established in 1932 and had become one of the most experimental schools in the Eight Year Study" (p. 141). For Zirbes, Klohr tells us, "the arts should be a major core running throughout the curriculum" (p. 141). So Zirbes has much in common with many women Progressives that were explored in the previous chapter who also embraced the arts. Klohr tells us that Zirbes

> drew heavily on the arts—art, music, dance and drama. She worked closely with her friend and colleague, Ross Mooney, in his research into the nature of creativity. Her leadership in the 1952 national Granville Conference on Creativity best illustrated this persistent interest in the arts. (p. 144).

Another Progressive educator who is not often remembered is Florence B. Stratemeyer. Martin Haberman (1996) writes about his memories of this remarkable woman. Haberman tells us:

> Stratemeyer first came to Teachers College as a young woman from Detroit. From 1924–1965 she served on the T.C. faculty. Her ability to remember students' ideas was legendary. I can recall several instances in classes, which frequently numbered 200 in size, when she would respond to a student's comments by saying something like, "That's a very interesting comment, John. How does it reconcile with the comment you made in the paper you wrote last month." (p. 165)

Haberman's recollections of Stratemeyer's almost heroic capacity to remember what students wrote about are quite something indeed. This too is part of the mentoring process. Much of the time, Haberman tells us, Stratemeyer liked to point out contradictions in students' ideas. Haberman also points out that Stratemeyer "taught us to respect our ideas" (p. 171). It seems from Haberman's recollections that Stratemeyer encouraged students to clarify and hammer out their ideas. One of the more striking comments that Haberman remembers about Stratemeyer is that she would ask: "On what basis do you say that?" (1996, p. 169). A seemingly commonsensical question, but not so. Writing, for Stratemeyer, was of utmost importance as Haberman points out when he says that she "had events called 'opportunities to write' rather than tests" (p. 171). Haberman says that reading her comments "was exhausting"

(p. 170). As it should be. But these are the often overlooked aspects of mentoring.

Another Teachers College professor of note is Alice Miel. Louise Berman (1996) remembers Miel's "frequent advice to search, to think about what can be, and then to eliminate" (p. 174). Most of the note taking done in scholarly writing is thrown out, but not many people talk about this process. Like Stratemeyer, Miel was interested in language. Berman comments

> She loved language and committed care in using it. Interested in the total communication process—speaking, listening, writing, and editing—she listened with the intent of entering the world of the speaker and helping the person bring forth meanings which may heretofore have been silent, or unclear. (p. 178)

The scholarly life is both the writerly and speakerly life, if you will, and Miel cultivated both of these things in her students. It is not easy to teach the scholarly craft to doctoral students. Writing is a terribly complex art and not easily taught. Berman's memories of Miel are mostly about writing. Berman says, "According to Alice, persons should be scholars of language" (pp. 178–179). The language with which we write is often overlooked. The focus on language is one that is not often thought through enough. Scholars must make language come alive. Thinking through ideas means also thinking through the words used to express those ideas. Both Miel and Stratemeyer were interested in words, ideas, and language.

Biography as memory is an interesting way to get at history. Memories, however, are never straightforward or clear. What people remember about their mentors is perspectival. When one does not question what a memory is, though, one tends to believe that what is remembered is what actually happened. Memory is a tricky thing because memory is never exact. The modernist position on memory is that it is a straightforward event, that what is remembered is what actually happened. But memory is not so clear or straightforward.

Petra Munro Hendry: Poststructural Life History

There are other ways to think about memory and here I am thinking of the work of Petra Munro (1998b) (now Petra Munro Hendry) in her notable book titled *Subject to Fiction: Women Teachers' Life History Narratives and the Cultural Politics of Resistance*. Munro writes a poststructural life history of three women teachers and in the process questions what memory and history are.

Munro takes a very different approach to issues of memory and history than Kridel et al. (1996). Munro questions basic issues that turn on the notion of self, the idea of memory, and the idea of history. Even narrative is questioned. These questions are all poststructural ones and turn on issues around uncertainty. Munro is not so sure that one can get at the truth of memory and she is not so sure that narrative is an avenue to clear recollection since it is "subject to fiction," as the title of her book suggests. So if the stories that we tell about ourselves are fictions, what to make of our memories? If our memories are "subject to fiction," what then? And how do ethnographers proceed if their subjects are telling fictions? This is one of the most interesting points of Munro's book. Another interesting thing that Munro does in the book is intertwine her own life history narrative with that of her subjects, so students learn about her life story along with the life histories of her subjects. This is a poststructural move. The traditional form of ethnography is one where the researcher removes herself from that which she researches. Contrarily, Munro says, "By placing [herself] within this work [she] hope[s] to avoid the decontextualization and detachment, so often found in social science research, that perpetuate the myth of objectivity and neutrality" (p. 17). Students learn about Munro's life history alongside the life history of her subjects, and this serves to complicate her study. The collective portraits of three teachers (Agnes, Cleo, and Bonnie) tell much not only about the subjects at hand but also about Munro as a researcher. Munro reports that what she found when studying these women is not what she thought she would find. In fact, her own projections got in the way of figuring out that these women were not who she wanted them to be. Scholars want to identify with their subjects but when they do not, disappointment sets in. The lesson students learn from studying Munro's work is that researchers do not know what will emerge when studying others.

Although Munro, in *Subject to Fiction*, wanted her subjects to reject patriarchy outright, they did not, and this is disappointing for Munro. However, Munro comes to terms with the contradictory ways these women teachers negotiated patriarchy during their tenure as teachers. Munro comments that the women teachers she interviewed "simultaneously reject[ed] dominant discourses as well as accommodate[d] them" (p. 35). Contradictions are not easy to reconcile. In fact, the poststructural position, as Munro points out, is one that does not work to reconcile opposites. People are bundles of opposites. Munro's women teachers—as she suggests—are both complicit in their own gender oppression at the same time that they are also active in trying to undo the very gender oppression in which they are complicit. The poststructural approach to history is a complex one. Subjects are not who you think they are.

Two Psychobiographies: Interior Lives Torn Asunder

Emerging from recent work on biographies of women teachers are two notable books dealing with the ruins of the psychic interiors of teachers. I would consider these books psychobiographies because both deal with inner psychic struggles. First, I will discuss the work of Judith P. Robertson and Cathryn McConaghy's (2006) edited collection on Sylvia Ashton-Warner titled *Provocations: Sylvia Ashton-Warner and Excitability in Education* and then turn to Paula M. Salvio's (2007) provocative book titled *Anne Sexton: Teacher of Weird Abundance*. Both of these texts shock and surprise. These books shock because the reader might begin to wonder whether either of these women (Sylvia Ashton-Warner and Anne Sexton) belonged in classrooms at all. Their behavior in the classroom was unscrupulous and inappropriate. These biographies tell stories of people who are psychic wrecks and as Wilfred Bion (1994) put it "hastily organized improvisation[s] of...personalit[ies]" (p. 74). Both Ashton-Warner and Sexton suffered from mental breakdowns, maybe even psychotic breaks. They were less than professional with their students and crossed boundaries—including sexual boundaries. Historically, teacher biographies have been about heroic teachers. And there is nothing wrong with that in and of itself. But psychobiographies—although they might deal with love—also deal with hate. Psychobiographies deal both with what is called positive transference and negative transference. It is the negative transference and acting out that becomes problematic, especially for classroom teachers. It is one thing to have negative transference (hatred toward others), but it is another thing entirely to act it out (beat students, yell at them, or sexually abuse them). Marjorie Theobald (1999) talks about the fantasy of women teachers as "angel[s] in the classroom" (p. 19) and teacher stories as "grand narrative[s] of emancipation" (p. 20). Theobald asks: Why is it that teachers should be angels? What is behind this fantasy? This is a gendered construction no doubt but also a psychological projection. Teachers are hardly "angels in the classroom" (Theobald, p. 19). They are complicated. These psychobiographies allow us to rethink our own anxieties and fears.

Judith Robertson and Cathryn McConaghy on Sylvia Ashton-Warner

Sylvia Ashton-Warner's life story is rather shocking. Today scholars are acknowledging that she was no "angel in the classroom" (Theobald, p. 19). This is what is brought to light in the brilliant and most provocative—to use their title—work edited by Judith Robertson and Cathryn McConaghy (2006). Students learn from Alison Jones (2006) that according to Lynley Hood that "Sylvia had been abused [sexually] by two teachers as a child" (p. 26). When people experience sexual abuse as children—if they do not go through extensive therapy and work through the abuse—they can repeat this abuse with others, which is exactly what Ashton-Warner did. Alison Jones says that Ashton-Warner had "charged feelings toward her small pupils" (p. 25). And these small pupils were five and six years old! Sue Middleton (2006) reports that Ashton-Warner had deep-seated problems that stemmed from her troubled relationship with her mother. Middleton tells us

> Ashton-Warner's mother had also suffered miscarriages and infant deaths. Sylvia herself had been named after one of the dead babies and felt, as she said in *I Passed This Way*, that she…sometimes felt like a ghost. (p. 49)

This ghostly personality was also a cruel one as she acted out her childhood wounds in the classroom. She beat her students, even with "the strap" (Jones, 2006, p. 27). And her students suffered bruises (p. 27) from these beatings. It is clear that Ashton-Warner projected onto her students all of her hatreds and intense (sexual) feelings. It is the acting out of these feelings that is the problem here. When psychoanalysts treat patients they don't like or even patients that they fall in love with, they are taught to not engage in what is called "countertransference"—or acting out. Teachers also experience countertransference in the classroom as they too can fall in love with or hate their students. But to act out these feelings is highly problematic. And it is this acting out that got Ashton-Warner in hot water. Alison Jones comments

> The physical passions expressed in Sylvia's classrooms would be highly suspect today, and Sylvia would be told in no uncertain terms that positive intimacy with her children was not allowed. Any suggestion that good teaching of small children might elicit fleshly desires to hold and be held would be considered unethical, immoral and even illegal. (p. 25).

What makes this all so terrible is that these children, were—well—children. These were elementary school-aged students. That is what makes this disgraceful. So, as Cathryn McConaghy and Judith Robertson (2006) put it, Ashton-Warner has been called a demon and a maniac (p. 1). Why study and write about a demon and maniac? Perhaps because she teaches us something about ourselves. She forces us to look at our own issues. Not all women teachers are nurturing. Ashton-Warner was outright mean and sexually abusive. This psychobiography certainly cracks through stereotypes one might have of elementary school teachers. To cover over her behavior, Ashton-Warner imbibed both drink and drugs. Cathryn McConaghy tells us that Ashton-Warner

> disclosed in a letter to her friend Barbara Dent: "a sherry before school in the morning and one after lunch...somehow the woman must keep going" (p. 83). Who painted her out to be an "angel in the classroom" (Theobald, 1999, p. 19) when clearly she was a "demon?" (p. 1)

Paula Salvio on Anne Sexton

Like Ashton-Warner, Anne Sexton—Paula Salvio (2007) tells us—suffered excesses and was also a demon (p. 6). Like Ashton-Warner, Sexton suffered sexual abuse and also sexually abused her daughter and stepped over lines in her classroom. Like Ashton-Warner, Sexton suffered from breakdowns and, as Salvio puts it, "serious mental illness that defied diagnosis and cure" (p. 2). She suffered addictions (p. 2) and took to the bottle as she drank before faculty meetings at Boston University. And it seems too that her personality was—as Bion (1994), puts it, "hastily organized" (p. 74). Salvio reports that Sexton suffered from "self evacuation" (p. 12). Salvio states, "In fact, Sexton goes on to say, "it comes down to the terrible truth that there is no true part of me...I suspect that I have no self so I produce a different one for different people" (p. 12). Now, this differs from the poststructural position whereby the self is multiple. Mental illness is not the same as the poststructural self. The mentally ill self is completely shattered (Salvio, p. 12). To say that there is no self means that whatever part of the ego that was once syntonic was somehow obliterated; the loss of ego is the loss of self. When people suffer sexual abuse as children they learn to abandon their egos—or shatter their egos—as a defense mechanism. When one abandons the ego and dissociates from the scene of abuse one obliterates all feeling and memory of the event. This defense mechanism—which serves to protect the psyche—later in life becomes the downfall of the psyche. Salvio tells us that Sexton "was indeed perceived by many as a teacher perpetually in error" (p. 23). In a remarkable passage by Sexton's friend Maxine Kumin, Salvio reports

> "One of the things I learned from my loving relationship with Anne," recalls Kumin, "was not to fear mental illness, not to be afraid of people who are in the grip of it. She was never anything but real to me. Even crazy, she was still Anne." (p. 58)

Sexton suffered not only from psychotic breaks but also from suicidal ideation. Eventually she killed herself. Sexton worked on her mental illness through her poetry; she was one of the greats of the 20th century. Her poetry is profoundly autobiographical, and at times crazy. She opened the door for many poets.

Did Sexton belong in the classroom? Salvio raises this question throughout her book. And yet, she says, "Anne Sexton has been a provocative intellectual companion" (p. 6) for her. Both Sexton and Ashton-Warner were provocateurs.

One of the interesting things about Salvio's book is that this psychobiography is not something one would expect to show up in the "canons of curriculum" (p. 7). And why would that be so? Historians of education have focused mostly on teacher educators. Sexton was a poet, not a teacher educator. But why shouldn't we study Sexton? Was she not an educator? Salvio, like Pinar (2009b) and Hendry (2011), broadens the curricular conversation. Who counts as an educator? Curriculum historiography, recall, differs from traditional educational history because it opens up these other avenues for study. Anne Sexton should be studied alongside other educators, even if she was not a teacher educator.

The other interesting thing about Salvio's book is that alongside the narrative about Sexton, she engages in an autobiographical counternarrative and inserts herself into the story, much as Petra Munro (1998b) inserted her counternarrative into the life histories of the teachers whom she studied. This tells us how interrelated biography and autobiography are. Why, one wonders, was Salvio drawn to Sexton? It is no accident that Salvio worked on Sexton. In a way, Salvio identifies with Sexton as she says

> Sexton has haunted me over the years because as I moved in closer to her teaching life, her pedagogy began to look so ordinary to me—so uncanny, so frighteningly familiar. I grew up in the New England suburbs in Sexton's poetry. My parents are contemporaries of Sexton. (p. 8)

But later on in the narrative, Salvio begins to wonder whether she even likes Sexton and wonders whether she should be doing a biography of her at all. This tension in the narrative makes for very interesting reading. It is a remarkable book indeed and raises many questions unthought in the history of American curriculum. Both Salvio's and Robertson and McConaghy's (2006) books are groundbreaking because they shatter expectations and open the conversation onto a new plane. Biographies are not always about nice people, nor should they be.

Salvio wonders why people like Anne Sexton and other women educators are peripheral to the discussions of curriculum studies. She states

> I began to speculate why Sexton's teaching had been left so unexplored—and why other female figures like Sylvia Ashton-Warner, Jane Adams [sic], and Maria Montessori appear as mere background figures in the canons of curriculum studies. (p. 7)

When studying the work of traditional educational history students can better understand Salvio's worry. These women are seemingly on the edges of the historical scene, and if they are mentioned, they are mentioned in passing or referenced in footnotes. But there are other questions too. When talking about the "canons of curriculum studies" who gets talked about and who decides who is in the canon? Or are there—as Salvio puts it—canon(s) of curriculum?

Lawrence Cremin (1988) tells us that publishing houses in the late 19th century (mostly located in New York City) published only a certain kind of biography. Cremin tells us

> Biographies were meant to instruct through exemplary lives; the fiction [novels that were published during this period] was meant to instruct through plots that ended in the triumph of middle-class values.... most books remained didactic. (p. 428)

The biographies of Ashton-Warner and Sexton certainly do not represent the "triumph of middle-class values." If these biographies had been written in the late 19th century they probably would not have been published.

Deborah Britzman on Anna Freud and Melanie Klein: Biography as Intellectual History

The study of curriculum history must be continually broadened. Deborah Britzman (2003) has done just this in her work on Anna Freud and Melanie Klein. Why Anna Freud and Melanie Klein? These women are considered founding mothers of psychoanalysis. But could they also be considered founding mothers of Progressive education? Could they be considered founding mothers of curriculum? Yes. Many of us work in the interstices between curriculum theory and psychoanalysis and draw on both Anna Freud and Melanie Klein.

It is interesting that Britzman calls her work histories of learning. The histories she traces are psychoanalytic. She is doing what I would consider to be intellectual histories of psychoanalytic educators. And certainly both Anna Freud and Melanie Klein are two important historical figures for our work in curriculum studies, especially for those of us who do work in psychoanalytic theory. Britzman's book, *After-Education: Anna Freud, Melanie Klein, and Psychoanalytic Histories of Learning*, fascinates. For Britzman both Anna Freud and Melanie Klein have something to teach about the vicissitudes of psyche. The book focuses more on Anna Freud than Melanie Klein, but Britzman even-handedly writes about both. Britzman is doing an intellectual biography of both of these women as she tells us what their major contributions have been as they relate to education. Britzman's thesis gets stated early on in the book as she claims

> My orientation to the trouble in education is a patchwork of Anna Freud's insistence that education is made from all sorts of interference, and Melanie Klein's argument that the desire for creativity and construction emerges from destruction and negativity. (p. 9)

Anna Freud and Melanie Klein couldn't be more different in psychoanalytic orientation. Anna Freud's focus is on defense mechanisms and undoing them to make the unconscious, conscious (that is what Britzman calls interference) while Melanie Klein's focus is more on the unconscious (ph)antasy—the *ph* designates unconscious fantasy—and the destructive sides of human beings. Anna Freud's work reminds me of the work of theologian Meister Eckhart who always looked for the good in us and worked from a position of the *via positiva*. Melanie Klein, on the other hand, reminds me of Augustine's theology of the *via negativa*. Eckhart believed that human beings are innately good while Augustine believed that human beings have to overcome original sin.

Britzman suggests that for Anna Freud learning is about the willingness of the person to adapt (p. 60) to reality. She puts it this way:

> Anna Freud, however, saw the work of the human in more adaptive terms, for while a human is subject to flights of fantasy and to wishful thinking, all signals of instinctual

conflict, she believed that the trauma of the Oedipal conflict could be resolved with an acceptance of reality. (p. 60)

Anna Freud worked around the notion of the ego and the defense mechanisms that block people from becoming whole.

Britzman reports on the two founding mothers of psychoanalysis—Anna Freud and Melanie Klein—without taking sides as she argues that both have something important to offer educators. Britzman tells us

> Melanie Klein asks us to accept an inaugural negativity at the heart of psychical design—a time before education that nonetheless still exerts influence. This kernel of negativity creates, for Klein, our urge for reparation, the gradual translation of inchoate demands and feelings of persecution into affectation, the desire to think of and care for the other. (p. 12)

Like Augustine's original sin—which must be worked through—Britzman argues that for Klein the negative "must be overcome" so that patients can learn to love and experience what Klein calls "gratitude" (p. 12). In no way does Klein suggest that the ego must submit to the norms of society however. She argues that children are highly destructive and need to work through this destruction. The paranoid-schizoid phase must be worked through so that the psyche can also work through what Klein calls the depressive position toward reparation and finally gratitude. The repair that the young psyche has to make is with the mother.

Britzman's interesting thesis of the book, too, concerns the "afterwardness" of education. Drawing on the German *Nacherziehung*—which Sigmund Freud uses—Britzman tells us that this word gets "wrongly translated" as "re-education" (p. 4). *Nacherziehung* should be translated, rather—as Britzman tell us—as "after-education" (p. 4) because she states that Freud suggests that people need to be educated again because there is "an original flaw made from education: something within its very nature has led it to fail" (p. 4). Thus, there is an afterwardness to getting educated. Students have to start all over again because education fails us.

I want to make the point here that I include Britzman's work in this section on curriculum history because I think what she offers is a biographic portrait of two historical figures who have had impact not only on psychoanalysis but also on the field of curriculum studies. It is most unusual to see these two women considered part of the canon of curriculum studies. Britzman's work helps us better understand why Anna Freud and Melanie Klein clearly belong in our canon of curriculum.

Morris on Melanie Klein: Biography as Intellectual History

My book *Jewish Intellectuals and the University* (2006) also looks at Melanie Klein as a historical figure who should be considered in studies of curriculum. Her curriculum was the psyche. I do a biographical sketch of Klein as a Jewish intellectual and show that like other Jewish intellectuals—and here I am thinking of the struggles that Maxine Greene (1998) had at Columbia, Teachers College—Klein felt estranged (p. 79). Maxine Greene (1973) early in her career wrote *Teacher as Stranger* perhaps because, like Klein, she too felt estranged as a Jewish woman in an Ivy League school that had a long history of anti-Semitism.

I suggest in my book that Klein

> was an outsider in Viennese culture as a Jew, she was [also] an outsider within the psychoanalytic movement because her ideas were heterodox and bizarre even for other analysts. Klein's notions of phantasy, the early arrival of the Oedipus Complex, greed, and the primacy of the mother...brought her much scorn. (p. 80)

Klein's ideas were shocking to other analysts, and still today her ideas are not wholly acceptable in the American psychoanalytic community. For educators especially, Klein is invaluable because she questions stereotypes of the child. For Klein, children "are not innocent" (Morris, p. 81). For Klein, "a child who rips up her doll may be annihilating her mother!" (p. 81).

Neither Anna Freud nor Melanie Klein graduated from a university (Morris, p. 81). Being disaffiliated from a university was what probably allowed these women to do intellectually groundbreaking work. Women—especially Jewish women—were not exactly welcomed in European universities in the early part of the 20th century.

Who Is Included in Curriculum Historiography?

While Anna Freud and Melanie Klein were not school teachers or teacher educators, they were both what I would consider Progressive women educators and should be included in the study of curriculum historiography. Both women founded important schools of thought (one could argue that Anna Freud founded ego psychology and Melanie Klein founded object-relations theory) that directly impact the history of curriculum studies since many curriculum theorists work at the interstices of curriculum and psychoanalytic theory. (For more on this see volume 2.) Anna Freud and Melanie Klein should be included in our study of curriculum history alongside other women who also were not teachers or teacher educators per se.

Intellectual History and Biographic Portrait(s) of Maxine Greene

One of the most important and beloved educationists of our time is Maxine Greene. There are two notable edited books that I would like to explore here that highlight the life and work of Maxine Greene. One is titled *A Light in Dark Times: Maxine Greene and the Unfinished Conversation*, which is co-edited by William Ayers and Janet Miller (1998), and the other book is titled *The Passionate Mind of Maxine Greene: 'I Am…Not Yet'*, which is edited by William F. Pinar (1998a). What I would like to do here is paint in broad brush strokes some of the highlights from these books.

William Pinar compares Maxine Greene to many well-known intellectuals of our time. In the Ayers and Miller (1998) collection, Pinar says of Greene

> No, like Adorno, like Said, like Woolf, Maxine Greene remains the stranger, the one in exile, thinking of what might be next, not playing to our gaze, not collapsing, as a more ordinary mortal might, into our admiration for her. How *does* she think of herself? She asked that question that morning [at the LSU Hill Memorial Library in 1996]. Toward the end of the speech. "Who am I?" she posed, half to us, half to herself, then paused before the answer: "I am who I am not yet." (p. 120)

Greene is an intellectual who, as Pinar suggests, carved out a unique and lasting place in the intellectual archives of our times. One of the distinguishing characteristics of Greene's work, says Pinar (1998a), is that like other New York intellectuals like Susan Sontag, Greene is a generalist. Pinar comments

> New York intellectual culture at mid-century was typified by intellectual generalists: Edmund Wilson, Paul Goodman, and Harold Rosenberg. There were as well important literary critics such as Lionel Trilling, Irving Howe, Mary McCarthy, and Philip Rahv, who shared with the generalists an interest in exploring diverse contemporary topics in their writings. (p. 3)

Pinar places Greene's work in the company of these New York intellectuals. And when one studies Greene's work one can easily see this connection as Greene draws on many different kinds of writers and artists, philosophers, and educationists to make her points. "Keeping up" with Greene, as William Ayers (1998a) puts it, is difficult. She seems always to be ahead of everyone, both in conversation at the dinner table as well as in her books. The issue of her being a generalist is an important one, especially for curriculum theorists. One of the hallmarks of curriculum studies is that it, too, is the work of generalists. This is what makes our field so broad and so exciting. And it is to Maxine Greene that curriculum scholars owe a debt of gratitude. Without her work, ours would not be what it is. In fact, Wendy Kohli (1998) remarks

> Maxine has made the field more hospitable for many of us who draw on continental philosophy, the arts, literature, feminism, and discourses of the "other," to do our work. Perhaps this is one of her finest, most powerful contributions: the *openings* she created for others, particularly for women. (p. 187)

Kohli points out that Greene was housed in a department of philosophy of education at Columbia and had to come in through the back door, as it were, because women were not welcomed in departments of philosophy of education. And, too, the kind of work she was doing was considered anathema at the time.

One of the key words in Wendy Kohli's quote above is the italicized word *"openings."* Greene not only opened the way for curriculum scholars to do the kind of interdisciplinary work that they do, but also, as a professor, she psychically opened spaces for people. Nancy Lesko (1998) tells us

> The strongest and clearest response to being a student in Maxine's class was registered through my body. When I left her class at about 7 pm on Mondays and walked the two blocks to my temporary home in Teachers College family housing, I walked more erect, breathed more deeply, my shoulders moved easily back and down and I felt greater *openness* [emphasis mine] in my chest. (p. 241)

What is it about Greene's work that allows for this openness? How is she different from most professors, most intellectuals? What is it that she teaches that allows for this opening to occur? Well, Lesko tells us that Greene "explained on the first night that the literature on the syllabus was not about teaching and schools. Rather, 'reading literature (a work of imagination) is a way to illuminate some aspects of life'" (p. 239). Lesko makes an important point here. Let us rephrase what Greene said in Lesko's syllabus: curriculum studies is not about teaching per se, and it is not about schools per se—this is Greene's point and it is one that allows for openings to occur. One way of shutting down the conversation in curriculum is to focus too narrowly on schools and on teaching—a point that William Pinar has made repeatedly throughout his life's work. (Of course curriculum scholars are concerned also with schools and teaching.) Curriculum studies, and here curriculum historiography, should be about opening up the conversation, not shutting it down. Lawrence Cremin (1988) also makes this point, especially in his historiographies, because they are social histories that are not in any way narrow or parochial.

Maxine Greene broadens and opens the conversation by engaging works of literature, the arts, and philosophy. This interesting interconnection of sources—which is most unusual for philosophers—is what allows the feeling of openness that Lesko writes about. Greene allows us to breathe again and to become more open to a wide variety of sources to think through issues of education. Education—as a broad concept—is one that she is concerned with. Greene suggests throughout her work that students get at issues of education partly through studying fiction. What is it about studying fiction that allows us to breathe more openly?

During Maxine Greene's tenure at Teachers College, nobody was doing work like this. Philosophy—for most philosophers—meant studying Plato, Aristotle, Hume, and the rest. For Greene philosophy meant studying characters in novels, going to art galleries, and reading people like Albert Camus. Greene allows us to think more broadly about every segment of curriculum studies, including history. Maxine Greene moves beyond issues of teaching and schools to capture the richness of education. William Ayers (1998b) says of Greene that she "was gleefully blurring genres" (p. 6). Can the study of the history of curriculum "gleefully blur genres"? These biographic portraits of Maxine Greene teach that in order to move the field forward scholars have to break open old boundaries of what counts as history, what counts as curriculum, and who counts as a curriculum theorist. Poets, psychoanalysts, political theorists—like, say, Hannah Arendt—or anthropologists like Margaret Mead and Ruth Benedict should be included in our studies (Morris, 2009). What about women composers and conductors like Nadia Boulanger? Well, she too has been written about in the context of curriculum as she was a groundbreaker and opened the doors to women in the music world (Morris). Like other women intellectuals, though, she is remembered as a teacher, not as an intellectual or composer or conductor. Similarly Petra Munro (1998a) points out that Jane Addams was not remembered as an intellectual but as a social worker. Maxine Greene would welcome the discussion of these women intellectuals, these women artists, who usually get left out of the "canons of curriculum," as Paula Salvio (2007) puts it. William Ayers (1998b) says of Maxine Greene—in the spirit of the openness of the disciplines—that her "field of study [was] lived situations" (p. 6). Shouldn't the history of curriculum too be about the study of lived situations? Ayers goes on to tell us

> Philosophy, anthropology, literature, psychology, science, the arts—[Maxine insisted on] knocking down barriers, insisting on her right (and ours) to use everything—any discipline, any curriculum, any encounter—as nourishment, as a source to pose our questions, confront our problems. (p. 6)

Ayers's words capture the brilliance and vitality of Greene's intellectual contributions. Like Greene, Dwayne Huebner, Paul Klohr, and William Pinar—also push students to study broadly and draw on everything, to dare to be generalists.

Tom Barone (1998) comments on the "sheer number of references from literary works" (p. 139) that Greene draws upon in a book called *Releasing the Imagination*. Barone says

> One gauge of her commitment to the discovery through literature of meanings that would "otherwise have been inaccessible" (1977, p. 294) is the sheer number of references from literary works which are sprinkled so liberally throughout her essays and chapters. Indeed, in one book of 198 pages (*Releasing the Imagination*, 1995) Greene manages to weave into her text relevant thoughts and excerpts from no less than 78 literary works. (p. 139)

Greene's erudition is quite astounding. What strikes me about Greene's work is the use she is able to make from the sources she cites. Citing the work of others is one thing but making use of what is cited is something altogether different. Greene is able to not only make use of others' writings, but also she is able to make her readers think differently about life after reading her work. This is what Barone is saying about Greene.

Which writers are important to Greene? Well, it depends on how you read her and what you are looking for. Nancy Lesko (1998) comments that Greene's writers are "Emerson, Mann, Hawthorne, Melville, Thoreau, Douglass, Twain, Chopin, Morrison, Fitzgerald, Ellison, among others" (p. 239). Denise Taliaferro (1998) comments that Greene's writers are "Ralph Ellison, Zora Neale Hurston, Richard Wright, Martin Luther King Jr., Paula Giddings, Ntozake Shange… Alice Walker and Toni Morrison" (p. 91). Morris (1998) claims that Greene's writers are "Jean-Paul Sartre, Simone de Beauvoir, Albert Camus, Alfred Schutz, Soren Kierkegaard and Maurice Merleau-Ponty" (p. 124). Whose Greene? Whose writers? Which Greene? Which writers? Lesko's Greene is a different Greene from Taliaferro's. The richness of Greene's work and the richness of interpretation around her work is a testament to the depth and breadth of her thinking. And this can only happen when one is, as Wendy Kohli (1998) says of Greene, a "voracious and responsible reader" (p. 186). Kohli makes an interesting point here about reading responsibly. She argues that Greene "keeps up with intellectual developments in many fields, particularly in philosophy, cultural studies, literary theory and educational thought" (p. 186). William Ayers (1998b) says, "Doing philosophy with Maxine Greene could be—had to be—both exhausting and exhilarating. Keeping up was the first challenge" (p. 5).

Memory Work: Boyd Bode, George Counts, Philip Jackson, and Paul Klohr

In recent years there have been notable books in the field of curriculum studies that examine biographic portraits of men. Now, many of these men are rather well known and have been written about by traditional historians. Men tend to become more well known than women probably because men are written about more than women. The biographic portraits of Boyd Bode, George Counts, Philip Jackson, and Paul Klohr are all found in Kridel, Bullough, and Shaker's (1996) *Teachers and Mentors*. I have chosen to share with readers portraits of these particular men because their work best exemplifies the experimental nature of curriculum studies. What strikes me about *Teachers and Mentors* is that readers come to know these figures through the memories of former students of these scholars. Earlier I discussed some of the memories that former students had of notable women Progressives; here I want to explore the memories that former students had of notable male figures in our field. *Teachers and Mentors* explores biography as memory, which is an often overlooked aspect of studying curriculum history. How do we remember our teachers? This is an important and often ignored question. The memories of our teachers clearly shape our scholarship. But more traditional historians are usually not too interested in memories of their subjects because they feel that memories are unreliable and shifty. Historical methodology tends to constrain what it is that historians can do. More liberal historians, like Kridel, Bullough, and Shaker, take the memories of their mentors seriously and share liberally those memories with readers. So what I want to do here is share with students some memories—which are found in the *Teachers and Mentors* book—former students had of Boyd Bode, George Counts, Philip Jackson, and Paul Klohr.

Boyd Bode

I would like to begin with the memories of Kenneth Winetrout (1996) who says of Bode that he was mostly concerned with "the social responsibilities of education and educators" (p. 74). What does it mean to be a socially responsible educator? Educating others is always social work because we teach against a larger sociohistorical backdrop. Bode, Winetrout tells us, "would council the professorate to reach out to other disciplines" (p. 77). Bode was an earlier pioneer in curriculum who began the conversation around the importance of interdisciplinary study. The best way to be socially responsible would be to try to get at social issues through as many intellectual avenues as possible. Perhaps today some take the interdisciplinary nature of our field for granted, but it was scholars like Boyd Bode who opened the doors for us to do this kind of work. Thinking education socially suggests also that scholars must think more broadly. As George Herbert Mead (1964) suggested, the self is always already social. Thus, scholars must work at understanding the self as it is situated in the social. This means studying history, sociology, culture. Education must be understood against the larger sociohistorical scene.

For Bode the democratic nature of education was all, as Winetrout points out. Craig Kridel and Robert Bullough (2007), in their book *Stories of the Eight-Year Study*, say of Bode that "progressive schools, he insisted, must lead their pupils to oppose dictatorship and make democracy 'a way of life,' and he defined democracy as 'continuous extension of common interest'" (p. 183). Bode was writing in the 1930s when dictatorships were on the rise in Europe. Many people like Bode who were involved in the Eight-Year Study were concerned about the problems of dictatorships in Europe. During the Eight-Year Study and during the years in which Bode taught and wrote, Kridel and Bullough comment

> The situation in Europe was increasingly frightening as well. The growing appeal of fascism, with its glorification of youth, horrified the PEA Commission members. The German Youth Movement gave new meaning to the social importance and political potential of adolescents. Eight Year study staff—most notably Bruno Bettelheim, Fritz Redl, Peter Blos, Erik Erikson, and Walter Langer—had fled Austria and Germany for refuge in the United States. (p. 35)

Bode's interest in democracy probably was, in part, a reaction to what was going on in Europe. And perhaps people become more concerned with issues around democracy when their own freedoms are threatened. A kind of fascism was also on the rise in the United States during WWI. Woodrow Wilson violated civil liberties, as historian John Cooper (2009) reminds. Cooper says

> During the war, Wilson presided over an administration that committed egregious violations of civil liberties. He pushed for passage of the Espionage Act, which punished dissident opinions, and he refused to rein in his postmaster general, who indiscriminately denied use of the mails to dissenting publications, particularly left-wing ones. He likewise acquiesced in his attorney general's crackdown on radical labor unions. (p. 11)

Fascism at home is—in some ways—harder to see because it is right in front of us. If we are to be socially responsible—as Bode suggests—Americans must come to terms with the underside of American history.

Bode's writings on democracy might have been a response to the historical memory of Wilson's violations of civil liberties as well as the rise of fascism abroad. When civil liberties are threatened, people become more interested in the meaning of democracy, and curriculum studies scholars have had a long history of writing about democracy (probably because schools are hardly democratic places). Today, one of the largest topics of debate in the political sector of the field turns on the meaning of democracy and how education and democracy are impacted by the loss of civil liberties.

George Counts

Another curriculum theorist who was concerned with the intersections of politics and education was George Counts. Counts has been written about by many educational historians, and we won't reiterate what we already know about him (Cremin, 1988; Kliebard, 2002; Pinar et al., 1995). What I do want to do here is discuss some memories that Lawrence Cremin (1996) shares with readers about Counts that might give us new insights. Cremin, who was a student of Counts, recalls

> Counts' office was the perfect site of the Socratic teacher. The walls were crammed with books, pamphlets, and periodicals arranged on the shelves that rose to the ceiling, while tables held stacks of recent publications, especially newspapers and magazines. Counts worked at a rolltop desk, with pictures of Abraham Lincoln and John Dewey above it. He smoked incessantly, mostly a pipe and occasionally a cigar. (p. 238)

I cite this passage because it gives us clues into Counts' reading habits. Of course, one would expect a scholar of such eminence to be surrounded by books, but to hear Cremin in his own words talk about Counts makes it all come to life. Young scholars should be inspired to work with books piled all over the place, with bookshelves from the floor to the ceiling jammed with books. How else can one become a scholar? Cremin (1996) says of Counts

> [He] must have read everything on every side of every educational issue; and, as he made his recommendations, I would dutifully note them, with every expectation of turning to them promptly. But I never came close to catching up. The longer I knew him and the more we talked, the greater the gap between the burgeoning list and my actual achievement. (pp. 238–239)

Cremin's books have bibliographies that are miles long. Counts' influence on him was immense. Think of Cremin's (1988) *American Education: The Metropolitan Experience, 1876–1980*. Probably in the back of Cremin's mind are those extensive lists of books that Counts suggested he read. Cremin (1996) comments on taking a class with Counts at Teachers College, and he tells us that Counts had the students read "history, sociology, and political economy" (p. 239). Counts had his students do interdisciplinary work. Reading widely is key to becoming an intellectual.

Philip Jackson

A scholar who has helped his students think more broadly is Philip Jackson. One of his former students, David Hansen (1996), shares memories with us of being in one of Jackson's classes at the University of Chicago. Interestingly, Hansen tells us

> This is what most endures from my memories of Jackson's classroom: that the project of learning to think for oneself is not a sideshow to life, it *is* life itself, in fact how we treat this text and one another's ideas for the next hour is *decisive* for the kinds of people we will become. Jackson's approach promoted the moral obligation of respect for authors, in the sense of trying to understand what they were saying. (p. 130)

Jackson honored the text. Where does that sense of obligation to honor a text come from? One of the reasons that students study in the academic disciplines is to honor those who came before us. Our ideas, then, spring from reading the works of others. Without studying the past students do not know how to invent a future. Students have a professional obligation to think historically about the field. Students owe a debt of gratitude to all of the scholars who paved the way for us.

David Hansen comments that "the titles of Jackson's courses are telling: Dewey as educator, Wittgenstein as educator, Wordsworth and Coleridge as educators" (p. 133). This is a fascinating approach to education. Like Maxine Greene, Philip Jackson obviously felt that education was broader than issues around instruction per se. Philosophers and poets interested Jackson. What do students learn from philosophers and poets about educational issues? How do they educate us? Philosophers and poets think differently about lived experience. To think philosophically is to think abstractly and almost poetically. To think poetically is to think philosophically as poetry raises the big questions of life and death. Jackson was interested in the big questions. David Hansen remarks that Jackson "has long been taken with the broad, complex question of how we should perceive and describe our everyday human experience" (p. 133). Perhaps one way to get at the everyday is through abstract and poetic language. Using common sense language and colloquialisms—ironically—obfuscates. Like Alice Miel, Jackson was interested in language—as philosophy and poetry are about language. David Hansen also remarks that Philip Jackson had a "long term love affair with poetry, painting [and the] arts" (p. 135). The arts have played such a crucial role in the work of curriculum theorists as students have learned from our study so far. Recall that many of the women Progressive educators like Jane Addams, Caroline Pratt, Marietta Johnson, Margaret Naumburg, and Maxine Greene also had a "long term love affair"—to use Hansen's phrase—with the arts. Younger scholars in curriculum studies who do arts-based education should study these theorists so they understand how their interests tie into the work of their academic ancestors. Advancing curriculum from an arts-based perspective means studying the past and understanding the history of the arts in our field.

Paul Klohr

Finally in this section I want to share with readers some memories that Robert Bullough (1996) has of Paul Klohr. Bullough comments that Klohr's courses

> were messy and challenging, genuinely counter-cultural. Reading lists were long and included items from diverse disciplines and included obscure writers working well outside the mainstream of education... . Klohr took seriously the charge of Joseph Schwab that the curriculum field was "ahistorical." (p. 260)

Paul Klohr was interested—as Bullough tells us—in having his students read literatures that were not usually taught in curriculum classes. This is an important point. Reading books that seemingly have little to do with education forces students to make connections between "obscure" literature and the field of curriculum studies. Studying obscure texts leads to new thoughts and new connections to education. To get away from rehashing what has already been done students might try reading things that are unusual. This is risky, especially for younger professors who are not yet tenured. But a field can only advance if thought progresses in new directions.

Klohr worried about the ahistorical nature of curriculum studies. This has been a longstanding problem. When education courses focus on methods and teaching strategies, objectives and standards, the field moves nowhere. Without projects of historicality this field cannot advance. Students need to think historically about whatever their projects may be.

Robert Bullough explains that Paul Klohr worked around what he called "gestalts" (p. 260). Klohr wanted his students to study "work being done on the edges of the disciplines" (p. 260). Thinking on the edge. This is a profound way to think. Scholars must be willing to take risks, to think on the edge. This edge work is done through the study of texts that make us think otherwise. How to think otherwise? Bullough comments that Klohr had his students read Philip Rieff—a well-known Freudian interpreter. Bullough remarks that the students wondered why they would be reading Rieff in a curriculum class. Klohr taught that "education is understood as more than schooling, more than getting and keeping control over a classroom of rambunctious students" (p. 260). For Klohr, reading broadly—like reading Philip Rieff—opens vistas. Klohr taught his students about intellectual freedom. And it is this intellectual freedom that makes curriculum studies such an interesting, complex, and avant-garde field. No other field is as wide open and exploratory as this. And this wide openness and exploratory nature of the field have a history. Robert Bullough makes an interesting point in this regard as he says

> Traditions cannot be given; instead they are lived and in the living they are offered. Just as Professor Klohr made his dream available to us, it was made available to him by his mentors, Harold Alberty and Hank Hullfish who encountered it in their mentor, Boyd H. Bode. (p. 263)

The generations continue on and on. Klohr "made his dreams available" to others. Fields are transgenerational and students should honor the generations before us who made our work possible.

Biographic Portraits: Joseph Schwab, William Heard Kilpatrick, and Harold Rugg

Three notable books that I want to explore here are about well-known figures in the field of curriculum studies mentioned above. I am thinking of Alan Block's (2004) *Talmud, Curriculum, and the Practical: Joseph Schwab and the Rabbis*; John Beineke's (1998) *And There Were Giants in the Land: The Life of William Heard Kilpatrick*; and Roland Evans's (2007) *This Happened in America: Harold Rugg and the Censure of Social Studies*. Biographies such as these can deepen our understanding of the contributions made by these men to the field of curriculum studies.

Alan Block on Joseph Schwab

Alan Block—a well-known curriculum scholar—has done much work in the intersections between Jewish studies and curriculum theory. Block's (2004) book makes the connection between Schwab's Jewish identity and his academic work. This is a unique book that advances our knowledge of Schwab because of this connection made by Block as he argues that "Schwab spoke, to, from a silenced and invisible Jewish tradition" (p. 6). Block says that Schwab is like the rabbis of old who studied the Talmud and argues that "there is always another use and interpretation of text because what is at stake is not final knowledge but daily practice" (p. 14). Schwab's call toward the practical can been seen against the ancient Jewish tradition of learning. Jewish ethics is based on doing, not on knowing only. The heart of Jewish ethics is doing good deeds. This is the point Block is trying to make about Schwab. More than anything else, for Schwab, education should be about doing good deeds and doing things that make a difference. Knowledge that changes lives is the knowledge of most worth for Schwab. Schwab argued that the curriculum field was moribund, not because it was ahistorical but because it was too theoretical. Heubner, as Pinar et al. (1995) point out, argues just the opposite: That the trouble with the curriculum field—at least in the 1960s and before—was that it was not theoretical enough.

Block makes a very Deweyan point when talking about what Schwab was up to when he says

> As Schwab argued, education divorced from the lives of its students is a meaningless enterprise and has no value. For such an education, there is no perceived use, nor can it be exchanged for anything that could be deemed valuable. Nothing is acquired.

> The classically oriented liberal arts curriculum proved irrelevant to children for whom liberal arts held no meaning. (p. 39)

The call toward the practical, for Schwab, Block tells us, was meant to correct this problem of a seemingly meaningless education. This was also the point that Dewey made in his writings. Dewey did not suggest that the liberal arts curriculum had no place in students' lives; he just wanted it to be made relevant to the lives of students so that they would get something out of it. And so, too, this is the point that Block is making about Schwab. Block states

> The field of curriculum has been forever dominated by the discourses derived from Greek, Roman, and Christian principles and by practices and methods that derive from those principles. These are the principles found in the works of Socrates, Plato, Aristotle, Augustine, Aquinas and Descartes. (p. 10)

Block speaks here of the Great Books Tradition. He makes an important and overlooked point about which students need to be more conscious: Where do our traditions of learning come from? Do students give this enough thought?

Block comments on Schwab's difficulties working at the University of Chicago, which was "a hostile environment" for Jews (p. 9). And since he worked in such a hostile environment—like so many other Jews in the academy (Morris, 2006)—he hid his Jewishness and submerged it in his academic work. During the early to mid-20th century Jewish intellectuals were almost forbidden to talk about their Jewish identities or make use of their Jewish identities in their academic work (Morris). When Maxine Greene was a professor at Columbia, for example, talking about one's Jewish identity just wasn't done, it wasn't acceptable. Most of the Ivy League institutions in the United States have had a history of anti-Semitism (Morris), and so talking about one's Jewish identity was highly risky.

Erudition and study are highly valued in the Jewish tradition. Erudition is built into the tradition of Judaism. One might make, therefore, a similar argument about Maxine Greene that Block makes about Schwab. What is Jewish about Greene? Well, that is a book for another time. But the question is an interesting one and further work on this subject needs to be done.

William Heard Kilpatrick

Let us turn to the work of John Beineke (1998) and his study of William Heard Kilpatrick. Beineke argues that Kilpatrick straddled between the

Reconstructionists (like Counts and Rugg) and the more child-centered progressives (like Dewey.) Beineke puts it this way:

> Kilpatrick can be placed at the midpoint of the social reconstructionist spectrum. While never embracing the more extreme elements of the movement—such as indoctrination, the class struggle, and Marxism—he did, during the 1920s, anticipate portions of social reconstructionist thought. There was, admittedly, a mild radicalism in his thinking, but it was tempered by a reflective, Deweyan philosophical process. (p. 233)

Like Kilpatrick, Jane Addams was rather suspicious of Socialism and Marxism because it seemed too dogmatic (Elshtain, 2002). And like Kilpatrick, Addams too was highly political but did not want to label herself Marxist because she did not trust the Marxists. And yet again, she was friends with many Marxists and Socialists like John Reed and Lincoln Steffens.

What exactly does Beineke mean by calling Kilpatrick a "mild" radical? Does this mean that Kilpatrick was sort of radical but sort of not? This mild radical, Beineke tells us—along with other professors—wrote a manifesto to Franklin Roosevelt about the poor condition of the public schools in New York City. Beineke explains:

> Soon after the election of 1932, The Kilpatrick Discussion Group began working on a "manifesto," as they termed it, to send to President-Elect Roosevelt. Counts, Childs, Paul Hanna, and William C. Bagley worked on a rather lengthy first draft…. It began by describing the plight of American children, stating that one-fourth of those in New York City schools were suffering from malnutrition…. The manifesto stated that educators could not stand by while such conditions continued unabated. (p. 212)

Roosevelt, however, surprisingly turned a deaf ear. Kilpatrick thought that Roosevelt was a "private school snob" and had little interest in public education. It is disturbing to see how deeply historical the distain for public school is in American culture. No Child Left Behind (NCLB) and Race to the Top are policies made up by people who obviously have disdain for the public school, distrust teachers, and dislike children.

Kilpatrick, during WWI, compared "Columbia to German universities" (Beineke, p. 93). Recall that Woodrow Wilson clamped down on free speech and freedom of the press. And so too did the president of Columbia University, Nicholas Murray Butler. Historian Jay Martin (2002) says that the clamp down on intellectual freedom at Columbia began with a thwarted visit to campus by Ilya Tolstoy. Martin tells us

> In February 1917, an incident occurred that, it seemed to many, might lead to the beginning of the curtailment of free speech at Columbia. Count Ilya Tolstoy had been invited by a student society to speak at the university... . Then, with the acknowledged support of President Butler, the chair of Slavonic Languages prevented Tolstoy from lecturing, by withdrawing permission for him to use a university building. (p. 269)

Censorship and dismissals of professors at Columbia who dared to speak out against the war were all too common. Tolstoy wrote much about peace, and Jane Addams was highly influenced by Tolstoy's writings as she traveled around the globe lecturing on peace.

The reason Kilpatrick compared Columbia to German universities was that he thought that the firings and censorship were fascist. Beineke (1998) points out that Kilpatrick linked "Germany's 'war attitude' directly to German education" (p. 91). The Prussian tradition of education was one of "unquestioning obedience" to school officials and to the state (Beineke, p. 91). Many of the scholars at the New School for Social Research, such as Adorno, Frenkel-Brunswik, Levinson, and Sanford wrote a well-known study of German obedience titled *The Authoritarian Personality* (1950/1993). This study was an attempt to try to understand what drove the Germans to become Nazis and to annihilate six million Jews. One conclusion from this study was that Germans were taught obedience not only in schools but also in churches and by stern authoritarian fathers. The need for an authoritarian leader—Hitler—was so ingrained in the German psyche, these authors contend, that it made sense that they followed Hitler's lead and did whatever he told them to do (Morris, 2001). This book, *The Authoritarian Personality*, was later roundly critiqued for its simplistic thesis and sweeping generalizations about authoritarian fathers. Surely not all Germans were raised by authoritarian fathers and even if they were, how does that lead to the annihilation of six million Jews (Morris)?

Kilpatrick's political views are important to consider when studying his contribution to progressive education. His left-leaning views were also evident in his project method and in the way he thought about freedom of the intellect and education in general. His project method is a testament to intellectual freedom. Beineke (1998) tells us an interesting story of how Kilpatrick came to the project method. Beineke says

An episode related to him that summer by Otis Ashmore of Chatham Academy in Savannah, Georgia, dramatically changed Kilpatrick's view of the educative process. Ashmore told of leaving his students unattended one day for a brief period of time. A visitor came by the classroom looking for Ashmore and found the students so engaged in their lesson that they were working without supervision. "I did not see that far into the future then," Kilpatrick wrote, "but this 1892 suggestion led to the 1918 'Project Method.'" (p. 22)

Kilpatrick, Beineke says, was "opposed to any form of…awards, honors, or grades" (p. 103). And he was opposed to a "curriculum set in advance" (p. 107). Kilpatrick wanted to encourage students to do intellectual work for its own sake. And certainly, grades get in the way of intellectual work because grades only make students nervous and filled with anxiety. To have preset objectives (as did Ralph Tyler, for instance) thwarts creativity and intellectual freedom—this is what Kilpatrick meant by the troubling idea of a set curriculum. Students do not know where their intellectual labors will take them. If teachers begin to set objectives, students will never be able to truly do the intellectual work that will free thought and, as Maxine Greene (1995) might put it, "release the imagination."

Here I am also reminded of the pedagogical labors of both Philip Jackson and William Pinar. Pedagogically, both men create the conditions whereby intellectual exploration becomes a possibility. David Hansen (1996) tells us

> There was no lesson plan detectable in Jackson's approach, no set of passages or ideas in the reading we had to cover… . We simply had no idea what passages would become the center of our talk, nor what ideas would emerge… . In time, it became apparent that each class was destined to be an adventure into the unknown. (p. 129)

Scholarship—for the intellectual—is an "adventure into the unknown"—to use Hansen's phrase. There is no telling where ideas might lead and it is best to follow hunches and intuition rather than trying to force things. This is the way that Jackson taught his courses. And for doctoral students who are used to a scripted and highly structured lesson plan, this approach must be not only puzzling but also frustrating. Thinking is not following a script and neither is teaching.

Harold Rugg

Another Progressive educator affiliated with Teachers College (and a colleague of Kilpatrick) was Harold Rugg. A biography of Rugg by Ronald Evans

(2007) titled *This Happened in America* gives students insight into Rugg's political struggles while at Columbia. The title of Evans's book is interesting in that it suggests that things like banning school textbooks don't happen here. One might think that things like burning text books only happen in places like Nazi Germany. But things like that do happen here. It is interesting that banning and burning are not that dissimilar. Both mean getting rid of—one way or another. Rugg's social studies textbooks were banned from use in many public schools during WWII because they were thought to be too radical and too critical of capitalism. Evans tells us

> At the peak of their popularity, the Rugg textbooks were censured by a media storm fed by conservative patriots and business groups who, in an un-American fashion, did not want school children, or their parents for that matter, raising questions about the basic structures of American life and the capitalist economic system. (p. xv)

These "conservative patriots" accused Rugg of spreading Communist propaganda. But according to Evans, Rugg wasn't Communist and the textbooks in question were hardly radical. Evans says that Rugg's books were "relatively moderate in outlook.... and typical of many progressive school textbooks of the era" (p. 101). Nonetheless, Rugg's "inclusion in *The Red Network: A Who's Who of Radicalism for Patriots*" (p. 147) did him in. *The Red Network* was put together by one Elizabeth Dilling, who, Evans tells us, was a "self-described super Patriot" (p. 147). Evans points out, "The attack on Rugg, on his ideas and school materials, was perhaps the first major battle of what I have previously termed the war on social studies" (p. xv). To critique the sociopolitical landscape of American culture has always been dangerous business in a country that cherishes conservative "family values." And to bring to the attention the wrongs and gross inequities in this society to students and their families has always been thought to be anathema by conservatives even today.

One of the interesting things students learn from studying Evans's biography of Rugg is about his struggle working in textile mills. The horrible experience that Rugg had in a textile mill shaped his ideas on the problems of industry, capitalism, and inequity. Evans tells us

> After leaving high school and prior to attending Dartmouth College Rugg worked in a textile mill and was directly exposed to the realities of modern industry. From 1902 to 1904 Rugg was employed by the Parkhill Manufacturing Company and was engaged in various departments of the cotton manufacturing business. (p. 6)

Working in a textile mill Rugg experienced firsthand the rough life of working-class people.

One of the most fascinating things about Rugg is that not only was he interested in politics but he was also interested in the arts. This is something that people forget when they lump Rugg with the social Reconstructionists. And this is the problem with putting people into categories like social reconstruction. This category tends to erase other contributions made outside of politics. Evans says Rugg

> blamed the pragmatists, including John Dewey, Charles Peirce, and William James, for an overemphasis on experimental inquiry and problem solving with too little attention to feeling appreciation, and contemplation. (p. 117)

This citation is curious because Dewey (2005) was clearly interested in the arts, and his book *Art as Experience* was a groundbreaking contribution to "appreciation and contemplation" of the arts as they are experienced in the everyday. At any rate, Evans says that Rugg felt that "artists and writers should lead the way" (p. 114). Perhaps Rugg's experience with the Greenwich Village crowd (Cremin, 1988) influenced him more so than his Teachers College colleagues.

J. Wesley Null on Isaac Leon Kandel

J. Wesley Null (2007) has written an interesting biography of Isaac Leon Kandel titled *Peerless Educator: The Life and Work of Isaac Leon Kandel*. Kandel was a critic of Progressive education. He taught at Teachers College alongside George Counts and Harold Rugg. Null states that Kandel "began to argue against radical Progressives like Counts, Kilpatrick, Childs, and Rugg during the Depression" (p. 166). Kandel, says Null, was a "democratic traditionalist" (p. 3) and was known for his work in comparative education. Null says that Kandel is a forgotten figure in the history of curriculum because he was a traditionalist. By this Null means that Kandel was a Great Books scholar. Null explains:

> He believed in tradition, but he was by no means wed to the past. Kandel valued the high standards of scholarship set by ancient writers like Plato and Aristotle, but he was by no means an elitist who shied away from the challenge of democratic education. Kandel believed in liberal education for all. (p. 3)

And yet "the charge of 'elitism' was a common criticism that Kandel had to deal with" (p. 277). Kandel was highly skeptical of Dewey's work because he felt that Dewey did not value the liberal arts tradition. But clearly this is not the case. Dewey embraced the liberal arts and he wanted to make the liberal arts more meaningful for young people, he wanted to link the liberal arts tradition to lived experience.

Kandel had some things in common with Dewey, in fact. Null states that Kandel's "view of an educated person is someone who can see all of the academic disciplines in their entirety and as they relate to one another" (p. 14). Dewey would not disagree with this position. However, Null paints Dewey and the Progressives out to be anti-intellectual throughout his biography of Kandel. His position is not dissimilar from Diane Ravitch's (2001). Ravitch, too, reads the Progressives as anti-intellectual. Clearly, this is a gross misreading.

Kandel was interested in the moral and ethical implications of education. Null tells us that Kandel felt that "education has been and always will be a social, moral, and political enterprise" (p. 10). Null contends that the "foundation of Kandel's understanding of liberal curriculum is ethics" (p. 20). Kandel drew on a variety of disciplines to make his points. Null explains:

> He sought to integrate the fields of political science, philosophy, history, sociology, and economics by focusing specifically on education and the practice of teaching. Moreover, he searched throughout his career to integrate the aspirations of various countries into a worldwide view of curriculum. (p. 21)

Kandel believed that students should study broadly but should also learn "a common cultural heritage" (p. 9). Null intimates in the book that Kandel ostracized himself from the Progressives at Teachers College because of his conservative tendencies. Kandel had to wait some thirteen years to get a professorship at Teachers College and Null suggests that this could have partly been because of anti-Semitism. Kandel was, Null tells us, the first Jewish faculty member at Teachers College.

William G. Wraga on Alexander James Inglis

William G. Wraga (2007) has written an interesting biography of Alexander James Inglis whose "work has remained relatively obscure" (p. 1). The interesting thing about Inglis is that he started his academic career as a traditionalist—much like Kandel—but did an about face, studying at Teachers College—to become a Progressive educator. Wraga explains

> He began his career as a Latin teacher, coauthored three Latin textbooks...translated Cicero's Essays on Friendship. In 1907, he entered Teachers College, Columbia University, to pursue his interests in the teaching of ancient and modern languages. Four years later, however, Inglis emerged from Teachers College as a progressive experimentalist. According to one of his students, Inglis spent the remainder of his career repudiating his academic traditionalist formative years. (p. 2)

It is highly unusual that someone would turn their backs on their own educational formation. As a student at Wesleyan University, Inglis was steeped in the classics. But there must have been something about Teachers College that turned him toward more Progressive ideas. Wraga does not tell us what this turn was about, but one can speculate that the Progressive atmosphere at Teachers College must have excited the young Inglis. He went on to write an important book called the *Principles of Secondary Education* in 1918. Wraga tells us that Inglis's book "represents an application to education of hallmarks of American pragmatism: commitment to the method of science, to democracy, and to the reconstruction of traditional patterns of action in response to changing social realities" (p. 49). This is quite a far cry from the traditional curriculum Inglis was steeped in while at Wesleyan as he studied "Logic, Advanced Logic, Introduction to Philosophy, Ancient and Medieval Philosophy, Modern Philosophy" (pp. 13–14). What drew Inglis to the Progressives remains an open question. He couldn't be more opposite from Isaac Leon Kandel (see Null, 2007), who remained wedded to the classics and was a fierce proponent of them throughout his entire academic career.

Autobiography as Historical Text

Is the 21st century history? It is if you make it so. Is autobiography history? It is if you make it so. Autobiography teaches us much about history. I argue that biography and autobiography are forms of history. Some might be puzzled as to why I think autobiography has anything to do with history. But it does. When students study autobiographies they learn much about the historical period in which these books were written. Autobiographies teach us much not only about race, class and gender but also about history. And many women—who get left out of traditional histories—find a home in autobiography. Men tell their tales too of course and historically autobiography began as a male genre. Many mark Augustine's *Confessions* as the first important autobiography (e.g., see Anderson, 2004). Linda Anderson does some remarkable work for us as she tells us in brief about major patterns and trends of autobiography, and interestingly enough she calls autobiographers "historians of the self" (p. 18). She tells us that Augustine's *Confessions* "is often thought of as the origin of Western autobiography" (p. 18).

Two words to ponder on here in relation to autobiography: confession and testimony. These are two major components of autobiographical work. Foucault (1979) had trouble with the concept of confession. In *Discipline and Punish* he argues that confession is—in the religious sense—a form of control. One can, though, confess to a crime. One can confess one's sins. But a confessional can also be a personal narrative that dares to reveal what is perhaps secret, private, or painful. The term I like better, though, is "testimony." A testimony is an autobiography. Testify is also a sort of spiritual concept. But it doesn't have to be. Testimony is also a word used in trauma studies. Victims testify in court, yes, but people testify—in a more metaphoric way—when telling their stories. Storytelling is autobiography.

William Pinar brought autobiography into the conversation of curriculum in the 1970s. Pinar wants us to think about "psychic movement," as a sort of going back and forth between the past and present between analysis and synthesis of lived experience. The progressive, regressive, analytic, and synthetic are the movements of *currere* (for more on this, see Pinar, 1994). Students must think of their lives as always open to change and movement. Now, for Pinar autobiography means, most importantly, theorizing around a life in an open-ended way whereby the self is in relation to the Other and to the larger sociopolitical landscape. This is a difficult task. Writing an autobiography requires some real soul searching, and as Celia Hunt (2000) says, autobiography "involves self-exposure [as we]…place ourselves and our views not only on the page but 'on the line'" (p. 50). Writing one's life is risky. What to tell and what not to tell. Secrets or the truth.

Max van Manen and Bas Levering (1996) have written a very interesting book, in fact, on childhood and secrets. Van Manen and Levering state,

> Keeping secrets and sharing secrets are unique human experiences. Yet the experience of secrecy is complex, multilayered, and multi-dimensional. For example, clandestine actions, sacred practices, stashing a cache, veiling ones' eyes, masking an intention, covering a deception, disguising an emotion, sheltering a treasure—all of these expressions in one way or another describe secrecy. (p. 10)

Autobiography is always already about negotiating secrets. It is a tricky genre indeed. Secrets come up as an issue, especially if people write about what troubles them, or if they have been, say, abused as children or struggle with traumatic pasts. People write autobiographies because they feel driven to do so. There is a need to tell the story and sometimes this need comes from some deep psychic wound. It is no accident, then, that autobiography and psychoanalysis go hand in hand.

There are all kinds of autobiographies. As Linda Anderson (2004) tells us, Augustine wrote a spiritual autobiography whereas Rousseau, wrote a secular (p. 43) autobiography. Autobiography is not a monolithic genre. Here I list types of autobiography: pathography (autobiographies of illness); traumatic autobiographies (stories of abuse or oppression); postcolonial autobiographies (what happens to the victims of colonialism); poststructural autobiography (a Beckettian antinarrative); feminist autobiography, working-class autobiography, autobiography and race, autobiography and place, queerly done autobiography, and so forth.

Edmund C. Short and Leonard J. Waks

Edmund C. Short and Leonard J. Waks (2009), in their book *Leaders in Curriculum Studies: Intellectual Self-Portraits*, explore the autobiographies of scholars who belong to the generation of those born during the Great Depression or shortly thereafter. Readers are introduced to autobiographic portraits of such people as Michael Apple, Miriam Ben-Peretz, Louise M. Berman, F. Michael Connelly, William Doll, Elliot Eisner, John Elliot, Ivor F. Goodson, Maurice Holt, M. Francis Klein, Herbert M. Kliebard, William F. Pinar, William A. Reid, William H. Schubert, Edmund C. Short, Malcolm Skilbeck, Laurel Tanner, and Michael F. D. Young. What becomes apparent are the multiple ways in which these scholars understand curriculum theory. Reba N. Page (2009) points out

> The last common thread in the essays is the oft-noted lack of consensus within the field about how curriculum is best conceptualized. The decades of the 1960s and 1970s were a theoretically vital period—"fertile," Berman says—and a variety of theoretical perspectives were developed: Bill Reid and Decker Walker's elaboration of Schwab's emphasis on the practical and deliberation; Bill Pinar's reconceptualism; the "new" sociology of curriculum of Michael Apple and Michael F. D. Young; the turn to curriculum history, made by Herb Kliebard, Laurel Tanner, and Ivor Goodson. (p. xiii)

Upon reading these autobiographic portraits one better understands the multiplicities of interpretations of curriculum theory. Some writers are more interested in practice; others are more interested in theory; some combine both. It is interesting to note that there is little agreement on what curriculum theory is. Many of the writers—in Short and Waks—talk about teachers with whom they studied or traditions of thought they have followed throughout their careers. I will share a few of these autobiographic portraits with readers.

Michael Apple (2009) talks of studying with Dwayne Huebner. Apple tells us,

> Very few doctoral students had finished with Dwayne. He was demanding (of himself as well as his students) and he was among the most creative critical curriculum scholars in the history of the field.... He sent me away with a list of more than fifty books to read—in philosophy, social theory, literature and literary theory, and curriculum history. (p. 2)

Huebner's (1999) work is highly interdisciplinary. He was interested in a vast range of topics, ranging from the importance of language to aesthetics, from history to politics, from theology to curriculum history. It is clear that he wanted his students to study all of these disciplines as Apple suggests.

Apple comments on his own work as he states

> I am not simply a "neo-Marxist," a "sociologist," a "critical curriculum scholar," or someone in "critical theory" or "critical pedagogy." Nor am I someone whose roots can be traced simply to something like "phenomenology meets Marxism." As I showed in the list of my early influences, a commitment to the arts—written, visual, and tactile—and to an embodied and culturally/politically critical aesthetic, have formed me in important ways as well. (p. 11)

Thus, when people peg Michael Apple as a critical theorist, they are missing all of these other influences on his work. Apple's work is highly theoretical, historical, and political and yet there is more to him than this.

F. Michael Connelly's work could be seen in direct contradistinction to Apple's. Connelly was a student of Joseph Schwab and so he is interested in the practical. Connelly (2009) states that he is interested in "personal practical knowledge, narrative inquiry, cross-cultural educational links between China and Canada" (p. 40). Although Connelly states that he considers himself to be theoretically minded, his "school based studies" are rooted in the practical everyday lives of teachers (p. 11). Connelly tells us

> I continue to read abstract, philosophical work and I think of myself as having a theoretical turn of mind. Yet I have not been part of the movement to text and post-modern theorizing that has come to characterize curriculum studies.... My lack of engagement with these debates is mildly principled on the grounds that there is little to be gained for the practice of curriculum. (p. 45)

Connelly's work toward the practical couldn't be more different from the work, say, of William Doll who, in the Short and Waks collection, talks about his turn toward postmodernism. Doll (2009) states

> At Redlands (Director of Teacher Education), I became serious about studying the emerging *new sciences*, particularly as represented in the works of Ilya Prigogine.... In his (with Isabel Stengers) *Order out of Chaos* (1984), Prigogine draws heavily on the philosophy of A.N. Whitehead. Down the road from Redlands...is the California School of Theology.... There, again, serendipitously, I was introduced, via John Cobb and David Griffin, to the word and concept "postmodernism." (p. 61)

Doll, later in his career, became known for his work in both chaos theory and postmodernism—two highly theoretical fields of study.

Another interesting autobiographic portrait in the Short and Waks collection is that of curriculum historian William H. Schubert (2009b) who states

> One of my major concerns has been the *ahistorical* and *atheoretical* nature of teaching and curriculum. Despite the transformation of emphasis from curriculum development to curriculum studies, from institutional facilitation to understanding diverse cultures of curriculum, there remains a staunch absence of theory and history. (p. 170)

William Schubert, Ann Lynn Lopez Schubert, Thomas P. Thomas, and Wayne M. Carroll (2002) have written a remarkable historical book on the field of curriculum studies, which has come out in its second edition, and it is called *Curriculum Books: The First Hundred Years*. Each historical epoch in the book is divided into three sections. The first section deals with the broader world historical backdrop against which curriculum books were written; the second section deals with the curriculum books written during a particular era; and the third section is a bibliography of books. What is striking about the book is the vast knowledge base these writers have not only of the curriculum books but also of the world historical backdrop against which they are placed. These writers talk about everything from the arts to sports, from scientific discoveries to film, from radio to poetry, and they couch it all against issues of race and gender. Quite a remarkable achievement. This book is deeply historical.

Another curriculum scholar in the Short and Waks collection is William F. Pinar. As a student of Don Bateman, Paul Klohr, and Dwayne Huebner, Pinar's intellectual trajectory reflects the intellectual freedom his teachers taught him. Pinar is highly interdisciplinary and is interested in a variety of theoretical positions. Pinar (2009a) states

> It was during my early years at Rochester that I fastened onto autobiography as a means to recast curriculum theory.... From the phenomenological I moved—as did many others—to poststructuralist understandings of subjectivity and society, influenced by Foucault (at first through Taubman), then later by Derrida and Deleuze.... Only in recent years have I recoiled from what now seems to me an excessive textualism in post-structuralism, undertaking a reconstruction of humanism. (p. 148)

What is missing from this list is Pinar's interest and concern with history. Like Schubert, Pinar has been highly critical of a field that seems both ahistorical and atheoretical.

Carlos Alberto Torres

Carlos Alberto Torres (1998) has compiled autobiographic portraits in his book titled *Education, Power, and Personal Biography: Dialogues with Critical Educators*. Here students are introduced to a variety of scholars like Michael Apple, Samuel Bowles, Martin Carnoy, Paulo Freire, Herbert Gintis, Henry A. Giroux, Maxine Greene, Gloria Ladson-Billings, Henry Levin, Jeannie Oakes, and Geoff Whitty. Torres tells us why he grouped these scholars together as he states that "they all represent a sample of progressive educators employing all sorts of approaches including Critical Theory, Marxism, Neo-Marxism, Game Theory, postmodernism, postpositivism, Feminism, and theories of race/ethnicity, class, and gender" (p. 5). Here I would like to share a few autobiographic portraits with readers. One of the writers that struck me is Paulo Freire in his description of how he came to write *Pedagogy of the Oppressed*. Freire (1998) states

> I began *Pedagogy of the Oppressed* with the title. *Pedagogy of the Oppressed* is possibly the most didactically well-organized book that I have written.... When I began...I discovered that a large part of it was written on the notecards of which I spoke earlier. So, I would organize these cards on top of my table according to titles and I would always discover the following: that between notecard number four and number five—I numbered all of them—there was a void. It was a void I needed to fill. (p. 95)

It is always interesting to take note of the way in which a scholar works. For Freire notecards seemed to help him organize his thoughts. Freire also comments that when writing *Pedagogy of the Oppressed* he was obsessed (p. 95).

Another critical theorist of note is Henry A. Giroux, who comments on his intellectual influences. Giroux (1998a) states

> So, Paulo [Freire] and Stanley's [Aronowitz] works completely changed my perception of problems in education, particularly regarding positivism, ideology, the role of the state, and the politics and culture of capitalism. Martin Carnoy's work was also very important for me in the early stages of my work. Bowles and Gintis were enormously influential.... . Phil Corrigan and Roger Simon were very important in my own self-formation, Antonio Gramsci increasingly played a prominent role. (pp. 135–136)

Later on in the piece, Giroux comments that he too has been highly influenced by a variety of feminist thinkers. Scholars' work does not come out of a vacuum. Scholars are influenced by the work of others.

Maxine Greene (1998), in Torres's collection, tells us

> My thinking, I realize, is divergent. I have a great deal of imaginative literature stored in my experience.... . It is hard for me not to find illustrations of philosophic arguments, claims, abstractions in the particularities of art forms.... . In Social Philosophy and Education, we read Arendt, Habermas, Foucault, Adorno, others—but also Don DeLillo's novel, *White Noise,* for the purpose of giving students an opportunity for a concrete encounter with a highly mystified, technologized, consumerized culture. (p. 169)

Maxine Greene's work is highly literary and highly philosophical. She intersperses the philosophical with the literary. During her tenure at Columbia University, Teachers College, this approach to philosophy of education was highly unusual. Greene—as was discussed earlier—has opened the door to many of us to do interdisciplinary work.

Janet L. Miller: Sounds of Silence Breaking

Janet L. Miller (2005) writes about the craft of autobiography in her book titled *Sounds of Silence Breaking: Women, Autobiography, Curriculum.* First, she situates herself historically in the field of curriculum studies as she states

> I had first heard Maxine [Greene] and Jim [Macdonald], as well as Dwayne Huebner, Donald Bateman, and Paul Klohr, present or facilitate sessions at the 1973 curriculum

theory conference at the University of Rochester, where Madeleine Grumet and I were master's degree students, studying with William Pinar. (p. 17)

Miller did her dissertation on the work of Maxine Greene and was managing editor for the *Journal of Curriculum Theorizing* from 1978 through 1998. Miller studied with both William Pinar and Paul Klohr. Miller was surrounded by highly influential scholars during the early days of the reconceptualization. Miller was one of the earliest scholars to do feminist autobiography in the field of curriculum studies. In *Sounds of Silence Breaking* she offers a retrospective of her work from the 1970s on. Her work shifted over the years from feminist concerns to poststructural ones. Miller's interests have turned on doing feminist autobiography and more recently she has made the poststructural turn and discusses what she terms "feminist poststructuralist autobiography." Describing feminist poststructural autobiography Miller claims, "I struggle to engage in forms of narrative and autobiographical inquiry that do not present single, essentialized, or unified representations of 'self,' 'identity,' 'woman,' or 'experience,' for example" (p. 89). Writing autobiography in a poststructural fashion requires us to think anew about the notions of self. For poststructuralists, selves, identities, the notion of women, and experience all become complicated. None of these terms can foreclose on themselves. All is shifting, in motion. This makes the task of writing autobiography difficult because the self is not one thing. And there are multiple stories to tell. Miller states

> I've been persuaded by poststructural feminist claims that subjects and "voices" are irreducibly multiple.... I now consider fragmentation as suggestive of openings, crossings, and spaces in and through which to disrupt notions of authoritative and "finalized" discourses or identity constructions. (p. 6)

Writing autobiography in a poststructural fashion requires one to rethink the self as multiple, Miller tells us. She goes on to state that the self is fragmented and so too is the art of autobiography because the storyline of an autobiography is not the final story. How to write an autobiography that is fragmented, non-unitary, and multiple?

Miller goes on to state that in her most recent work she has "queered" the notion of autobiography. Drawing on queer theory Miller states, "Queered autobiography suggests a focus on a range of sexualities as well as racialized and classed identities that exceed singular and essential constructions of 'student' or 'teacher,' with fixed attributes of 'masculine' or 'feminine'" (p. 223). Miller's work has moved away from her concerns of getting out from under the thumb of patriarchy to complicating the very ideas that make identities possible. Queering autobiography makes us think differently about the entire genre of autobiography. What kind of autobiographies are possible if we queer them? Miller states "I could queer both the subject and the forms that autobiography typically [take] in educational settings" (p. 219). Miller critiques teacher autobiographies that appear to be seamless or linear (p. 149), and the same goes for collaborative work as Miller has been engaged in many collaborative projects over the course of her career.

History, Trauma, Autobiography

Recently in the field of curriculum studies scholars are beginning to combine history, trauma, and autobiography. This form of writing differs greatly from, say, the traditional form of autobiography that has been about heroic white Euro-centric males. Conversely, more recent autobiographies by women tell tales of heartbreak and struggle.

More specifically, I want to explore the works of three curriculum scholars: Ming Fang He (2003), who writes of her struggles growing up during the Cultural Revolution in China in a book titled *A River Forever Flowing: Cross-cultural Lives and Identities in the Multicultural Landscape*; Xin Li (2002), who writes also of her struggles during the Cultural Revolution in her book titled *The Tao of Life Stories: Chinese Language, Poetry, and Culture in Education*; and my book (2008), *Teaching Through the Ill Body: A Spiritual and Aesthetic Approach to Pedagogy and Illness*. I group these three autobiographies together because they all demonstrate that autobiography is also historical and all three describe forms of trauma.

Both He's and Li's books are especially important because students learn about what people—especially teachers—experienced during the Cultural Revolution in China. This is an event that many Americans know little about. Reading these women's stories is heartbreaking and shocking. The story of self, for both of these women, is also the story of China's human rights abuses.

Most Americans—I would venture to say—have little historical memory of the Cultural Revolution in China because many of us never learned about it in school. If readers want to know more about this historically tragic event, read He and Li. I want to explore highlights and trends from these books. What strikes me about both of these women is that they have tremendous inner strength and a life force that allowed them to somehow get through those terrible years and to become, later, professors of education. Both books are amazing testimonies to the human spirit and the life force.

Dominick LaCapra (2001) writes of "empathetic unsettlement" when studying trauma (p. xi). Students of history need to have empathy for those who suffered terrible trauma, and yet our empathy can only be partial because the experience of trauma is so personal. And yet empathy is a must.

The River and the Knot

What interests me about He and Li is that both use metaphors to hold their stories together. He uses the metaphor of the river to hold her story together, to give her story a center, when the center cannot hold. Likewise, Li uses the metaphor of the knot, or knot work, to hold together a story where the center cannot hold.

Both He and Li write about the central place that reading had for them in the midst of utter chaos and horror. Xin Li tells us, in a most powerful and eloquent way,

> My love of reading has never weakened throughout my life. In the Cultural Revolution when culture was revolutionized, I read. In the years on the farm [read labor camp] where I was supposed to get rid of my former "book knowledge," I read. When I myself decided not to read any more in order to avoid the painful turmoil caused by the striking contrasts between books and reality, I still couldn't refrain from reading. Even when my father tried to take away my books forbidden by the government, I read. (p. 24)

Li's love of books is a testament to words and the power of words. Words help people survive utter horror. Words are powerful indeed. Words certainly helped Xin Li survive. During the Cultural Revolution people were beaten, tortured, and killed for reading what was forbidden.

Ming Fang He tells us that her father, who was a teacher, was beaten and kept in solitary confinement for not toeing the party line. He says

> My father was confined in a little dark room in the school compound to confess his antirevolutionary teaching. There were ten small rooms in that compound where teachers' children used to play hide-and-seek. The Red Guards were watching the gates in turns. Uncle Li, the physics teacher who graduated from Qinghua, the most prestigious University in China then, who was denounced as a rightist in 1957, was kept in a dark room next door to my father's. I remember that all those rooms smelled of rust and rotten wood, and were full of spider webs. (p. 34)

Ming Fang He was a child when she witnessed all of this. Childhood memories, when they are traumatic, are very difficult to psychologically negotiate. Ming Fang He often talks about feeling as if she is in exile still. I wonder whether a child who is exiled—to a labor camp—ever psychically leaves that labor camp? Is this the feeling of continual exile?

Ming Fang He explains more about the Cultural Revolution as she tells us,

> As eleven and twelve-year-old girls, we were encountering torture, violence, and madness almost every day. We could see: wives reporting their husbands…sons fighting ruthlessly against their fathers or mothers…brothers spying on each other…"revolutionary" students sending their teachers to "reforming farms" or dark rooms and repaying their teachers' kindness with enmity and cruelty. (p. 5)

A counterrevolutionary (p. 3) was someone who didn't agree with Mao Zedong's politics. Ming Fang He tells us that millions of people disappeared for re-education (p. 3). The Cultural Revolution sounds like an Orwellian hell where love meant hate and freedom meant oppression. Revolutionary meant reactionary in this case. People were spat on, pianos destroyed, dresses cut up, people were beaten and broken, houses invaded, china destroyed. The stories in this book go on and on and the reader is dumbfounded at the sheer insanity of it all. Out of a bizarre Orwellian scene Ming Fang He describes a day in her grandmother's town. She comments

> In my grandmother's hometown, early every morning the loudspeaker played…. Before each meal, people would line up piously in front of Mao's pictures, wave the Little Red Book for ten minutes for the "morning consultation with Chairman Mao," and wish Chairman Mao good health and an eternal life. Before people went to sleep they would line up in front of the picture again and perform the "late progress report to Chairman Mao." (p. 41)

And if people did not do these things, then what? They were probably reported and disappeared, tortured or killed.

Like He, Li tells us about her experience in the labor camps, called farms. She explains,

> Tears and wood ashes were all over my face: tears from both the smoke of the wood fire and from the frustration. In winter, I had many cuts on my hands from the chilly wind and the heavy manual labor. In summer, I had to face mosquito bites, fleas, leeches, and other insects. In the spring, cold water in the rice fields froze my legs,

causing them to turn red first, then completely purple. In the autumn harvesting summer fields and planting winter fields broke my back. I was often sick. (p. 19)

Most Americans live such soft lives compared to what these Chinese women had to suffer during the Cultural Revolution. Most Americans know little about working in labor camps and being exiled. Li and He are today professors of education and they certainly have things to teach us about struggle and hardship. This suffering that they both experienced comes through in their storytelling. Storytelling is not soft, as some might think. Storytelling—of this sort—can be very powerful and can teach us about experiences that cannot be gotten at by abstract concepts alone. How to capture suffering in language? Sometimes it is best captured through story.

Suzette Henke (2000) writes about what she calls "shattered subjects" (p. xv) and suggests that shattering is captured through narrative. Henke suggests that the narrative can serve as a form of "scriptotherapy" (p. xv). I wonder whether the writing of these stories served any cathartic purpose for these women. One can only guess that at some level it did. Writing out trauma sometimes helps. But sometimes it makes things worse. In any case, reading traumatic life stories raises many questions about the readers' interaction with such texts. How does one respond to others who write out of such trauma? What does it do to the readers' psyche to respond to the trauma of the other? Or can one respond at all? Yes, one can respond by reading more and writing about what one has read in response. Moreover, what these narratives do is open a space to do historical work. Students need to study historical texts on the Cultural Revolution so as to better understand this horrific event. It is our obligation to study these horrific acts of inhumanity, not as voyeurs, but as students of history.

Autobiography as Pathography

There are many ways to be traumatized. War. Famine. Revolution. And illness. There are many ways to write autobiographies: stories of great men, conversion experiences, out-of-body experiences, near-death experiences. A traumatic autobiography that deals with illness is called a pathography and there aren't too many of these in curriculum studies. My book (2008) *Teaching Through the Ill Body: A Spiritual and Aesthetic Approach to Illness and Pedagogy* deals with illness through a Jungian lens. Theorizing the self is no easy task. The book is couched between the study of aesthetics—mainly poetry, painting, and music—and Buddhist spirituality. There is a real struggle at hand to think through illness in these various registers. I weave between two times—scripts and what are called (post)scripts—to complicate the narrative and to show that autobiography is in no way linear. The book is also historical in that it deals with history of the self. Everyone has their own histories and memories that emerge as time sweeps us into the future. Autobiography is inherently historical—as the self has a history. The self is an historical self. And that is partly what this book shows.

Drawing on Adrienne Rich's phrase "diving into the wreck" (2013, p. 147), I say,

> American education runs counter to diving into the wreck of illness. History is about victors. But being sick is not about being a victor it is about being a victim. The voices of the losers are squashed out of history because historians do not think that they are reliable. Pathographies attempt to put those voices back into the historical record. An individual's memory is part of that historical record. (p. 194)

Memory is part of history and thus it must be considered to be historical. People are inherently historical beings because our memories give us a sense of time and space. The stream of life is one of memory. What else is there? When people dismiss autobiography as not being rigorous enough or not being real scholarship, they do not understand what is most important about scholarship: the study of the self. What could be more important than understanding our own histories?

One of the key points that I make in this pathography is about the importance of compassion (2008). I draw on the Buddhist idea of the Bodhisattva (the compassionate one). Compassion is an educative idea. A concept easy enough to grasp, but difficult to actually act upon in life. People who suffer from illness in American culture tend to get shunned. Schooling teaches little about compassion. Schooling teaches fear and meanness. Repeatedly and ruthlessly testing young children teaches them to be mean and to fear adults. Where is compassion modeled in school?

Like Xin Li (2002), I turned to books (art and music) for solace during the worst period of my illness. I say

> In times of great turmoil and stress, I return again and again to the same writers, the same poets, and the same ideas. I have returned to my Anne Sexton, my Kenneth Patchen, my Mark Rothko, my Steve Reich and to Buddhism. To make sense of darkness, these artists, poets and Wisdom figures give me strength. (p. 196)

The point of writing the pathography is an altruistic one: to offer company in bad times. Getting sick can make you feel utterly isolated but through reading the struggles of others, one finds some solace and company. You will notice in the list of people I mention above, one of them is Anne Sexton. Recall Paula Salvio's (2007) book on Sexton. Reading Sexton's poetry alongside Salvio's biographic portrait of her helps the reader to read less naively. Readers get a better understanding of what Sexton is up to in her poetry by studying Salvio. Sexton's poetry is difficult to read because it is so raw and it is about so much suffering. Her poetry is highly autobiographical and much of it is about the body, the body in pain, the body depressed. These, as Salvio points out, are not usual topics in education circles. These are taboo topics. And certainly a pathography is also a taboo topic for educators because there is no place for illness in the academy. It is especially a hard place to survive when illness strikes because the tenure clock ticks regardless.

History, Place, Autobiography

Another interesting way of doing autobiography is through the intersections of history and place. Three significant studies reflect the interconnection of history, place, and autobiography. I would like to explore Reta Ugena Whitlock's (2007) *This Corner of Canaan: Curriculum Studies of Place and the Reconstruction of the South*; Brian Casemore's (2008) *The Autobiographical Demand of Place: Curriculum Inquiry in the American South*; and Laura Jewett's (2008) *A Delicate Dance: Autoethnography, Curriculum, and the Semblance of Intimacy*.

The South is, as Whitlock says, both an attraction and an aversion (p. 19). Casemore comments on both the "idyllic fantasy of Southern community" (p. 2) as well as the Southern history of "racism, misogyny and homophobia" (p. 39). The beauty of the landscape in the South—Live oaks, moss haunted trees, and lush greenery—obscures and covers over a hideous history. Students need to continually study the history of the South so as not to fall into nostalgia, as Casemore, Whitlock, and Jewett insist. Nostalgia is highly reactionary as it erases historical memory and makes what was bad good. Whitlock says that the South must not "remain unconfronted" (p. 1). Casemore claims that, especially for white Southerners, the history of racism is one of denial (p. 28) and this denial must be confronted. Likewise Jewett suggests that white people might begin to study the history of racism through—interestingly enough—"learning zydeco dancing" (p. 1). Zydeco dancing can serve as a site of cultural memory.

Jewett teaches her readers about race relations through her ethnographical work in the Creole world of zydeco dance. She explores issues that turn on what "Ida B. Wells (1892/1993) calls...'white Delilahs,' these temptresses who deploy their smiles to lure black men into self destructive unions). In his play *Mad Heart*, Amiri Baraka (1969/1998) calls us 'Devil Ladies'" (p. 97). Jewett reminds us that African American men were lynched for being falsely accused of raping white women. The "rape myth," Jewett reminds us—as does William Pinar (2001)—was one of the most common "reasons" whites lynched blacks. Jewett is a white woman who enjoys dancing with Creole black men and through the dance, the horrors of history seep through the zydeco. So Jewett's book is about history, and it is about her own self-exploration of "the relationship between black masculinity and white femininity" (p. 2). This study deals with the complexities of gender, race, place, history, and identity. Thinking autobiographically, then, is thinking through all of these complexities.

These complexities are also taken up by Casemore, especially around his own white masculinity and the ways in which he must confront the history of white males in the South. Casemore says, "Therefore, reading relationships between gender identifications and racial/racist identifications, I hope to illuminate the South's gendered pedagogy of whiteness and its racialized pedagogy of gender" (p. 39). For both Casemore and Jewett race and gender are intertwined. As both Casemore and Jewett are white, they work to understand whiteness and what that means in the context of Southern history. There must be a sense of shame on the part of whites when they think through their history, especially if they were born in the South. Although neither Casemore nor Jewett directly raises the issue of shame, I wonder whether it should be a topic that needs to be worked through psychologically when studying the South. Being born in the South as a white person comes with a lot of historical baggage that must be, as Whitlock puts it, confronted.

For Whitlock, the issue of queerness gets raised as she talks about queerness and religious fundamentalism in one breath. The reader wonders, how can these seeming incompatibles go together? How does Whitlock psychologically manage these—what I think are schizoid—parts of herself? From my reading of Whitlock's book, it seems that she holds what is irreconcilable in tension and never attempts to resolve her queerness and her fundamentalism. So the question for Whitlock is how to think through the history of the South against her own curious personality of being queerly fundamental, or a queer fundamentalist. Whitlock calls the South a place that is inhabited by "neo-confederates" (p. 31). How to live in such a place as a queer woman? Clearly, Whitlock seems torn between loving and loathing the South. She talks about the "lure of home" and her "aversion" (p. 19) to the history of this home. There is no other place in the United States that is so schizophrenic and so haunted. Terrible things happened in the South; a history that many Southerners are all too eager to forget. But these three curriculum scholars won't let us forget and for that I applaud Whitlock, Casemore, and Jewett.

History, Memory, Autobiography

Mary Aswell Doll, Delese Wear, and Martha Whitaker (2006) have co-written a marvelous book titled *Triple Takes on Curricular Worlds* that fleshes out three interrelated themes: history, memory, and autobiography. Mary Doll introduces the book and tells us that *Triple Takes* "web[s] our various selves with the networks that surround us, not unlike a rhizomatic structure" (p. 2). This book—as Doll tells us—deals generally with

> work in memory and reflection to engage the serious issues of our time.... Examining our own histories, as one way of confronting historical and contemporary dimensions of our country's ideological and economic forces [which]...keeps us focused on the personal which is political. (pp. 2–3)

What strikes me here are the intertwining themes of memory, history, and the personal. The argument Doll makes is that one cannot think the historical without thinking through autobiography. The home of the self is where we understand the world around us.

Triple Takes is organized in such a way that each writer takes a theme, say, boundaries, disgrace, distance, and tells us what their "take" on this theme is. Each theme, then, has three takes by three different writers. Hence, triple takes. These scholars write from an autobiographic perspective to get at historical and social issues. Martha Whitaker writes about the history of Sri Lankan struggles; Mary Doll writes about apartheid South Africa. Postcolonial theory informs both of their work. Delese Wear and Mary Doll both draw on fiction in order to better understand history, and both do autobiographical work that helps us to understand where they are coming from on a more personal level. The book raises some important questions about the intersections between history and fiction. This is a rather postmodern question in that one begins to wonder whether history and fiction are more related than we would like to think. Is history fictioned? Is fiction history?

Students learn about the history of South African apartheid in Doll's chapter, through the unpacking of "Nadine Gordimer, Andre Brink, Athol Fugard and J. M. Coetzee" (p. 49). Studying South African fiction encourages us to also study South Africa historically. I suggest that students read historians and novelists side by side so as to better understand the history of apartheid.

Students learn from studying both Doll and Wear that fiction allows us to reflect not only on history but—as Doll puts it—also to have more self-reflexivity (p. 2). Studying fiction teaches us about history and ourselves as we respond to texts. Our responses bring up autobiographical issues.

I want to focus on two chapters in *Triple Takes*. First, I want to look at Doll's work on the theme of disgrace, and second, I want to unpack Wear's chapter on the theme of distance. Keep in mind that these themes (disgrace and distance) have everything to do with the complex intersections of history, memory, and autobiography.

Doll's work draws on postcolonial theory to unpack South African fiction. This raises some interesting questions about the uses of postcolonial theory and autobiography. When Doll writes about teaching postcolonial novelists like Nadine Gordimer and J. M. Coetzee, for example, she asks her students to reflect on race in their own lives. Doll reports that her students—on the West Bank of New Orleans—aren't exactly cosmopolitan. Teaching parochial students about race is a problem because white students do not want to confront their own white privilege not to mention their own racism. Resistance is the first problem. But race issues in New Orleans—although they are not the same as in apartheid South Africa—are certainly problematic. New Orleans, like many cities in the South, is highly segregated. You might say that Louisiana has its own sort of apartheid going on. Recall Hurricane Katrina. This horrific event tells you something about race relations in Louisiana. Teaching South African fiction, as Doll points out, brought up in her own students the terrible history of race relations in New Orleans. The South can never escape its history. And white Southerners, for the most part, have a difficult time confronting their own history. What postcolonial fiction does, Doll tells us, is "complexify Eurocentric conceptions of heroism and history" (p. 57). Eurocentric history tells one tale, postcolonial history tells another tale altogether. What students learn from studying the postcolonial is, as Doll suggests, "disjunction, displacement, and disorientation" (p. 57). History, place, and race issues emerge from Doll's teaching South African fiction. Similar issues emerge in the work of Casemore and Jewett. Race, place, identity, and history all come up in the work of these scholars. This shows how autobiography is always already couched in the middle of other issues, especially historical ones.

Delese Wear's chapter on the theme of distance in the book *Triple Takes* brings up some other issues that turn on autobiography, fiction, and memory. Wear's writing is autobiographical as well as historical. Wear draws on her own memories of growing up on a farm in rural Missouri. Currently Wear teaches in Ohio and memories of growing up on a farm inform her current "urban dweller" (p. 71) life. A key to her thinking is found in the following sentence: "But I can become my Missouri farm self without going to the farm when I imagine the farm" (p. 70). Memory and imagination are two interconnecting ideas for Wear. She talks about her farm life and growing up in the "beauty of the endless fields of corn and wheat, the dust billowing behind [her]…in the narrow dirt road [hearing]…the hum of a tractor" (p. 71). She tells us that she wants to "collapse worlds" (p. 70), bringing closer together seemingly distant worlds of the farm and her memories of it. Wear writes about the concept of distance, especially when traveling back to see her mother on the farm. She is at a distance from her mother as she has moved away to an urban setting. But this distance can be bridged through the play of imagination. Distance between two people shrinks (p. 70) as one imagines what other peoples' lives might be like, Wear tells us. What is life like for her mother on the farm, she wonders?

Wear teaches medical students. Through reading fiction together with her students, Wear believes that the students might be able to develop more sensitivity when treating patients. Literature can teach this art of sensitivity to others. She suggests that studying characters in novels might help medical students better understand that all of their patients have stories to tell. The patient is "someone with a story" (p. 70).

Medical humanities is a field within medical education that attempts to humanize medical students through the study of the humanities, for example, literature. As medicine becomes more and more technological, doctors feel a growing distance between themselves and their patients. Technology, as Plato might put it, is both cure and poison. Medical technology poisons our relations but cures what ails us—maybe. One of the interesting points that Wear makes in her piece is that the use of images can help us to become more human. Wear says

> I think that the more images they [doctors] have the more they are likely to wonder about their patients and the meanings patients' various illnesses have in lives lived outside of examining rooms. I think they are more likely to be compassionate: L. *com*, together + *pati*, to suffer. (p. 74)

The root of the word "imagination" is image. Images freely associated can help us to uncover unconscious material. The Jungians say: go to the images (in dreams) and you will find out what you need to do in your life.

Imaginative literature, for both Wear and Doll, serves to teach students about the care of Others. Imaginative literature, too, for Maxine Greene (1995) helps students to better understand the Other in relation to the self. If the imagination is arrested or stultified, people cannot be compassionate toward Others. Compassion and imagination go hand in hand.

Historically speaking, an issue not often dealt with in curriculum studies is the tension between the rural and the urban—this is an issue that Wear raises in her chapter on the theme of distance in *Triple Takes*. The Progressive movement, historically, has been associated with the urban, not the rural. However, recall that Chautauqua was associated with the rural, not the urban. The Populist Party, which some associate with Progressivism, was agrarian. There has not been much discussion in curriculum history about agrarianism. Wear's piece gives us a bit of an insight—a small window—into agrarianism and the love of the land. What must it be like, then, for the urban dweller to reimagine life on the farm? Historian Douglas Brinkley (2009) unearthed a marvelous quote by Teddy Roosevelt about the farmer:

> No nation has ever achieved permanent greatness unless this greatness was based on the well-being of the great farmer-class, the men [and women I would add] who live on the soil,.... For it is upon their welfare, material and moral, that the welfare of the rest of the country ultimately rests. (p. 133)

Teddy Roosevelt had a tremendous respect for the land—as he was, as Brinkley points out, "The Wilderness Warrior" (the title of Brinkley's book). The rural life was appealing to Roosevelt and thanks to him—through his conservation efforts— national parks have not been destroyed by developers.

There has always been a tension between the rural and the urban, and I wonder whether that tension is felt in an embodied way by someone who straddles both of these worlds. I contend that people drive a wedge too deeply between the rural and the urban. There are rural aspects to the urban—think of Central Park in New York City—and there are urban aspects to the rural—think of a university in the middle of cow pastures.

In sum I would suggest that students read *Triple Takes* if they are interested in unpacking ideas around disgrace and distance, especially as they interconnect to history, memory, and autobiography. There are other themes in the book as well such as boundaries, fear, forgiveness, light, and motherhood, which are all equally as interesting. This book approaches curriculum in such a way that history and autobiography are tightly woven.

Intellectual Retrospectives: Dwayne Huebner and Ted Aoki

I want to explore two remarkable books that trace the intellectual histories of two remarkable curriculum scholars: *The Lure of the Transcendent: Collected Essays by Dwayne E. Huebner*—which is edited by Vikki Hillis and collected by William F. Pinar (1999)—and *Curriculum in a New Key: The Collected Works of Ted T. Aoki*, which is edited by William F. Pinar and Rita Irwin (2005). I want to unpack some of the major themes that emerge from the work of both Huebner and Aoki to show where they converge and where they diverge.

Huebner and Aesthetics

Sprinkled throughout Huebner's work one finds many references to aesthetics. Clearly, he thought that aesthetics could change the conversation of curriculum to better the human condition. Huebner (1999) states, "Students need to have opportunities to approach parts of the world in many ways…to symbolize it via art and the aesthetic disciplines" (p. 7). He made this claim in 1959 and the year is significant because there were few people in curriculum circles at that time who talked about curriculum in the context of the arts. Recall that John Dewey and Harold Rugg were some of the first educationists to talk about the importance of the arts. Maxine Greene and Elliot Eisner were also two early pioneers in this area. In 1962 Huebner talks about the notion of difference in the context of art as he says "for art deals with differences and idiosyncrasies" (p. 25). Now, this is a remarkable sentence because the notion of difference did not become common academic fare until around the 1990s. Today, the idea of difference is all the rage. In 1962 Huebner anticipated the importance of this concept. Not only that, he taught us about what artists do. To be recognized as an artist, one must have a unique and recognizable style and that is what difference is. And yet Americans have a difficult time with the notion of difference. People who are "different" have a hard time. Scholars can talk about the abstract notion of difference all day long, but on a concrete level, many people don't like others who are different. Huebner says in 1962 that "the arts...are also ways of exploring the world" (p. 58). Juxtapose this to what other curriculum scholars were saying. Ralph Tyler (1949) suggested that teaching was about controlling children. The world for Tyler was foreclosed. The craze for standardized testing is an extension of Tyler's rationale. Our battles with National Council for Accreditation of Teacher Education (NCATE; an accrediting agency) are a Tylerian nightmare.

Conversely, Huebner opened up spaces for students to explore and find things out about themselves through the artistic senses. Huebner tells us

> Aesthetic exploration and expression require heightened sensitivity to the sensory components of experience. Awareness of colors, shapes and their interrelationships necessary for the visual artist, as is sound and rhythm for the musical artist. Awareness of the sensory aspects is heightened by increased participation in expressive activity. (p. 59)

Huebner approaches the arts in a philosophical way. He talks about the deeper issues that undergird artistic production. Not many educationists—who do arts-based inquiry—do this.

Not only does Huebner talk about painting (or the visual arts) he also talks here about music. Music is still an underdeveloped topic of discussion in curriculum circles. My book *On Not Being Able to Play: Scholars, Musicians and the Crisis of Psyche* (2009) is one of the few full-length texts on music and its intersection with curriculum studies. Most curriculum scholars who write on the arts today write on the visual arts. Maxine Greene (1995) focuses mostly on literature as an art form.

Huebner talked also about the importance of "storytelling, poetry, drama, short stories, and novels" (p. 49) in 1962. How forward thinking he was! Students might think that storytelling—for example—is something new in curriculum—well it isn't. Huebner was talking about this some 40 years ago. To tell a good story is to be, as Tom Barone (2000) would later put it, a "strong poet" (p. 119). Huebner also comments on dance as an important art form and anticipates the work of scholars like Donald Blumenfeld Jones, Mary Beth Cancienne, and Celeste Snowber.

Aoki and Aesthetics

Like Huebner, Ted Aoki (2005) has written about the importance of the arts in the context of curriculum scholarship. In "Toward Curriculum Inquiry in a New Key (1978/1980)," Aoki states

> Whether we agree with A. J. Magoon that educational research is in a crisis stage, there are no doubt noteworthy indications of search efforts for alternative research possibilities in education. The convening of this conference, Phenomenological Description: Potential for Research in Art Education, is in itself such an indication. (p. 89)

The arts—in the context of phenomenology—allow educationists to get at the aesthetic through philosophy. A philosophical approach to the arts was anticipated by Huebner, but Aoki's take on the arts turns on the phenomenological. A phenomenological approach is one that focuses on how one feels about something. What does it feel like to work in the arts? What does it feel like to play music or to hear jazz?

Aoki writes about jazz in a 1990 essay titled "Sonare and Videre: A Story, Three Echoes and a Lingering Note" (also found in the 2005 collection). In the context of music, Aoki talks of achieving a "sonorous clearing" (p. 369). In the Heideggerian (1962) sense the concept of clearing means to have an intellectual breakthrough. Aoki tells us that upon interviewing the trumpeter named Bobby Shew,

> When we asked Bobby Shew, "When does an instrument cease to be an instrument?," he offered us a thoughtful response: "When music to be lived calls for transformation of instrument and music into that which is bodily lived." In these remarks, he gives us in the field of curriculum a reason to reflect upon the ambience within which we have been toiling as curriculum workers. What Bobby Shew has done for us is to open up a sonorous clearing so that we might recognize instrumental words in curriculum and seek curriculum words that can sound and resound in an inspirited way. (p. 369)

This is a most remarkable passage. Aoki asks students to rethink curriculum as a musical curriculum, to rethink words as sounds and music.

Language

For both Aoki and Huebner the care of language takes on new meaning. Both Aoki and Huebner harken back to scholars like Alice Miel (called the scholar of language) and Florence Stratemeyer, who wrote so many comments on student papers that she became almost a "co-author" with the student (Kridel, Bullough, & Shaker, 1996). To think of words as music (see Aoki above) is also important to minimalist composer Steve Reich (Morris, 2009). Reich talks about what he calls "speech melody" (Morris, p. 129) as he listens to the inflections of people's voices and sentences and writes his music around those inflections. Aoki and Reich have something in common. Aoki thinks of language through music and music as a language and so too does Reich. At the close of many of Aoki's pieces (like musical pieces) he uses the phrase "lingering notes." This phrase could be read in two ways: that which lingers are footnotes that leave an impression, or that which lingers are words that resonate like musical notes.

Alongside music, it is clear that Aoki loved poetry as many of his pieces are highly poetic. And he talks about the importance of poetry throughout his work. Aoki (2005) poetically says, "Earth, measure, temple, mouth, echoes, to speak/to say—these are the polyphonic strands of poetry" (p. 375). Aoki is a visionary as is Huebner. So ahead of their time—both of them. Poetry as a way to speak curriculum is a gift to younger scholars and to the field, to a field once considered moribund, as Joseph Schwab put it.

Both Aoki and Huebner brought vision and vitality to curriculum studies. Aoki opened "sonorous clearings" and Huebner "lured" us into the "transcendent," especially when it came to the arts and the importance of rethinking curriculum as a field more opened to artistic expression. To get at the artistic soul of curriculum, scholars must begin to think differently about doing educational theory. Curriculum studies scholars are indebted to Huebner and Aoki. Recall too that the doors were opened for Huebner and Aoki by their foremothers who also embraced the arts and their intersection to education. Think about our Progressive foremothers: Caroline Pratt, Margaret Naumburg, Jane Addams, and Anna Julia Cooper. Students of curriculum studies must not forget these women as they, too, opened clearings for the arts and education. There is an historical continuity in our field that is often forgotten or bifurcated by the ghettoization of women in the field and it would be prudent for our readers to remember our foremothers and forefathers.

History, Poststructuralism, and Lacanian Psychoanalysis

More so than Aoki, Huebner was very interested in historicity and the historical nature of our work. On the other hand, Aoki brings into the curriculum conversation poststructuralism and Lacanian psychoanalysis, two interests that diverge from Huebner. Although both Huebner and Aoki clearly studied the work of Martin Heidegger, only Aoki moves into the realm of what some would call "French Heideggerianism" or what is known as poststructuralism. Derrida, for example, is called a French Heideggerian. I argue in a piece on Heidegger that without Heidegger there would be no Derrida (2002). Derrida's work would not have been what it was without his study of Heidegger. At any rate, Aoki states the importance of many poststructural thinkers as he says "Foucault (1972), Derrida (1978), Lyotard (1984), and Deleuze and Guattari (1987) [have led to] new stirrings" (p. 184). Aoki recognizes the importance of poststructuralists for the field of curriculum studies. And of all of these thinkers it is Derrida who most resonates with Aoki's thinking.

Aoki (2005) draws on the work of Jacques Lacan—which Huebner does not do—to talk about the concepts of "verticality and horizontality" (p. 325). For Aoki, verticality and horizontality move "us to the metonymic space…the space between representational discourse and nonrepresentational discourse, into what Homi Bhabha, a postcolonial scholar, calls a 'third space of ambivalent construction'" (p. 325). The space in-between the vertical and horizontal is where curriculum work gets done for Aoki, and this is a sort of virtual, metaphorical space. This is the space of ambiguity, not of Tylerian or Cartesian certainty. For Pinar (2007) these terms—verticality and horizontality—take on a different meaning. He suggests that verticality is a study of the historicity of the field, especially as it gets re-presented through the "concrete and embodied" in "biographical studies and volumes of collected works" (p. xiv) while horizontality concerns "analyses of present circumstances" (p. xiv). So if students think Aoki and Pinar together one might say that curriculum studies explores spaces in-between the past and the present and between our biographic and collective lives.

Politics and Spirituality: Huebner and Aoki

The political is especially important to Huebner (1999). Interesting for Huebner, the political is intimately tied to the spiritual. In fact, in 1962 Huebner talks about issues of power by drawing on theologian Paul Tillich. And in 1961, in a discussion on elementary curriculum, Huebner talks much about the notion of responsibility and guilt. These two concepts are both political and spiritual. Moreover, Huebner's politico-spirituality, if you will, is Heideggerian. Huebner states,

> Responsibility comes not from a sense of burden but of a sense of guilt. Responsibility comes because we have become so curious about the world, so excited about our participation in it, so involved with those who share our space and time, that we wish to continue our existence, the existence of those who share it with us and indeed to continue the world itself. (p. 11)

Derrida also takes up the notion of responsibility throughout his work. Heidegger's student Emmanuel Levinas also talks about responsibility. Huebner brought this word—responsibility—into the curriculum conversation in 1961. Later on curriculum scholars like David Jardine—who is also a Heideggerian—and Peter Trifonas—who is Derridean—also make much of the notion of responsibility. Responsibility, Derrida often says, deserves response. And this response is both political and spiritual. Furthermore, the spiritual is—for Huebner—at once political (the work of the everyday) as well as transcendent (the "lure of the transcendent"). The transcendent, for Huebner, is squarely located in the concrete. Huebner—again drawing on Heidegger—argues in 1966 (when talking about the responsibilities of supervisors) that "the word 'responsibly' is used in the sense of being aware of one's obligations as an historical being.... To be responsibly responsive, then, is to be aware of the history and destiny of the given situation" (p. 120). The transcendent is, thus, historical. The "lure of the transcendent" is not the lure into some distant world above, but rather the transcendent—for Huebner—is always already grounded in history and our responsibility to think historically. This, too, was Heidegger's (1962) point: If being is time, then being must be thought of in all its historicity because time is history. Recently curriculum scholar Sharon Todd (2009) will take up Levinas's work—which I will examine later—to suggest that it is our responsibility to study the history of the negative, the history of tragedy. Levinas was a Holocaust survivor. This is why he was interested in grappling with the negative.

Unlike Todd, Huebner's (1999) work turns on wonder and awe (p. 1) as did Aristotle's. Philosophy, Aristotle said, begins in wonder. So too for Huebner. Curriculum theory begins in wonder. And this wonder and awe for Huebner are spiritual. He talks of mystery (p. 8). This too is a spiritual word. It is interesting that Huebner talks about the notion of "moreness." Huebner states,

> There is more than we know, can know, will ever know. It is a "moreness" that takes us by surprise when we are at the edge and end of our knowing. There is a comfort

in that "moreness" that takes over in our weakness, our ignorance, at our limits or end. (p. 403)

Derrida often talks about a remainder that is left over after thinking through things. There is always something left over, something "more," something else, some loose ends, a trace. But for Huebner, what is left over—this "moreness" as he calls it—is more of a spiritual notion than Derrida's remainders.

Like Huebner, Aoki's politico-spirituality is Heideggerian. Aoki (2005) tells us the "curriculum implementation is a political act" (p. 121). And when this implementation has instrumental purposes we have reached a "serious crisis" (p. 137). Aoki draws on the Frankfurt School political theorists to make a connection between philosophy and the problems of instrumentality in curriculum. Aoki states

> In our search flowing from our questioning, we have come to know some Continental European scholars who did not succumb to the persuasions of logical positivism expounded by members of the Vienna Circle as did North American scholars. Among these is Jürgen Habermas, a German scholar affiliated with the Frankfurt School. He, together with others such as Horkheimer, Marcuse and Adorno, announced what they saw as a serious crisis in the Western intellectual world so dominated by instrumental reason based on scientism and technology. (p.137)

Curriculum theorists and educational philosophers like Wendy Kohli, Peter McLaren, Henry Giroux, Michael Apple, and others are also influenced by the Frankfurt School, in one way or another. Aoki's concerns about politics differs from these other critical theorists because his is a more spiritual politic (what I call the "politico-spiritual"). Aoki and Huebner are both interested in the politico-spiritual.

Aoki (2005) writes about the importance of responding—like Huebner. Aoki says, "Pedagogic listening [is]…a responding to others" (p. 211). Aoki, unlike Huebner, makes much of the notion of listening, and later on Brent Davis (1996) will take up this theme in his book on mathematics and curriculum theorizing.

Aoki is also interested in the Heideggerian notions of indwelling (p. 159) and dwelling (p. 161). Later on, David Jardine too will take up these concepts throughout much of his work. Indwelling and dwelling are spiritual words as they suggest the contemplative.

Intellectual Retrospective: *The Journal of Curriculum Theorizing*

William Pinar (1999b) edited a collection of articles taken from the *The Journal of Curriculum Theorizing* (JCT) titled *Contemporary Curriculum Discourses: Twenty Years of JCT*. This is an important historical document. It is an intellectual retrospective of the curriculum field. Pinar comments that JCT is *"the* avant-garde journal, not only in North American curriculum studies, but perhaps in all of education" (p. xi). The book documents what Pinar considers to be representative of the most avant-garde work in the curriculum field from 1979 to 1996. What strikes me about the book is that the pieces reflect various segments of the field that would later become major configurations. These scholars, in other words, anticipated the major configurations of the field-to-come, as Derrida might say. The book includes twenty-nine articles from JCT. I cannot discuss all of them here, but rather, I would like to comment on only a few. The book explores curriculum as various text(s): historical, ecological, political, autobiographic, biographic, gendered, spiritual, psychoanalytic, literary, poststructural, and postcolonial. The book is an interesting study, then, in multiple configurations of the field. Many of these configurations were already in place during the 1970s; many of them—over the years—have grown significantly. Today psychoanalytic theory, ecological theory, and postcolonial theory—in the intersections of curriculum theory—have grown into major configurations of the field. (For more on these see Volume 2 of *Curriculum Studies Guidebook*.)

William Pinar says "the book [*Contemporary Curriculum Discourses*] is intended also to encourage beginning students to remake a field that—in our time—we helped to refashion" (p. xiii). The only way to remake a field is to study its history. I highlight a few pieces from *Contemporary Curriculum Discourses* here.

Jo Anne Pagano: The Historicality of the Structure of a Discipline

In an interesting piece titled "The Curriculum Field: Emergence of a Discipline," Jo Anne Pagano (1999) writes

> Typical of the period was the 1961 symposium held at Johns Hopkins that was addressed solely to the issue of the disciplinary status of education. The prevailing

> opinion among participants in the debate was that education was not, and logically could not be, a discipline, and that curriculum theory was, in principle, impossible. (p. 82)

Those of us who take for granted that there is a field called curriculum studies need to know that historically there has been much resistance to acknowledging this. Pagano notes that these kinds of attitudes existed in the 1960s. Well, perhaps these attitudes exist today as well. Like curriculum studies, women's studies programs—at least in the early 1970s—were also not respected and not thought to be legitimate fields of study. The connection here between women's studies and curriculum studies is an important one. Education—and so too curriculum studies—has always been seen as women's work, and misogyny has played a role in the disregard of our field. Some of our colleagues within colleges of education do not see what curriculum scholars do as legitimate because they are blinded by scientism. Many of them—mostly in departments of teaching and learning or educational psychology—think that what curriculum studies scholars do is not really "research." Research to them means statistics, numbers, empiricism, hard data. It is a tiring battle especially for younger scholars who are new to academe. Any avant-garde field within academe has to fight these kinds of battles. The academy is a place where knowledge is conserved. The new is always suspect. Curriculum studies, though, is a vibrant field and has survived the onslaught of conservative politics. Interestingly, there is much discussion today—as Pagano raised this question in 1981—around what constitutes a discipline. The question becomes more pronounced when scholars feel that their discipline is under attack. Pagano suggests

> What is needed here is a need to reconceptualize "discipline" in terms of sociointellectual communities. This means that in order to identify and characterize a disciplinary community, we must attend not only to subject matter, theoretical propositions, and research methodology, we must be equally attentive to social networks and boundaries that are constituted by scholars in the field. (p. 83)

This is the point of William Pinar's (2010) Canon Project. Although it seems that there is much resistance to this project, Pinar's concern is that the curriculum studies field remains "self-conscious of its historic" content (p. 530). The point is not to canonize some and exclude others—in the sense of the traditional canon—but to make sure that curriculum scholars understand the history of the various configurations of the field. The Canon Project is a way to map what Jo Anne Pagano talked about in the quotation above. She suggests that fields are made up of "sociointellectual communities" and "social networks" (p. 83). Pinar's Canon Project serves to historicize these sociointellectual communities and social networks. However, as Pinar (2010) points out, many are resistant to this project. Pinar states

> Partly to contradict the presentism that accompanies such splintering [in the field] at the 2007 annual meeting of the American Association for the Advancement of Curriculum Studies I advocated, and the General Membership accepted, a Canon Project, enabling us to structure a scholarly field self-conscious of its historic concerns. Given its hijacking by opponents at the 2008 meeting, the Canon Project appears blocked, at least for the moment. (p. 530)

The Canon Project is another way to archive our field. The hijacking of the Canon Project is, in part, because participants of the conference are reacting to the word "canon" as it suggests a body of knowledge that serves to exclude. But this is not what the Canon Project is about. The purpose is not to exclude but to remind us of our own history.

The American Association for the Advancement of Curriculum Studies is also something that students of curriculum should know about. Annual conferences are held in the United States. And there is a journal attached to the conference that is another important outlet for curriculum scholars, *The Journal of the American Association for the Advancement of Curriculum Studies*. Along with this conference, IAACS—the International Association for the Advancement of Curriculum Studies—has conferences all over the world. This organization is also of importance because it works to internationalize the field. These are examples of what Jo Anne Pagano calls "sociointellectual communities" (p. 83) that help us to, as Pinar (1999b) puts it, make and remake (p. xiii) our field.

Eco-Spirituality: David Smith, Florence Krall, and David Jardine

In Pinar's (1999b) *Contemporary Curriculum Discourses*, there are three scholars who do what I would call "eco-spirituality." David Smith, Florence Krall, and David Jardine all work toward attaining a more ecologically sustainable and spiritual world. There is something almost mystical about working in ecology and there is an ecological element in working through spirituality.

David Smith (1999) writes about collapsing the false dichotomy between self and Other. Smith states that scholars must work toward the "abandonment of Self and Other" (p. 465) in the spirit of Eastern mystic and theologian

Nagarjuna, who argued that everything is co-arising with everything else. The idea that everything is in everything (or co-arising) is a Buddhist notion of the inter-dependence of all things. Self and Other, for Nagarjuna, sets up a false dichotomy. Derrida (1976) notes in his work *Of Grammatology* that in dualisms like this (self and other) one term is always favored over another. Hence, for Smith—on a spiritual and ecological register—the self is one with the other and one with the world.

Florence Krall (1999) also collapses the self and Other as she says, "I am the bird, free and beautiful" (p. 1). She goes on to say, "I become: the canyon, the forest, the path winding up, crossing others, fading into the future" (p. 3). Krall says that people live "at the interface of two worlds with eyes to see both. Which am I?" (p. 2). An ecological consciousness is one that is able to merge two worlds into one: the cosmic consciousness of the universe. And in that cosmic consciousness, everything is in everything else.

Like Krall and Smith, David Jardine (1999) writes that human beings are part of the "vibrant and crawling interrelatedness and resonances of the earth… [people are] the intertwining kinship of things" (p. 264). And like Smith, Jardine draws on a Buddhist notion—mindfulness—to get at our "rootedness in earthy experiences…[which is] the belonging—together of things" (p. 264). Jardine is also a Heideggerian scholar and it is no accident that many Heideggerians become ecologists. There is much in Heidegger that is ecological.

Now, the poststructuralists, however, will find problematic the idea that self and other are one. Emmanuel Levinas and Jacques Derrida argue that there is radical alterity between people and that my "I" cannot be reduced to your "You." The I-Thou relation about which Martin Buber wrote is one of radical alterity. The poststructural position around alterity and the more eco-spiritual position on the collapse of self and other (or the interconnection of all things) are irreconcilable. What would a poststructural eco-spirituality look like? Well, that's for a later discussion. But for now, it is enough to point out that these three scholars (Smith, Krall, and Jardine) have shifted the curriculum conversation toward the eco-spiritual and have opened up worlds for others to do work in these areas. Ecology and spirituality have grown into large configurations in the field.

Henry Giroux, Shirley Steinberg, Joe Kincheloe, and Philip Wexler: The Sociopolitical

In *Contemporary Curriculum Discourses*, students are introduced to the scholarship of four curriculum scholars who work in the sociopolitical.

Shirley Steinberg and Philip Wexler, today, have taken a politico-spiritual turn as Steinberg emphasizes the idea of "radical love" (a phrase coined by Paulo Freire) and Wexler who has turned toward Jewish mysticism. But the pieces represented in Contemporary Curriculum Discourses reflect more of the sociopolitical. The late Joe Kincheloe was a political scholar and one of the few—besides Dewey—to try to make vocational education an intellectual enterprise. He also worked with Shirley Steinberg on the notion of postformal thought. Postformal thought is a critique of Piaget's work and its normalizing tendencies. Steinberg and Kincheloe worked to build the Paulo and Nita Freire Project for International Critical Pedagogy at McGill University before Kincheloe's untimely death.

Steinberg's (1999) piece in Contemporary Curriculum Discourses deals with gender issues and especially the way in which toys—namely Barbie dolls—script gender for children. Steinberg states: "It is no surprise that toys reinforce the feminization of the early childhood teacher…the new Teacher Barbie is an instructor of a preschool" (p. 478). There are power relations here—which Steinberg comments on—in the way in which Barbie gets scripted. Gender roles are tightly prescribed. A Barbie doll isn't just a Barbie doll. Barbie is symbolic: she disciplines and patrols gender boundaries. Barbie is political. Steinberg anticipated an entire configuration of the field—cultural studies in the intersection of curriculum theory—that has taken off since she wrote this piece.

Henry Giroux, like Shirley Steinberg, has recently taken a turn toward cultural studies and this turn was also anticipated in his earlier work on the sociopolitical. In Contemporary Curriculum Discourses, Giroux (1999) talks much about using the "dialectic" to try to think together the "social and the personal, history and private experience" (p. 11). Theodore Adorno—a member of the Frankfurt School to which many political scholars are indebted—made much of the notion of the dialectic as he warned against dogmatism and taking rigid stands on political issues. Adorno understood on a visceral level the problem of rigid thinking as he fled from the horrors of Nazi Germany. Hitler's ideology was all about rigidity and dogmatism. And, too, Robert Musil (1979), in his novel A Man Without Qualities, writes about the problems of rigid identity and its relation to the rise of nationalism. Musil anticipated the horrors of Nazi Germany. Rigid thinking leads to totalitarianism and fascism.

Thinking through dialectics avoids the problems of rigidity and dogmatism. How to think, as Giroux (1999) says, the "social and the personal" (p. 11) together? Giroux teaches that it is "dominant ideology" (p. 12) that blinds us. The only way to get a handle on ideology—Giroux teaches—is through the study of history. So on this point Giroux and Pinar are in agreement.

Like Giroux, Philip Wexler (1999) is interested in the sociopolitical as it gets instantiated in "social change movements" (p. 129). More recently, Wexler has turned toward Jewish mysticism.

For Wexler, one of the problems of culture is being blinded by capitalist ideology. Wexler states that "the most insightful intellectuals see prevailing social arrangements and patterns of culture as partial, deceptive, and socially oppressive" (p. 129). Like Giroux, Wexler argues that scholars must think in terms of a dialectic. Wexler looks to the Frankfurt School to help unpack what this might mean. Wexler puts it this way:

> Neither the critique of cultural knowledge as ideology, nor the idealization of a working-class culture, nor the simple assertion of emancipatory belief, can provide a theory of education for social change. A recognition of the dialectic of culture is required... . [understanding] a complex tension between materialist and idealist moments, the Frankfurt school, offers insight into this dialectic. (p. 135)

The dialectic—as a way of thinking—also includes changes in the self. Wexler talks about the importance of changes in "personal commitments" and "cultural mobilization" (p. 141). To change larger social structures, one must change the self as well. Individuals must change to make "social change movements" (p. 129) possible, Wexler tells us.

Auto/Biography: Shigeru Asanuma, Madeleine Grumet, and Janet Miller

In *Contemporary Curriculum Discourses* (Pinar, 1999b), three scholars of note (Shigeru Asanuma, Madeleine Grumet, and Janet Miller), work on autobiography and biography. These scholars suggest that both the self and the social need to be studied together. This is also the case with Giroux and Wexler. The self is never isolated from the social surroundings into which it is thrown. But it is here that the similarities between these three scholars end. Asanuma (1999) talks about doing autobiographical work through the concept of what he calls "seikatsu tsuzurikata" (p. 151). Asanuma explains that this term "was born out of political oppression in Japan before World War II" (p. 151). Asanuma explains

> More than half of the population in Japan lived in rural areas before the war and most of them suffered by being exploited by the land owners in the tenant farm system. The tsuzurikata teacher aimed at awakening social consciousness among students by having them write down essays reflecting on their social situation. (p. 155)

Asanuma compares tsuzurikata to currere. Autobiography, for both Asanuma and Pinar—who was the first scholar to use the word "currere" in the field of curriculum studies—means self-study in the context of the social. Pinar (1994) often uses the term "psycho-social" to explain what he is doing in his own work. Michael Littleford (1999)—also a notable scholar, who I will discuss in a moment—uses the phrase "cultural psychoanalysis" to suggest that working on the self is also working on culture and that culture and the self cannot be separated. Unlike Littleford and Pinar, however, Asanuma is not doing psychoanalysis. Tsuzurikata—a Japanese form of autobiography—is at once political and artistic (p. 154). Students are taught to engage in "artistic expression" (p. 154) of their political situation. The pairing of the political and the aesthetic has a history in curriculum studies. Think back to the Progressive women educators discussed earlier (Caroline Pratt, Jane Addams, Anna Julia Cooper, Margaret Naumburg). These women were all interested in both politics and the arts; Dwayne Huebner talks throughout his work of the importance of both the political and aesthetic; Ted Aoki also talks throughout his work of the importance of the political and aesthetic as well. One wouldn't think that these two things (the political and aesthetic) go hand in hand. Many artists—like the abstract expressionists—had little, if any, interest in politics. Conversely, political scholars—like the Marxists—are rarely interested in the arts.

At any rate, the concept of tsuzurikata, as explained by Asanuma, emerged around social stress. When a situation becomes unbearable, people need to think about who they are in order to find a way out of their terrible situation. Recall the writings of Xin Li and Ming Fang He. Both suffered through the Chinese Cultural Revolution and wrote through that oppression using narrative inquiry. Are people driven to write about the self when the very psychic structure of the self is threatened by external circumstances? Perhaps.

One of the first scholars in the field to take autobiography seriously as a way to theorize curriculum is Madeleine Grumet. Together she and William Pinar worked in the 1970s to reconceptualize the field. Grumet (1999) writes, in her eloquent piece titled "Autobiography and Reconceptualization," in *Contemporary Curriculum Discourses*, that "I organize my story as

I organize my world" (p. 27). Grumet, throughout this piece, talks much about the importance of the concrete and the importance of being embodied in the concrete. Grumet states, "The reconceived curriculum is reclaimed by what Merleau-Ponty calls the body-subject. It is the relation of the knower to the known (and to the unknown) that is manifested in the concrete images of lived worlds" (p. 27). Embodiment is not merely an abstraction, it is made concrete, Grumet tells us, by focusing on the "particular person" (p. 24) who is also part of a larger culture. The person—who is embodied—has a particular part to play in the larger culture—which is what Grumet suggests when she says that thinking through the self is also a way to "organize my world" (p. 27). The self is always already a social self. But too this self is embodied. Grumet suggests that scholars must consider the unconscious aspect of knowing to get at the (un)known. One can get at the (un)known through the study of psychoanalysis, which is exactly where her work turns in her 1988 book *Bitter Milk*.

Janet Miller (1999)—in *Contemporary Curriculum Discourses*—wrote a piece called "The Evolving Educational Consciousness." Miller—who was the managing editor of JCT for many years—talks about the importance of biography, and she draws on Maxine Greene's work throughout her piece. Recall, Janet Miller and William Ayers (1998) edited a book that features biographic portraits of Maxine Greene. It is important to note that the Ayers and Miller edited collection was published in 1998—some 18 years after Miller wrote her piece in the collection *Contemporary Curriculum Discourses* on what she called the "biographic vignette" (p. 35). Miller suggests that the biographic and the autobiographic interweave as she states: "Questions arise from my own biographic experience" (p. 31). So the biographic for Miller means self-study and the study of the Other. Miller wrote her dissertation on Maxine Greene and has been invested in her work for many years. Miller is also concerned with gender issues and states that "we must expose the bases of the predicaments of women, as Maxine Greene so eloquently reminds us" (p. 39). Gender in its intersection with curriculum theory has been a well-defined configuration of the field for many years, although it has gone through some major changes since the 1990s. Today, gender in its intersection with curriculum studies also includes queer theory and masculinity studies. The study of gender should include as many gender(s) as there are colors of the rainbow. Gender should be thought of in terms of the multiple. (I devote an entire chapter to gender issues in this volume.)

For Miller, then, the biographic situation is engendered. But not only this. She also remarks that the biographic situation also brings up "philosophical, psychological, and sociological considerations" (p. 36). The study of the self is also the study of culture.

Psychoanalysis and Depth Psychology: Michael Littleford and Mary Aswell Doll

Psychoanalysis is not monolithic. There are many psychoanalytic schools such as the Freudian, post-Freudian, Kleinian, and object-relations. Depth psychology refers to Jungian and post-Jungian theory. Michael Littleford (1999)—who draws on what she calls "cultural psychoanalysis"—and Mary Aswell Doll (1999)—who is a post-Jungian—both write interesting pieces in *Contemporary Curriculum Discourses* that foreshadow major configurations of the field-to-come (as Derrida would put it).

Michael Littleford writes about social action and democracy, which are not usually used in the context of psychoanalysis. What she tries to show in this piece is that psychoanalysis needs to be the study of the social and the political. However, most Freudian scholarship and post-Freudian scholarship deal with interpsychic and intrapsychic problems. Psychoanalysts rarely write about politics. Although Freud was interested in problems of the father and other male traumas (i.e., the Oedipus complex), he mostly focused on the inner workings of the psyche through dreams and the unconscious. Freud was also interested in the larger culture as he did study group mentality, especially as he witnessed Austrians embrace Hitler as the Germans marched into Austria.

Littleford argues that psychoanalysis needs to become a cultural theory. She blends social activism with psychoanalysis. Littleford states, "Self-reflection [should be]...a complement of responsible social action" (p. 116). A more political psychoanalysis is what Littleford calls for. Understanding the self through psychoanalysis means people must make the world better through action. But there is more to it than that. Littlefield makes the argument that the point of "social and political emancipation is the release of the creative imagination" (p. 18). In 1995, Maxine Greene will write a book titled *Releasing the Imagination*. But Greene is not interested in psychoanalysis but rather in the literary and the artistic. Littleford tells us that curriculum studies scholars might consider reading "Blake and Whitman, the philosophers of the imagination, and the most inclusive aspects of contemporary feminism" (p. 119).

One contemporary feminist who is also Jungian is Mary Aswell Doll. She wrote an important piece in *Contemporary Curriculum Discourses* titled "Beyond the Window: Dreams and Learning." Doll (1999) writes about the child in symbolic and even mythic terms as she says that she sees "the child as an archetype" (p. 106). Doll is post-Jungian. The term "archetype" suggests a collective pattern across time and culture. This is a very different way of talking about psyche than Freudian or object-relations theory. Students can trace Doll's intellectual interests back to this article as many of the key ideas like "myth, fairytale, the bible and literature" will later permeate all of her scholarly work, especially in her more recent book *Like Letters in Running Water: A Mythopoetics of Curriculum* (2000). The Jungian, the mythological, and the literary are three through lines that Doll has been working on throughout her academic career. Doll says that for Jung the "unconscious is a poetic not a scientific reality" (p. 107).

Doll states that "the archetypal child recurs through time to remind us of our poetic origins" (p. 109). Poetic origins are unearthed through the study of dreams. Doll uses the interesting idea of "dream window" (p. 111). The dream window, Doll says, "enables the dreamer to see a poetic image, another imagined reality of the self" (p. 111). The dream window is unlike a real window because the real window, Doll claims, is a "barrier to reflection in the psychological sense" (p. 111). The real window directs one's gaze outside the self. The dream window, contrarily, directs one's gaze inside the self. Doll argues that people need to get "beyond the window" and down into our interior selves. The point of education, then, is "to lead in" (p. 112), and to pull out, as in the Latin root *educare* (which means to pull or lead out). Dreams are a major theme in depth psychology. Students learn from Doll to go back beyond our "dream windows" so as to discover our identities.

Postcolonialism: Cameron McCarthy

Cameron McCarthy (1999) wrote "The Palace of the Peacock: Wilson Harris and the Curriculum in Troubled Times" in *Contemporary Curriculum Discourses*. McCarthy was one of the first scholars in curriculum studies to draw on postcolonial literature. Curriculum in its intersection with postcolonial theory has grown into a significant configuration of the field. McCarthy anticipated the importance of the postcolonial. McCarthy begins his piece by saying that students need to get "beyond the quaint particularisms of the Wild West and the Rest" (p. 365). By this he means that one should not think of the colonial as the Western world (who are the oppressors) and colonized third world countries (who are oppressed by the Western world). The postcolonial situation is much more complicated than this, McCarthy intimates. The center and the periphery, says McCarthy, are not so clear cut (p. 368).

McCarthy suggests studying the postcolonial through reading fiction. Drawing on the work of Edward Said, McCarthy suggests that students read third world and first world fiction side by side. McCarthy states

> We might read Joseph Conrad's *Heart of Darkness* by the light of Chinua Achebe's *Things Fall Apart*; Daniel Defoe's *Robinson Crusoe* through the eyes of J. M. Coetzee's *Foe* or Derek Walcott's *Pantomime*; Shakespeare's *Tempest* under the microscope of George Lamming's *The Pleasures of Exile*. (p. 375)

The issue that is raised here concerns the canon. Scholars should not simply toss out Western books and read only non-Western or third world authors. McCarthy argues that scholars need to study colonial literature alongside literature written by those who are colonized. McCarthy suggests that scholars study colonial literature with suspicion. Critique is called for when studying colonial works.

McCarthy comments that he has "reached a kind of exhaustion with a certain usage of the language of difference" (p. 366). Difference—as an abstraction—can serve to veil and cover over what it feels like to live under the shadow of Empire. Rather, by studying fiction—McCarthy argues—students can better understand the postcolonial. Mary Doll, Delese Wear, and Martha Whitaker (2006) study J. M. Coetzee's (1999) novel *Disgrace* in their book *Triple Takes* (as readers remember from our earlier discussion) to better understand the postcolonial. Fiction tells us much about history. What does history, in turn, teach us about fiction?

When thinking the postcolonial some scholars argue that the postcolonial is not exactly "post." Many countries today are still colonized. And colonized peoples who have been liberated from their oppressors still suffer psychologically from being colonized.

Intellectual Retrospective of the Purdue (2006) Conference

Erik Malewski (2010) edited the collected papers of the 2006 Purdue Conference in his collection *Curriculum Studies Handbook: The Next Moment*. Although the point of the conference was to write about the current state of the field, that current (next) moment is already in the past. I see his collection as an intellectual retrospective. Some of the participants' papers were not included in his volume because of the angry diatribe that occurred during a session that impacted the whole conference. This angry diatribe is commented upon in many of the papers that Malewski collected in this volume. William Pinar (2010) reports

> By the "logic" of identity politics, in which utterances are reduced to their identity politics subtexts, the fact that this event followed a speech by a lesbian and a response by a homosexual man (c'est moi) it was "obviously" a homophobic repudiation of sexual minorities disguised in racial drag. (Given that the other discussant was Jewish the event "must" be decoded as anti-Semitic as well.) There is no acknowledgment of Jews or lesbians (or women generally: we "must" add misogyny to the list of identity transgressions). (p. 531)

What ensued, then, was not exactly a scholarly discussion but a rant session. William Pinar comments here,

> At one point during the conference, acting as if the event were a demographic exercise, a Latina audience member complained that she was not represented. A senior African American scholar (herself on the program as a discussant) followed suit, complaining that in racial terms curriculum studies had not changed in 30 years, a fantastical claim given the centrality of race and antiracism obviously occupy in the field.... What the event generated was the excess of contemporary identity politics: self-indulgent indignation substituting for scholarship. (p. 529)

Others in Malewski's collection comment on this event. Jennifer Gilbert (2010) remarks that "conflicts over theoretical and political commitments erupted" (p. 63). Patti Lather (2010) called what happened a "breakdown" (p. 74). Lather thought that the breakdown was due to a sort of Bergamo "in group/outgroup" mentality. Janet Miller (2010) felt "worried with/in tensions" again of the Bergamo in and out groups. Madeleine Grumet (2010) referred to "the provocation" at the conference. Like Janet Miller, Madeleine Grumet says that "it is the next step that I worry about" (p. 408).

Intellectual Retrospective of Curriculum Visions

William Doll and Noel Gough (2002) co-edited a book titled *Curriculum Visions*. This book—like Erik Malewksi's (2010) *Next Moment* collection—is about where the field is moving in the future. But as I read it, ironically, many of the scholars in the book talk about understanding the past and understanding history. The *vision* and lesson of the book are that if scholars are going to talk about where the field is going, studying the past matters. The book is a kind of paradox. To have vision you must look back. Noel Gough begins the collection by stating

> If curriculum visions are to be generative—that is, if we are to be in a position to negotiate visions of curriculum futures worth working for—we must accept that we stand at the center of our own histories. (p. 5)

What would the center of our history be? I leave this as an open question.

Here, I share with you—from *Curriculum Visions*—three pieces in the book.

1. William Doll Jr.: "Ghosts and the Curriculum"
2. William F. Pinar: "Robert Musil and the Crisis of European Culture in America"
3. Deborah Britzman: "The Death of Curriculum?"

William Doll Jr.: "Ghosts in the Curriculum"

William Doll's (2002) "Ghosts and the Curriculum" is an important piece, especially for students who are interested in the history of issues of control (p. 28) and method (p. 30) in curriculum studies. Doll states that students must "dig deeply into the history and concept of curriculum as a word and idea" (p. 24). The ghosts of control (p. 28) and method (p. 30) go far back behind industrialization, Doll tells us. Doll teaches that ghostly words—that haunt our curriculum even today—can be traced back to the 1500s with Peter Ramus, "the man who spent virtually all his adult life 'methodizing' knowledge" (p. 30). Why Ramus? Why now? Well, students must know that the word "curriculum," as Doll points out, first appeared in one of Ramus's books titled *Professio Regia*. The curriculum was a "sequential course of study" (p. 31). Sequence means order. And this order, Doll says, was "designed to bring an 'orderliness' to teaching" (p. 31). Interestingly enough, Doll points out that the book *Professio Regia* took off in Calvinist areas in Europe. Calvinists love orderliness and the "control Calvin felt all Christians should bring to their lives" (p. 31). Doll brilliantly ties Calvin and Ramus to one of the major problems of teacher education: methods courses. Doll says that methods courses serve to control and "yield efficient 'short-cuts' to the way knowledge is structured and acquired" (p. 33). The "blessed rage for order" (Tracy, 1996) can be traced back to the 1500s.

The common schools in the United States had an underlying agenda: Protestantism (the "ghost" as Doll puts it of Calvin). And the common schools' other underlying agenda has been to—as Foucault (1979) would put it—discipline and punish. Schools are holding cells for children. Doll argues, then, that ghosts haunt schooling. Doll suggests that educationists must think about the uses and abuses of control. Doll suggests that students study chaos and complexity theory. Scholars can invent a vision of the future for curriculum through chaos. Chaos is a far cry from control. William Doll has been working in chaos and complexity science for some time now and has contributed much to the field by way of this work.

William F. Pinar: "Robert Musil and the Crisis of European Culture in America"

Like William Doll's piece in *Curriculum Visions*, William F. Pinar's piece looks to the past to help us understand our present predicament. Pinar (2002) points out that there are parallels between our current educational nightmare, as he calls it elsewhere, and the nightmare that was Vienna at the fin de siècle. Schools in Vienna were just as oppressive as they are in America. Pinar points out

> Then as now the educational system [in Vienna had a]...curriculum unrelated to lived experience. Schooling produced constant weariness and boredom in the youth of Vienna. To escape this formalized, institutionalized world where "business was business," many students went to coffeehouses, the same ones frequented by artists and bohemians. They found a vital and spontaneous self-expression absent in their classrooms. (p. 103)

The coffeehouse culture in Vienna is very much alive today. People come into coffeehouses and stay for hours on end reading, studying, talking, smoking. Racks abound with international papers that you can peruse; or you can choose to sit and sip quietly. America doesn't have this kind of culture, at least not in most cities where Starbucks has corporatized the coffeehouse.

Education happens in coffeehouses, indeed. Poets write. Artists draw. Intellectuals study. There is something almost magical about a coffeehouse. A Viennese intellectual who did not frequent coffeehouses was Freud (Morris, 2006). Was it the clatter of dishes, or the interruptions that bothered him? Perhaps Freud did not frequent Viennese coffeehouses because of anti-Semitism. Jews were not exactly welcomed in public places in Vienna. Freud also did not like to hear people practicing the piano and had little use for music (Gay, 1998). So if music was playing in a coffeehouse or on the street outside of a coffeehouse, he probably felt annoyed.

William Pinar (2002) writes about a well-known European intellectual, Robert Musil. For Musil "literary art" expressed "the inner life of the felt word" (p. 105), says Pinar. Musil was a great novelist. And he used words, Pinar suggests, to explore both his own biographic situation as well as his place in history. Pinar tells us that "Musil emphasized the contextual—biographic—significance of these 'living thoughts'" (p. 106). In Musil's (1979) novel *The Man Without Qualities*, readers learn about the dangers of dogmatic thinking and nationalism; readers learn about the dangers of having a firm identity; readers learn about the problems of rigid identities, superiority, nationalism and fascism. Musil intuited what was to come later on in history (recall that I touched on Musil earlier). Surefootedness marched right into the heart of Vienna and this was called the Anschluss. Hitler's armies marched right in as their native son—Hitler—was welcomed home with open arms (Gay, 1998).

Pinar (2002) comments that "Musil chose what he viewed as the indirectness of literary art, an art which seemed to him to resemble, in its narrative structure, the indirectness, the mystery, of life itself" (p. 105). Studying Musil is studying history. Pinar is impressed with Musil's love of words and artistic sensibilities. Maxine Greene (1995) has always drawn on literature to inform education. And it is through literature that students learn about educational questions and as Pinar says even questions of "the mystery of life itself" (p. 105). Throughout his career, Pinar has been drawn to novelists like Virginia Woolf, painters like Jackson Pollock, filmmakers like Pier Paolo Passolini. Art teaches much about history.

Deborah Britzman: The Death of Curriculum?

Deborah Britzman's (2002) piece in *Curriculum Visions* is curiously called "The Death of Curriculum?" This is a rather puzzling title. But that is Britzman's intent: to disturb and puzzle. She disturbs our thought in order to get us to think otherwise. This is her brilliance indeed. Like William Doll she talks about ghosts and the curriculum. But Britzman's ghosts are not Doll's ghosts. Britzman explains that there are "other ghosts who haunt the curriculum, not so much by their presence, but by their absence...[the] forgotten figures like Melanie Klein, Robert Musil, Wilfred Bion, and, of course, Sigmund Freud" (p. 93). You will notice that one of Britzman's ghosts is Robert Musil. For

Pinar (2002), too, Musil is an important historical figure. Britzman suggests that upon studying these historical figures

> They noticed something that the moribund curriculum foreclosed, namely, the problem of what it is to work through woeful disregard and be called to notice something about the dignity of vulnerability in the confusion of our times. While none of them asked the question—Why curriculum?—they did notice something difficult about knowledge and thinking that will be put to use. (p. 93)

For Britzman, knowledge is not something one has but something that one loses, or something that gets lost. It is loss that interests her more than anything here. She says, "Can we imagine the lost curriculum? How does one come to mourn the losses that go under the name curriculum?" (p. 92). What curriculum scholars lose are the memories of these forgotten ones like Musil and Klein. The point here is not that scholars must all draw on Musil and Klein, no. But perhaps scholars could look more to historical figures to better understand our own situatedness and, as Britzman puts it, the "confusion of our times" (p. 93). Studying the past is as important—if not more so—than studying contemporaries. Who do scholars forget when talking about curriculum? And what do scholars lose—Britzman wants to know—when our ancestors are forgotten? How to know the past? The elusive work of history remains a mystery. Historians have their methods—but William Doll warns us about the way in which methods—to use Britzman's phrase here—"foreclose" the curriculum (p. 93). Curriculum historiography—unlike traditional educational history—is not bound by method. As inheritors of the Progressive project, curriculum scholars who work on the past do so in experimental ways not bound by rigid academic rules. Working on the past can be the work of the avant-garde if that work pushes the boundaries of knowledge. Opening up one portal of history always closes another. But study history we must. Britzman comments, "Monday's curriculum cannot decide the confusion of our times" (p. 96). Monday is a symbol of the future, or perhaps a near present. Thinking in the near present or even only in the future will never lead us out (*educare*). Scholars are only led out through the understanding that studying our own past opens and closes at once our thoughts. The path not chosen is the path that is lost. Britzman anticipated long ago the kind of curriculum history that was—as Derrida would put it—to come. The historical study of trauma is inherently about the study of loss and recently many curriculum scholars have turned toward the study of historical trauma and the loss that goes hand in hand with such trauma. Before 1996, not too much was written in curriculum around loss and trauma. But in the last, say, ten years more scholars are working on this aspect of curriculum history.

Historical Retrospective: Turning Points

The second edition of *Turning Points in Curriculum: A Contemporary American Memoir*, co-written by J. Dan Marshall, James T. Sears, Louise Anderson Allen, Patrick A. Roberts, and William H. Schubert (2007) is a monumental work of curriculum historiography. This book is highly unusual in that it offers to us a variety of source material that complicates what it is that historiography can be. The book is couched in the larger sociocultural and sociopolitical landscape of world history. Curriculum books are explored in detail since WWII. Cultural history is explored. Personal memories of curriculum "workers" are explored. The authors write: "We favor the term curriculum *work* over curriculum *studies, theory,* or *development.* To us, the broader notion of *work* allows for variations that include reflection, study, theorizing, construction, inquiry, and deliberation" (p. v). Interspersed among world history, cultural history, and personal memoirs are primary source documents that serve as turning points in the field. Alongside curriculum books, readers encounter such topics as IBM, the Roman Catholic Church, homophile and gay liberation movements, tennis, NASA, popular music, and big tobacco. Alongside these, readers encounter everything from theater, to TV, from film to scientific developments, from baseball to Barbie dolls, from fiction to crack cocaine, from AIDS to musicals. The book is highly complex in format as well as in content. Along the way students meet such curriculum workers such as Arthur Wellesley-Foshay, Louise Berman, Louis J. Rubin, Michael Apple, Janet Miller, Alex Molnar, Henry Giroux, Tom Barone, Mary-Ellen Jacobs, Susan Edgerton, Peter Hlebowitsh, Petra Munro, and Bill Watkins.

Early on in the book the writers point out who has been left out of curriculum history. They state

> Reflecting on the first 50 years of curriculum work finds racial, intellectual, gendered, and other voices largely invisible—a term used perceptively by the African-American scholar W. E. B. Du Bois (1903). Du Bois wrote on a host of curricular topics…yet his work is rarely cited in curriculum literature. Other African-American voices (Carter G. Woodson [1933] Benjamin Mays, Horace Mann Bond [see Urban, 1992], and Allison Davis [1929] are missing too. (p. 13)

Since the 1970s curriculum theorists have been working hard to incorporate these missing voices. At any rate, *Turning Points* is an excellent historiography that captures competing voices and competing memories of the field of curriculum since WWII.

Auto/Biography: Portrayals of Practice

William Ayers

William Ayers (2010) has written a remarkable autobiographic portrait of his journey as a teacher in *To Teach: The Journey of a Teacher*. This book is in its third edition and is certainly an inspiring and uplifting portrayal of teaching. Interestingly enough, Ayers claims "greatness in teaching, too, requires a serious encounter with autobiography" (p. 137). Ayers intimates that the most important thing about being a teacher is knowing who you are. He suggests throughout the book that teachers are not technicians and teaching is not about how-tos. For Ayers teaching is a "moral act" and an "intellectual challenge" (p. 45). He talks much about the ethicality of teaching and the responsibility teachers have toward their students. And he says of students that they teach us as well. Ayers comments, "Teachers must understand that even as they teach, they will be taught" (p. 90). Teaching should never be an authoritarian act whereby teachers dictate to students and students passively take in the lessons of the day. For Ayers "teaching is relational and interactive. It requires dialogue, give-and-take, back-and-forth. It is multidimensional" (p. 29). Ayers suggests that teachers must get to know students and try to understand where they are coming from. Teachers must try to understand students' backgrounds. In essence, teachers must learn the cultures of their students. Ayers explains:

> Culture is an important window into a child, an essential part of any bridge's blueprint, and effective teachers must learn to be lifelong students of culture.... Their workshop is the students themselves, their families and neighborhoods, and ever wider circles embracing larger and larger communities. (p. 88)

In order to study culture, one must also study history. This is why auto/biography is an inherently historical act. To understand culture(s) of students one must study the history of those cultures. It is not enough to reach out to students; teachers must study what is important to students as well. For Ayers, teaching begins with student interests. Ayers asks, "What knowledge and experiences are most worthwhile" (p. 34)? Teachers can only know this if they study the culture of the child, Ayers intimates. When teaching children, Ayers suggests, there is a certain "urgency" (p. 2) at hand. And for Ayers teaching is not simply about knowledge—although of course learning subject matter is of the utmost importance—teaching is about relationship, "love and hope" (p. xi). It is not enough to teach classes but teachers must both love their subject matter and love the children they are teaching. But the act of teaching is not an easy one, especially in light of state-mandated scripted curricula and standardized testing. Ayers speaks to these problems: "Our foundational belief in the value of every human life is contradicted by many kinds of contemporary efforts that are sold as 'reform'—closing schools, privatizing the public space, testing children relentlessly" (p. 9). Ayers argues that teachers must "work" these "contradictions" in order to have a "more hopeful teaching life" (p. 10). Sorting out the contradictions is what makes teaching a difficult challenge. But Ayers remains upbeat. At the end of the day, Ayers maintains that teaching is a noble profession, no matter what problems teachers encounter. One must understand the self, Ayers tells us, in order to understand the task of teaching. And in order to understand the self teachers must delve into their own histories to figure out who they are.

Gregory Michie

Gregory Michie (2009) has written a remarkable book titled *Holler if You Hear Me: The Education of a Teacher and His Students*. Michie states: "I wrote this book as a memoir of my teaching" (p. 199). But there is more. Readers learn in this book about the struggles of a white male teacher teaching Mexican American children on the south side of Chicago. In the beginning of the book Michie admits that he knows little about Mexican American culture or history. But as the book moves along he feels compelled to study this culture seriously in order to be better able to teach. Michie states

> I also had to commit myself to learning more about the historical, political, and economic developments—both in Mexico and in the U.S.—that had brought them to where they were, and the current issues that continued to affect them. I couldn't teach kids to honor and respect their rich legacy as Mexicans and as working people, if I only did so in vague terms myself. (p. 93)

Michie points out that in order to teach these children successfully he had to understand their culture historically. It is not enough to be able to relate to students, but one must dig deeper and try to understand their culture as well. Unfortunately, Michie points out, the history books from which the children studied in school did not in any way reflect their own culture. In fact, when Mexicans were discussed in their history texts they were often seen as "villains or victims" (pp. 80–81). One wonders what this does to a student's sense of self. Certainly, it must make Mexican students feel badly about themselves. Michie speaks to issues of cultural identity as he states that the Mexican American children "could feel the Mexican part of themselves slipping away" at school (p. 82). But Michie was determined not to allow this to happen as he found ways to relate to these children and foster their sense of identity. One of the most remarkable events in his classroom was teaching Sandra Cisneros's 1984 book *The House on Mango Street*. Michie thought that his students would be more involved in the reading of the book if they were to make an audio tape of the book and read it out loud. So he took them to a recording studio to do just that. The children loved this assignment and were so enthralled at the chance to record their voices that they wrote a letter to Cisneros telling her about their school project and how much they identified with her book. Cisneros actually came to their school to give a talk on her writings and the children were awed by her. Michie states, "The vignettes in *The House on Mango Street* never failed to conjure up memories from the girls' own lives, and we spent as much time sharing those as we did reading the book" (p. 64). Michie states that if children do not see themselves "reflected in the curriculum" they will not be engaged in their learning (p. 198). And if children are not reflected in their curriculum they feel that they do not count. Their identities are erased. But if teachers bring to the class materials that do reflect the students' culture, children might be more engaged in their learning—as was the case here. It is interesting to note that upon reading Cisneros's book, these children began thinking about their own lives and their own histories. Michie honored these children's memories and talked about them in his classroom. Michie also got involved in teaching media studies and engaged in another innovative teaching strategy as he had Mexican American children make a video describing the problems of gangs. Michie states,

> Perhaps the most powerful statements my students have made on gangs have come in the form of dramatic video productions, which often grow out of open-ended scripting assignments, such as "a scene on a street corner" or "a conversation among family members." (p. 148)

Michie related better to his students by having the students make their own video and deal with the issue of gangs through the use of video. This brought the classroom to life and allowed the students to explore their own identities and the problems they face daily. Like Ayers (2010) Michie says that teaching is "a reciprocal endeavor: You guide and are guided, show and are shown, speak and listen, receive as much as you give" (p. 200). Both Ayers and Michie bring democracy into the classroom; they bring life into their classrooms.

Chris Liska Carger

In a book titled *Dreams Deferred: Dropping Out and Struggling Forward*, Chris Liska Carger (2009) tells the tragic story of a Mexican American boy who drops out of high school in his sophomore year. This book is unlike Michie's (2009) uplifting tale of mentoring Mexican Americans and successfully teaching them about their identity formations. Carger's book is a tragic tale of a boy who drops out, not so much because of his own failings—Carger intimates—but because of a larger systemic failing of our educational system. Carger states

> I wrote to try to find closure, to make sense of the educational failures I witnessed. Not Alejandro's failure so much as the failures of educators with Alejandro and the sea of Alejandros, whose stories wallow in the schools of the cities and towns of our nation. (p. 5)

Carger's "partial biography" (p. 4) of a Mexican American youth dropping out of school is a tragedy. Even though Carger says she wanted to find closure after writing this ethnography, she did not. Carger struggled as a sort of mentor figure to Alejandro as she tutored him when he was in elementary school. She followed his story throughout his high school years and beyond and wrote this heartfelt ethnography that does not have a happy ending. Alejandro moves from low-paying job to low-paying job, has very poor literacy skills, and can barely fill out job applications. Carger tries to get Alejandro back into an academic setting but to no avail. Alejandro wants to work and make money to support an infant he had when he was just sixteen years old. He marries and divorces his wife, develops a drinking problem, and struggles to make ends meet throughout his young adult years. Carger interviews not only Alejandro but all the members of his family over the course of at least ten years. Carger is not afraid to be intimate with this family and to write about her long-lasting bonds she formed from doing this ethnography. It is truly a heart-wrenching tale. Carger in no way blames the victim in this story. Clearly, from Carger's perspective the school system is to blame for Alejandro's dropping out. Carger explains

> Alejandro's dropping out was not a response to a particular crisis situation; it was not linked to a sudden change in personality due to, for example, drug use. Slowly, after years of frustrating school experiences that were disconnected to his home life, Alejandro eventually "shut down" and gradually closed the door on education himself. (p. 138)

Not only was school "frustrating" for Alejandro, "no one at Alejandro's school seemed to notice his crisis" (p. 11). Alejandro fell through the cracks as do so many other Mexican American children. In fact, Carger points out, "It is estimated that close to 50% of Latino families experience their male children dropping out of school, establishing this ethnic subgroup as having the highest dropout rate in America" (p. 3). Wretched school buildings, irrelevant curriculum, and uncaring teachers—according to Carger—all play a role in these staggering statistics.

Carger tells us that if one child in a family drops out, the likelihood that siblings will drop out is high. But this was not the case for Alejandro's siblings. In fact, his dropping out had the opposite effect on his siblings. They went on to be successful in school because they did not want to be like their brother. Part of this, too, had to do with the humiliation Alejandro's parents felt at his dropping out. Carger states that Alma, Alejandro's mother, and "her husband truly saw Alejandro's dropping out as a humiliation for their family" (p. 10). The other children in the family did not want to add to this humiliation. They continued on successfully in school. Carger, the ethnographer, voices strong emotions while writing up her findings. She states, "There are times I find myself wanting to pull Alejandro out of the mudslide of a meaningless education, a social disaster, that has left him as an unskilled laborer with low literacy and few employment prospects" (p. 7). This book is a moving and heartbreaking account of a Mexican American dropout who has nowhere to go with his life and yet he still struggles to find better work for himself.

Brian Schultz

Brian Schultz (2008) tells the uplifting tale of children attending Carr Academy while living in the Cabrini Green Housing Projects in Chicago in his book *Spectacular Things Happen Along the Way: Lessons from an Urban Classroom*. This is a courageous story of children in the fifth grade fighting to get a new school built because the one they attend is in wretched shape. Brian Schultz engages in what he calls social justice curriculum where he allowed the students to build their own curriculum around the problems of the school. Schultz explains

> Teachers teaching for social justice maintain a curricular stance rooted in and relevant to the lives of students. With a focus on critical, multicultural, antiracist, and antioppressive perspectives teachers focus on meaningful hands-on, experiential, and participatory activities. (p. 127)

As a white teacher teaching all African American students, Schultz had to negotiate issues of privilege and power. He turned the classroom upside down as students took the lead and built their curriculum around getting a new school and getting the word out about the horrible conditions of Carr Academy.

Schultz tells us that it was Joseph Schwab who influenced his pedagogy the most. Schultz says, "Schwab contended that for deliberative processes between all stakeholders to be meaningful and worthwhile, a practical approach to curriculum is necessary to meet the situational needs of students" (p. 21). Students deliberated over their situation and took it upon themselves to write letters, build a website, make a DVD and a video about the conditions in which they were being schooled. The students understood that they had to know the history of their school and so they studied this history. Schultz explains: "The class agreed that the first step included researching the history of Carr Community Academy and investigating the potential for getting a new school built" (p. 42). Schultz's pedagogical practices were influenced by Project Citizen, which builds curricula on democratic principles "encouraging teachers and students to engage in citizen action and public policy change" (p. 9). This is the story of a teacher who really cared about his students and allowed his students to work out life problems in the classroom rather than follow state-mandated scripted curricula. This story is a courageous one in that Schultz took a risk by not teaching to the test and not following scripted curricula.

The students were highly engaged in their learning about the school's history. They essentially drove the curriculum. This takes a lot of courage on the part of the teacher to give over the control of the class to students. In the process, disciplinary boundaries were broken open. Schultz explains: "The students' action plan became the epicenter of the entire curriculum for the remainder of the school year. Every subject lost its compartmentalization, becoming integrated and integral in solving the problem" (p. 7). The students were highly successful in understanding their problem and even getting the attention of many politicians and the media. Eric Zorn of the *Chicago Tribune* wrote a story about the children; State Representative Willie Delgado visited the children; the U.S. Department of Education responded to them; ABC and NBC interviewed the children, and NPR did a special on the children on *This American Life*. Ralph Nader visited the children and wrote an article about the situation that got international attention. The attention the children received is astounding. What they didn't get, however, was their new school. Carr Academy was eventually closed and the kids were transferred to another school. Schultz comments that the children were well aware that discrimination played a part in their plight. Schultz states, "Questions about racial discrimination were on students' minds, and the space provided allowed Room 405 to get closer to answering them" (p. 38). This story is both uplifting and tragic. The students fought for their rights and for the right to learn in a decent environment. The world was listening to them but still they were powerless against the forces of the Chicago Public School system. That they didn't get their new school is shocking given all the national attention this story got.

Ming Fang He and JoAnn Phillion

Ming Fang He and JoAnn Phillion (2008) co-edited an important book titled *Personal~Passionate~Participatory Inquiry into Social Justice Education*. These co-editors explain

> This book draws together work which demonstrates three distinct and interconnected qualities: *personal~passionate~participatory*. Each is personal, compelled by values and experiences researchers bring to the work. Each is passionate, grounded in a commitment to social justice....Each is participatory, built on long term, heart-felt engagement, and shared efforts. (pp. 1–2)

This is a profoundly inspiring book written by scholars who discuss their oppressions and ways in which they work to get beyond their oppressions. Their writing is indeed personal and passionate; these educators all fight for social justice in the process. Personal stories allow these researchers to understand themselves, to understand oppression and to write through that oppression. This collection includes the writings of African American women, Native American women, white working-class women, immigrant women. This book deals with issues such as teenage pregnancy, sweat shops, disability, and suicide.

Some of the stories we read about are these: Sonya Jefferson (2008) explores stories of generational memories of racial discrimination, especially in educational settings; Advis Dell Wilkerson (2008) explores racism and sexism being a teenage "mom" (p. 34); Wynnetta Scott-Simmons (2008) explores oral history and jump rope as a tool of resistance (p. 72) to racism; Angela Haynes (2008) explores white working-class life, women's oppression, and the problems of poverty. Co-editors Ming Fang He and JoAnn Phillion comment

> Personal~passionate~participatory inquiry draws on an array of research traditions: action research, teacher research, self study, life history, teacher lore, participatory inquiry, narrative inquiry, and cross-cultural and multicultural narrative inquiry. Many of these traditions can be traced back to practitioner research. (p. 12)

These writers are not merely victims, they are fighters. One of the most interesting tools of resistance is jump rope, as Wynnetta Scott-Simmons explains. She states

> The Hambone chant symbolizes that heritage [the African American heritage], the lessons, and the triumph. The Hambone is a story of community, connection, resistance, and survival. It is a jump rope rhyme that speaks of possibility, of dreams, of hopes. (p. 72)

There is nothing insignificant about jumping rope. One might think that it is just child's play, but children know things and know how to fight back against racism and oppression. Jumping rope can be a political act. Children are not merely victims, they are fighters too.

Curriculum as Historical Trauma: Witnessing

A major shift in curriculum history within the last ten years has been the turn toward the history of trauma. Curriculum theorists have shifted their focus, especially since 9/11. Catastrophes such as 9/11 raise questions about the purposes of historiography, memory, and testimony. While traditional educational history continues to be narrowly focused on the school, curriculum historiography has moved in another direction. The field of curriculum historiography as it relates to trauma is becoming increasingly broader, more sociopolitical and sociopsychoanalytic. Questions around the schoolhouse are of importance of course. But historical trauma is a pedagogy of catastrophe. This pedagogy of catastrophe opens up what it is that scholars must talk about in education. We can no longer talk about school or education without taking into consideration the larger backdrop of the catastrophic times in which we live.

James Watson (2002) comments on the problematics of studying philosophy against atrocities such as Auschwitz. Watson explains:

> If, on the other hand, the practice of teaching continues with the customary assumptions of the Western philosophical tradition [and I would add to this the tradition of curriculum history] and acts as if nothing has happened to problematize these assumptions, the Auschwitz legacy will claim another victory. (p. 105)

The study of the school must be contextualized against the larger historical scene. Children who come to school have parents and grandparents who might be survivors of the Holocaust. How are teachers to understand our pupils if they haven't a clue about their backgrounds? What does school mean to a child whose parents suffer from the haunting of their own memories? What does school matter to a child whose parents or grandparents suffer and psychologically project that suffering onto their children? Transgenerational trauma is a real and current danger (Morris, 2001). If scholars continue to talk about educational history or curriculum history as the study of the school in and of itself without also taking into account the horrors that have transpired not only in the 21st century—but also in the 19th and 20th centuries—ignorance prevails. Our traumas are historical and what our grandparents suffered gets passed down through generations via psychological transference (Morris). It is important to explain that one of the problems of studying catastrophes is the tendency to compare one to the other and lump them together as if they are all the same. When a Holocaust survivor talks about her experiences, others might be reminded of their own ancestral traumas like slavery, or the Armenian massacre, Columbine, Vietnam, or the Iraq war. Making comparisons is natural enough, but highly problematic. I explain that "the Holocaust was not merely a humanitarian tragedy, it was rather a specifically Jewish one. It was not a tragedy like other tragedies" (2001, p. 120). In Holocaust studies, the issue of comparability is highly problematic. Neoconservatives like to compare the Holocaust to some other tragedy so as to erase and unwrite history, to sort of level the playing field. Each catastrophe has its unique history. Slavery has its unique history in the United States and should not be compared to the Holocaust. But again, the natural tendency is to compare. All historical traumas are not the same, and it is very important to keep this in mind especially when reading texts that discuss many different tragedies (e.g., see Simon, Rosenberg & Eppert, 2000). It is important not to collapse one tragedy onto another one. On a concrete level, historical traumas are different and this difference must be kept intact. Alterity—as a radical form of difference—must be thought through when talking about the horrors of our time. Each particular horror has a particular history. This particularity is important to keep in mind when studying curriculum as historical trauma.

Trauma: History, Memory and Testimony

Thinking about curriculum against a larger sociohistorical lens means rethinking the purposes of doing historiography in the first place. What is the point of studying the history of curriculum? What does it mean to study curriculum history under the shadow of the object of trauma? In his monumental and groundbreaking book *The Gender of Racial Politics and Violence in America*, William Pinar (2001) states: "In one sense, this book is a project of 'historical witness,' a project that intersects with a more general preoccupation in the West with the remembrance of traumatic historical events" (p. 5). The key term in Pinar's passage is the concept "witness." To be a witness to history means to seriously study history. Pinar suggests that if an antiracist pedagogy is only about changing attitudes and beliefs, the eradication of racism is a lost cause. Racism is much deeper than attitudes. Racism is a historical problem. Pinar tells us

> What is melancholic for me...is to live among and teach white people who remember nothing, who perceive "racism" as merely attitudinal, and as common among black folks as among white, and, most surprisingly, having nothing to do with them. (p. 5)

Racism, as Pinar teaches, must be taught historically, otherwise scholars continue to perpetuate the status quo. Pinar's text is a study of the history of lynching and prison rape. These are two subjects that are difficult to think through and perhaps considered anathema to many school people. Issues of both race and gender, as Pinar teaches, are of importance when studying the history of lynching and prison rape.

Not all witnesses to lynchings were merely passive observers. Some, like Ida B. Wells, were actively engaged in the eradication of lynching (Pinar, 2001). Witnesses also have agency. Lynching has a particular history in the United States and more to the point, in the South, although there were some lynchings in the North. Roger Simon (2005) says that we must "bear witness to specific histories of violence" (p. 4). The key word here is "specific." The tragedy of the American South is a unique one and must be studied as such. For students who are interested in studying racism and the South, Pinar's (2001) book is a good place to begin. The book is incredibly detailed and the details disturb. Most American schoolchildren have never heard of lynching or if they have they do not know what it means. In the South lynching is one of those taboo topics not talked about or it is glossed over. Studying Pinar's book teaches that histories of horror demand attention. There is no glossing over in Pinar's book. His is a serious historical study of the terrible things that have gone on, especially in the American South—and to some extent in the North as well. So when scholars study issues around racism, they need to also include studying the history of lynching.

Traumatic history raises other significant questions. For what purposes do we study history? Roger Simon, Sharon Rosenberg, and Claudia Eppert (2000) suggest that historical trauma can bring about "reparation and reconciliation" (p. 3). So the purpose of doing traumatic historiography is to repair (reparation) and bring people together (reconciliation). Is it possible to repair the psychological damage of being a Holocaust survivor? Is it possible to reconcile with Germans who were complicit in the Holocaust? Is reconciliation a possibility at all? To reconcile is to forgive. Reconciliation leads to forgiveness, which in turn leads to forgetfulness. Lawrence Langer " points out that redemptive strategies serve as psychological defense mechanisms against pain" (Morris, 2001, p. 10). While Roger Simon (2000) talks of the "possibilities of hope" (p. 5) in studying traumatic history (of the Holocaust) I write against hope and offer what I call a "dystopic curriculum" (2001, p. 9) that is a "testament to despair" (p. 9). Hope, I argue, is a problematic idea because it covers over and glosses over the reality of trauma. Hope is an enlightenment idea that needs problematizing and rethinking.

When history—or the idea of history—is separated from memory—or the idea of memory, "commemorative practices," as Claudia Eppert (2002) points out, become "disembodied, threatening to become abstractions" (p. 46). Historiography as abstraction is particularly problematic as the abstraction or objective writing tends to remove human emotion and feeling from the text. In the case of German, non-Jewish historians, this issue of objectivity—or abstraction—became a well-known heated debate between Martin Broszat (German, non-Jewish historian) and Saul Friedlander (Jewish historian). Broszat argued for what he called a "plea for historicization" (cited in Morris, p. 131). Broszat was arguing that German historians must remove their own feelings and emotions from their work and write up their histories in an objective fashion. Friedlander, on the other hand, saw this move as one of the many ways Germans tried to erase their own complicity in the Holocaust. To separate the historians' memory from history—especially if they have lived through that history—is highly problematic. If one lives through a historical event, one cannot simply erase the memory of it, and this memory of it affects the ways in which the scholar writes historiography. To objectify history is a way to erase what happened.

Objectification also serves to undermine the suffering of the victims. Karen Anijar and Barbara Mascali (2002) argue that there is always a danger of the Holocaust "being made into a fetishized artifact" (p. 250). An artifact is an object and the fetish is an obsession. Roger Simon (2000) comments, "Whose and what memories matter, not abstractly, but viscerally, requiring my attention and vigilance, speaks volumes about the terms on which lives of others come into view" (p. 12). Historiography of trauma, then, might be written in a more visceral way. But for the historian, as John Weaver (2002) points out, the problem of "method" prevents history writing from being visceral. Weaver says that method serves to silence victim's voices and testimonies (p. 157). And as William Doll (2005) writes, method has always been about control. Historians, through their writing, work to control "whose and what memories matter" (Simon, Rosenberg, & Eppert, 2000, p. 12). Historians control what it is that gets archived. Historians control our past, or our memory of it (Weaver, 2002). And when this past is especially embarrassing, historians—on the wrong side of history—erase what they don't want us to remember.

But what about that unremembered stuff of history? What about the testimonies of victims about whom we never hear? Roger Simon (2005), speaking of Jules Michelet, says that he understands "the historian's implication in the ongoing formation of culture" (p. 2). A scholar can shape culture through leaving behind texts. Scholars, then, must write texts, as William Pinar (2001) puts it, that "honor the dead" (p. 32). Not only do historians and other scholars shape culture, they too have already been shaped by the culture into which they are thrown. The social construction of historical writing means two things: culture shapes scholars as scholars shape culture. The shaping of culture is a social construction. To construct a past is to reconstruct the past. And to reconstruct something means that the scholar works through his or her own psychological baggage. Historiography is always perspectival and hardly objective. The perspective of the historian is psychological. And to have psychological baggage means that the scholar also has psychological blinders. But what happens to the unconscious content of historiography? How is it that historians can write histories of horror at all? And how can readers understand the reconstructed histories handed down to them when historians are just as baffled by these catastrophes as are their readers? Thus, reconstructions of traumatic histories are, as I point out, "beyond understanding and representation" (2001, p. 6). And Karen Anijar and Barbara Mascali (2002) ask: "How could we possibly subject incomprehensibility to analysis?" (p. 250). How do scholars write about something they cannot possibly understand?

Sharon Todd (2009) comments that scholars should be focusing not on what is good and decent, joyful and triumphant, but rather on man's inhumanity to man. Todd tells us that scholars must study "the imperfection of humanity" (p. 6). Scholars must study what it is that makes people vicious and murderous. Psychoanalyst Harold F. Searles (2005) talks about the problem of murderous rage. What is murderous rage and where does it come from?

James Watson (2002) suggests that scholars can learn from Theodor Adorno, especially when he speaks of what he calls "reified consciousness" (pp. 112–113). A reified consciousness is akin to the hardening of the arteries of the mind. Reified consciousness tends toward parochialism, nationalism, egotism, and, as Adorno suggests, murder. Is this the seat of murderous rage? The notion of purity is one of reified consciousness. This term—purity—stands out as a Nazi legacy. A reified consciousness gets rid of whatever it cannot deal with. This is what being rigid means. A rigid person cannot deal with nuance or accept ambivalence. A rigid person cannot psychologically manage the other. The easiest and most expedient way to deal with the thing that troubles is to get rid of it. The Jews were thought to be vermin who tainted the purity of German culture. The easiest and most expedient way to purify German culture was to rid it of vermin, the Jews. As James Watson points out "reified consciousness...tends toward violence" (p. 113). Thus, violence begins in rigidity. This rigidity is the inability to manage opposites, others, differences, disagreements, dislikes. Rigidity is the inability to handle the negatives: anger, resentment, despair, revenge. Thinking through these negatives and working through them psychologically is one way not to end up with a reified consciousness, not to end up in a violent situation. But then again there is more to violence than just reified consciousness. Why people kill baffles. At the end of the day, why people are so violent remains an open question. Freud tried to figure this out as he argued that all of us have aggression in us—what he called the death drive. People who do not at least acknowledge this aggression are a danger.

Studying violence, William Pinar (2001) suggests, serves to unsettle (p. 24) the self. The unsettling is what might break through a reified consciousness. To be unmoored by reading is powerful. This is the purpose of studying historical trauma, to be unmoored so as to acknowledge not only the reality of past wrongs but to also acknowledge within ourselves our own capacity for hatred and aggression. Thinking through historical trauma means, as Roger Simon puts it, "psychic shattering" (p. 18). Studying traumatic historiography is not only about reconstructing the self, it is also about reconstructing the social and political.

When speaking of the unspeakable Montreal Massacre—where 14 women were gunned down at the University of Montreal because the gunman claimed that "feminists were ruining his life" (Rosenberg, 2000, p. 76)—Sharon Rosenberg comments,

> The massacre has put violence against women as a social and political issue in the domain of public discussion, in a manner unprecedented in Canada. Indeed, I would argue, the force of the memorial legacy of the Massacre has come to depend upon its being read as symbolic of a "larger problem" that requires social and political address. (p. 76)

Violence, then, involves psychic, social, and political address. Roger Simon (2005) says, "We will have to consider a form of public history that opens one to both the demand, and responsibility to, the alterity of the historical experiences of others" (p. 4). Scholars make private lives public by writing about them and studying them. People live in time and space, they live in a sociopolis. The context around which people live their lives is that public space that Simon refers to above. So our address must be in writing. It is not enough to march on the frontlines. But one must archive that march. It is the archive that remains. And it is this archive that shapes how others will remember.

Why Remember?

Why remember at all? Grace Feuerverger (2002), a child of Holocaust survivors, says that people remember and archive memories in order to "speak for those who cannot speak" (p. 15). William Pinar (2001) says that scholars should "work to avenge their murders" (p. 32). I suggest that scholars write about historical trauma out of "an ethical commitment" (2001, p. 3). Roger Simon (2005) says scholars write out of the "obligations of remembrance" (p. 2). Historical trauma is not easy to write about and it is not easy to study either. Curriculum history is one of remembrance. And curriculum theorists who work historically have heeded the call to remember.

· 5 ·

POLITICAL CURRICULUM CONCEPTS

Introduction

Curriculum scholars study politics in a variety of ways. The aim of this chapter is to examine in broad strokes what it is that curriculum scholars are currently discussing in the context of politics. Such topics include the problematics of neoliberalism and the way in which neoliberalism has affected schooling practices as well as neoconservatism and the battles over whose knowledge is of most worth. Neoliberalism and neoconservatism are right-wing agendas that many curriculum studies scholars try to untangle so as to undo. Many argue that schools need to become places of democracy, but neoliberalism and neoconservatism do not lend themselves to democratic practices. Some curriculum scholars approach these problematics through poststructural politics mostly using the works of Michel Foucault and Jacques Derrida. Others turn to critical theory to unpack the problematics of neoliberalism and the way that neoliberal policies have made schools undemocratic places. I will examine current curriculum debates around issues of fascism, authoritarianism and militarism in their relations to neoliberal politics. Toward the end of the chapter I explore the politics of postformalism, the problems of school shootings, and what I call the politics of emotion. Throughout the chapter I will be discussing the problems of standardized testing (No Child Left Behind and Race to the Top).

Neoliberalism

Here I introduce students to curriculum scholars who define neoliberalism and the problematics of neoliberalism in the context of schooling. Michael Peters (2009) states

> Neoliberalism in the popular sense is a label for what is commonly understood as the doctrine of political and economic liberalism and set of policies originating in the 1970s that wielded together classical political theory as exemplified by the Mont Pelerin Society after WWII and neoclassical economic theories that became identified with the so-called Chicago school under Milton Friedman in the 1960s. (p. xxvii)

Neoliberal policies are right wing, in that all is reduced to the free market with little government intervention (like social programs). The market takes precedence over democratizing practices such as welfare programs that serve the poor. The neoliberal school of thought is not unlike the idea that people can lift themselves up by their own bootstraps, as it were, and do not need the help of government. Henry Giroux (2004) explains

> Neoliberalism has indeed become a broad-based political and cultural movement designed to obliterate public concerns and liquidate the welfare state, and make politics everywhere an exclusively market-driven project… . Its supporting political culture and pedagogical practices also put into play a social universe and cultural landscape that sustain a particularly barbaric notion of authoritarianism. (p. xxiii)

Giroux's critique of neoliberalism is also a critique of the Bush administration. Under Bush, as Giroux points out, many civil liberties were taken away, especially after 9/11. School policies like NCLB were hardly democratic since high-stakes testing and the close monitoring of teachers were more akin to authoritarianism than democracy. Ross Collin and Michael W. Apple (2010) comment:

> Many of the school reforms proposed and implemented by business friendly figures in the neoliberal state, includ[ed] high-stakes standardized testing, school choice programs, and slowed growth in governmental spending on K–12 public education…. [E]vidence suggests that the expansion of school choice programs and educational markets correlates with increased segregation of schools by race and class. (p. 39)

It becomes clear—especially as students move through this discussion—that neoliberal policies impact schools in negative ways. Standardized testing is a practice of the homogenization of knowledge. This is in no way a democratic practice. If anything, it shuts down conversation and discourages dissent. The resegregation of public schools is hardly democratic and is a result—as Collin and Apple point out—of school choice programs.

The Globalizing Effects of Neoliberalism

Neoliberalism has had globalizing effects. David Harvey (2005) explains:

> Deregulation, privatization, and withdrawal of the state from many areas of social provision have been all too common. Almost all states, from those newly minted after the collapse of the Soviet Union to old-style social democracies and welfare states such as New Zealand and Sweden, have embraced...some version of neoliberal theory.... Post-apartheid South Africa quickly embraced neoliberalism. (p. 3)

The deregulation of the market is what led to what is now being called the Great Recession. The social policies that President Franklin D. Roosevelt put in place during the Depression began to unravel under the Reagan and Thatcher administrations. This unraveling caused great harm to the poor and underclass especially. But more than this, neoliberalism has been embraced globally, as Harvey points out, with detrimental effects to the poor. In fact, Marvin J. Berlowitz and Nathan A. Long (2003) tell us, "Neoliberal policies and legislations have dramatically impacted the most vulnerable of the world's children, impoverishing them and often leading to their violent conscription into sweatshops, the sex industry, and the armed forces" (p. 163). What is most insidious here is that neoliberal policies have hurt children. Not only have these policies hurt children in the ways described above but these policies have hurt children in their school settings. Many argue that standardized testing does violence to children by putting them in a situation where they are fearful all the time. Fear is not conducive to learning. The structure of children's knowledge base has become so narrow that when they get older they will not know how to maneuver in a complex world. On the globalizing effect of neoliberalism, Michael Apple (2010) suggests

> Neoliberal, neoconservative and managerial impulses can be found throughout the world cutting across both geographical boundaries and even economic systems. This points to the important "spatial" aspects of globalization. Policies are "borrowed"

and "travel" across borders in such a way that these neoliberal, neoconservative, and managerial impulses are extended throughout the world. (p. 2)

The globalizing effect of neoliberalism is devastating for the poor, as I have pointed out. But these policies also affect people of color and women. Neoliberalism hurts mostly minorities and the underclass because it undermines social programs that are meant to help these constituencies.

Kenneth J. Saltman (2003) also examines the effects of the globalization of neoliberalism. He states

> Corporate globalization, which should be viewed as a doctrine rather than as an inevitable phenomenon, is driven by the philosophy of neoliberalism. The economic and political doctrine of neoliberalism insists upon the virtues of privatization and liberalization of trade and concomitantly places faith in the hard discipline of the market. (p. 3)

Neoliberals seek to privatize all social programs. Here in the United States that would have detrimental effects not only on the poor but also on the elderly and on public school students as well. During the Bush administration there was talk of privatizing social security; Bush suggested that people should put their monies in the stock market. Neoliberals would like to see public schools privatized and some already are. This defeats the whole purpose of public education. Shelia Landers Macrine (2003) suggests

> Ultimately, neoliberalism serves to justify an educational system that enhances the emerging American economy of service managers, franchise workers, entrepreneurs, and venture capitalists that sit on a huge underclass of burger wrappers and security guards, certainly not what the "promise of a literate" society intended. (p. 205)

Neoliberal policies, in other words, undermine chances that newly graduated students have of making a decent wage and having a meaningful livelihood. Too many students upon graduation find terrible employment or cannot find jobs at all. Without social programs young people do not have many options in a weakened economy.

Neoconservatism

Neoconservatism is an offshoot of neoliberalism but has more to do with questions of literacy than anything else. Neoconservatism is about whose knowledge is of most worth. Neoconservatives want children to have a conservative education, which means studying the classics and leaving out multicultural literatures. Michael Apple (2006) explains

> Among the policies being proposed under this ideological position are mandatory national and statewide curricula, national and statewide testing, a "return" to higher standards, a revivification of the "Western tradition," patriotism, and conservative variants of character education.... Behind it as well—and this is essential—is a fear of the "Other." (p. 39)

Later on Apple tells us that William Bennett's (1996) *The Book of Virtues: A Treasury of Great Moral Stories* is part and parcel of the neoconservative agenda. When scholars ask the question whose knowledge is of most worth, for conservatives that knowledge is of the Western traditional canon. Of course, there is nothing wrong with studying the classics, but there are many other literatures (multicultural literatures) that are worth studying as well. An integrated canon would be a more liberal approach to education where students study the classics alongside the multicultural literature.

Some other books in the neoconservative tradition would be Allan Bloom's (1988) *The Closing of the American Mind*, Diane Ravitch's (2001) *Left Back: A Century of Battles Over School Reform*, and E. D. Hirsch's (1988) *Cultural Literacy: What Every American Needs to Know*.

Poststructuralism and Politics: Michel Foucault and Jacques Derrida

Here I will touch on what it is curriculum scholars are commenting on when drawing on poststructuralists in the context of politics. Mainly I will be looking briefly at what curriculum scholars are discussing around the work of Michel Foucault and Jacques Derrida, two poststructural scholars who write about politics. First, I begin with an examination of what it is that curriculum scholars are talking about in the context of Foucault and politics.

Michael Peters (1996) examines the problematics of neoliberalism in the context of Foucault's notion of governmentality. Peters explains

> Foucault's work provides resources for understanding what I am going to call the *paradox* of the neoliberal state: the paradox is that while neoliberalism can be regarded as a doctrine concerning the self-limiting state, under neoliberal market policies the state has become more powerful. The understanding of this paradox can be fruitfully approached through Foucault's notion of governmentality. (p. 81)

Schools have been dominated by neoliberal politics. Schools are tightly controlled by the use of high-stakes testing. School teachers are under strict supervision and constant surveillance. The school curriculum is a conservative one and the idea that schools and the market should be linked are neoliberal ideas. The schools, in other words, are highly governed (Foucault's notion of governmentality) by neoliberal politics. Peter's point above is that although neoliberal policy limits government, ironically schools are highly governed and highly controlled by neoliberal policies.

Foucault (1983) explains what he means by governmentality when he states

> This word [government] must be allowed the very broad meaning it had in the sixteenth century. "Government" did not refer only to political structures or to the management of states; rather it designated the way in which the conduct of individuals or of groups might be directed: the government of children, of souls, of communities, of families, of the sick…. To govern, in this sense, is to structure the possible field of action of others. (p. 221)

High-stakes testing and the standardization of knowledge are ways to govern children. The strict supervision and surveillance that teachers are under are ways to govern them. Governmentality is a word that suggests control and power. As Foucault says, it concerns "the conduct of individuals" and "structure[s] the possible field of action of others" (p. 221). Neoliberal governmentality, as Peters puts it, is a form of control and a form of power.

Other curriculum scholars also comment on Foucault's notion of governmentality. Thomas S. Popkewitz and Marie Brennan (1998) suggest, "The notion of governmentality provides a way to consider the concept of power as deployment" (p. 20). Bernadette Baker (1998) puts it this way: "The art of governing required a kind of 'governmentality' related to the role of the state as a definer, watcher, and manager of difference" (p. 132). Thus governmentality is a form of control and power over the conduct of others. Related ideas are found in Foucault's (1979) *Discipline and Punish: The Birth of the Prison*. Foucault uses the terms "macro" and "micro-physics of power" (p. 160) in talking about "disciplining" others (especially prisoners, inmates of mental institutions, and school children). A way to punish and to control others and exercise power (because for Foucault power is exercised) over others and to govern others (hence governmentality) is to

> adjust the mechanisms of power that frame the everyday lives of individuals; an adaptation and a refinement of the machinery that assumes responsibility for and places

under surveillance their everyday behaviour, their identity, their activity, their apparently unimportant gestures. (p. 77)

Control and surveillance are ways to govern and control the conduct of others. A micro-physics of power is a way of controlling every movement of an individual including gestures. In the context of teaching, Foucault remarks,

> The same movement was to be found in the reorganization of elementary teaching: the details of surveillance were specified and it was integrated into the teaching relationship. The development of the parish schools, in the increase in the number of their pupils, the absence of methods for regulating simultaneously the activity of a whole class, and the disorder and confusion that followed from this made it necessary to work out a system of supervision. (p. 175)

Supervision and surveillance are ways of governing both children and their teachers. One effect of governmentality is that—in Foucault's words—it "normalizes" (1979, p. 183). For students who are interested in an in-depth treatment of Foucault's notion of governmentality I suggest that they consult a book co-edited by Michael Peters, A. C. Besley, Marc Olssen, Susanne Maurer, and Susanne Weber (2009) titled *Governmentality Studies in Education*. Governmentality is a highly complex idea that I have only touched on here. One can see how neoliberal governmentality plays out in our current school systems and the detrimental effects that governmentality has had not only on children but also on teachers.

Poststructuralism and Politics: Jacques Derrida

Derrida is known for his work on what has been called "deconstruction." Deconstruction is a way to read texts in exegetical fashion, providing a close reading of philosophers and literary writers. Traditional analytic philosophers have shunned Derrida and do not consider what he is doing real philosophy. Instead, Derrida's work has been mostly embraced by English and curriculum scholars. Although Derrida focuses much on the art of reading and writing, the art of deconstructing texts (analyzing them and making something of them), he is also known to be a highly political writer. Much of his work deals with the politics of the university. He also deals with the politics of the Other, of responsibility, of duty, of understanding difference and the politics of difference, the politics of hospitality, and more. Curriculum scholars comment on Derrida's work as it relates to politics and to education. Michael Peters and Girt Biesta (2009) tell us

Derrida came to influence a range of radical educators, including Henry Giroux, Gregory Ulmer, Peter Trifonas, Denise Egea-Kuehne, Patti Lather, Gayatri Chakravorty Spivak, Gert Biesta, Michael Peters and many others. His legacy in education and pedagogy will continue to grow as educators, teachers, and students continue to explore the complexity and fullness of his opus and its significance to politics and pedagogy. (pp. 9–10)

Some noteworthy books students might consult if they are interested in the connections among Derrida, politics, and education are these: Peter Pericles Trifonas's (2000) *The Ethics of Writing: Derrida, Deconstruction and Pedagogy*, Michael Peters and Gert Biesta's (2009) *Derrida, Deconstruction, and the Politics of Pedagogy*, Peter Trifonas and Michael Peters' (2005) co-edited book *Deconstructing Derrida: Tasks for the New Humanities*, and Gert Biesta and Denise Egea-Kuehne's (2001) co-edited book *Derrida and Education*.

Denise Egea-Kuehne and Gert Biesta point out that when educationists were first introduced to Derrida, most focused on his work on literary texts. Egea-Kuehne and Biesta state

> Although some scholars have acknowledged the possible political implications of deconstructive writing pedagogy (e.g., Knoper 1989), it is true that this first "wave" of the reception of deconstruction in education has been primarily "technical" in its narrow focus on literary analysis. (p. 4).

The books that are mentioned above, however, deal mostly with Derrida's concern with politics. So one might say that the second wave of scholars interested in Derrida's work are interested in the connections among curriculum studies, deconstruction, and politics.

When turning to Derrida's texts one can see just how interested in politics he was. One of Derrida's main concerns is the politics of the university. Derrida (1995) states

> My belonging to the institution of the university [has]…never been a comfortable relation of identification…. Yet it is true that the critique, let us call it the political critique, that I have on occasion undertaken of the institution remained either "private," empirical, more or less spontaneous. (p. 14).

Derrida's political critique of the university, however, does not seem to be spontaneous or private as he makes his claims public throughout much of his writing. He is highly critical of the nondemocratic nature of higher education and the institution of the university. He is highly critical of the problem of censorship within this institution as well as the little freedom that professors have. He writes about the possibility of a "democracy to come" (1995, p. 338) in universities. What this signifies is that democracy in the university is not yet. It has not yet arrived. But the job of the professor is to work to undo undemocratic practices in the university so as to make this "democracy to come" possible. Michael Peters (2009) points out that Derrida also explores the notion of "democracy to come" in the realm of global politics. Peters explains

> Derrida maintains that since technics have obliterated "locality," the future of democracy must be thought of in global terms. It is no longer possible to be a democrat "at home" and wait to see what happens "abroad." In emphasizing a world democracy, Derrida suggests that the stakes of "democracy to come" can no longer be contained within frontiers. (p. 74)

For Derrida, the world is not yet a democratic place but people must work to make it so. Derrida's ideas on democracy dovetail the interests of postcolonial scholars and scholars who do work on cosmopolitanism.

Another political concept for Derrida is responsibility, which he talks about much throughout his work. Derrida (1995) remarks, "Each time a responsibility (ethical or political) has to be taken, one must pass by way of antinomic injunctions, which have an aporetic form, by way of a sort of experience of the impossible" (p. 359). The aporia of which Derrida speaks is like a conundrum without resolution. Ethical and political decisions must pass by way of this conundrum. Ethical and political decisions, in other words, are impossible because they are difficult. But at the end of the day one must come to a decision. Julian Edgoose (2001) says of this impossible responsibility:

> One *must* decide. Here the third aporia—the *aporia of urgency*—comes into play. Ethical decisions cannot wait—a decision *has* to be made.... One *has* to decide, but a just decision is impossible—this very mad impossibility makes justice possible. Derrida claims that justice, based upon a radical openness to alterity, can be persevered only as a result of the aporias of suspension, undecidability, and urgency. (p. 129)

What Edgoose drives home here is that for Derrida, politics—the politics of responsibility, justice, decision making, and so forth—only come by way of difficulty of the undecidable. But finally a decision must be made. If decisions come too easily they might have unfortunate consequences. A decision that passes through the motions of the aporia might have a chance to have better ethical consequences.

Derrida's concept of duty is connected with his notions of the Other and of hospitality. He states, "The *same duty* also dictates welcoming foreigners [the Other] in order not only to integrate them but to recognize and accept their alterity: two concepts of hospitality that today divide our European and national consciousness" (1992, p. 77). The Other must be welcomed, not shunned. There is no room for xenophobia in a place where people practice hospitality. It is a duty to be hospitable to the Other, Derrida says throughout his work. Gert Biesta (2009) comments that for Derrida "the ethicopolitical horizon of deconstruction can be described as a concern for the other.... . Deconstruction is an affirmation of what is wholly other" (p. 15). The wholly Other is the foreigner about whom Derrida speaks. The absolute alterity of the Other is something that must be kept intact, not collapsing the Other onto the self. The self and the Other are different from each other. It is this difference that Derrida embraces, especially in his notion of hospitality. Hospitality is a political move. To be hospitable to the wholly Other is both political and ethical. However, Derrida knows how difficult it is for people to be hospitable to the wholly other because of the problems of racism and nationalism. Derrida (1992) comments, "There is *today* the same feeling of imminence, of hope and of danger, of anxiety before the possibility of other wars with unknown forms [terrorism], the return to old forms of religious fanaticism, nationalism, or racism" (p. 63). Racism is an ongoing problem in Europe as well as around the world. This too is why democracy is not yet. But people must work on "democracy to come"—this is Derrida's hope and his politic.

Patti Lather (2004) comments on the difficulty of doing deconstructive work and on the difficulty of working on Derrida. She states that "the practical politics of putting deconstruction to work entail a sort of getting lost as an ethical relationality of non-authoritarian authority to what we know and how we know it" (p. 7). Later on in this chapter I will tease out the complicated meanings of authoritarianism, fascism, and totalitarianism as they relate to thinking of curriculum politically. But for now let us ask whether authorities can be non-authoritarian in Derrida's eyes? This is yet another example of the impossibility of the aporia. At the end of the day authorities must work to be democratic (non-authoritarian) even though "democracy is to come." The many aporetic ethical situations in which people find themselves lend to "getting lost," as Lather (p. 7) puts it. But getting lost is part of the work of politics. Nothing is straightforward in a deconstructive reading of politics; rather everything is complex and highly difficult. The work at hand is hard but it must be done. In the context of education, Derrida would suggest that all places of education must be made more democratic and more free. And yet, scholars work inside of institutions that are not yet democratic nor are they free.

Critical Theory, Politics, and Curriculum Studies

Here I turn to a discussion on critical theory and what it is that curriculum theorists are currently debating. Peter McLaren (2005) suggests that scholars who work in the area of critical theory need to carefully study the writings of Marx. McLaren tells us that "the Marxist tradition has been woefully absent from critical pedagogy" (p. 35). Scholars who work in critical theory must return to Marx in order to enrich their thought. It is the scholar's responsibility and obligation to study primary sources to better understand historically from whence ideas spring. McLaren points out, "Marxism is seen from this perspective as a failed experiment and the teaching of Marx is viewed as something that should be put to rest since the persistence of capital appears to have rendered the old bearded devil obsolete" (p. 34). McLaren's concern is that critical theory has been domesticated (p. 33). Intellectual laziness (Gramsci, 2000) might be what prevents scholars from going back to study primary sources. And as Antonio Gramsci teaches, the study of Marx is a cure for that intellectual laziness. Gramsci states, "Karl Marx is for us a master of spiritual and moral life, not a shepherd wielding a crook. He is the stimulator of mental laziness, the arouser of good energies which slumber and which must wake up for the good fight" (p. 39). One of the reasons Marx is the "stimulator of mental laziness" is that he is a difficult read: there is nothing easy about Marx. When speaking of Marxism, however, several problems emerge. It is to this point that Deb Hill (2007) speaks. She suggests that the problem of class has been superseded by other pressing concerns like race and gender. Moreover Hill states

> The latter [class] is now even branded by some as a "negative" form of struggle, allegedly representative of an "essentialist" and "totalizing" (totalitarian) political vision. Collective ascriptions such as "the masses" or "the bourgeoisie" are now regarded as outdated and ubiquitous terminology with little or no practical meaning. (p. 2)

When scholars examine terms such as "the masses"—as Hill points out—charges of essentialism are at hand because it is not clear what "the masses" means. Who are the masses? Class—as it gets separated out from race and gender—also might be seen as problematic. Ideally all three signifiers—race, class, gender—should be examined together. But most scholars in the field of curriculum studies tend to focus on class or race or gender.

Class is a useful and important idea that continually needs unpacking. Peter McLaren (2005) tells us that "class struggle is now perilously viewed as an outdated issue" (p. 29). But class is not an outdated issue at all. In the United States there is a huge gap between the very wealthy and the very poor. When the economy turns bad, class becomes an important issue. Today many Americans are struggling to keep their jobs, to make ends meet, to survive. The majority of Americans are no longer middle class but working class. The terms "proletariat" and "bourgeoisie"—although coined in another era—are of use even today. These terms not only have practical meaning but they also have theoretical usefulness. Scholars who have never had to struggle to make ends meet might think that class struggle is a useless idea. However, there is a real struggle among working-class people to just get by. There is little time for leisure in a life that is consumed by the time clock. Losing a job means losing the means to take care of oneself. Homelessness is a real problem, not only in the United States but also globally. These issues go back to Marx. Taking care of the poor is a human right. If students study Marx carefully they will find these issues raised, albeit in another time and place (19th century Germany).

What must the scholar do to make Marx applicable to the present? How are writings from the 19th century of use to us today? In response, they are of use if scholars want to make them useful. It is an easy dismissal to say that notions of class struggle are useless today. It is an easy dismissal to launch the charges of essentialism when talking about the working class and the rest. Essentialism is a charge that can be launched against almost any idea.

Peter McLaren (2005) remarks that much of his academic work is devoted to "introduc[ing] Marxist scholarship into the field of critical pedagogy" (p. 35). More than any other curriculum scholar, McLaren has led us back to primary sources; as was mentioned earlier, he calls for a return to Marx, just as Jacques Lacan called for a return to Freud. And yet the majority of critical theorists do not cite Marx, according to McLaren.

For McLaren, like Marx, reform is not enough. Revolution is a must. During the Bush presidency, many were asking when the revolution would occur. No revolution occurred. One might argue, however, that the election of Barack Obama was a revolution of sorts. And yet many of Obama's policies—most particularly his educational policies—are the same as Bush's or perhaps even worse. Obama's Race to the Top is disheartening. This policy calls for more standardized testing. McLaren (2005) warns that "there is also a movement to develop international standardized tests, creating pressures toward educational convergence and standardization among nations" (p. 28). In educational institutions—whether schools or universities—teachers and professors have little power. If scholars dare put up what Gramsci (2000) calls "the good fight" (p. 39), punishment, humiliation, or termination is at hand. So scholars march in lock-step out of fear. Henry Giroux (2007) talks about the "university in chains" (p. 2). But there is more to it than that. Working in an atmosphere that is akin to a totalitarian regime is a felt, visceral, and embodied experience. Scholars obey. And so many of us are complicit in what Gramsci called a "strong bourgeois society" (p. 30). Gramsci comments

> In one of the stories in *The Jungle Book* Rudyard Kipling shows discipline at work in a strong bourgeois society. Everyone obeys in the bourgeois state. The mules in the battery obey the battery Sergeant, the horses obey the soldiers who ride them. The soldiers obey the lieutenant, the lieutenants obey the regimental colonels. (p. 31)

One way to combat a totalizing administration is through scholarship. Paulo Freire (1996) states that writing "has also become a duty that I cannot reject, for it is a political project that must be met" (p. 2). It is our duty as scholars to write, to publish, to study. After all, it is the writing that matters, it is the writing that will outlive us and it is the writing that will hopefully change (at least something) about the world. The daily pettiness and confrontations with totalizing administrators must be documented, commented upon, and critiqued. Remember that Marx (1978) called for "a ruthless critique of everything existing" (p. 13). One of the reasons that education professors are so loathed—at least by some—is that we are the ones who critique the very institutions of which we are a part. But the only way to change institutions is to challenge the very structure upon which they are built. Marx states that "the criticism must not be afraid of its own conclusions, nor of conflict with the powers that be" (p. 13).

Peter McLaren (2005) calls for a "rematerialized critique" (p. 9). The question remains: What would that "rematerialized critique" look like through the eyes of Marx and how do scholars make use of that critique in our current sociopolitical situation? A few passages from Marx might be helpful here. A powerful passage by Marx (1978) is this:

> That men must be in a position to live in order to be able to "make history." But life involves before everything else eating and drinking, a habitation, clothing and many other things. The first historical act is thus the production of the means to satisfy these needs, the production of the material itself. (pp. 155–156)

Most middle-class people take it for granted that there is enough food to eat, that they have a place to sleep and clothes to wear. But when disaster strikes awakening occurs. After a disaster—like the catastrophic earthquake that struck Haiti in January of 2010 and killed some one hundred thousand people or more—people realize that nothing can be taken for granted. This complacency that many of us have—until something terrible happens to us—must be ruptured. *Organic* intellectuals—the kind of intellectuals about whom Gramsci (2005, p. 6) spoke—might know what it means to live in dire straits more than those of us who work comfortably in the academy.

Marx argues that "the formation of ideas [comes] from material practice" (p. 164). The materiality of a person's world shapes thought. The fact that Paulo Freire grew up knowing hunger in a real and painful way must have shaped the scholar that he became. Freire (1996) speaks of the "geography of my hunger" (p. 17). The term "geography" suggests that hunger is not only felt in the stomach but as a world, as a place, as a terrible psychic place. Fighting hunger is something that many of us will never know or experience. But there are many Americans today—and children too—who fight hunger. A rematerialized critique, about which McLaren speaks, must take account of hunger first and foremost.

A rematerialized critique must also deal with issues of working. More than any other topic, Marx spends most of his time on work, the work of the working class. Working is a material reality. And if working conditions are highly problematic, the worker suffers. Marx was most concerned with this kind of suffering. Marx puts it this way:

> Not only are they [the workers] slaves of the bourgeois class, and of the bourgeois State; they are daily and hourly enslaved by the machine, by the over-looker, and, above all, by the bourgeois manufacturer himself. The more openly the despotism proclaims gain to be its end and aim, the more petty, the more hateful and the more embittering it is. (p. 479)

Today the minimum wage is the equivalent of slave labor. There must be a better way to work in the world. Minimum wage jobs can only pay for less than adequate rental apartments, or trailers. In these less than adequate abodes rodents, insects, and squalor prevail. Marx says

> Man returns to living in a cave, which is now, however, contaminated with the mephitic breath of plague given off by civilization and which he continues to occupy only *precariously*, it being for him an alien habitation, which can be withdrawn from him any day—a place from which, if he does not pay, he can be thrown out any day. For this mortuary he has to *pay*. (p. 94)

The landlord is the lord of the land while the tenant is at the whim and mercy of the landlord. This issue is not only about apartment dwellers. It is also about homeowners whose homes are under foreclosure. "Foreclosure" is the watchword of the decade. This is a word that was hardly ever uttered since the Great Depression but today foreclosures are common.

A rematerialized critique, as McLaren calls for, also concerns a myriad of problematics. Scholars might study matters of hunger, work, and home to advance the field. There are some curriculum scholars working in all three of these areas but still more needs to be done. McLaren's call for rematerialization concerns the basic staples of living. These should be pressing concerns especially for members of a privileged group—university professors—who might forget what it means to live without the basics.

And so I ask whither Marx? I use the word "whither" purposely here as Marx himself used the word in his piece "Ruthless Critique" as he states that "all the more confusion reigns about the 'whither'" (p. 13). During the Great Recession Marx's work and writings could have been of use. But still, many are unconvinced. Jacques Derrida (1994) says, "Perhaps people are no longer afraid of Marxists" (p. 50). To counter Derrida here, I would venture to say that people are, in fact, still afraid of Marxism. The fear is well founded when it is put in the context of the disasters of Communism and the catastrophes of Stalin and Mao. It is difficult for some to disentangle Communism and totalitarian states from Marx's own writing, which is hardly totalitarian.

Marx even warned against the problematic of dogma in "Ruthless Critique." The dialectic that Marx called for is one way to avoid dogmatism because there is always another thought to consider. Dogma cannot tolerate two opposing ideas that are thought together. Dogma is the way of religious fundamentalism. And ironically enough, Deb Hill (2007) points out that those unconvinced by Marxism worry about its tendency toward fundamentalism (p. 2). Clearly, Marx can be interpreted in a variety of ways. But a close reading of Marx hardly bespeaks fundamentalism. Indeed, any theory can become a sort of fundamentalism. Marxism will not go away. Jacques Derrida (1994) points out that the specter (p. 11) of Marx continues to haunt. Derrida suggests that Marx is not dead, nor is Marxism.

The Politics of Knowledge Production: Freire and Gramsci

For both Freire and Gramsci, reading and writing are political acts. One cannot be a scholar without writing. And the scholar cannot write if she does not read. Not only this. Knowledge production is political. The production of knowledge for both Freire and Gramsci means making new meaning out of old ideas, studying the past in order to create a future. Freire (2005) states that reading is a "composition between reader and writer in which the most profound significance of the text is also the creation of the reader" (p. 55). Reading and writing also have to do with the production of identity. Identity formation shifts with reading and writing. Identity formation is also political. How the reader sees the world and writes about the world can change it. Freire (1996) states

> FOR ME, WRITING HAS BECOME A DEEP PLEASURE, [caps in original] just as it has also become a duty that I cannot reject, for it is a political project that must be met. The joy of writing fills all my time. It fills my time when I write, when I read and reread what I have written, when I receive the first galleys to be corrected, and when I receive the first still-warm copy of the book from the publishing house. (p. 1)

For Freire there is joy in the process of writing. But more than this he feels that writing is a duty and a political act. Changing the world means writing about what is wrong with it. Reading is not enough.

Quintin Hoare (2005) describes Gramsci's struggles when he was imprisoned in Fascist Italy. Hoare states

> He was 35 years old. At his trial of 1928, the official prosecutor ended his peroration with the famous demand to the judge: "We must stop this brain from working for twenty years!" But, although Gramsci was to be dead long before those twenty years were up, released, his health broken only in time to die under guard in a clinic rather than in prison, yet for as long as his physique held out his jailers did not succeed in stopping his brain from working. The product of those years of slow death in prison were the 2,848 pages of handwritten notes. (p. xviii)

What astonishes is that despite the imprisonment—or maybe because of it—Gramsci wrote an enormous amount; luckily, it was smuggled out of the prison cell, and that is why today his *Prison Notebooks* are available. Perhaps it was this experience that drove Gramsci to write. Like Freire, Gramsci felt that writing was a political act, a duty, a responsibility. But writing must not be what Freire (1996) terms "historically anesthetized" (p. 21). Writing must be historically situated and historically informed. The study of history, then, is paramount to the study of subject matter, no matter what that subject might be. It is not enough, for example, to talk about race if one only talks about attitudes and beliefs. One must treat the subject of race historically.

Gramsci (2000) goes one step further by calling for a study of "the history of research, the history of this immense epic of the human spirit." (p. 67). Scholars need to study the history of their own scholarship and periodically review and revise the ways in which ideas are formed and conclusions are made. Scholarship must continually be historically analyzed so as to make sure that ideas continue to push boundaries; the only way to push boundaries is to keep pushing backward (into one's own history and the history of the culture into which one is thrown) and forward into the future.

Like Gramsci, Freire was a victim of exile. Donaldo Macedo and Ana Maria Araujo Freire (2005) remind us:

> Paulo Freire was in exile for almost sixteen years precisely because he understood education this way and because he fought to give a large number of Brazilians access to an asset traditionally denied them: the act of reading the world by reading the word. (p. xv)

Literacy is political. Peoples can change their history only if they can read their worlds. Unpacking the world through reading, as Paulo Freire teaches, is an imperative. For both Freire and Gramsci reading and writing require much discipline. Both of these scholars make much of the notion of discipline. Good reading and writing practices come from dedication and discipline that are rather difficult to sustain. Reading and writing are not occasional things we do as scholars; reading and writing are our life's work. And this life work takes an incredible amount of discipline. In order to write anything at all, scholars must study. Freire (2005) says

> Studying is a demanding occupation, in the process of which we will encounter pain, pleasure, victory, defeat, doubt, and happiness. For this reason, studying requires the development of rigorous discipline, which we must consciously forge in ourselves. (p. 52)

Disciplined reading and writing practices are a must, as Freire points out. Road blocks will be present, says Freire. But if scholars work long and hard enough happiness is afoot. Freire considers the act of writing part of his occupation and part and parcel of his being. As Freire (1996) says, writing is a duty (p. 1) and an obligation.

Like Freire, Gramsci too felt that intellectual work required a great amount of discipline. In fact, Peter Mayo (2004) points out that Gramsci had an "obsession with discipline and rigor" (p. 12). But for Gramsci (2000), this discipline is of a certain kind. Gramsci draws a distinction between what he calls "bourgeois discipline" and "socialist discipline" (p. 32). Doing the work of the state is a form of bourgeois discipline. Slaves of the state do others' bidding. The scholar with a socialist bent does her own work and that work is for the good of all. It is important to note that Gramsci points out, "Whoever is a socialist or wants to become one does not obey: he commands himself, he imposes a rule of life on his impulses" (p. 32). And this discipline and "rule of life" is a way to "free oneself from a state of chaos" (p. 59). Gramsci's ideas on discipline are radically different from those of Foucault. For Foucault discipline went hand in hand with punishment. For Foucault (1979) discipline might be akin to what Gramsci calls "bourgeois" (p. 32) discipline, which is punishment. Gramsci also refers to this kind of discipline as "authoritarian" (p. 32). Authoritarian institutions abound. The university might be seen as authoritarian. As I mentioned earlier, Jacques Derrida (1995) is highly critical of the university because it is not yet a democratic place. He criticizes censorship, especially in the university.

For Freire, Gramsci, and Derrida, it is the intellectual who must write and publish. But as Richard Hofstadter (1963) points out, "All academic men [and women] are not intellectuals; we often lament this fact" (p. 26). Many academics are simply functionaries. The abuse of power by administrators is rampant in academic institutions. Administrators operate under what Foucault (1979) calls a "micro-physics of power" (p. 26). And this power is not possessed but exercised (p. 26). But too for Foucault power can also be productive (p. 27). A good example of this is that "power produces knowledge" (p. 27). The person who writes produces knowledge and if this knowledge is political it can have an impact against the despotism of the institution at hand. For Foucault power is not a top-down affair, it is circular and everybody has a certain amount of power at certain times. Power is a shifting terrain. Power can be made use of if one writes through and about the issues and also situates those issues historically and contextually. What goes on inside of institutions reflects the larger historical and social landscape.

To "accredit" means to standardize. Institutions rely on, need, accreditation. But knowledge that is standardized is hardly productive. Gramsci (2000) notes this fact as he states that "on the whole the average urban intellectuals are very standardized" (p. 308). Hence, standardization is hardly a new problem. Plus standardization is highly anti-intellectual and as Richard Hofstadter (1963) points out anti-intellectualism—especially in American culture—is not new either. Hofstadter tells us

> The American mind [if there is such a thing] was shaped in the mold of early modern Protestantism. Religion was the first arena for American intellectual life, and thus the first arena for an anti-intellectual impulse.... The feeling that ideas should above all be made to work, the disdain for doctrine and refinements in ideas, the subordination of men of ideas to men of emotional power or manipulative skill are hardly innovations of the twentieth century; they are inheritances from American Protestantism. (p. 55).

Now, to be fair, Hofstadter points out also that American Protestantism was not always anti-intellectual, and certainly today there are strands of Protestantism as well as Catholicism—in academic theology—that are not anti-intellectual. But the main problem Hofstadter sees in religion is its fundamentalist impulse (p. 55). He compares fundamentalism to "quasi-fascism" (p. 132).

For Freire (2001) intellectuals must develop what he calls "epistemological curiosity" (p. 32). Curiosity is hardly practical. Curiosity is a state of mind. This state of mind leads scholars to come to certain thoughts while disregarding others. The material that is thrown out is as important as the material that is kept. But coming to decisions about what to keep and what to throw away—in intellectual work—hardly concerns practicality. To be curious about something means to grope in the dark. It is in this groping that the work is done.

The ultimate point of intellectual work for Gramsci and for Freire is revolution. Our contemporary, Peter McLaren (2005), suggests, too, that critical theory should be revolutionary, not reformist. Revolution—according to Gramsci—cannot come about without intellectuals, Stanley Aronowitz (2002) reminds us. Aronowitz points out that for Gramsci:

> The intellectuals are not to be conceived of as the technicians of power but as its sinews. No class in modern society, he argues, can organize itself for power—for the war of maneuver, that is, revolutionary activity—without the participation of intellectuals whose ultimate task is to embody the unity of theory and organization. It is they who contest the institutions of civil society, the trade unions, as well as the universities. (p. 117).

To "contest the institutions of civil society" is our duty, as Freire might put it. Not only should we contest but scholars should also try to find new ways of being in the world; scholars should attempt to rebuild a better society. It is not enough to protest; something better must be built. This building comes about primarily through ideas. Scholars fight battles via ideas first. Gramsci knew that most battles are ideological. And it is in the schools where these ideological battles are fought. Stanley Aronowitz explains:

> Gramsci devotes considerable attention to education, among other institutions, because, even under fascism, schools are primary sites for achieving mass consent for social rule. The great Gramscian, Louis Althusser, argues that among the State's ideological apparatuses, as opposed to the repressive apparatuses (law, courts, police, army, and prisons), educational institutions are the most important. The school is the State institution *par excellence*. (p. 113)

Power, for Gramsci, comes about through the shaping of ideas. But school children get shaped the way the state wants them to be shaped. Today, this problem is made more pressing by what we see happening to children in terrorist organizations who are brainwashed to engage in suicide bombings in the name of religion. Children tend to believe what adults tell them. And if terrorists are telling children that they will go to heaven if they blow themselves up along with their enemies, they will want to do this.

Gramsci understood that wars are fought not only by fire power but also by ideas and their persuasiveness. This is what he termed "hegemony." Carmel Borg, Joseph A. Buttigieg, and Peter Mayo (2002) explain:

> Modern bourgeois civilization, in Gramsci's view, perpetuates itself through the operations of hegemony—i.e. through the operations of a vast network of cultural organizations, political movements, and educational institutions that instill its conception of the world and its values in every capillary of society. (p. 8)

In America, the underlying lesson of schooling is that students should become good consumers. The point of going to school is to get a job. The point of getting a job is to make money. The university calls its students customers and students expect to be treated as such. So if the customer is always right, faculty lose professional autonomy.

The children are not the problem, however. Scholars should be careful, as Henry Giroux (2003) points out, not to demonize (p. xvii) them. Adults in America have created this culture of consumerism and this needs to be undone. Children grow up, Giroux tells us, where

> Ardent consumers and disengaged citizens provide fodder for a growing cynicism and depoliticization of public life at a time when there is an increasing awareness not just of corporate corruption, financial mismanagement, and systemic greed, but also of the recognition that a democracy of critical citizens is being replaced quickly by a democracy of consumers. (p. xix).

Schooling in this country is about miseducating the young to think that consuming is what really matters. What matters, for Giroux, is that schooling should be about building democracy, building community, engaging citizens to live better lives.

Gramsci's War of Position

For Gramsci, Benedetto Fontana (2002) points out, the only way to fight oppressive powers is through a "war of position." Fontana explains:

> Thus, a war of position, that is, ideological, cultural, and intellectual struggle becomes necessary to overcome the established order. Radical social and political change in the West involves sociocultural and socioeconomic "trench warfare," whose purpose is to undermine the "ethico-political" and ideological structures of society. (p. 30)

What is striking about the war of position, as Gramsci calls it, is that it is a war not of brute force but of ideas. So people must understand the ideas of others before fighting a war of position because a war of position is, in essence, a war of ideas.

Curriculum Debates over Fascism(s)

Here I want to speak to issues around fascism(s) that are raised by political scholars. Generally speaking political scholars have returned to discussions on fascism in light of our current historical situation as a post-9/11 culture. The concerns that these scholars have reflect the larger problematics of neoliberal politics discussed earlier. A key term for both McLaren and Giroux is totalitarianism (which can be understood as a form of fascism). When the United States went to war in Iraq a new totalitarian era arrived, according to McLaren and Giroux. Henry Giroux (2007) comments

> State violence and totalitarian power, which historically have been deployed against marginalized populations—principally Black Americans—have now, at least in the

> United States, become the rule for the entire population, as life is more ruthlessly regulated and increasingly placed in the hands of military and state power. (p. 25)

If students are to understand the word "totalitarian," a historical study of the term becomes necessary. One of the most well-known books on totalitarianism is Hannah Arendt's (1979) *The Origins of Totalitarianism*, upon which neither Giroux nor McLaren draws. Both Giroux and McLaren seem to use the terms "totalitarianism" and "fascism" in a broad sense. But these words have histories that need to be unpacked.

In my book on the Holocaust (2001), I point out that fascism is a word that has a very specific meaning for Germans. Former East Germans accused former West Germans of being fascist. East German Communists claimed that their major concern was for the working class and that they had nothing to do with the Holocaust. Nevertheless many East Germans were anti-Semitic and were complicit in the Holocaust, although they claimed that theirs was an anti-Fascist government. But even if they were anti-Fascist, they were also anti-Semitic and were complicit—as were former West Germans—in the annihilation of European Jews. For Germans, especially then, Fascism had a particular meaning that was directed at former West Germans by former East Germans.

Like the Germans, the Italians tend not to use the term "Fascism" in a broad or generic sense. As Roger Griffin (2008) points out, "With very few exceptions both Italian and German non-Marxist historians of fascism and Nazism, respectively, have avoided the generic term [fascism] altogether" (p. 186). Still, most political theorists in the field of curriculum studies use the term "fascism" in the generic, not historically specific, sense. Philip Morgan (2006) points out

> There are, of course, good and understandable reasons why it is largely the Anglo-Saxon "outsiders," lacking any direct involvement in these national "historians', controversies," who went for comparative and "generic" analysis of fascism. For Germany, Italy and France, countries with unpalatable "fascist" or "fascist collaborating" recent pasts, their historians have naturally been preoccupied with dealing with these pasts and explaining and understanding them in terms of national historical development. (p. 157)

For most readers unfamiliar with these so-called historians' debates some explanation is needed. During the 1980s especially, historians of Nazi Germany were caught up in what they called the *Historikerstreit* or the historian's debate (Morris, 2001). Here, the main issue turned on comparability. The question is whether the Holocaust can be compared to other mass annihilations. In the 1980s many thought that comparing one tragedy with another leads down the slippery slope to revisionism. Revisionist historiography—for Holocaust historians—means to unwrite or whitewash history.

German historians who were complicit or sympathetic with the Nazi regime wrote their histories so as to unremember the past and justify their own complicity. In Vichy France, Nazi collaboration was widespread. Many French historians have had a difficult time coming to terms with Vichy, and so it took much longer for the French to write about their own complicity than, say, the former West Germans. So too, the Austrians. They claimed after the war that they were victims of the Nazi regime. But in fact the Austrians had an enormous role in the Holocaust as many of Hitler's henchmen were Austrian (Morris, 2001). Austria wasn't the only collaborating country. I comment, "Raul Hilberg (1992) reminds us that collaborating countries included Italy [especially the Fascists], Bulgaria, Romania, Hungary, Slovakia, Croatia, Norway, France, and the Netherlands" (p. 153). Many of these countries had their own brand of fascism. Walter Laquer (1996) tells us that Romania's "Iron Guard [especially during the 1930s] under Corneliu Codreanu was the most radical of the European fascist movements" (p. 84). Laquer says that "Fascism in Hungary was surprisingly strong [again during the 1930s]" (p. 84). And then there were also the Croatian fascists (Laquer). Recently in France, Jean-Marie Le Pen's *National Front* is fascist, as pointed out by Tamir Bar-On (2006), Roger Griffin (2008), and Robert O. Paxton (2004).

The point being made here is that there seems to be a historical continuum of Fascism from the 1920s—with the advent of the Italian Fascists—on through World War II and even beyond that into the 1990s and still even today. Fascism seems to remain a continual problem and continual force with which to be reckoned, not only in Europe but also all over the world. Robert O. Paxton asks a good question about the earliest versions of Fascism. Interestingly enough, he suggests that the American Ku Klux Klan was one of the earliest Fascist organizations. Paxton says

> A debate has arisen about which country spawned the earliest Fascist movement. France is a frequent candidate. Russia has been proposed. Hardly anyone puts Germany first. It may be that the earliest phenomenon that can be functionally related to fascism is American: the Ku Klux Klan. (p. 49)

This is a surprising statement, especially for Americans who more than likely would have guessed that Germany and/or Italy would have been considered the first Fascists. Right here on our own soil, fascism(s) spreads.

Critical theorists like McLaren and Giroux seem to suggest that fascism equals neoliberalism. But Kevin Passmore (2006) warns that when Marxists speak of a "core of fascism" (p. 174)—such as neoliberalism—this produces theoretical problems. Is there really a core to fascism and can it be reduced to neoliberalism? No. It is much more complex than that as many historians of fascism seem to suggest. And this is the problem with much critical theory today. The discussions on fascism—in education—do not take into account the historicity of the term, nor do critical theorists cite historians who work in what is called fascist studies. Some of the key historians in this area, as Tamir Bar-On tells us, are "Ernst Nolte, Renzo De Felice, Zeev Sternhell, James Gregor and Stanley Payne…[and] Roger Griffin" (p. 87). There seems to be a gaping hole in the study of fascism in the field of curriculum studies. Most political theorists in education ignore the work being done in fascist studies, which has been ongoing since at least the 1960s.

Comparability and Fascism(s)

It is important to address the issue of comparability in relation to fascism(s). John Weaver (2001) warns that in the context of the Holocaust, Ernst Nolte's position—which is one of comparability—is highly problematic. Weaver states

> Nolte's references to the Gulag system, Pol Pot in Kamphuchea, or Armenians in Turkey were seen as ploys to lessen the contemporary significance of the Holocaust rather than to contextualize the Holocaust within a broader world history perspective. Indeed, by making these references and drawing inferences from these other genocidal events, Nolte constructed a crude hierarchy of genocides, in which the Holocaust, when compared to the killing fields of Kampuchea and the Gulag Archipelago, was neither unique nor very high on his scale of destruction. (p. 64)

The question here is this: Can historians compare one genocide with another without sliding down the slippery slope to revisionism? Can scholars put the Holocaust, as Weaver suggests, "in a broader world history perspective" (p. 64) without erasing the uniqueness and historical particularity of this horrific event? For those who do comparative studies, this is the key problematic.

If historians resort to the generic use of the term "fascism," they face this problem as well: a generic use of this term erases the historical particularity of the event. Robert O. Paxton suggests that if scholars use comparisons in the study of fascism(s) they might follow the lead of Marc Bloch who "reminded us [that comparison] is most useful for eliciting differences" (p. 20). The generic term "fascism," however, tends to—as Walter Laquer (1996) points out—obliterate differences. Laquer says

> The use of the term *fascism* with regard to Nazi Germany also obliterates the important differences between the two regimes [Fascist Italy and Nazi Germany] and the fact that leading authorities on the subject, such as K. D. Bracher and Renzo De Felice, were among the most outspoken opponents of the use of the generic term *fascism* provides, at the very least, food for thought. (p. 7)

The Generic Use of the Term "Fascism"

The case against the generic use of fascism is a convincing one, and yet many scholars who do fascist studies resort to the generic use and draw on comparisons without making enough of the historical specificity of events. Let us consider again the work of Ernst Nolte and also of Roger Griffin. The approach taken by both Nolte and Griffin toward fascism is highly problematic. It was Ernst Nolte who suggested that scholars search for the root of fascism. Roger Griffin (2008) explains that it was Nolte who "popularised" what he called "the fascist minimum" (p. 185). Now this quest for the so-called fascist minimum is taken up by Roger Griffin as he suggests that fascism can be reduced to a few descriptors that can apply to many historical cases. Griffin (2006) suggests that fascism(s) all have a "minimum core ideology of national rebirth (palingenesis) that [embraces] a vast range of highly diverse concrete historical permutations" (p. 29). This so-called fascist minimum is highly problematic because it seems to gloss over historical particularity, reducing or erasing highly complex phenomena.

This is not unlike Holocaust debates. The Holocaust was an extremely complicated historical catastrophe. When scholars ask why it happened, they do not really know. And scholars certainly should not reduce the causes of the Holocaust to one thing (like the fascist minimum). There were many factors that caused the Holocaust. In particular, I am reminded of the Goldhagen controversy (Morris, 2001) where Goldhagen tried to reduce the cause of the Holocaust to "eliminationist anti-Semitism" (p. 136). Goldhagen said the reason the Germans did what they did is because they wanted to. For this simplistic explanation Goldhagen was roundly criticized by the historical community. There were many reasons that the Holocaust happened. Studying possible reasons historians give for the rise of Nazi Germany, scholars should not try to reduce the cause of this historical event to one thing. In my book on the Holocaust, I state:

> In Goldhagen's notes in his book, he takes to task every major Holocaust historian and argues that their ideas are completely misguided. He says that ordinary Germans did not kill because they were coerced, which is what Sarah Gordon argues (p. 490); they did not kill because they were "blind followers of order" (p. 490) which is what Friedlander, G. P. Gooch, Stanley Milgram, and Hannah Arendt argue; they did not murder because of "social psychological pressure" (p. 490) which Goldhagen suggests is Browning's contention; they did not kill because they were "petty bureaucrats" (p. 490) which is Heim and Aly's and Mommsen's position. (2001, p. 137)

Goldhagen's argument is that Germans killed because they wanted to. This simple explanation will not do. Reducing any historical event to one thing is counterintuitive.

Educational scholar Heinz Sunker (1997) makes a similar mistake when trying to explain the Holocaust, wanting to reduce the cause of the Holocaust to one thing. He suggests that the "folk community [was]...the foundation" of National Socialism (p. 7). He explains

> In relation to the development of what can be defined in a preliminary sense as political culture in this period, the ideology of the folk community constitutes the most important reference point. It connected the demands of nationalism, organic thinking, a fetishization of totalization, so that ultimately racism was bound up together with a repressive social order. Folk community as National Socialism's ideology of formation was the foundation of the fascist dictatorship. (p. 7)

What is troubling about this citation is that Sunker suggests that there is actually a foundation or root to National Socialism. However, there were many reasons the Holocaust occurred. Reducing the Holocaust to the rise of a "folk community" does not sufficiently explain the complexities of the Holocaust.

Sunker uses the phrase "fascist dictatorship." This is another problem. Recall that in the context of Germany, fascism means the former West Germany, not the East. Former East Germans considered themselves Communist and accused the West of fascism. So in Germany, the term "fascism" has a specific meaning. But remember too that the Communists were just as complicit in the Holocaust as the so-called fascists.

Against Generic Fascism

Robert O. Paxton (2004) writes that there is no essence to fascism (p. 21). As Roger Eatwell (2006) points out, although "Sir Ian Kershaw, who is willing to concede that there were major ideological affinities between Nazism and Fascism, [he] finds no place for discussion of generic fascism" (p. 105). When educational scholars use the term "fascism" it seems to be mostly used in its generic sense, and this is problematic. Peter McLaren (2006)—in the context of the abstract term "difference"—argues that this term is "unhinged from its historical embeddedness" (p. 31). The same argument can be made about the generic use of the term "fascism"—it too is ahistorical. And yet it seems that McLaren (2005) uses fascism in its generic sense in the context of neoliberalism and the "steady movement toward fascism" (p. 11) of the United States. Robert O. Paxton cautions that "war government under fascism is not the same as the democracies' willing and temporary suspension of liberties" (p. 157). The problem with using fascism in the context of the United States is that it is, as Robert O. Paxton points out, "sloppy usage" (p. 21) of a term that has a history. But the question remains: is neoliberalism fascism? No. Neoliberalism is a terrible thing because it makes the rich richer and exploits everyone else. But it is a global problem that cannot be reduced to the generic sense of the term "fascism." The Bush administration was not the same as fascist Italy under Mussolini. Walter Laquer (1996) is careful to qualify the use of the term "fascism" and points out that—in the context of Nazi Germany and Stalinist Russia—"not everyone who opposes further immigration is a fascist; not every anti-Semite is a fascist; and not every ultranationalist is a fascist" (p. 7). But on the other hand, a terrible person might be all of these things—xenophobic, anti-Semitic and nationalistic—and be a fascist too.

Alexander de Grand (2006) points out that Roger Griffin "frees himself from the lists of attributes that other historians use by limiting the linkage [to fascism] to one point in ideology" (p. 97). Fascism is a style of government that has, as Alexander de Grand points out, "lists of attributes" (p. 97). As opposed to Roger Griffin and Ernst Nolte—who argue that there is a core to fascism—Robert O. Paxton argues that fascism is made up of a network of things. Paxton explains, "Fascism in action looks much more like a network of relationships than a fixed essence" (p. 207). What is this network? What makes up the relationships of a fascist regime? These are the questions raised by scholars who look for multiple—not singular—causes for the rise of oppressive governments.

Nationalism as an Ingredient of Fascism

When educationists describe neoliberalism they often use terms that historians use to describe fascist regimes. Political theorists often do not contextualize historically the terms that they use. Here I discuss some of the ingredients that go into the making of fascism. One such ingredient is nationalism. Robert O. Paxton, Roger Griffin (2006; 2008), Walter Laquer (1996), Hannah Arendt (1979), Richard Hofstader (1963), and Stanley Payne (1995)—to name but a few—all agree that nationalism is an important facet of fascism. But Peter Fritzsche (2006) argues, "It is important to keep in mind that fascism in Italy and Germany succeeded precisely because it was different from traditional fascism" (p. 111). There are historic and geographic differences between Italian and German fascism(s). And certainly there have been more fascist governments than only Italy and Germany. In fact, various countries that have been oppressed by fascist regimes have had very different histories; those differences should be noted, not obfuscated through comparisons. Jeffrey Bale (2006) tells us that scholars like Roger Griffin point out that fascism is not just a European phenomenon. But most scholars of fascism focus on European fascism, Bale reports. Walter Laquer discusses fascist regimes in Italy, Germany, Spain, Romania, Croatia, and Hungary; Robert O. Paxton discusses fascism in France, Russia, Germany, Spain, Portugal, Romania, and the phenomenon of the Ku Klux Klan in the United States; Hannah Arendt focuses mostly on Nazi Germany and Stalinist Russia; Roger Griffin (2008) talks about apartheid South Africa, Chile, Spain, Austria, and France. Griffin argues

> Fascism is a copious taxonomic pot into which Nazi Germany, Francisco Franco's Spain, Apartheid South Africa, Augusto Pinochet's Chile, Jean-Marie Le Pen's plans for the renewal of France, and Jorg Haider's ideal Austria can be thrown [in] without too much intellectual agonizing over definitional or taxonomical niceties. (p. 183)

But there should be intellectual agonizing over what these differing versions of fascism mean in these very different countries. Can scholars—with intellectual integrity—simply throw all of these fascism(s) into the same pot? Perhaps Griffin doesn't mean that all of these fascism(s) are literally the same, but by making such sweeping comparisons Griffin suggests that they basically are all alike, when clearly they are not. Each of these countries has a unique history of fascism. The uniqueness of each should be studied with care.

Militarism as a Facet of Fascism

Another facet of fascism that many scholars agree upon is that fascism is militaristic. The state becomes militarized in fascist governments. Stanley Payne (1995) tells us that militarization is a main feature of fascism:

> Together with the drive for mass mobilization went one of the most characteristic features of fascism, its attempt to militarize politics to an unprecedented degree. This was done by making militia groups central to the movement's organization and by using military insignia and terminology in reinforcing the sense of nationalism and constant struggle. (p. 12)

Giroux (2004) writes about the increasing militarization of the U.S. government in the context of the university and public education. For instance, Giroux says that teachers and scholars work in a "military-corporate-industrial-educational-complex" (p. 34). For Giroux, the university and the public school have both been militarized. To a certain extent this is true. Public school students are under surveillance by police and are scrutinized like never before. University professors too are under surveillance, especially—as Peter McLaren (2006) points out—those who are Marxist. McLaren puts this into historical perspective when he states

> Of course, Marxist analysis is being linked to "anti-Americanism." The Cold War basically drove Marxism out of mainstream intellectual life in the U.S. Some Marxist scholars inhabit the universities, but they are under close scrutiny, especially after September 11. (p. 62)

It is not only Marxist scholars who are under scrutiny after 9/11. All left-wing scholars had to worry under the Bush regime. Henry Giroux (2007) writes that under Bush "corporatist and military tendencies [emerged] within both the university and the wider society" (p. 1). What became increasingly alarming was the government's urging citizens to spy on each other to try to figure out if the enemy (after 9/11) was within. Homegrown terrorists seemed to be everywhere lurking, according to Bush. Both Giroux (2003) and McLaren (2005) comment on the advent of spying under the Bush regime. Alarmingly, McLaren reports that the

> Department of Homeland Security along with its secret police now has the right to wiretap anyone's phone it wants without a court order, to search any home without a warrant... to secretly monitor people's finances, purchases, library or internet use with sophisticated electronic and computer eavesdropping equipment. (p. 64)

Militarization means control and surveillance. McLaren, who comments on the increased militarization of the state under Bush, compares Bush to Hitler. Perhaps this comparison is farfetched. But still, the Bush administration was awful and what McLaren reports in the above citation certainly reminds one of Nazi Germany. However, certainly Nazi Germany and the United States—under the Bush regime—are not the same thing.

Alexander de Grand (2006) also points out that under Mussolini, the Italian State was also militarized as "the fascist motto was not 'think and judge for yourself', but rather 'believe, obey, fight'" (p. 96). This unquestioning obedience to the government is what the Bush regime wanted, and they too wanted an unquestioning fighting force to go into Iraq under the concocted evidence that Saddam Hussein had weapons of mass destruction.

Fundamentalism and Fascism

Fundamentalism is another facet of fascism. Bush wanted people to believe in him unthinkingly because, as McLaren (2005) points out, Bush thought that God spoke to him. Bush was a fundamentalist of sorts. McLaren says

> For most of us who would like to see foreign and domestic policy run by carefully considered deliberation based on sound intelligence and critical analysis, a faith-based presidency presents a crisis of inestimable proportions. You can't run the world on the supreme confidence that your views are right because they are guided by God. (p. 3)

Bush and Hitler are not the same, yet there are uncanny similarities between them, especially on the issue of prophecy. Hitler also said that God spoke to him (Morris, 2001). And interestingly enough Hannah Arendt (1979) points out that many dictators "have the habit of announcing their political intentions in the form of prophecy" (p. 349). I point out in my book on the Holocaust:

> Hitler (1923) says "Thus did I believe that I must act in the sense of the almighty Creator: by fighting against the Jews I am doing the Lord's work" (p. 25). Hitler really believed that he had been called, like a prophet, to carry out the will of God. He uses words like Providence over and over again [in *Mein Kampf*] to suggest that the Final Solution was fated by God. (2001, p. 214)

Here, Hitler sounds like a fundamentalist. And certainly many have commented on the links between religious fundamentalism and fascism (McLaren, 2005; Reynolds & Webber, 2009; Giroux, 2007; Payne, 1995; Laquer, 1996).

Today, Americans especially worry about Islamic fundamentalism and terrorist attacks. But not all Muslims are terrorists, and this is something that people on the right—especially Christian fundamentalists—do not understand. Anti-Muslim sentiment and xenophobia are on the rise in the United States since 9/11. Some might think that the link between fundamentalism and fascism is new, especially with the advent of Islamic terrorists. But Walter Laquer tells us otherwise. He states

> In the Middle East, Radical Islam is a rising force and has a striking overlap with fascism. But this *clerical fascism* is not a new phenomenon, as the term was used in Italy as far back as 1921 to describe those advocating a synthesis between Catholicism and the dynamic new political movement headed by Benito Mussolini. During World War II, clerical Fascist regimes ruled Slovakia and Croatia. (p. 5)

A few points here about the above citation. Most of us know little about clerical fascism during the 1920s either in the Middle East or in places like Slovakia and Croatia. Americans are so narrowly educated. Few of us have any knowledge of international affairs. American news tells us very little about what is really going on in the world. A second point I would like to make here is that it is a well-known fact for many European scholars that the Catholic Church supported Mussolini—and Hitler for that matter. Protestant churches also supported the Nazis (Morris, 2001). Probably not many Americans know this. Again, not all Catholics or Protestants are fundamentalists or fascists, but some are. The unbending, rigid, parochial, and militant attitude of fundamentalists leads to violence. History teaches us this.

What is worrisome today is Sarah Palin and her Tea Party followers. This Tea Party movement in the United States is yet another example of fundamentalism. These people are xenophobic, homophobic, racist, and the rest. The Tea Party movement has arisen at this time in history in direct reaction to the election of the first black president of the United States, Barack Obama. Since this movement is relatively new, it is hard to say what they are capable of doing.

Historically, many fundamentalist churches have supported hate speech. Stanley Payne (1995) points out the connection between Mussolini and the Vatican. Payne tells us

> For Mussolini, the final achievement in the creation of a political structure was to sign a concordat with the Church, which would in effect bring the blessing of Italy's most influential institution. Overt, often intense, hostility between church and state had existed since unification in 1860, but as early as 1922 the Vatican had indicated

> it would not oppose a Mussolini government and appreciated Fascism's role in the defeat of the left. Latern Pacts in 1929 completed the system. (p. 119)

When organized religions support dictatorships trouble abounds because organized religions bring with them millions of supporters. It is these millions of supporters who are worrisome.

Historians comment on the rise of fascism and the way in which the millions of people who support dictators are, in some ways, more frightening than the dictator. As historian Robert O. Paxton (2004) points out, "No dictator rules by himself" (p. 119). Robert Soucy (2006) remarks that Alexander de Grand emphasizes that what makes Italy's fascist regime frightening "were the large numbers of social conservatives and cultural traditionalists who poured into the movement after 1920" (p. 213). Paxton warns

> The image of the all-powerful dictator personalizes fascism, and creates the false impression that we can understand it fully by scrutinizing the leader alone. This image, whose power lingers today, is the last triumph of fascist propagandists. It offers an alibi to nations that approved or tolerated fascist leaders, and diverts attention from the persons, groups, and institutions who helped him. (p. 9)

I would like to point out that these examples from history show that religious fundamentalists in America—in many ways—mirror fundamentalism(s) in countries like fascist Italy. Still fundamentalism(s) are not the same. Peter McLaren (2005) and Henry Giroux (2009) try to elucidate these problems in the United States, but they do not give historical examples in much detail to buttress their points.

Violence and Fascism

Another key ingredient to fascism is violence. European fascism arose in Italy—as Robert O. Paxton (2004) discusses—with WWI. As Paxton says, after experiencing violence during WWI, people wanted to solve their problems through the use of more violence. Violence begets violence. William F. Pinar's (2001) work on lynching and prison rape suggests that there was something sexual about lynching. Is there a sexual component to violence? Perhaps sometimes there is. And, too, students learn from studying the history of Nazi Germany that there was something sexually sadistic about torturing people (Morris, 2001). Sadistic behavior is also sexual. War is sadism. Robert Paxton says that "fascism's deliberate replacement of reasoned debate with immediate sensual experience transformed politics, as the exiled German critic Walter Benjamin was the first to point out, into aesthetics. And the ultimate fascist experience, Benjamin warned in 1936, was war" (p. 17). Hitler had a way of seducing people by pounding his fist on the podium, ranting and raving. There was a violent and sexual "aesthetic," if you will, to his political rants. Watching footage of him is always shocking because today that kind of behavior in the United States would never be acceptable. Americans like politicians to be calm, cool, and collected. Americans do not like drama in Congress, unlike the British, who in Parliament carry on so. Americans, recall, are of Puritan stock and this means that anger—at least being irate—is not an acceptable emotion. But Hitler raved on and on and the Germans obviously liked it. It seems that all of Europe liked it.

Why were there so many collaborating countries during the Holocaust? Walter Laquer (1996) suggests that today "the cult of the Fuhrer and the Duce has gone out of fashion" (p. 93). But who knows what tomorrow will bring? In dire economic times dogma wins elections. Hitler was the master of dogma. Nuance and ambivalence on the political stage are beside the point when people can't pay the rent or buy food. George Bush had little nuance and seemed certain of his principles. Dogmatic. Bush was never wrong—at least in his mind. And this reminds us of a comment made by Hannah Arendt (1979) about dictators. She says, "The chief qualification of a mass leader has become unending infallibility; he can never admit an error" (pp. 348–349). Bush never admitted error. Right-wing conservatives loved Bush because whatever he did he seemed sure about. The Iraq war was one of the biggest blunders in the history of the United States, but Bush never admitted that he was wrong. Hannah Arendt comments that in Hitler's *Mein Kampf*, he "stated that to be successful, a lie must be enormous" (p. 439). The Bush administration told the American people—told the world—"an enormous lie" about Hussein's so-called weapons of mass destruction.

No Dissension in a Fascist Regime

Another key ingredient of fascist regimes is that they do not tolerate dissension. During times of war and during times of conservative administrations in the United States, dissension is also vilified. Dissension was not tolerated during the years of Woodrow Wilson and WWI. Dissension was not tolerated during the Iraq war and the Bush years. During the regimes of Stalin and Mao dissension could get you disappeared, tortured, or murdered. And this is the meaning of a totalitarian regime: total power over everything, including dissenters.

During the Bush administration, Peter McLaren (2006) commented, "It is very likely that the Bush gang will make more concerted effort to root out dissension in the universities" (p. 36). Under conservative regimes, Henry Giroux (2007) remarks that "faculty are increasingly being stripped of their autonomy and critical capacities, silenced in the governance process" (p. 8). John Dewey and others founded the American Association of University Professors (AAUP) to serve as a watchdog group to protect faculty. But the AAUP has little power. Left-leaning faculty are under watch and constantly under surveillance. But still a totalitarian regime is more than the stripping away of the right to dissent.

In Europe, many Jewish intellectuals were not only not allowed to dissent, but they also were murdered for doing so. In the place of Jewish professors who were fired or murdered during the Nazi regime, Max Weinreich (1999) tells us that "Hitler's professors" were hired. Weinreich explains that these professors wrote,

> A good many thousands of books, pamphlets, and documents [which] provide ample evidence that there was participation of German scholarship in every single phase of the crime.... Nazi policies were drawn into the work for more than a decade: physical anthropology and biology, all branches of the social sciences and the humanities. (p. 7).

During the Holocaust dissenters were fired, many killed, while those who were complicit were rewarded with academic positions. And what disturbs here is that Hitler's scholars justified theory to commit mass murder. John Weaver (2001) reminds us that the former East German historians (who were in cahoots with the Stasi police) were responsible for the arrest of students who questioned them. Robert O. Paxton (2004) points out that in Italy a similar scene took place among academics. Paxton reports

> When university professors [in Mussolini's Italy] were required to take an oath to the regime during the academic year 1931–32 only 11 out of 1,200 refused. Only after the racial legislation of 1938...did a significant number of intellectuals emigrate. (p. 140)

Did these professors take this oath out of fear or peer pressure or did they actually like Mussolini's policies? Alexander de Grand (2006) tells us that the Italian Fascists also "used racial criteria to purge both Jews and Jewish influences. In their purge of Jewish literature, the ban was extended back to

1850" (p. 96). How can a book written in 1850 be considered dangerous? This shows that paranoia and hate can drive people to do the most absurd things, like getting rid of books that were written more than a hundred years ago.

University professors weren't the only ones under surveillance during the Hitler years. School children, in Hitler's Germany, were also under surveillance and sent to "camps" to learn obedience and to learn the ways of the Nazis (Dudek, 1997; Schiedeck & Stahlmann, 1997; Harvey, 1997). Jürgen Schiedeck and Martin Stahlmann tell us

> Camps also had a lot in common when it came to the teaching topics, regardless of a camp's special orientation. For example, topics almost everywhere included the 'Fuhrer', the 'movement', 'national Socialist philosophy' and the Versailles Treaty. Sports (of a paramilitary nature) also played a major role as a self-evident part of the daily routine.... . Wearing a uniform and weapons practice were also obligatory. (p. 56)

In the United States the push for physical education and sports during the early 1900s was really about the crisis of masculinity. Boys are made more masculine by playing sports. Teddy Roosevelt had much to do with the masculinization of politics. Being a real man meant hunting, killing, being a sportsman (Haraway, 1989). Real men are not scholars, they are athletes and fighters.

At any rate, these so-called camps in Nazi Germany were meant to make men of boys and made certain that these boys were loyal to the Nazi cause. Taking children away from their parents was a way to control them. Peter Dudek (1997) claims, "A policy of nationalizing youth education [was] to counteract the traditional childrearing institutions of the school and the family, and thus enforce the national-socialist demands for total control over all youth and all phases and areas of life" (p. 41). The Nazis left no stone unturned. No child was left behind. Camp made sure that all children were indoctrinated fully into Nazi ideology.

And then there were the other camps for the "uneducable" (Sunker, 1997, p. 25). These were concentration camps. Unbelievable as it is, the Nazis murdered their own children if they were uneducable or disabled. Jürgen Schiedeck and Martin Stahlmann (1997) report, "Although officially called remand camps, both Moringen and Uckermark were actually concentration camps, with Moringen being responsible for the death of at least fifty-nine youths" (p. 61). This is a little known fact among most Americans. And it is an example of what can happen to people who are considered different. Difference was clearly not acceptable in any of these fascist/authoritarian regimes.

New Fascisms

Today many talk of new fascism(s). It seems that fascism—in whatever stripe—never seems to go away. One begins to wonder why this phenomenon continues. Many of these new fascists are right-wing extremists—and they come in many stripes. Some scholars suggest that it has become increasingly difficult to pinpoint who these people are because of the internet and cybercrime. For example, Roger Griffin (2008) suggests that the new face of fascism(s) is "predominantly rhizomatic (and hence largely faceless)" (p. 202). Griffin calls new fascism "slime mould" (p. 192) because it is like a "weather resistant organism" (p. 200) that keeps coming back in different hard-to-pin-down forms. Today radical Islamic terrorists—who behead and burn people alive—are emerging around the globe like a cancer. It seems that there is no stopping them. But it is not only Islamic terrorists that give us pause. Home-grown terrorists like neo-Nazis, skinheads, and the Aryan Brotherhood are right here on U.S. soil.

Roger Griffin tells us about other fascism(s). He states,

> One symptom of the extreme right's rhizomatic structure is an ecumenicalism unthinkable in the "fascist" era, expressed both in the way web-linkages exist in cross-currents of influence detectable between diffuse currents of fascism such as universal Nazism, Christian Identity, Third Positionism and the New Right. (p. 199)

Griffin points out that these groups are international and continue to spread because of the internet. And the facelessness of these new groups in some ways causes more uneasiness than the black shirts of Italy, for example. If these terrorists are indeed faceless, it is hard to know how to find them and what to do about them. During what scholars call the classical era of fascism the enemy was clear. A black shirt obviously was a fascist. Today, this is not the case. However, Martin Durham (2008) suggests that there are fascists who are identifiable. Clearly, Osama Bin Laden was not faceless. Durham points out that "America neo-Nazi…William Pierce…looks not toward leaderless resistance but to a centralized organisation" (p. 102). Durham argues that there are two kinds of fascism(s) today: one has a face and a structure; the other is faceless and amorphous. David Duke—former wizard of the Ku Klux Klan—has a well-known face, especially for people who live in Louisiana. But ISIS is faceless and indeed amorphous.

Walter Laquer (1996) points out that fascism(s) are not only in the United States but are everywhere. He states,

> In France, Russia, Italy, and Austria, the parties of the extreme right are among the strongest. By adopting certain aspects of contemporary youth culture (such as the skinheads), neofascist groups have been able to gain a foothold in Europe. (p. 5)

But not all youngsters are drawn to terrorist organizations. As Giroux (2003) points out, since Columbine "a whole generation of youth have been labeled as superpredators" (p. xiv). Not all young people shoot school children. However, Walter Laquer reminds us that "Nazism and Italian Fascism appeared as the movement of Youth; to wit, the Italian anthem was 'Giovinezza' (Youth)" (p. 29). Universities in Germany and Austria—during WWII—were hotbeds of anti-Semitism (Morris, 2001). Still sweeping generalizations are not accurate.

Today scholars talk about "postfascist" (Bar-On, 2006, p. 88), "microfascisms" (Roy, 2008, p. vii), "proto-fascism" (Giroux, 2004, p. 17), "neofascist" (Laquer, 1996, p. 5), or "creeping fascism" (Giroux, p. 11). Of these concepts, postfascism is the least helpful. Fascism is not "post." Post suggests that fascism is over; it's not over, it seems to stay with us and morph into a variety of forms as Griffin's (2008) metaphor of "slime mould" suggests (p. 192). Hatreds abound. Anti-Semitism continually emerges and so too does racism.

Political scholars in curriculum studies tend not to look at hate groups like the neo-Nazis or skinheads—but rather focus on neoliberalism as the main force of (what they consider to be a form of fascism)—as I pointed out earlier. Many critical theorists tend to argue that the U.S. government is fascist. What they tend not to examine are hate groups—especially if they are youth hate groups. Critical theorists are so worried about not demonizing youth, as Giroux (2003) puts it, that they have missed what is right before their eyes. There are youth militias, neo-Nazi youth, and youth skinheads here in the United States.

Critical theorists in the United States and Canada focus mostly on the problems of neoliberalism to the exclusion of youth hate groups. But neoliberalism is not the whole story. Moreover, neoliberalism is not new. Scholars trace neoliberal tendencies back to the Hoover administration. Adam Cohen (2009) reminds us that Herbert Hoover was all about the free market. There are striking similarities between the Hoover administration and the G. W. Bush administration. Cohen reminds us that during the Depression

> the nation was crying out for the government to respond, but President Herbert Hoover refused to acknowledge the seriousness of the crisis. "I am convinced," he said in the spring of 1930, "we have passed the worst." As the Great Depression held

on for year after brutal year, Hoover began to concede that the crisis was real, but he still refused to provide the sort of relief that was needed. His free-market ideology taught him that private enterprise should be the source of all solutions, and his near-religious commitment to "rugged individualism" convinced him that giving aid to the Depression's victims would morally damage them. (p. 2)

Many neoliberals today continue to think in Hooveresque fashion. Neoliberals seem to think that the market will take care of itself without any government intervention. Again, neoliberalism is not the only problem at hand politically.

I argue that scholars of education must study youth groups who are fascist—like the neo-Nazis or skinheads—without demonizing youth. The fear of demonizing (p. xvii) youth—as Giroux (2003) puts it—blinds critical theorists to other kinds of fascism(s) with which young people are engaged. There are many kinds of problems that need to be studied. School shootings need to be studied more, for example. There are two notable books in education about school shootings such as Julie Webber's (2003) *Failure to Hold: The Politics of School Violence* and Douglas Kellner's (2008) *Guys and Guns Amok: Domestic Terrorism and School Shootings from the Oklahoma City Bombing to the Virginia Tech Massacre*. I encourage students to read these primary texts closely to get a better handle on violence in youth culture(s).

Totalitarianism(s), Militarism(s): Continued Patterns in Political Scholarship

Peter McLaren and Henry Giroux aren't the only education scholars talking about education against the backdrop of totalitarianism or fascism. Wayne Ross (2004), Kenneth Saltman (2003; 2007), David Gabbard (2003), Kaustuv Roy (2008), Stanley Aronowitz (2000), Julie Webber (2003), Douglas Kellner (2008), Enora Brown (2003; 2007), Pauline Lipman (2003; 2007), Joe Kincheloe (2008), Donaldo Macedo (2006), Sandy Grande (2004), Shirley Steinberg (2007), and Marvin Berlowitz and Nathan Long (2003)—for starters—all talk about education in the context of authoritarianism, militarism, and neoliberalism. Henry Giroux (2004) has written a book titled *The Terror of Neoliberalism: Authoritarianism and the Eclipse of Democracy*. What is implied in this title is that neoliberalism is a form of terrorism and that neoliberalism is a form of authoritarianism. But this form of authoritarianism surely isn't the same as a true totalitarian government like Nazi Germany or Stalinist Russia.

Again, terms like "totalitarianism" and "terror" are used generically by political scholars in curriculum studies.

An important book that many political theorists draw on—especially Kenneth Saltman (2007)—is Naomi Klein's (2007) *The Shock Doctrine: The Rise of Disaster Capitalism*. Kenneth Saltman's edited collection is titled similarly *Schooling and the Politics of Disaster*. Saltman acknowledges Naomi Klein as the inspiration for his edited collection. For students who are interested in a hard-hitting look at the problematics of neoliberal policy and the problems of the ongoing privatization of public services, Naomi Klein's book is a must read and a real "shock" to use her term. Klein (2007) tells us that the Bush administration used disasters in order to, for example, privatize public schools. Hurricane Katrina in New Orleans is one such disaster upon which Klein draws. Klein tells us

> In sharp contrast to the glacial pace with which the levees were repaired and the electricity grid was brought back online, the auctioning off of New Orleans' school system took place with military speed and precision. Within nineteen months, most of the poor residents still in exile, New Orleans' public school system had been almost completely replaced by privately run charter schools. (p. 6)

In the media, news anchors turned Katrina—a catastrophe—into a good thing. They suggested that the New Orleans public school system actually benefited from Katrina. But what the news anchors did not tell us is that according to Naomi Klein "New Orleans teachers used to be represented by a strong union; now the union's contract had been shredded, and its forty-seven hundred members had all been fired" (p. 6). This is an example, Klein tells us of "disaster capitalism"; this is the way the Bush administration shamefully capitalized on disaster. Many of the political writers in curriculum studies I mention above comment on the ongoing concern of the privatization of public services, especially the privatization of public schools.

To make what is public private is a way to control the kinds of ideas that are taught to our children. A for-profit private school can do as it pleases. Neoliberals want total control over schools, over ideas, and over what gets taught to our children. Peter Taubman (2009), in his important book titled *Teaching by Numbers: Deconstructing the Discourse of Standards and Accountability in Education*, suggests that the hidden curriculum of No Child Left Behind is an economic one. NCLB is a for-profit institution. Taubman states

> Although corporate interests were clearly involved in the formation of No Child Left Behind, they were not explicit. At the state level, the business community is

deeply and visibly involved in the formulation of policy, and its involvement is clear in the language used to articulate the policies. That involvement has been incredibly lucrative for corporations invested in educational resources, such as Pearson Education, Kaplan, and McGraw-Hill, and for individuals, like Sandy Kress, an architect of NCLB, who has made millions lobbying for some of those companies (Emery and Ohanlan). (p. 67)

Textbooks published by these companies whitewash and water down history. These kinds of textbooks are not meant to be serious intellectual contributions; they are meant to make money. Erudition has nothing to do with profit. But clearly, these textbook companies are out to make profits.

Not only is NCLB a for-profit institution, the entire standardized testing industry is out to make the profit as well. Standardized testing is big business. Pepi Leistyna (2007) concurs with Peter Taubman (2009) on the issue of the profitability of NCLB. Leistyna remarks

> Embracing what is in fact an old neoliberal approach dressed up as innovative reform, the political machinery behind NCLB has effectively disguised the motivations of a profit-driven industry. Schools now give nearly 50 million tests per year and the annual value of this market ranges from $400 million to $700 million. (p. 147)

These political scholars have done some important work unearthing the money-making aspect of NCLB. Imagine the human cost of test taking on millions of children every year. Standardized tests have nothing to do with teaching children to be caring, concerned, and informed citizens. On a related note, Antonia Darder (2002) points out that there is much money to be made in phonics textbooks. Phonics is hardly what Freire had in mind when he talked about literacy. At any rate, Darder says, "While Sacramento is busy setting up mandates for the implementation of a phonics curriculum in the schools, the marketing divisions of corporations that publish phonics texts…are revving their engines for multi-million-dollar sales" (pp. 11–12). Phonics is big business and is hardly intellectual. Stanley Aronowitz (2000), who is highly critical of standardized testing, suggests that real academic scholars are interested in erudition, not standardization. He asks:

> Why do some choose academic professions rather than more remunerative occupations in business or in technosciences such as molecular biology or computer science?…The answers, in these times, are culturally startling: some people abhor corporate life and don't care about making more money than they need to live in reasonable comfort, and they enjoy reading, writing, research, and teaching. (p. 13)

Corporations are dictating to education scholars, even in the universities, how they should teach and what textbooks to use (i.e., Pearson and edTPA). Aronowitz tells us in the corporatized university, college courses of most worth—"are useful to the corporate order" (p. 126). If college classes have no use value for the corporate order then they are cut. Philosophy departments disappear. The liberal arts are certainly viewed as the stepsister of the academy (Mary Doll, personal communication). In *Jewish Intellectuals and the University* (2006), I suggest that even the founders of colleges like Leland Stanford and Andrew Carnegie thought that the university was not a place for real intellectual work: the purpose of the university should be to serve corporate interests; the university should be practical and not theoretical. What use is theory? Carnegie and Stanford wondered. The only theory of any use for corporations is economic theory. The rest—at least for Stanford and Carnegie—was a waste of time. And yet today both of these institutions (Stanford and Carnegie Mellon) honor the liberal arts and certainly honor theoretical fields of study. Not only that, Carnegie Mellon is known for its fine arts program, especially its drama program. Ironically, Andrew Carnegie had little interest in the arts. Richard Hofstadter (1963)—in talking about these same tycoons—reports that Vanderbilt "is reported to have read one book in his life, *Pilgrim's Progress*, and that at an advanced age" (p. 258). What is valued in the United States is not how erudite people are but how rich people are. And this is where Marxist scholarship becomes particularly important. Scholars have to have a way to unpack what is wrong with this corporate mentality, and Marxism helps us to understand these problems; this is one of the reasons why Peter McLaren's work is so important, for example. He is perhaps the only political scholar today in the field of education who suggests that critical theorists return to Marx. Likewise, I suggest that scholars return to the work of Hannah Arendt (1979). Her book titled *The Origins of Totalitarianism* is one of the most important books on the subject of totalitarianism in the 20th century, but it is often overlooked by political scholars in curriculum studies with a few exceptions. Kaustuv Roy (2008) is clearly indebted to Arendt in his work. I will discuss Roy's work later.

Defending Public Schools

Wayne Ross (2004) argues that scholars need to defend public schools. But the question here is what are educationists defending them from?—an encroaching totalitarianism (p. xvii). Kenneth Saltman (2007) says, "By reducing the politics of education to its economic functions, [i.e., making schooling into a form of job training or corporatizing schooling] neoliberal educational thinking has deeply authoritarian tendencies" (p. 14). When schooling is built on the business model or becomes like a business or is thought of as business, Saltman claims authoritarianism is at hand. The idea that everything can be reduced to business is as old as industrialization. Richard Hofstadter (1963) reminds us of "the famous remark of Calvin Coolidge: 'The business of America is business'" (p. 237). The idea that schooling can be reduced to business is not new. But the idea that schooling as business is authoritarian—as Saltman claims—does not fit into the classic definitions of authoritarianism (Arendt, 1979). There is nothing in Arendt's description of authoritarian regimes that has to do with business practices. But what Saltman seems to be getting at is that when the total idea of schooling is reduced to business it is this totalizing mentality that becomes problematic. Totalizing and totalitarian, however, might not be the same thing. Saltman uses the word "totalitarianism" in its generic form.

Schooling is not business and should have nothing to do with business or making profits. Privatizing public schools in order to make profits is clearly wrong. But using the term "totalitarian" in the context of schooling in the United States' troubles. Perhaps totalitarianism in the context of neoliberal schooling needs more qualification.

Kaustuv Roy (2008) says that neoliberalism is a form of "neo-plantation[ism]" (p. xvii). Roy suggests that relations—under neoliberal government—are those of master and slave. Roy argues that this plantation (as a metaphor) has gone global in fact. The metaphor of the plantation (for neoliberal governments) is unusual for political theorists. It captures the problems of economic slavery that most people(s) of the world suffer because of free market ideology. Roy says

> On the neoplantation [read neoliberalism], market theology and the commodity as the measure of all things belong to a certain pathology within whose horizons the militarization of society becomes the inevitable deployment of desire, from [which] proceeds the war on the human. (p. xvii)

In his acknowledgements, Roy mentions Hannah Arendt. Roy's "war on the human" is akin to Arendt (1979), who states, "The totalitarian attempt at global [read Roy's global plantation] conquest and total domination has been the destructive way out of all impasses. Its victory may coincide with the destruction of humanity [read Roy's 'war on the human']" (p. viii).

Neoliberalism is, as Hobbes might put it, a war of all against all. This is the bigger point that both Roy and Arendt make. Both are pessimistic about our future. As long as market forces are "free" and regulations of banks are undone, as long as what is public becomes private, and as long as global inequities continue, there is little to celebrate. And this is why scholars like Wayne Ross (2004) talk about the need to defend public schools.

Neoliberalism, Totalitarianism, Militarism, and the Public Schools

One of the ongoing themes in the political sector of the field is the worry of militarization, as I mentioned earlier. Many political scholars comment on the ways in which neoliberalism, totalitarianism, and militarism go hand in hand with schooling. Think back to our earlier discussion of totalitarianism and fascism because militarization is part and parcel of these disastrous forms of governing. It is not only Peter McLaren and Henry Giroux who worry about militarization and schooling; many more can be added to the list—for example, see Douglas Kellner (2008), Kenneth Saltman and David Gabbard (2003), or Marvin Berlowitz and Nathan Long (2003). In fact, readers might consult Kenneth Saltman and David Gabbard's edited collection titled *Education as Enforcement: The Militarization and Corporatization of Schools*. Kenneth Saltman explains the title of his book here. He states

> What I am calling "Education as Enforcement" understands militarized public schooling as part of the militarization of civil society that in turn needs to be understood as part of the broader social, cultural, and economic movements for state-backed corporate globalization that seek to erode public democratic power and expand and enforce corporate power. (p. 3)

What is striking in this passage is the term "enforcement." This is a concept not used very much, if at all, in the political sector of the field. What is being enforced is free market ideology in its complicity with militarization. But what exactly is being militarized in the context of schooling? Saltman tells us

> Military generals running schools, students in uniforms, metal detectors, police presence, high-tech ID card dog tags, real time internet-based surveillance cameras, mobile hidden surveillance cameras, security consultants, chainlink fences, surprise searches—as U.S. public schools invest in record levels of school security. (p. 1)

The level at which the schools have been militarized, according to Saltman, is total. Totalization=militarization=corporatization=public schools. And this is exactly what schools should not be. Not only are schools becoming militarized, schoolchildren are, as Douglas Kellner (2008) suggests, "being preyed upon by the military that has returned thousands of dead soldiers in body bags from U.S. intervention in Afghanistan and Iraq" (p. 81). Marvin Berlowitz and Nathan Long (2003) tell us that working-class youth join the military because they feel that they have so few economic options in life. These youth see the military as a paycheck and a chance to see the world. They do not know what war means or what killing people or seeing people being killed really means, and many do not even think about it until it's too late. War is romanticized. Billboards abound with soldiers in crisp uniforms with the caption "courage" or "bravery" or "honor" or "duty." Be all that you can be, the army mantra goes. One would think that after the nightmares of the 20th century—that is, the horrors of the world wars, Vietnam, and the rest—that people wouldn't romanticize war. But they do. Youth are especially vulnerable. I am reminded of what Martin Berlowitz and Nathan Long tell us about JROTC. They state

> The advocates of JROTC, who are endeavoring to transform their schools into military academies, target these "urban underclass" schoolchildren for recruitment. Defense Department guidelines for JROTC specifically seek "the less affluent large urban schools" and populations who are "at-risk." These children are trapped by a form of economic conscription referred to as the "push-pull phenomenon," in which they are pushed by poverty and racism and pulled by the promise of military benefits. (p. 167)

Many of these youth think that nothing bad will happen to them and in fact they can't wait to dress up in their crisp new military uniforms. They want to carry guns because that image is glamorized on TV and in the movies. But they do not think through the consequences of actually shooting another human being. The bottom line is that these youth feel that they have no options once they are out of school. What jobs are to be had? Most of these youngsters can't afford college and so what real choices do they have? The military gives them a choice and a paycheck—and as Douglas Kellner (2008) points out—these kids are also given a body bag (p. 81).

Class, Control, and the Politics of Emotion

In this final section three issues are addressed that emerge in the recent literature: class, control, and what I call the politics of emotion. For political scholars class—as a category—is a key interest. This is not surprising. But what is surprising—as I mentioned earlier—is that many comment that the concept "class" tends to get ignored by educationists (Fine & Weis, 1998; Brantlinger, 2003; Weis, 2008, Howard, 2008; McLaren, 2000). For example, Peter McLaren claims

> Because capital has itself invaded almost every sphere of life in the United States, the focus of the educational left has been distracted from the great class struggles that have punctuated this century and now rests almost entirely on an understanding of asymmetrical gender and ethnic relations. Although this new focus is important, class struggle is now perilously viewed as an outdated issue. (p. 32)

The exploration of "gender and ethnic relations" is not, in fact, new. If students trace curriculum history back to at least the 1970s, they will learn that scholars have been working in these areas at least since then, if not before. There does, however, seem to be a trend among curriculum scholars that class, as McLaren points out, is beside the point. But there are other ways to get at class as well and feminists have known this for a long time. Although the primary category for feminist analysis has historically been gender, class can also be examined from a feminist perspective. Marxists historically have left out gender, and some complain that critical theory is, as Joe Kincheloe (2007b) points out, seen as a "White North American (and often European) 'thing'" (p. 11). Sandy Grande (2004) contends

> Critical theorists have failed to recognize and, more importantly, to theorize the relationship between American Indian tribes and the larger demographic imaginary. This failure has severely limited their ability to produce political strategies and educational interventions that account for the rights and needs of American Indian students. (p. 1)

Along with Grande, Kincheloe suggests that critical theorists have much to learn from "subjugated knowledges" and should make an effort to "engage people of African, Asian, and indigenous backgrounds" (p. 11). Sandy Grande calls for a "red pedagogy" (as the title of her book suggests).

Adam Howard (2008) argues that class—as a category of study—is taboo (p. 16). Perhaps class is not taboo so much as something people take for granted and don't bother thinking about. Also it must be noted that the working class is not monolithic. Marxists are not all of a piece either. None of these categories is monolithic. I would suggest that students who are interested in issues of class consult the primary texts of Adam Howard (2008), Lois Weis (2008), Ellen Brantlinger (2003), Michelle Fine together with Lois Weis (1998), Peter McLaren (2000), Henry Giroux (1996), Joe Kincheloe (2007a), and Shirley Steinberg (2007).

Postformal Thinking: Undoing Control

Joe Kincheloe, Shirley Steinberg, and Patricia Hinchey (1999) edited a collection of essays on what they call "postformal thought." Here, they critique the formalism of Piaget and developmental psychology. Developmental psychology has historically been—according to these scholars—a form of controlling children and "normalizing" them. This is another way that scholars are talking about control. (See also the work of Gaile Cannella [2008], Gaile Cannella & Radhika Viruru [2004], Joe Kincheloe and Shirley Steinberg [1999, Marianne Bloch and Thomas Popkewitz [2005], Lourdes Diaz Soto [2005] on their critiques of Piaget and what they call "formal" thinking.) Postformal thinking is political, as well as poststructural. But primarily postformalism is political.

The scholars mentioned above all write about the way in which developmental psychology via Piaget attempts to fit children into certain predisposed categories. If children don't fit in these categories they are considered abnormal. This stance can also be seen in what is called "ego psychology" in the work of Anna Freud and Heinz Hartmann. Ego psychology, like formalism, is a way to normalize and control peoples' eccentricities and to erase difference. Ego psychology and developmental psychology pathologize.

Joe Kincheloe and Shirley Steinberg (1999) argue that developmental psychology via Piaget is classist and racist. These scholars tell us

> Metaphorical constructs and meaning-making frameworks brought to school by African American, Latino, or other children who do not come from white middle-class backgrounds are often dismissed as developmentally inappropriate. (p. 59)

Who is to say what is developmentally appropriate? Kincheloe and Steinberg point out that there are power issues at stake here. Many people do not like difference and whatever appears different—including children who are different (read not white and not middle class)—is pathologized. Pathologizing is political as well as psychological. Gaile Cannella (2008), interestingly, points out that developmental psychologists need to rethink the notion of development. Cannella states that an "assumption underlying child development is the conviction that all human beings grow and develop in a predetermined manner" (p. 47). These predetermined phases of development were invented by a white male scholar (Piaget) who saw the world through his white privilege and by his class privilege. Radhika Viruru (2001) says that many poor children in India eat out of garbage cans. How can they fit into Piaget's white Western male elitist vision? Viruru says that "so much of early childhood education and care is written in the language of affluence and privilege that it is far removed from the realities of so many children" (p. 19). Piagetian thought is, thus, highly problematic.

The Politics of Emotion

Critical theorists do not often deal with the issue of emotions. But as Joe Kincheloe (2007b) points out, it was Paulo Freire who—in the context of critical theory—talked about the notion of "radical love" (p. 9). Kincheloe tells us that "radical love [is]…the foundation that grounds my conception of critical pedagogy" (p. 10). Shirley Steinberg (2009) explains that radical love is the kind of love that is extremely difficult. Difficult love is the love that is nearly impossible. What this suggests is that doing the work of critical theory—if grounded in Freire's notion of radical love—is extremely difficult. And this is what Peter McLaren means when he talks about not watering down critical theory by skipping over difficult intellectual and emotional issues. If teachers are really doing their jobs they must engage—as Megan Boler (1999) puts it—in a pedagogy of discomfort. Engaging in political theorizing is emotional. As Joe Kincheloe says, "From a critical perspective emotion is one of the many ways we know the world" (p. 7). And if one is truly paying attention to the vast inequities of this world, anger—as Shirley Steinberg poignantly points out—is the appropriate response. Steinberg (2007) calls for a "pedagogy of insubordination" (p. ix). Steinberg goes on to say

> Refusing to compromise to the standards-wielding, neo-liberal pedagogical pundits [the writers of her edited collection on critical pedagogy] are engaged in a pedagogy

of insubordination. Insubordination borne by the fact that we have been violated by conservatives, liberals, quasi-critical pedagogues, and just about everyone who doesn't get *it*. And therein lies the proverbial rub: there is no *it*. Critical pedagogy isn't formulaic, it isn't stagnant, and it isn't an *it*... . Critical pedagogy has the right to be angry, and to express anger. (p. ix)

It is exactly this anger—Julie Webber (2003) tells us—that kids are not allowed to express in school. Pent-up anger leads to school shootings, according to Webber. A "policy of containment" (p. 193)—that is containing kids' emotions—leads to violence. A violent atmosphere leads to violent acts. Henry Giroux's (2003) adults have abandoned an entire generation of kids because they are treated like criminals.

Both Henry Giroux (2003) and Kaustuv Roy (2008) comment that fear is part and parcel of being an American since 9/11. Living in constant fear can only lead to bad things. Giroux suggests that it is not only that kids live in fear, but that adults fear kids. Kids have become school shooters. But they are not alone. A man flew a plane into an IRS building because he hated the IRS; a biologist at the University of Alabama opened fire on six of her colleagues, killing three of them, because she didn't get tenure. And at Georgia Southern University a professor's wife shot and killed her husband because he was cheating on her. Violence is pervasive in American culture. This is Michael Moore's point in his film *Bowling for Columbine* (2002). Douglas Kellner (2008), William Pinar (2001), and Julie Webber (2003) all point out that gender and the crisis of masculinity have something to do with violent actions. As Julie Webber remarks, violence is a form of rage. Anger and rage are two different things. There is appropriate anger—and there is inappropriate and murderous rage (Searles, 2005). Rage is, as Julie Webber says, symptomatic of "a failure to hold."

Standardized testing is violent. Any attempt to standardize people and or knowledge is symbolically violent. Peter Taubman (2009) argues that under NCLB (and I would add Race to the Top) teachers today feel worthlessness (p. 128), shame (p. xi), and are held in contempt (p. 138) in American culture. Schooling is little more than "paint by numbers" (p. 1).

School teachers and professors have rarely been held in high regard in America. Perhaps during Franklin Roosevelt's administration professors who advised Roosevelt and made up what was called the "brain trust" (p. 7) altered this pattern a bit, as Adam Cohen points (2009) out. But by and large educators are not valued and in fact are scorned because—and this is worth repeating—as Calvin Coolidge said "the business of America is business" (cited in

Hofstadter, 1963, p. 237). NCLB and Race to the Top are built on a business model, which means schools are businesses and the business of school is not school but business. Taubman (2009) claims that teachers have so bought into the business model that they have given in to NCLB and have allowed this to happen. However, William Ayers (2004a; 2004b) suggests that despite the horrors of NCLB and the ever-increasing march toward standardization, teachers must hold onto the idea of hope. Ayers (2004a) says we must "teach consciously for ethical action" (p. 13) and we must find "the moral heart of teaching" (2004a, p. xi) and work "toward [building] a moral universe" (2004a, p. 11). But Sharon Todd (2009) is not so sure that this way of thinking helps us out of our current conundrum. Todd emphasizes that scholars must study our inhumanity and our aggressions.

· 6 ·

MULTICULTURAL CURRICULUM CONCEPTS

Introduction

In this chapter I will explore a brief overview of multicultural education. I will also examine a variety of theoretical frameworks for studying multicultural education. The major threads of multiculturalism in this chapter turn on whiteness studies, Latino/a studies, Islamophobia, Black/Feminist/Womanist studies and disability studies.

Overview of Multicultural Education

Christine Bennett (2011) writes that multicultural education has its roots in what Horace Kallen termed "cultural pluralism." Bennett explains:

> The concept of cultural pluralism was developed early in the 20th century by democratic philosopher Horace Kallen…and has been transformed by scholars of color such as Carter G. Woodson (1933/1969), W. E. B. Du Bois (1961), Jack Forbes (1973), Ronald Takaki (1989), and Richard Ruiz (1991). (p. 90)

The term "cultural pluralism" came about in response to large waves of immigrants coming to the United States from Europe. Although many immigrants wanted to hold onto their cultures, they had to become Americanized. Donna M. Gollnick (2011) suggests that minority cultures had to "adapt to an Anglo-conformity system" (p. 39). While adherents of cultural pluralism applauded difference on the surface, assimilation was key. One wonders whether today the underlying message to new immigrants is "Anglo-conformity" (Gollnick, p. 39). Since 9/11 new immigrants are feared, especially by the right wing. Whereas at the turn of the 20th century, immigrants were not so much feared as they were shunned.

By the 1940s, Donna M. Gollnick explains, "intergroup education" (p. 34) arrived on the scene. In Europe WWII was raging on and millions of Jews were being annihilated. Intergroup education, then, was—as James Banks (2004) points out—a response to anti-Semitism. Therefore, intergroup education was of particular interest to American Jews. Gollnick writes that intergroup education was led by "the National Conference on Christians and Jews, the American Council on Education (ACE), the Anti-Defamation League, the American Jewish Committee, and the National Education Association" (p. 34). What is striking here is that intergroup education was concerned with the problem of anti-Semitism. Today multicultural literature rarely deals with Jewish issues or with anti-Semitism. Although Jews are a minority culture in the United States, they are not, for the most part, treated in the multicultural literature.

James Banks (2004) argues that intergroup education had little to do with multicultural education. He states that although intergroup education is an antecedent to multicultural education it is "not an actual root of it" (p. 12). Thus, Banks points out,

> The current [multicultural] movement is directly linked to the early ethnic studies movement initiated by scholars such as G. W. Williams (1882–83) and continued by individuals such as W. E. B. Du Bois (1935), Woodson (1919/1968), Bond (1939), and Wesley (1935). (p. 12)

The field today has moved in different directions from the ethnic studies movement that Banks writes about in the above citation. Today the field is much broader and more inclusive than the earlier ethnic studies movement.

In the 1950s and 1960s Cameron McCarthy (2011) points out that "policies of assimilation lost credibility" (p. 50). But James Banks (2011) argues to the contrary. Banks explains,

> The Western nations were characterized by myriad racial, cultural, ethnic, religious, and linguistic diversity when the Ethnic revival movements emerged in the 1960s and 1970s. However, they were dominated by an *assimilationist* ideology.... The older nation-states in Western Europe—such as the United Kingdom (Carby, 1982), France, Germany, and The Netherlands—were also dominated by an assimilationist ideology. (p. 11)

Assimilationist ideology is evident today in many countries. Against the backdrop of 9/11 the acceptance of difference becomes a challenge for those on the right. 9/11 has turned back many of the gains made by multicultural education. Today people are afraid of the Other.

In the 1950s and 1960s Christine Bennett (2011) points out that multicultural education was a "response to the Civil Rights Movement...that developed into a Black Power movement and spread to include many other minority groups, including women" (p. 88). Minority groups began to demand that their voices be heard. Black studies, Latino/a studies, and disability studies can be traced back to the civil rights movement.

Cameron McCarthy (2011) suggests

> Blacks and other oppositional racial minorities had begun to champion a radical pluralism (Berlowitz, 1984). It is in this context of radical black discontent with American schooling that educational policy makers began to forge a "new" discourse of multiculturalism. (p. 50)

Black studies emerges as a discipline, then, during the civil rights movement (McCarthy, 2011; Gollnick, 2011). Today scholars of multiculturalism examine black studies in relation to whiteness studies which I examine in this chapter.

Etta Ruth Hollins (2011) writes that James Banks in the late 1960s became the authority (p. 64) on multicultural education. In the 1970s Carl Grant popularized multicultural education (p. 64). Together Banks and Grant worked to "facilitate the development of an integrated curriculum at the elementary and secondary levels and to maintain departments of ethnic studies at the college and university level" (Hollins, p. 64).

Today most colleges of education offer courses in multicultural education at both the undergraduate and graduate levels. Ideally, though, multicultural ideas should be woven throughout the curriculum. James Banks (2004) tells us

> Baker (1977), J. A. Banks (1973), Gay (1971), and Grant (1973, 1978) have each played a significant role in formulating and developing multicultural education in

the United States. Each of these scholars was heavily influenced by the early work of African American scholars and the African American ethnic studies movement. (p. 12)

For more on African American scholars turn to the chapters in this volume called "Curriculum as Historical Concept" (part 1, part 2, and part 3) as I have provided a detailed account of the contributions African American scholars have made to curriculum history.

James Banks (2004) reports that multicultural education was also influenced early on by many other scholars of varying ethnicities. He states

> Scholars who are specialists in other ethnic groups—such as Carlos E. Cortez (1973, 2002, Mexican Americans), Jack D. Forbes (1973, American Indians), Sonia Nieto (1986, Puerto Ricans), and Derald W. Sue (1981, Asian Americans)—also played early and significant roles in the evolution of multicultural education. (p. 12)

Early on multicultural education was an inclusive discipline. Today more groups have been included in the multicultural canon such as disabled peoples and the LGBTQ communities. (For more on the LGBTQ community turn to the chapter on gender in this volume.)

Sonia Nieto (2011) points out that some scholars feel that multicultural education has become, in fact, too inclusive. Nieto states

> While most scholars in the field have in recent years broadened the scope of multicultural education…others believe that being so inclusive diminishes the original purpose of multicultural education, which was to provide an equal education for marginalized students of color (Gay, 2003). (p. 86)

The field of multicultural education has become increasingly complex and increasingly diverse. The study of race is not enough. One could argue that the original purpose of multicultural education can be found in intergroup education. The main theme of intergroup education was the eradication of anti-Semitism. Some scholars do not see a connection between intergroup education and multicultural education, but clearly intergroup education was a form of multiculturalism. Today people live in an increasingly multicultural world and the inclusiveness of the field should be embraced, not dismissed. Marc Chun, Susan Christopher, and Patricia J. Gumport (2000) argue

> While there may be no simple or easily accepted definition of multiculturalism, the term generally refers to the collective fields of African American (or black) studies, Asian-American studies, Chicano or Latino studies, and Native American

studies, as well as women's studies and queer studies. We note here, however, that multiculturalism is frequently assumed to be synonymous with race or ethnic studies. (p. 228)

To this list I would also add whiteness studies, disability studies (which includes both physical and mental disabilities), and masculinity studies. The way in which scholars define what counts as multiculturalism harkens back to the question Herbert Spencer raised: What knowledge is of most worth? This is a political question. Who gets included or excluded from the multicultural canon is political. There are, in fact, many multicultural canons. What is attractive about the above citation about multiculturalism is the notion that scholars should study collective fields. And this is what makes the study of multiculturalism complex.

Theoretical Frameworks

Before I examine the collective fields of multiculturalism, I will explore different theoretical frameworks that undergird the study of multiculturalism. Steinberg and Kincheloe (2009) and Steinberg (1997) flesh out complex theoretical frameworks of multicultural education. These scholars suggest that there are five different theoretical frameworks that scholars use while exploring multicultural issues: conservative monoculturalism, liberal multiculturalism, pluralist multiculturalism, left-essentialist multiculturalism, and critical multiculturalism.

Conservative monoculturalism is what is known as the Great Books Tradition. Here students study the Western canon only. Whose knowledge is of most worth? White, European/Euro-American males. Here scholars teach that the Western canon is a "universally civilizing influence" (Steinberg, 2009, p. 4). Conservative scholars feel that multiculturalism is an "enemy of Western progress" (Steinberg, p. 4).

Liberal multiculturalism stresses the common humanity (Steinberg, 2009) of all peoples. This is an assimilationist position. Here, all diverse groups of people must melt into the Anglo-Saxon norm in the United States. This version of multiculturalism does not honor difference and blames victims when they face hardships. There is little discussion in liberal multiculturalism on the problematic of "structural adversities" (Steinberg, p. 4).

Pluralist multiculturalism "focuses more on race, class, and gender differences" (Steinberg, p. 4). However the study of differences here means to "exoticize" difference. Curiously this form of multiculturalism "avoids use of the concept of oppression" (Steinberg, p. 4). Exoticizing difference Others. The erasure of oppression is a form of denial.

Left-essentialist multiculturalism essentializes or reifies the categories of race, class, and gender. Scholars suggest that "race, class, and gender categories consist of a set of unchanging priorities (essences)" (Steinberg, 2009, p. 4). However, race, class, and gender are historically produced and are socially constructed and always change meaning because of historical context. Another curious thing about this particular framework is, as Steinberg points out, that "only authentically oppressed people can speak about particular issues concerning a specific group" (p. 4). However, nobody owns knowledge. Scholars must approach others' knowledges and oppressions with care and without appropriating knowledge for academic gain.

Critical multiculturalists study issues of power, politics, and oppression. The goal here is the "elimination of human suffering" (Steinberg, 2009, p. 5). This version of multiculturalism is concerned with race, class, and gender oppressions. Most important, critical multiculturalists are concerned with "modes of resistance" (p. 5) against oppressive powers. People are not merely victims. This is a crucial point that critical multiculturalists raise. Critical multiculturalists trace their history back to "the evolving theoretical position emerging in the Frankfurt School of Critical Theory in the 1920s" (Steinberg, p. 5). Further, critical multiculturalists study the problems of whiteness and the role that whiteness plays in the lives of the oppressed.

Like Steinberg, Peter McLaren (1997) suggests that scholars engage in what he calls "revolutionary multiculturalism" (p. 11). McLaren writes that revolutionary multiculturalism is akin to critical multiculturalism. Like critical multiculturalists, revolutionary multiculturalists study whiteness and white privilege. Unlike critical multiculturalists, revolutionary multiculturalists see people as revolutionary agents. Further, McLaren argues "for the disassembly and destruction of whiteness and advocates its rearticulation as a form of critical agency dedicated to struggles in the interests of the oppressed" (p. 276). McLaren also suggests that scholars should not engage in "celebrating whiteness in any form" (p. 276). He advocates the "abolition of whiteness" (p. 276). This is a curious position.

Whiteness is often left out of other versions of multiculturalism mentioned above. But if whiteness is left out of the discussion, issues of power and oppression do not get discussed. It is not enough to study minority groups. Scholars must study minority groups and whiteness so as to get a better understanding of the interrelations between whiteness and the suffering of oppressed groups.

George J. Sefa Dei (2008) offers another potential framework for the study of multiculturalism, although he says that his position on what he calls anti-racist pedagogy has little to do with multiculturalism. Anti-racist pedagogy, as Dei suggests, deals with on-the-ground change. Dei comments

> The core of anti-racism resides in concrete action to bring about systemic change. Anti-racism can be defined as a discursive and political practice to address the myriad forms of racisms and the intersections with other forms of oppression. Anti-racism addresses the systematic and institutional dimensions of racism as well as drawing attention to more than the overt forms of racist acts lodged in individual actions. (p. xix)

Dei insists that scholars engage in on-the-ground resistance to racism. He also tackles institutionalized racism(s). These issues are of importance especially to critical multiculturalists (see Kincheloe & Steinberg, 1997a; May & Sleeter, 2010) and revolutionary multiculturalists (see McLaren, 1997).

David Gillborn (2005) explains anti-racist pedagogy as follows:

> Anti-racism has developed as an overtly radical and oppositional approach that stands apart from self-consciously liberal and consensual "multicultural" schools of thought. This approach to anti-racism has been especially prominent among radical scholars in the UK, Canada, Australasia and South Africa (see, for example, Dei et al., 2004). Elements of this same critique are present in some versions of "critical multiculturalism" and, increasingly, within race critical scholarship. (p. 112)

Anti-racist pedagogy is in some ways like anti-colonial theory put forth by George J. Sefa Dei. One of the things that Dei worries about is that abstract discussions about racism and colonialism leave out concrete suffering of human beings. He does not, however, suggest that scholars dismiss the discursive. Rather, the study of the discursive must go hand in hand with an examination of the material suffering of people. This same kind of argument is made when talking about poststructuralism. Some argue that poststructuralism is too abstract and has little to do with on-the-ground suffering. However, some versions of poststructuralism are political and have everything to do with human suffering. (See the discussion on the work of Jacques Derrida in the previous chapter on "Curriculum as Political Concepts.")

Whiteness Studies

When studying multiculturalism it is imperative that scholars examine whiteness. Of course whiteness is not a stand-alone category because it intersects with gender, class, sexuality, religion, and so forth. Since I deal with gender, class, sexuality, and religion in other chapters, I will not treat them here. Rather, I will focus on whiteness with the understanding that it is a socially constructed concept that intersects with other categories. Here I trouble the notion of whiteness in the context of multiculturalism. Whiteness is about power and privilege. Yet, many white people do not think about their whiteness at all. It is a taken-for-granted category that remains invisible to many white people. Whiteness is a problem that scholars must untangle. Joe Kincheloe and Shirley Steinberg (1997a) write about whiteness in the context of critical multiculturalism. These scholars state

> Whiteness study in a critical multicultural educational context should delineate the various ways such material effects shape culture and institutional pedagogies and position individuals in relation to the power of reason. Understanding these dynamics is central to the curricula of black studies, Chicano studies, post-colonialism and indigenous studies. (p. 211)

In a critical multicultural framework it is not enough to examine black studies, Chicano studies, post-colonialism and indigenous studies—as Kincheloe and Steinberg (1997a) point out—without studying whiteness. Some more conservative versions of multiculturalism leave out whiteness altogether. But whiteness is inextricably related to power. And power relations are important to grapple with.

For example, power struggles get played out in universities. White professors—who outnumber black professors—have the power to make decisions related to tenure and promotion. White professors have the power to turn down colleagues who go up for tenure because they work in, say, black studies or in post-colonialism. Conservative white professors might feel that black studies is not relevant to academic discourse. Or some conservative white professors might think that writing about indigenous studies does not advance one's discipline.

When women's studies emerged on the scene, many male professors did not see the value in studying women's issues and argued that women's issues are not academic. In the early years of women's studies, many women who went up for tenure were turned down because their knowledge was not valued by white male colleagues. The upshot of this discussion is that when scholars talk about whiteness they are also talking about power. Who has the power to decide what knowledge counts? This is indeed a political question.

David Roediger (2005) writes that there is a wedge between whiteness studies and critical whiteness studies. He argues that it is not enough to merely add white people to the multicultural canon. Roediger explains

> The critical study of whiteness is not whiteness studies. We should reject the term's implication that whites are just another group to be welcomed at the table of multiculturalism and instead continue to direct our attention to who owns and designs the table. (p. 219)

The notion of whiteness needs to be unpacked. And as I stated above, whiteness means power. And whiteness means privilege. How do white people undo their privilege? Or are white people unaware of their privilege and power?

Nelson Rodriguez (2000), like David Roediger, thinks that scholars need to be critical of whiteness and not just add it to the multicultural canon. Rodriguez writes:

> Here, I agree with historian David Roediger's (1994) assertion that "if it does not involve a critique of whiteness, the questioning of racism often proves shallow and limited" (p. 13). Bringing whiteness *inside* multiculturalism no longer enables the latter to remain exclusively focused on the "Other" as well as continue to be devoid of critical analyses of whiteness as an invisible norm. (p. 3)

The teaching of multicultural education includes teaching about whiteness and the power whites have over minority groups. If multicultural education is only about the Other, one takes the risk of exoticizing minorities and exonerating whites. If scholars are to understand oppression and oppressive practices, they must study whiteness with a critical eye. The problem with approaching whiteness, though, is that students in teacher education programs—who are mostly white females—might be resistant to thinking about whiteness. Teaching whiteness is a challenge. Some students see the teaching of whiteness as white bashing. Some students put up psychological barriers when issues of whiteness come up in the classroom. They become angry, feel insulted and victimized.

Peter McLaren (1997) argues

> When North Americans talk about race, they inevitably refer to African-Americans, Asians, Latino/as, and Native Americans to the consistent exclusion of

> Euro-Americans.... I want to argue instead that we need also to put our emphasis on the analysis of white supremacist ideology and practice. (p. 10)

It is important to note here that when McLaren writes about white supremacy he is not only writing about thugs, he also is talking about everyday white America. McLaren suggests—perhaps too aggressively—that there is no redeeming value in being white. It is this kind of thinking that sets up an antagonistic relation with white students. To state that every white person in the United States is a white supremacist is an extreme position. There are certainly other ways of talking about whiteness in classroom situations. All white people are not white supremacists. Christine Sleeter and Peter McLaren (1995) write

> We locate the current struggle in our schools in the larger efforts of white supremacist, patriarchal capitalism to condition the public's consciousness of everyday life, to create the borders of what is considered the meaningful universe of its citizens, and to tacitly privilege the manner in which everyday life is framed and coded. (p. 9)

Sleeter and McLaren argue that white supremacist patriarchal capitalists are ruining our schools. Training students to be efficient workers in a capitalist society is the hidden curriculum in American schools. Students are also implicitly taught that the patriarchy knows what is best for all students. But things could be otherwise. Feminists have been writing about these issues for decades. America is a consumerist capitalist patriarchy where whiteness is privileged, maleness is privileged. Curriculum workers need to undo white power and privilege. Curriculum workers need to teach students that education is not about getting a job. Education is about social justice, democracy, and freedom. Education is about undoing white power and privilege.

Ruth Frankenberg (2005) writes

> Whiteness refers to a set of locations that are historically, socially, politically, and culturally produced and, moreover, are intrinsically linked to the unfolding relations of domination. Naming "whiteness" displaces it from the unmarked, unnamed status that is itself an effect of dominance. Among the effects on white people both of race privilege and of the dominance of whiteness are their seeming normativity, their structured invisibility. (p. 6)

Unexamined issues of whiteness, for Frankenberg, are linked to domination. Notice in the above citation the number of times Frankenberg uses the term "domination" to describe whiteness. Whiteness is domination. And yet it does not have to be. But first, Frankenberg teaches that whites must "name" their whiteness. Until whites name their whiteness they cannot undo domination because they cannot see it.

Virginia Lea and Erma Jean Sims (2008) argue

> Whiteness is a complex, hegemonic, and dynamic set of mainstream socio-economic processes, and ways of thinking, feeling, believing, and acting (cultural scripts) that function to obscure the power, privilege, and practices of the dominant social elite. (pp. 1–2)

Whiteness is a way of being-in-the-world. And this way of being includes "ways of thinking, feeling, believing, and acting," as Lea and Sims suggest. White people think that they are entitled because they are white. But if white people do not think through their whiteness and the privileges that come with being white they obscure their power, as Lea and Sims point out. Whites decimated Native Americans, put Japanese Americans in internment camps, enslaved and lynched black people, founded militias to combat Latino/a immigration. The point of studying whiteness is to undo white privilege, to undo domination, to undo negative power relations. Michael Apple (1998) speaks to these issues as he says

> Focusing on whiteness can simply generate white guilt, hostility, or feelings of powerlessness. It can actually prevent the creation of those "decentered unities" that speak across differences and that can lead to broad coalitions that challenge dominant cultural, political, and economic relations. (p. xi)

Apple goes on to say that when approaching the topic of whiteness with students, teachers must be sensitive to these problems of anger and guilt that white students might feel. Teachers must address their students' anger and their guilt and help them work through these emotions so as to move on to more productive ways of relating to others. Apple writes that whiteness must be "interrupted, and transformed" (p. x). Like Apple, Nelson Rodriguez (1998) argues that when scholars teach about whiteness they will be able "to rethink and live whiteness in progressive ways" (p. 32). Henry Giroux (1998b) remarks,

> Defining "whiteness" largely as a form of domination, such scholarship, while rightly unmasking whiteness as a mark of ideology and racial privilege, fails to provide a nuanced, dialectical, and layered account of whiteness that would allow white youth and others to appropriate selective elements of white identity and culture as oppositional. (p. 43)

Giroux, Apple, and Rodriguez all agree that teaching about whiteness can lead to working toward social justice and undoing harmful white practices. For these three scholars whiteness does not have to mean domination, it can mean other things. Recall the earlier discussion about the work of Peter McLaren (1997). He suggests that there are no redeeming qualities about whiteness. Remember, he calls for the "abolition of whiteness" (McLaren, p. 276). How is that possible or helpful?

Whiteness is not only an American problem, it also is a global problem, as Paul Carr and Darren Lund (2009) point out. These scholars suggest

> Not merely the opposite of black, white has been a signifier for global racial supremacy—good against evil, lightness versus darkness and benevolence over malevolence—and in English, it symbolizes cleanliness, kindness, serenity, and youth. White is associated with Europe, the conqueror, while black is inexorably fused to colonial notions of the "dark continent" of Africa. (p. 46)

White racism is indeed a global problem. Postcolonial literature discusses these problems. Historically colonizers have been, for the most part, white. Catherine Kroll (2008) points out

> White narratives frequently assume credit for the origins of "civilization," and the building of a national infrastructure (Fanon, 1963: 51). For many in the majority culture, what constitutes civilization is defined according to Eurocentric norms. As Toni Morrison has argued, from its very ideological origins, American identity was predicated on a self-definition that was exclusionary. (p. 34)

College courses in Western Civilization or the history of Western philosophy or the Classics are examples of what counts as civilized knowledge in the academy. A counter-curriculum might offer, rather, courses in indigenous knowledges, feminist knowledges, queer theory, or disability studies. It is important to study all kinds of knowledges—including Western philosophy or the classics—but with a critical eye. The notion of civilized knowledge must be interrogated. Who decides who is "civilized?" What counts as "knowledge?" These are political questions. Canon formation must be deconstructed and analyzed carefully because what students learn in school shapes the way they see the world. If students only see the world through Eurocentric eyes or Euro-American eyes they are only getting part of the picture. An integrated curriculum—where students study European texts alongside indigenous texts—will give students a broader knowledge base. Building a more inclusive curriculum is what multiculturalism is about.

Ladislaus Semali (1998) comments

> The curriculum of whiteness is approximately as follows: white, Western, "civilized," male, adult, urban, middle class, heterosexual, and so on. This profile has monopolized and dominated all other curriculums, including the definition of humanity in mainstream Western imagery. (p. 181)

Curriculum is a "symbolic form of representation" (Pinar et al., 1995). Who gets represented in the curriculum? Who is excluded? Again these are political questions. Those who are powerful decide what counts as knowledge. Those who are powerful decide what the curriculum should be. As Semali suggests the "curriculum of whiteness" is the curriculum that counts. A conservative education is one where students study only the writings of white men. The Great Books Tradition was invented by white men. Philosophy, theology and the classics are all troubled disciplines because these are colonizing white disciplines.

Shirley Steinberg and Joe Kincheloe (2009) suggest that students study a different kind of curriculum that questions what Semali (1998) calls "the curriculum of whiteness" (p. 181). Steinberg and Kincheloe argue

> A critical pedagogy of whiteness produces a counter-history grounded on the deconstruction of a whitewashed official history. Such a counter-history opens questions for discussion and research—questions about the deracialization of early Christianity; the possible whitening of ancient Egypt…and the bleaching of particular authors of African descent in the European literary canon… . Such historical whitewashing conveys debilitating messages to contemporary blacks and other non-whites, teaching them to believe that they are intellectually inferior to whites. (p. 15)

Steinberg and Kincheloe point out that by studying only white texts, people of color—who are not represented in the curriculum—suffer from invisibility. People of color suffer from being erased from history. Women too get erased from history. People of color and women, then, might internalized this invisibility. But counter-histories, as Steinberg and Kincheloe point out, serve to undo invisibility. Minority literatures are resistance literatures. Minority literatures are oppositional literatures. Scholars must keep in mind that people are not just victims. Multiculturalism also should be about resistance.

Joe Kincheloe and Shirley Steinberg (1997a) write that the notion of whiteness is ephemeral. They state

> The ephemeral nature of whiteness as a social construction begins to reveal itself when we understand that the Irish, Italians and Jews have all been viewed as non-white in

> particular places at specific moments in history. Indeed, Europeans prior to the late 1600s did not use the label black to refer to any race of people, Africans included. (pp. 211–212)

Although the notion of race is a social construction, there are material consequences of being or appearing to be non-white. People of color suffer from discrimination and violence. White people do not suffer from these humiliations in their everyday lives. White people who do not think about their own white privilege do not think about the suffering of others or claim that the suffering of minorities has little to do with them. Many whites are blinded by their privilege. Kincheloe and Steinberg point out that "whiteness as a socio-historical construct is constantly shifting" (p. 208). What is considered white in some countries might be considered black in other countries. And as the above quote suggests, peoples who are today considered to be white were, at one time, considered to be black. Biracial peoples might be considered to be black in some situations while in others they might be considered white.

Henry Giroux (1998b) takes the discussion of whiteness in another direction. He argues that some whites today see themselves as victims of racial discrimination. Giroux tells us

> For conservative ideologues, whiteness has been appropriated as a badge of self-identity and fashioned as a rallying point for disaffected whites who claim they are the victims of reverse racism in a country that is becoming increasingly racially diverse and hybridized. Under attack by multiculturalists, radicals, feminists, gays, lesbians, and other subordinate groups, whites feel besieged and persecuted. (p. 42)

Scholars see this same kind of thinking among German youth who feel that they are the victims of the Holocaust (Morris, 2001). German youth complain that they are sick and tired of learning about the Holocaust. They feel that this constant reminder of the terrible deeds done by their elders has little to do with them. They do not want to hear any more about the Holocaust because they had nothing to do with it. The more that this horrific tragedy is talked about in school the more German youth feel like victims.

In America, as Giroux points out in the above citation, white men feel that they are the victims in a multicultural society. Some white men feel that people of color steal jobs from them, get scholarships to college while whites are left behind. These white men feel that affirmative action is a form of reverse racism. What they really fear is the loss of their own privilege. These white men have difficulties acknowledging difference. In the reelection of

President Obama, the Romney camp was shocked that they lost. Republicans are threatened by the rising tide of immigration and of being overtaken by minorities. Romney's hope of becoming president was dashed. Republicans feel that they are the victims.

Michael Apple (1998) tells us

> It may be unfortunate, but it is true that many Whites still believe that there is a social cost attached to being white rather than being a person of color. Whites are the "new losers" in a playing field that they believe has been leveled now that the United States is a supposedly basically egalitarian, color-blind society. Since "times are tough for everybody," policies to assist "underrepresented groups"—such as affirmative action—are unfairly supporting "non-Whites." (p. ix)

Teaching courses on multiculturalism is difficult, in part, because many white students complain that they are being bashed. White students, thus, are reluctant to engage multicultural literature. They are defensive and they are angry. Whiteness is not something they want to study or hear about. Many white students—both male and female—feel victimized in courses on multiculturalism.

Cameron McCarthy (1995) speaks to these issues. He states

> The post-civil rights era is the era of the displaced and decentered white subject. White students on college campuses find themselves positioned as the antagonists in an unpredictable racial drama in which middle class subjects speak in the voice of the new oppressed—a progeny spawned in an era of the discourse of racial resentment and reverse discrimination. (p. 247)

Indeed, white students resent having to take courses in multiculturalism. White students often do not want to engage the material of multiculturalism because they resent it. They do not understand why whiteness must be studied. It would be easier for them to only study minority cultures because then they would not have to think about their own complicity in a racist society.

Sonia Nieto (2011) writes about critiques of multiculturalism coming from the right wing. One of their "fears" is "the shrinking of the Western canon, particularly at colleges and universities (Bloom, 1988), or…that American common culture is being sacrificed at the altar of diversity, resulting in the hatred of Whites and increased divisiveness (D'Souza, 1991; Hirsch, 1987; Ravitch, 1990)" (Nieto, (2011), p. 86). The Western canon is by no means shrinking. It is being critiqued and deconstructed. But few scholars want to be rid of the Western canon. The Western canon should be studied but it should be studied alongside minority literatures. The question of the canon is complex indeed. Few scholars would advocate throwing out one canon for another. Few scholars advocate teaching only minority literatures. The point is not to do a compensatory history but to critique what books come before us (i.e., the Western canon) and integrate minority literatures into that history.

Latina/o Studies

Latinas/os are sometimes referred to as Hispanic. The notion of Hispanic is highly problematic because it essentializes. Hispanic identity can mean many different things. Manning Marable (2002) explains that this term "Hispanic" was invented by the United States Census Bureau. Marable writes

> The term [Hispanic] was imposed on a population of 16 million people reflecting divergent and even contradictory nationalities, racialized ethnicities, cultural traditions, and political loyalties: black Panamanians of Jamaican or Trinidadian descent, who speak Spanish; Argentines of Italian or German descent; anti-Castro, white, upper-class Cubans in Miami's Dade County; impoverished Mexican-American farm workers in California's Central Valley; and black Dominican service and blue-collar workers in New York's Washington Heights. (p. 13)

Hispanic is a signifier for blacks, whites, upper class, working class, or poor. Hispanic, too, refers to people of differing nationalities, countries, and so on. The term "Hispanic" reifies notions of race, culture, ethnicity, and class. Hispanic means many different things to many different peoples. The term "Hispanic" is an umbrella term that is supposed to cover all of these disparate peoples. The term "queer"—as in queer theory—serves a similar purpose. Queer is an umbrella term that is supposed to cover lesbians, gays, bisexuals, transsexuals, transvestites, and so forth. The problem with the term "queer" is that it does not capture the differences between and among these groups of people. One could say the same thing about the term "Hispanic." Hispanic does not capture the differences of all the various groups of people it is supposed to name. All Hispanics are not the same.

Francisco Vazquez and Rodolfo Torres (2003) ask

> What is in a name? Could the invisibility of Latino/as be attributed to their sheer diversity of nationalities, races, ethnic groups, and religions? Perhaps the difficulty in representing them is that they do not lend themselves to an easy portrayal. (p. 3)

Vazquez and Torres go on to state, "We also have Hispanics, Latino/as, Raza, Cuban Americans, Puerto Ricans and Nuyoricans, Mexicans, Mexican Americans, Spanish Americans, Chicano/as, Indio/as, Tex Mex, Manito/as Cholo/as, Pocho/as" (p. 3). Vazquez and Torres suggest that Hispanics come from Spain while Latinas/os come from Latin American countries. Latinas/os are the fastest growing minority in the United States. Latinas/os are becoming a powerful force in national elections. Politicians know that the Latina/o vote for President Obama's reelection was overwhelming. The Republicans, for the most part, want Latinas/os to be deported while at the same time they want to hire illegal aliens to do work for deplorable wages.

George Martinez (2011) explains:

> Latinos recently became the largest minority group in the United States. African-Americans may therefore be about to give up political clout to Latinos. This prospect has generated tension between African-Americans and Latinos.... Specifically, the legal construction of Mexican-Americans as white has generated tensions that form a barrier to coalition building. (p. 481)

Mexicans and Mexican Americans are also thought of as being brown, not white. Neil Foley (2011) points out that in the 1930s Hispanics were considered to be "non-white" (p. 369). Who is considered white and who is considered nonwhite changes over time. Race is socially constructed and changeable.

The notion of hybridity complicates even more the discussion of race, ethnicity, and culture in the context of Chicana/o identities. C. Alejandra Elenes (2003) tells us that people who live "in between U.S. and Mexican culture(s)" (p. 191) draw on the notion of borderlands to describe Chicana/o identity. Elenes states

> The educational history of Chicanas/os in the twentieth century is one of legal battles to end school desegregation and to implement bilingual and multicultural education.... For the Chicana/o movement, access to education meant not only the literal access of bodies into the classroom, but also to a curriculum where Chicana/o history, culture, politics, and identity were central. (pp. 192–193)

Still, though, in the United States, public school curriculum focuses on Euro-American culture. The underlying message of public school curricula is assimilation. However, on college campuses one finds that ethnic studies has become more prominent. Elenes explains

> Chicana/o Studies curriculum and scholarship has advanced in directions that were not envisioned by the Chicana/o Studies pioneers. Feminist and Queer Theory, for example, have transformed the discipline from its narrow male focus. Additionally, many Chicana/o scholars are contributing to new theoretical frameworks such as poststructuralism and postmodernism. (p. 193)

The notion of hybridity lends itself nicely to poststructural thought. Recall that Chicanas/os feel that they have hybrid identities and live in the borderlands. It was Gloria Anzaldúa—Elenes points out—who brought the term "borderlands" into the discussion. Anzaldúa also contributed to the conversation by introducing the term "mestiza." Here the "mestiza identity is located in the interstices of Mexican/Chicano culture, patriarchy, homophobia, and Anglo-American domination" (Elenes, p. 196). Anzaldúa (2002) emphasizes the need to build bridges between peoples of different backgrounds.

Earlier in this discussion Vazquez and Torres (2003) suggested that Latinas/os are invisible even though they are the largest growing minority in the United States (p. 1). These scholars suggest that this invisibility might be due to the vast differences among Latinas/os. However, Antonia Darder, Rodolfo Torres, and Henry Gutierrez (1997) argue that in the 1960s during the civil rights movement the discussion was mostly about blacks and whites. Darder, Torres, and Gutierrez suggest

> If we consider the literature of the civil rights era and the era of multiculturalism, what is consistently reflected are deeply racialized discourses grounded in black and white categories. As such, this has perpetuated a dimension of invisibility with respect to the role of Latino scholarship. (p. xiv)

Juan Perea (2011) argues similarly. He states

> Only a few writers even recognize that they use a Black/White paradigm as the frame of reference through which to understand all racial relations…because the Black/White binary paradigm is so widely accepted, other racialized groups…are often marginalized or ignored altogether. (p. 336)

So this black/white paradigm could account for the invisibility of Latinas/os in discussions on race. Race is so much more complicated than the black/white paradigm. Biracial peoples are still not discussed much in the literature of multiculturalism. Biracial peoples complicate the notion that race is one thing. There is no pure race. There is no clear-cut dualism between black and white. "Hybridity" is a good term not only for exploring Chicanas/os but also for discussing biracial identity.

Angharad Valdivia (2005) remarks

> Latinas/os challenge commonsense and theoretical notions of race and ethnicity. Often referred to as the "brown race," Latina/os supposedly fall somewhere between Eurocentric and black Afrocentric racial categories. The muddled ethnoracial space signified by brownness means, among other things, impurity and contamination in relation to the pure poles of blackness and whiteness. (p. 307)

But the notions of black and white are not pure. Furthermore, who is considered black and white changes over time. The meanings of black and white change when borders between nations are crossed. What is considered black in one country might be considered white in another country. It is disturbing to think that Latinas/os are thought to "contaminate," as Valdivia (2005) puts it. Not only are Latinas/os thought of as a form of contamination—by racists—they have been "the object of a politics of surveillance" (Valdivia, p. 311) since 9/11. All brown bodies—if you will—are under surveillance. Brown bodies are thought to be potential terrorists.

Millions of Latinas/os immigrate to the United States every year. The United States is the land of immigrants. But many Americans are xenophobic and want to stop the tide of immigration. Marcelo M. Suárez-Orozco, Carola Suárez-Orozco, and Desirée Baolian Qin (2005) write

> Over the course of the last century, immigration to the United States has become thoroughly dominated by the Latin American experience. More than half of all immigrants originate in Latin America, the vast majority from Mexico. Nearly a third of the foreign-born population in the United States today is of Mexican origin. (p. x)

One of the reasons that immigration is such a contentious issue in the United States is because the majority of people who come here are considered brown. Racism is rampant in the United States. The major reason right-wing whites do not want Mexicans or Latin Americans here is because they are racist. Immigrants from Canada are not treated the same as immigrants from Latin America. Immigrants from Canada are mostly white. One must wonder why border patrol issues seem to be a concern only on the border between Mexico and the United States and not the border between the United States and Canada. Borders are racialized places. Nancy Brown Diggs (2011) reports that

Mexicans suffer from virulent forms of racism once in the United States. Diggs tells us

> Day laborers are "jeered by suburbanites, harassed by Minuteman vigilantes and hounded by communities with police crack-downs, anti-loitering statutes, and mass evictions," says Lawrence Downes. "Contractors cheat them. People beat them up and fire-bomb their homes." (p. 51)

When European immigrants came to this country in the early 20th century they were not treated like this. Of course these immigrants had to contend with xenophobia, anti-Semitism, and so forth. But they were not thought of as potential terrorists. One of the reasons Mexicans are treated so poorly here is they are thought of as potential terrorists.

Leo Chavez (2008) writes about what he calls "The Latino Threat Narrative" (p. 2). Chavez states

> The Latino Threat Narrative posits that Latinos are not like previous immigrant groups, who ultimately became part of the nation. According to the assumptions and taken-for-granted "truths" inherent in this narrative, Latinos are unwilling or incapable of integrating, of becoming part of the national community. Rather, they are part of an invading force from south of the border that is bent on reconquering land that was formerly theirs (the U.S. Southwest) and destroying the American way of life. (p. 2)

Why should immigrants have to assimilate? Why should they blend in with Anglo culture? They should not have to assimilate. If Latinas/os do not assimilate and, rather, hold onto their traditions, rituals, and culture how does this destroy America? In Europe, even before the Holocaust—especially in Germany and Austria—Jews were also seen as invaders. Germans thought that Jews were not able to be fully German and were not thought to be citizens of Germany but rather parasites. The irony here is that when Jews did attempt to assimilate, Germans became more fearful because they could not tell who was Jewish and who was not (Morris, 2001). In the United States, Germany, and Austria (especially in the 1930s and 1940s) difference was not welcomed (Morris, 2001; Soto, 2011). Conservatives want to conserve their own culture, they want to conserve their traditions, and they want foreigners to also conserve Anglo culture at the expense of their own culture. Assimilation erases the culture of the Other. This is colonization. But again since 9/11 Mexicans and Latin Americans are seen as terrorists (Chavez, 2008; Bender, 2011). Steven Bender explains

> In the days following the September 11 terrorist attacks, reports emerged of hate crimes, discrimination, and profiling directed at Arab Americans, Arabs, and Muslims in the United States. Yet, Latinas/os are not immune from these negative sentiments. Given their societal construction as violent, foreign, criminal-minded, dis-loyal, and as overrunning the border, Americans are beginning to similarly construct Latinas/os as a terrorist threat. (p. 204)

All brown people in the United States are seen as potential terrorists—especially by right-wing conservatives. Thus, whether or not Latinas/os assimilate into Anglo culture, they are still seen as a threat to the United States.

Lourdes Diaz Soto (2011) suggests that there is a "panic over immigration" (p. 10). Soto explains

> The panic over immigration continues to create an inhospitable and dangerous environment for Latino/a children and families. The perspectives and the experiences from the northern neighbors (United States) and the southern neighbors (Mejico) are quite varied. In the north the organized militia and fringe groups continue to demonize immigrants. In the south families struggle as their livelihood is replaced by powerful multinational corporations. (p. 10)

It is not only "organized militia and fringe groups" who "demonize" immigrants. Well-respected television commentators like Lou Dobbs also demonize immigrants. Everyday people demonize immigrants, too. The United States is virulently racist. The rise of the Tea Party movement should give us pause. Even though President Obama was reelected does not mean racism suddenly disappears.

Celia Jaes Falicov (2005) reports that when immigrants do come to the United States they do not —for the most part—give up their native traditions and cultures but rather

> most immigrant families manage to maintain contacts with their culture of origin and to reinvent old family themes while carving out new lives. New acculturation theories reflect this dynamic of continuity and change, rather than the traditional "either/or" linear theory of abandoning one culture to embrace the other. Terms such as *binationalism, bilingualism, biculturalism,* and *cultural bifocality* describe dual visions. (p. 199)

As Falicov points out, most immigrants live in two worlds or have to negotiate between two worlds. They assimilate and yet they do not assimilate. This is a postmodern position indeed. Immigrants have hybrid identities. Marcelo M. Suárez-Orozco (2005)) attributes this hybrid identity to "the relative ease and accessibility of mass transportation...and the new globalized communication and information technologies" (p. 73). Thus, immigrants can hold onto their native cultures because they can be in touch with family and friends who live across the border. With the advent of Skype, cell phones and so forth, immigrants can live in two worlds at once (i.e., the virtual world and the world they newly inhabit).

Although immigrants can live in two worlds at once, schooling has devastating consequences for youth. Schooling in the United States forces youth to assimilate and give up their native cultures. Even if young people assimilate in school, they can hold onto their cultures, but the struggle is difficult. Antonia Darder (2010) claims

> Public schooling has functioned as a deeply colonizing force in the lives of bilingual/bicultural children and their communities. Toward this end, traditional classroom pedagogy and curriculum have been used to systemically strip away the primary cultures and languages of racialized communities, replacing them, instead, with an assimilative "American" identity. (p. xiii)

Education has had a long history of colonizing others. But people can resist the assimilative nature of schooling. People are not merely victims of colonization. Youth fight back. Yet, sometimes forms of resistance—like dropping out of school—backfire. Julio Cammarota (2011) writes

> School holds a different meaning for Latinos than for Latinas; it is a place in which they are policed, contained, and treated as if they are a social and criminal threat. This experience of containment makes them feel uneasy in social/public spaces and willing to avoid or resist the uncomfortable feeling of being perceived as a menace. Their responses are often drawn from certain notions of urban masculinity that find meaning in rebelling against mainstream life and institutions such as schools. (p. 433)

Young males "rebel" by "cutting class" and eventually drop out. Latinos have a high drop-out rate compared with other youth groups. Latinas, on the other hand, tend to stay in school and finish and go onto college. Dropping out of school does not help young males make their way in American society. What is striking here is the reaction Latinos have to schooling. They know it is colonizing, even—as Cammarota says—racist. Latinos/as cannot relate to the texts used in school because they are not represented in these texts.

Lourdes Diaz Soto (1997) argues, "The advocates of cultural conservatism, the 'enemies within,' have also helped devalue bilingualism/biculturalism by advocating a knowledge base that is Anglo-centric" (p. 7.) Lourdes Diaz Soto says that "the concerted effort to mandate English-only is synonymous with an America that is for whites-only" (p. 6). In many public schools "activities aimed at punishing children for speaking their native language still persist in contemporary America" (Soto, p. 6). When children internalize these negative reactions to their cultures they begin to believe that they are inferior to whites. This self-hatred is a psychological phenomenon that many colonized people suffer. If a child is told over and over that her language is inferior or her culture is not important, after a while she begins to believe it and so begins the process of self-loathing. The phenomenon of self-loathing and shame is also seen in the GLBTQ (gay, lesbian, bisexual, transgendered and queer) community. If a gay person is told enough times that he is sick or disgusting eventually he will begin to believe this. Heteronormativity and homophobia go hand in hand. Heteronormativity is a colonizing force that the GLBTQ community has to fight every day. This is probably why in the GLBTQ community—especially among young people—suicides are not uncommon. (For more on this turn to the chapter on "Gender Curriculum Concepts.")

Christine Sleeter (1997) reports that conservative Americans feel that bilingualism is "anti-American" (p. xii). Sleeter writes

> Multicultural and bilingual education connect to political issues involving voice and power, not just in schools but also in the wider society. Even though good bilingual education promotes educational achievement and English acquisition, it also supports bilingualism, which many monolingual Americans regard as anti-English and anti-American. (p. xii)

In Europe children learn to speak many languages because countries are in close proximity to each other. Multilingual Europeans are far more advanced than North Americans on the issue of language. However, in Germany during the Holocaust Yiddish was seen as the "secret language of the Jews" (Gilman cited in Morris, 2001) and non-Jewish Germans feared this. They feared this because they thought the Jews were conspiring against them. Instead the Germans annihilated six million Jews. Yiddish is a dying language because of the Holocaust. When peoples are decimated so too is their language.

Antonia Darder (2010) argues that the English-only mandate practiced in public schools is a way to commit "linguistic genocide" (p. xiii). Darder writes

> Given the significant role of the primary language in the development of identity and a sense of belonging, linguistic genocide, as an outcome of cultural invasion, is clearly one of the most devastating consequences faced by bilingual and bicultural students. (p. xiii)

Darder points out that when peoples lose their language, identity is destroyed. Language is inextricably tied to one's identity. And if language is taken away so too is part of one's identity. If schools are ever to become noncolonizing they must respect differences in culture, language, and identity. School teachers must teach a more inclusive curriculum. But as Lourdes Diaz Soto and Haroon Kharem (2010) point out, language, identity, and culture are related to power. Those in power (white people) want to keep that power. And this is done through an assimilationist agenda. Conservative Americans think that if the curriculum becomes more inclusive white America will lose its power. But this is not just an American problem. Lourdes Diaz Soto and Haroon Kharem argue

> Scholars have struggled with how language issues can ultimately be an integral part of power issues. Pennycook (1998), for example, describes how English around the world is not only at the "heart of colonialism" but is also deeply interwoven with the discourses of colonialism. (p. 9)

Resistance against colonizing powers is difficult, but not impossible. The real problem here is that children have little say in how they are to be educated. Teachers have little power to change public school curriculum as the curriculum is mandated by the state.

Islamophobia

Since 9/11 the term "Islamophobia" has come to the attention of Americans. However, this is not a new term. Marc Helbling (2012) points out

> While the term "Islamophobia" had appeared as early as the 1920s, it became extremely popular in the 1990s (Allen, 2006: 68–71). According to Otterbeck and Bevelander (2006) the term appeared for the first time in 1918 in France. (p. 4)

There has been a long history in France of tensions with Muslims. One need only to think of France's colonization of Algeria.

Islamophobia means the fear (phobia) of people (who call themselves Muslims) who practice Islam. Although this is an irrational fear, it has real, material consequences for Muslims. Fazal Rizvi (2005) writes about "anti-Muslim sentiment" (p. 171):

> Even before September 11, the rise of Anti-Muslim sentiment was widely noted not only in the United States but in Europe as well. Partly in order to overcome the limitations of the black-white dualistic framework for understanding racism, a number of theorists, particularly in Europe, had begun to speak of *Islamophobia*, a term designed to highlight the specificities of contemporary forms of racism directed against Muslims. (p. 171)

Recall that Antonia Darder, Rodolfo Torres, and Henry Gutierrez (1997) suggest that "black and white categories" (p. xiv) erased the importance of studying other groups, like Latinas/os. Similarly, Muslims do not fit into the black and white "dualistic framework" (Rizvi, 2005, p. 171) and tend to get erased from academic discussions on racism. Scholars who study and write about multicultural education tend not to treat Islamophobia with a few exceptions (e.g., see Kincheloe & Steinberg [2000]; Kincheloe, Steinberg, & Stonebanks [2010]; McCarthy, Crichlow, Dimitriadis, & Dolby [2005]).

Rizvi points out

> In a major report, the highly influential Runnymede Trust (1998) in England defines "Islamophobia as dread, hatred and hostility towards Islam and Muslims by a series of 'closed views' that imply negative or derogatory stereotypes and beliefs to Muslims." (p. 171)

Islamophobia has much in common with anti-Semitism. Jews (although not seen as a race) have to contend with irrational phobias, hatred, discrimination. Simply put, anti-Semitism is hatred of Jews. Islamophobia is hatred of Muslims. Scholars debate reasons why these groups of people are so hated. But no rational answers can be given.

Nathan Lean (2012) writes

> The predominant sentiment among many right-wing Americans regarding Muslims... is that they are not welcome in "our" country. Such ferocity and dogged nationalism are predicated on the assumption that Muslims are immigrants and that the religion of Islam is not a fluid or borderless belief system, but rather originates from afar and [Muslims have]...invaded the United States. (p. 5)

Recall that Leo Chavez (2008) writes that Latinas/os are seen as an "invading force" (p. 2) in the United States. The right-wing in the United States sees both Latinas/os and Muslims as invaders.

A key word in the above quote is "immigrant." Muslims, like Latinas/os are seen as immigrants. Deepa Fernandes (2007) writes, "Given the direct connections that have been made in the media between immigrants and terrorists, the fact that the government now treats immigration as an issue of homeland security is barely questioned" (p. 29). Not all immigrants are terrorists and not all terrorists are immigrants. There are homegrown terrorists in the United States who are not Muslims and who are not Latinas/os. And yet anyone who has dark skin is now subject to interrogation by the U.S. government. Anyone who appears to be Muslim is subject to interrogation, arrest, detention, and so forth. Anny Bakalian and Mehdi Bozorgmehr (2009) state

> Immediately after the attacks [of 9/11], individuals who appeared to be Middle Eastern or had Arabic- or Islamic-sounding names became the scapegoats of Americans' anger and vengeance. Balbir Singh Sodhi was the first murder victim of the backlash because his traditional Sikh looks—*dastaar* (turban) and *Kesh* (unshorn hair)—were confused with Osama Bin Laden's *Kaffiyeh* (male headdress) and beard. Ironically, Sikhs are neither Arab nor Muslim. (p. 1)

People who appear to be Arabs are targets. What does it mean to appear to be Arab? Christopher Stonebanks (2004) writes about the phenomenon of what he calls "Pan-terrorist-Arabism" (p. 88). Stonebanks asks

> How is it that an Iranian, a Pakistani, an Indian, a Sikh, an Afghani, or any other dark-skinned person from this vast region have all become Arabs, or more accurately, Arabs with possible links to terrorism? Are we witnessing the creation of some sort of Pan-Arabism or Pan-terrorist-Arabism? (pp. 87–88)

These cultures in the above citation are not the same. But Americans who are miseducated, as Kincheloe and Steinberg (2004) put it, tend to see dark-skinned foreigners as Arab terrorists. Part of the problem, too, is that xenophobes see all foreigners as possible terrorists. Xenophobes do not know the difference between one culture and another. Manning Marable (2002) comments that this discrimination and hatred also apply to other non-Arab peoples. Marable reports, "In Seattle and other West Coast cities, dozens of Hawaiians, Central Americans, South Asians, and even American Indians have been subjected to verbal insults and harassment because they 'appear' to be vaguely 'non-American'" (p. 308). The inability to tolerate difference is part of the problem. Islamophobes—like homophobes—(those who cannot psychologically manage sexual difference) project hatred onto the other.

Nathan Lean (2012) writes that even when Muslims become citizens or are born in a country that is intolerant of Muslims, they are still thought of as immigrants or foreigners. Lean reports

> American and European Muslims, born in the United States and countries like France and Britain, are, to Islamophobes, just as foreign as immigrants. Even if they may be naturalized or natural-born citizens, they are cast into the larger pot of strangeness. (p. 6)

A parallel problem occurred in Germany—even before the Holocaust. Germans did not recognize Jews as citizens even if they were (Morris, 2001). Jews were seen as foreigners even in their homelands.

Today those who seem to be strange, as Nathan Lean puts it, are targeted as possible terrorists. In fact, the airlines have discriminated against so many people that several of them have been sued. Anny Bakalian and Mehdi Bozorgmehr (2009) write

> Airline profiling of Middle Eastern and Muslim American passengers has led to the settling of discrimination suits. In June 2004, upon allegations that Delta Airlines had discriminated against travelers appearing to be of Middle Eastern, Arab, or South Asian descent, the airline opted for a settlement. (p. 5)

Part of the problem is that Americans are uneducated about other cultures. For more on this, students should consult the book titled *The Miseducation of the West: How Schools and the Media Distort Our Understanding of the Islamic World*, which is co-edited by Joe Kincheloe and Shirley Steinberg (2004). What do young people learn in schools about other cultures? Probably very little. American news channels are highly controlled and viewers learn very little about other cultures when watching, say, CNN. Ibrahim Abukhattala (2004) points out

> Also, Western writers and news anchors use the terms *Arab* and *Muslim* interchangeably, although they are not necessarily the same: not every Muslim is Arab, nor is every Arab Muslim. In fact, Arabs comprise less than 15 percent of the whole population of the Islamic world, and considerable numbers of Arabs are Jews or Christians. (p. 160)

Americans are undereducated when it comes to Arabic cultures. American schooling is about getting students to score high on standardized tests. These tests serve only to undereducate youth. And the media are also partly to blame for "the miseducation of the West" as Kincheloe and Steinberg put it. Michael

Giardina (2010) reports that the right-wing media have bashed Muslims and Islam publicly. Giardina tells us

> Right-wing media personalities, in particular, fanned the flames of intolerance, such as when Ann Coulter (2001) wrote in a *National Review* article, just days after the [9/11] tragedy, that the United States "should invade their countries, kill their leaders and convert them to Christianity." (p. 135)

Interestingly enough, before 9/11 Arabs were considered to be—as Nadine Naber (2008) puts it—white. After 9/11 Arabs became nonwhite (pp. 1–2). Naber explains

> Some scholars have argued that the aftermath of September 11 consolidated the racialization of the category "Arab/Middle Eastern/Muslim" as a signifier of nonwhite Otherness or that a "racialization of Islam" has underlain the post-9/11 backlash against persons perceived to be Arab, Middle Eastern, South Asian, and/or Muslim. (pp. 1–2).

One can better understand from this example that the notion of race is indeed socially constructed and changeable. Recall that Latinas/os in different time periods or in different settings are considered nonwhite and some are considered white. According to George Martinez (2011) Mexicans are considered to be white (by the government). In the 1930s, however, Neil Foley (2011) points out that Hispanics were seen as "nonwhite" (p. 369). Race is changeable depending on history, culture, and geography.

How Arabs and Muslims are represented in texts or in popular culture makes a difference in the way they are treated. Many people demonize Arabs in texts or in images or in popular culture. This demonization through mis-representation has a long history. Fazal Rizvi (2005) writes, "Indeed, as Miles (1989, 18) points out, the European image of Islam first emerged in the eleventh and twelfth centuries and involved portraying the Islamic Other as 'barbaric, degenerate and tyrannical'" (p. 171). Stereotypes of Muslims are not new. And these stereotypes are ingrained in European culture. Like Muslims, Jews were considered to be degenerate peoples even before the Holocaust (Morris, 2001). A degenerate people, then, produces degenerate art (e.g., Gustav Mahler's music was considered degenerate in Austria).

Joe Kincheloe and Shirley Steinberg (2010) report, "In the Western tradition of teaching about, writing about, researching, and representing Islam, Europeans have positioned Muslims as the irrational, fanatic, sexually enticing, and despotic other" (p. 3). Kincheloe and Steinberg suggest that teachers need to find ways to not misrepresent Muslims. They argue that teachers must "construct a liberatory framework to teach against Islamophobia" (p. 3). After 9/11 this task is a difficult one. Victims' families and friends still might be too raw or too unwilling to listen to those who teach against Islamophobia (Kincheloe & Steinberg). Islamophobes cling to their preconceived notions. How do teachers and scholars teach people to stop hate?

Jehanzeb Dar (2010) reports on the ways in which Islamophobia is represented in popular culture. Dar comments, "In his book *Reel Bad Arabs* (2001), Jack Shaheen documented and discussed over 900 Hollywood films to expose the industry's unapologetic degradation and dehumanization of Muslims and Arabs" (p. 100). Dar uncovers astounding evidence of the hatred of Muslims and Islam in Hollywood. Hollywood has been historically an institution of fear of the Other. There is a long history in Hollywood of misrepresenting or demonizing gays and lesbians as well (Faderman & Timmons, 2006). People who watch films are influenced by what they see or by what they do not see. Film has a huge impact on people and can shape their worldviews.

Misrepresentations of Arabs and Muslims have material consequences. Louise Cainkar (2008) reports

> Twenty-five of the thirty-seven known government security initiatives implemented between September 12, 2001, and mid-2003 either explicitly or implicitly targeted U.S. Arabs and Muslims (Tsao and Gutierrez 2003). These measures included mass arrests, secret and indefinite detentions, prolonged detention of "material witnesses," closed hearings, secret evidence, government eavesdropping on attorney-client conversations. (p. 53)

Tram Nguyen (2005) reports that people (after 9/11) were detained but did not know why they were detained. Nguyen goes on to say that "no names of those detained were released, and none was connected to terrorist-related activity" (p. xvii). These detentions remind us of Japanese internment camps in the United States during World War II. One might think that these kinds of things do not happen in the United States, but they do. And it seems that government officials under G. W. Bush had learned nothing from the past. These acts of "indefinite detentions" (Cainkar, 2008) are hardly constitutional. Civil liberties vanished after 9/11. Institutionalized racism, misrepresentations, stereotypes, and miseducation have much to do with the way Arabs, Muslims, and other peoples were treated after 9/11. Joe Kincheloe and Shirley Steinberg (2010) explain, "Little elementary or secondary school material devoted to historicizing or contextualizing the Islamic world and its relation with the West appeared in the first two years after the tragic events of 9/11" (p. 5). Islamophobia is rampant in the United States and in Europe. And as Kincheloe and Steinberg (2004) point out, much of Islamophobia is due to being miseducated. Standardized testing has little to do with learning about real-world politics and institutionalized racism. Much of American culture is anti-intellectual. Much of American culture is parochial. Much of American culture is intolerant and xenophobic. If our children were educated differently, perhaps America would become a less racist society. This is the point that is driven home by Kincheloe and Steinberg (2004; 2010). As long as Americans continue to miseducate our children this country will remain racist. Perhaps, too, scholars must move beyond the notion of tolerance and work to understand difference. The study of Others must be historical, as Kincheloe and Steinberg (2010) suggest. Islamophobia will continue to haunt America if Americans do not change the U.S. educational system.

Black/Feminist/Womanist Studies

Jacqueline Bobo, Cynthia Hudley, and Claudine Michel (2004) write that black studies came about during the civil rights movement. These scholars comment that black studies was "born of social unrest" (p. 3) Bobo, Hudley, and Michel argue that black studies deals with "issues of social, educational, and economic disparities, defining curricula vitally engaged with present-day societal issues" (p. 4) Two key terms are important to black studies scholars: "resistance" and "resilience" (Bobo, Hudley, & Michel, p. 4). What is important to note here is that black scholars emphasize that blacks are not merely victims of social oppression. Rather, they fight back. For black intellectuals, then, writing is a form of what William Watkins (2005) calls "protest thought" (p. 1). An ongoing trend in black studies is the importance of connecting theory to social activism. It is not enough to theorize. Black studies scholars want to interrupt oppressive practices on the ground. James Jennings (2004) comments

> "COMMUNITY SERVICE" and related efforts to develop programmatic linkages with neighborhood institutions and organizations represent a key component in the theory and pedagogy of Black studies. Research paradigms that include community service and civic involvement reflect the description of Black studies as a discipline that is "descriptive, critical, and prescriptive," to use the words of Professor Manning Marable. (p. 35)

Theory and social activism go hand in hand for black studies scholars. It is important to note that many scholars, however, are not interested in social activism. But for black studies scholars this is a hallmark of their work. Black studies scholars want to interrupt the status quo on the ground in real-life situations.

When black studies emerged as a discipline it was mostly a male endeavor. But many women were involved in the early years to help build this new discipline. Stanlie M. James, Frances Smith Foster, and Beverly Guy-Sheftall (2009) write

> Although Black women had been instrumental in helping establish Black Studies, the field remained male centered, while Women's Studies privileged middle-class white women as the norm for what it meant to be female. Because Black Studies and Women's Studies failed to adequately address the unique experiences of women of African descent in the United States and around the world, a few brave women created a new field—Black Women's Studies. (p. xiii)

William Watkins (2005) comments that in the 1970s black women developed what is called black feminist studies. Watkins reports, "Black women found themselves racially marginalized in the Women's movement and sexually oppressed in the male-dominated Black Liberation Movement" (p. 23). Watkins tells us that it was Audre Lorde who initiated the black feminist movement. It is important to note that Watkins calls Lorde a militant black woman (p. 23). Thus, black feminist thought has an edge to it. Some black women, however, are uncomfortable with the term "feminism" because it is associated with white women. Patricia Hill Collins (2000) tells us, "Large numbers of African American women reject the term 'feminism' because of what they perceive as its association with whiteness" (p. 63). Following Alice Walker (2006), these women prefer to use the term "womanist" (p. 19). Many African American women want to drive a wedge between the terms "feminist" and "womanist," but Alice Walker—who coined the term "womanist"—uses these terms interchangeably. Walker tells us that a womanist is "[a] black feminist or feminist of color" (p. 19). Following Walker I use these terms interchangeably.

Black feminist thought could be compared to queer theory in that this movement is also a militant movement in that it emerged during the early years of the AIDS epidemic, and queers were angry and militant because the government did nothing to help develop research to cure AIDS because it was thought in the early 1980s that AIDS was a gay disease. Militant responses do not come out of nowhere. Militant responses are angry, emotional. Black women who formed the black feminist movement did so out of anger.

Like the founders of the black studies movement, founders of the black feminist movement linked together theory and social activism. Patricia Hill Collins (2000) tells us

> Denied positions as scholars and writers which allow us to emphasize purely theoretical concerns, the work of most Black women intellectuals has been influenced by the merger of action and theory. The activities of nineteenth-century educated Black women intellectuals such as Anna J. Cooper, Frances Watkins Harper, Ida B. Wells-Barnett, and Mary Church Terrell exemplify this tradition of merging intellectual work and activism. (p. 33)

For more on these women cited above turn back to the historical chapters in this volume as I have dealt with many of these women in detail.

Historically, intellectuals were thought to be white Anglo-Saxon men (Morris, 2006). Living in a patriarchy it is hard to escape misogyny. Some men feel that women cannot be intellectuals; this attitude comes out of misogyny. Black women intellectuals have to fight on two counts: on being black and on being female. Black women intellectuals have to contend with both racism and sexism. The problems continue in the academy as some conservative white racist scholars do not think that black women intellectuals are doing legitimate scholarship. When a new discipline arrives on the scene in academe conservative scholars are resistant to it. As I stated earlier, women's studies—when it first appeared on the scene in academe—was not thought to be a legitimate field. Women who wrote about women's issues were sometimes denied tenure because it was thought—by sexist colleagues—that research on women's issues was not real scholarship. The question of whose knowledge is of most worth comes into play. Who decides what "real" scholarship is? The powerful. What counts as knowledge is highly political.

Black feminist studies is a rich field. One of the hallmarks of this field is the interconnection between theory and activism. Barbara Smith (1995) discusses the kinds of social activism in which black feminists are involved. She states

> Some of the issues we have worked on are reproductive rights, equal access to abortion, sterilization abuse, health care, child care, the rights of the disabled, violence against women, rape, battering, sexual harassment, welfare rights, lesbian and gay rights, educational reform. (p. 263)

Many scholars in the academy do not have the time to get involved in social activism, but black feminist scholars make time to get involved outside the academy and in the world where social justice is carried out. Black feminists are engaged in social justice education on the ground. This is no easy task because of all the demands made on scholars inside the academy. Black feminist intellectuals want to change the world not only through their words but also through their actions. Gloria Joseph (1995) reports

> Black feminist theory is a theory of change with black feminist pedagogy being the change agent in and outside the classroom—wherever education takes place… . Black feminist theory challenges Marxist theory to consider race as a primary contradiction, and it challenges feminists (white feminist theorists) to recognize the automatic dual oppression of sexism and racism… . Black feminists ask Marxist and white feminists, "Is our liberation going to be part of your revolution?" (p. 468)

Black women intellectuals have hardly been a topic of discussion in Marxist scholarship. William Watkins' (2005) scholarship is an exception. And white feminists have had a long history of racism. This is partly the reason that black feminists had to carve out their own territory and found their own discipline. Rochelle Brock (2005) writes about the importance of agency and empowerment for black students and professors alike. Here, she continues in the tradition of black feminist thought by focusing on social activism while doing theory. Brock tells us

> Black student empowerment and Black revolutionary thought are two dynamics that are complementary. The dynamics between the two make it possible for the world not to be some place where we must be tolerated… . Instead, we look at the world as something, given the right tools, we can change. Empowerment is agency. Agency is the ability to act on and change our world/environment. (p. 92)

Note in the above citation that Brock points out that toleration is not enough. If scholars really want to understand people they have to study cultures historically. Racism must be studied historically. The problem is that racism is so entrenched, not just in the United States, but around the world.

Annette Henry (2005) points out that in the academy black feminist thought is absent. Curriculum scholars are particularly interested in groups who have been "largely ignored" (Henry, p. 101). Our task is to bring to the curriculum marginalized groups of people. Our task is to shed light on cultures and peoples who get left out of the official curriculum.

Colleges of education are notoriously conservative. The hidden agenda in conservative institutions is to conserve tradition. Tradition is a loaded concept that suggests that white male scholarship is the only scholarship that is worth studying. Breaking with tradition and inventing different canons of knowledge within the academy are difficult to do. Black feminist thought breaks with tradition and brings to the fore black women intellectuals who have historically been left out of the official canon.

Many black feminist scholars write about the problem of the official canon (white, male, European or Euro-American) and write about knowledge production. Toni Morrison (1993) comments

> For some time now I have been thinking about the validity or vulnerability of a certain set of assumptions conventionally accepted among literary historians and critics and circulated as "knowledge." This knowledge holds that traditional, canonical American literature is free of, uninformed, and unshaped by the four-hundred-year-old presence of, first, Africans and then African-Americans in the United States. (pp. 4–5)

Morrison suggests that in order to understand who we are as Americans we must acknowledge that "black presence is central to any understanding of our national literature" (p. 5). In the academy some scholars who work in conservative disciplines like philosophy and the classics are still resistant to deconstructing the problem of Eurocentrism and are resistant to including marginalized peoples in their work. (Western) philosophy—as a discipline—is particularly troubling because this field erases women and people of color. Epistemology—or the study of knowledge—is a male domain, even though feminists have been writing about this problem for over a decade. Whose knowledge counts? What knowledge is of most worth? Black feminists understand the problem of the Western canon and work to undo the racist and sexist underpinnings of the traditional canon. Patricia Hill Collins (2000) tells us

> Maintaining the invisibility of Black women and our ideas not only in the United States, but in Africa, the Caribbean, South America, Europe, and other places where Black women now live, has been critical in maintaining social inequities. Black women engaged in reclaiming and constructing Black women's knowledges often point to the politics of suppression that affect their projects. (p. 3)

The academy is a political place. Conservative scholars engage in this suppression of knowledge. The tenure process is a process of suppression. Who decides what knowledge counts? The powerful. White male knowledge, white Eurocentric knowledge is still considered superior by conservative scholars. The Great Books Tradition is still valued—by conservative scholars—over marginalized knowledges.

Rochelle Brock (2005) writes about her struggles as a black feminist working inside the academy. She states, "I have continually analyzed the pain Black women experience living in a society which methodically devalues, dehumanizes, and disempowers them" (p. xvi). Brock writes about the ways in which the academy devalues her work and her engagement with knowledge production. She tells us that the academy constrains her knowledge (p. xvi). One's identity and one's knowledge are inextricably tied. To constrain one's knowledge, then, is to constrain one's identity. How can a scholar produce knowledge if she is constrained? Black feminist intellectuals have had a long history of writing against the grain. Violet Eudine Barriteau (2009) addresses these problems. She states

> Black feminist scholarship underlines the importance of using lived experience as a criterion for generating knowledge. These experiences should be used to validate knowledge claims and to create or refute generalizations. This insistence that theory should be built "from the ground up" rejects Western philosophy's fascination and faith in rationality, objectivity and theory that move from the abstract to the concrete. (p. 421)

Curriculum theorists believe that intellectual work and knowledge building are inextricably tied to interiority (e.g., see Pinar et al., 1995). Knowledge is embodied and as Munro Hendry (2011) puts it engendered. Knowledge building has to do with race, class, and gender. The history of Western philosophy is about generating knowledge in a disembodied fashion. Even if male philosophers talk about the body they do so in a disembodied way.

Joyce E. King (2005) calls for a "transformative [Black] education" (p. 5). King says

> A goal of transformative education and research practice in Black education is the production of knowledge and understanding people [we]...need to rehumanize the world by dismantling hegemonic structures that impede such knowledge. (p. 5)

The production of knowledge is about power. As I mentioned earlier, in the academy power plays a big role in granting tenure and promotion. Who decides what knowledge counts when going up for tenure or promotion? White, male elites decide. Institutionalized racism has a lot to do with denying tenure and promotion to black intellectuals. Institutionalized sexism too has much to do with denying black women intellectuals tenure. These "hegemonic structures" must be "dismantled" (King, p. 5).

Disability Studies

Disability studies is not often a topic of scholarly debate in the context of multicultural education. Lennard J. Davis (2002) tells us that "the majority of academics do not consider disability to be part of their social conscience" (p. 35). Although multicultural scholars discuss the importance of alterity they rarely think through this concept against the backdrop of disability. Lennard J. Davis writes about Michael Berube's response to disability studies. Berube, although the father of a child with Down Syndrome, "thinks of his resistance to disability studies as 'a piece with a larger and more insidious cultural form of resistance'" (p. 35). People are resistant to study disability because becoming disabled is the unthinkable. Scholars can write about alterity but in the context of disability they do not want to think about it. Berube, Davis tells us, "calls this 'the politics of disavowal,'" which he links to "the psychological distance most people put between themselves and disability" (p. 35). Thus, disability is hard to think about. Most people who are not disabled do not want to think about disability because they are afraid of it. Disabled people are shunned because able-bodied people cannot think the unthinkable. Able-bodied people engage in what is referred to as "ableism," which Davis suggests is "an equivalent to better known terms like racism and sexism" (p. 35). Able-bodied people are blind to their own privilege. And in many respects being able bodied is not unlike white privilege. Tobin Siebers (2008) claims

> The ideology of ability is at its simplest the preference for able-bodiedness. At its most radical, it defines the baseline by which humanness is determined, setting the measure of body and mind that gives or denies human status to individual persons.... it is discriminatory and exclusionary. (p. 8)

Disabled people, then, are outcasts. Able-bodied people are in denial about disability because it is too emotionally difficult to think about. If people are not confronted with disability they would rather not think about it. As curriculum scholars it is imperative that disability studies be integrated into our discussions on difference and alterity. Scholars must bring into the canon more studies on the disabled. Curriculum scholars must think about the ways in which disabled people are excluded from our literatures. Margaret Price (2011) comments that "academic discourse abhors mental disability" (p. 8). She goes on to say, "Ableism contributes to the construction of a rigid, elitist, hierarchical, and inhuman academic system" (p. 8). The academic system into which curriculum scholars are thrown rarely includes scholarship on disabled peoples. Disability studies tends to get ghettoized if it is dealt with at all. But outside of curriculum theory, disability studies "has been recognized as an academic discipline in its own right" (Roulstone, Thomas, & Watson, 2012, p. 3).

Dan Goodley (2011) writes, "Disability affects us all, transcending class, nation, wealth. The notion of TAB—Temporarily Able Bodied—recognises that many people will at some point become disabled (Marks, 1999a: 18)" (p. 1). People who are able bodied rarely think that they will become disabled as they get older. Able-bodied people are thus "Temporarily Able Bodied" (Goodley, p. 1). Our bodies eventually break down. Goodley points out that 150 million disabled peoples are children. Teachers must have a better understanding of what disabled children experience.

A Brief Historical Overview

Colin Barnes (2010) writes

> Hafter (1968) has pointed out that in medieval Europe disability was associated with evil and witchcraft.... Protestant reformer Martin Luther (1483–1546) proclaimed that he saw the Devil in a profoundly disabled child. If these children lived, Luther recommended killing them. (p. 21)

The Nazis heeded Luther's call and exterminated disabled children and adults (Morris, 2001). Barnes, drawing on the work of Wolfensberger, writes, "During the 1939–45 war…between 80,000 and 100,000" disabled people were exterminated (p. 26). Barnes (2010) also writes about the eugenics movement and suggests that eugenicists were "concerned mainly with what they saw as racial degeneration through the birth of disabled children" (p. 26). In Nazi Germany, Jews too were thought to be racially degenerate (Morris, 2001).

Alan Roulstone, Carol Thomas, and Nick Watson (2012) tell us

> Disability studies can trace its origins to the organizations of disabled people whose voices emerged in the late 1960s and who shared ideas drawn from other previously excluded groups such as African Americans in the US, black and other minority ethnic groupings elsewhere, women, and lesbians and gay men. (p. 3)

Black studies, queer theory, and disability studies are disciplines that express much discontent with the status quo. These disciplines are all concerned with issues of social justice and equity. Scot Danforth and Susan Gabel (2006) claim that disability studies is a form of "protest literature" (p. 6). Black feminist studies too is thought to be a protest literature (Watkins, 2005).

Paul K. Longmore and Lauri Umansky (2001) report that during the 1970s the history of disability was treated as a "compensatory initiative" (p. 16). Longmore and Umansky tell us

> A celebratory and compensatory initiative appeared among activists and advocates beginning in the 1970s. As with any group denied a significant place in history, people with disabilities claimed heroes: Beethoven was deaf! Milton was blind! Franklin Delano Roosevelt had polio!..... This heritage hunting often unwittingly reinforced oppressive mainstream heralding of disabled people who had "overcome" their disabilities to almost miraculous effect. (p. 16)

Disability scholars critique the status quo. Not all disabled people overcome their disability but this is the only narrative that many able-bodied people can deal with.

In the 1980s disability scholars "concentrated largely on the myriad patterns of abuse, discrimination, and oppression in the history of people with disabilities" (Longmore & Umansky, 2001, p. 17). Longmore and Umansky also state that "more recently" disability scholars focus on disabled people not as victims but as "agents in their own lives" (p. 17).

Theoretical Frameworks

In disability studies scholars utilize different theoretical frameworks or models to better understand ways to approach disabilities. Here I will briefly discuss the medical model, the social model, the cultural studies model, and the critical studies model.

John Davis (2012) tells us that the medical model

> pathologized children who failed to meet standardized developmental targets, viewed disability as the natural consequence of impairment rather than being caused by society, ignored the structural and cultural barriers that blocked disabled children's inclusion...into society. (p. 415)

The medical model tends to normalize children. Davis discusses Piaget's stages of development that dovetail with the medical model. The upshot of this discussion of Piaget is that if children do not fit into certain developmental categories or do not reach age-related milestones they are considered abnormal. Abnormal children are then placed in special education classrooms where they are segregated from children who are "normal." Davis points out that so-called abnormal children—or children with disabilities—were historically thought to be a "threat to society" (p. 415). Lennard J. Davis (2002) says, "The medical model treats disability as a disease in need of a cure" (pp. 40–41). The so-called cure suggests that disabled people need to become more like 'normal' people. Disease is associated with abnormality.

As against the medical model, the social model places emphasis on the way in which society treats people who are different. Dan Goodley (2011) states

> While we may identify people as having physical, sensory, cognitive or mental health impairments, disability studies place the problems of disability in society… . If we locate disability in the person, then we maintain a disabling status quo. In contrast, by viewing disability as a cultural and political phenomenon, we ask serious questions about the social world. (p. xi)

The social model examines the ways in which disabled people are Othered and marginalized. The social model looks at the way able-bodied people discriminate against disabled people. This discrimination is institutionalized much like the way racism, sexism, and classism are also institutionalized. Bradley Lewis (2010) remarks

> [Today] disability activists resist these individualizing and medicalizing approaches by reframing disability as a social restriction and oppression rather than simply a medical problem. Emphasizing a social model…they call attention to the fact that much of the suffering of different bodies comes from social exclusion, isolation, and lack of opportunity. (p. 161)

Institutionalized discrimination against disabled persons causes suffering. Dismantling institutionalized discrimination is a key to undoing this suffering. Schools that separate disabled children from able-bodied children are part of the problem. When children are placed in special education classrooms they feel that they are inferior to children who are in mainstream classes. Disability studies scholars feel that disabled children should not be excluded from their peers. This exclusion makes children suffer. They begin to think of themselves as outcasts. Tobin Siebers (2008) comments

> The social model opposes the medical model by defining disability relative to the social and built environment, arguing that disabling environments produce disability in bodies and require interventions at the level of social justice…. Without returning to a medical model, which labels individuals as defective, the next step for disability studies is to develop a theory of complex embodiment that values disability as a form of human variation. (p. 25)

Siebers points out that the major problem with the medical model is that it treats disabled people as defective. Rather, Siebers suggests that disability is part of a broad spectrum of what it means to be human. Humanizing disabled people is what the social model attempts to do. The medical model dehumanizes disabled people. Disabled people are more concerned with social injustice and the unfair treatment they receive by able-bodied people. Disabled people are certainly not defective. This discussion again is, at bottom, about the way in which people have a hard time managing difference psychologically. Able-bodied people fear the disabled because they know at some deep level that they too could become disabled. Or able-bodied people shun the disabled because they represent otherness. Otherness is feared. Thus, disabled people are shunned, discriminated against and treated as subhuman.

Tom Shakespeare (2010) reports

> While the problems of disabled people have been explained historically in terms of divine punishment, karma or moral failing, and post-Enlightenment in terms of biological deficit [i.e., the medical model], the disability movement has focused attention onto social oppression, cultural discourse, and environmental barriers. (p. 266)

Blaming the victim is not uncommon. To suggest that someone is disabled because they deserve it is reprehensible. To suggest that someone with a disability is a victim of bad karma is unconscionable. To suggest that disabled people deserve God's wrath is immoral. Disability can strike anyone. Why people are born disabled or become disabled later in life is a mystery. Some disabilities are caused by living in toxic environments, for example, pesticides or herbicides. The human body is complex and oftentimes doctors do not understand why people are born disabled or become disabled.

Carol Thomas and Mairian Corker (2002) critique the social model for not taking into account gender. These scholars claim that "disability is fundamentally gendered" (p. 19). These scholars also note, "This in turn, makes one alert to the significance of other dimensions of social oppression associated with 'race', age, sexuality, class and so forth" (p. 19). Disability, then, is engendered, raced, classed. Disabled people are thus treated differently—and worse—if they are women, if they are people of color and/or poor. Karen Beauchamp-Pryor (2012) suggests, "Disabled people are not a homogeneous social group, and the social model is criticized for neglecting experiences of disablism based on gender, ethnicity, sexuality, age and class" (p. 178). Thus, the social model is not complex enough to take into account the various ways people can be discriminated against. Discussions of race, class, gender, sexuality have to go hand in hand with discussions on disability. Chris Bell (2010) offers a harsher critique still. Bell states

> I would like to concede the failure of Disability Studies to engage issues of race and ethnicity in a substantive capacity, thereby entrenching whiteness as its constitutive underpinning. In short, I want to call a shrimp a shrimp and acknowledge Disability Studies for what it is, White Disability Studies. (p. 374)

Earlier in this chapter I discussed the problems of whiteness and of white privilege. The critiques around whiteness apply to disability studies as well. The question here, though, is how to integrate race into scholarly debates on disability. It is well documented, as Nirmala Erevelles (2006) points out, that African Americans, Latina/os, and Native Americans are often placed in special education classrooms because of racism. Erevelles claims, "What is clearly apparent is that public education has used the concepts of difference, deviance, and disability synonymously to justify the exclusion of certain student populations in an attempt to adhere to demands of normativity" (p. 366). Clearly, the terms "difference," "deviance," and "disability" do not mean the same things. Disabled people are not deviant, they are not criminals. The term "difference" is not pejorative. Disabled people do not have to be excluded from classes because they are disabled. Putting disabled people in ghettos will not solve anything; in fact it makes things worse.

Cultural Disability Studies

David Bolt (2012) tells us

> Cultural disability studies is an explicitly interdisciplinary field, synthesizing, as it often does, scholarship in both disability and forms of cultural production…a critical appreciation of disability can greatly inform cultural representations, be they literary, filmic, artistic, musical. (p. 287)

For Bolt disability is not deviant. Disability is not bad, nor is it something to be feared. Thinking disability and cultural studies together is an important advance in both fields. It is interesting to note that in 2014 two films, *The Theory of Everything* and *Still Alice*, explored the problems of ALS and Alzheimer's disease. Both lead actors won Oscars for their performances. Bringing sympathetic portrayals of disabilities teaches audiences—who watch films like these—about these diseases and perhaps through educating audiences via film people can become more empathetic.

Critical Disability Studies

Margrit Shildrick (2012) writes about CDS or critical disability studies. CDS includes thinking about disability through "feminism, postmodernism, queer theory, critical race theory...phenomenology of the body and psychoanalysis" (p. 32). Of these various theoretical frameworks, Shildrick claims that postmodernism is the most controversial. Postmodernism, many believe, is about the nature of discourse and not materiality. However, some versions of postmodernism are political and therefore lend themselves to materiality. Derrida and Foucault are highly political and are not just interested in word games. Their theories have real-life consequences.

Lennard J. Davis (2002), Mairian Corker and Tom Shakespeare (2002) write about disability studies and postmodernism. Lennard J. Davis, for example, suggests that the notion of disability (as an identity) is "inherently unstable" (p. 5). Davis writes that "disability is an amorphous identity with porous boundaries" (p. 36). He also suggests that disability is a social construction and highly changeable. These are some of the hallmarks of a postmodern sensibility. Disability is not a monolithic category but a multiplicity, as Michel Serres (1995), Gilles Deleuze and Felix Guattari (2000), might put it.

What Counts as a Disability?

Able-bodied people attach the term "disability" to people who they think are disabled. But some people (who are thought to be disabled by others) do not like this label and do not believe that they are, in fact, disabled. A good example of this is deafness. Many people who are deaf do not believe that they are, in fact, disabled (Davis, 2002; Baynton, 2010; Siebers, 2008; Scully, 2012). Lennard J. Davis tells us

> Even within the disability rights movement itself, notions about who falls into the category of the "disabled" are unclear. For example, many Deaf activists do not consider themselves disabled. Rather, the Deaf think of themselves as a linguistic minority like Latinos or Asians. (p. 37)

That deaf people do not think of themselves as disabled might come as a surprise to some.

Margaret Price (2011) wants to argue that mentally ill people are disabled. Price says that "disabilities of the mind" (p. 5) are usually left out of most discussions on disabilities. Price, therefore, wants to "broaden the field of DS and…critique…the field's longstanding emphasis on physical and sensory impairments" (p. 5). However, Peter Beresford (2012) argues

> While terms like mentally disabled and psychiatric disability are used in some countries and in some contexts, this has not been the general way in which service users/survivors have described themselves or been described. (p. 155)

Beresford (2012) suggests that mental illness tends to be seen as something different from disability. The literature on mental illness differs from the literature on disability studies. Scholars who write about mental illness are for the most part psychologists, psychiatrists, and psychoanalysts. These scholars are interested in the way the mind works or does not work. Much of the literature on disability studies, on the other hand, tends to focus on the way the body works or does not work.

Sasha Scambler (2012) writes about whether chronic illness can be considered as a disability. Scambler writes that chronic illnesses "are often relegated to the sidelines in mainstream disability studies texts" (p. 136). Most writing on chronic illness comes out of the discipline of sociology, Scambler tells us. The medical humanities and the genre of pathographies grapple with chronic illness but chronic illness is rarely considered to be a disability (Morris, 2008). But one can become disabled because of a chronic illness. And so because of this, Scambler would like to see chronic illness explored in the literature on disability.

· 7 ·

GENDER CURRICULUM CONCEPTS

Introduction

When studying literature(s) on gender, there are three directions I would like to take. I would like to explore feminism, masculinity studies, and queer theory. Although I separate out feminism, masculinity studies, and queer theory for the sake of organization, these concepts—in their intersections with curriculum studies—are interrelated. Thinking feminism, masculinity studies, and queer theory together is the goal of this chapter. But before thinking these interrelated concepts together it makes sense to think about them one at a time.

Feminism(s) and Gender(s)

I should note at the outset that there are many different kinds of feminism(s). Feminism has a long and rich history. The literature(s) on feminism(s) is extensive. I offer here only glimpses of what is going on in the contemporary scene.

Leila Villaverde (2008) has written a helpful primer on feminism. For students who are new to feminism, Villaverde's book is an excellent introduction.

Villaverde tells us that there are important differences in the way scholars talk about gender. She states

> The 1980s and the 1990s marked the true arrival of gender studies in the literature and in academic circles. Much debate exists about the switch to "gender studies" from "women's studies" or the use of the compound programmatic title, such as "women's and gender studies." (p. 71)

Gender is the main concept in the feminist literature. When feminists talk about gender, little consensus is at hand. Feminism(s) come in many stripes. I want to talk about curriculum scholars who write about feminism(s) and gender(s). These are vague signifiers but nonetheless they can be useful. There is a long history in curriculum studies around feminism(s) and gender(s). In the 1970s William Pinar, Janet Miller, Madeleine Grumet, and Peter Taubman—to name a few—broke ground in this area (Pinar, Reynolds, Slattery, & Taubman, 1995). Here I want to explore more current discussions on these concepts.

A Brief Aside: A Feminist Life

For students who want to know what it means to live a feminist life, read Sandra Gilbert and Susan Gubar's *The Madwoman in the Attic*. The original date of publication was 1979; the reissue of the book in 2000 signals its importance. Gilbert and Gubar bring feminist issues into the everyday and talk about what many women experience, especially in academe. Sandra Gilbert says

> Remember the old feminist device of the mental "click" that you experience when you find yourself confronting what used to be called sexism? By the time I ran into Susan [Gubar] in the elevator, I'd encountered a tap-dance worth of potential clicks, without paying much attention to them. Click: what was I doing in graduate school anyway? demanded one of my professors at Columbia when he found out that my husband was teaching in Columbia College.... Click: there was absolutely no chance of my getting a job at Davis because nepotism rules were inviolable, explained one of my husband's colleagues.... Click: and that was only right, chimed in another, because it wouldn't be fair if there were "two salaries in one family." Click: I gave up. (p. xvii)

Like Gilbert, many women tend to ignore or bury these kinds of indignities that happen on a daily basis in academe. You get used to it. Or maybe you don't! Gilbert's "clicks" are very useful. Sexism is alive and well.

Curriculum Scholars, Feminism(s), and Resistance

Let us begin with Kathleen Weiler. Weiler (1998)—in her remarkable book *Country Schoolwomen: Teaching in Rural California 1850–1950*—explains that at one time feminist writing focused on the ways in which women were made to feel invisible (like the examples Gilbert gives above); more recently feminists avoid talking about women as mere victims of patriarchy but as fighters. Weiler tells us

> In the 1960s, historians writing from an explicitly political, feminist perspective began a project to recover women's lives from the *oblivion* [emphasis mine] to which they had been relegated. These histories tended to emphasize the oppression of patriarchal practices and sexist ideology. Subsequent women's histories turned to the question of resistance. (p. 5)

This is an important shift in feminist thought. Women are not merely victims but they are also fighters. Women need to fight the good fight, as Gramsci would put it. The more you try to erase somebody from history, the more that somebody comes back fighting. This is what Freud called Eros. Eros, or the life force, is what makes people want to survive and want to be seen and heard, not pushed into a corner or erased or made to feel invisible. Women are life givers; men seem to forget that. Or perhaps that is exactly what they fear. What men fear they push away.

Women are victims of patriarchy. Women are victims of a system of discrimination and misogyny. Feminists, however, fight against these practices. Margaret Smith Crocco, Petra Munro (now Munro Hendry), and Kathleen Weiler (1999) write about these issues in their book *Pedagogies of Resistance: Women Educator Activists, 1880–1960*. The issue of resistance is important for these three scholars. However, being a resistor doesn't mean that you win the fight; it means you put up a fight.

Not all women resist. Some do and some don't. This is one of the points of *Pedagogies of Resistance*. Women, as Petra Munro (1998b) tells us in her book, live contradictory and complicated lives. Eloquently, Munro points out

> I would maintain that it is precisely the loss of the unitary subject that is necessary for a political revisioning of resistance and agency. The fragmentation of the subject provides new ways to reconceive gender and to reimagine concepts like the subject that are central to theorizing feminism. (p. 37)

Two key ideas for Munro are contradiction [read non-unitary subject] and resistance. Nobody lives a straightforward life. Nobody is "unitary." It is simplistic to think that all women take up the feminist creed because they do not. Some women—and men I might add, as Munro points out—surprise us. People are a bundle of contradictions and complications. Contradictions are hard to think through because people are not easy to understand. Not all women resist patriarchy. Perhaps at some level they do resist patriarchy but on other levels they are complicit with patriarchy—this is Munro's point. Can it be that some women are complicit in their own oppressions? Yes. Men too can be complicit in their own oppressions. Women, for example, can fight and give up simultaneously. This is exactly what Sandra Gilbert (2000) talked about with her "clicks." She fights back through writing but then at the same time she tells us that she "gave up" (p. xvii). The majority of women academics end up in institutions where teaching loads are heavy. White men get the golden jobs still. Many women trudge along teaching too many classes, serving on too many committees, barely having enough time to do scholarship.

Like Munro (1998b), Leslie Bloom (1998) points out why women especially live contradictory lives. Bloom explains

> Because of women's long history of material marginalization, patriarchal oppression, colonization, physical abuse, and the psychological damage of being demeaned by the pervasive hierarchical structuring of the sexual differences male/female, women have internalized many negative and conflicted ideas about what it means to be a woman. (p. 5)

Bloom is suggesting here that women suffer psychological wounds that men—for the most part—do not. Of course, men have their own issues. But men are still in a position of power to hurt and do damage. The big problem here is the institution of patriarchy and the systemic damage it does to women. White—and I should add heterosexual—men, even if they are conflicted, do not suffer the same oppressions as women.

It is important to note that not all women are the same. White middle-class women do not suffer the same oppression as working-class women of color, for example. White working-class lesbian women do not suffer the same oppression as working-class women of color. Eve Sedgwick (2003) says, "Nature and essentialism are, and have always been, the defining ruses of repression/prohibition" (p. 11). Human nature is a social construction. Nature—as in the wild—is socially constructed. Gender is a social construction; sexuality is a social construction—which is the point that Judith Butler

(1990) makes in *Gender Trouble*. Butler writes about the idea of "woman" and how complex—and socially constructed—that term is. Butler states

> If one "is" a woman, that is surely not all one is; the term fails to be exhaustive, not because a pregendered "person" transcends the specific paraphernalia of its gender, but because gender is not always constituted coherently or consistently [as it]…intersects with racial, class, ethnic, sexual and regional modalities of discursively constituted identities. (p. 3)

The language used by Butler in terms of discourse makes some feminists nervous. If discussions of gender sound at all postmodern—the concept discourse is part of the postmodern lexicon—skeptics of postmodernism, Elizabeth St. Pierre and Wanda Pillow (2000) tell us, doubt the usefulness of such theory. St. Pierre and Pillow suggest

> Many feminists believe poststructural feminism is more concerned with language and discourse [a la Judith Butler] than with working to improve the everyday oppressions women suffer. The conversation around the poststructural subject in feminism is complex, and no resolution is in sight, according to poststructural feminists. (p. 7)

Petra Munro (1998b), Leslie Bloom (1998), Judith Butler (1990), and Eve Sedgwick (2003)—all of whom I would consider poststructural feminists—are indeed concerned with the materiality of suffering, the real-world suffering that women face. One can be both poststructural and concerned about the everyday. To describe the everyday, theory and abstractions are necessary, otherwise one gets trapped in using everyday language. Judith Butler puts it this way:

> Gender is the repeated stylization of the body, a set of repeated acts within a highly rigid regulatory frame…. A political genealogy of gender ontologies, if it is successful, will deconstruct the substantive appearance of gender into its constitutive acts and locate and account for those acts that create the appearance of a naturalistic necessity. (p. 33)

Gender—as a social construction—is used to regulate behavior, as Butler suggests here. But this is difficult to comprehend if you think that gender is natural or is predetermined by nature or biology. Even biology is a social construction and this too is Butler's point. The effects of gender, as Suzanne de Castell and Mary Bryson (1997, p. 97) put it, are real but the concept "gender" shifts over time.

Representation

Sue Middleton and Kathleen Weiler (1999) caution us to unpack the ways in which "women are represented in discourse...precisely because of the patriarchal nature of ideology and language" (p. 3). The issue of representation is a complex one. To represent something means to re-present something. That which is re-presented gets mediated through culture. Since ours is a patriarchal culture, patriarchy filters the way people see everything. Sometimes people are duped by patriarchy and buy into it. But feminism asks us to think otherwise. Isn't this what Maxine Greene (1995) asks us to do? To see the world otherwise? To be "wide awake"—as Greene puts it—means seeing differently. But then again, who is awake after all? Can people ever cut through culture to see things differently? To re-present something is to make something reappear, and each time something reemerges it changes. Every turn of phrase changes what it is that one is attempting to describe. The idea of gender is mediated through culture. That culture is webbed into a particular history. Steven Seidman (1997) states

> By not considering the "historical, cultural, and ideological" contexts in which gender circulates—the heterosexual imaginary—feminist theories of gender not only are contradictory but also leave heterosexuality as the unsaid on which gender depends. (p. 177)

Gender needs to be contextualized against history. Discussions on gender need to deconstruct this "heterosexual imaginary." Otherwise the concept of gender will seem static and it is not, in fact, static but continually changing.

Whose Gender?

Gender is a role that we are assigned by our culture. One can choose to act out that role or not. But it is not as simple as that. Since women and men are thrown into a particular culture it is hard to see what role they are playing and what role they've been assigned and what choices they have to undo assigned gender roles. Conservatives want to keep gender roles polarized. A man is a man and a woman a woman. But a man can be a woman if he chooses and a woman can be a man if she chooses. Feminism(s) gets pushed to the brink when gender is turned on its head. Judith Kegan Gardiner (2002) tells us

> Some scholars also perceive crises in feminism and gender theories as these fields try to accommodate the increasingly sophisticated insights of postmodernist and

queer theories and those that demonstrate how racialized formations and sexuality construct and are constructed through gender. (p. 9)

Feminist postmodernists push the limits of thought. Feminists of the more modernist bent can be rather conservative. Some feminists are homophobic. Some feminists are racist and/or anti-Semitic. The point here is that all feminists are not the same, and those who cling to modernism are probably resistant to the changes that postmodern theories bring about.

Gender and Race

William Pinar (2001; 2006) brings together the queering of gender in the intersection of race throughout his work. He argues, for example, that "the crisis of gender is racialized" (2001, p. 2) and that white men must queer their "inner topography of white masculinity" (2006, p. 7) to understand difference and to integrate that difference into the psyche and not "split it off" and negatively project it onto an object (2006, p. 3). It is interesting that Pinar (2001) begins his book that deals with the "gender of racial politics" by saying

> As a feminist man it is clear to me that I must confront my own manhood, understood of course not essentialistically, but historically, socially, racially, in terms of class and culture…. I employ the method of *currere* in search for a passage out of the impasse, in this individual life which shares with others the dilemma of being an American, a white man, in my case, an American white man who is queer. (pp. 1–2)

Pinar (2001) queers gender first off by calling himself a feminist. He goes on to mix these categories—gender and race—together so as to knock down the false boundaries put up between these concepts. Gender is not a stand-alone category. Pinar (2001) suggests that gender is raced. Race is gendered. A man can be both feminist and queer. All categories must be turned on their heads in order to make any headway—as it were—in theorizing. This is what postmodern feminism(s) are about. The groundbreaking work of the scholars discussed thus far opens up concepts by turning them upside down.

Gender and Technology

When scholars think about gender in the context of our work at our computers, what does this mean? A few remarks are at hand. Lelia Villaverde (2008) writes about "gender/cyberfeminism" (p. 12). But what would this be?

If gender is erased via cyberspace—which it is—what happens to feminism without the category of gender? When teaching online courses gender gets erased, race gets erased, the body and much of the personality get erased as well. Or, people seem different on the screen than they are in real (face to face) life. People take on different personalities once online. Or maybe not. But cyberspace partly serves to erase. Suzanne de Castell and Jennifer Jenson (2007) have written interesting things about gender and cyberspace. When children play games in cyberspace, interesting things happen, de Castell and Jenson tell us. Children make up lives, change identities, genders, species even. The imagination can run wild in cyberwild (worlds).

Girls and Feminism(s)

Another interesting book for students to consult about gender and feminism(s) is an edited collection by Pamela Bettis and Natalie Adams (2009). I mention their book titled *Geographies of Girlhood* because they suggest that the concept of 'girls' is missing from feminist debates. I think this is an important discussion to have. Bettis and Adams say

> We were frustrated with the feminist researchers who took what were some "women's issues" and transplanted them onto the lives of girls. For some feminist researchers, all identity discussions must be located in concerns for racial, ethnic, and social-class inequities... . But if you listen closely, these global concerns are not found in the everyday talk of teenage girls when they walk through the hallways. (p. 2)

Perhaps scholars—when thinking through feminism(s)—could consider rethinking why the notion of "girls" is missing from feminist debates. Instead of ignoring children, scholars should listen to them and include them into these kinds of discussions. Gaile Cannella and Radhika Viruru (2004)—two of the most interesting early childhood scholars today—have often commented in their work that researchers do not listen to children. Often children are made into victims or objects by adults who have little time to listen. Or they are turned into criminals, as Henry Giroux (2003) has pointed out.

Masculinity Studies

In this second brief section, I will discuss what is called masculinity studies. This is a subspecialty of gender studies. Michael Kimmel (2002) argues

> Masculinity studies is a significant outgrowth of feminist studies and an ally to its older sister in a complex and constantly shifting relationship.... masculinity studies can be informed by a feminist project to interrogate different masculinities, whether real (as in corporeal) or imagined (as in representations in texts). (p. ix)

What is a "real" masculinity? Aren't all forms of masculinity—to use Kimmel's word—"imagined?" It is true enough that masculinity studies "can be informed by a feminist project" (Kimmel, p. ix), but both Sally Robinson (2002) and Sander Gilman (2004) caution that masculinity studies and feminism(s) have different histories and should be thought of as two different and competing areas. For example, Sally Robinson tells us

> The problem with lumping masculinity studies in with women's studies or ethnic studies is that masculinity—unlike femininity or blackness—already equates with power, so the empowerment model of women's or ethnic studies is embarrassingly inappropriate. (p. 142)

Kimmel does suggest that masculinity studies must address the power and privilege that men (white men) have so as to try and undo the abuses of that power. Still, masculinity studies is not the other half—as it were—of women's studies. Sander Gilman suggests "Masculinity is not simply a parallel construct to femininity but has its own complex history" (p. 7). Yet, masculinity and femininity are related terms; masculinity is only so because of its opposite, femininity. One term is defined against the other. Without the notion of femininity there would not be a notion of masculinity. Perhaps in some cultures and in some historical periods these words did not exist. But these are loaded terms in this culture and they are, indeed, interrelated. Harry Brod (2002) puts it this way:

> For I believe that gender is not an attribute of individuals at all, but a relational category. That is to say, it is a theoretical mistake to think that one can analyze women's lives and men's lives separately and then simply synthesize the results of these analyses into an analysis of gender. This sort of "separate spheres" model of gender misses precisely the core of the reality of gender, that gender is a socially constructed category formed precisely in and through the interplay of genders. (p. 165)

When one studies feminism(s) together with masculinity studies, there is much to be learned not only about the relationship between femininity and masculinity but, more important, scholars also learn about their differences. Perhaps scholars should think in terms of relations-of-difference in the context of gender(s).

I see masculinity studies—when talking about men—like whiteness studies. Both of these studies are dealing with issues of power and privilege. Understanding one's own privilege and power is not an easy thing to do when you are blinded by it. Most white men are, indeed, blinded by their own power and privilege. Studying masculinity studies is a good first move to help men undo their power and privilege. The only way that white men can relate to the Other (whether that Other is a woman and/or person of color or queer) is to understand their own positionality. Most white men do not want to get into these issues because they don't see that they are issues in the first place. Harry Brod (2002) contends, "Men, as do whites, have a vested interest in not asking questions about the sources of their privileges. Any form of oppression maintains itself in power in part by masking how it operates" (pp. 162–163). (Masc)ulinity "masks" its own privilege and in doing so masks its (oppressive) relation to women. Interestingly enough, Michael Kimmel (2002) suggests that—in talking of relations—

> American men define their masculinity, not as much in relation to women, but in relation to each other. Masculinity is largely a homosocial enactment. "Women have, in men's minds, such a low place on the social ladder of this country that it's useless to define yourself in terms of women," noted playwright David Mamet. "What men need is men's approval." (p. 5)

David Mamet's remarks reflect the strikingly misogynist problem with patriarchy. If women are so "low on the social ladder," why do men bother having relations with women at all? Certainly, not all men think that women are inferior. Perhaps Mamet's statement reflects his own anxieties. Ironically, some men identify so strongly with women that they want to become women! Plenty of men in the French Quarter in New Orleans dress the part so perfectly that you can't tell whether you are looking at a man or a woman or a man in women's clothes or a transsexual. This is the trouble with gender, or what Judith Butler (1990) calls "gender trouble."

Michael Kimmel (2002) asks: "Why do so many contemporary American men feel that they have to 'prove it' all the time" (p. 2)? They have to "prove" they are men so that people won't think them effeminate or homosexual. Imagine the pressure a male elementary school teacher is under to "prove" his masculinity. Most elementary school teachers are women. And when a man arrives on the scene, problems arise. Some feel that men are not supposed to teach elementary school. This is a woman's domain. If men do teach elementary school, they are thought of as either gay or strange. Male elementary school teachers' lives are made difficult by people who are uncomfortable in their own sexuality.

Masculinity, Heteronormativity, and Hegemony

Masculinity and heteronormativity are usually thought of together. To be a "real" man means to be a straight man. However, plenty of masculine men are gay. But are men considered masculine if they are not straight? Michael Warner (1999) tells us

> So much privilege lies in heterosexual culture's exclusive ability to interpret itself as society. Het culture thinks of itself as the elemental form of human association, as the very model of inter-gender relations, as the indivisible basis of all community. (p. xxi)

So for "het" society, masculinity means straight man. For het culture, there is no such thing as a masculine gay man. Gay men—in the eyes of homophobes—are just gay. Gay men—in the eyes of homophobes—are always already effeminate because they are gay.

R. W. Connell (2005) talks about what he calls "hegemonic masculinity" (p. 81). He explains

> I emphasize that terms such as "hegemonic masculinity" [meaning straight men] and "marginalized masculinities" [meaning gay men] name not fixed character types but configurations of practice generated in particular situations in a changing structure of relationships. Any theory of masculinity worth having must give an account of this process of change. (p. 81)

Hegemonic masculinity, then, symbolizes straight patriarchal power while marginalized masculinity (i.e., gay men) refers to men who are subject to this power. Although Connell emphasizes the changing nature of these groups, it is still the case that straight men always have the power to oppress gay men as well as women. Connell makes an important point about what he means when he talks about hegemony. He states, "It is the successful claim to authority, more than direct violence, that is the mark of hegemony (though violence often underpins or supports authority)" (p. 77). Power undergirds this "claim to authority" more than anything else. This power, although ideological, is also material. Gay men are subject to gay bashing or even murder, as in the case of Matthew Shepard, not to mention thousands of other beatings and murders of gay people that occur worldwide. Straight men who appear to be gay but are not, however, are also subject to gay bashing. So straight men aren't always in the position of power. This is what Connell means by "configurations of [material] practice" (p. 81). These practices shift and change depending on particular circumstances. Connell is right to not essentialize what he calls hegemonic masculinity or marginalized masculinity because no group is static and power relations are changeable. Still, at the end of the day straight [white] men occupy a position of unparalleled power and are responsible, by and large, for the oppression(s) of many marginalized groups of people.

Masculine Women, Androgyny, and the Posthuman

And what of masculine women? Judith Halberstam (1998) writes:

> I am trying to explain why, as a culture, we seem to take so little interest in female masculinity and yet pay a considerable amount of attention to male femininity.... . In actual fact, there is remarkably little written about masculinity in women, and this culture generally evinces considerable anxiety about even the prospect of manly women. (p. xi)

"Manly" women might be anathema, but, as Jim Sears (1999) points out, "early childhood teachers appear to have more tolerant attitudes for tomboy-like behaviors among girls than for sissified behaviors of boys" (p. 8). Why is it seemingly okay to be a tomboy but not a masculine (adult) woman? Halberstam rightly points out that hardly anybody pays attention to issues around masculine women. Of course there are plenty of histories of lesbian women, notably the work of Lillian Faderman (1999) and others. But in the context of gender studies, masculine women—as a topic—doesn't emerge in the discourse much. Halberstam is one of the few scholars to write about this. I have addressed some of these issues in some of my work (1998; 2002b). I wrote a piece—for the Anzaldúa and Keating (2002) collection—called "Young Man Popkin." In this piece I talk about being misidentified by others. People don't know whether to call me sir or ma'am. Androgyny is a strange way to live a life. Felicity Haynes (2001) tells us that there is a "foundation for Androgynous Studies" (p. 9). She explains that this foundation called the

> [International Foundation for Androgynous studies] (IFAS) was established in 1998 to redress...injustices and inform more people about those who share mixed traits of both male and female. IFAS sees the danger in normalizing certain physiognomies as stereotypically male or female and trying to make anyone who appears different meet

those norms. It is trying to draw attention to exclusive normalizing practices that pathologize the "queer." (p. 9)

These "normalizing practices" begin with very young children. And these normalizing practices are very damaging psychologically. If someone does not fit into a polarized gender role, trouble is ahead. Why is it that some become frustrated when they cannot figure out if a person is a woman or a man? Being androgynous is made difficult by insensitive people who cannot deal with difference. Is there room in either feminist studies or masculinity studies for the androgynous? I leave this an open question.

Not all feminists are happy about this turn to masculinity studies. Robyn Wiegman (2002) remarks

> By the end of the decade [of the 1990s]…conference presentations and articles began appearing quite forcefully [that] critiqued feminist interest in studying masculinity because of the way it seemed to reproduce the centrality of "man" against which women's studies as a broad, interdisciplinary field had long defined itself. (p. 36)

Masculinity studies can be used to recenter "man," if you will. But scholars can work to queer the masculine by decentering man. Donna Haraway (1997), in *Modest_Witness@_Second_Millennium.FemaleMan©_Meets_OncoMouse™*, decenters men, queers, genders, species, and machines. Haraway says that "the lines among human, machine, and organic nature are highly permeable and eminently revisable" (p. 14). Merging human, machine and nonhuman animals is the hallmark of what is called posthumanism, which is an offshoot of postmodernism. A more modernist way of thinking is that computers are separate from humans, mice live separately from people, and females and males are different. But Haraway merges all of these things together. Haraway's insights are striking.

The Trouble with the Feminist Focus on the Masculine

Lelia Villaverde (2008) cites Alfredo Mirande who

> alerts us to the ways that masculinity studies could also be and is being used as a strategy to undermine women's studies programs and to move toward a more generic (instead of inclusive) gender studies, to weaken feminist studies, or to reinscribe heterosexism. (p. 77)

If scholars are using masculinity studies to indeed "undermine women's studies" and or "reinscribe" heterosexism, then there is a problem. There are scholars who use theory abusively in every field. You can use theory to justify whatever you want to. But there are scholars who are doing masculinity studies in order to better understand what power and privilege mean and do want to understand relations with others better. So masculinity studies does not always serve to undermine women's studies. Again, though, scholars have to be careful too because some will always want to reappropriate theory for their own advantage even at the expense of others. Scholars must never use theory to recenter the center or to reappropriate the work of others so as to further demean them.

Heterosexist Privilege, Masculinity, and the Arts

Heterosexist privilege is also linked to what scholars call the crisis of masculinity (see Pinar, 2001). The crisis of masculinity is about what it means to be a "real" man. Manhood—whatever that is—is a fantasy. Men feel that they have to live up to that fantasy. When they don't, they either feel that they are not man enough or they fear that they might be called effeminate. What is it that men so fear in women that they have to do everything not to be like them? Sander Gilman (2004) writes about what he calls "fat boys" in his book *Fat Boys: A Slim Book*. He argues that being fat is a threat to a man's masculinity. Gilman says that "the very notion of a hobbled masculinity seems to be built in the image of the fat man" (p. 19). But when you look at football players, many of them are hugely fat and hugely macho. Hardly anyone doubts football players' masculinity.

I wonder whether men doubt their own masculinity more if they are in (what are considered) women's professions. For example, male ballet dancers—see the 2000 film *Billy Elliot*—must have a time of it defending what they do. Or again, male elementary school teachers must have a difficult time of it. Dancing and teaching elementary school are considered—at least for the past one hundred years—to be women's professions.

Jacques Le Rider (1993) talks about the "fantasy" of the "feminized writer and artist" (p. 112). Le Rider tells us

> The fantasy of the feminized writer and artist recurs in a good many representatives of 1900s modernism. Thomas Mann wrote in *Tonio Kroger* (1903), "All in all, is an artist a man? Ask the 'woman'"! I think that we artists all share a little in the fate of those "doctored" papal singers. Lou Andreas-Salome noted in her 1898 essay on "The

Humanity of Women": "It is not by chance that feminine traits are so often found in artists, or that they are so often accused of being effeminate." (p. 112)

Being an artist, as Le Rider points out, means being less than a man. Are artists who are men not considered manly because the arts are thought of as soft? Do male writers have to also defend their masculinity? Counter-examples abound. Hemingway was a man's man. F. Scott Fitzgerald, a man's man. Thomas Wolfe, a man's man. Artists? Picasso, very manly. Michael Kimmel (2006) talks about the rough and rugged Ashcan School. Recall, that I discussed the Ashcan artists in the historical section of the book. I talked about the gritty quality of life that these artists wanted to depict with the rise of industrialization. Kimmel adds another dimension. He suggests that the Ashcan School is a good example of art-as-masculine. Kimmel says

> Ashcan School members like George Bellows, Robert Henri, and John Sloan challenged European painterly conventions of beauty with their stark evocations of the brutal reality of urban life, as in Bellows's painting of boxing matches or Remington's romanticized visions of Indian slaughter and cowboy life. Whether painting the hurly-burly of the city streets or the rugged coast of Maine, Bellows's energetic style and rough-hewn subject matter brought appreciation from male viewers who felt excluded by dandified aesthetes. (p. 99)

Is an "aesthete" queer? Is a dandy queer? Were the Ashcan artists manly men? The Ashcan artists—and here I am thinking in particular of George Bellows—painted toughness, ruggedness, the grim and grit of the city. One must wonder, then, whether painters' subjects are related to the way in which they deal with their own crises of masculinity. Jessica Benjamin (1988) has an interesting psychoanalytic way of interpreting this crisis of the masculine:

> The boy develops his gender and identity by means of establishing discontinuity and difference from the person to whom he is most attached. This process of disidentification explains the repudiation of the mother that underlies conventional masculine identity formation, and results in a kind of "fault line" running through the male achievement of individuality. (pp. 75–76)

Benjamin suggests that the boy must repudiate the mother in order to become a man. But why? Why the need to repudiate at all? Why can't a boy love his mother and still become a man? What is the underlying fear of the female that makes men push themselves far away from anything female? This fear of the female is so irrational as to be nonsensical. But fears are not only fantasy, they have real material consequences. The boy's fear of his own femininity gets negatively projected onto women. William Pinar (2006) attributes sexism and racism not to the repudiation of the mother so much as the repudiation of the father. Pinar says

> We must re-experience our subjective relation to the internalized father not as disavowed, competitive, and contentious (as "cursed"), but as symbiotic and "incestuous" (homosexual not homosocial). In such an enfleshed restructuring of the inner topography of white masculinity, we might welcome the opposite sex and race within our own psyche. (p. 7)

Pinar's call for symbiosis with the father and his call for homosexual identification with the father are in contradistinction to Jessica Benjamin's (1988) call for the repudiation of the mother. Both of these scholars suggest psychical work needs to be done so as to work through the crisis of masculinity.

Queer Theory

In the final section of this chapter, I will be discussing queer theory. It was William Pinar (1998b) who first introduced queer theory to the field of education. But many in the field are reluctant, if not outright hostile, to queering curriculum. Despite ongoing homophobia and heterosexism, queer theory is here to stay. William Pinar points out

> Homophobia (not to mention heterosexism) is especially intense in the field of education, a highly conservative and often reactionary field. Still, the closet is being emptied, identities are being declared, practices and theories are being challenged, and...new [theories]...formulated. (p. 2)

Queer theory has been all the rage in the discipline of English for at least fifteen years. It is a highly popular field outside of education. As Pinar states above, many of our colleagues in the discipline of education are reactionary and homophobic. Colleges of education—in the United States—are notoriously Republican. And most Republicans are notoriously homophobic (with the exception of the Gay Republicans).

Homosexuality is nothing new. Homosexuals have been here—and so too have bisexuals, intersexuals, transgendered peoples—for a very, very long time. Several interesting historians to read on homosexuality are John Boswell (1981; 1995), Christine Downing (1989), Lillian Faderman and

Stuart Timmons (2006), and Foucault (1990). I suggest students read—for starters—Foucault's *The History of Sexuality: An Introduction, Volume 1*. John Boswell (1995) points out

> It may be helpful to recognize that same-sex unions in the Western tradition are by no means a bizarre aberration. Many cultures other than Western ones have recognized and institutionalized same-sex unions—Japanese warriors in early modern times, Chinese men and women under the Yuan and Ming dynasties, Native Americans from a number of tribes (mostly before white domination), many African tribes well into the twentieth century, and residents (both male and female) of the Middle East, South-East Asia, Russia, other parts of Asia, and South America. (p. xxvi)

We're here, we're queer—get used to it! This is the mantra of queer activists. We are your next-door neighbor. But for homophobes today, thinking about the next-door neighbor as queer is almost too much. We are your children too!

Barney Frank—who is quite frank about his partner Jim—is an openly queer politician. I bring him up because of the insight he has about notoriously homophobic people (many of whom are Republican). He talked on MSNBC about the many anti-bullying laws that the U.S. government has passed. Many victims of bullying are gay kids. Frank said that (some) Republicans and junior high school students have something in common: they are both bullies. He said that kids watch the behavior of these so-called respected senators who bully. Kids then think bullying is an acceptable behavior. Anti-bullying laws do little if kids witness senators bullying people. Julie Webber (2003) points out that school shootings might, in part, be caused by boys being teased for being gay, or seemingly gay. Name calling and teasing are certainly not benign. Homophobic kids can be quite dangerous. Homophobia, of course, is a historical and cultural concept. John Boswell (1981) tells us

> Among ancient peoples who acknowledged the likelihood and propriety of erotic interest between persons of the same gender it was often assumed that men who loved other men would be more masculine than their heterosexual counter-parts, by the logical (if unconvincing) argument that men who loved women would become like women, i.e., effeminate. (p. 24)

But in today's culture men who love other men are hardly viewed as being masculine.

Queer histories of women are hard to find because, as John Boswell (1995) puts it, male historians tend to write about men. If students want an alternative history, I suggest reading Christine Downing's (1989) work. She writes about lesbian identity historically and interestingly tells us

> The word *lesbian* seems to have been used once in the modern sense in the sixteenth century, but this definition did not gain currency until late in the nineteenth century. Indeed, in the 1928 edition of the *Oxford English Dictionary* "lesbian" is still defined as applying to the Aegean island, to a particular kind of mason's rule, and to a principle of judgment that is pliant and accommodating. (pp. 7–8)

It is astonishing that the term "lesbian" dates back to the 16th century. Today, queer theorists use the phrase "GLBTQ" to capture a rainbow of sexualities (gay, lesbian, bisexual, transgendered, queer). Still there are more sexualities like intersexed or hermaphrodites who for some reason are left out of this queer umbrella. In the queer theory literature transgendered people cross dress. Transsexuals have sex change operations. On the street, though, people who are not academics collapse transgendered and transsexual to mean the same thing. Some queer people do not like any of these terms and would rather just use the word "queer." And others do not like that word—queer—at all because it brings back too many awful Stonewall memories. Stonewall is a bar in New York City where—many years ago—gay men were bashed by police, arrested en masse, and repeatedly called queer and faggots. Stonewall is today a sort of sacred watering hole for gay men. It is an historic landmark for gay men.

Erasure of Queer Women from History

Queer women tend to get erased from history. Why should this be surprising? Women—of all stripes—have been erased from history, or their images completely distorted by male writers. I point out that Holocaust scholarship deals with gay men, but not many scholars have written about lesbians who were also victims of Hitler's regime (2001). It is as if queer women didn't even exist.

Lillian Faderman has written much on the history of lesbian culture. Students should consult Faderman's book co-written with Stuart Timmons (2006) called *Gay L.A.: A History of Sexual Outlaws, Power Politics, and Lipstick Lesbians*. Faderman and Timmons suggest from the title of their work that gay people are outlaws. William G. Tierney (1997), in his book titled *Academic Outlaws: Queer Theory and Cultural Studies in the Academy*, also considers gay/queer people to be outlaws. And Ellis Hanson (1999) writes about queer theory in the context of what he calls "out takes." The title of his book is *Out Takes: Essays on Queer Theory and Film*. I mention the titles of these books to bring up a few issues. First, notice the word "out." Out is a loaded word in queer culture. Being out means basically being honest about who you are. The term "out" is a reference to the closet. Let me explain. Being out of the closet means you are out—or open—about your sexuality. To be out is to be outside the law (as in outlaws) and being out means also to be taken out, erased, as in an out-take from films. The edited-out portions of film are of interest to Ellis Hanson who states

> The outtake raises the possibility that to be taken out—to be taken out to the movies, to be taken out of the movies—is often to be taken in (perhaps knowingly), to be seduced for better or for worse by the spectacle of one's own disappearance—which is to say, one's own constitution—as a subject. (p. 19)

To be taken out of the movies, to be written out of history, to be edited out of history, or misrepresented in a text, for Hanson, means also to make an absent subjectivity present. So queers are like Houdini. Queers are a disappearing act. Others force our disappearance. Be invisible. But, ironically, our absence makes our presence stronger. What is it to have an invisible identity?

Lillian Faderman and Stuart Timmons (2006) write about Hollywood stars who had to have their sexual orientations taken out—if you will—of the public eye. Hollywood tried—in the 1930s—to make all queer actors appear straight. Faderman and Timmons comment

> By the mid 1930s, the film industry, already financially hit by the depression, had reason to panic about the pressure that churchly groups were exerting in the studios to make movies that were "100 percent pure or else," as the *Hollywood Reporter* lamented. (p. 53)

The language of "100 percent pure" reminds me of Nazi Germany. Aryans were pure, Jews were diseased. The Christian Right in the United States uses this kind of language today, too, to talk about immigrants. To be 100 percent American means no foreigners allowed. The English only movement is also about being 100 percent American. Hispanics are the largest growing minority population in the United States—so they are feared by xenophobes. So, 100 percent really means 100 percent hatred of the Other. Today the 100 percenters are members of the Tea Party movement.

Homophobia, Xenophobia, Patriarchy and Heteronormativity

There are plenty of homophobes and xenophobes, not only in rural places but also in big cities, even in Los Angeles, as Faderman and Timmons (2006) tell us. Despite fierce homophobia, Faderman and Timmons claim,

> We discovered that, historically, more lesbian and gay institutions started in Los Angeles than anywhere else on the planet, and that L.A.'s multifaceted, multiracial, and multicultural lesbian and gay activism continues to have tremendous worldwide impact…. we wondered how such a history could have been discounted or left uncommemorated. (p. 3)

Gays and lesbians have been erased from history. Erasure goes on in everyday life all the time, especially when it comes to acknowledging queer sexualities. When people say things like "We don't think of you as part of the gay community, you are just you!", this is erasure. This is homophobia. This is like saying, "I don't see race, I just see people." This is erasure. This is racism. If you don't see race and you don't see queerly then you erase people's personal and collective histories. Everybody who lived in San Francisco in the late 1970s remembers when Harvey Milk was murdered. He was an out gay politician and spoke out for gay rights. A typically homophobic response to Milk's murder is this: "Well, I lived in San Francisco in the 1970s but I knew nothing about Harvey Milk, that was that a gay thing, and I'm not gay." Erased from history.

Hollywood has a history of erasing history. Hollywood has a history of whitewashing history. Think of the 1939 film *Gone With the Wind*. The romanticization of the "old" South is really about keeping intact racism. In Hollywood in the 1930s, Faderman and Timmons (2006) point out that filmmakers felt forced to cover up and out take or take out actors' sexuality if they were queer. Hollywood has always been Disneyfied and sanitized. It has only been since 1982, with films like *Personal Best* (1982), *Brokeback Mountain* (2005), *Boys Don't Cry* (1999), *The Hours* (2002), and *Milk* (2008), that Hollywood has dared to produce films about gay and lesbian people. Still, for the most part Hollywood is a rather conservative institution. The bottom line for Hollywood is the bottom line. What makes money is what gets produced.

The concept "queer" implies that GLBTQ histories are alike. Well, they aren't. And our lived experiences are not alike either. Alexander Doty (1993) notes:

> I want to construct "queer" as something other than "lesbian," "gay," and "bisexual"; but I can't say that "lesbian," "gay," and "bisexual" *aren't* also "queer." I would like to maintain the integrity of "lesbian," "gay," and "bisexual" as concepts that have specific historical, cultural, and personal meanings. (p. xvii)

Queer theory signifies a shift away from the gay/lesbian movement, say, of the 1970s or earlier. This shift occurred in the 1980s when the AIDS crisis exploded. The response to this deadly virus, on the part of government officials and right wingers, was a no-response because AIDS was thought to be a gay disease. Queer theory was born out of this no-response. Queer theory is a movement of anger and resistance to heteronormativity and homophobia.

When scholars study race, they study white privilege and power so as to be better able to undo white privilege and power. Likewise, when scholars study sexuality—and in this case queer sexualities—heteronormativity must be studied to be better able to undo heteronormativity. Scholars must work to undo the privilege and power of heteronormativity. Heteronormativity goes hand in hand with homophobia. There is no place for homophobia on, as Michael Warner (1993) might say, a "queer planet."

Hetero-norm-ativity. Hidden in this concept is the word "norm." To be heterosexual is considered normal while any other sexuality is not. This term—"heteronormativity"—implies also power and privilege. To be heterosexual means having the power to discriminate, demean, and belittle. It's hard to be queer, especially in the United States. Queer theorists, however, counter heternormativity. Queering norm(ativity) means undoing that which is considered normal. America is a conformist culture. In many ways—partly because of our Puritan history—America is much more conservative than Canada. To conserve culture means conserving the normal. And the normal in American culture is the heteronormal. Anything outside of the heteronormal is abnormal. America does not like the ab-normal. But queer theorists intervene. Mary Louise Rasmussen (2006) points out, "Within this queer theoretical framework [as she draws on both Foucault and Butler], gender and sexual identities are perceived as unstable performances, constantly mediated by relations of power and open to possibilities of change" (p. 4). The performativity of queerness suggests that queerness is a fluid concept, one that constantly changes in relation to heteronormativity. Still, heteronormativity is a strong force in our culture and still the norm is the hetero.

Gay Marriage?

Within queer circles, there is much debate about gay marriage. Now, if you really are queer, this idea has got to sound ludicrous. Marriage is a normalizing practice. Why would someone who is queer want to get married, just like a straight person? Others in the GLBTQ community are very excited about the Supreme Court ruling on gay marriage. Still some queer activists suggest that gay marriage is just another hetero-normative demand. If we really want to claim difference, then, well, let's be different. Dennis Carlson (1998) says

> Queerness also has changed the gay credo, "we're just like you," and proudly and defiantly asserted the right and even importance of being different. It is a bold assertion from the margins, a declaration that we do not want to be normalized. (p. 110)

The quickest way to be normalized is through marriage. If gay people get married, isn't that simply mimicking straight people? Some queer activists suggest that marriage couldn't be a more conservative and heteronormative act. Queer activists argue that they do not want to imitate the straight lifestyle and marriage represents everything that is heteronormative. Michael Warner (1999) comments on gay marriage. He states

> No one was more surprised by the rise of the gay marriage issue than many veterans of earlier forms of gay activism. To them, marriage seems both less urgent and less agreed upon than such items as AIDS and health care, AIDS prevention, the repeal of sodomy laws, antigay violence, job discrimination, immigration, media coverage, military antigay policy, sex inequality, and the saturation of everyday life by heterosexual privilege. Before the election of Bill Clinton, in 1992, marriage was scarcely a blip on the horizon of queer politics. (p. 84)

The idea of marriage is patriarchal. Queer theorists argue that marriage is a system of domination and control. Marriage, historically, has not been a democratic institution but an autocratic one. To be a wife means to be someone's property. Marriage can become, as Ellis Hanson (1999) says, a form of "sexual oppression and normalization" (p. 4). Hanson says

> Queer theory submits the various social codes and rhetorics of sexuality to a close reading and rigorous analysis that reveal their incoherence, instability, and artificiality, such that sexual pleasure or desire, popularly conceived as a force of nature that

transcends any cultural framework becomes instead a performative effect of language, politics and the endless perversity and paradox of symbolic (which is also to say historical and cultural) meaning. The very word *queer* invites an impassioned, even angry resistance to normalization. (p. 4)

In this context, then, marriage is a totalizing system, culturally reproduced and historically situated. Our culture is so blinded by its own rules and mores that we cannot see what is right in front of us. Marriage is a cultural construct that is rule-bound. People cannot, however, be controlled by rules and mores. This was Freud's (1961) lesson in *Civilization and Its Discontents*. Marriage pretends to civilize. But human beings are animals and animals cannot be civilized without some backlash.

The point of queer theory is to fight normalization, abuse, violence, and discrimination. But in order to do this, queer theorists can't just march down the street with picket signs. Doing queer theory also means writing about it. The ferocity of the AIDS crisis and the way in which the GLBTQ community is demeaned or completely ignored have made people stand up and stand out and act out and act up. Queering the political means being angry. Sue Ellen Case (2000) speaks to these points as she states

> The rise of the fundamentalist right demanded a new, more aggressive political activism. The failure of government institutions to respond to the need for AIDS treatment became more and more reactionary. ACT UP, formed in the late 1980s in New York, produced "live" agitprop street performances within a coalition. (p. 34)

Since the onset of AIDS, people can no longer be passive or complacent. What strikes me about American culture today is that you rarely hear about AIDS any more. It is as if it doesn't exist. A taboo disease. Patti Lather and Chris Smithies (1997) have written eloquently about the AIDS crisis. Working with women with AIDS changed Lather's theoretical approach to scholarship. AIDS unmoors. And it was this unmooring that led Lather to turn toward poststructuralism. There are no certainties in the world of AIDS. Poststructuralism helps to articulate a world without certainties.

Women and Queer Theory

Women who work in queer theory tend to get overshadowed—once again—by men. The irony is that "queer theory" was coined by women but appropriated by gay urban male theorists. William Turner (2000) writes about the "mothers of queer theory" below.

> [Dinitia] Smith's article identifies Sedgwick and Butler as the founding mothers of queer theory, but it was feminist film theorist Teresa de Lauretis who first used the term "queer" in 1991 to describe her intellectual endeavors. Lauretis came to queer theory via questions about the ability of women to speak about and otherwise represent themselves using a language and conceptual framework that men had created...that took little account of women, except as commodities for exchange. (p. 5)

Although Eve Sedgwick, Judith Butler, and Teresa de Lauretis are cited often enough in the literature on queer theory, many scholars comment on the ways in which queer theory is associated with white, middle-class, urban (homosexual) males. Ironically, critical theory is often associated with white urban middle-class (heterosexual) males (see Pinar, 1998b). Critical theory and queer theory are hardly bedfellows! One could invent a "critically" queer theory. Only a few scholars mention the importance of social class in connection with queer theory (Warner, 1993; Moraga, 2000; Henderson, 2007). Perhaps this is an area that neo-Marxist curriculum scholars could flesh out.

What is it about the scholarly world that continually makes women—of all stripes—invisible? In the GLBTQ community, women are mostly forgotten or ignored. Misogyny is a problem within the GLBTQ community, just as it is in the straight community. The appropriation of patriarchy is evident in the lesbian world as historians comment on butch-femme role playing that goes on (see Lillian Faderman, 1999). The butch-femme dynamic, especially among couples who are of the baby boomer age, polarizes gender. Playing butch-femme is not queer at all. Eve Sedgwick comments on what she calls the "mainstream gay and lesbian culture" (Sedgwick et al. 2002, p. 253). Sedgwick says

> I don't know how to map queer thought, but it certainly seems to me that gay and lesbian culture—mainstream gay and lesbian culture, which mostly means white gay male culture—has gotten a lot less queer, and way less interesting. (p. 254)

To be in the mainstream is not queer at all. Queerness moves against the mainstream. But like every other group, there are conservative strains of the GBLTQ community.

Elitist Queers, Organic Intellectuals, and Other Queers

Erica Meiners (1998) claims that there is an "elitism in queerness" (p. 124). Are academics the only people who grapple with queer theory? Perhaps. What disturbs is that organic intellectual queers, coffeehouse queers, working-class queers get left out of the academic discussion. Organic intellectual queerness is something that scholars must work on.

Meiners is also troubled by the white privilege of queer theorists. Is queer theory, again, a white thing? Or is it that once again women get left out of the discussion? Joseph Boone (2000) says that the key problem in queer theory is that women get erased, which is

> one of the pitfalls often attributed to the concept of queer: for this omission repeats the same elision of much queer theory and praxis, from which many women, have at times felt excluded or, in spite of their participation, rendered more or less invisible by a movement that is most often associated, especially in the media with white, urban gay men. (p. 8)

Even in the gay community, women get left out of the discussions. Misogyny shapes the gay community, just as it does the straight community. Erica Meiners asks: "Who is acceptable in these new Nations [or communities], who isn't, and who gets to mark the territories? Which practices, identity markers, or identifications, count?" (p. 123). Who counts as queer? What does the concept of community mean when talking about queerness? When straight people want to claim that they are queer what does that mean? Can anybody be queer? If they can, then queer is empty of meaning. Gloria Anzaldúa and AnaLouise Keating (2002) co-edited a collection called *This Bridge We Call Home*. There was much debate about who should and should not be in the collection. Many of the writers were upset when white people were included, when men were included. But Anzaldúa's point in the book is that we need to build bridges across communities and form coalitions. Many of the writers were not happy with this. There was much fighting (during internet communication) even over the title of the book. Anzaldúa (2002) states

> [This book] questions the term *white* and *women of color* by showing that whiteness may not be applied to all whites, as some possess women-of-color consciousness, just as some women of color bear white consciousness.... . Today categories of race and gender are more permeable and flexible than they were for those of us growing up prior to the 1980s. *This Bridge We Call Home* invites us to move beyond separate and easy identifications. (p. 2)

So is whiteness a state of mind for Anzaldúa? Is queerness a state of mind? In part, it is. However, the material realities of living in a body that is continually being threatened with being gay bashed is not just a state of mind. There are real material consequences to looking like a boy-girl or a girl-boy. There is a price to pay for looking like a boy-girl or girl-boy. Shirley Steinberg (2000) raises similar questions when she asks: "Are we all queer? Are our lovers or partners queer? Are we straight? What is straight? Is queer 'bent' if straight is—well—straight?...Queerness is a part of all of us" (p. viii). A straight person could be queerly "bent." But, on the other hand, straight people have privileges and power over people who actually do live queer lives. A straight person does not have to worry about walking into the women's room and having people tell you to get out because they simply cannot believe you are a woman. A straight person does not have to constantly struggle with a body that does not seem to fit one's gender or sex. To be bullied, teased, and threatened and in some cases murdered because of the way you (queers) look is not something that straight people have to put up with. So you can call yourself queerly straight or bent straight but straight people still have all the privileges of heteronormativity.

To Assimilate or not to Assimilate: That Is the Question

Sue Ellen Case (2000) points out that "antiassimilation[ism]" can be traced back before the advent of queer theory. Case explains

> The tradition of antiassimilation, then, could be perceived as emanating from a 1970s working-class butch feminism, rather than a late 1980s New York queer coalition. Embedded in camp irony and wit (a discourse some writers of lesbian history deny to lesbians), these shared moments of Dorothy Allison and Bertha Harris at the feminist writer's institute could promote the kind of move that would embrace the insult of queer, in order to retrieve a contestatory site for political intervention. (p. 25)

Antiassimilationist thinking is usually attributed to queer urban males. But Case tells a different story.

Queering the Curriculum

There are important queer collections in curriculum studies that I have touched on in this discussion. I reiterate here what books you might consult if you are interested in the inter(sex)ions of queerness and education.

Read William F. Pinar's (1998d) *Queer Theory in Education*; Susan Talburt and Shirley Steinberg's (2000) *Thinking Queer: Sexuality, Culture, and Education*; Patti Lather and Chris Smithies (1997) *Troubling the Angels: Women Living with HIV/AIDS*; Nelson M. Rodriguez and William F. Pinar's (2007b) *Queering Straight Teachers: Discourse and Identity in Education*; William J. Letts and James T. Sears (1999) *Queering Elementary Education: Advancing the Dialogue about Sexualities and Schooling*; Suzanne de Castell and Mary Bryson's (1997) *Radical In(Ter)ventions: Identity Politics and Difference/s in Educational Praxis*; William G. Tierney's (1997) *Academic Outlaws: Queer Theory and Cultural Studies in the Academy*; Susan Talburt's (2000) *Subject to Identity: Knowledge, Sexuality, and Academic Practices in Higher Education*; William F. Pinar's (2006) *Race, Religion, and a Curriculum of Reparation: Teacher Education for a Multicultural Society*; and William F. Pinar's (2001) *The Gender of Racial Politics and Violence in America: Lynching, Prison Rape, & the Crisis of Masculinity*; Mary Louise Rasmussen's (2006) *Becoming Subjects: Sexualities and Secondary Schooling*; Kate Evans's (2002) *Negotiating the Self: Identity, Sexuality, and Emotion in Learning to Teach*. The books I have listed here will give students a good start in trying to understand how curriculum studies can be queered.

Mixing up Gender and Sexuality

Judith Halberstam (1998) writes about the

> perils for passing FTM in the men's room [which] are very different from MTF in the women's room. On the one hand, the FTM in the men's room is likely to be less scrutinized because men are not quite as vigilant about intruders as women.... On the other hand, if caught, the FTM may face some version of gender panic from the man who discovers him...The MTF, by comparison, will be more scrutinized in the women's room but possibly less open to punishment if caught. (p. 25)

Here, Halberstam is talking about transsexual peoples. FTM (female to male) means women who work surgically to become men; MTF (male to female) are males who work surgically to become women. Surgical procedures to alter gender and sexual identities might seem to be the most queer thing anybody would ever want to do. However, there are criticisms about these surgical procedures. Some argue that these surgeries are the least queer thing you can do because surgery serves to normalize. Cherrie Moraga (2000) states

> What's hard for me to understand about the transgendered movement and transgenderism is the conviction that you have to fuck up your body to fit a fucked up world.

> I understand people making those choices because they ain't going to change that world…but the idea of societally enforced mutilation still makes me really outraged. (p. 79)

What Moraga calls transgenderism I call transsexualism. Transgender means changing clothes, performing drag without surgery. Transsexualism is surgery and swapping sexual identity with the help of a surgeon. Is getting a sex change operation, then, an act of normalization or is it queer? To live in a body that isn't the body that you should have or the body that you think you should have can drive you to do extreme things. When you look in the mirror and see a man when you are a woman and people are always calling you 'sir,' what to do about it? There is always a "gender panic"—as Halberstam (1998, p. 25) puts it—in the women's room when a masculine woman walks in. What is this panic about? Society is gender polarized and gender policed.

Living Beside Gender Polarizations

Eve Sedgwick (2003) has this marvelous notion of what she calls "the beside" (p. 8). Living on "the beside," in the context of queerness, is living beside gender polarizations. Living on "the beside" is living queerly. Queer is "the beside." It is not something that one can pin down easily, it does not fit neatly into any categorization, and nobody can figure it out. It is, as Susan Talburt (2000) says—in the context of lesbian identities—the "unrepresentable" (p. 9).

Like Sedgwick's notion of "the beside" here I am thinking of an interesting collection edited by Felicity Haynes and Tarquam McKenna (2001) called *Unseen Genders: Beyond the Binaries*. The key word here is "beyond." This word "beyond" is like Sedgwick's "beside." Sedgwick tries to get beyond dualistic thought and argues for "nondualist thought" (p. 1). Haynes and McKenna examine genders that bend our perceptions. Getting "beyond binaries" is nondualistic thinking. A good example of nondualistic-and-beyond-the-binary-thinking is the hermaphrodite. Haynes (2001) tells us

> Hermaphroditism has been pathological to such a degree that it is invisible and unthinkable to many doctors as well as lay people and teachers. Hermaphrodites or intersex persons, are those born with physiological characteristics of both male and female. (p. 4)

Doctors perform what critics are now calling "genital mutilation" or "a type of surgery known as IGM...mostly making AIS and CAH chromosomal males into genital females" (p. 7). Is this genital mutilation and if so is it unethical and/or criminal? Who decides what you should be if you are born on the "beside" or you are born "beyond the binaries"? Why can't people be both/and? Or whatever? Well, obviously in this heteronormative culture people must be either/or; there is no room for in-betweens. Who is having the "gender panic" (Halberstam, 1998, p. 25) now? Doctors, parents? The medical community is notoriously conservative (Delese Wear, personal communication). They want to conserve gender and sexuality as if gender neatly aligns with sexuality. Gender doesn't always match sexuality and sexuality doesn't always match gender, and if you try to force these to go together through genital mutilation you are asking for "gender trouble" (Butler, 1990). These surgeries civilize. Ah, but then civilization is discontented, as Freud (1961) points out. Civilization is what kills us. What kills us—queerly speaking—is depression, anxiety, internalized hatred, shame, paranoia, and the rest. Michael Warner (1999) points out, "So even an expanded catalog of identities can remain blind to the ways people suffer, often indiscriminately, from gender norms, object-orientation norms, norms of sexual practice, and norms of subjective identification" (p. 39). Heteronormativity and the policing of the abnormal by reactionary heterosexuals cause people to painfully embrace queerness. Being queer comes with a price tag and that price tag is pain.

Shame, Paranoia, and Trust

According to Douglass Crimp (2002), Eve Sedgwick's most important contribution to queer theory is the concept of shame. For Sedgwick being queer means living with shame. Crimp says, "Schematically, Sedgwick suggests that shame is what makes us queer" (p. 64). Well, perhaps for some.

Kate Evans (2002), in a discussion of being a homosexual teacher, reminds us that "how feelings, or emotions, are implicated in the process of being in relation to other people" (p. 3) and count especially when you are continually discriminated against. Evans argues that "emotions and negotiation are linked through emotional work" (p. 4). Emotions, however, are not that easy to untangle as many of them are unconscious. Things linger. Repressions break through.

Childhood and Being on Edge

Childhood experiences of teasing, especially for gay children, is terrible. Being teased is bound to cause psychological problems. The problem with living the GLBTQ life is that you are always on edge because of the possibility of a violent encounter with homophobes. This violence can be verbal, but it can also be physical. When you know that at any moment you could be gay bashed, you live in a state of alert, 24–7. That changes the chemical structures of your brain. Living in a fight-flight mode and living in a state of constant stress is not healthy. Heterosexuals do not have to live like this. You don't have to live with danger hanging over your head at every moment if you are straight. Jim Sears (1999) tells us

> Meanwhile, a college student is kidnapped, robbed, burned, beaten, and tied in scarecrow fashion to a wooden ranch post on a windswept Laramie range, abandoned to die alone. His generation—like mine and those before—suffers from the silence, neglect, denial, and reproach in dummy-down elementary curricula that too often are intellectually vacuous, politically sedate. (p. 4)

Matthew Shepard was beaten to death because he was gay. This is who Jim Sears is talking about in the above citation. And it's not only gay men who are brutalized. The entire GLBTQ community has to always be on alert. I cite below another example of the kinds of violence that queers have to deal with on a daily basis. Suzanne de Castell and Mary Bryson (1997) tell us

> We have come to this point in educational institutions and no less in educational discourses/practices, when cries of "Fag!" ring through virtually every school corridor, students are assaulted and sometimes killed in their schoolyards, where racism flourishes as productively in staffrooms and professional journals, in faculty lounges and board offices, as in the classroom and in the curriculum. And as female students and teachers who dare to contest male privilege are greeted with catcalls of "man-hating-dyke" or, only slightly less awful, "feminist"—a label not so long ago invoked in Montreal as a warrant for fourteen murders but since celebrated and parodied in university skits. (p. 5)

The Montreal massacre as it is now called is one of the most horrific shootings in Canadian history. A male student opened fire on women because he claimed that feminists ruined his life. The word "feminist"—for people who are willfully ignorant—is a supposed code word for lesbian and that is why many straight women are hesitant to call themselves feminists. Feminism doesn't mean lesbianism; many feminists historically have been homophobic, racist, and classist. Lesbians are as hated as gay men by homophobes. The hatred is deep and has a long history. Homophobia is always present, in every classroom and down every hallway, as de Castell and Bryson (1997) point out. William Turner (2000) states:

> Introducing the topic of queer theory is as simple as pointing to violence. After a century of civil rights work by and for African Americans and nearly a half-century of civil rights work by and for queers, including some significant gains in public policy, the culture of liberalism in the United States leaves ample permission for the most hideous forms of violence against racial and sexual minorities. Three murders within a year—James Byrd, dragged behind a pickup truck in Texas; Matthew Shepard, pistol-whipped and left hanging from a fence in Wyoming; and Billy Jack Gaither, beaten and immolated on a pyre of tires in Alabama—illustrate the point well enough. (p. 1)

Again, this example demonstrates that the concept of race intersects with the concept of gender, and violence is linked to racialized gender and the gender of race, as William Pinar (2001) points out. Living with the constant threat of violence is living in continual turmoil, chaos, and fear. Because of being under constant threat psychological problems emerge such as paranoia, fear, shame, the inability to trust, posttraumatic stress syndrome, and depression.

In the introduction to his edited collection *Queer Theory in Education*, William Pinar (1998d) speaks to the issues I am addressing here, namely violence. Pinar says that he has put his edited collection together as a form of memory work. Pinar states

> In memory of those who have been murdered and beaten in gay bashings, those exterminated in the Holocaust, those who struggle(d) to survive in families whose "values" justify sadism, for all those who have died of and are living with AIDS, you are with us here. We acknowledge all those who have come before us, especially those whose courage has now made possible a certain (if slight and problematical) clearing of the public space for us to speak. It is long past time for us to speak. Will our colleagues in education hear us? (p. 2)

Our colleagues in academe hear what they want to hear. The rest they shut out. So, mostly queers get shut out. Those of us on the front lines teach our students about GLBTQ issues no matter how uncomfortable it is for them or, for that matter, for us.

Queer people are not all tragic figures. Queer people are not merely victims of homophobia. Queer people write books, give lectures, march on the front lines, study and teach the young. Ours is a public pedagogy, a queer pedagogy that queers the curriculum. And queer teachers have to build up defense mechanisms in order to take the insults and the sneers from the back of the classroom or the gossip in the hallway. If scholars do not teach queer literature(s) then they simply reinscribe the heteronormative canon and once more make queer people invisible. And what about the kids sitting in our classes? Some of them must be GLBTQ. Queer theory courses are not exactly welcomed on more conservative college campuses. Susanne Luhmann (1998) says

> Immense moral panic erupts over the discovery that lesbians and gays educate our children. Intense, sometimes even violent, contestations occur over the curricular inclusion of the study of sexuality in general, or of lesbian and gay content in particular. (p. 142)

Luhmann says here that "moral panic erupts" over issues of sexuality. Everyone it seems is in a panic about sexuality. Is sexuality the most taboo topic still?

Sexuality Matters

People write out of their race, class, gender, and sexuality. William Tierney (1997) suggests that when teaching the works of GLBTQ writers, teachers need to address the sexuality of the writer and not gloss over it as if it doesn't matter. Tierney states

> Those who reject the so-called flaunting of one's sexual orientation readily agree that to understand T. S. Eliot, for example, we must examine his conversion to Catholicism, or to comprehend the work of Richard Wright we should know that he was African American. And yet the sexual orientation of Henry James, Walt Whitman, or Willa Cather often escapes scrutiny because such information is presumably irrelevant. (p. xv)

It's not that sexual orientation is irrelevant, it is that teaching about sexual orientation causes panic, either "moral panic" (Luhmann, 1998, p. 142) or "gender panic" (Butler, 1990, p. 25), or a generalized anxiety panic.

Knowing the biography of the writer makes for more interesting reading. But there is more to it than that. Knowing the biography of the writer makes students and teachers better readers. Reading queerly means taking into account the importance of studying sexuality alongside gender, race, and class.

· 8 ·

LITERARY CURRICULUM CONCEPTS

Introduction

In this chapter I will explore the interconnections between reading, writing, and thinking; writing and the imagination; what I call "eco-poeisis," identity and difference; memory and history as they pertain to the literary; and finally the cathartic effects of reading, writing, and thought.

I want to stress the word "literary" and not "literacy." Work in literacy is different from work around the literary. This is not a chapter on literacy. This is a chapter on the literary and the way in which scholars of curriculum work around literary texts. The earliest precedents for work on the literary can be found in William F. Pinar's (1994) scholarship, especially on Virginia Woolf and his important piece "Death in a Tenured Position," which is in his collection of essays titled *Autobiography, Politics and Sexuality: Essays in Curriculum Theory, 1972–1992*.

Maxine Greene—throughout all of her work—brought literature to the fore when teaching as a philosopher of education at Columbia University. Maxine Greene (1978) changed the "landscape"—to use her word in her book *Landscapes of Learning*—of philosophy of education and curriculum studies from the very beginning of her writings. Scholars owe a debt of gratitude to Pinar and Greene for opening doors for many of us to work on the literary in the field of curriculum studies.

Reading, Writing, and Thought: Interrelations

In a book on reading, writing, and thought called *How We Work*, which is co-edited by myself, Mary Aswell Doll, and William F. Pinar (1999b), William F. Pinar begins the conversation with these thoughts. He states that scholars must

> reflect on the conditions in which we read, write, and learn realizing how intertwined—even simultaneous, it sometimes seems—these are. By such reflection and self-report we hope to encourage readers to become more aware of how they work, what conditions support not just productivity but contemplation: thinking that moves beyond the calculation of means to ends, learning that deepens and widens our understanding of our work, of education, of who we are in this historical moment. (p. xiii)

This chapter addresses the very questions that Pinar raises here. Let us dwell for a moment on Pinar's profound citation above and think about what he is saying in the context of our own scholarly work. What strikes me about this citation is that Pinar suggests that scholars need to find the conditions that will allow us to do our best work. What might those conditions be? Being in an intellectual environment might be the first place to start. In America, however, most universities are hardly intellectual places. How do scholars work in the corporate university? Where do scholars find inspiration to do good work? Good scholarly work is of a literary quality. It is not just about putting ideas down on paper. The language used to express these ideas must be carefully crafted. Scholars might find the conditions to do this work outside the halls of academe. Many colleagues work at home, in coffee houses, renting rooms in hotels, or in their basements. Inspiration to do this kind of work is found at conferences or by studying the work of others. Some of us are lucky enough to find stable workplaces, at home or in coffee houses. But others are in continual exile. Hannah Arendt, Walter Benjamin, and Paulo Freire were all exiles. And yet they were able to write important and beautiful texts. Derrida remarked that he traveled in order to think. He found travel the only way to jar his thinking so he lived in a constant state of movement in order to do his work. Most people find travel exhausting and discombobulating. Others find solace.

The other important point that Pinar makes in the above citation dovetails with what Paulo Freire says about scholarly work. Both agree that reading, writing, and thought are interconnected. Freire (2005)—in an important book called *Teachers as Cultural Workers: Letters to Those Who Dare Teach*—notes

> We must remember that there is a dynamic movement between thought, language, and reality that, if well understood, results in a greater creative capacity. The more we experience the dynamics of such movement, the more we become critical subjects concerning the process of knowing, teaching, learning, reading, writing, and studying. (p. 3)

For Freire the literary must be political and the literary must work to liberate the oppressed. For Freire, the point of reading, writing, studying, and thinking is to better understand the conditions of oppression that stultify not only work but also life. Scholars read, write, and study to live more freely and to better understand the political landscape that keeps us prisoners of our own consciousness. An overlooked aspect of Freire's work is about writing and the process of writing and reading. Most commentators focus on his politics but skip over the literary. It is important for students to read Freire, keeping in mind both the political and literary aspects of his work. His scholarship on writing is profound. Students not familiar with Freire should begin with Freire's *Teachers as Cultural Workers*, which is a remarkable book.

Derrida (1995) remarks, "No text opens itself immediately to everyone" (p. 176). Derrida teaches throughout his work that understanding is a process of delay. This too is the lesson of psychoanalysis. What comes before us takes time to digest. Some things are never understood. But sometimes glimmers of light come through. William Pinar (1999b) comments on students' unwillingness to read. Pinar states that "for many is a deep resistance to thinking, to learning, or writing. This resistance is often psychological, but it is also cultural" (p. xiii). Students are not the only ones who do not want to read, write, or think. Some tenured colleagues stop reading.

Teaching comes directly out of writing and studying. Being a scholar means that one must do all of these things. In fact, Freire says it is our duty to write. In his book called *Letters to Cristina: Reflections on My Life and Work*, Freire (1996) states

> FOR ME, WRITING HAS BECOME A DEEP PLEASURE [capitals in original] just as it has also become a *duty* [emphasis mine] that I cannot reject, for it is a political project that must be met. (p. 1)

The word "duty" is striking. It is our duty as scholars to write. Reading, writing, and thought are inextricably tied.

Derrida talks about the process of writing throughout his work. I would encourage students to study Derrida if they are interested in discussions about the complexities of writing. Here I will just cite one example from Derrida about the way in which good writing takes off—seemingly on its own—going in its own direction. Writing has a mind of its own! Derrida (1978) states

> It is because writing is *inaugural*, [emphasis in the original] in the fresh sense of the word, that it is dangerous and anguishing. It does not know where it is going, no knowledge can keep it from the essential precipitation toward the meaning that it constitutes and that is, primarily, its future. (p. 11)

Writing has a mind of its own, indeed. As Derrida says, writing has a future (p. 11). The future is when the text is finished—if it is ever finished. To write is to engage in an adventure.

Cultivating Scholarship

Our future(s) and our past(s) are understood through what Alberto Manguel (2010) calls "cultivation" (p. 164). He points out that the concept of cultivation is related to both gardening and reading. Manguel states

> Gardening and reading have a long association. In 1250, the chancellor of the cathedral of Amiens, Richard de Fournival, imagined a book-cataloging system based on a horticultural model. He compared his library to an orchard wherein his fellow citizens might gather "the fruits of knowledge." (pp. 164–165)

Reading, writing, and thinking must be cultivated like a garden, or the mind withers like a dying plant. Cultivation is an ongoing process, one that should never end. But too many people do not read. Ironically, some scholars have given up on writing and thinking because of the strains of university life. William Pinar (1994) wrote about this in his piece "Death in a Tenured Position." The entire process of tenure, Pinar suggests, is deadly. Going up for tenure is a killing game. There are no gardens in the university, only dead places. The only garden left might be kinder-garden; but standardization and constant testing overwhelm the child. So where do students and scholars get the inspiration to read, write and think? Mostly from intellectual friends and reading good books. Building a library is the most important task of the scholar. But today with iPads, iPhones, and Nooks people do not build libraries so much as read things on computer screens. What will this do to the cultivation of our intellectual garden(s)? This remains an open question.

Good Books

Why cultivate intellectual gardens? Harold Bloom (2001) suggests that "we read, frequently, if unknowingly, in quest of a mind more original than our own" (p. 25). A writer who had an original mind was Antonin Artaud (1988). Yes, Artaud was schizophrenic. He was quite mad really. But in that madness is such depth and, at times, such lucidity. Artaud wrote mostly about theater. He also wrote about his own withering mind when he was lucid enough to write. His work is a fascinating study in thinking differently. I am not romanticizing his madness or suggesting that schizophrenics are by nature brilliant. Schizophrenia does not make one brilliant. Artaud, for example, was brilliant before the onset of illness.

Maxine Greene (1995)—drawing on Virginia Woolf—suggests that reading good books should help to "break through the cotton wool of 'nondescript' daily life" (p. 23). Woolf's phrase speaks. Woolf is referring to the thickness (or cotton wool) of boredom and triviality. Books help us not to be bored. This is why I try to find good books so I am not bored and am not filling my mind with cotton wool.

Maxine Greene and Mary Aswell Doll

Maxine Greene knows more about literature than almost anybody in the field of curriculum studies. Her literary references are scattered throughout all of her work. She is certainly one of the most original minds—as Harold Bloom (2001) puts it—in the field. Not only is she original but she is also profound. She has a tremendous grasp of the literary and uses the literary to come to profound insights about the human condition. Perhaps her most well-known use of the literary is Wallace Stevens's *The Man with the Blue Guitar*. Greene (1995) says

> I think of Wallace Stevens's "man with the blue guitar," the guitar that symbolizes imagination. The guitarist speaks of throwing away "the lights, the definitions" and challenges his listeners to "say of what you see in the dark" (Stevens, [1937], 1964, p. 183). These are the listeners who have been asking him to "play things as they are," because it is disruptive to look at things as if they could be otherwise. (p. 15)

To play things otherwise is a theme that runs throughout Greene's work. But how does one see things otherwise? Reading good books helps us see things otherwise.

Mary Aswell Doll's (2000) *Like Letters in Running Water: A Mythopoetics of Curriculum* is certainly an excellent book that helps us see otherwise. Like Greene, Doll has an extensive and erudite grasp of the literary. In her book she writes about three kinds of "heads": "blockheads" (p. 1) "splitheads" (p. 81), and "fountainheads" (p. 145). Doll explains

> My book is divided in sections offering a reinterpretation of the Buddha's three types of people. People who are like letters carved in rock [blockheads]…are those who easily give way to anger and retain their anger for a long time…People who are like letters written in sand [splitheads]…are those who give way to anger but whose angry thoughts quickly pass away…[and] People who are like letters in running water [fountainheads] are those who do not retain their passing thoughts and whose minds are always clear. (p. xix)

All three sections of Doll's book are filled with literary references that describe these different types of people.

Let us dwell on blockheads and fountainheads for a moment. If you are a blockhead—as Doll puts it—you let anger get the best of you. Being blocked, or being a blockhead, also means that you are guarded by too many psychological defense mechanisms that get in the way of writing and thinking. If you are a fountainhead you let the water run through you and give in to whatever happens. Being a fountainhead—as Doll notes—also allows you to free associate in the psychoanalytic sense.

What ties Greene and Doll together is the profound nature of their writings and their use of the literary. But more than this, both draw on literary figures whom they love, and this is made evident in their reimagining these literary figures throughout their work. Alberto Manguel (2010) points out, "Henry James coined the phrase 'the figure in the carpet' for the recurrent themes that runs through a writer's work like a secret signature" (p. x). Two excellent collections of essays that trace Maxine Greene's "figure[s] in the carpet," as James puts it, are these: *The Passionate Mind of Maxine Greene: 'I am…not yet,'* which is edited by William F. Pinar (1998b), and *A Light in Dark Times: Maxine Greene and the Unfinished Conversation*, which is co-edited by William C. Ayers and Janet L. Miller (1998). These secondary sources are both excellent readers on Greene's work and help students to find those "figure[s] in the carpet" about which Henry James' comments (cited in Manguel, 2010, p. x).

Delese Wear

Many curriculum theorists who work in the realm of the literary often talk about the ways in which imaginative fiction makes us think differently and crack open our universe(s). I want to briefly comment on different ways of cracking open our worlds (through literature). Delese Wear (2006)—who has spent her career as a curriculum theorist teaching literature to medical students—tells us that "I picked up J. M. Coetzee's *Disgrace* after a friend told me that I would be terribly disturbed by it" (p. 59). Allowing a book to disturb us is one way to crack open worlds. Many do not like to read disturbing things. Imaginative fiction allows readers to enter disturbing worlds. What happens to readers psychologically when they are disturbed by something? Readers get jolted out of their comfort zones. This is one way of getting out of that "cotton wool" that Maxine Greene (1995) writes about. Cotton wool does not allow people to see what is disturbing; it fogs vision.

Historical fiction is a great pedagogical tool in that it opens us not only to the past—even if it is fictionalized—it also opens readers to emotions otherwise unexplored. So if you want to learn about how disturbing this world is, Delese Wear (2006) would suggest that you study fiction. Wear has devoted her life to the study of fiction in the hopes of making medical students more human. Medical school, like the military, often works to dehumanize people as a way to prepare students for the coming storm. Once thrown into the world of the hospital, fragile personalities can crack. The world of the hospital and of illness is a hard and disturbing world. How better to prepare medical students for the disturbing world of illness than through the teaching of disturbing fiction. People often think that reading fiction is a way to escape the world. Well, yes, it can be used in that way. But as many curriculum theorists point out, reading fiction is a way to get deeper into the world.

Toby Daspit

One of the most poetic writers in the field of curriculum studies today is Toby Daspit (1999). One of Daspit's most movingly profound—and I should add—disturbing pieces is about the death of his brother. I suggest students of curriculum read Daspit's piece titled "'Nothing's Died: It Just Got Buried': Theory as Exhumation, as Duty Dance." Daspit, in his piece about the death of his brother, tells us

> My oldest brother died fifteen years ago in a car accident. The last night I remember with him was one of chess at midnight (and after), beer (lots of beer), and loud, omnipresent music (Rolling Stones, Doors, etc.). He left a wife and two daughters, and two parents...and three brothers...and one sister. (1999, p. 74)

Daspit returns throughout his piece to the metaphor of "midnight chess" as a way to remember his brother. He says toward the end of the piece that "this is why I must return to the tomb, to midnight chess. To reinvent a theory for dying, a theory for living" (p. 77). The theme of midnight chess is moving as Daspit takes us back to that terrible night when his brother was killed in a car accident. Curriculum theory as poetry is Toby Daspit. And his poetry comes out of this disturbing experience of his brother's death. This is a touchstone of all of his work. But Daspit is not morbid. He says he wants not only to invent a theory for dying but also one for living. Dying and living go hand in hand. Curriculum studies is a place where dying is discussed.

Gary Rasberry

Poet and curriculum theorist Gary Rasberry (2001), in his book titled *Writing Research/Researching Writing: Through a poet's I*, suggests that the purpose of reading and writing is to be unhinged (p. xix). Rasberry writes about being unhinged in the context of obsession. He explains

> Obsession is desire unhinged, or so we say. Not usually used in curricular terms. Yet, it seems an appropriate word to use in the context of our work as writers and teachers and researchers; it lends itself to our becoming curious. (p. xix)

Scholars should write about obsessions, Rasberry suggests. If Rasberry is right, if "desire" gets "unhinged" from the moorings of the ego, what kind of writing would that produce? Desire sometimes has no object as it is Id unleashed. Or if it does have an object, it tends to be irrational. Let us be irrational for a while. Let us write the irrational. Is this not what poetry is? But scholars can put the irrational to work, as Martha Nussbaum (1995) points out in her book called *Poetic Justice: The Literary Imagination and Public Life*. Nussbaum suggests

> The purpose of this book is to describe the ingredient of public discourse that Whitman found missing from his America and to show some roles it might play in our own. It grows out of the conviction, which I share with Whitman, that storytelling and literary imagining are not opposed to rational argument, but can provide essential ingredients in a rational argument. (p. xiii)

Rational arguments are emotional too. Plato had it all wrong. He separated the emotional from the rational, but in fact, the two go together, hand in glove. People get ideas about what constitutes justice—as Nussbaum teaches—from their emotional and poetic lives. Like medical students, law students need to study imaginative literature to understand better the human condition, which is more often than not insane. Our lives lead us down crazy paths. Rationality doesn't always help us understand this world. Of course rational decisions are important, but many of those rational decisions about justice are, in fact, based on emotion. I suggest that the seat of justice is emotion, not rationality. Why do people not like to see dogs tortured? Because it twists our guts and makes us emotionally sick. Why does child abuse bother us? Not because it is irrational, but because it makes us emotionally sick to see a child tortured or humiliated. Justice is about emotion and this is part of Nussbaum's point. Nussbaum has something in common with Delese Wear. Wear argues that medical students need to study fiction so as to become more humane; Nussbaum suggests that law students need to study fiction so as to become more humane.

Peter Appelbaum

Peter Appelbaum (2008)—in his award-winning book called *Children's Books for Grown-Up Teachers: Reading and Writing Curriculum Theory*—talks about the way in which imaginative fiction for children teaches scholars about how to be more humane. Appelbaum argues that children's fiction allows us to "weird" the curriculum (p. 1). He wants to adopt a novel [a spin on children's novels and taking a novel approach] educational theory that "weird[s]" the curriculum. Appelbaum comments: "A new discourse of educational theory: weirding, poaching, the feed, vision, stinks, cyborg selves, consumer culture, dark matter, jazz, aliens" (p. 1). Imaginative fiction written for children, Appelbaum declares, teaches much about the world(s) people inhabit. Appelbaum's point is that children's fiction can be profound. Scholars need to pay attention to children's literature because they can learn from it. Many might think, Appelbaum seems to suggest, that there is nothing profound about children's imaginative fiction because it is—well—written for children and what could be profound about that? Children are profound, Appelbaum argues, and books written for them reflect this. Readers need to navigate carefully through Appelbaum's book to figure out what weirding and poaching mean, and to find out more about "the feed" and "stinks." Appelbaum wants to take something that is seemingly everyday and overlooked—children's literature—and show how strange it is. Through the strangeness—or what he calls "weirding"—world(s) can be turned upside down.

The other important aspect of Appelbaum's book—especially for students of curriculum studies—is that he does a careful overview of the field of curriculum studies and couches his work in a solid literature review. He weaves his book in such a way as to show that he knows the conversation that has come before him. Curriculum scholars who have done work around the literary are cited and worked on. So the book is rich with references to our curricular history, especially for those of us who have worked with the literary. This book is especially helpful for students of curriculum studies who want to know who has done work on the literary in our field. But not only that, Appelbaum also offers an original thesis and certainly makes us think differently about the possibilities of reading with children rather than looking down on them, as so many people do. Children are so disrespected in our culture (Giroux, 2003). So too is their literature. But Appelbaum warns us not to take this demeaning approach to children or to their literary world(s). Children's literary world(s) have much to offer to scholars. Children's books should be taken seriously.

Dennis Sumara

Like Appelbaum, Dennis Sumara (1996)—in his book called *Private Readings in Public: Schooling the Literary Imagination*—has written a marvelous text on reading imaginative fiction and the ways in which this fiction serves to "present a disrupted world" (p. 35). If imaginative fiction does not disrupt a world then it is not worth reading. Sumara suggests that good fiction will turn readers upside down. Sumara's book on reading fiction is one of the best in the field because it is rich with theory and metaphor. Too, this book sets the stage for Sumara's later work on chaos theory and poststructuralism. Sumara tells us that "reading literary fictions—means being prepared to have the order of one's life rearranged" (p. 9). Suddenly it seems—after reading a good novel—the world changes. Not too many books change our worlds. But when readers find a book that does, Sumara suggests that rereading is in order. Continually coming back to a book over time opens us to new readings. Books that readers come back to over the years also serve as what Sumara calls a "commonplace" (p. 49) book. A commonplace book is a place holder for us to return to throughout our lives. A commonplace book is one where scholars write in the margins, take copious notes, and reread to write in the margins again and make new meanings. Drawing on Michael Ondaatje's novel *The English*

Patient (1992), which was also subsequently made in 1996 into a film, Sumara tells us

> Therefore, although the English patient calls *The Histories* [by Herodotus] his "commonplace" book, and although it is true that it forms a commonplace for ideas, thoughts, and reflections and other artifacts, the actual commonplace is not to be found in the book, but rather in the *relationship* he has with the book. (p. 49)

Sumara suggests that readers have relationships with writers. Books are living things for Sumara, not dead texts. Readers should treat books as living things and remember that people wrote them, not computers. This is especially a problem with college textbooks because some of them are written in such a dead style that it seems that a computer wrote the book, not a living, breathing person. Think of those large, bulky, academic Psychology 101 texts you studied—or rather memorized—as an undergraduate. Can students have a relationship with these kinds of textbooks? These books are about gathering facts and disconnected information about things. Memorizing facts from a poorly written textbook will teach students little. Readers cannot have relationships with bad books.

Sumara suggests that students can have relationships with good books and especially with imaginative fiction. Sumara talks much about Ondaatje's *The English Patient* as one of the books he loves and comes back to over and over again. Some students think that there is no purpose in rereading books. Once read, that's that. But not so for Sumara. There is much to be learned in rereading books. The problem is finding books worth rereading. Good novels—or novels that readers can build a relationship with—are few and far between. But one day the reader will find a book that she can't put down and this is the one that might become a commonplace book.

Writing and Grief Work

Louise de Salvo (2000)—who is one of Sumara's favorite writers—tells us something interesting about the way in which Virginia Woolf thought about her novels. De Salvo says

> When Virginia Woolf contemplated the literary works she had created, she realized that in writing each she had tried to recover something or someone she had lost. Using the term *novel* for her creations, she realized, was inadequate. Instead, she believed each of her works, more properly, should be termed *elegy*—a lamentation for the dead. (p. 53)

De Salvo captures so well the profundity of Woolf's literary world(s). Fiction, as "a lamentation for the dead," turns the reader's world upside down. Rainer Maria Rilke (1995) wrote the "Duino Elegies," which I highly recommend to students. Recall the work of Toby Daspit (1999) and Mary Aswell Doll (1995) who both write about the deaths of their brothers—these are elegies. Another form of elegy is my book *Curriculum and the Holocaust: Competing Sites of Memory and Representation* (2001). I explore German non-Jewish fiction and German Jewish fiction to find out the different ways that both former East and West Germans represent the Holocaust in imaginative fiction. In the early years after the Holocaust, turning the Holocaust into fiction was thought to be anathema. But after time passed, more and more people began writing literary works about the Holocaust as a way of expressing their grief and their loss. These fictions are all elegies in one way or another. Again, whenever a writer deals with traumatic histories, he or she is actually writing an elegy, what Virginia Woolf calls—according to Louise de Salvo (2000)—a "lamentation for the dead" (p. 53).

Madness and Writing

Students might think that novels that are lamentations or elegies are a form of madness! Why write novels for the dead? The dead are with us in our memories and books should honor those memories. Novels about loss serve a particular purpose—they can help us grieve. Is this madness? Perhaps. The grief process can be likened to going mad. If you have ever lost a parent, partner, or a child you feel as if the rug has been pulled out from under you. Loss is a feeling of madness. Derrida (1995) suggests that "A 'Madness' Must Watch Over Thinking" (p. 339). There is a certain amount of madness, then, in thought itself. To think is to be—in a way—mad. To think differently is to think like the mad. Andrew Gitlin and Marcia Peck (2005), in their book titled *Educational Poetics: Inquiry, Freedom, and Innovative Necessity*, suggest

> Understood in this way, commonsense stands in the way of madness, when madness is seen as our ability to move beyond the everyday and to see the world anew, unencumbered by the norms of what is supposed to be desirable and right. As opposed to fearing this madness, our focus on commonsense suggests that we think about the relationship between commonsense and the cultural self (how many texts begin with a plea for madness?). (p. 24)

Gitlin and Peck carefully qualify what they mean by madness when they say that it is a way of thinking that allows us to "move beyond the everyday" (p. 24). They argue that commonsense gets us bogged down. Recall, this is what Virginia Woolf—according to Maxine Greene (1995)—calls "the cotton wool of everyday life" (p. 23). Antonin Artaud (1988) writes:

> The belly evokes surgery and the Morgue, the construction yard, the public square, and the operating table. The body of the belly seems made of granite or marble or plaster, but a plaster that has set. There is a compartment for a mountain. (p. 67)

Clearly these are the words of a madman. But Michel Foucault in his *History of Madness* (2006) remarks:

> What then is madness, in its most general but most concrete form, for anyone who immediately challenges any hold that knowledge might have upon it? In all probability, nothing other than *the absence of an oeuvre* [emphasis in the original]. (p. xxxi)

So according to Foucault's definition of madness, then, Artaud—since he had an oeuvre—should not be called mad. If he had not had an oeuvre, then he might be considered mad. For Foucault, people who are Othered and excoriated because they are strange have been medicalized, pathologized, and diagnosed as insane. But these historical constructs (i.e., insanity) appeared in the history of medicine at a particular juncture. Before this juncture, the mad were not medicalized, diagnosed, and treated like criminals. Anyone who knows Foucault's (2006) work, knows that he takes us through a complicated European history of insane asylums. The shocking thing is that these insane asylums were not just far-away institutions in place and time, they existed right here in the United States. And right up until the 1950s—according to Darby Penny and Peter Stastny (2008)—mental institutions treated patients like prisoners and tortured them. Much of their book documents case studies from Willard State Hospital in New York. This book shockingly reveals that most of the patients who were committed were not insane; many of them were women or immigrants who had little power or little say over being committed. Once committed they were held like prisoners for the remainder of their lives. They were also tortured when they misbehaved or spoke out about the institution. Penny and Stastny tell us

> Hydrotherapy, where people were submerged and confined for long periods of time in cold or tepid baths [was used to calm patients down but really was a way to torture

> them]... . Metrazol shock "treatment" [was] introduced in 1937...[which] induced violent seizures; these were replaced a few years later by electroshock "therapy." The jolts that were supposed to tear people out of various altered states quickly became known for their brutality and the way they wiped out memories, sometimes entire periods of life. (p. 109)

This digression on madness has a point. The above citation shows that people who are considered strange or odd because they hear voices or see things that are not really there, or people who think differently from others, are punished for being different. The psychiatric community has a long history of (mis) treating its patients, according to Foucault (2006) as well as the authors I cite above, Penny and Stastny.

Carl Leggo

Curriculum theorist and poet Carl Leggo (2005) says

> As a part of my ongoing investigation of the experience of "living poetically," I have recently been researching the biographies of poets like Dylan Thomas and Anne Sexton and asking the question, Why do poets *not* live more poetically? Many poets have been alcoholic, suicidal, insane and violent. (p. 441)

What does it mean, exactly, to live poetically? Artist, poets, writers, creative people create from strange places—places of insanity even. Perhaps being insane fuels the art. Perhaps mental illness helps people see the world differently and helps them to live poetically. Living poetically does not mean living a clean, healthy life necessarily. Poetic living means living deeply and experiencing the depth of pain and suffering, as well as joy and happiness. Living poetically does not mean being happy all of the time. Living poetically means entering altered states of mind. To write a good poem or novel you have to think in ways that alter the states of mind of your readers. If a novel does not allow people to live in novel ways, then the writing isn't very good. Let us think more like Artaud!

Writing, Reading, and Imagination

The imagination is often taken for granted. Some do not realize that to see the world is to imagine it. Even when doing action research, a most empirical task it seems, the scholar must imagine her world. Patricia H. Hinchey (2008) states

> From an interpretivist perspective [which I would consider the seat of imagination], then, things of the world have no meaning in and of themselves; all meaning is assigned by human observers. It follows that because every human's perspectives are shaped by personal [or I would say imaginary] history, cultures, interests, beliefs, and so on, perceptions of the same event or object will vary. (p. 23)

Hinchey suggests that there is no direct way to see the world. There are no things-in-themselves—as Kant once put it. The world is mediated by perception and imagination. People live in the space of the imaginary and Hinchey calls for interpretation of this space. In order to interpret the world, first and foremost, one needs to be able to draw on the imagination.

Noreen B. Garman (2007) talks of the symbolic nature of scholarly work. Like Hinchey, she uses the word "interpretivist" in the context of symbol formation. Garman states

> Interpretivists are concerned with symbolic meaning and various forms of representation that help the reader [writer or researcher] better understand the phenomenon under study. Thus interpretivists do not claim that their research portrayals *correspond* [emphasis in the original] to a general reality. (p. 2)

Correspondence theories of reality presuppose that the observer can directly perceive the world. Most poststructural researchers have problems with this position because they argue that the world is mediated through the lens of perception and imagination. People imagine the world to be what it is. To see the world symbolically, as Garman puts it, is to imagine the world in symbols. Garman does emphasize the role of the imagination in doing research as both she and Maria Piantanida title their interesting book, *The Authority to Imagine: The Struggle toward Representation in Dissertation Writing* (2007). One of the biggest blocks students have in doing research is wanting to get it right. Of course students should want to get it right; researchers should try to understand the world. However, understanding the world—via imagination and symbol formation—changes perceptions of the world. These changing perceptions do not make the interpretations wrong—unless they are dead wrong. How far can interpretation be pushed?

Max van Manen

A marvelous book students might consult on writing and the imagination is edited by Max van Manen (2005), and it is titled *Writing in the Dark: Phenomenological Studies in Interpretive Inquiry*. The title of van Manen's book tells the tale. To write in the dark is to not know where one is going. This is psychological. Researchers do not know where they are going when they write because the unconscious blinds—indeed researchers are "writing in the dark," as van Manen puts it.

Phenomenology is about how things appear to us in the world. Our experience of how things appear to us is highly personal. The difficulty for phenomenologists is to explain how two people can communicate their personal experiences to each other. If our experiences are personal, there seems to be an interminable abyss between one mind and another. People never really do communicate with one another. People talk past one another.

In a psychoanalytic sense people are talking to symbolic (imagined) parents. Freud suggests that people are always embedded, as it were, in the family romance even as adults. Ironically, people unconsciously seek out (a sort of double of) the parent who gave them the most grief—in new relationships. This is what Freud called repetition compulsion. People compulsively repeat bad things that happened to them as children. Our world(s) are imagined. For Freud fantasy (via imagination) is the human condition.

Van Manen argues that writing and reading entail imaginative thought because "we take leave of the common world that we share with others. We step out of one world, the ordinary world of daylight, and enter another, the textorium, the world of the text" (p. 3). The "textorium" is the imaginary world of the writer. Every piece of writing—whether it is report writing or fiction writing—is imaginative. Entering this textorium means entering into someone else's imaginary world. To write a text means that the writer uses her imagination to fix letters on a page or screen. To read a text also means that the reader uses her imagination to try to understand the world of another.

An interesting question van Manen and Bas Levering (1996) ask, in the context of reading and writing, is this: "Where exactly do we go when we read or write? Where do we go back to?" (p. 240). People always already go back to childhood. People live out imaginary relationships with parents—whether they are dead or alive. So our relation with texts has much to do with our relation with our own family romance(s).

Van Manen and Levering (1996) suggest that children live in secret worlds. Van Manen and Levering point out, "Secrets are always relational. Secrets are commentaries about human relationships as well as emotional commentaries about the relation of the person to his or her inner self or inner life" (p. 13). When researchers read a book—whether it is a scholarly text or imaginative fiction— a secret world is opened to us too. And the secret worlds of texts might unconsciously bring up questions about childhood. It might seem that scholars pick up books willy-nilly, but scholars read things for reasons unbeknownst to them. The unconscious pull toward certain kinds of books has everything to do with the relations with our parents and our family romances.

What scholars choose to write about, too, is not willy-nilly. The choices made—concerning what to write about—are unconscious. The unconscious—whatever that is—directs our private internal world. This is the lesson learned from psychoanalysis. The Jungians and Freudians agree on this principle. People are not the masters of their psychic houses. If this is the case, why scholars write and read what they do forever remains a mystery, a secret. One of the exciting things about good writing, is that scholars always seem to surprise themselves.

Linda Laidlaw

Linda Laidlaw (2005), in her book *Reinventing Curriculum: A Complex Perspective on Literacy and Writing*, asks an interesting question about writing as she wonders: "What happens when children begin to write?" (p. xiii). Well, first off, they begin to engage their imaginations. They express on paper their imaginary worlds. Sometimes these imaginary worlds, though, are not innocent and sweet. Melanie Klein (1940/1975; 1946/1984)—one of the pioneers of child therapy and object relations theory—took note of the violence with which children played with dolls, especially children who seemed particularly disturbed by something. These imaginary play sessions with children that Klein observed led her to explore two basic psychological phases that children move through when growing up. The first phase she called the "paranoid schizoid" phase, and she argued basically that before the child can distinguish between one object and another, she lives in a sort of psychotic state. This psychosis leads the child toward paranoia about the mother. The mother, who for a moment slips away—whether psychically or literally—leads the child to phantasize (the ph designates unconscious fantasy) that the mother is trying to annihilate her. The child works through these bad feelings, gets depressed about them, and feels guilty thinking the mother capable of infanticide. Thus the child wants to repair this damage—what Klein calls "reparation"—and moves on into the second phase Klein calls the "depressive position." Here, the child is able to distinguish between her own phantasies and what is really going on in the relationship with the mother. The dilemma for Klein is that all of this happens in the preverbal stage. How can people know what children think when they cannot talk? Klein's theories were based on watching children play rather meanly with toys. She witnessed shocking acts of violence that children committed against imaginary figures.

Most curriculum scholars who write in the area of what I call the literary have little interest in Melanie Klein. But the connections among writing, reading, the imagination, and the psyche—as it gets formed especially in early childhood—are crucial. The missing link in the study of the literary is the psychoanalytic. Perhaps one could read imaginative literature side by side with psychoanalytic theory so as to get a fuller picture of what is going on when a child begins to write, which brings us back to Laidlaw's question. Let us repeat it here: "What happens when a child begins to write?" (p. xiii). Now, think of this in the context of this discussion about Melanie Klein. If the child remains in the paranoid schizoid phase, she will write crazy and mean things. If the child moves through the depressive phase, she will write about repairing (what Klein called reparation) the relationship with her mother. But, at the end of the day, what happens when a child begins to write remains a mystery.

Curriculum Theorists Drawing on Imaginative Literature

I drive a wedge between literacy and the study of the literary. In recent curriculum scholarship there seems to be a turn toward the literary (engaging with literary fiction) and a turn away from literacy (which is about *how to* read). Curriculum theorists, generally speaking, are not interested in how-tos. I am not saying, however, that curricularists are not interested in how to read. This is a given. Much recent work done in curriculum scholarship concerns literary fictions. Through reading imaginative literature, scholars theorize the major themes of curriculum studies, for example, race, class, gender, and so forth. Now some might argue that the differences between literacy and the literary are small. But I do not think so. Of course—as I stated at the outset of this chapter—there is a long history in curriculum studies of using imaginative fiction to raise theoretical questions. Today many more scholars use imaginative fiction to discuss curricular issues than they did even just ten years ago. This configuration of curriculum studies is continually on the move and continually growing. For a moment let us document some of the fiction writers upon which curriculum theorists draw. Dennis Sumara (1996) is especially fond of Michael Ondaatje. Delese Wear (2006) draws on a vast range of fiction writers, but two that caught my attention are J. M. Coetzee (p. 59) and Susan Sontag (p. 72). Mary Aswell Doll (2006) draws on a vast array of fiction writers, far too many to mention here. But a few that caught my attention are these: Edgar Allan Poe (p. 12), Katherine Mansfield (p. 13), Samuel Taylor Coleridge (p. 14), Charlotte Perkins Gilman (p. 14), and Jack London (p. 14). Mary Aswell Doll (2000) also draws on William Faulkner (p. 12), Toni Morrison (p. 46), and Richard Wright (p. 46), among many, many others. Rebecca Luce-Kapler (2004), in her book (which we will examine more closely in a while) titled *Writing With, Through, and Beyond the Text: An Ecology of Language*, explores such writers as "Emily Carr, Kate Chopin, and Margaret Bourke-White" (p. xiii). Maxine Greene (1995) draws on a vast array of fiction writers—far too many to mention here but a few that caught my attention are these: Emily Dickinson (p. 22), Virginia Woolf (p. 23), Toni Morrison (p. 38), Denise Levertov (p. 29), Henry James (p. 67), and Louisa May Alcott (p. 91).

Eco-Poesis

Reading, writing, and thinking are not done in a vacuum. Although these experiences can be highly personal, the personal is always already in relation to something or someone. There is—as Rebecca Luce-Kapler (2004), Gary Rasberry (2001), and Linda Laidlaw (2005) all point out—an ecological dimension to reading, writing, and thinking. Scholars read, write, and think in relation-to-the-world. Thus, reading, writing, and thinking are ecological acts. Reading, writing, and thinking are what I call eco-poetic. Rebecca Luce-Kapler interestingly remarks, "I would further add, thinking of David Abram's work in philosophy and ecology, that the locations and situations in which we write, especially ones that link us to the non-human world, also influence our work" (p. xiii). David Abram's (2010) book *Becoming Animal: An Earthly Cosmology* is marvelous. His phrase "becoming animal" is borrowed from the work of Deleuze. Abram suggests that people need to understand that human beings are human animals. And human animals are in relation to nonhuman animals. Abram remarks, "We cut ourselves off from the necessary nourishment of contact and interchange with other shapes of life, from antlered and loop-tailed and amber-eyed beings whose resplendent weirdness loosens our imaginations" (p. 7). Some scholars read, write, and think—as human animals—in contact with nonhuman animals—our dogs and cats, for example. Animals are everywhere. However, people seem to block them out of their vision, as Abram points out. Luce-Kapler writes about "an ecology of language" as the title of her book suggests. This ecology of language is also the ecology of the language of nonhuman animals. People are related to nonhuman animals through language, although the language of animals remains mysterious. Birds chirp, cats meow, and dogs bark. Each of these creatures has a language. Scholars need to pay more attention to these creatures as they could affect our work. Luce-Kapler states that the nonhuman world does indeed affect our work. This nonhuman world could be the world of trees, rocks, mountains, dirt even. Reading, writing, and thinking happen with feet on the ground; the ground is made from dirt.

Like Luce-Kapler, Gary Rasberry (2001) remarks

> In our textual dwelling together, it is often form that provides the underpinnings of our coming together and coming apart. Sometimes this shaping and creating, this unfolding of form is an ecological movement—a deepening—*waiting for the moon to find a form that signals the planet's giving way to an inevitable shape born out of light* [emphasis in original]. (p. 19)

Rasberry and Luce-Kapler are both poets and certainly write in a poetic fashion. Here, Rasberry speaks of form, the moon, and light. These are three key words that tie his passage together with reading, writing, and thinking. Scholars do these activities in-a-place and that place is the earth. At night the moon seems—at times—to be lit up. The light from the moon can be very bright indeed. Is this when the poet works, at night? Place, sound, light, and darkness are all ecologically related to reading, writing, and thinking. This is Rasberry's point. There is a magic to writing. Rasberry captures this magic in the above citation.

Like Rasberry, Linda Laidlaw (2005) makes reference to reading, writing, and thinking in the context of the ecological. She states, "Living systems, such as ecosystems, human beings, brains, and writing classrooms are 'open' systems, open to a flow of energy and materials that moves through the system" (p. 33). In order to access this open system, however, one has to be open to it—psychologically. Being open to writing and being open to the world happens after much study and much work. The "flow," as Laidlaw terms it, only comes about after much study and work. If the writing does not come, there is no flow. Flow in writing only comes when you have something to say. This "something" comes from studying the work of others and spending time with books.

To Love Books

Let us talk about our time with books. If scholars love what they are reading, they might be inspired to speak to these writers—metaphorically—through their own writing. Having conversations with books is what scholarship is. Joe L. Kincheloe (2005) talks about Freire's notion of radical love in the context of reading books. Kincheloe tells us

> I returned to my dorm room [while in college] with the book [Freire's *Pedagogy of the Oppressed*]. I imagined Paulo working with the Brazilian peasants, teaching them to read the word and the world, developing generative themes that connected education to their everyday lives. Reading deep into the night, I noted the scholars Paulo referenced: Herbert Marcuse, Erich Fromm, Karl Marx, Georg Lukacs, Simone de Beauvoir, Frantz Fanon [and many more].... I promised myself that I would read all of these people. (p. xiv)

Kincheloe was devoted to Paulo Freire's work and carried it on at McGill University at the Paulo and Nita Freire Project for International Critical Pedagogy before his untimely death. What strikes me in the passage above is that Kincheloe was so devoted to Freire that he felt obligated to read all the scholars whom Freire loved and quoted. Kincheloe read the books he cites above out of a sense of "radical love"—to use Freire's phrase.

Like Kincheloe, Denise Taliaferro (1999) writes about reading her "mothers" who gave her the courage to write about her own work in the context of race. Taliaferro explains

> In an intellectual context, then, my mothers nurture me, take care of me, love me through the work that they do to disrupt, to rebel against the discourses that invisible-ize us and make me impossible. It is the mother tongue—the love words and ideas of Anna J. Cooper, Mary Church Terrell, Ida B. Wells, Assata Shakur, Angela Davis [and more].... that forges, that creates the spaces of my existence. (p. 49)

Like Kincheloe, Taliaferro talks about reading and writing in the context of love. If scholars read writers they love, they love the work even more. Read writers you love, read people on your tree, as it were, and you will find that your writing will take off on the wings of a dove!

A curriculum scholar who writes on the wings of a dove and loves books is Dennis Sumara (2002), who I have talked a little about already. Sumara tells us

> Because I like to re-read my favorite books, I sometimes develop strong identifications with whom Eco (1994) calls the "model author"—the persona the reader invents to represent the flesh and blood author. With books I come to love, these model authors attain mythical status, becoming fantastical, larger than life. (p. 11)

One of the things that strikes me about Sumara's passage above is that he points out that beloved authors are inventions. Readers do not know who these writers really are—on a personal level (unless, of course, readers know the writers personally). Readers fantasize about the writers they love. Fantasy, for Freud, is reality. Thus, all of us live in fantasy worlds.

The books that people love are probably well written. Writing well, and even poetically, in the context of doing scholarship, is, for Freire, an imperative. It is not enough to have ideas, you have to be able to communicate those ideas well and care about language. Freire (1996) declares, "The aesthetic dimension of language should concern only artists, not scientists, is false. It is the duty of all those who write to write beautifully.... read authors who write well and beautifully" (p. 80). Curriculum scholars, then, must write beautifully, as Freire puts it. Ideas need to be fleshed out poetically. Scientists—as Freire says—should also write beautifully. Social scientists too should take up Freire's call to write beautifully. In order to write beautifully—as Freire insists—writers must foster what Maxine Greene (1995) calls a "poetic use of our imagination" (p. 4). Tom Barone (2000)—drawing on Harold Bloom—calls for scholars to become "strong poets" (p. 125). Barone explains

> A strong poet is someone who refuses to accept as useful the descriptions of her life written by others. Instead, the strong poet is a strong storyteller, continuously revising her life story in the light of her own experience and imagination. The strong poet constantly redescribes her past interactions with the world around her, constantly reinvents her *self*. (p. 125)

The strong poet is an ecological poet if she is in touch with "her past interactions with the world around her," as Barone puts it. Storytelling happens in the context of place (or the world, as Barone suggests). Scholars who are storytellers and strong poets know that the place into which they are thrown is part of the story they tell. Moreover, for Barone, the strong poet is also a political poet who is "necessarily a social being and a moral agent" (p. 125). It is not enough to write poetically. One must engage poetics with a sense of responsibility (p. 125). Some insist on a political aesthetic (Kumar, 1999). Freire (1996) also insists that writing is a "political project" (p. 1).

Identity and Difference

Let us begin this section with a passage from Walter Benjamin's (1997) *One-Way Street*. He states the following:

> *Child reading* [emphasis in the original].—You are given a book from the school library. In the lower classes they are simply handed out. Only now and again do you dare to express a wish. Often, in envy, you see coveted books pass into other hands. At last desire was granted. For a week you were wholly given up to the soft drift of the text, that surrounded you as secretly, densely and unceasingly as snowflakes. You entered with limitless trust. (p. 71)

Let us unpack some of the words here that relate to reading and identity. It is significant that Benjamin titles his piece "Enlargements" (p. 71). And it is also significant that a child is reading and not an adult. The child's identity is "enlarged," so to speak, in the following ways: she opens herself to trust, secrets, wishes, desires, and even envy. Is it possible that reading can evoke so many feelings? And is it the case that our identities are wrapped up in emotions? Yes. Indeed. Without the ability to express emotion our identities are somehow compromised. The child in this passage explores all of these emotions from simply opening a book. It is not enough to merely hand out any book to a child. The child must choose what to read. Shouldn't teachers ask the child what she wants to read? William Heard Kilpatrick's project method comes to mind. Teachers following the project method ask children what they want to read and study. Shouldn't children have a choice in what books they would like to read? Dewey approaches Kilpatrick's method with caution, however. He suggests that children need much guidance. For Dewey teaching the liberal arts curriculum is paramount. Dewey argues, though, that teachers have to make connections to children's lives if they are to learn anything.

A child's identity is built from relations, and reading books is like building relations—as Dennis Sumara (1996) so artfully points out. Books make a great impact on our identities. If one identifies with a text, the experience can be glorious. If not, the experience can be hideous. But what does it mean to relate to a book? The reader—when reading literary fiction—looks for characters who are like herself. Is this really a good thing? Or should readers try to identify with characters who are not like them? This is the challenge of the text. Mary Aswell Doll (2006) discusses this issue. She explains:

> Teaching literature, I often get the complaint from undergraduates, "I just can't relate to this." Conversely, they say, "I really like this because I could relate." How ordinary, unsophisticated, sophomoric, moronic, is this idea that that which is familiar is only to which I can relate. What the relating is about, of course, is usually heteronormativity, Eurocentrism, phallologism, or any other "ism" of any established norm that prevents mind travel. (p. 27)

In order to relate to a character who is not like us takes sophistication, as Mary Aswell Doll points out. But not only this. In order to relate to a character who is not like us means that readers understand the concept of difference. People are radically different from each other. It is to this radical difference that readers must turn. An ongoing discussion in curriculum studies, for at least the last fifteen years, has been around this notion of difference. The problem with this idea is that it is an abstraction and means little in the face of the real Other. Someone—or a character in a novel—who is of a different race, class, and/or gender must not be shunned but embraced. But people tend to look for sames; perhaps readers should look for not-sames, as Mary Aswell Doll suggests. Doll says that "disidentity" "give[s] meaning its edge and being its worth" (p. 76). Can one accept that the Other is not at all like us? That is the challenge before us when reading.

Let us think about the writer for a moment. Rebecca Luce-Kapler (2004) suggests, "Writing enriches our lives, helps us to understand who we are and teaches us to bring closer attention to the world and even, perhaps, to change it" (p. xii). Writing teaches us about our identity, Luce-Kapler suggests. Writing teaches us to learn about ourselves in relation to the world, to others, and to other texts. It is not enough to look in the mirror and say, ah, I know who I am. I only know who I am in contradistinction to the Other and against the backdrop of the world.

Every person and every character in a text is wholly Other to us. Nobody is like anybody. Perhaps the problem is the mirror. But identity is made only in relation to difference. I am who I am because the other is Other to me. Identity is only found in difference. The concepts of identity and difference are difficult not only to conceptualize but also to emotionally understand. The challenge is to know that everybody is different. Maxine Greene (1995) suggests

> Imagination [in reading and writing] may be a new way of decentering ourselves, of breaking out of the confinements of privatism and self-regard into a space where we can come face to face with others and call out, "Here we are." (p. 31)

To decenter the self is to suggest that Otherness is also within. The decentered Id is something about which Jean Laplanche (1999) explores in his work. The Id is not a thing, nor is it a place. The Id is a symbol for the Otherness within our own psyches. The center cannot hold because there is no center. The mind is wholly Other.

When Maxine Greene (1995) talks about the problem of "breaking out" of "privatism" she is on the mark. The only way to understand the world is to work through solipsism and to be in relation to the wholly Other. Reading imaginative fiction helps us to break out of our own world and move toward relations-in-the-world.

Delese Wear (2006) writes about the "polymorphous" "culture of literature" (p. 72). Literature is polymorphous because people are polymorphous. Martha Nussbaum (1995) takes this discussion one step further as she states, "I defend the literary imagination precisely because it seems to me an essential ingredient of an ethical stance that asks us to concern ourselves with the good of other people whose lives are distant from our own" (p. xvi). Understanding difference, then, for Nussbaum, is an ethical imperative. Reading imaginative fiction is one of the best ways to get to know people who are not like us. Books open new worlds to readers.

Returning to the Library

What about our libraries? What kind of places are libraries? The job of the scholar is to build a library. That is certainly part of the work that makes reading and writing exciting. Over the years we can trace our interests in the books we find in our own libraries.

Let us think about Alberto Manguel's (2006) book *The Library at Night* for a moment. He states that libraries are all about identities. We build our identities through the building of our libraries. What happens when these libraries are destroyed for one reason or another? Manguel tells us

> In Mexico and Central America, particularly, the great libraries and archives of the pre-Columbian peoples were systematically destroyed by Europeans, both to deprive them of an identity and to convert them to the religion of Christ. (pp. 117–118)

The connection between the library and an identity of a peoples is important. When libraries are destroyed, peoples are destroyed. When the Nazis burned books written by Jews, Jewish culture was also destroyed. Books must be powerful things if people want to purposefully destroy them. The word is a powerful thing.

Memory/History

The literary is inextricably tied to memory and to history. Paulo Freire (1996) tells us that "when we write, we cannot ignore our condition as historical beings" (p. 3). People do not write by stepping outside of history. Writers are deeply embedded into particular histories. And histories are linked with memories. Dennis Sumara writes about reading imaginative fiction in relation to his family's involvement in World War II. Sumara (2002) states, "My readings of Anne Michael's (1996) novel *Fugitive Pieces* [allowed me to] interpret a historical relationship to my ancestors, focusing on my parents' emergence from events of WWII" (p. xvii). Reading imaginative literature fosters a deeper understanding of our own identities, our families, and our relationships with historical events. Not only this, reading imaginative fiction—especially historical fiction—allows us to experience a deeper sense of emotion than, say, reading history text books. Imaginative fiction should be read alongside historical works. Although historians are bound by methodologies that restrict their own emotional engagement with their texts, they have much to teach us about the past. If historians were not bound by method, could they write in a more literary style? What difference would it make if they did? David Abram (2010) writes about the deadness of much scientific writing and suggests that there are "*other* [emphasis in the original] styles of discourse that stir the senses from their slumber" (pp. 69–70). Abram argues that the way scholars write about things matters. This reminds of me of what Freire (1996) says about the duty to write beautifully—no matter what discipline you are in. The beauty of the language used impacts the way readers read texts. But not only beauty. When authors are writing about something horrific—like the Holocaust—it is also the duty of writers to capture the horror in language. This horror must be communicated in such a way as to not gloss over the horror of the horror. The descriptive arts, as I shall call them, must pay homage to the dead by getting at the historical truths of what happened. This requires the novelist to study history and write in such a way to capture this history but in an imaginative sense. The writer of imaginative fiction must write in such a way to capture the reader's attention and draw her into the text viscerally. There was much debate in the 1960s after the Holocaust whether or not it was even ethical to turn horror into poetry (Adorno, 1993). But what is the alternative? Silence?

Where does that get us? Nowhere. Today, these kinds of debates are far into the past, and as the years go by people have fewer reservations about turning the Holocaust into imaginative fiction or poetry. But after the war was over, this debate understandably created a great stir, especially in the Jewish community.

Like Freire (1996), Morris, (2001), and Sumara (2002), Mary Aswell Doll (1999) says that she writes out of "memories, dreams, hints, hunches, gestures, notions, forgotten pearls" (p. 2). Beautifully stated indeed! Academic writing can become more literary if scholars take Doll's advice. Writing out of our own senses includes the "forgotten pearls." But how to write about something forgotten? Academic writing can become more literary and it should if scholars are to engage readers. Through the reading of literary texts perhaps these forgotten pearls will come back. Much of what scholars are driven to write about comes out of repressed memory. Perhaps after writing things out those forgotten pearls will come back to us. Why is the forgotten a pearl? Freud suggested that gems—as it were—of wisdom are found in the not-said, not the said. What is not said is what is forgotten. But readers can get the forgotten pearls back through studying, reading, and engagements with literary texts. Rebecca West (2006) tells us, "My memory is certainly in my hands. I can remember things only if I have a pencil and I can write with it and I can play with it" (p. 256). Do our hands have a memory? A musician will tell you, yes. Even if you learned a piece of music as a young child, as an adult your hands will remember where to go and what to do. It really is quite remarkable that the hands do have a memory. Memory might not be in our heads, but in our hands. Remarkable.

Memory is also found in other places as well. Alberto Manguel (2006) tells us

> By housing as many books as possible under one single roof the librarians of Alexandria also tried to protect them from the risk of destruction that might result if left in what were deemed to be less caring hands (an argument adopted by many Western museums and libraries today). Therefore, as well as being an emblems of man's [sic] power to act through thought, the Library [in the original] became a monument intended to defeat death, which, as poets tell us, puts an end to memory. (p. 32)

The library is a storehouse of memory. This is Manguel's point. When people vanish, the library will keep our memories (in the form of books and articles) in a storehouse. This is partly why it is important to write: to be remembered and leave a mark on the world. People certainly do not want to be forgotten. Books are memories; they are memories of the way writers perceive the world around us. Future generations will read our books—hopefully—

and learn something about the past that they did not know before. Scholars and fiction writers make history by writing books. Books can change history and shape history. Perhaps our books will make a small impact on the world in our absence. The library—as Manguel points out—is "a way to defeat death" (p. 32).

Writing and Healing

Many academics do not like to write. But writing is healing. Let us begin in the company of Louise de Salvo (2000) who has written a book on this topic titled *Writing as a Way of Healing: How Telling Our Stories Transforms Our Lives*. De Salvo says

> Writing is a *very sturdy ladder out of the pit* [emphasis in the original]. I like that metaphor very much. For it says that though there's a pit, there's a way out that's safe and strong and dependable. That all you have to do when you're in the pit is to remember that writing's there. And use it as a way to reach safety and freedom. (p. 8)

Like de Salvo, Freud suggests that when you have a problem to write it out and write it out again. Perhaps all of our books are repetitions of a problem. Writing books and reading books for that matter are ways to work through emotional issues. At any rate, de Salvo finds that writing is salvific. Is it the case that writing can save us from ourselves? Yes. Or maybe not. It might not be that "safe and sturdy ladder" for everybody. I found that many Holocaust survivors who wrote about their experiences did not find salvation, but rather committed suicide (2001). Writing can be both—as Plato would put it—a poison and a cure. But writers press on anyway with the hope that writing will heal our wounds. Yet some wounds never go away. Still we press on. Alan Block (1999) says

> I write because it cures me; I write because it comforts me; I write because it produces me. Writing has become a way of life. Writing is the dialogue in which I engage with myself so that I might produce some interesting ideas that will get me through the days. (p. 103)

For Block, then, writing is a curative, not a poison. For Block writing is all. His entire life is wrapped up in writing. This is as it should be for the scholar. And not only this. Block writes in a literary fashion, his writing is beautiful; he takes great care with language in all of his work and it is a pleasure to read.

Can we work to collapse the scholarly and literary? Can we think these two things together instead of driving them apart? Much of our schooling teaches us that academe—if it is social science or science—is not literary and has nothing to do with the care of language (Abram, 2010). Abram suggests that his (mis)education turned him away from the sensuous world and turned off his senses altogether. He had to work to reeducate himself after leaving school to get retuned to the natural and sensual world. The science that Abram studied in school seemed dead because the language used to describe the science seemed dead, and so it made his relation to the world deadening. Language affects our entire being. So let us take better care of our language. Let us be more literary. Gary Rasberry (2001) talks about a "therapeutic catharsis" (p. xix) in the context of curriculum studies and the poetic. Can curriculum studies become more poetic? For Rasberry, the two (curriculum studies and the poetic) are one. He answers Freire's (1996) call toward the beautiful. Another poetic curriculum theorist is Rebecca Luce-Kapler (2004), if you recall from our previous discussion. Like Rasberry, Luce-Kapler is truly a poet. She does not drive a wedge between the art of poetry and the art of curriculum theorizing. Moreover, Luce-Kapler suggests that writing is healing, and she too draws on the work of Louise de Salvo to describe this healing process. Luce-Kapler declares

> In her examination of the healing effects of writing, Louise de Salvo (1999) described how Virginia Woolf believed that moments of profound insight come from writing about a thoughtful examination of psychic wounds. Such a process makes us aware of ourselves, our relationships to others and our place in the world and helps to heal our sense of fracture and disconnection. (p. 81)

Scholarship can serve these healing functions. The healing also comes about through the care of language and the careful use of language. Scholarship is not merely about ideas, it is about writing those ideas down in such a way that others can connect to them and perhaps be healed by them. Curriculum studies, in particular, is indeed healing.

REFERENCES

Abbas, N. (2005). Introduction. In N Abbas (Ed.), *Mapping Michel Serres* (pp. 1–9). Ann Arbor: University of Michigan Press.

Abram, D. (2010). *Becoming animal: An earthly cosmology*. New York: Vintage.

Abukhattala, I. (2004). The new bogeyman under the bed: Image formation of Islam in the Western school curriculum and media. In J. L. Kincheloe & S. R. Steinberg (Eds.), *The miseducation of the West: How schools and the media distort our understanding of the Islamic world* (pp. 153–170). Westport, CT: Praeger.

Adams, H. (2009). *Tom and Jack: The intertwined lives of Thomas Hart Benton and Jackson Pollock*. New York: Bloomsbury.

Addams, J. (1997). From "A function of the social settlement" (1899). In L. Menand (Ed.), *Pragmatism: A reader* (pp. 273–286). New York: Vintage.

Adorno, T. (1966/1993). *Negative dialectics*. (A. B. Ashton, Trans.). New York: Continuum.

Adorno, T., Brunski-Frenkel, E., Levinson, D. J., & Sanford, R. N. (1950/1993). *The authoritarian personality*. Studies in Prejudice Series. New York: W.W. Norton.

Agacinski, S. (2003). *Time passing: Modernity and nostalgia* (J. Gladding, Trans.). New York: Columbia University Press.

Alter, R. (1991). *Necessary angels: Tradition and modernity in Kafka, Benjamin, and Scholem*. Cambridge, MA: Harvard University Press.

Anderson, L. (2004). *Autobiography: The new critical idiom*. New York: Routledge.

Anijar, K., & Mascali, B. (2002). How can we speak at all? In M. Morris & J. A. Weaver (Eds.), *Difficult memories: Talk in a (post) Holocaust era* (pp. 249–265). New York: Peter Lang.

Anzaldúa, G. E. (2002). Preface: (Un)natural bridges, (un)safe spaces. In G. E. Anzaldúa and A. Keating (Eds.), *This bridge we call home: Radical visions for transformation* (pp. 1–5). New York: Routledge.

Anzaldúa, G. E. & A. Keating (Eds.). (2002). *This bridge we call home: Radical visions for transformation*. New York: Routledge.

Aoki, T. (2005).*Curriculum in a new key: The collected works of Ted T. Aoki* (W. F. Pinar & R. L. Irwin, Eds.). Mahwah, NJ: Lawrence Erlbaum.

Appelbaum, P. M. (2008). *Children's books for grown-up teachers: Reading and writing curriculum theory*. New York: Routledge.

Appelfeld, A. (1994). *Beyond despair: Three lectures and a conversation with Philip Roth* (J. M. Green, Trans.). New York: Fromm.

Apple, M. (1998). Foreword. In J. L. Kincheloe, S.R. Steinberg, N. Rodriguez, & R. E. Chennault (Eds.), *White reign: Deployment of whiteness in America* (pp. ix–xiii). New York: St. Martin's Griffin.

Apple, M. (2006). *Educating the "right" way: Markets, standards, God, and inequality*. New York: Routledge.

Apple, M. (2009). On being a scholar/activist in education. In E. C. Short & L. J. Waks (Eds.), *Leaders in curriculum studies: Intellectual self-portraits* (pp. 1–13). Rotterdam: Sense.

Apple, M. (2010). Global crises, social justice, and education. In M. Apple (Ed.), *Global crises, social justice, and education* (pp. 1–24). New York: Routledge.

Arendt, H. (1979). *The origins of totalitarianism*. New York: Harcourt Brace.

Arendt, H. (1994). *Essays in understanding, 1930–1954: Formation, exile, and totalitarianism*. New York: Schocken.

Aronowitz, S. (2000). *The knowledge factory: Dismantling the corporate university and creating true higher learning*. Boston: Beacon.

Aronowitz, S. (2002). Gramsci's theory of education: Schooling and beyond. In C. Borg, J. Buttigieg, & P. Mayo (Eds.), *Gramsci and education* (pp. 109–120). Lanham, MD: Rowman & Littlefield.

Artaud, A. (1988). *Antonin Artaud: Selected writings* (S. Sontag, Ed.). Berkeley: University of California Press.

Asanuma, S. (1999). The autobiographical method in Japanese education. In W. F. Pinar (Ed.), *Contemporary curriculum discourses: Twenty years of JCT* (pp. 151–167). New York: Peter Lang.

Ayers, W. (1998a). Doing philosophy: Maxine Greene and the pedagogy of possibility. In W. C. Ayers & J. L. Miller (Eds.), *A light in dark times: Maxine Greene and the unfinished conversation* (pp. 3–10). New York: Teachers College Press.

Ayers, W. (1998b). I search, you search, we all search: Biography and the public voice. In C. Kridel (Ed.), *Writing educational biography: Explorations in qualitative research* (pp. 235–244). New York: Garland.

Ayers, W. (2004a). *Teaching the personal and the political: Essays on hope and justice*. New York: Teachers College Press.

Ayers, W. (2004b). *Teaching toward freedom: Moral commitment and ethical action in the classroom*. Boston: Beacon.

Ayers, W. (2010). *To teach: The journey of a teacher.* New York: Teachers College Press.

Ayers, W. & Miller, J. (Eds.) (1998). *A light in dark times: Maxine Greene and the unfinished conversation.* New York: Teachers College Press.

Bakalian, A., & Bozorgmehr, M. (2009). *Backlash 9/11: Middle Eastern and Muslim Americans respond.* Berkeley: University of California Press.

Baker, B. M. (1998). "Childhood" in the emergence and spread of U.S. public schools. In T. S. Popkewitz & M. Brennan (Eds.), *Foucault's challenge: Discourse, knowledge, and power in education* (pp. 117–13). New York: Teachers College Press.

Bale, J. M. (2006). Fascism and neo-fascism: Ideology and "groupuscularity." In R. Griffin, W. Loh, & A. Umlands (Eds.), *Fascism past and present, West and East: An international debate on concepts and cases in the comparative study of the extreme right* (pp. 78–86). Stuttgart: Ibidem-Verlag.

Banks, J. A. (2004). Multicultural education: Historical development, dimensions, and practice. In J. A. Banks & C. A. McGee Banks (Eds.), *Handbook of research on multicultural education* (2nd ed., pp. 3–29). San Francisco: Jossey-Bass.

Banks, J. A. (2011). Multicultural education: Dimensions and paradigms. In J. A. Banks (Ed.), *The Routledge international companion to multicultural education* (pp. 9–32). New York: Routledge.

Bankston, C. L., & S. J. Caldas. (2009). *Public education: America's civil religion: A social history.* New York: Teachers College Press.

Barnes, C. (2010). A brief history of discrimination and disabled people. In L. J. Davis (Ed.), *The disability studies reader* (pp. 20–32). New York: Routledge.

Bar-On, T. (2006). A critical response to Roger Griffin's "fascism's new faces." In *Fascism past and present, West and East: An international debate on concepts and cases in the comparative study of the extreme right* (pp. 87–93). Stuttgart: Ibidem-Verlag.

Barone, T. (1998). Maxine Greene: Literary influences. In W. F. Pinar (Ed.), *The passionate mind of Maxine Greene: 'I am...not yet'* (pp. 137–147). New York: Falmer.

Bar-On, T. (2000). *Aesthetics, politics, and educational inquiry: Essays and examples.* New York: Peter Lang.

Barone, T. (2001). *Touching eternity: The enduring outcomes of teaching.* New York: Teachers College Press.

Barriteau, V. E. (2009). The relevance of black feminist scholarship: A Caribbean perspective. In S. M. James, F. S. Foster, & B. Guy-Sheftall (Eds.), *Still brave: The evolution of black women's studies* (pp. 413–434). New York: Feminist.

Baynton, D. (2010). "A silent exile on this earth": The metaphorical construction of deafness in the nineteenth century. In L. J. Davis (Ed.), *The disability studies reader* (pp. 33–51). New York: Routledge.

Beauchamp-Pryor, K. (2012). Visual impairment and disability: A dual approach towards equality and inclusion in UK policy and provision. In N. Watson, A. Roulstone, & C. Thomas (Eds.), *Routledge handbook of disability studies* (pp. 178–192). New York: Routledge.

Beineke, J. A. (1998). *And then there were giants in the land: The life of William Heard Kilpatrick.* New York: Peter Lang.

Bell, C. (2010). Is disability studies actually white disability studies? In L. J. Davis (Ed.), *The disability studies reader* (pp. 374–382). New York: Routledge.

Bender, S. W. (2011). The war on terrorism and its consequences for Latinas/os. In R. Delgado & J. Stefancic (Eds.), *The Latino/a condition: A critical reader* (2nd ed., pp. 204–207). New York: New York University Press.

Benjamin, A. (2005). Boredom and distraction: The moods of modernity. In A. Benjamin (Ed.), *Walter Benjamin and history* (pp. 156–170). New York: Continuum.

Benjamin, J. (1988). *The bonds of love: Psychoanalysis, feminism, and the problem of domination.* New York: Pantheon.

Benjamin, W. (1997). *One-way street.* New York: Verso.

Benjamin, W. (2006). *Selected writings: Vol. 4: 1938–1940* (E. Jephcott et al., Trans.). Cambridge, MA: Belknap/Harvard University Press.

Bennett, C. (2011). Genres of research in multicultural education. In C. A. Grant & T. K. Chapman (Eds.), *History of multicultural education: Vol. 1: Conceptual frameworks and curricular issues* (pp. 88–132). New York: Routledge.

Bennett, W. (1996). *The book of virtues: A treasury of great moral stories.* New York: Simon & Schuster.

Beresford, P. (2012). Psychiatric system survivors: An emerging movement. In N. Watson, A. Roulstone, & C. Thomas (Eds.), *Routledge handbook of disability studies* (pp. 151–164). New York: Routledge.

Berlin, I. (1997). *The proper study of mankind: An anthology of essays.* New York: Farrar, Straus & Giroux.

Berlowitz, M. J., & Long, N. A. (2003). The proliferation of JROTC: Educational reform or militarization. In K. J. Saltman & D. Gabbard (Eds.), *Education as enforcement: The militarization and corporatization of schools* (pp. 163–174). New York: RoutledgeFalmer.

Berman, L. (1996). Alice Miel: Exemplar of democracy made real. In C. Kridel, R. V. Bullough Jr., & P. Shaker (Eds.), *Teachers and mentors: Profiles of distinguished twentieth-century professors of education* (pp. 173–183). New York: Garland.

Berson, R. K. (2004). *Jane Addams: A biography.* Westport, CT: Greenwood.

Bettis, P. J., & Adams, N. G. (2009). Landscapes of girlhood. In P. J. Bettis & N. G. Adams (Eds.), *Geographies of girlhood* (pp. 1–16). Mahwah, NJ: Lawrence Erlbaum.

Beyer, L. E. (2000). *The arts, popular culture, and social change.* New York: Peter Lang.

Bhabha, H. K. (1994). *The location of culture.* New York: Routledge.

Biesta, G. (2009). Deconstruction, justice, and the vocation of education. In M. A. Peters & G. Beista (Eds.), *Derrida, deconstruction and the politics of pedagogy* (pp. 15–37). New York: Peter Lang.

Biesta, G., & Egea-Kuehne, D. (2001). (Eds.). *Derrida and education.* New York: Routledge.

Bion, W. (1994). *Cogitations.* London: Karnac.

Birkerts, S. (2006). *The Gutenberg elegies.* New York: Farber & Farber.

Black, M. S. (2005). Mexican American education: An elementary school case study. In L. M. Burlbaw & S. L. Field (Eds.), *Explorations in curriculum history* (pp. 261–280). Greenwich, CT: Information Age.

Bleich, D., & Holdstein, D. H. (Eds.). (2001). *Personal effects: The social character of scholarly writing*. Logan: Utah State University Press.

Bloch, M. N., & Popkewitz, T. S. (2005). Constructing the parent, teacher, and child: Discourses of development. In L. D. Soto (Ed.), *The politics of early childhood education* (pp. 7–32). New York: Peter Lang.

Block, A. A. (1999). "Johnny's in the basement, mixing up the medicine," or I'll trade you two metaphors for a metonymy. In M. Morris, M. A. Doll, & W. F. Pinar (Eds.), *How we work* (pp. 101–114). New York: Peter Lang.

Block, A. A. (2004). *Talmud, curriculum, and the practical: Joseph Schwab and the rabbi's*. New York: Peter Lang.

Bloom, A. (1988). *Closing of the American mind*. New York: Simon & Schuster.

Bloom, H. (2001). *How to write and why*. New York: Simon & Schuster.

Bloom, L. (1998). *Under the sign of hope: Feminist methodology and narrative interpretation*. Albany, NY: SUNY.

Bobo, J., Hudley, C., & Michel, C. (Eds.). (2004). *The black studies reader*. New York: Routledge.

Bock, G. (2006). Women's history and gender history: Aspects of an international debate. In S. Morgan (Ed.), *The feminist history reader* (pp. 104–115). New York: Routledge.

Bohan, C. H. (2004). *Go to the sources: Lucy Maynard Salmon and the teaching of history*. New York: Peter Lang.

Boler, M. (1999).Feeling power: Emotions and education. Newyork: Routledge.

Bollas, C. (1997). Christopher Bollas. In, A. Molino (Ed.), Elaborate selves: Reflections and reveries of Christopher Bollas, Michael Eigen, Polly Young-Eisendrath, Samuel and Evelyn Laevchli, Marie Coleman Nelson (pp. 11–60). Newyork: The Hawthorne Press.

Bolt, D. (2012). Social encounters, cultural representation and critical avoidance. In N. Watson, A. Roulstone, & C. Thomas (Eds.), *Routledge handbook of disability studies* (pp. 287–297). New York: Routledge.

Boone, J. A. (2000). Go West: An introduction. In J. A. Boone, M. Dupuis, M. Meeker, K. Quimbly, C. Sarver, D. Silverman, & R. Weatherston (Eds.), *Queer frontiers: Millennial geographies, genders, and generations* (pp. 3–20). Madison: University of Wisconsin Press.

Borg, C., Buttigieg, J. A., & Mayo, P. (2002). Introduction. Gramsci and education: A holistic approach. In C. Borg, J. Buttigieg, & P. Mayo (Eds.), *Gramsci and education* (pp. 1–24). Lanham, MD: Rowman & Littlefield.

Boswell, J. (1981). *Christianity, social tolerance, and homosexuality*. Chicago: University of Chicago Press.

Boswell, J. (1995). *Same-sex unions in premodern Europe*. New York: Vintage.

Bowers, C. A. (1995). *Educating for an ecologically sustainable culture: Rethinking moral education, creativity, intelligence, and other modern orthodoxies*. Albany, NY: SUNY.

Brady, E. H. (1996). The congruity of professing and doing. In C. Kridel, R. V. Bullough Jr., & P. Shaker (Eds.), *Teachers and mentors: Profiles of distinguished twentieth-century professors of education* (pp. 59–69). New York: Garland.

Brantlinger, E. (2003). *Dividing classes: How the middle class negotiates and rationalizes school advantage*. New York: RoutledgeFalmer.

Brinkley, D. (2009). *The wilderness warrior: Theodore Roosevelt and the crusade for America*. New York: Harper.

Britzman, D. P. (2002). The death of curriculum? In W. E. Doll Jr. & N. Gough (Eds.), *Curriculum visions* (pp. 92–101). New York: Peter Lang.

Britzman, D. P. (2003). *After-education: Anna Freud, Melanie Klein and psychoanalytic histories of learning*. Albany, NY: SUNY.

Brock, R. (2005). *Sista talk: The personal and the pedagogical*. New York: Peter Lang.

Brod, H. (2002). Studying masculinities as superordinate studies. In J. K. Gardiner (Ed.), *Masculinity studies & feminist theory: New directions* (pp. 161–175). New York: Columbia University Press.

Brown, E. A. (2003). Freedom for some, discipline for "others": The structure of inequity in education. In K. J. Saltman & D. Gabbard (Eds.), *Education as enforcement: The militarization and corporatization of schools* (pp. 127–151). New York: RoutledgeFalmer.

Brown, E. A. (2007). The quiet disaster of No Child Left Behind: Standardization and deracialization breed inequality. In K. J. Saltman (Ed.), *Schooling and the politics of disaster* (pp. 123–140). New York: Routledge.

Bullough, R. V., Jr. (1996). Professional dreams and mentoring: A personal view. In C. Kridel, R. V. Bullough Jr., & P. Shaker (Eds.), *Teachers and mentors: Profiles of distinguished twentieth-century professors of education* (pp. 257–67). New York: Garland.

Butler, J. (1990). *Gender trouble: Feminism and the subversion of identity*. New York: Routledge.

Cainkar, L. (2008). Thinking outside the box: Arabs and race in the United States. In A. Jamal & N. Naber (Eds.), *Race and Arab Americans before and after 9/11: From invisible citizens to visible subjects* (pp. 46–80). New York: Syracuse University Press.

Cammarota, J. (2011). Going to school: "Two struggles." In R. Delgado & J. Stefancic (Eds.), *The Latino/a condition* (2nd ed., pp. 433–439). New York: New York University Press.

Cannella, G. S. (2008). *Deconstructing early childhood education: Social justice and revolution*. New York: Peter Lang.

Cannella, G. S., & Viruru, R. (2004). *Childhood and postcolonialization: Power, education, and contemporary practice*. New York: RoutledgeFalmer.

Carger, C. L. (2009). *Dreams deferred: Dropping out and struggling forward*. Charlotte, NC: Information Age.

Carlson, D. (1998). Who am I? Gay identity and a democratic politics of the self. In W. F. Pinar (Ed.), *Queer theory in education* (pp. 107–119). Mahwah, NJ: Lawrence Erlbaum.

Carr, P., & Lund, D. (2009). The unspoken color of diversity: Whiteness, privilege, and critical engagement in education. In S. Steinberg (Ed.), *Diversity and multiculturalism: A reader* (pp. 45–55). New York: Peter Lang.

Case, S.-E. (2000). Toward a butch-feminist retro-future. In J. A. Boone, M. Dupuis, M. Meeker, K. Quimby, C. Sarver, D. Silverman, & R. Weatherston (Eds.), *Queer frontiers: Millennial geographies, genders, and generations* (pp. 23–38). Madison: University of Wisconsin Press.

Case, V. (1948). *We called it culture: The story of Chautauqua*. New York: Doubleday.

Casemore, B. (2008). *The autobiographical demand of place: Curriculum inquiry in the American South.* New York: Peter Lang.

Chavez, L. R. (2008). *The Latino threat: Constructing immigrants, citizens, and the nation.* Stanford, CA: Stanford University Press.

Chiarelott, L. (2006). *Curriculum in context.* Belmont, CA: Thomson Wadsworth.

Chun, M., Christopher, S., & Gumport, P. J. (2000). Multiculturalism and the academic organization of knowledge. In R. Mahalingam & C. McCarthy (Eds.), *Multicultural curriculum: New directions for social theory, practice, and policy* (pp. 223–241). New York: Routledge.

Cohen, A. (2009). *Nothing to fear: FDR'S inner circle and the hundred days that created modern America.* New York: Penguin.

Cohen, S. (1999). *Challenging orthodoxies: Toward a new cultural history of education.* New York: Peter Lang.

Collin, R., & Apple, M. (2010). New literacies and new rebellions in the global age. In M. Apple (Ed.), *Global crises, social justice, and education* (pp. 25–60). New York: Routledge.

Collins, P. H. (2000). *Black feminist thought: Knowledge, consciousness, and the politics of empowerment* (2nd ed.). New York: Routledge.

Connell, R. W. (2005). *Masculinities.* Berkeley: University of California Press.

Connelly, M. F. (2009). Bridges from then to now and from them to us: Narrative threads on the landscape of "the practical." In E. C. Short & L. J. Waks (Eds.), *Leaders in curriculum studies: Intellectual self-portraits* (pp. 39–54). Rotterdam: Sense.

Connelly, M. F., He, M. F., & Phillon, J. A. (Eds.). (2008) *The Sage handbook of curriculum and instruction.* Los Angeles: Sage.

Cooper, A. J. (1888/1892). *A voice from the South.* New York: Oxford University Press.

Cooper, J. M. (2009). *Woodrow Wilson: A biography.* New York: Alfred Knopf.

Corker, M., & Shakespeare, T. (2002). Mapping the terrain. In M. Corker & T. Shakespeare (Eds.), *Disability/postmodernity: Embodying disability theory* (pp. 1–17). New York: Continuum.

Cremin, L. A. (1961). *The transformation of the school: Progressivism in American education, 1876–1957.* New York: Vintage.

Cremin, L. A. (1988). *American education: The metropolitan experience, 1876–1980.* New York: Harper & Row.

Cremin, L. A. (1996). George S. Counts as a teacher: A reminiscence. In C. Kridel, R. V. Bullough Jr., & P. Shaker (Eds.), *Teachers and mentors: Profiles of distinguished twentieth-century professors of education* (pp. 237–243). New York: Garland.

Crimp, D. (2002). Mario Monez, for shame. In S. M. Barber & D. L. Clark (Eds.), *Regarding Sedgwick: Essays on queer culture and critical theory* (pp. 57–70). New York: Routledge.

Crocco, M. S., Munro, P., & Weiler, K. (1999). *Pedagogies of resistance: Women educator activists, 1880–1960.* New York: Teachers College Press.

Cuban, L. (2003). *Why is it so hard to get good schools?* New York: Teachers College Press.

Cuban, L., & Shipps, D. (Eds.). (2000). *Reconstructing the common good in education: Coping with intractable American dilemmas.* Stanford, CA: Stanford University Press.

Culler, J. (1982). *On deconstruction: Theory and criticism after structuralism.* Ithaca, NY: Cornell University Press.

Culler, J. (2011). *Literary theory: A very short introduction.* New York: Oxford Press.

Danforth, S., & Gabel, S. L. (Eds.). (2006). *Vital questions facing disability studies in education.* New York: Peter Lang.

Dar, J. (2010). Holy Islamophobia, batman! Demonization of Muslims and Arabs in mainstream American comic books. In J. L. Kincheloe, S. R. Steinberg, & C. D. Stonebanks (Eds.), *Teaching against Islamophobia* (pp. 99–110). New York: Peter Lang.

Darder, A. (2002). *Reinventing Paulo Freire: A pedagogy of love.* Boulder, CO: Westview.

Darder, A. (2010). Foreword. In L. Diaz Soto & H. Kharem (Eds.), *Teaching bilingual/bicultural children: Teachers talk about language and learning* (pp. xi–xiv). New York: Peter Lang.

Darder, A., Torres, R. D., & Gutierrez, H. (Eds.). (1997). *Latinos and education: A critical reader.* New York: Routledge.

Daspit, T. (1999). "Nothing's died: it just got buried": Theory as exhumation, as duty dance. In M. Morris, M. A. Doll, & W. F. Pinar (Eds.), *How we work* (pp. 71–77). New York: Peter Lang.

Davis, B. (1996). *Teaching mathematics: Toward a sound alternative.* New York: Garland Publishing.

Davis, J. (2012). Conceptual issues in childhood and disability: Integrating theories from childhood and disability studies. In N. Watson, A. Roulstone, & C. Thomas (Eds.), *Routledge handbook of disability studies* (pp. 414–425). New York: Routledge.

Davis, L. J. (2002). *Bending over backwards: Disability, dismodernism and other difficult positions.* New York: New York University Press.

De Botton, A. (2004). *The art of travel.* New York: Vintage International.

De Castell, S., & Bryson, M. (Eds.). (1997). *Radical in(ter)ventions: Identity, politics and difference/s in educational praxis.* Albany, NY: SUNY.

De Castell, S., & Jenson, J. (Eds.). (2007). *Worlds in play: International perspectives on digital games research.* New York: Peter Lang.

De Certeau, M. (1988). *The practice of everyday life.* Berkeley: University of California Press.

De Grand, A. (2006). Griffin's new consensus: A bit too minimal? In R. Griffin, W. Loh, & A. Umland (Eds.), *Fascism past and present, West and East: An international debate on concepts and cases in the comparative study of the extreme right* (pp. 94–98). Stuttgart: Ibidem-Verlag.

De Salvo, L. (2000). *Writing as a way of healing: How telling our stories transforms our lives.* Boston: Beacon.

Dei, G. J. S. (2008). *Racists beware: Uncovering racial politics in contemporary society.* Rotterdam: Sense.

Deleuze, G., & Guattari, F. (2000). *Anti-Oedipus: Capitalism and schizophrenia* (R. Hurley, M. Seem, & H. R. Lang, Trans.). Minneapolis: University of Minnesota Press.

Derrida, J. (1976). *Of grammatology.* (G. C. Spivak, Trans.). Baltimore: Johns Hopkins University Press.

Derrida, J. (1978). *Writing and difference.* (A. Bass, Trans.). Chicago: University of Chicago Press.

Derrida, J. (1992). *The other heading: Reflections on today's Europe.* (P.-A. Brault & M. Nass, Trans.). Bloomington: Indiana University Press.

Derrida, J. (1994). *The specters of Marx: The state of debt, the work of mourning, and the new international.* New York: Routledge.

Derrida, J. (1995). *Points: Interviews, 1974–1994*. (P. Kamuf, Trans.). Stanford, CA: Stanford University Press.

Derrida, J. (1996). *Archive fever: A Freudian impression* (E. Prenowitz, Trans.). Chicago: University of Chicago Press.

Derrida, J. (2002). *Negotiations: Interventions and interviews, 1971–2001* (E. Rottenberg, Trans.). Stanford, CA: Stanford University Press.

Dewey, J. (1899). *The school and society*. Chicago: University of Chicago Press.

Dewey, J. (1902). *The child and the curriculum*. Chicago: University of Chicago Press.

Dewey, J. (1916/1966). *Democracy and education*. New York: Free.

Dewey, J. (1951). The construction of the good. In M. H. Fisch (Ed.), *Classic American philosophers* (pp. 360–380). Englewood Cliffs, NJ: Prentice-Hall.

Dewey, J. (1974). *On education: Selected writings* (R. Archambault, Ed.). Chicago: University of Chicago Press.

Dewey, J. (1991). *How we think*. Buffalo, NY: Prometheus.

Dewey, J. (2005). *Art as experience*. New York: Penguin.

Diggs, N. B. (2011). *Hidden in the heartland: The new wave of immigrants and the challenge to America*. East Lansing: Michigan State University Press.

Doll, B. (2009). The path stumbled upon. In E. C. Short & L. J. Waks (Eds.), *Leaders in curriculum studies: Intellectual self-portraits* (pp. 55–65). Rotterdam: Sense.

Doll, M. A. (1995). *To the lighthouse and back: Writings on teaching and living*. New York: Peter Lang.

Doll, M. A. (1999). Beyond the window: Dreams and learning. In W. F. Pinar (Ed.), *Contemporary curriculum discourses: Twenty years of JCT* (pp. 106–113). New York: Peter Lang.

Doll, M. A. (2000). *Like letters in running water: A mythopoetics of curriculum*. Mahwah, NJ: Lawrence Erlbaum.

Doll, M. A. (2006). Curriculum: Introduction. In M. A. Doll, D. Wear, & M. Whitaker (Eds.), *Triple takes on curricular worlds* (pp. 27–28). Albany, NY: SUNY.

Doll, M. A. (2011). *The more of myth: A pedagogy of diversion*. The Netherlands: Sense.

Doll, M. A., Wear, D., & Whitaker, M. (2006). *Triple takes on curricular worlds*. Albany, NY: SUNY.

Doll, W. E. (1993). *A post-modern perspective on curriculum*. New York: Teachers College Press.

Doll, W. E. (1998). Curriculum and concepts of control. In W. Pinar (Ed.), *Curriculum and new identities* (pp. 295–324). New York: Garland.

Doll, W. E. (2002). Ghosts and the curriculum. In W. E. Doll Jr. & N. Gough (Eds.), *Curriculum visions* (pp. 23–70). New York: Peter Lang.

Doll, W. (2005). The culture of method. In W. Doll Jr., M. J. Fleener, D. Trueit, & J. St. Julien (Eds.), *Chaos, complexity, curriculum, and culture: A conversation* (pp. 21–75). New York: Peter Lang.

Doll, W. E., Jr. & Gough, N. (Eds.). (2002). *Curriculum visions*. New York: Peter Lang.

Doty, A. (1993). *Making things perfectly queer: Interpreting mass culture*. Minneapolis: University of Minnesota Press.

Downing, C. (1989). *Myths and mysteries of same sex love*. New York: Continuum.

D'Souza, D. (1991). Illiberal Education. The politics of Race and Sex on Campus. Newyork: Free.

Dudek, P. (1997). National-Socialist youth policy and the labour service: The work camp as an instrument of social discipline. In H. Sunker & H.-U. Otto (Eds.), *Education and fascism: Political identity and social education in Nazi Germany* (pp. 36–53). London: Falmer.

Durham, M. (2008). Palingenesis and the rebirth of the study of fascism. In R. Griffin, W. Loh, & A. Umland (Eds.), *Fascism past and present, West and East: An international debate on concepts and cases in the comparative study of the extreme right* (pp. 99–103). Stuttgart: Ibidem-Verlag.

Duster, A. M. (Ed.). (1970). *Crusade for justice: The autobiography of Ida B. Wells.* Chicago: University of Chicago Press.

Eagleton, T. (2003). *After theory.* New York: Basic.

Eagleton, T. (2013). *How to read literature.* New Haven, CT: Yale University Press.

Eatwell, R. (2006). The nature of fascism: [O]r essentialism by another name? In R. Griffin & A. Umland (Eds.), *Fascism past and present, West and East: An international debate on concepts and cases in the comparative study of the extreme right* (pp. 104–109). Stuttgart: Ibidem-Verlag.

Eco, U. (1995). *Six walks in the fictional woods.* Cambridge, MA: Harvard University Press.

Eco, U. (2012). *Experiences in translation* (A. McEwen, Trans.). Toronto: University of Toronto Press.

Edgoose, J. (2001). Just decide! Derrida and the ethical aporias of education. In G. J. Biesta & D. Egea-Kuehne (Eds.), *Derrida & education* (pp. 119–133). New York: Routledge.

Egea-Kuehne, D., & Biest, G. J. (Eds.). (2001). *Derrida and education* (pp. 1–11). New York: Routledge.

Elenes, C. A. (2003). Reclaiming the borderlands: Chicana/o identity, difference, and critical pedagogy. In A. Darder, M. Balodano, & R. D. Torres (Eds.), *The critical pedagogy reader* (pp. 191–210). New York: Routledge.

Elshtain, J. B. (2002). *Jane Addams and the dream of American democracy: A life.* New York: Basic.

Eppert, C. (2002). Throwing testimony against the wall: Reading, relating loss and responsible/responsive learning. In M. Morris & J. Weaver (Eds.), *Difficult memories: Talk in a (post) Holocaust era* (pp. 45–67). New York: Peter Lang.

Eppert, C., & Wang, H. (Eds.). (2008). *Cross-cultural studies in curriculum: Eastern thought, educational issues.* New York: Lawrence Erlbaum.

Erevelles, N. (2006). Deconstructing difference: Doing disability studies in multicultural educational contexts. In S. Danforth & S. L. Gabel (Eds.), *Vital questions facing disability studies in education* (pp. 363–378). New York: Peter Lang.

Evans, K. (2002). *Negotiating the self: Identity, sexuality, and emotion in learning to teach.* New York: RoutledgeFalmer.

Evans, R. W. (2007). *This happened in America: Harold Rugg and the censure of social studies.* Charlotte, NC: Information Age.

Faderman, L. (1999). *To believe in women: What lesbians have done for America—A history.* New York: Houghton Mifflin.

Faderman, L., & Timmons, S. (2006). *Gay L.A.: A history of sexual outlaws, power politics, and lipstick lesbians.* New York: Basic.

Falicov, C. J. (2005). Ambiguous loss: Risk and resilience in Latino immigrant families. In M. M. Suárez-Orozco, C. Suárez-Orozco, & D. B. Qin (Eds.), *The new immigration: An interdisciplinary reader* (pp. 197–206). New York: Routledge.

Fernandes, D. (2007). *Targeted: Homeland security and the business of immigration.* New York: Seven Stories.

Feuerverger, G. (2002). My Yiddish voice. In M. Morris & J. A. Weaver (Eds.), *Difficult memories: Talk in a (post) Holocaust era* (pp. 13–23). New York: Peter Lang.

Fine, M., Burns, A., Torre, M. E., & Payne, Y. A. (2008). How class matters: The geography of educational desire and despair in schools and courts. In L. Weis (Ed.), *The way class works: Readings on school, family, and the economy* (pp. 225–242). New York: Routledge.

Fine, M., & Weis, L. (1998). *The unknown city: The lives of poor and working-class young adults.* Boston: Beacon.

Fink, L. (1997). *Progressive intellectuals and the dilemma of democratic commitment.* Cambridge, MA: Harvard University Press.

Finkelstein, B. (1998). Revealing human agency: The uses of biography in the study of educational history. In C. Kridel (Ed.), *Writing educational biography: Explorations in qualitative research* (pp. 45–59). New York: Garland.

Fisch, M. H. (Ed.). (1951). William James. In *Classic American philosophers* (pp. 128–165). Englewood Cliffs, NJ: Prentice-Hall.

Fish, S. (2011). *How to write a sentence and how to read one.* New York: Harper.

Flinders, D. J., & Thornton, S. J. (Eds.) (2004). *The curriculum studies reader* (2nd ed.). New York: RoutledgeFalmer.

Foley, N. (2011). Mexican Americans and the Faustian pact with whiteness. In R. Delgado & J. Stefancic (Eds.), *The Latino/a condition: A critical reader* (2nd ed., pp. 369–372). New York: New York University Press.

Fontana, B. (2002). Hegemony and rhetoric: Political education in Gramsci. In C. Borg, J. Buttigieg, & P. Mayo (Eds.), *Gramsci and education* (pp. 25–40). Lanham, MD: Rowman & Littlefield.

Foucault, M. (1979). *Discipline and punish: The birth of the prison* (A. Sheridan, Trans.). New York: Vintage.

Foucault, M. (1983). Afterword. The subject and power. In H. L. Dreyfus & P. Rabinow (Eds.), *Michel Foucault: Beyond structuralism and hermeneutics* (pp. 208–226). Chicago: University of Chicago Press.

Foucault, M. (1988). *Madness and civilization: A history of insanity in the age of reason.* New York: Vintage.

Foucault, M. (1990). *The history of sexuality: An introduction: Vol. 1.* New York: Vintage.

Foucault, M. (1994). *The order of things: An archaeology of the human sciences.* New York: Vintage.

Foucault, M. (2003). *"Society must be defended": Lectures at the College de France, 1975–1976* (D. Macey, Trans.). New York: Picador.

Foucault, M. (2006). *History of madness.* New York: Routledge.

Frankenberg, R. (2005). *White women, race matters: The social construction of whiteness.* Minneapolis: University of Minnesota Press.

Franklin, B. M. (Ed.). (2000). *Curriculum and consequence: Herbert M. Kliebard and the promise of schooling*. New York: Teachers College Press.

Freire, P. (1996). *Letters to Cristina: Reflections on my life and work* (D. Macedo, with Q. Macedo & A. Oliveira, Trans.). New York: Routledge.

Freire, P. (2001). *Pedagogy of freedom: Ethics, democracy, and civic courage*. Lanham, MD: Rowman & Littlefield.

Freire, P. (2004). *Pedagogy of indignation*. Boulder, CO: Paradigm.

Freire, P. (2005). *Teachers as cultural workers: Letters to those who dare teach* (Exp. ed., D. Macedo, D. Koike, & A. Oliveira, Trans.). Boulder, CO: Westview.

Freud, S. (1961). *Civilization and its discontents* (J. Strachey, Ed. & Trans.). New York: W. W. Norton.

Fritzsche, P. (2006). Fascism and illiberalism. In R. Griffin, W. Loh, & A. Umland (Eds.), *Fascism past and present, West and East: An international debate on concepts and cases in the comparative study of the extreme right* (pp. 110–114). Stuttgart: Ibidem-Verlag.

Gabbard, D. (2003). Education is enforcement! The centrality of compulsory schooling in market societies. In K. J. Saltman & D. Gabbard (Eds.), *Education as enforcement: The militarization and corporatization of schools* (pp. 61–78). New York: RoutledgeFalmer.

Gadamer, H.-G. (1975). *Truth and method*. New York: Seabury.

Gardiner, J. K. (Ed.). (2002). *Masculinity studies & feminist theory: New directions*. New York: Columbia University Press.

Garman, N. B. (2007). Imagining an interpretive dissertation: Voice, text, and representation. In N. B. Garman & M. Piantanida (Eds.), *The authority to imagine: The struggle toward representation in dissertation writing* (pp. 1–15). New York: Peter Lang.

Garman, N. B., & Piantanida, M. (Eds.). (2007). *The authority to imagine: The struggle toward representation in dissertation writing*. New York: Peter Lang.

Garrison, J. (1997). *Dewey and Eros: Wisdom and desire in the art of teaching*. New York: Teachers College.

Gawande, A. (2002). *Complications: A surgeon's notes on an imperfect science*. New York: Picador.

Gay, P. (1998). *Freud: A life for our time*. New York: W.W. Norton.

Giardina, M. D. (2010). Barack Obama, Islamophobia, and the 2008 U.S. presidential election media spectacle. In J. L. Kincheloe, S. R. Steinberg, & C. D. Stonebanks (Eds.), *Teaching against Islamophobia* (pp. 135–157). New York: Peter Lang.

Giddings, P. J. (2008). *Ida: A sword among lions: Ida B. Wells and the campaign against lynching*. New York: HarperCollins.

Gilbert, J. (2010). Reading histories: Curriculum theory, psychoanalysis, and generational violence. In E. Malewski (Ed.), *Curriculum studies handbook: The next moment* (pp. 63–72). New York: Routledge.

Gilbert, S. M., & Gubar S. (2000). *The madwoman in the attic: The woman writer and the nineteenth-century literary imagination*. New Haven, CT: Yale University Press.

Gillborn, D. (2005). Anti-racism: From policy to praxis. In Z. Leonardo (Ed.), *Critical pedagogy and race* (pp. 111–126). Malden, MA: Blackwell.

Gilman, S. L. (2004). *Fat boys: A slim book*. Lincoln: University of Nebraska Press.

Gilmore, G. E. (2002). Introduction: Responding to the challenges of the progressive era. In G. E. Gilmore (Ed.), *Who were the progressives?* (pp. 3–24). New York: Bedford/St. Martin's.

Gilmore, L. (2001). *The limits of autobiography: Trauma and testimony.* Ithaca, NY: Cornell University Press.

Giordano, G. (2005). *Wartime schools: How World War II changed American education.* New York: Peter Lang.

Giroux, H. A. (1996). *Fugitive cultures: Race, violence and youth.* New York: Routledge.

Giroux, H. A. (1998a). Henry A. Giroux. In C. A. Torres (Ed.), *Education, power, and personal biography* (pp. 129–157). New York: Routledge.

Giroux, H. A. (1998b). White noise: Toward a pedagogy of whiteness. In K. Myrsiades & L. Myrsiades (Eds.), *Race-ing representation: Voice, history, & sexuality* (pp. 42–76). Lanham, MD: Rowman & Littlefield.

Giroux, H. A. (1999). Dialectics and the development of curriculum theory. In W. F. Pinar (Ed.), *Contemporary curriculum discourses: Twenty years of JCT* (pp. 7–23). New York: Peter Lang.

Giroux, H. A. (2003). *The abandoned generation: Democracy beyond the culture of fear.* New York: Palgrave Macmillan.

Giroux, H. A. (2004). *The terror of neoliberalism: Authoritarianism and the eclipse of democracy.* Boulder, CO: Paradigm.

Giroux, H. A. (2007). *The university in chains: Confronting the military-industrial-academic complex.* Boulder, CO: Paradigm.

Gitlin, A., & Peck, M. (2005). *Educational poetics: Inquiry, freedom, and innovative necessity.* New York: Peter Lang.

Gollnick, D. M. (2011). Multicultural education. In C. A. Grant & T. K. Chapman (Eds.), *History of multicultural education: Vol. 1: Conceptual frameworks and curricular issues* (pp. 34–48). New York: Routledge.

Goodley, D. (2011). *Disability studies: An interdisciplinary introduction.* Los Angeles: Sage.

Goodson, I. (1998). Storying the self: Life politics and the study of the teacher's life and work. In W. F. Pinar (Ed.), *Curriculum: Toward new identities* (pp. 3–20). New York: Garland.

Goodson, I. F., & Marsh, C. J. (1996). *Studying school subjects: A guide.* London: Falmer.

Gordimer, N. (2003). Being a product of your dwelling place. In M. Arana (Ed.), *The writing life: Writers on how they think and work: A collection from the* Washington Post *book world* (pp. 59–63). New York: Public Affairs.

Gordon, L. D. (1990). *Gender and higher education in the progressive era.* New Haven, CT: Yale University Press.

Gough, N. (2002). Voicing curriculum visions. In W. E. Doll Jr. & N. Gough (Eds.), *Curriculum visions* (pp. 1–22). New York: Peter Lang.

Gramsci, A. (2000). *The Antonio Gramsci reader: Selected writings, 1916–1935* (D. Forgacs, Ed.). New York: New York University Press.

Gramsci, A. (2005). *Selections from the Prison Notebooks.* (Q. Hoare & G. N. Smith, Eds. & Trans.). New York: International.

Grande, S. (2004). *Red pedagogy: Native American social and political thought.* New York: Rowman & Littlefield.

Grant, C. A., & Chapman, T. K. (2011). Introduction to volume one. In C. A. Grant & T. K. Chapman (Eds.), *History of multicultural education: Vol. 1: Conceptual frameworks and curricular issues* (pp. 1–9). New York: Routledge.

Gray, J. (2001). In the name of the subject: Some recent versions of the personal. In D. H. Holdstein & D. Bleich (Eds.), *Personal effects: The social character of scholarly writing* (pp. 51–76). Logan: Utah State University Press.

Green, A. (1999). *The work of the negative*. New York: Free Association.

Greene, M. (1973). *Teacher as stranger: Philosophy for the modern age*. New York: Wadsworth.

Greene, M. (1978). *Landscapes of learning*. New York: Teachers College Press.

Greene, M. (1995). *Releasing the imagination: Essays on education, the arts, and social change*. San Francisco: Jossey-Bass.

Greene, M. (1998). An autobiographical remembrance. In W. F. Pinar (Ed.) *The passionate mind of Maxine Greene* (pp. 9–12). London: Falmer.

Griffin, R. (2006). Fascism's new faces (new facelessness) in the "post-fascist" epoch. In R. Griffin, W. Loh, & A. Umland (Eds.), *Fascism past and present, West and East: An international debate on concepts and cases in the comparative study of the extreme right* (pp. 29–67). Stuttgart: Ibidem-Verlag.

Griffin, R. (2008). *A fascist century: Essays by Roger Griffin* (M. Feldman, Ed.). New York: Palgrave Macmillan.

Gros, F. (2014). *A philosophy of walking*. New York: Verso.

Grumet, M. R. (1999). Autobiography and reconceptualization. In W. F. Pinar (Ed.), *Contemporary curriculum discourses: Twenty years of JCT* (pp. 24–30). New York: Peter Lang.

Grumet, M. R. (2010). Response to Nina Asher: Subject position and subjectivity in curriculum theory. In E. Malewski (Ed.), *Curriculum studies handbook: The next moment* (pp. 403–409). New York: Routledge.

Grumet, M. R., & Pinar, W. F. (2006). *Toward a poor curriculum*. Troy, NY: Educator's International.

Haberman, M. (1996). Florence B. Stratemeyer: Teacher educator. In C. Kridel, R. V. Bullough Jr., & P. Shaker (Eds.), *Teachers and mentors: Profiles of distinguished twentieth-century professors of education* (pp. 163–172). New York: Garland.

Halberstam, J. (1998). *Female masculinity*. Durham, NC: Duke University Press.

Ham, D. N. (2005). Foreword. In M. C. Terrell, *A colored woman in a white world* (pp. 7–21). Amherst, NY: Humanity.

Hamacher, W. (2005). "Now": Walter Benjamin on historical time. In A. Benjamin (Ed.), *Walter Benjamin and history* (pp. 38–68). New York: Continuum.

Hansen, D. T. (1996). In class with Philip W. Jackson. In C. Kridel, R. V. Bullough Jr., & P. Shaker (Eds.), *Teachers and mentors: Profiles of distinguished twentieth-century professors of education* (pp. 127–138). New York: Garland.

Hanson, E. (1999). *Out takes: Essays on queer theory and film*. Durham, NC: Duke University Press.

Haraway, D. J. (1989). *Primate visions: Gender, race, and nature in the world of modern science*. New York: Routledge.

Haraway, D. J. (1997). *Modest_Witness@_Second_Millennium.FemaleMan©_Meets_OncoMouse*™: *Feminism and technoscience*. New York: Routledge.

Hartman, G. (1982). *Saving the text: Literature, Derrida, philosophy.* Baltimore: Johns Hopkins University Press.

Harvey, D. (2005). *A brief history of neoliberalism.* New York: Oxford University Press.

Harvey, E. (1997). Youth welfare, social crisis and political reaction: Correctional education in the final phase of the Weimar Republic. In H. Sunker & H.-U. Otto (Eds.), *Education and fascism: Political identity and social education in Nazi Germany* (pp. 81–101). London: Falmer.

Hauser, M. E. (2006). *Learning from children: The life and legacy of Caroline Pratt.* New York: Peter Lang.

Hawley, J. D. (2008). *Theodore Roosevelt: Preacher of righteousness.* New Haven, CT: Yale University Press.

Hayles, N. K. (1999). *How we became posthuman: Virtual bodies in cybernetics, literature, and informatics.* Chicago: University of Chicago Press.

Hayles, N. K. (2005). *My mother was a computer: Digital subjects and literary texts.* Chicago: University of Chicago Press.

Haynes, A. (2008). A quiet awakening: Spinning yarns from granny's table in the rural south. In M. F. He & J. Phillion (Eds.), *Personal-passionate-participatory inquiry into social justice education* (pp. 127–143). Charlotte, NC: Information Age Publishing, Inc.

Haynes, F. (2001). Introduction. In F. Haynes & T. McKenna (Eds.), *Unseen genders: Beyond the binaries* (pp. 1–16). New York: Peter Lang.

Haynes, F., & McKenna, T. (Eds.). (2001). *Unseen genders: Beyond the binaries.* New York: Peter Lang.

Hayot, E. (2014). *The elements of style: Writing for the humanities.* New York: Columbia University Press.

He, M. F. (2003). *A river forever flowing: Cross-cultural lives and identities in the multicultural landscape.* Greenwich, CT: Information Age.

He, M. F., & Phillion, J. (Eds.). (2008). *Personal~passionate~participatory inquiry into social justice education.* Charlotte, NC: Information Age.

He, M. F., Phillion, J., Chan, E., & Xu, S. (2008). Immigrant students' experience of curriculum. In M. F. Connelly, M. F. He, & J. Phillion (Eds.), *The Sage handbook of curriculum and instruction* (pp. 219–239). Los Angeles: Sage.

Heidegger, M. (1962). *Being and time* (J. Macquarrie & E. Robinson, Trans.). New York: Harper & Row.

Helbling, M. (2012). Islamophobia in the West: An introduction. In M. Helbling (Ed.), *Islamophobia in the West: Measuring and explaining individual attitudes* (pp. 1–18). New York: Routledge.

Henderson, L. (2007). Queer visibility and social class. In K. G. Barnhurst (Ed.), *Media: Media queered. Visibility and its discontents* (pp. 198–216). New York: Peter Lang.

Hendry, P. M. (2010). Response to Denise Taliaferro-Baszile: The self: A bricolage of curricular absence. In E. Malewski (Ed.), *Curriculum studies handbook: The next moment* (pp. 496–499). New York: Routledge.

Hendry, P. M. (2011). *Engendering curriculum history.* New York: Routledge.

Henke, S. A. (2000). *Shattered subjects: Trauma and testimony in women's life-writing.* New York: St. Martin's.

Henry, A. (2005). Black feminist pedagogy: Critiques and contributions. In W. H. Watkins (Ed.), *Black protest thought and education* (pp. 89–105). New York: Peter Lang.

Hill, D. (2007). *Hegemony and education: Gramsci, post-Marxism and radical democracy revisited.* Lanham, MD: Rowman & Littlefield.

Hinchey, P. H. (2008). *Action research: Primer.* New York: Peter Lang.

Hinitz, B. (2002). Margaret Naumburg and the Walden School. In A. R. Sadovnik & S. F. Semel (Eds.), *Founding mothers and others: Women educational leaders during the progressive era* (pp. 37–59). New York: Palgrave.

Hirsch, E. D., Jr. (1988). *Cultural literacy: What every American needs to know.* New York: Vintage.

Hlebowitsh, P. (2007). *Foundations of American education.* Dubuque, IA: Kendall/Hunt.

Hoare, Q. (2005). Introduction. In Q. Hoare & G. N. Smith (Eds.), *Antonio Gramsci: Selections from the prison notebooks* (pp. xvii–xcvi). New York: International.

Hofstadter, R. (1955). *The age of reform: From Bryan to F.D.R.* New York: Vintage.

Hofstadter, R. (1963). *Anti-intellectualism in American life.* New York: Vintage.

Hofstetter, M. F. (2001). *The romantic idea of a university: England and Germany, 1770–1850.* New York: Palgrave

Hollins, E. R. (2011). Beyond multicultural education. In C. A. Grant & T. K. Chapman (Eds.), *History of multicultural education: Conceptual frameworks and curricular issues* (pp. 64–68). New York: Routledge.

Horowitz, H. L. (1999). *The power and passion of M. Carey Thomas.* Chicago: University of Illinois Press.

Howard, A. (2008). *Learning privilege: Lessons of power and identity in affluent schooling.* New York: Routledge.

Huebner, D. E. (1999). *The lure of the transcendent: Collected essays by Dwayne E. Huebner* (V. Hillis, Ed., W. F. Pinar Collector). Mahwah, NJ: Lawrence Erlbaum.

Hunt, C. (2000). *Therapeutic dimensions of autobiography in creative writing.* London: Jessica Kingsley.

Jackson, P. W. (1998). *John Dewey and the lessons of art.* New Haven, CT: Yale University Press.

Jackson, P. W. (2002). *John Dewey and the philosopher's task.* New York: Teachers College Press.

Jacoby, R. (1997). *Social amnesia: A critique of contemporary psychology.* New Brunswick, NJ: Transaction.

James, S. M., Foster, F. S., & Guy-Sheftall, B. (Eds.). (2009). *Still brave: The evolution of black women's studies.* New York: Feminist.

James, W. (1998). *Pragmatism and the meaning of truth.* Cambridge, MA: Harvard University Press.

Jardine, D. W. (1998). *To dwell with a boundless heart: Essays in curriculum theory, hermeneutics, and the ecological imagination.* New York: Peter Lang.

Jardine, D. W. (1999). A bell ringing in the empty sky. In W. F. Pinar (Ed.), *Contemporary curriculum discourses: Twenty years of JCT* (pp. 262–277). New York: Peter Lang.

Jardine, D. W., Friesen, S., & Clifford, P. (2006). *Curriculum in abundance.* Mahwah, NJ: Lawrence Erlbaum.

Jefferson, S. (2008). Stitched from the soul: An auto/biographical inquiry of a black woman principal. In M. F. He & J. Phillion (Eds.), *Personal~passionate~participatory inquiry into social justice education* (pp. 23–36). Charlotte, NC: Information Age.

Jennings, J. (2004). Theorizing black studies: The continuing role of community service in the study of race and class. In J. Bobo, C. Hudley & C. Michel (Eds.), *The black studies reader* (pp. 35–40). New York: Routledge.

Jennings, M. (2006). Introduction. In W. Benjamin (Ed.), *The writer of modern life: Essays on Charles Baudelaire* (pp. 1–25). Cambridge, MA: Belknap/Harvard University Press.

Jewett, L. M. (2008). *A delicate dance: Autoethnography, curriculum, and the semblance of intimacy.* New York: Peter Lang.

Johnson, K. A. (2000). *Uplifting the women and the race: The educational philosophies of social activism of Anna Julia Cooper and Nannie Helen Burroughs.* New York: Garland.

Johnston, I. (2003). *Re-mapping literary worlds: Postcolonial pedagogy in practice.* New York: Peter Lang.

Jones, A. (2006). Sex, fear, and pedagogy: Sylvia Ashton-Warner's infant room. In J. P. Robertson & C. McConaghy (Eds.), *Provocations: Sylvia Ashton-Warner and excitability in education* (pp. 15–32). New York: Peter Lang.

Joseph, G. (1995). Black feminist pedagogy and schooling in capitalist white America. In B. Guy-Sheftall (Ed.), *Words of fire: An anthology of African-American feminist thought* (pp. 462–471). New York: New.

Kammen, M. (1990). *People of paradox: An inquiry concerning the origins of American civilization.* Ithaca, NY: Cornell University Press.

Kellner, D. (2008). *Guys and guns amok: Domestic terrorism and school shootings from the Oklahoma City bombing to the Virginia Tech massacre.* Boulder, CO: Paradigm.

Kent, S. K. (2006). Mistrals and diatribulations: A reply to Joan Huff. In S. Morgan (Ed.), *The feminist history reader* (pp. 184–188). New York: Routledge.

Kimmel, M. (2002). Foreword. In J. K. Gardiner (Ed.), *Masculinity studies & feminist theory: New directions* (pp. ix–xi). New York: Columbia University Press.

Kimmel, M. (2006). *Manhood in America: A cultural history.* New York: Oxford University Press.

Kincheloe, J. L. (2004). Introduction. In J. L. Kincheloe & S. R. Steinberg (Eds.), *The miseducation of the West: How schools and the media distort our understanding of the Islamic world* (pp. 1–23). Westport, CT: Praeger.

Kincheloe, J. L. (2005). Introduction. In P. Freire, *Teachers as cultural workers: Letters to those who dare teach* (pp. xli–xlix). Boulder, CO: Westview.

Kincheloe, J. L. (2007a). City kids—not the kind of students you'd want to teach. In J. L. Kincheloe & K. Hayes (Eds.), *Teaching city kids: Understanding and appreciating them* (pp. 3–38). New York: Peter Lang.

Kincheloe, J. L. (2007b). Critical pedagogy in the twenty-first century: Evolution for survival. In P. McLaren & J. L. Kincheloe (Eds.), *Critical pedagogy: Where are we now?* (pp. 9–42). New York: Peter Lang.

Kincheloe, J. L. (2008). *Knowledge and critical pedagogy: An introduction.* New York: Springer.

Kincheloe, J. L., Slattery, P., & Steinberg, S. R. (2000). *Contextualizing teaching: Introduction to education and educational foundations.* New York: Longman.

Kincheloe, J. L., & Steinberg, S. R. (1997a). *Changing multiculturalism*. London: Open University Press.

Kincheloe, J. L., & Steinberg, S. R. (1997b). Who said it can't happen here? In J. L. Kincheloe, S. R. Steinberg, & A. Gresson (Eds.), *Measured lies: The bell curve examined* (pp. 3–47). New York: St. Martin's.

Kincheloe, J. L., & Steinberg, S. R. (1999). A tentative description of post-formal thinking: The critical confrontation with cognitive theory. In J. L. Kincheloe, S. R. Steinberg, & P. H. Hinchey (Eds.), *The post-formal reader* (pp. 55–90). New York: Routledge.

Kincheloe, J. L., & Steinberg, S. R. (2000). Constructing a pedagogy of whiteness for angry white students. In N. M. Rodriguez & L. E. Villaverde (Eds.), *Dismantling whiteness: Pedagogy, politics and whiteness* (pp. 178–197). New York: Peter Lang.

Kincheloe, J. L., & Steinberg, S. R. (2004). *The miseducation of the west. How schools and the media distort our understanding of the Islamic world*. New York: Praeger.

Kincheloe, J. L., & Steinberg, S. R. (2010). Why teach against Islamophobia? Striking the empire back. In J. L. Kincheloe, S. R. Steinberg, & C. D. Stonebanks (Eds.), *Teaching against Islamophobia* (pp. 3–27). New York: Peter Lang.

Kincheloe, J. L., Steinberg, S. R., & Hinchey, P. H. (Eds.). (1999). *The post-formal reader: Cognition and education*. New York: Falmer.

Kincheloe, J. L., Steinberg, S. R., & Stonebanks, C. (Eds.). (2010). *Teaching against Islamophobia*. New York: Peter Lang.

King, J. E. (2005). A transformative vision of black education for human freedom. In J. E. King (Ed.), *Black education: A transformative research and action agenda for the new century* (pp. 3–17). Mahwah, NJ: Lawrence Erlbaum.

Klein, M. (1940/1975). *Love, guilt and reparation and other works 1921–1945*. New York: Delacorte/Seymoure Lawrence.

Klein, M. (1946/1984). *Envy and gratitude and other works, 1946–1963*. New York: Free.

Klein, N. (2007). *The shock doctrine: The rise of disaster capitalism*. New York: Picador.

Kliebard, H. M. (1995). *The struggle for the American curriculum, 1893–1958*. New York: Routledge.

Kliebard, H. M. (1999). *Schooled to work: Vocationalism and the American curriculum, 1876–1946*. New York: Teachers College Press.

Kliebard, H. M. (2002). *Changing course: American curriculum reform in the 20th century*. New York: Teachers College Press.

Klinkenborg, V. (2013). *Several short sentences about writing*. New York: Vintage.

Klohr, P. (1996). Laura Zirbes: A teacher of teachers. In C. Kridel, R. V. Bullough Jr., & P. Shaker (Eds.), *Teachers and mentors: Profiles of distinguished twentieth-century professors of education* (pp. 139–145). New York: Garland.

Kohli, W. (1998). A situated philosopher. In W. F. Pinar (Ed.), *The passionate mind of Maxine Greene: 'I am...not yet'* (pp. 180–189). New York: Falmer.

Kohn, J. (1994). Introduction. In H. Arendt, *Essays in understanding, 1930–1954: Formation, exile, and totalitarianism* (pp. ix–xxxi). New York: Schocken.

Krall, F. R. (1999). Living metaphors: The real curriculum in environmental education. In W. F. Pinar (Ed.), *Contemporary curriculum discourses: Twenty years of JCT* (pp. 1–6). New York: Peter Lang.

Kridel, C. (1998). *Writing educational biography: Explorations in qualitative research.* New York: Garland.

Kridel, C. (Ed.). (2010). *Encyclopedia of curriculum studies.* Los Angeles: Sage.

Kridel, C., & Bullough, R. V., Jr. (2007). *Stories of the Eight-Year Study: Re-examining secondary education in America.* Albany, NY: SUNY.

Kridel, C., Bullough, R. V., Jr., & Shaker, P. (Eds.). (1996). *Teachers and mentors: Profiles of distinguished twentieth-century professors of education.* New York: Garland.

Kridel, C., & Newman, V. (2003). A random harvest: A multiplicity of studies in American curriculum history research. In W. F. Pinar (Ed.), *International handbook of curriculum research* (pp. 637–650). Mahwah, NJ: Lawrence Erlbaum.

Kroll, C. (2008). Imagining ourselves into transcultural spaces: Decentering whiteness in the classroom. In V. Lea & E. J. Sims (Eds.), *Undoing whiteness in the classroom: Critical educultural teaching approaches for social justice activism* (pp. 29–46). New York: Peter Lang.

Kumar, A. (Ed.). (1999). *Poetics/politics: Radical aesthetics for the classroom.* New York: St. Martin's Press.

LaCapra, D. (2000). *History and reading: Tocqueville, Foucault, French studies.* Toronto: University of Toronto Press.

LaCapra, D. (2001). *Writing history, writing trauma.* Baltimore: Johns Hopkins University Press.

Lagemann, E. C. (2000). *An elusive science: The troubling history of educational research.* Chicago: University of Chicago Press.

Laidlaw, L. (2005). *Reinventing curriculum: A complex perspective on literacy and writing.* Mahwah, NJ: Lawrence Erlbaum.

Laplanche, J. (1999). *Essays on otherness.* New York: Routledge.

Laquer, W. (1996). *Fascism past, present, future.* New York: Oxford University Press.

Lather, P. (2004). Applied Derrida: (Mis)reading the work of mourning in educational research. In P. P. Trifonas & M. A. Peters (Eds.), *Derrida, deconstruction and education: Ethics of pedagogy and research* (pp. 3–16). Malden, MA: Blackwell.

Lather, P. (2010). Response to Jennifer Gilbert: The double trouble of passing on curriculum studies. In E. Malewski (Ed.), *Curriculum studies handbook: The next moment.* New York: Routledge.

Lather, P., & Smithies, C. (1997). *Troubling the angels: Women living with HIV/AIDS.* Boulder, CO: Westview.

Lea, V., & Sims, E. J. (2008). Undoing whiteness in the classroom: Different origins, shared commitment. In V. Lea & E. J. Sims (Eds.), *Undoing whiteness in the classroom: Critical educultural teaching approaches for social justice activism* (pp. 1–28). New York: Peter Lang.

Lean, N. (2012). *The Islamophobia industry: How the right manufactures fear of Muslims.* London: Pluto.

Leggo, C. (2005). The heart of pedagogy: On poetic knowing and living. *Teachers and Teaching: Theory and Practice, 11*(5), 439–455.

Leistyna, P. (2007). No corporation left behind. In K. J. Saltman (Ed.), *Schooling and the politics of disaster* (pp. 141–157). New York: Routledge.

Le Rider, J. (1993). *Modernity and crises of identity: Culture and society in fin-de-siècle Vienna* (R. Morris, Trans.). New York: Continuum.

Lesko, N. (1998). Feeling the teacher: A phenomenological reflection on Maxine Greene's pedagogy. In W. F. Pinar (Ed.) *The passionate mind of Maxine Greene: 'I am...not yet'* (pp. 238–246). London: Falmer.

Letts, W., & Sears, J. T. (Eds.). (1999). *Queering elementary education: Advancing the dialogue about sexualities and schooling.* Lanham, MD: Rowman & Littlefield.

Levinas, E. (2001). *Existence & existents* (A. Lingis, Trans.). Pittsburgh, PA: Duquesne University Press.

Lewis, B. (2010). A mad fight: Psychiatry and disability activism. In L. J. Davis (Ed.), *The disability studies reader* (pp. 160–176). New York: Routledge.

Li, X. (2002). *The Tao of life stories: Chinese language, poetry and culture in education.* New York: Peter Lang.

Lipman, P. (2003). Cracking down: Chicago school policy, and the regulation of black and Latino youth. In K. J. Saltman & D. Gabbard (Eds.), *Education as enforcement: The militarization and corporatization of schools* (pp. 81–101). New York: RoutledgeFalmer.

Lipman, P. (2007). Feasting on disaster: Urban school policy, globalization and the politics of disaster. In K. J. Saltman (Ed.), *Schooling and the politics of disaster* (pp. 87–99). New York: Routledge.

Littleford, M. S. (1999). Curriculum theorizing and the possibilities and conditions for social action: Toward democratic community and education. In W. F. Pinar (Ed.), *Contemporary curriculum discourses: Twenty years of JCT* (pp. 114–127). New York: Peter Lang.

Longmore, P. K., & Umansky, L. (2001). Disability history: From the margins to the mainstream. In P. K. Longmore & L. Umansky (Eds.), *The new disability history: American perspectives* (pp. 1–29). New York: New York University Press.

Lorde, A. (1997). *The cancer journals.* San Francisco: Aunt Lute.

Luce-Kapler, R. (2004). *Writing with, through, and beyond the text: An ecology of language.* Mahwah, NJ: Lawrence Erlbaum.

Luhmann, S. (1998). Queering/querying pedagogy? Or, pedagogy is a pretty queer thing. In W. F. Pinar (Ed.), *Queer theory in education* (pp. 141–156). Mahwah, NJ: Lawrence Erlbaum.

Macdonald, J. B. (1995). *Theory as a prayerful act: The collected essays of James B. Macdonald* (B. J. Macdonald, Ed.). New York: Peter Lang.

Macedo, D. (2006). *Literacies of power: What Americans are allowed to know.* Cambridge, MA: Westview.

Macedo, D., & Freire, A. M. A. (2005). Foreword. In P. Freire, *Teachers as cultural workers: Letters to those who dare teach* (pp. vii–xxvi). Cambridge, MA: Westview.

Macrine, S. L. (2003). Imprisoning minds: The violence of neoliberal education or "I am not for sale!" In K. Saltman & D. Gabbard (Eds.), *Education as enforcement: The militarization and corporatization of schools* (pp. 203–212). New York: RoutledgeFalmer.

Malewski, E. (Ed.). (2010). *Curriculum studies handbook: The next moment.* New York: Routledge.

Malpas, J. E. (2007). *Place and experience: A philosophical topography*. New York: Cambridge University Press.

Manguel, A. (1996). *A history of reading*. New York: Penguin.

Manguel, A. (2006). *The library at night*. New Haven, CT: Yale University Press.

Manguel, A. (2010). *A reader on reading*. New Haven, CT: Yale University Press.

Marable, M. (2002). *The great wells of democracy: The meaning of race in American life*. New York: Basic.

Marcus, L. (1994). *Auto/biographical discourses: Theory, criticism, practice*. New York: Manchester University Press.

Marcus, L. (Ed.). (1999). *Sigmund Freud's The Interpretation of Dreams: New interdisciplinary essays*. Manchester, UK: Manchester University Press.

Marsh, C. J., & Willis, G. (2007). *Curriculum: Alternative approaches, ongoing issues*. Upper Saddle River, NJ: Pearson/Merrill Prentice Hall.

Marshall, J. D., Sears, J. T., Allen, L. A., Roberts, P. A., & Schubert, W. H. (2007). *Turning points in curriculum: A contemporary American memoir*. Upper Saddle River, NJ: Pearson/Merrill Prentice Hall.

Martin, J. (2002). *The education of John Dewey: A biography*. New York: Columbia University Press.

Martinez, G. A. (2011). African Americans, Latinos and the construction of race: Toward an epistemic condition. In R. Delgado & J. Stefancic (Eds.), *The Latina/o condition: A critical reader* (pp. 481–483). New York: New York University Press.

Marx, K. (1978). *The Marx-Engels reader* (R. C. Tucker, Ed.). New York: W. W. Norton.

May, S., & Sleeter, C. E. (2010). *Critical multiculturalism: Theory and praxis* (pp. 1–16). New York: Routledge.

May, V. M. (2007). *Anna Julia Cooper, visionary black feminist*. New York: Routledge.

Mayo, P. (2004). *Liberating praxis: Paulo Freire's legacy for radical education and politics*. Westport, CT: Praeger.

McCarthy, C. (1995). The problem with origins: Race and the contrapuntal nature of the educational experience. In C. E. Sleeter & P. L. McLaren (Eds.), *Multicultural education, critical pedagogy, and the politics of difference* (pp. 245–268). Albany, NY: SUNY.

McCarthy, C. (1998a). The uses of culture: Canon formation, postcolonial literature, and the multicultural project. In W. F. Pinar (Ed.), *Curriculum: Toward new identities* (pp. 253–262). New York: Garland.

McCarthy, C. (1998b). *The uses of culture: Education and the limits of ethnic affiliation*. New York: Routledge.

McCarthy, C. (1999). The palace of the peacock: Wilson Harris and the curriculum in troubled times. In W. F. Pinar (Ed.), *Contemporary curriculum discourses: Twenty years of JCT* (pp. 364–378). New York: Peter Lang.

McCarthy, C. (2011). Multicultural approaches to racial inequality in the United States. In C. A. Grant & T. K. Chapman (Eds.), *History of multicultural education: Vol. 1: Conceptual frameworks and curricular issues* (pp. 49–63). New York: Routledge.

McCarthy, C., Crichlow, W., Dimitriadis, G., & Dolby, N. (2005). Introduction: Transforming contexts, transforming identities: Race and education in the new millennium. In

C. McCarthy & W. Crichlow (Eds.), *Race, identity and representation in education* (pp. xv–xxvii). New York: Taylor & Francis.

McCluskey, A. T. (1999). Introduction. In A. T. McCluskey & E. M. Smith (Eds.), *Mary McLeod Bethune: Building a better world. Essays and selected documents* (pp. 3–19). Bloomington: Indiana University Press.

McConaghy, C. (2006). Teaching's intimacies. In J. P. Robertson & C. McConaghy (Eds.), *Provocations: Sylvia Ashton-Warner and excitability in education* (pp. 63–94). New York: Peter Lang.

McConaghy, C., & Robertson, J. P. (2006). Sylvia Ashton-Warner: Reading provocatively from subject to theory. In J. P. Robertson & C. McConaghy (Eds.), *Provocations: Sylvia Ashton-Warner and excitability in education* (pp. 1–14). New York: Peter Lang.

McFarland, G. W. (2001). *Inside Greenwich Village: A New York City neighborhood, 1898–1918.* Amherst: University of Massachusetts Press.

McGerr, M. (2003). *A fierce discontent: The rise and fall of the progressive movement in America.* New York: Oxford University Press.

McKnight, D. (2003). *Schooling, the Puritan imperative, and the molding of an American national identity: Education's errand into the wilderness.* Mahwah, NJ: Lawrence Erlbaum.

McLaren, P. (1997). *Revolutionary multiculturalism: Pedagogies of dissent for the new millennium.* Boulder, CO: Westview.

McLaren, P. (2000). *Che Guevara, Paulo Freire, and the pedagogy of revolution.* Boulder, CO: Rowman & Littlefield.

McLaren, P. (2005). *Capitalists & conquerors: A critical pedagogy against empire.* Boulder, CO: Rowman & Littlefield.

McLaren, P. (2006). *Rage and hope: Interviews with Peter McLaren on war, imperialism, and critical pedagogy.* New York: Peter Lang.

Mead, G. H. (1964). The social self. In A. J. Reck (Ed.), *Selected writings: George Herbert Mead* (pp. 142–149). Chicago: University of Chicago Press.

Meiners, E. (1998). Remember when all the cars were Fords and all the lesbians were women? Some notes on identity, mobility, and capital. In W. F. Pinar (Ed.), *Queer theory in education* (pp. 121–140). Mahwah, NJ: Lawrence Erlbaum.

Michie, G. (2009). *Holler if you hear me: The education of a teacher and his students.* New York: Teachers College Press.

Middleton, S. (2006). "I am my own professor": Sylvia Ashton-Warner as New Zealand educational theorist 1940–60. In J. P. Robertson & C. McConaghy (Eds.), *Provocations: Sylvia Ashton-Warner and excitability in education* (pp. 33–62). New York: Peter Lang.

Middleton, S., & Weiler, K. (1999). Introduction. In K. Weiler & S. Middleton (Eds.), *Telling women's lives: Narrative inquiries in the history of women's education* (pp. 1–6). Buckingham: Open University Press.

Milkis, S. M. (2009). *Theodore Roosevelt, the progressive party, and the transformation of American democracy.* Lawrence: University of Kansas Press.

Miller, J. (1999). Women: The evolving educational consciousness. In W. F. Pinar (Ed.), *Contemporary curriculum discourses: Twenty years of JCT* (pp. 31–41). New York: Peter Lang.

Miller, J. (2005). *Sounds of silence breaking: Women, autobiography, curriculum*. New York: Peter Lang.

Miller, J. (2010). Response to Ruben A. Gaztambide-Fernandez: Communities without consensus. In E. Malewski (Ed.), *Curriculum studies handbook: The next moment* (pp. 95–100). New York: Routledge.

Mitchell, T. (2000). Turning points: Reconstruction and the growth of national influence in education. In L. Cuban & D. Shipps (Eds.), *Reconstructing the common good in education: Coping with intractable American dilemmas* (pp. 32–50). Stanford, CA: Stanford University Press.

Molino, A. (Ed.). (1997). Christopher Bollas. In *Elaborate selves: Reflections and reveries of Christopher Bollas, Michael Eigen, Polly Young-Eisendrath, Samuel and Evelyn Laeuchli, Marie Coleman Nelson* (pp. 11–60). New York: Hawthorne.

Moraga, C. (2000). An interview with cherric Moraga: Queen reservations; or, Art, identity, and politics in the 1991s. IN, J. A. Boone, M. Dupuis, M. Meeker, K. Quimbly, C. Sarrer., D. Silverman & R. Weatherston (Eds.), Queen frontiers: Millennial geographies, genders, and generations (pp.64–83) Massm, WI: The University of Wiseinsin.

Morgan, P. J. (2006). Recognizing the enemy. In R. Griffin, W. Loh, & A. Umland (Eds.), *Fascism past and present, West and East: An international debate on concepts and cases in the comparative study of the extreme right* (pp. 156–160). Stuttgart: Ibidem-Verlag.

Morgan, S. (2006). Introduction: Writing feminist history: Theoretical debates and critical practices. In S. Morgan (Ed.), *The feminist history reader* (pp. 1–48). New York: Routledge.

Morris, M. (1998). Existential and phenomenological influences on Maxine Greene. In W. F. Pinar (Ed.), *The passionate mind of Maxine Greene: 'I am...not yet'* (pp. 124–136). New York: Falmer.

Morris, M. (2001). *Curriculum and the Holocaust: Competing sites of memory and representation*. Mahwah, NJ: Lawrence Erlbaum.

Morris, M. (2002a) Curriculum theory as academic responsibility: The call for reading Heidegger contextually. In M. Morris & J. A. Weaver (Eds.), *Difficult memories: Talk in a (post) Holocaust era* (pp. 227–247). New York: Peter Lang.

Morris, M. (2002b). Young man Popkin. In G. Anzaldúa & A. Keating (Eds.), *This bridge we call home: Radical visions for transformation* (pp. 137–144). New York: Routledge.

Morris, M. (2006). *Jewish intellectuals and the university*. New York: Palgrave Macmillan.

Morris, M. (2008). *Teaching through the ill body: A spiritual and aesthetic approach to pedagogy and illness*. Rotterdam: Sense.

Morris, M. (2009). *On not being able to play: Scholars, musicians and the crisis of psyche*. Rotterdam: Sense.

Morris, M., Doll, M. A., & Pinar, W. F. (Eds.). (1999). *How we work*. New York: Peter Lang.

Morris, M., & Weaver, J. (Eds.). (2002). *Difficult memories: Talk in a (post)Holocaust era*. New York: Peter Lang.

Morrison, T. (1993). *Playing in the dark: Whiteness and the literary imagination*. New York: Vintage.

Munro, P. (1998a). Engendering curriculum history. In W. F. Pinar (Ed.), *Curriculum: Toward new identities* (pp. 263–294). New York: Garland.

Munro, P. (1998b). *Subject to fiction: Women teachers' life history narratives and the cultural politics of resistance*. Buckingham: Open University Press.

Munro, P. (1999). Political activism as teaching: Jane Addams and Ida B. Wells. In M. S. Crocco, P. Munro, & K. Weiler (Eds.), *Pedagogies of resistance: Women educator activists, 1880–1960* (pp. 19–45). New York: Teachers College Press.

Musil, R. (1979). *The man without qualities* (E. Kaiser, Trans.). London: Secker & Warburg.

Naber, N. (2008). Introduction: Arab Americans and U.S. racial formations. In A. Jamal & N. Naber (Eds.), *Race and Arab Americans before and after 9/11: From invisible citizens to visible subjects* (pp. 1–45). New York: Syracuse University Press.

Nash, R. J. (2004). *Liberating scholarly writing: The power of personal narrative*. New York: Teachers College Press.

Naumburg, M. (1953). *Psychoneurotic art: Its function in psychotherapy*. New York: Grune & Stratton.

Naumburg, M. (1987). *Dynamically oriented art therapy: Its principles and practice*. Chicago: Magnolia Street.

Newman, J. W. (2006). Experimental school: Experimental community: The Marietta Johnson School of Organic Education in Fairhope, Alabama. In S. F. Semel & A. R. Sadovnik (Eds.), *"Schools of tomorrow," schools of today: What happened to progressive education?* (pp. 67–101). New York: Peter Lang.

Nguyen, T. (2005). *We are all suspects now: Untold stories from immigrant communities after 9/11*. Boston: Beacon.

Nidiffer, J. (2003). From whence they came: The contexts, challenges, and courage of early women administrators in higher education. In B. Ropers-Huilman (Ed.), *Gendered futures in higher education: Critical perspectives for change* (pp. 15–34). Albany, NY: SUNY.

Nieto, S. (2011). Multicultural education in the United States: Historical realities, ongoing challenges, and transformative possibilities. In J. A. Banks (Ed.), *The Routledge international companion to multicultural education* (pp. 79–95). New York: Routledge.

Nietzsche, F. (1967). *The genealogy of morals: Ecce homo*. New York: Vintage.

Novoa, A. (2001). Texts, images, and memories: Writing "new" histories of education. In T. S. Popkewitz, B. M. Franklin, & M. A. Pereyra (Eds.), *Cultural history and education: Critical essays on knowledge and schooling* (pp. 45–66). New York: RoutledgeFalmer.

Null, J. W. (2007). *Peerless educator: The life and work of Isaac Leon Kandel*. New York: Peter Lang.

Nussbaum, M. C. (1995). *Poetic justice: The literary imagination and public life*. Boston: Beacon.

Nye, A. (1994). *Philosophia: The thought of Rosa Luxemburg, Simone Weil, and Hannah Arendt*. New York: Routledge.

Olney, J. (1998). *Memory-narrative: The weave of life-writing*. Chicago: University of Chicago Press.

Pagano, J. A. (1999). The curriculum field: Emergence of a discipline. In W. F. Pinar (Ed.), *Contemporary curriculum discourses: Twenty years of JCT* (pp. 82–105). New York: Peter Lang.

Page, R. N. (2009). Foreword. In E. C. Short & L. J. Waks (Eds.), *Leaders in curriculum studies: Intellectual self-portraits* (pp. ix–xvi). Rotterdam: Sense.

Paris Review. (2006). Truman Capote, The art of fiction. In *The Paris Review Interviews: Vol. 1*. New York: Picador.

Parkerson, D. H., & Parkerson, J. A. (2001). *Transitions in American education: A social history of teaching*. New York: RoutledgeFalmer.

Passmore, K. (2006). The essence of fascism. In R. Griffin, W. Loh, & A. Umland (Eds.), *Fascism past and present: West and East. An international debate on concepts and cases in the comparative study of the extreme right* (pp. 352–359). Stuttgart: Ibidem-Verlag.

Paxton, R. O. (2004). *The anatomy of fascism*. New York: Vintage.

Payne, S. G. (1995). *A history of fascism, 1914–1945*. Madison: University of Wisconsin Press.

Penny, D., & Stastny, P. (2008). *The lives they left behind: Suitcases from a state hospital attic*. New York: Bellevue Literary.

Perea, J. F. (2011). The black/white binary paradigm of race. In R. Delgado & J. Stefancic (Eds.), *The Latino/a condition: A critical reader* (pp. 335–342). New York: New York University Press.

Peters, M. A. (1996). *Poststructuralism, politics and education*. Westport, CT: Bergin & Garvey.

Peters, M. A. (2009). Introduction: Governmentality, education and the end of neoliberalism. In M. A. Peters, A. C. Besley, M. Olssen, S. Maurer, & S. Weber (Eds.), *Governmentality studies in education* (pp. xxvii–xlviii). Rotterdam: Sense.

Peters, M. A., Besley, A. C., Olssen, M., Maurer, S., & Weber, S. (Eds.). (2009). *Governmentality studies in education*. Rotterdam: Sense.

Peters, M. A., & Biesta, G. (2009). Introduction: The promise of politics and pedagogy. In M. A. Peters & G. Biesta (Eds.), *Derrida, deconstruction, and the politics of pedagogy* (pp. 1–13). New York: Peter Lang.

Peters, M. A., & Biesta, G. (Eds.). (2009). *Derrida, deconstruction, and the politics of pedagogy*. New York: Peter Lang.

Phillips, A. (2013). *One way and another: New and selected essays*. New York: Hamish Hamilton.

Pinar, W. F. (1994). *Autobiography, politics and sexuality: Essays in curriculum theory, 1972–1992*. New York: Peter Lang.

Pinar, W. F. (Ed.). (1998a). *Curriculum: Toward new identities*. New York: Garland.

Pinar, W. F. (Ed.). (1998b). *The passionate mind of Maxine Greene: 'I am…not yet'*. New York: Falmer.

Pinar, W. F. (1998c). Notes on the intellectual: In praise of Maxine Greene. In W. C. Ayers & J. L. Miller (Eds.), *A light in dark times: Maxine Greene and the unfinished conversation* (pp. 108–121). New York: Peter Lang.

Pinar, W. F. (Ed.). (1998d). *Queer theory in education* (pp. 1–47). Mahwah, NJ: Lawrence Erlbaum.

Pinar, W. F. (1999a). Introduction. In M. Morris, M. A. Doll, & W. F. Pinar (Eds.), *How we work* (pp. xiii–xvii). New York: Peter Lang.

Pinar, W. F. (Ed.). (1999b). *Contemporary curriculum discourses: Twenty years of JCT*. New York: Peter Lang.

Pinar, W. F. (2001). *The gender of racial politics and violence in America: Lynching, prison rape, & the crisis of masculinity*. New York: Peter Lang.

Pinar, W. F. (2002). Robert Musil and the crisis of European culture in America. In W. E. Doll Jr. & N. Gough (Eds.), *Curriculum visions* (pp. 102–110). New York: Peter Lang.

Pinar, W. F. (2004). *What is curriculum theory?* Mahwah, NJ: Lawrence Erlbaum.

Pinar, W. F. (2006). *Race, religion, and a curriculum of reparation: Teacher education for a multicultural society.* New York: Palgrave.

Pinar, W. F. (2007). *Intellectual advancement through disciplinarity: Verticality and horizontality in curriculum studies.* Rotterdam/Taipei: Sense.

Pinar, W. F. (2009a). The primacy of the particular. In E. C. Short & L. J. Waks (Eds.), *Leaders in curriculum studies: Intellectual self-portraits* (pp. 143–152). Rotterdam: Sense.

Pinar, W. F. (2009b). *The worldliness of a cosmopolitan education: Passionate lives in public service.* New York: Routledge. Taylor & Francis.

Pinar, W. F. (2010). The next moment. In E. Malewski (Ed.), *Curriculum studies handbook: The next moment* (pp. 528–533). New York: Routledge.

Pinar, W. F. (2012). *What is curriculum theory?* (2nd ed.). New York: Routledge.

Pinar, W. F., & Pautz, A. E. (1998). Construction scars: Autobiographical voice in biography. In C. Kridel (Ed.), *Writing educational biography: Explorations in qualitative research* (pp. 61–72). New York: Garland.

Pinar, W. F., Reynolds, W. M., Slattery, P., & Taubman, P. M. (1995). *Understanding curriculum: An introduction to the study of historical and contemporary discourses.* New York: Peter Lang.

Polsky, S. (2005). Down the K. hole: Walter Benjamin's destructive land-surveying of history. In A. Benjamin (Ed.), *Walter Benjamin and history* (pp. 69–87). New York: Continuum.

Popkewitz, T. (2001). The production of reason and power: Curriculum history and intellectual traditions. In T. Popkewitz, B. Franklin, & Miguel Pereyra (Eds.), *Cultural history and education: Critical essays on knowledge and schooling* (pp. 151–186). New York: Routledge-Falmer.

Popkewitz, T., & Brennan, M. (1998). Restructuring of social and political theory in education: Foucault and a social epistemology of school practices. In T. S. Popkewitz & M. Brennan (Eds.), *Foucault's challenge: Discourse, knowledge, and power in education* (pp. 3–35). New York: Teachers College Press.

Price, M. (2011). *Mad at school: Rhetorics of mental disability and academic life.* Ann Arbor: University of Michigan Press.

Ranciere, J. (1991). *The ignorant schoolmaster: Five lessons in intellectual emancipation* (K. Ross, Trans.). Stanford, CA: Stanford University Press.

Rasberry, G. W. (2001). *Writing research/researching writing: Through a poet's I.* New York: Peter Lang.

Rasmussen, M. L. (2006). *Becoming subjects: Sexualities and secondary schooling.* New York: Routledge.

Ravitch, D. (2001). *Left back: A century of battles over school reform.* New York: Touchstone/Simon & Schuster.

Readings, B. (1999). *The university in ruins.* Cambridge, MA: Harvard University Press.

Reese, W. J. (1999). Foreword. In H. M. Kliebard, *Schooled to work: Vocationalism and the American curriculum, 1874–1946* (pp. ix–xi). New York: Teachers College Press.

Reese, W. J. (2000). Public schools and the elusive search for the common good. In L. Cuban & D. Shipps (Eds.), *Reconstructing the common good in education: Coping with intractable American dilemmas* (pp. 13–31). Stanford, CA: Stanford University Press.

Reese, W. J. (2005). *America's public schools: From the common school to "no child left behind."* Baltimore: Johns Hopkins University Press.

Reynolds, K. C. (2002). Charlotte Hawkins Brown and the Palmer institute. In A. R. Sadovnik & S. F. Semel (Eds.), *Founding mothers and others: Women educational leaders during the progressive era* (pp. 7–17). New York: Palgrave.

Reynolds, W. M., & Webber, J. A. (Eds.). (2009). *Expanding curriculum theory: Dis/positions and lines of flight*. Mahwah, NJ: Lawrence Erlbaum.

Rich, A. (2013). *Diving into the wreck: Poems, 1971–1972*. New York: W.W. Norton.

Richards, S., & Lemelle, S. J. (2005). Pedagogy, politics, and power: Antinomies of the black radical tradition. In W. H. Watkins (Ed.), *Black protest thought and education* (pp. 5–31). New York: Peter Lang.

Rieser, A. C. (2003). *The Chautauqua movement: Protestants, progressives, and the culture of modern liberalism*. New York: Columbia University Press.

Rilke, R. M. (1995). *Ahead of all parting: The selected poetry and prose of Rainer Maria Rilke* (S. Mitchell, Ed. & Trans.). New York: Modern Library.

Rizvi, F. (2005). Representations of Islam and education for justice. In C. McCarthy, W. Crichlow, G. Dimitriadis, & N. Dolby (Eds.), *Race, identity, and representation in education* (pp. 167–178). New York: Routledge.

Robertson, J. P., & McConaghy, C. (Eds.) (2006). *Provocations: Sylvia Ashton-Warner and excitability in education*. New York: Peter Lang.

Robinson, S. (2002). Pedagogy of the opaque: Teaching masculinity studies. In J. K. Gardiner (Ed.), *Masculinity studies & feminist theory: New Directions* (pp. 141–160). New York: Columbia University Press.

Rodriguez, N. M. (1998). Emptying the content of whiteness: Toward an understanding of the relation between whiteness and pedagogy. In J. L. Kincheloe, S. R. Steinberg, N. M. Rodriguez, & R. E. Chennault (Eds.), *White reign: Deploying whiteness in America* (pp. 31–62). New York: St. Martin's Griffin.

Rodriguez, N. M. (2000). Projects of whiteness in a critical pedagogy. In N. M. Rodriguez & L. E. Villaverde (Eds.), *Dismantling white privilege: Pedagogy, politics, and whiteness* (pp. 1–24). New York: Peter Lang.

Rodriguez, N. M. (2007). Preface: Just queer it. In N. M. Rodriguez & W. F. Pinar (Eds.), *Queering straight teachers: Discourse and identity in education* (pp. vii–xiii). New York: Peter Lang.

Rodriguez, N. M., & Pinar, W. F. (Eds.). (2007). *Queering straight teachers: Discourse and identity in education*. New York: Peter Lang.

Roediger, D. (2005). Defending critical studies of whiteness but not whiteness studies. In M. Marable (Ed.), *The new black renaissance: The souls anthology of critical African-American studies* (pp. 218–220). Boulder, CO: Paradigm.

Rosenberg, S. (2000). Standing in a circle of stone: Rupturing the binds of emblematic memory. In R. I. Simon, S. Rosenberg, & C. Eppert (Eds.), *Between hope & despair: Pedagogy and the remembrance of historical trauma* (pp. 75–89). New York: Rowman & Littlefield.

Ross, E. W. (2004). General editor's introduction: Defending public schools, defending democracy. In D. A. Gabbard & E. W. Ross (Eds.), *Education under the security state* (pp. xi–xviii). New York: Teachers College Press.

Roulstone, A., Thomas, C., & Watson, N. (2012). The changing terrain of disability studies. In N. Watson, A. Roulstone, & C. Thomas (Eds.), *Routledge handbook of disability studies* (pp. 3–11). New York: Routledge.

Rousmaniere, K. (1999). Where Haley stood: Margaret Haley, teacher's work, and the problem of teacher identity. In K. Weiler & S. Middleton (Eds.), *Telling women's lives: Narrative inquiries in the history of women's education* (pp. 147–161). Buckingham: Open University Press.

Roy, K. (2003). *Teachers in nomadic space: Deleuze and curriculum.* New York: Peter Lang.

Roy, K. (2008). *Neighborhoods of the plantation: War, politics and education.* Rotterdam: Sense.

Royce, J. (1951). The nature of community. In M. H. Fisch (Ed.), *Classic American philosophers* (pp. 200–211). Englewood Cliffs, NJ: Prentice-Hall.

Sadovnik A. R., & Semel, S. F. (Eds.). (2002). *Founding mothers and others: Women educational leaders during the progressive era.* New York: Palgrave.

Sallis, J. (2006). *Topographies.* Bloomington: Indiana University Press.

Saltman, K. J. (2003). Introduction. In K. J. Saltman & D. Gabbard (Eds.), *Education as enforcement: The militarization and corporatization of schools* (pp. 1–23). New York: RoutledgeFalmer.

Saltman, K. J. (Ed.). (2007). *Schooling and the politics of disaster.* New York: Routledge.

Saltman, K. J., & Gabbard, D. (Eds.). (2003). *Education as enforcement: The militarization and corporatization of schools.* New York: RoutledgeFalmer.

Salvio, P. M. (2007). *Anne Sexton: Teacher of weird abundance.* Albany, NY: SUNY.

Scambler, S. (2012). Long-term disabling conditions and disability theory. In N. Watson, A. Roulstone, & C. Thomas (Eds.), *Routledge handbook of disability studies* (pp. 136–150). New York: Routledge.

Schiedeck, J., & Stahlmann, M. (1997). Totalizing experience: Educational camps. In H. Sunker & H.-U. Otto (Eds.), *Education and fascism: Political identity and social education in Nazi Germany* (pp. 54–80). London: Falmer.

Schubert, W. H. (2009a). *Love, justice, and education: John Dewey and the utopians.* Charlotte, NC: Information Age.

Schubert, W. H. (2009b). What's worthwhile? Playing with ideas in loving company. In E. C. Short & L. J. Waks (Eds.), *Leaders in curriculum studies: Intellectual self-portraits* (pp. 165–177). Rotterdam: Sense.

Schubert, W. H., Schubert, A. L. L., Thomas, T. P., & Carroll, W. M. (2002). *Curriculum books: The first hundred years* (2nd ed.). New York: Peter Lang.

Schultz, B. (2008). *Spectacular things happen along the way: Lessons from an urban classroom.* New York: Teachers College Press.

Scott, J. W. (1999). *Gender and the politics of history* (Rev. ed.). New York: Columbia University Press.

Scott-Simmons, W. (2008). Self, others, and jump rope communities: Oral history of the triumphs of African American women. In M. F. He & J. A. Phillion (Eds.), *Personal–*

passionate-participatory inquiry into social justice in education (pp. 71–91). Charlotte, NC: Information Age.

Scully, J. L. (2012). Deaf identities in disability studies: With or without us? In N. Watson, A. Roulstone, & C. Thomas (Eds.), *Routledge handbook of disability studies* (pp. 109–121). New York: Routledge.

Searles, H. F. (2005). *Collected papers on schizophrenia and related subjects*. London: Karnac.

Sears, J. T. (1999). Teaching queerly: Some elementary propositions. In W. J. Letts IV & J. T. Sears (Eds.), *Queering elementary education: Advancing dialogue about sexualities and schooling* (pp. 3–14). Lanham, MD: Rowman & Littlefield.

Sedgwick, E. K., Barber, S. M., & Clark, D. L. (2002). This piercing bouquet. An interview with Eve Kosofsky Sedgwick. In S. M. Barber & D. L. Clark (Eds.), *Regarding Sedgwick: Essays on queer culture and critical theory* (pp. 243–262). New York: Routledge.

Sedgwick, E. K. (2003). *Touching, feeling: Affect, pedagogy, performativity*. Durham, NC: Duke University Press.

Segal, H. (2000). *Dream, phantasy and art*. London: Routledge.

Seidman, S. (Ed.). (1997). *Queer theory: Sociology*. Malden, MA: Blackwell.

Selden, S. (1999). *Inheriting shame: The story of eugenics and racism in America*. New York: Teachers College Press.

Semali, L. (1998). Perspectives of the curriculum of whiteness. In J. L. Kincheloe, S. R. Steinberg, N. M. Rodriguez, & R. E. Chennault (Eds.), *White reign: Deploying whiteness in America* (pp. 177–190). New York: St. Martin's Griffin.

Serres, M. (1995). *Genesis* (G. James & J. Nielson, Trans.). Ann Arbor: University of Michigan Press.

Serres, M. (2000). *The troubadour of knowledge* (S. F. Glaser & W. Paulson, Trans.). Ann Arbor: University of Michigan Press.

Shakespeare, T. (2010). The social model of disability. In L. J. Davis (Ed.), *The disability studies reader* (pp. 266–273). New York: Routledge.

Shanks, M. (1991). *Experiencing the past: On the character of archaeology*. New York: Routledge.

Shildrick, M. (2012). Critical disability studies: Rethinking the conventions for the age of postmodernity. In N. Watson, A. Roulstone, & C. Thomas (Eds.), *Routledge handbook of disability studies* (pp. 30–41). New York: Routledge.

Short, E. C., & Waks, L. J. (2009). *Leaders in curriculum studies: Intellectual self-portraits*. Rotterdam: Sense.

Siebers, T. (2008). *Disability theory*. Ann Arbor: University of Michigan Press.

Simon, R. I. (2005). *The touch of the past: Remembrance, learning, and ethics*. New York: Palgrave Macmillan.

Simon, R. I., Rosenberg, S., & Eppert, C. (Eds.). (2000). *Between hope and despair: Pedagogy and the remembrance of historical trauma*. New York: Rowman & Littlefield.

Sleeter, C. E. (1997). Foreword. In L. D. Soto, *Language, culture, and power: Bilingual families and the struggle for quality education* (pp. ix–xiii). Albany, NY: SUNY.

Sleeter, C. E., & McLaren, P. L. (Eds.). (1995). *Multicultural education, critical pedagogy and the politics of difference*. Albany, NY: SUNY.

Smith, B. (1995). Some home truths on the contemporary black feminist movement. In B. Guy-Sheftall (Ed.), *Words of fire: An anthology of African-American feminist thought* (pp. 255–267). New York: New.

Smith, D. G. (1999). Identity, self, and other in the conduct of pedagogical action: An East/West inquiry. In W. Pinar (Ed.), *Contemporary curriculum discourses: Twenty years of JCT* (pp. 458–473). New York: Peter Lang.

Smith, J. S. (2006). *Building new deal liberalism: The political economy of public works, 1933–1956*. New York: Cambridge University Press.

Soto, L. D. (1997). *Language, culture, and power: Bilingual families and the struggle for quality education*. Albany, NY: SUNY.

Soto, L. D. (Ed.). (2005). *The politics of early childhood education*. New York: Peter Lang.

Soto, L. D. (2011). *Latina/o hope*. New York: Springer.

Soto, L. D., & Kharem, H. (2010). Engaging the world of teacher preparation on behalf of bilingual/bicultural learners. In L. D. Soto & H. Kharem (Eds.), *Teaching bilingual/bicultural children: Teachers talk about language and learning* (pp. 7–18). New York: Peter Lang.

Soucy, R. J. (2006). What is meant by "revolutionary" fascism? In R. Griffin, W. Loh, & A. Umland (Eds.), *Fascism past and present, West and East: An international debate on concepts and cases in the comparative study of the extreme right* (pp. 212–218). Stuttgart: Ibidem-Verlag.

Southern, D. W. (2005). *The progressive era and race: Reaction and reform, 1900–1917*. Wheeling, IL: Harlan Davidson.

Spring, J. (2010). *American education*. New York: McGraw-Hill.

Stack, S., Jr. (2004). *Elsie Ripley Clapp (1879–1965): Her life and the community school*. New York: Peter Lang.

Steinberg, S. R. (1997). The bitch who has everything. In S. R. Steinberg & J. L. Kincheloe (Eds.), *Kinderculture: The corporate construction of childhood* (pp. 207–218). Boulder, CO: Westview.

Steinberg, S. R. (1999). Early education as a gendered construction. In W. F. Pinar (Ed.), *Contemporary curriculum discourses: Twenty years of JCT* (pp. 474–482). New York: Peter Lang.

Steinberg, S. R. (2000). Preface: Getting here. In S. Talburt & S. Steinberg (Eds.), *Thinking queer: Sexuality, culture and education*. New York: Peter Lang.

Steinberg, S. R. (2007). Where are we now? In P. McLaren & J. L. Kincheloe (Eds.), *Critical pedagogy: Where are we now?* (pp. ix–x). New York: Peter Lang.

Steinberg, S. R. (2009). Diversity? Multiculturalism? Moving tolerance and tokenism to a critical level. In S. R. Steinberg (Ed.), *Diversity and multiculturalism: A reader* (pp. xi–xiii). New York: Peter Lang.

Steinberg, S. R., & Kincheloe, J. L. (2009). Smoke and mirrors: More than one way to be diverse and multicultural. In S. R. Steinberg (Ed.), *Diversity and multiculturalism: A reader* (pp. 3–22). New York: Peter Lang.

Stonebanks, C. (2004). Consequences of perceived ethnic identities. In J. L. Kincheloe & S. R. Steinberg (Eds.), *The miseducation of the West: How schools and the media distort our understanding of the Islamic world* (pp. 87–102). Westport, CT: Praeger.

St. Pierre, E. A. (2000). Inquiry among the ruins. In E. A. St. Pierre & W. S. Pillow (Eds.), *Working the ruins: Feminist poststructural theory and methods in education* (pp. 1–24). New York: Routledge.

St. Pierre, E. A., & Pillow, W. S. (Eds.). (2000). *Working the ruins: Feminist poststructural theory and methods in education*. New York: Routledge.

Suárez-Orozco, M. M., Suárez-Orozco, C., & Qin, D. B. (Eds.). (2005). *The new immigration: An interdisciplinary reader*. New York: Routledge.

Sumara, D. J. (1996). *Private readings in public: Schooling the literary imagination*. New York: Peter Lang.

Sumara, D. J. (2002). *Why reading literature in school still matters: Imagination, interpretation, insight*. Mahwah, NJ: Lawrence Erlbaum.

Sunker, H. (1997). Political culture and education in Germany. In H. Sunker & H.-U. Otto (Eds.), *Education and fascism: Political identity and social education in Nazi Germany* (pp. 1–14). London: Falmer.

Sunker, H. & Otto, H.-U. (1997). Volk community: Identity formation and social practice. In H. Sunker & H.-U. Otto (Eds.), *Education and fascism: Political identity and social education in Nazi Germany* (pp. 15–35). London: Falmer.

Sword, H. (2012). *Stylish academic writing*. Cambridge, MA: Harvard University Press.

Talburt, S. (2000). *Subject to identity: Knowledge, sexuality, and academic practices in higher education*. Albany, NY: SUNY.

Talburt, S., & Steinberg, S. R. (Eds.). (2000). *Thinking queer: Sexuality, culture and education*. New York: Peter Lang.

Taliaferro, D. M. (1998). Signifying self: Re-presentations of the double-consciousness in the work of Maxine Greene. In W. F. Pinar (1998), *The passionate mind of Maxine Greene: 'I am…not yet'* (pp. 89–98). New York: Falmer.

Taliaferro, D. (1999). On writing my love child. In M. Morris, M. A. Doll, & W. F. Pinar (Eds.), *How we work* (pp. 41–54). New York: Peter Lang.

Taliaferro-Baszile, D. (2010). In Ellisonian eyes, what is curriculum theory? In E. Malewski (Ed.), *Curriculum studies handbook: The next moment* (pp. 483–499). New York: Routledge.

Tanner, D., & Tanner, L. (2007). *Curriculum development: Theory into practice*. Upper Saddle River, NJ: Pearson/Merrill, Prentice Hall.

Tanner, L. (1997). *Dewey's laboratory school: Lessons for today*. New York: Teachers College Press.

Taubman, P. M. (2009). *Teaching by numbers: Deconstructing the discourse of standards and accountability in education*. New York: Routledge.

Theobald, M. (1999). Teachers, memory and oral history. In K. Weiler & S. Middleton (Eds.), *Telling women's lives: Narrative inquiries in the history of women's education* (pp. 9–24). Philadelphia: Open University Press.

Thomas, C., & Corker, M. (2002). A journey around the social model. In M. Corker & T. Shakespeare (Eds.), *Disability/postmodernity: Embodying disability theory* (pp. 18–31). New York: Continuum.

Thoreau, H. D. (2000). *Walden and civil disobedience*. New York: Houghton Mifflin.

Tierney, W. G. (1997). *Academic outlaws: Queer theory and cultural studies in the academy*. London: Sage.

Todd, S. (2009). *Toward an imperfect education: Facing humanity, rethinking cosmopolitanism.* Boulder, CO: Paradigm.

Torres, C. A. (1998). Introduction to dialogues with critical educators. In C. A. Torres (Ed.), *Education, power, and personal biography: Dialogues with critical educators* (pp. 1–20). New York: Routledge.

Tracy, D. (1996). *Blessed rage for order: The new pluralism in theology.* Chicago: University of Chicago Press.

Trifonas, P. (2000). *The ethics of writing: Derrida, deconstruction, and pedagogy.* Lanham, MD: Rowman & Littlefield.

Trifonas, P. P., & Peters, M. A. (Eds.). (2004). *Derrida, deconstruction and education: Ethics of pedagogy and research.* Malden, MA: Blackwell.

Trifonas, P. P., & Peters, M. A. (Eds.). (2005). *Deconstructing Derrida: Tasks for the new humanities.* New York: Palgrave Macmillan.

Turner, W. B. (2000). *A genealogy of queer theory.* Philadelphia: Temple University Press.

Tyack, D. (1974). *The one best system: A history of American urban education.* Cambridge, MA: Harvard University Press.

Tyack, D. (2003). *Seeking common ground: Public schools in a diverse society.* Cambridge, MA: Harvard University Press.

Tyler, R. W. (1949). *Basic principles of curriculum and instruction.* Chicago: The University of Chicago Press.

Urban, W. J. (1998). Black subject, white biographer. In C. Kridel (Ed.), *Writing educational biography: Explorations in qualitative research* (pp. 103–111). New York: Garland.

Urban, W. J. (2000). *Gender, race, and the national education association: Professionalism and its limitations.* New York: RoutledgeFalmer.

Valdivia, A. N. (2005). Geographies of Latinidad: Deployment of radical hybridity in the mainstream. In C. McCarthy, W. Crichlow, G. Dimitriadis & N. Dolby (Eds.), *Race, identity, and representation in education, second edition* (pp. 307–317). New York: Routledge.

Van Manen, M. (Ed.). (2005). *Writing in the dark: Phenomenological studies in interpretive inquiry.* Manitoba, Canada: Althouse.

Van Manen, M., & Levering, B. (1996). *Childhood's secrets: Intimacy, privacy, and the self reconsidered.* New York: Teachers College Press.

Vazquez, F. H., & Torres, R. D. (Eds.). (2003). *Latino/a thought: Culture, politics, and society.* New York: Rowman & Littlefield.

Villaverde, L. E. (2008). *Feminist theories and education.* New York: Peter Lang.

Viruru, R. (2001). *Early childhood education: Postcolonial perspectives from India.* London: Sage.

Waite, C. L. (2001). DuBois and the invisible talented tenth. In K. Weiler (Ed.), *Feminist engagements: Reading, resisting, and revising male theorists in education and cultural studies* (pp. 33–46). New York: Routledge.

Walker, A. (2006). Womanist. In L. Phillips (Ed.), *The womanist reader* (p. 19). New York: Routledge.

Warner, M. (Ed.). (1993). *Fear of a queer planet: Queer politics and social theory.* Minneapolis: University of Minnesota Press.

Warner, M. (1999). *The trouble with normal: Sex, politics, and the ethics of queer life*. New York: Free.

Washington, M. H. (1988). Introduction. In A. J. Cooper, *A voice from the South*. New York: Oxford University Press.

Watkins, W. H. (2001). *The white architects of black education: Ideology and power in America 1865–1954*. New York: Teachers College Press.

Watkins, W. H. (Ed.). (2005). *Black protest thought and education*. New York: Peter Lang.

Watras, J. (2002). *The foundations of educational curriculum and diversity, 1565 to the present*. New York: Pearson.

Watras, J. (2004). *Philosophic conflicts in American education, 1893–2000*. New York: Pearson.

Watras, J. (2008). *A history of American education*. New York: Pearson.

Watson, J. (2002). Philosophy and reified consciousness in the age of genocide. In M. Morris & J. A. Weaver (Eds.), *Difficult memories: Talk in a (post)Holocaust era* (pp. 105–115). New York: Peter Lang.

Wear, D. (2006). Shrinking distance. In M. A. Doll, D. Wear, & & M. Whitaker, *Triple takes on curricular worlds* (pp. 70–75). Albany, NY: SUNY.

Weatherston, R. (2000). An interview with Cherrie Moraga: Queer reservations; or, art, identity, and politics in the 1990s. In J. A. Boone, M. Dupuis, M. Meeker, K. Quimbly, C. Sarver, D. Silverman, & R. Weatherston (Eds.), *Queer frontiers: Millennial geographies, genders, and generations* (pp. 64–83). Madison: University of Wisconsin Press.

Weaver, J. A. (2001). *Rethinking academic politics in (re)unified Germany and the United States*. New York: RoutledgeFalmer.

Weaver, J. A: (2002). Silence of method. In M. Morris & J. A. Weaver (Eds.), *Difficult memories: Talk in a (post)Holocaust era* (pp. 157–170). New York: Peter Lang.

Webber, J. (2003). *Failure to hold: The politics of school violence*. Lanham, MD: Rowman & Littlefield.

Weibe, R. H. (1967). *The search for order, 1877–1920*. New York: Hill & Wang.

Weiler, K. (1998). *Country schoolwomen: Teaching in rural California, 1850–1950*. Stanford, CA: Stanford University Press.

Weiler, K. (Ed.). (2001). *Feminist engagements: Reading, resisting, and revising male theorists in education and cultural studies*. New York: Routledge.

Weinreich, M. (1999). *Hitler's professors: The part of scholarship in Germany's crimes against the Jewish people*. New Haven, CT: Yale University Press.

Weis, L. (Ed.). (2008). *The way class works: Readings on school, family, and the economy*. New York: Routledge.

West, R. (2006). Rebecca West (1981). In *The Paris review: Interviews, Volume 1* (pp. 228–274). New York: Picador.

Wetzsteon, R. (2002). *Republic of dreams: Greenwich Village: The American Bohemia, 1910–1960*. New York: Simon & Schuster.

Wexler, P. (1999). Body and soul: Sources of social change and strategies of education. In W. F. Pinar (Ed.), *Contemporary curriculum discourses: Twenty years of JCT* (pp. 128–150). New York: Peter Lang.

White, H. (1999). *Figural realism: Studies in the mimesis effect*. Baltimore: Johns Hopkins University Press.

Whitlock, R. U. (2007). *This corner of Canaan: Curriculum studies of place and the reconstruction of the South*. New York: Peter Lang.

Wiebe, R. H. (1967). *The search for order, 1877–1920*. New York: Hill & Wang.

Wieder, A. (1998). Trust and memory: Explorations in oral history and biography. In C. Kridel (Ed.), *Writing educational biography: Explorations in qualitative research* (pp. 113–119). New York: Garland.

Wieder, A. (2003). *Voices from Cape Town classrooms: Oral histories of teachers who fought apartheid*. New York: Peter Lang.

Wiegman, R. (2002). Unmaking: Men and masculinity in feminist theory. In J. K. Gardiner (Ed.), *Masculinity studies & feminist theory: New directions* (pp. 31–59). New York: Columbia University Press.

Wilkerson, A. D. (2008). Teen mom: A black feminist inquiry. In M. F. He & J. A. Phillion (Eds.), *Personal~passionate~participatory inquiry into social justice education* (pp. 37–51). Charlotte, NC: Information Age.

Winetrout, K. (1996). Boyd H. Bode: The professor and social responsibility. In C. Kridel, R. V. Bullough Jr., & P. Shaker (Eds.), *Teachers and mentors: Profiles of distinguished twentieth-century professors of education* (pp. 71–79). New York: Garland.

Winfield, A. G. (2007). *Eugenics and education in America: Institutionalized racism and the implications of history, ideology, and memory*. New York: Peter Lang.

Wittgenstein, L. (1977). *Culture and value* (P. Winch, Trans.). Chicago: University of Chicago Press.

Wraga, W. G. (2007). *Progressive pioneer: Alexander James Inglis (1879–1924) and American secondary education*. New York: Peter Lang.

Young, E. F. (1900). *Isolation in the school*. Chicago: University of Chicago Press.

Young-Bruehl, E. (1998). *Subject to biography: Psychoanalysis, feminism, and writing women's lives*. Cambridge: Harvard University Press.

Zimmerman, J. (2002). *Whose America? Culture wars in the public schools*. Cambridge, MA: Harvard University Press.

Zurier, R. (2006). *Picturing the city: Urban vision and the Ashcan school*. Berkeley: University of California Press.

INDEX

A

Abbas, N., 11
ableism, 330
Abram, D., 389, 396, 399
absolute monism, 63
Abukhattala, I., 321
Academic Outlaws, 356
accredit, 262
Adams, H.B., 107, 150
Adams, N., 346
Addams, J., 35, 42, 58, 83, 90, 99, 101, 108, 110, 111, 121, 122, 123, 124, 127–28, 134, 138, 145–47, 170, 180
Adler, M., 16
Adorno, T., 216, 241, 396
After-Education, 165
Agacinski, S., 27, 28
ahistoricism, 24–25
AIDS, 325, 359, 361
Allen, L.A., 228
Alter, R., 32
alterity, 238
American Association for the Advancement of Curriculum Studies, 214
American Association of University Professors (AAUP), 147, 278
American Civil Liberties Union, 147
American Council on Education, 156
American Education: The Metropolitan Experience 1876–1980, 59, 78, 175
American Federation of Labor (AFL), 128–29
American Federationist, 128
American Populist Progressives, 112
American Protestantism, 263
And There Were Giants in the Land, 178
Anderson, L., 188
androgyny, 350–51
anger, 292
Anijar, K., 240, 241
Anne Sexton, 160

anti-intellectualism, 87, 90, 93
anti-racist pedagogy, 301
anti-Semitism, 167, 179, 269, 281, 319
Anzaldúa, G., 312, 350, 363, 364
Aoki, T., 205, 207, 208, 209–11, 18
Apartheid, 201–2
aporia of urgency, 253
Appelbaum, P., 379–80
Appelfeld, A., 49
Apple, M., 189, 246, 247, 249, 305, 309
Arabs, 322
archiving the ancestors, 27–28
Arendt, H., 22, 26, 266, 272, 274, 277, 285, 286, 287, 372
Aristotle, 210
Aronowitz, S., 263, 264, 284
art
　difference and, 205
　masculinity and, 352–54
Art as Experience, 96, 184
Artaud, A., 375, 383
Aryan Brotherhood, 280
Asanuma, S., 217–20
Ashcan Art Movement, 134, 141–42, 353
Ashmore, O., 182
Ashton-Warner, S., 160, 161–62
assimilationist ideology, 297, 314
Augustine, 165, 166, 187, 188
The Authority to Imagine, 385
The Authoritarian Personality, 181
authoritarianism, 18, 245, 246, 286
auto, 52
The Autobiographical Demand of Place, 199
autobiography, 18, 39, 43–44
　and the common good, 51
　curriculum history and, 41
　feminist poststructuralist, 193
　gender and, 49–50
　historical and literary, 50–51
　as historical text, 186–88
　history and, 194–95, 199–201, 201–5
　interiority and, 51
　as pathography, 197–99
　place and, 199–201

queered, 193
race and, 49
teacher, 194
theorizing as historical text, 47–49
trauma and, 194–95, 197
tsuzurikata, 218
types of, 188
William Pinar and, 187
Autobiography, Politics and Sexuality, 371
Ayers, W., 46, 168, 171, 219, 229, 232, 293, 376

B

Bakalian, A., 320, 321
Baker, B., 250
Bale, J., 272
Banks, J., 296, 297, 298
Bankston, C., 66
Baraka, A., 200
Barbie dolls, 216
Barnard College, 84
Barnes, C., 331
Bar-On, T., 267, 268, 281
Barone, T., 45, 102, 148, 171, 206, 392
Barr, J., 81
Barriteau, V.E., 329
Bateman, D., 191
Baynton, D., 337
Beauchamp-Pryor, K., 335
Becoming Animal, 389
Bederman, 55
Beineke, J., 178, 179
Being and Time, 25
Bell, C., 335
Bellamy, F., 82
Bellows, G., 141, 353
Bemis, E., 112
Bender, S., 314–15
Benjamin, J., 353, 354
Benjamin, W., 23, 30, 31, 32, 37, 41, 42, 45, 46, 277, 372, 393
Bennett, C., 295, 297

Bennett, W., 249
Beresford, P., 337
Berlin, I., 53
Berlowitz, M.J., 247, 288
Berman, L., 158
Berson, R., 121, 146, 147
Berube, M., 330
beside, 366
Besley, A.C., 251
Bethune, M.M., 120, 123, 130–31
Bethune-Cookman College, 120
Bettis, P., 346
Between Hope and Despair, 34
Beyer, 102
Bhabha, H.K., 13, 209
Biesta, G., 251, 252, 254
Billy Elliot, 352
Bin Laden, O., 280
biography, 18, 39, 115
    culture and, 47
    curriculum history and, 41
    educational, 45
    history and, 43–44
    as memory, 155, 158
    partial, 232
    Sigmund Freud and, 44–45
    teacher, 160
Bion, W., 160, 162, 226
Birkerts, S., 2, 7
Birth of a Nation, 109, 110
Bitter Milk, 219
Black, M.S., 73
black feminist studies, 325
black studies, 297, 302, 324–30
Bleich, D., 6
Bloch, M., 269, 290
Block, A., 36, 69, 70, 178–79, 398
blockages, 30
blockheads, 376
Bloom, A., 249
Bloom, H., 7, 309, 375, 392
Bloom, L., 342, 343
Bobbitt, F., 39, 55, 85
Bobo, J., 324

Bock, G., 114
Bode, B., 172, 173–74
Bodhisattva, 198
Bohan, C., 108, 119, 120, 123, 142
Boler, M., 291
Bollas, C., 115, 116
Bolt, D., 335
Bond, H.M., 52, 124
The Book of Virtues, 249
books, love of, 391–92
Boone, J., 363
borderlands, 312
Borg, C., 264
Borgos, J.L., 10
Boston University, 162
Boswell, J., 354, 355
Bowers, C., 51
Bowling for Columbine, 292
Boys Don't Cry, 358
Bozorgmehr, M., 320, 321
Brady, E.H., 156
Bragg, L., 35, 42
Brantlinger, E., 289
Brennen, M., 250
Brinkley, D., 104, 105, 106, 107, 204
Britzman, D., 164–66, 224, 226–28
Brock, R., 327, 329
Brod, H., 347, 348
Brokeback Mountain, 358
Broszat, M., 38, 239
Brown, C.H., 80, 149
Bryan, W.J., 110, 136
Bryn Mawr, 108, 120, 132
Bryson, M., 343, 368, 369
Buber, M., 215
Bull Moose Party, 104
bullying, 355, 364
Bullough, R.V., Jr., 155, 156, 172, 173, 176, 177, 208
Burgess, J.W., 107
Burroughs, N.H., 118
Bush, G., 246, 248, 256, 271, 273, 274, 277, 278, 283
Bush, G.W., 281, 323

butch-femme role playing, 362
Butler, J., 343, 348, 359, 362, 367, 370
Butler, N.M., 180
Buttigieg, J.A., 264

C

Cainkar, L., 323
Caldas, S., 66
Cammarota, J., 316
The Cancer Journals, 48
Cannella, G., 290, 291, 346
Canon formation, 306
Canon Project, 213–14
Capote, T., 14
The Cardinal Principles of Secondary Education, 85
Carger, C.L., 232
Carlson, D., 360
Carnegie, A., 101, 285
Carnegie Mellon University, 153
Carr, P., 306
Carr Community Academy, 234, 235
Carroll, W.M., 190
Casals, P., 97, 146
Case, S.-E., 361, 364
Case, V., 135, 136, 137
Casemore, B., 199, 203
Catholicism, 263
Chan, E., 75
Changing Course, 54
chaos thoery, 190
Charters, W.W., 39, 55, 85
Chatham Academy, 182
Chautauqua, 134, 204
    literary circles at, 135–37
    music at, 135
    popular education and, 137
    problems with, 137–38
    as a rural movement, 134–34
Chavez, L., 314, 319
Chevy Chase School, 79
Chiarelott, L., 102

Chicago Teachers Federation, 82, 128
Chicago Tribune, 235
Chicano Education in the End of Segregation, 74
Chicano studies, 302
The Child and the Curriculum, 58
child therapy, 387
Children's Books for Grown-Up Teachers, 379
Christopher, S., 298
Chun, M., 298
Cisneros, S., 231
City and Country Progressive School, 129, 139, 150
civic education, 63
civil liberties, 246
Civilization and Its Discontents, 361
Clapp, E.R., 121, 129–30
class, 55, 255, 256, 289–90
clerical fascism, 275
Clifford, P., 93, 94
The Closing of the American Mind, 249
Codreanu, C., 267
Coetzee, J.M., 202, 222, 377, 388
Cohen, A., 281, 292
Cohen, S., 28, 32, 35, 58
Collin, R., 246
Collins, P.H., 325, 326, 328
colonialism, 301
Columbia University, 84, 107, 179, 181, 183, 371
Columbine High School, 281
common school, 17, 66–67, 71–73, 73–76
Connelly, M.F., 16
common curriculum, 68
common good, 62–65, 66
common schools, 62–65, 78
commons, 51
Commons, J.R., 112
Comparative Studies in Society and History, 114
confession, 187
Confessions, 187
Connell, R.W., 349, 350
Connelly, F.M., 189–90

conservative monoculturalism, 299
constellations, 30contextualizing, 103
Contemporary Curriculum Discourses, 212, 215, 217, 220, 221
control, 251, 290–91
Cooke, P., 119
Coolidge, C., 286, 292
Cooper, A.J., 57, 80, 116, 117, 118, 119, 122, 124, 125, 133, 143–45
Cooper, J.M., 108, 109, 147, 174
Corker, M., 334, 336
correspondence theories of reality, 385
Country Schoolwomen, 33, 341
Counts, G., 79, 101, 133, 172, 174–75, 184
Cremin, L., 59, 60, 64, 71, 78, 79, 90, 103, 104, 111, 117, 138, 139, 152, 153, 164, 170, 174, 175, 184
Crichlow, W., 319
Crimp, D., 367
critical multiculturalists, 300
critical pedagogy, 255, 256
critical theory, 255–59, 362
critical whiteness studies, 303
Crocco, M.S., 116, 118, 123, 126, 341
Crunden, R.M., 70
Cuban, L., 36, 62, 63
Culler, J., 10
Cultural Literacy, 249
cultural memory, 199
cultural pluralism, 295–96
cultural psychoanalysis, 220
Cultural Revolution (China), 194–96, 218
culture, 47
currere, 12, 187, 218
curriculum
    anti-intellectual, 88
    Christian principles and, 69
    common. *See* common curriculum
    dystopic, 239
    gendered, 124–25. *See also* gender curriculum
    hidden, 66
    historical trauma and, 236–38
    historiography. *See* historiography, curriculum
    humanities and, 14
    imaginative literature and, 388–89
    as interdisciplinary study, 3
    literary. *See* literary curriculum
    movement and, 2
    multicultural. *See* multicultural curriculum
    political. *See* political curriculum
    (post)reconceptualization of. *See* (post)reconceptualization
    queering, 364–65
    social sciences and, 14
    studies, 255–59
    theorists, 139–40
    theorizing, 9–11
    witnessing and, 155
Curriculum and the Holocaust, 382
Curriculum Books: The First Hundred Years, 17, 190
Curriculum in a New Key, 205
curriculum studies. *See* curriculum
Curriculum Studies Handbook, 222
The Curriculum Studies Reader, 16
Curriculum: Toward New Identities, 12
Curriculum Visions, 223–24
cyberfeminism, 345

D

Dalcroze Eurhthmics, 153
Damrosch, W., 135
Danforth, S., 332
Dar, J., 323
Darder, A., 284, 312, 316, 317, 318, 319
Dartmouth College, 183
Daspit, T., 377–78, 382
Daughters of the American Revolution, 147
Davis, B., 211
Davis, J., 332
Davis, L.J., 330, 333, 336, 337
de Botton, A., 5

de Castell, S., 343, 346, 368, 369
de Certeau, M., 16
de Fournival, R., 374
de Grand, A., 271, 274, 276, 278
de Lauretis, T., 362
de Salvo, L., 398, 399
Deconstructing Derrida, 252
Dei, G.J.S., 301
Deleuze, G., 336, 389
Delgado, W., 235
A Delicate Dance, 199
Democracy and Education, 58
depth psychology, 220–21
Derrida, J., 4, 6, 18, 26, 209, 210, 211, 212, 215, 245, 259, 262, 301, 382
  the Other and, 254
  poststructuralism and politics, 251–55
  writing and, 372, 373, 374
Derrida and Education, 252
Derrida, Deconstruction, and the Politics of Pedagogy, 252
Descartes, R., 52–53
deschooling, 74
developmental psychology, 290
Dewey, A., 83
Dewey, J., 9, 58, 60, 61, 66, 68, 77, 79, 83, 88, 91, 92, 94, 99, 106, 111, 123, 147, 153, 156, 184, 393
  academic disciplines and, 102–3
  the arts and, 96, 102, 137
  chaos and, 97–98
  Chautauqua and, 134
  everyday world and, 96–97
  Isaac Leon Kandel and, 185
  the negative and, 97
  notion of experience and, 95–96
  the personal and the social, 98
  protection of faculties, 278
  the social and, 100–2
  study of culture, 114
  thought and, 100
dialectic, 217
dialogic exchange, 61
difference, 18, 205, 271, 371, 393–94

Diggs, N.B., 313, 314
Dilling, E., 183
Dimitriadis, G., 319
disability studies, 299, 330–31
  critical, 336
  cultural, 335–36
  defining disabilities, 336–37
  historical overview of, 331–32
  as protest literature, 332
  theoretical frameworks of, 332–35
Discipline and Punish, 187, 250
disgrace, 202, 222
Disgrace, 377
disidentity, 394
dislodged, 2
distance, 202, 203
diving into the wreck, 198
Dobbs, L., 315
Dodd, W., 71
Dodge, M., 134, 139, 140, 144
Dolby, N., 319
Doll, M.A., 201, 202, 203, 204, 220–21, 222, 285, 372, 375–76, 382, 389, 393, 394, 397
Doll, W., 53, 190, 223, 224–25, 240
Doty, A., 358
Douglass, F., 130
Down Syndrome, 330
Downing, C., 354, 356
Dreams Deferred, 232
D'Souza, D., 309
Du Bois, W.E.B., 56, 119, 122, 123, 228
Dudek, P., 279
Duke, D., 280
Durham, M., 280
Duster, A., 126, 127
dwelling, 211
dystopic curriculum, 239

E

Eagleton, T., 4, 8
Eastman, C., 141, 147

Eastman, M., 147
Eatwell, R., 271
Eckhart, M., 165
Eco, U., 8, 10
eco-poeisis, 18, 371, 389–90
eco-spirituality, 214–15
Edgoose, J., 253
edTPA, 285
educare, 221, 227
education
    the arts and, 143–54
    civic, 63
    colonization of others, 316
    discrimination against minorities, 73–76
    disciplinary status of, 212–13
    as an elusive science, 85
    as enforcement, 287
    humanitarian, 74
    moral and religious purposes of, 70
    multicultural, 156
    perception of women, 78
    public, 67
    religion and, 78
    salons and, 140
    the social and, 102–3
    Southerners and, 71–73
    as women's work, 213
Education as Enforcement, 287
Education, Power, and Personal Biography, 191
educational biography, 45
Educational Poetics, 382
Egea-Kuehne, D., 252
ego psychology, 290
Eight-Year Study, 156, 157
Elenes, C.A., 311, 312
elitist queers, 363–64
Elshtain, J.B., 83, 121, 124, 127, 128, 145, 147, 180
An Elusive Science, 84
Emerson, R.W., 6
emotion, 289–90, 291–93
empathetic unsettlement, 195
empiricism, 89

Encyclopedia of Curriculum Studies, 17
Engendering Curriculum History, 35, 55, 80
The English Patient, 381
epistemological curiosity, 263
epistemology, 328
Eppert, C., 33, 238, 239, 240
Erevelles, N., 335
Eros, 341
Espionage Act, 174
The Ethics of Writing, 252
eugenics, 39
Evans, K., 367
Evans, R.W., 138, 178, 182, 184

F

Faderman, L., 120, 123, 124, 125, 128, 129, 323, 350, 354, 356, 357, 359, 362
Failure to Hold, 282
Falicov, C.J., 315
fascism, 18, 174, 245, 266, 267
    against generic, 271
    comparability and, 268–69
    curriculum debates over, 265–68
    dissension and, 277–79
    fundamentalism and, 274–76
    generic use of term, 269–70
    militarism and, 273–74
    nationalism and, 272
    new, 280–82
    violence and, 276–77
fascist dictatorship, 270
fascist minimum, 269
Fat Boys, 352
fear, 292
Female Seminary, 125
feminism, 18, 220–21
    genders and, 339–40
    girls and, 346
feminist life, 340
feminist studies, 324–30
    curriculum scholars, 341–44

resistance and, 341–44
Fernandes, D., 320
Feuerverger, G., 242
fiction, 201–2
   postcolonial, 202
   South African, 203
Fine, M., 289
Fink, L., 70, 106, 110, 111
Finkelstein, B., 47
Fish, S., 2
Flinders, D., 16
Foley, N., 311, 322
formal thinking, 290
for-profit private schools, 283
Foster, F.S., 325
Foster, S. M., 325
Foucault, M., 10, 18, 30, 31, 34, 40, 225, 245, 249, 250, 251, 262, 355, 359, 383, 384
Founding Mothers and Others, 55, 79
fountainheads, 376
Frank, B., 355
Frankfurt School of Critical Theory, 211, 216, 300
Frankenberg, R., 304, 305
Franklin, B., 36
Freidlander, S., 239, 240
Freire, A.M.A., 261
Freire, P., 136, 191, 216, 257, 258, 260–65, 284, 372, 396, 397, 399
   radical love and, 291, 391
   scholarly work and, 373
   writing and, 262, 392
   as a victim of exile, 261
Frelinghuysen University, 143
French Heideggerainism, 209
Freud, A., 164–66, 167, 290
Freud, S., 36, 44–45, 132, 166, 220, 225–26, 226, 256, 341, 361, 367, 386, 398
Friesen, S., 93, 94
Fritzsche, P., 272
Fugitive Pieces, 396
fundamentalism, 274–76

G

Gabbard, D., 287
Gabel, S., 332
Gadamer, H.-G., 53
Gardiner, J.K., 344
Garman, N.B., 385
Garrett, M., 124
Garrison, 91, 92
Gay, P., 89, 226
Gay L.A., 356
gay marriage, 360–61
gender, 17, 55, 77, 219, 256, 342, 343
   the common school and, 71–73
   conflicting views on, 132–33
   curriculum and, 124–25
   the disciplines and, 84–85
   erasure of, 56–58
   polarizations, 366–67
   race and, 345
   redemption and, 77–78
   religion and, 78
   roles, 344–45
   sexuality and, 365–66
   technology and, 345–46
   vocational education and, 86–89
gender and ethnic relations, 289
gender curriculum, 339
   feminisms and, 339–40
   representation and, 344
The Gender of Racial Politics and Violence in America, 55, 80, 238
gender panic, 366, 370
gender trouble, 348, 367
Gender Trouble, 343
genital mutilation, 367
Geographies of Girlhood, 346
gestalts, 177
Giardina, M., 322
Giddings, P., 122, 130, 133
Gilbert, J., 223
Gilbert, S., 340, 342
Gillborn, D., 301
Gilman, C.P., 141

Gilman, S., 347, 352
Gilmore, G.E., 106
Gilmore, L., 54
Giordano, G., 87, 88
Giovanni, N., 48
Giroux, H., 192, 215–17, 246, 257, 264, 278, 282, 346
   Columbine High School and, 281
   disrespect of children and, 380
   fascism and, 268, 274
   fundamentalism and, 276
   militarism and, 273, 287
   totalitarianism and, 265, 266
   violence and, 292
   whiteness and, 305, 308
   youth and, 282
Gitlin, A., 382, 383
GLBTQ communities, 298, 317, 356, 358, 361, 362, 368
Goldenweiser, A., 153
Goldhagen controversy, 269
Goldman, E., 141
Gollnick, D.M., 296, 297
Gone With the Wind, 358
Gonzalez, G., 74
Goodley, D., 331, 333
Goodson, I., 49, 50, 84
Gordimer, N., 8, 202
Gordon, L., 120, 123, 124, 132
Gordon, S., 270
Gough, N., 223, 224
governmentality, 249–51
Governmentality Studies in Education, 251
Gramsci, A., 29, 45, 255, 257, 258, 260–65
   imprisonment in Fascist Italy, 260
   intellectual work and, 262
   power and, 264
   war of position, 265
Grande, S., 289, 290
Grant, C., 297
Gray, J., 5
Great Books Tradition, 16, 68, 112, 179, 184, 299, 307, 329
Great Recession, 247, 259

Green, A., 28, 97
Greene, M., 54, 102, 136, 140, 144, 167, 179, 182, 192, 193, 219, 220, 226, 344, 371, 372, 375–76, 377, 392
   biographic portraits of, 168–72
   imaginative literature and, 204, 394
   intellectual history of, 168–72
   literature as art, 206
   privatism and, 395
   Virginia Woolf and, 375, 383
grief work, 381–82
Griffin, R., 266, 267, 269, 271, 272, 280, 281
Grimke, C.F., 144
Gros, F., 3
Grumet, M., 6, 10, 12, 22, 217–20, 223
Guattari, F., 336
Gubar, S., 340
Gumport, P.J., 298
Gutierrez, H., 312, 319
Guy-Sheftall, B., 325
Guys and Guns Amok, 282
Gwinn, M., 124

H

Haberman, M., 157
Halberstam, J., 350, 365, 366, 367
Haley, M., 82, 83, 108, 123, 128, 129, 131–32
Hall, G.S., 123
Ham, D.N., 124, 130, 131
Hamacher, W., 30, 32
Hanson, D., 175, 176, 182
Hanson, E., 356, 357, 360
Harold, 144
Harraway, D., 104, 279, 351
Harris, W.T., 68, 74, 75, 82
Harrison, B., 130
Hartman, G., 10, 14
Hartmann, H., 290
Harvey, D., 247
Harvey, E., 279

Hauser, M., 123, 150
Hawley, J.D., 105, 107, 125
Hayles, N.K., 13
Haynes, A., 236
Haynes, F., 350, 366
Hayot, E., 15
Haywood, B., 147
He, M.F., 16, 75, 194–97, 218, 235–36
healing, 398–99
hegemonic masculinity, 349
hegemony, 264, 349–50
Heidegger, M., 25, 209
Helbling, M., 318
Henderson, L., 362
Hendry, P.M., 10, 23, 34, 35, 55, 57, 66, 79, 80, 82, 112, 123, 124, 126, 127, 158–60, 163, 329
Henke, S., 197
Henri, R., 142
Henry, A., 327
Heterodoxy Club, 134, 140–41
heteronormativity, 123, 317, 349–50, 358–59, 367
high-stakes testing, 250
Hilberg, R., 267
Hill, D., 255, 259
Hillis, V., 205
Hillman, J., 33
Hinchey, P., 290, 384
Hinitz, B., 58, 152, 154
Hirsch, E.D., 249, 309
Hispanic, 310
historical archive, 32–33
historical conjunctions, 30
historical trauma, 18, 33–34
historicality, 25–26
Historikerstreit, 266–67
historiography, curriculum, 6, 18, 21–23, 24–25, 37–38, 77, 155, 163, 170, 227
  autobiography and, 41–42
  biography and, 41–42
  educational history and, 59–60
  inclusion in, 167–68
  literary fiction and, 37

  memory work and, 40–41
  minorities and, 42, 56
  notion of the past and, 23–24
  rethinking, 34–36
  texts, 60–61
theorizing as autobiographic text, 54–56
  universal, 30–31
  women and, 42, 56
  women Progressive educators and, 113
history, 18, 371
  autobiography and, 194–95, 199–201, 201–5
  bringing to life, 46
  complexity of, 115–16
  cultural, 58
  educational, 59–60, 62–65
  erasure of queer women and, 356–57
  Eurocentric, 202
  fiction and, 201
  from below, 58
  of histories, 61
  intellectual, 164–66
  interpretation of, 23
  Lacanian Psychoanalysis and, 208–9
  of learning, 165
  materialist, 31
  memory and, 38–39, 396–98
  as multiplicity, 28–29
  narratives and, 29–31
  poststructuralism and, 208–9
  power and, 34
  racist ideologies and, 107
  rewriting, 72
  as social construction, 31–32
  Southern, 199–201
  trauma and, 194–95, 236–38
  witness and, 238
History of Madness, 383
The History of Sexuality, 355
Hitler, A., 267, 274, 277, 356
Hlebowitsh, P., 69
Hhoare, Q., 260
Hofstadter, R., 104, 106, 112, 138, 262, 263, 272, 285, 286, 293

Hofstetter, M., 70
Holdstein, D., 6
Holler if You Hear Me, 230
Hollins, E.R., 297
Holocaust, 7, 33, 39, 41, 43, 237, 266, 268, 269, 270, 274, 278, 308, 314, 321, 356, 382, 396, 397, 398
homogenous time, 31
homophobia, 80, 123, 317, 320, 349, 355, 358–59, 369
homosexuality, 80, 123
Hood, L., 161
Hoover, H., 281
horizontality, 209
Horowitz, H.L., 83, 120, 124, 131, 132
The Hours, 358
The House on Mango Street, 231
How We Think, 9
How We Work, 372
Howard, A., 289, 290
Hudley, C., 324
Huebner, D., 24, 25, 27, 29, 40, 42, 88, 171, 189, 191, 205–6, 208, 209–11, 218
Hull House, 58, 83, 90, 99, 113, 127–28, 129, 138, 147
humanism, 13
Hunt, C., 187
Hurricane Katrina, 283
hybridity, 312, 313

I

identity, 18, 371, 393–94
identity formation, 260
identity politics, 223
imaginative literature, 204, 388–89
indigenous studies, 302
industrial education, 86
Industrialists, 112
indwelling, 211
Inglis, A.J., 185
institutionalized racism, 323
intellectual retrospectives, 155
intergroup education, 296
Intergroup Education in Cooperating Schools, 156
International Foundation for Androgynous Studies, 350
interiority, 329
International Association for the Advancement of Curriculum Studies, 214
Iraq War, 277
Iron Guard, 267
Irwin, R., 205
Islamic fundamentalism, 275
Islamophobia, 318–24
I-Thou relation, 215

J

Jackson, P., 89, 90, 91, 96, 172, 175–76, 182
Jacoby, R., 114, 132
James, H., 376
James, S., 325
James, W., 60, 62, 63, 137
Jardine, D., 7, 93, 94, 210, 214–15
Jefferson, S., 236
Jennings, J., 324
Jennings, M., 23
Jenson, J., 346
Jewett, L., 199, 203
Jewish Intellectuals and the University, 36, 167, 285
Jewish mysticism, 216, 217
Johns Hopkins University, 107, 120
Johnson, G.D., 144
Johnson, K., 118, 122, 124
Johnson, M., 148–50, 153
Johnston, I., 2
Jones, A., 161
Joseph, G., 327
Journal of Curriculum Theorizing, 193, 212
JROTC, 288
Jung, C., 33, 65, 153
The Jungle, 106

K

Kallen, H., 84, 295
Kammen, M., 63, 89
Kandel, I.L., 184
Kant, E., 70, 385
Keating, A., 350, 363
Kellner, D., 282, 288, 292
Kent, S.K., 114
Kershaw, Sir I., 271
Kett, J., 149
Kharem, H., 318
Kilpatrick, W.H., 58, 79, 123, 179–82, 393
Kilpatrick Discussion Group, 180
Kimmel, M., 346, 347, 348, 353
Kincheloe, J.L., 102, 103, 215–17, 289, 290, 291, 299, 301, 302, 307, 308, 319, 320, 321, 322, 323, 324, 391
King, J.E., 329, 330
Klein, M., 164–66, 167, 226, 227, 387
Klein, N., 283
Kliebard, H., 36, 54, 58, 59, 78, 85, 86, 87, 88, 111, 174
Klinkenborg, V., 9
Klohr, P., 156, 171, 172, 176–77, 191, 193
Ku Klux Klan, 280
knowledge, 329
knowledge production, 260
Kohli, W., 169, 172
Kohn, J., 22
Krall, F., 214–15
Kridel, C., 17, 43, 44, 45, 60, 155, 156, 159, 172, 173, 208
Kroll, C., 306
Ku Klux Klan, 267, 272
Kumar, A., 392
Kumin, M., 163

L

Lacan, J., 209, 256
LaCapra, D., 37, 61, 195
Lagemann, E.C., 61, 84, 85, 88
Laidlaw, L., 387–88, 389, 390
Landscapes of Learning, 371
Langer, L., 239
Laquer, W., 267, 269, 271, 272, 274, 275, 277, 280, 281
Lather, P., 223, 254, 361
Latino/a studies, 73–74, 310–18
Latino Threat Narrative, 314
Le Pen, J.-M., 267
Lea, V., 305
Leaders in Curriculum Studies, 188
Lean, N., 319, 321
Left Back, 60, 249
left-essentialist multiculturalism, 300
Leggo, C., 384
Leistyna, P., 284
Le Rider, J., 352, 353
lesbianism, 80, 356
Lesko, N., 169, 171
Letters to Cristina, 373
Levering, B., 187, 386
Levinas, E., 63, 210, 215
Lewis, B., 333
Li, X., 194–97, 198, 218
liberal multiculturalism, 299
libraries, 395–96
The Library at Night, 395
life history, 49. 50
A Light in Dark Times, 168, 376
Like Letters in Running Water, 221, 376
Lincoln University, 143
literary curriculum, 371–74
Littleford, M., 220–21
Long, N.A., 247, 288
Longmore, P.K., 332
Lorde, A., 48, 325
Luce-Kapler, R., 389, 390, 394, 399
Luhmann, S., 370
Lund, D., 306
The Lure of the Transcendent, 205
Luther, M., 67
Luxemburg, R., 132, 133
lynchings, 116, 238, 239

M

Macdonald, J., 25
Macedo, D., 261
Macrine, S.L., 248
macro-physics of power, 250
Mad Heart, 200
madness, 382–84
The Madwoman in the Attic, 340
Malewski, E., 12, 13, 29, 30, 222, 223
Mallarmé, S., 30
Malpus, J.E., 4
Mamet, D., 348
The Man with the Blue Guitar, 375
A Man Without Qualities, 216, 226
Manguel, A., 7, 10, 11, 374, 376, 395, 397, 398
Mann, H., 64
Mao, Z., 196, 277
Marable, M., 310, 320, 324
Marcus, L., 50, 52
Marot, 123, 129, 138, 150, 151
Marsh, C., 84, 85
Marsh, C.J., 66
Marshall, D., 17
Marshall, J.D., 228
Martin, J., 101, 180, 181
Martinez, G., 311, 322
Marx, K., 86, 91, 255, 256, 258, 259, 285
Marxism, 180, 259, 273, 289
Mascali, B., 240, 241
masculine women, 350–51
masculinity, 349–50
    arts and, 352–54
    crisis of, 87
    feminist focus on, 351–52
    heterosexist privilege and, 352–54
masculinity studies, 18, 299, 346–49
mathematics education, 93, 94
Maurer, S., 251
May, V., 119, 125, 133, 143, 144, 301
Mayo, P., 262, 264
McCarthy, C., 50, 221–22, 296, 297, 309, 319

McCluskey, A., 120, 123, 130–31
McConaghy, C., 160, 161–62, 164
McGerr, M., 101, 106, 128, 129
McGill University, 216, 391
McKenna, T., 366
McKnight, D., 67, 71
McLaren, P., 255, 256, 257, 259, 263, 271, 282, 301
    class and, 289
    critical theory and, 291
    fascism and, 268
    fundamentalism, 276
    George Bush and, 278
    Marxism and, 285
    militarism and, 274, 287
    race and, 303–4
    revolutionary multiculturalism, 300
    surveillance and, 273
    totalitarianism and, 265, 266
    white supremacy and, 304
    whiteness and, 306
Mead, G.H., 99, 173
medical humanities, 203
Mein Kampf, 277
Meiners, E., 363
memory, 18, 48, 198, 371
    autobiography and, 201–5
    cultural, 199
    history and, 38–39, 201–5, 396–98
    purpose of, 40, 242–43
    trauma and, 238–42
memory work, 40–41
mentoring, 156
mestiza, 312
metahistories, 61
methods, 103, 240
Michael, A., 396
Michel, C., 324
Michelet, J., 240
Michie, G., 230–32
micro-physics of power, 250
Middleton, S., 115, 161, 344
Miel, A., 156, 158, 207
militarism, 18, 245, 282, 287–88

Milk, 358
Milkis, S., 104, 107
Miller, J., 10, 168, 192–94, 217–20, 223, 376
mindfulness, 215
Mirande, A., 351
The Miseducation of the West, 321
misogyny, 78, 81, 82, 84, 213, 362, 363
Mitchell, T., 72
Montreal Massacre, 242, 368
Moore, M., 292
Moraga, C., 362, 365, 366
morality, 69
moreness, 27
Morgan, J.P., 101
Morgan, S., 25, 31, 57
Morgan, T.J., 74
Morris, M., 7, 33, 36, 38, 43, 48, 65, 67, 79, 84, 97, 129, 146, 170, 194, 208, 225, 237, 239, 241, 267, 269, 326, 350, 372, 397
   Adolf Hitler and, 181, 274
   anti-Semitism and, 179, 281
   disability studies and, 337
   Holocaust and, 308, 314, 317
   Melanie Klein and, 167
   Nazism and, 275, 276, 331
   pathography and, 197–99
Morrison, T., 328
movement, 2
M Street High, 143
multicultural education, 295
   overview of, 295–99
   theoretical frameworks of, 299–301
multiculturalism, 18, 43, 156, 299, 309
Munro, P., 26, 29, 37, 43, 56, 58, 59, 113, 116, 118, 121, 123, 126, 127, 152, 163, 170, 341, 342, 343
murderous rage, 241
muscular Christianity, 125
Musil, R., 216, 225–26, 227
Muslims, 318, 319, 320, 322, 323
Mussolini, B., 271, 274, 275

N

Naber, N., 322
Nacherziehung, 166
Nader, R., 235
Nagarjuna, 215
Nash, R., 6
National American Women Suffrage Association, 108
National Council for Accreditation of Teacher Education (NCATE), 206
National Education Association, 81, 82
National Front, 267
National Socialism, 112, 270
nature of community, 99
Naumburg, M., 58, 79, 152–54
Nazism, 271, 275, 279, 331, 357, 395
neoconservativism, 245, 248–49
neoliberalism, 18, 245, 246–47, 271, 281, 281, 286, 287
   fascism and, 268
   globalizing effects of, 247–48
   public schools and, 287–88
neo-plantationism, 286
New Deal, 110
New Presbyterians, 125
New School for Social Research, 181
Newman, J., 148, 149
Newman, V., 43, 60
Next Moment, 223
Nguyen, T., 323
Nidiffer, J., 83
Nieto, S., 298, 309
Nietzsche, F., 62
No Child Left Behind, 180, 246, 283, 292, 293
Noddings, N., 16
Nolte, E., 268, 269, 271
Novoa, A., 29, 30
Null, J.W., 184, 186
Nussbaum, M., 378, 395
Nye, A., 128, 132, 133

O

Obama, B., 256, 275, 309, 315
Oberlin College, 143
object relations theory, 387
objectification, 240
objectivity, 6
Of Grammatology, 215
Ohio State University, 157
Olney, J., 48
Olssen, M., 251
On Not Being Able to Play, 206
Ondaatje, M., 380, 381, 388
The One and the Many, 62
One-Way Street, 393
Orff, C., 146
organic intellectuals, 45–46, 258, 363–64
Organic School, 148, 149
The Origins of Totalitarianism, 266, 285
Other, 63, 75, 86, 108, 114, 187, 204, 214, 215, 297, 300, 322, 323, 324, 333, 334, 348, 357, 383, 394, 395
  fear of, 65–66
  Jacque Derrida and, 254
  Latino/as and, 314
  multiculturalism and, 303
  sexuality and, 67
out, 357
Out Takes, 357

P

Pagano, J.A., 212–14
Page, R.N., 188
Paideia Proposal, 16
Palin, S., 275
Paris Review, 14
Parker Institute, 149
Parkerson, D., 69, 72, 82
Parkerson, J.A., 69, 72, 82
Parkhill Manufacturing Company, 183
partial biography, 232
Pasolini, P.P., 35, 42, 45, 226
The Passionate Mind of Maxine Greene, 168, 376
Passmore, K., 268
past, 23
Paterson Silk Workers Strike, 130
pathographies, 47, 197–99
patriarchy, 358–59
Paulo and Nita Freire Project for International Critical Pedagogy, 216, 391
Pautz, A., 52
Paxton, R.O., 267, 269, 271, 272, 276, 278
Payne, S., 272, 273, 274, 275
Pearson Education, 284, 285
Peck, M., 382, 383
pedagogies of resistance, 126
Pedagogies of Resistance, 341
pedagogy of insubordination, 291–92
Pedagogy of the Oppressed, 191–92, 391
Peerless Educator, 184
Peirce, C.S., 100
Penny, D., 383, 384
Perea, J., 312
Personal Best, 358
Personal~Passionate~Participatory Inquiry into Social Justice Education, 235
Peters, M., 246, 249, 251, 252, 253
phenomenology, 386
Phillips, A., 5
Phillon, J.A., 16, 75, 235–36
Piaget, J., 216, 290, 291, 332, 333
Piantanida, M., 385
Pierce, W., 280
Pilgrim's Progress, 285
Pillow, W., 343
Pinar, W., 6, 11, 12, 17, 21, 22, 43, 45, 52, 56, 72, 80, 85, 90, 105, 119, 127, 163, 169, 171, 182, 191, 205, 224, 340, 372
  autobiography and, 47, 48, 51
  Canon Project, 213–14
  Contemporary Curriculum Discourses, 212
  crisis of masculinity, 352
  currere, 187
  curriculum history and, 113
  disciplinarity and, 5

ethnographies, 89
gender, race, and, 55
George Counts and, 174
historical witness and, 238
historiography and, 42
Ida B. Wells and, 126–27
identity politics, 223
interiority and, 329
internationalization and, 16
Jackson Pollock and, 151–52, 154
Jane Addams and, 121
Janet Miller and, 193
lynching, violence and, 73, 116–17, 131, 200, 276
masculinity and, 108
Maxine Greene and, 168
movement and, 2
queer theory and, 354
racism and, 238
representation and, 307
repudiation of the father, 354
Robert Musil and, 225–26
self and, 7
tenure and, 374
verticality and, 24
violence and, 242, 292, 369
Virginia Woolf and, 371
the world stage and, 35
place, 199–201
Plato, 379
plea for historicization, 239
pluralist multiculturalism, 299–300
Poe, E.A., 389
Poetic Justice, 378
policy of containment, 292
political curriculum, 245
political scholarship, 282
politics, 255–59
of emotion, 18, 246
Jacques Derrida and, 251–55
poststructuralism and, 249–51
Pollock, J., 146, 150, 151–52, 154, 226
Polsky, S., 30
poor, 77

Popkewitz, T., 30, 250, 290
Populists, 106
postbiological, 13
postcolonialism, 13, 201, 202, 221, 302
postformal thought, 216, 290–91
postformalism, 18, 245
posthuman, 13, 350–51
postmodernism, 53–54, 190
(post)reconceptualization, 11–13
poststructuralism, 208–9, 301
    Jacques Derrida and, 251–55
    politics and, 249–51
    thought, 312
power, 34, 264
pragmatism, 99–100
Pratt, C., 79, 123, 129, 138, 150–52
Price, M., 331, 337
Principles of Secondary Education, 186
Prison Notebooks, 260
Private Readings in Public, 380
privatism, 395
Professio Regia, 224
progressive education, 18, 57–58, 78–80, 83, 91–95
    controversy about, 103–7
    debate about, 103–7
    politics and the arts, 126–27
    psychoanalysis and, 165
    women and, 77, 81, 117–22, 126–27
Progressive League, 148
Progressive movement, 101, 106, 112
    urban, 138–39
    women and, 107–11
Progressivism, 204
Project Citizen, 234
protest thought, 324
Protestantism, 67, 69
Provocations, 160
psychoanalysis, 5, 165, 208–9, 220–21
psychobiographies, 160
psychic moment, 187
psychic shattering, 242
psycho-social, 218
Public Education: America's Civil Religion, 66

Purdue Conference 2006, 29, 222–23
public schools
  defending, 285–87
  See also education
Pythagorean Theorem, 94

Q

Qin, D.B., 313
queer, 310
queer theory, 18, 193, 310, 354–56
  assimilation and, 364
  childhood and, 368–70
  critical theory and, 362
  curriculum and, 364–65
  erasure of queer women and, 356–57
  sexuality and, 370
  women and, 361–62
Queer Theory in Education, 369

R

Rabbit-Proof Fence, 74
Rabold, C., 149
race, 17, 55, 256
  the common school and, 71–73
  conflicting views on, 132–33
  erasure of, 56–58
  gender and, 345
Race to the Top, 180, 246, 256–57, 292, 293
racism, 75, 82, 156, 236, 239, 301, 313, 323, 326, 327, 330, 358
radical Islamist terrorists, 280
radical love, 216, 291, 391
rage, 292
Ramus, P., 224
Rancière, J., 32
rape myth, 200
Rasberry, G., 378–79, 389, 390, 399
Rasmussen, M.L., 359
Ravitch, D., 58, 60, 68, 85, 90, 185, 249, 309

Readings, B., 61
reconciliation, 239
Reconstructing the Common Good in Education, 62
The Red Network, 183
red pedagogy, 290
redemption, 71–73
  gender and, 77–78
  work and, 85–86
Reed, J., 180
Reel Bad Arabs, 323
Reese, W.J., 36, 62, 64, 69, 72, 73, 75, 77, 86, 87
Reich, S., 208
reified consciousness, 241
Reinventing Curriculum, 387
Releasing the Imagination, 171, 220
religion, 78
rematerialized critique, 257, 258, 259
reparation, 239
representations, 33
Rethinking Academic Politics, 34
revolution, 263
revolutionary multiculturalism, 300
Reynolds, K., 149, 274
Reynolds, W., 12, 17, 22, 85, 340
Rich, A., 198
Rieff, P., 177
Rieser, A., 134, 135, 136, 137, 142
Rilke, R.M., 382
A River Ever Flowing, 194
Rizvi, F., 319, 322
Roberts, P.A., 228
Robertson, J.P., 160, 161–62, 164
Robinson, S., 347
Rodman, H., 141
Rodriguez, N., 303, 305
Roediger, D., 303
Romney, M., 309
Roosevelt, F.D., 180, 247, 292
Roosevelt, T., 104, 105, 106, 107, 108, 110, 130, 136, 204, 279
Rosenberg, S., 33, 34, 238, 239, 240, 242
Ross, E.A., 112

Ross, W., 285, 287
Roulstone, A., 331
Rousmaniere, K., 123, 128, 131
Roy, K., 281, 285, 286, 287, 292
Royce, J., 99
Rugg, H., 55, 58, 79, 101, 133, 138, 182–84

S

Sadovnik, A., 36, 55, 58, 79, 80, 132
The SAGE Handbook of Curriculum and Instruction, 16
Said, E., 222
Sallis, J., 2, 11
Salmon, L., 58, 108, 119, 120, 123, 142
salons, 139–40, 144, 145
Saltman, K.J., 248, 283, 285, 286, 287, 288
Salvio, P., 35, 36, 47, 160, 162–64, 170, 199
Sanders, E., 106
Sartre, J.P., 52
Scambler, S., 337
Schiedeck, J., 279
school shootings, 18, 245
The School and Society, 58
Schooled to Work, 54, 86
Schooling and the Politics of Disaster, 283
Schubert, A.L.L., 190
Schubert, W.H., 17, 97, 190, 191, 228
Schultz, B., 233–35
Schwab, J., 178, 189, 234
Scott, J., 25
Scott-Simmons, W., 236
scriptotherapy, 197
Scully, J.L., 337
Searles, H.F., 241, 292
Sears, J.T., 228, 350, 368
Sedgwick, E., 342, 343, 362, 366, 367
Seeking Common Ground, 63
Segal, H., 126
Seidman, S., 344
Selden, S., 36
self, 12, 62, 67, 214, 215, 219
Semali, L., 307

Semel, S., 36, 55, 58, 79, 80, 132
Serres, M., 3, 15, 336
settlement houses, 83
Seven Sisters Colleges, 83
sexism, 55–56, 236, 326, 330
sexuality, 365–66, 370
Sexton, A., 35, 47, 162–64, 199
Shaheen, J., 323
Shaker, P., 155, 156, 172, 208
Shakespeare, T., 334, 336
shame, 367
Shanks, M., 115, 116
Shepard, M., 349, 368
shifting, 33
Shildrick, M., 336
Shipps, D., 36, 62, 63
The Shock Doctrine, 283
Short, E.C., 188–91
Siebers, T., 330, 333–34, 337
Simon, R.I., 33, 34, 41, 238, 239, 240, 242, 243
Sims, E.J., 305
Sinclair, U., 106
Slattery, P., 12, 17, 22, 85, 102, 103, 340
slavery, 237
Sleeter, C., 301, 304, 317
Smith, B., 326
Smith, D., 214
Smith, H.W., 110
Smith, J.S., 110
Smith, M.C., 113
Smith, M.R., 124
Smithies, C., 361
Sneeden, D., 39, 55, 85
social amnesia, 114
social change movement, 217
social efficiency, 85, 112
Social Gospel Movement, 121
Social Gospelers, 121, 125
Socialist Club, 148
Socialism, 106, 180
Sontag, S., 389
Sorbonne, 143

Soto, L.D., 290, 314, 315, 316, 317, 318
Soucy, R., 276
Sounds of Silence Breaking, 192, 193
Southern, D., 105, 107
Spectacular Things Happen Along the Way, 233
speech melody, 208
Spencer, H., 299
splitheads, 376
Spring, J., 33, 74, 75, 82
Sri Lanka, 201
Stack, S., 121, 130
Stahlmann, M., 279
Stalin, J., 277
Standard Oil Company, 106
standardization, 263
standardization of knowledge, 250
standardized testing, 247, 284, 292
Stanford, L., 285
Starr, E.G., 124
Stastny, P., 383, 384
Steffens, L., 180
Steinberg, S., 102, 103, 215–17, 290, 291, 299, 300, 301, 302, 307, 308, 319, 320, 321, 322, 323, 324, 364
Stevens, W., 375
Still Alice, 336
Stonebanks, C., 319, 320
Stonewall, 356
Stories of the Eight-Year Study, 173
storytelling, 392
St. Pierre, E., 343
Stratemeyer, F.B., 156, 157, 207
The Struggle for the American Curriculum, 78, 111
Suárez-Orozco, C., 313
Suárez-Orozco, M.M., 313, 315
Subject to Fiction, 158, 159
subjugated knowledge, 289
Sumara, D., 380–81, 388, 391, 392, 393, 396, 397
Sunker, H., 270, 279
surveillance, 251, 273, 279
Sword, H., 14

T

Taba, H., 155, 156
Taliaferro, D., 171, 391
Taliaferro-Baszile, D., 48
Talmud, Curriculum, and the Practical, 178
Tanner, D., 69
Tanner, L., 69, 92
The Tao of Life Stories, 194
Taubman, P., 12, 17, 22, 85, 283, 292, 293, 340
Tea Party, 275, 315, 357
Teacher as Stranger, 167
teachers
    assumed to be White, 80
    autobiographies, 194
    as intellectuals, 92
    perception as hysterical women, 82
    spinster, 79–80
Teachers and Mentors, 155, 172
Teachers as Cultural Workers, 373
Teachers College, 84, 85, 88, 123, 138, 156, 157, 158, 167, 170, 175, 182, 184, 185, 186, 192
Teaching by Numbers, 283
Teaching through the Ill Body, 47, 194, 197–99
technology, 345–46
Temporarily Abled Body (TAB), 331
Terrell, M.C., 119, 124, 130, 131
The Terror of Neoliberalism, 282
testimony, 41, 187, 238–42
textbooks, 284, 381
texts, interpreting, 8
textorium, 386
Theobald, M., 160, 161
The Theory of Everything, 336
thick description, 26
things-in-themselves, 385
thinking, 9
third space of ambivalent construction, 209
This American Life, 235
This Bridge We Call Home, 363
This Corner of Canaan, 199
This Happened in America, 178, 183

Thomas, C., 331, 334
Thomas, M.C., 35, 120, 124, 131, 132
Thomas, T.P., 190
Thoreau, H.D., 66
Thorndike, E.L., 85, 111
Thornton, S., 16
Tierney, W.G., 356, 370
Tillich, P., 209
time, 26–27, 31
Timmons, S., 323, 355, 356, 357, 358
To Teach: The Journey of a Teacher, 229
Todd, S., 210, 241, 293
Tolstoy, I., 181
Torres, C.A., 191–92
Torres, R., 310, 311, 312, 319
totalitarianism, 265, 266, 282, 285, 287–88
Toward a Poor Curriculum, 11, 12
Tracy, D., 224
traditional educational history, 21
Traditionalists, 112
The Transformation of the School, 103, 104
transgendered, 356, 366
transsexuals, 356, 365, 366
Transitions in American Education, 82
trauma
    historical, 236–38
    memory and, 238–42
    testimony and, 238–42
    transgenerational, 237
travel
    as metaphor, 1–5
    narrative, 2
Trifonas, P., 210, 252
Triple Takes and Curricular Worlds, 201, 202, 203, 204, 205, 222
Troy, E.W., 125
Truth, 117
Truth and Method, 53
tsuzurikata, 218
Turner, W., 362, 369
Turning Points in Curriculum, 17, 228

Tyack, D., 29, 36, 63, 64
Tyler, R., 182, 206

U

Umansky, L., 332
uncommon schools, 66
Underhill, A., 123
Understanding Curriculum, 13, 17, 24
United States Census Bureau, 310
university in chains, 257
University of California, 124
University of Chicago, 175, 179
University of Zurich, 120
Unseen Genders, 366
Urban, W., 52, 81

V

Valdivia, A., 313
van Manen, M., 187, 385–87
Vassar, 119, 120
Vazquez, F., 310, 311, 312
verticality, 24, 209
Vatican, 275
Village intellectuals, 139–40
Villaverde, L., 339, 345, 351
violence, 34, 242, 276–77, 292
Viruru, R., 290, 291, 346
vocational education, 85–86, 86–89, 90, 216
A Voice from the South, 143, 144
Von Ranke, L., 53

W

Waite, C., 56
Waks, L.J., 188–91
Walden School, 79, 152, 153
Walker, A., 325

Warner, M., 349, 359, 360, 362
Wartime Schools, 87
Washington, M.H., 119, 122
Watkins, W., 36, 75, 85, 324, 325, 327, 332
Watras, J., 36
Watson, J., 237, 241
Watson, N., 331
Wear, D., 201, 202, 203, 204, 222, 377, 379, 388, 395
Weaver, J., 34, 39, 53, 240, 268, 278
Weber, K.C., 274
Weber, S., 251
Webber, J., 282, 292, 355
Weiler, K., 33, 55, 57, 80, 81, 113, 115, 116, 118, 123, 126, 341, 344
Weinreich, M., 278
Weis, L., 289
Wells, I.B., 57, 80, 111, 120, 121, 122, 123, 126, 130, 133, 200, 238
Wesleyan University, 186
West, R., 397
Western canon, 309
Wetzsteon, R., 106, 140, 141, 146, 147, 150, 151, 152
Wexler, P., 215–17
Whitaker, M., 201, 222
White, H., 31, 32, 37
White, S.S., 110
The White Architects of Black Education, 36
white privilege, 363
whiteness, 364
whiteness studies, 299, 300, 301, 302–10
  curriculum of, 307
  domination and, 304
  masculinity studies and, 348
Whitlock, R.U., 199
Wiebe, R., 106, 107
Wieder, A., 46
Wiegman, R., 351
Wilkerson, A.D., 236
Willard State Hospital, 383

Willis, G., 66
Wilson, W., 108, 109, 174, 180, 277
Winetrout, K., 173
Winfield, A.G., 36, 39
witnessing, 18, 155, 236–38
Wittgenstein, L., 4, 5, 7, 30
Wobblies, 147
womanist studies, 324–30
women
  Black, 325
  as contaminants, 81–83
  erasure of, 78–80, 307
  labor unions and, 128–29
  masculine, 350–51
  as Progressive educators, 113–15, 117–22, 122–24
  the Progressive Movement and, 107–11
  queer theory and, 361–62
  socially constructed term, 343
  the university and, 83–84
  as victims of patriarchy, 341
women's clubs, 140–41
women's studies, 302
Women's Trade Union, 129
Woodson, C., 122
Woodward, E., 110
Woold, V., 226
Woolf, V., 371, 375, 382, 383
The Worldliness of a Cosmopolitan Education, 35
Wraga, W.G., 185–86
writing, 372–74, 392
  grief work and, 381–82
  healing and, 398–99
  madness and, 382–84
  as a political project, 392
  reading and imagination, 384–85
Writing as a Way of Healing, 398
Writing Educational Biography, 44
Writing in the Dark, 385
Writing Research/Researching Writing, 378

X

xenophobia, 358–59
Xu, S., 75

Y

Yale University, 149
Young, E.F., 64, 74, 75, 78, 82, 83
Young-Bruehl, E., 115

Z

Zimmerman, J., 71
Zirbes, L., 155, 156, 157
Zorn, E., 235
Zurier, R., 141, 142
zydeco dance, 200

Studies in the Postmodern Theory of Education

General Editor
Shirley R. Steinberg

Counterpoints publishes the most compelling and imaginative books being written in education today. Grounded on the theoretical advances in criticalism, feminism, and postmodernism in the last two decades of the twentieth century, Counterpoints engages the meaning of these innovations in various forms of educational expression. Committed to the proposition that theoretical literature should be accessible to a variety of audiences, the series insists that its authors avoid esoteric and jargonistic languages that transform educational scholarship into an elite discourse for the initiated. Scholarly work matters only to the degree it affects consciousness and practice at multiple sites. Counterpoints' editorial policy is based on these principles and the ability of scholars to break new ground, to open new conversations, to go where educators have never gone before.

For additional information about this series or for the submission of manuscripts, please contact:

> Shirley R. Steinberg
> c/o Peter Lang Publishing, Inc.
> 29 Broadway, 18th floor
> New York, New York 10006

To order other books in this series, please contact our Customer Service Department:

> (800) 770-LANG (within the U.S.)
> (212) 647-7706 (outside the U.S.)
> (212) 647-7707 FAX

Or browse online by series:
www.peterlang.com